A SYNOPSIS OF THE GOSPELS

PART I
THE SYNOPTIC GOSPELS WITH THE JOHANNINE PARALLELS

A SYNOPSIS OF THE GOSPELS

H. F. D. SPARKS

Part I. The Synoptic Gospels with the Johannine Parallels

Part II. The Gospel according to St John with the Synoptic Parallels

A
SYNOPSIS OF THE GOSPELS

PART I
THE SYNOPTIC GOSPELS
WITH THE JOHANNINE PARALLELS

H. F. D. SPARKS, D.D., F.B.A.

Oriel Professor of the Interpretation of Holy Scripture
in the University of Oxford

ADAM AND CHARLES BLACK
LONDON

FIRST PUBLISHED 1964
SECOND EDITION 1970
REPRINTED 1976
A. AND C. BLACK LTD.
35 BEDFORD ROW   LONDON WC1R 4JH

© 1964, 1970 HEDLEY FREDERICK DAVIS SPARKS

ISBN 0 7136 1069 7

Reproduced and printed by photolithography and bound in
Great Britain at The Pitman Press, Bath

PREFACE

THE suggestion that they should undertake a new Synopsis of the Gospels in English first came to the publishers from Canon C. B. Mortlock. He also suggested to them that I should be asked to prepare it. Throughout the period of preparation he has maintained a constant interest in the progress of the work ; and it is a pleasure now to be able to associate his name with it.

To the staff both of Messrs. A. & C. Black, the publishers, and of Messrs. R. & R. Clark, the printers, I owe a more than ordinary debt of gratitude for the patience and understanding with which they have received my repeated requests for re-setting (not infrequently of whole sections more than once) as the sheets were going through the press.

And to Mr. John Brown, the compositor, all users of the Synopsis will be indebted for the competence and care he has lavished on his task. My 'copy', alas, was never easy to decipher. But Mr. Brown has always managed to translate it into print, so that what should be parallel really is parallel—something much more difficult to do than many might suppose. Rarely in modern times can any book have been set by hand with greater devotion or greater skill.

H. F. D. SPARKS

THE RECTORY, WYTHAM, OXFORD
FEAST OF ST. JOHN THE EVANGELIST, 1963

INTRODUCTION

THE primary aim of this Synopsis is to enable the Greekless student of the gospels to read through any one of them continuously, in the English of the Revised Version, with the parallel passages in the other three printed in parallel columns alongside.

occur in all four gospels, and then sandwich in between them in the appropriate places the material that is in fact found between them in each separate gospel. A simple diagram should make this plain ('|||||||' represents the presence of material, '————' its absence):

Matt.	Mark	Luke	John
|||||||||||||	————	|||||||||||||	————
————	————	|||||||||||||	————
|||||||||||||	|||||||||||||	————	|||||||||||||

As is well known, the first three gospels share very much more in common with one another, both as regards subject-matter and the arrangement of that subject-matter, than they do, either individually or collectively, with the fourth. That is why we call them 'The Synoptic Gospels', why we recognise that there is a specifically 'Synoptic Problem' to solve, and why, in consequence, the majority of the synopses of the gospels in use to-day tend to concentrate on exhibiting the relationship between these gospels only, and either pay scant attention to the fourth or else ignore it completely. But that there is a relationship between all four gospels, as well as between the first three, is incontrovertible: in other words, there is a 'Four Gospel Problem' to solve, and not merely a 'Synoptic Problem'; and the most recent gospel scholarship has shown itself well aware of this problem and has concerned itself not a little with its solution.

This means that any synopsis of the gospels that is to be of more than limited value to the modern student must include the fourth gospel on equal terms with the other three. But that is more easily said than done. The obvious way to do it is to treat all four exactly alike—*i.e.*, first to set out opposite one another the parallel passages which

But the execution of such a plan, when it comes to the setting out of the actual material, is nothing like so simple, nor can the result be as satisfactory, as the above diagram might suggest. So long as we apply the plan to the Synoptics only, no serious complications arise. The amount of material shared in common by the Synoptics is very large indeed: a high proportion of it occurs in the same order in each of them: the 'fixed points', therefore, are many; and the result is that the 'sandwich' material for the most part falls naturally into place without posing the editor any problems about what order he is going to put it in. But as soon as John is added a radically different picture emerges. The amount of material shared in common by all four gospels is relatively small: very little of even this small amount occurs in the same order: the 'fixed points' are therefore few; and the result is that in the arrangement of the 'sandwich' material the widest possible discretion is left to the editor. Even where the 'fixed points' are fairly close together there is still considerable latitude. For example, two incidents which are shared in common by all four gospels, and which occur in the same order in all four, are The Feeding of the Five Thousand (Matt. 14 13-21 ‖ Mark 6 30-44 ‖ Luke 9 10-17 ‖ John 6 1-14) and Peter's Confession

(Matt. 16 13-20 ‖ Mark 8 27-30 ‖ Luke 9 18-21 ‖ John 6 66-69). In the Synoptics the complete series of incidents at this point works out as follows :

Matt.	Mark	Luke
The Feeding of the Five Thousand	The Feeding of the Five Thousand	The Feeding of the Five Thousand
Jesus walks on the Water	Jesus walks on the Water	——————
Healings in Gennesaret	Healings in Gennesaret	——————
A Question from the Scribes	A Question from the Scribes	——————
The Canaanitish Woman	The Syro-Phoenician Woman	——————
Healings by the Sea	The Healing of a Deaf-Mute	——————
The Four Thousand	The Four Thousand	——————
A Request for a Sign	A Request for a Sign	——————
The Leaven of the Pharisees	The Leaven of the Pharisees	——————
	The Healing of a Blind Man	
——————		——————
Peter's Confession	Peter's Confession	Peter's Confession

Here, it will be observed, there is no 'sandwich' material at all in Luke : the eight 'sandwich' incidents in Matt. and nine in Mark arrange themselves naturally in parallel throughout; and the editor has no problem. In John, however, there are two 'sandwich' incidents, and the sequence runs like this :

John

The Feeding of the Five Thousand
Jesus walks on the Water
In the Synagogue at Capernaum
Peter's Confession

The first 'sandwich' incident in John ('Jesus walks on the Water') is obviously parallel with the same incident in Matt. and Mark; but 'In the Synagogue at Capernaum' has no parallel. Where, then, if all four gospels are to be in parallel, should the editor place it in relation to the incidents in Matt. and Mark ? Should it go before 'Healings in Gennesaret' ? Or after it ? Or should the two be printed in parallel (on the ground that Capernaum was situated in the Gennesaret district, and that John expressly states that the incident in the synagogue took place 'on the morrow' after The Feeding of the Five Thousand) ? On the other hand, John distinctly implies that Peter's Confession followed straight after the synagogue incident, and that the two are intimately and causally connected. Should the editor, therefore, reserve 'In the Synagogue at Capernaum' until after 'The Healing of a Blind Man' in Mark, and put it immediately before Peter's Confession, in order to maintain and emphasize this Johannine connection, in spite of the statement that it took place 'on the morrow' after the Feeding ?

This kind of problem is repeated on a larger scale elsewhere. In fact it reaches such proportions that the inclusion of John must inevitably become an embarrassment to any editor who tries to construct a synopsis in this way; and, even if he is apparently successful, it is very doubtful whether the result can ever be regarded as a really satisfactory tool for the student, inasmuch as the ordering of so much of the contents must of necessity depend on the subjective judgement of one particular editor. Another editor might well prefer a quite different arrangement and with equal justification.

In constructing this Synopsis it has accordingly been thought best to cut the Gordian knot by presenting the material in two distinct parts. The present volume contains the text of the Synoptic Gospels with the Johannine parallels. If it is well received, it will be followed by another, which will contain the text of John with the Synoptic parallels. Only by some such expedient as this is it possible to combine the fulfilment of the primary aim of enabling each of the four gospels to be read through continuously in the light of the parallels in the other three, with the minimum of editorial idiosyncrasy.

Such an expedient, of course, does not eliminate entirely the necessity for some subjective judgements on the part of the editor. If it be asked, upon what principles, in this instance, the editor's subjective judgements are founded, the answer is: (1) upon what seems to be the natural logical or chronological order of the material, and (2) upon the commonly accepted order of the four gospels. Thus, 'The Lucan Prologue' stands at the very beginning as § 1, simply because it is a prologue (of the first three gospels, Luke alone has a prologue), and the Matthaean Nativity Narrative (§§ 2-6) precedes the Lucan (§§ 7-15) because it is customary to arrange the gospels in the order, Matthew-Mark-Luke-John.

And this order is also the order in which the texts of the four are presented in parallel—or, if we prefer it, horizontally. There are in the Synopsis four columns throughout, one for each gospel. These columns are always of the same relative width where there are parallels printed (e.g., § 113). Where there are no parallels printed, the column or columns with nothing in them contract (in order not to waste space) and the corresponding columns or column of text expand (*e.g.*, §§ 114, 115, and 122). The only exception occurs in those few cases where there is a parallel in the same gospel to print as well as parallels in other gospels, or where it has been thought advisable to print a parallel from outside the gospels altogether. In these cases, five, or even six, columns may be required (*e.g.*, §§ 66, 67, and 68); but in these cases the same conventions about the relative width of columns, and contraction and expansion, apply. However, although a parallel in the same gospel means in practice an additional column at that point, theoretically the additional column is nothing more than a sub-division of the original single column allocated to the gospel. To mark this distinction, columns containing parallels from the same gospel are separated by only a dotted line, instead of the standard 'rule' used to separate one gospel column from another (see again §§ 67 and 68). At the other extreme, a 'heavy rule' is used to separate the Synoptic columns from the John column, in order to remind the reader that this last column differs from the Synoptic columns in not offering a continuous text.

Thus, to read through a Synoptic gospel with the parallels, the student starts at the beginning (p. 3 for Matt., p. 11 for Mark, and p. 3 for Luke) and follows on from section to section. Whenever he comes to a section that does not continue the text of his gospel, he looks at the headline at the top of the page, and there he will find where to look for the continuation. For example, if he starts reading Luke in § 1 on p. 3, he will find that this section takes him only as far as verse 4 of the first chapter, but a glance at the headline will show him at once that for verse 5 he must turn to p. 6: he can then read continuously from Luke 1 5, in § 7 on p. 6, to Luke 4 30, in § 24 on p. 20; and so on, through §§ 26-31 on pp. 21 to 25, to where the Lucan text is resumed again in § 52 on p. 37. If, at any time, he wants to refer back, because the text of his gospel does not appear in the preceding section, he will find also in the headline a reference backwards to the page at which the text broke off —*e.g.*, if he is concerned with Luke 5 12-16, in § 52 on p. 37, and wants to look back to Luke 5 11, he will be directed by the headline to § 31 on p. 25.

It will be noted that parallels are printed in two sizes of type. Use of the larger (normal) size indicates that the parallels so printed occur in the same context. Use of the smaller size indicates that the context is different. It will be noted further (and this is a special feature of this particular Synopsis) that great care has been taken to ensure that identical or alternative words and phrases are printed *exactly* parallel. Naturally,

this results in a very large number of gaps in any passage which has a parallel, and in very much more total space being required than if the parallels had been printed simply as they stand without regard to correspondences in detail. But convenience in use should more than compensate for extra length. As the parallels have been arranged, the student has all the material set out in such a way that he can see at once which words and phrases in a passage occur in more than one gospel and which do not, and he has no need to search through up to (perhaps) twenty or so lines of text in the neighbourhood in order to discover what may, or may not, be relevant.

Another special feature of this Synopsis is the references. Occasionally a reference consists of just the chapter and verse numbers—*e.g.*, in § 73, '1 2' appears in the Mark column opposite Matt. 11 10 and Luke 7 27: in these cases attention is drawn to what is in fact a parallel, though for one reason or another it has not been printed in full. More frequently the chapter and verse numbers are preceded by '*cp.*' (='compare'): these are references proper, in no sense parallels, and of several kinds. Sometimes they draw attention to similar or comparable incidents or situations, as when Jesus is accused of blasphemy by 'the scribes' (§ 59) and by 'the high priest' (§ 242), or when He is said to have 'gone up into the mountain' and 'prayed' (see, for example, the references in § 114). Sometimes the point of comparison is theological rather than factual, as when the faith of the disciples is in question (see § 57), or when what is popularly known as a 'universalistic' note is struck (see § 53); and under this head should probably also be included those *motifs* which run through all the gospel material, such as the exhibition of 'fear' or 'amazement' by the bystanders after a miracle has been wrought (see § 59). At other times a reference may apply only to a single word or phrase, especially to words or phrases characteristic of the different evangelists: examples here are 'the holy city' as a synonym for Jerusalem (Matt. 4 5 and 27 53, but not elsewhere), 'the apostles' as a synonym for 'the twelve' (five times in Luke, once in Matt., once in Mark, but never in John: see § 177), and 'there shall be the weeping and gnashing of teeth' (six times in Matt., once in Luke, but not elsewhere: see § 103). The student is thus provided with what is virtually a miniature concordance to gospel usage; and he should find this of great help in learning to appreciate the stylistic peculiarities and theological preferences of the evangelists—a subject on which great stress is normally laid in modern study of the gospels. If his interests do not happen to tend that way, he can, of course, ignore the references completely. But in any case, he will soon discover from experience what sorts of references are worth pursuing from his own particular point of view, and what sorts are not, and treat them accordingly.

Wherever possible the division of the material into sections follows the paragraph divisions in the Revised Version. The exceptions are those comparatively rare instances where two or more gospels appear in parallel in the Synopsis but the Revised Version paragraphing differs between one gospel and another. Thus, in the Revised Version, Matt. 9 18-26 (The Healing of Jaïrus's Daughter and The Woman with an Issue of Blood) is given one paragraph only, but the parallels at Mark 5 21-43 and Luke 8 40-56 are each given three paragraphs: in the Synopsis there is a single section (§ 108).

The supplying of titles for sections in a work of this kind is always something of a problem. There are some titles which are so inseparably linked with their sections by custom that to attempt to change them would seem almost indecent (e.g., 'The Feeding of the Five Thousand'). On the other hand, there are many sections which have no generally agreed title, and some of these are so devoid of any obviously outstanding characteristic that to find any appropriate title at all is well-nigh impossible (e.g., § 151). And even when titles that are suitable in themselves have been found, there is the further probability that they will not mix happily with the titles of adjacent sections laid down by custom. It is hoped that the titles chosen will not be found unduly bizarre or uneven. When they seem unusual, there may well be a reason. For instance, § 254 bears the title 'The Penitent Malefactor', instead of the more usual 'The Penitent Thief': the reason is that the Revised Version text of the section refers to 'malefactors' and not to 'thieves'.

Finally, it may be asked, why has the Revised Version of 1881 been printed as the English text and not the more modern Revised Standard Version of 1946 or the New English Bible of 1961?

The simplest answer to this question may be given by quoting from the Revisers' own preface. The Revisers' commission, it will be remembered, was not to produce a new version, but to revise the Authorized Version, and, in doing so, 'to introduce as few alterations as possible . . . consistently with faithfulness'. One of the things they found amiss with the AV was what they stigmatized as 'a studied variety of rendering, even in the same chapter and context': this, they maintained, 'produced a degree of inconsistency that cannot be reconciled with the principle of faithfulness'; and they went on to confess to having had no hesitation in such cases in introducing alterations 'even though the sense might not seem to the general reader to be materially affected'. They explained this point as follows:

'When a particular word is found to recur with characteristic frequency in any one of the Sacred Writers, it is obviously desirable to adopt for it some uniform rendering. Again, where, as in the case of the first three Evangelists, precisely the same clauses or sentences are found in more than one of the Gospels, it is no less necessary to translate them in every place in the same way. These two principles may be illustrated by reference to a word that perpetually recurs in St. Mark's Gospel, and that may be translated either "straightway", "forthwith", or "immediately". Let it be supposed that the first rendering is chosen, and that the word, in accordance with the first of the above principles, is in that Gospel uniformly translated "straightway". Let it be further supposed that one of the passages of St. Mark in which it is so translated is found, word for word, in one of the other Gospels, but that there the rendering of the Authorised Version happens to be "forthwith" or "immediately". That rendering must be changed on the second of the above principles ; and yet such a change would not have been made but for this concurrence of two sound principles, and the consequent necessity of making a change on grounds extraneous to the passage itself.'

The importance of this approach, if we are choosing a version to serve as the basis for a Synopsis, is obvious. Yet the translators of the NEB deliberately repudiate it.

'We have not felt obliged (as did the Revisers of 1881)', they write in their Introduction, 'to make an effort to render the same Greek word everywhere by the same English word. We have in this respect returned to the wholesome practice of King James's men, who (as they expressly state in their preface) recognized no such obligation.'

And the most cursory study of the NEB makes the truth of this statement only too plain. For example, γραμματεύς occurs in the Greek gospels 59 times: in the RV it is uniformly translated 'scribe' (following the AV) ; but in the NEB it is variously translated 'lawyer' (31 times), 'doctor of the law' (22 times), 'teacher' (4 times), and 'teacher of the law' (2 times)—and the variants are to be found even in passages that are parallel (e.g., Matt. 16 21 ∥ Mark 8 31 ∥ Luke 9 22). Conversely (and the translators make no mention of this in their Introduction), the same English not infrequently does duty for different Greek: thus, 'lawyer' renders not only γραμματεύς (sometimes), but also νομικός (always—and both in parallel at Matt. 23 13 ∥ Luke 11 52 and Mark 12 28 ∥ Luke 10 25), while 'Jesus was at Bethany' renders both 'τοῦ δὲ Ἰησοῦ γενομένου ἐν Βηθανίᾳ' at Matt. 26 6 and 'καὶ ὄντος αὐτοῦ ἐν Βηθανίᾳ' in the parallel at Mark 14 3. Clearly, to construct a Synopsis on the basis of such a version, whatever be that version's merits for other purposes, would be irresponsible and culpably misleading.

By way of contrast with the NEB, which is a completely fresh translation, the Revised Standard Version is a revision—a revision, moreover, of the American Standard Version of 1901, which was in turn a very slight revision of the Revised

Version itself. It might therefore be supposed that, standing in such a direct line of descent, the RSV must necessarily be superior to the RV, and that it consequently has greater claims to serve as the basis for a modern Synopsis than the RV could possibly have.

Oddly enough, this very natural supposition is not borne out by the facts. Take, for instance, a single sentence from § 108. In the RV the parallels are:

Mark 5 29

And straightway the fountain of her blood was dried up.

This represents in the Greek:
Mark 5 29

καὶ εὐθὺς ἐξηράνθη ἡ πηγὴ τοῦ αἵματος αὐτῆς.

The RSV gives:
Mark 5 29

And immediately the hemorrhage ceased.

Here we note that according to the RSV rendering the only difference between Mark and Luke is 'hemorrhage' in Mark and 'flow of blood' in Luke: this reflects the difference in the Greek between πηγὴ τοῦ αἵματος and ῥύσις τοῦ αἵματος, and corresponds to the difference in the RV between 'fountain of her blood' and 'issue of her blood'. But there are two other differences in the Greek, both of which are reflected in the RV, but of which the RSV takes no account at all—viz., εὐθύς in Mark (RV 'straightway') as against παραχρῆμα in Luke (RV 'immediately') and ἐξηράνθη in Mark (RV 'was dried up') as against ἔστη in Luke (RV 'stanched'). And furthermore, the RSV's translation of ἡ πηγὴ τοῦ αἵματος αὐτῆς in Mark by 'the hemorrhage' passes over the word αὐτῆς (='her') altogether, and so creates the impression that there is an additional difference between Mark and Luke at this point, when in fact there is not.

If readability and conformity with modern idiom be regarded as the sole criteria for a version, there can be no doubt that the RSV has the advantage over the RV here: 'hemorrhage' is obviously a more meaningful and idiomatic expression than 'fountain of blood', and 'ceased' is even more obviously more modern than 'stanched'; and from this point of view the RSV's ignoring of the differences in the Greek between εὐθύς and παραχρῆμα, and between ἐξηράνθη and ἔστη, is a mere trifle, not to mention its passing over of αὐτῆς in Mark. Yet from the point of view of an editor of a Synopsis readability and conformity with modern idiom are by no means the sole criteria. What an editor of a Synopsis requires from a version above all else is

the clear and unambiguous reflection in English of the agreements and disagreements between the gospels as they exist in Greek. Compared with that the stylistic merits of a version are a secondary consideration. In the present passage, therefore, from the point of view of an editor of a Synopsis, the RV is patently preferable: all the differences in the Greek are clearly reflected in the RV, whereas in the RSV they are not; and one might press the argument even farther and claim that for the

Luke 8 44

And immediately the issue of her blood stanched.

Luke 8 44

καὶ παραχρῆμα ἔστη ἡ ῥύσις τοῦ αἵματος αὐτῆς.

Luke 8 44

And immediately her flow of blood ceased.

student even the RV's 'fountain of blood' and 'was dried up' have the advantage over the RSV's 'hemorrhage' and 'ceased' in that they are both more exact renderings of the Greek.

It was precisely this 'mechanically exact, literal, word-for-word translation' (which makes the RV such a satisfactory basis for a Synopsis), that those responsible for the RSV especially wished to avoid. In a pamphlet entitled *An Introduction to the Revised Standard Version of the New Testament*, published in 1946 by Members of the Revision Committee, Dr. Luther A. Weigle, the Chairman of the Committee, gave three reasons why the revision had been undertaken. The first of these reasons he stated thus:

'1. The English Revised Version of 1881 and its variant, the American Standard Version of 1901, lost some of the beauty and force which made the King James Version a classic example of English literature. They are mechanically exact, literal, word-for-word translations, which follow the order of the Greek words, so far as this is possible, rather than the order which is natural to English. Charles H. Spurgeon, the English preacher of the closing nineteenth century, put it tersely when he remarked that the Revised New Testament was "strong in Greek, weak in English". "The Revisers in their scrupulous and conscientious desire to be perfectly true to the Greek have . . . been too unmindful of the claims of their own language", was the comment of Dean Perowne. "They have sometimes been too literal, construing instead of translating; they have inverted the natural order of words in English in order to follow the Greek; and they have carried the translation of the article, and of the tenses, beyond their legitimate limits." A well-balanced and generally favorable article in the *Edinburgh Review* for July, 1881, concluded by saying: "The revisers were not appointed to prepare an interlinear translation for incompetent school-boys." These criticisms, which were made when the English Revised Version was published, apply as well to the American

Standard Version. These versions convey the meaning of the Scriptures more accurately than the King James Version, but they have lost much of its beauty and power.'

In other words, we are dealing in this matter with two incompatibles. The characteristics which commend a version for use in a Synopsis are not those which commend it for popular reading, and *vice versa*. The RV displays the former characteristics, the RSV (we may assume) the latter.

Lest, however, it be thought that the case for the RV as against the RSV depends entirely on the evidence of a single gospel passage, supported by a few chance remarks from one of the members of the American Revision Committee, it may be as well to add some further illustrative detail.

First, some more instances of inconsistency in translation in parallels—*i.e.*, instances where either the same Greek is translated differently in the RSV or different Greek is translated similarly: (1) Mark 12 43 (ἀμὴν λέγω ὑμῖν; RV 'Verily I say unto you'; RSV 'Truly, I say to you') ‖ Luke 21 3 (ἀληθῶς λέγω ὑμῖν; RV 'Of a truth I say unto you'; RSV 'Truly I tell you'); (2) Matt. 5 29 and 30 (βάλε ἀπὸ σοῦ· συμφέρει γάρ σοι . . .; RV 'cast it from thee: for it is profitable for thee . . .'; RSV 'throw it away; it is better that you . . .') ‖ Matt. 18 8 (βάλε ἀπὸ σοῦ· καλόν σοί ἐστιν . . .; RV 'cast it from thee: it is good for thee . . .'; RSV 'throw it from you; it is better for you . . .'); (3) Matt. 7 4 (πῶς ἐρεῖς; RV 'how wilt thou say?'; RSV 'how can you say?') ‖ Luke 6 42 (πῶς δύνασαι λέγειν; RV 'how canst thou say?'; RSV 'how can you say?').

'How can you say?' as the rendering of two different Greek expressions in the RSV in this last instance was doubtless prompted by stylistic considerations—the literal rendering in Matthew ('how will you say?') might well have seemed stilted, and so something like what anyone would normally say was substituted for it. And stylistic considerations are doubtless also the justification for the many other more idiomatic renderings in the RSV that so frequently replace 'mechanically exact, literal, word-for-word' renderings in the RV. Yet, for the student, there is loss here as well as gain. The student gets the feel of the gospels much better, and learns more about their language, from 'sons of the bridechamber' than from 'wedding guests', and from 'And his lord commended the unrighteous steward because he had done wisely' than from 'The master commended the dishonest steward for his prudence'—especially when, as in the last example, the RV adds a marginal note to the effect that 'the unrighteous steward' is in 'Gr. *the steward of unrighteousness*'.

The RSV gives no marginal note to its 'dishonest steward'. And marginal notes are on the whole much fewer in the RSV than in the RV (and fewer still in the NEB). Once again this is a loss for the student. For example, at Mark 9 41, in the passage about giving to drink a cup of water 'because ye are Christ's', the RV adds to 'because ye are' the note 'Gr. *in name that ye are*', thus making it plain that its rendering is a free one. The RSV renders 'because you bear the name of Christ' with no note; and with this we may compare the 'because you are followers of the Messiah' of the NEB, likewise without a note.

One other deviation of the RSV (and the NEB) from the practice of the RV also deserves mention in this connection. It is the disuse of italics. When words stood in their translation, which were not represented in the Greek but had been supplied, either to make sense or to bring out the sense, the Revisers continued the convention (well established through the various editions of the AV) of printing the words supplied in italics. As a result, what was not in the original stood out clearly from what was. In any case such a convention is useful; and it is particularly useful in parallels. Thus, in the RV we have:

Matt. 11 8	Luke 7 25
But what went ye out for to see? a man clothed in soft *raiment*? Behold, they that wear soft *raiment* are in king's houses.	But what went ye out to see? a man clothed in soft raiment? Behold, they which are gorgeously apparelled, and live delicately, are in king's courts.

in the RSV:

Matt. 11 8	Luke 7 25
Why then did you go out? To see a man [1] clothed in soft raiment? Behold, those who wear soft raiment are in kings' houses.	What then did you go out to see? A man clothed in soft raiment? Behold, those who are gorgeously apparelled and live in luxury are in kings' courts.

and in the NEB:

Matt. 11 8	Luke 7 25
Then what did you go out to see? A man dressed in silks and satins? Surely you must look in palaces for that.	Then what did you go out to see? A man dressed in silks and satins? Surely you must look in palaces for grand clothes and luxury.

[1] A difference in the underlying Greek text is involved here. As an alternative the RSV offers in the margin 'Or *What then did you go out to see? A man . . .*'

It should not, of course, be inferred from these remarks that because in general the RV provides a more satisfactory basis for a Synopsis than either the NEB or the RSV it is therefore perfect in all particulars.   The eagle-eyed will easily detect passages in the RV where identical words occur in parallel, but where the punctuation is different (*e.g.*, Matt. 12 45 ‖ Luke 11 26)—and for no apparent reason.   They will also notice occasional instances where precisely the same kind of inconsistency in rendering occurs as has been remarked on in the RSV, and which is so noteworthy a feature of the NEB: thus, in the passage set out in full on the previous page, ἰδεῖν is rendered in the RV by 'to see' at Luke 7 25 and by 'for to see' at Matt. 11 8 (the probable explanation here is that the Revisers revised the AV's 'for to see' in Luke but overlooked the necessity for revising it also in Matthew !   The American Standard Version of 1901, however, put this discrepancy right by reading 'to see' in both gospels.).   We have also to remember that since 1881 a number of hitherto unknown Greek manuscripts have been discovered and considerable advances made in the study of the text of the gospels.   Full advantage of these discoveries and advances has been taken in the RSV and in the NEB, both of which are consequently very much more up to date in this respect than is the RV.

Nevertheless, the fundamental point remains that what is primarily required of a version which is to serve as the basis in an English Synopsis is that it shall as clearly and unambiguously as possible reflect in English the agreements and disagreements between the gospels as they exist in Greek; and, judged by this criterion, neither the RSV nor the NEB can compare with the RV. If we are looking for a version to serve as the basis for a Synopsis, the RV's mechanical exactness and word-for-word literalness, the characteristics for which it has been so often abused (but which the Revisers themselves understood as 'faithfulness'), so far from being a drawback, become an outstanding and decisive recommendation.

TABLE OF CONTENTS

xv

F. THE PASSION AND RESURRECTION (§§ 225-259)

(i) The Prologue to the Passion (§§ 225-228)

(ii) In the Upper Room (§§ 229-234)

§		Matt.	Mark	Luke	John	Page

THE SYNOPTIC GOSPELS WITH THE JOHANNINE PARALLELS

§ 1. The Lucan Prologue

Luke 1 1-4

cp. 13 19 *ff.*	*cp.* 2 2 ; 4 14 *ff.*, 33 ; 16 20.	**1** Forasmuch as many have taken in hand to draw up a narrative concerning those matters which have been [1] fulfilled among us, **2** even as they delivered them unto us, which from the beginning were eyewitnesses and ministers of the word [*cp.* 4 32 ; 8 12 *ff.*: *also* 5 1 ; 8 11, 21 ; 11 28], **3** it seemed good to me also, having traced the course of all things accurately from the first, to write unto thee in order, most excellent Theophilus ; **4** that thou mightest know the certainty concerning the [2] things [3] wherein thou wast instructed.

[1] Or, *fully established*　　　[2] Gr. *words.*
[3] Or, *which thou wast taught by word of mouth*

cp. 4 41 ; 5 24, 38 ; *etc.*

A. The Birth and Childhood (§§ 2-15)

(i) The Birth and Childhood according to Matthew (§§ 2-6)

§ 2. The Genealogy of Jesus

Matt. 1 1-17		Luke 3 23-38
1 [1] The book of the [2] generation of Jesus Christ, the son of David [*cp.* 9 27 ; 12 23 ; 15 22 ; 20 30, 31 ; 21 9, 15], the son of Abraham. **2** Abraham begat Isaac ; and Isaac begat Jacob ; and Jacob begat Judah and his brethren ; **3** and Judah begat Perez and Zerah of Tamar ; and Perez begat Hezron ; and Hezron begat [3] Ram ; **4** and [3] Ram begat Amminadab ; and Amminadab begat Nahshon ; and Nahshon begat Salmon ; **5** and Salmon begat Boaz of Rahab ; and Boaz begat Obed of Ruth ; and Obed begat Jesse ; **6** and Jesse begat David the king. And David begat Solomon of her *that had been the wife* of Uriah ; **7** and Solomon begat Rehoboam ; and Rehoboam begat Abijah ; and Abijah begat [4] Asa ; **8** and [4] Asa begat Jehoshaphat ; and Jehoshaphat begat Joram ; and Joram begat Uzziah ; **9** and Uzziah begat Jotham ; and Jotham begat Ahaz ; and Ahaz begat Hezekiah ; **10** and Hezekiah begat Manasseh ; and Manasseh begat [5] Amon ; and [5] Amon begat Josiah ; **11** and Josiah begat Jechoniah and his brethren, at the time of the [6] carrying away to Babylon. **12** And after the [6] carrying away to Babylon, Jechoniah begat [7] Shealtiel ; and [7] Shealtiel begat Zerubbabel ; **13** and Zerubbabel begat Abiud ; and Abiud begat Eliakim ; and Eliakim begat Azor ; **14** and Azor begat Sadoc ; and Sadoc begat Achim ; and Achim begat Eliud ; **15** and Eliud begat Eleazar ; and Eleazar begat Matthan ; and Matthan	*cp.* 10 47, 48.	**23** And Jesus himself, when he began *to teach*, was about thirty years of age, *cp.* 18 38, 39 ; *also* 1 32. being the son (as was supposed) of Joseph, the *son* of Heli, **24** the *son* of Matthat, the *son* of Levi, the *son* of Melchi, the *son* of Jannai, the *son* of Joseph, **25** the *son* of Mattathias, the *son* of Amos, the *son* of Nahum, the *son* of Esli, the *son* of Naggai, **26** the *son* of Maath, the *son* of Mattathias, the *son* of Semein, the *son* of Josech, the *son* of Joda, **27** the *son* of Joanan, the *son* of Rhesa, the *son* of Zerubbabel, the *son* of [1] Shealtiel, the *son* of Neri, **28** the *son* of Melchi, the *son* of Addi, the *son* of Cosam, the *son* of Elmadam, the *son* of Er, **29** the *son* of Jesus, the *son* of Eliezer, the *son* of Jorim, the *son* of Matthat, the *son* of Levi, **30** the *son* of Symeon, the *son* of Judas, the *son* of Joseph, the *son* of Jonam, the *son* of Eliakim, **31** the *son* of Melea, the *son* of Menna, the *son* of Mattatha, the *son* of Nathan, the *son* of David, **32** the *son* of Jesse, the *son* of Obed, the *son* of Boaz, the *son* of [2] Salmon, the *son* of Nahshon, **33** the *son* of Amminadab, [3] the *son* of [4] Arni, the *son* of Hezron, the *son* of Perez, the *son* of Judah, **34** the *son* of Jacob, the *son* of Isaac, the *son* of Abraham, the *son* of Terah, the *son* of Nahor, **35** the *son* of Serug, the *son* of Reu, the *son* of Peleg, the *son* of

begat Jacob ; **16** and Jacob begat Joseph the husband of Mary, of whom was born Jesus, who is called Christ [*cp.* 27 17, 22].

17 So all the generations from Abraham unto David are fourteen generations ; and from David unto the ⁶ carrying away to Babylon fourteen generations ; and from the ⁶ carrying away to Babylon unto the Christ [*cp.* 11 2] fourteen generations.

¹ Or, *The genealogy of Jesus Christ*
² Or, *birth* : as in ver. 18.   ³ Gr. *Aram.*
⁴ Gr. *Asaph.*   ⁵ Gr. *Amos.*
⁶ Or, *removal to Babylon*   ⁷ Gr. *Salathiel.*

Eber, the *son* of Shelah, **36** the *son* of Cainan, the *son* of Arphaxad, the *son* of Shem, the *son* of Noah, the *son* of Lamech, **37** the *son* of Methuselah, the *son* of Enoch, the *son* of Jared, the *son* of Mahalaleel, the *son* of Cainan, **38** the *son* of Enos, the *son* of Seth, the *son* of Adam, the *son* of God.

¹ Gr. *Salathiel.*
² Some ancient authorities write *Sala.*
³ Many ancient authorities insert *the* son *of Admin* : and one writes *Admin* for *Amminadab.*
⁴ Some ancient authorities write *Aram.*

cp. **4** 25.

§ 3. The Birth of Jesus

Matt. 1 18-25

18 Now the ¹ birth ² of Jesus Christ was on this wise : When his mother Mary had been betrothed to Joseph, before they came together she was found with child of the ³ Holy Ghost. **19** And Joseph her husband, being a righteous man, and not willing to make her a public example, was minded to put her away privily. **20** But when he thought on these things, behold, an angel of the Lord appeared unto him in a dream [*cp.* 2 12, 13, 19, 22 ; 27 19], saying, Joseph, thou son of David, fear not to take unto thee Mary thy wife : for that which is ⁴ conceived in her is of the Holy Ghost. **21** And she shall bring forth a son ; and thou shalt call his name JESUS ; for it is he that shall save his people from their sins. **22** Now all this is come to pass, that it might be fulfilled which was spoken by the Lord through the prophet, saying,

  23 Behold, the virgin shall be with child, and shall
      bring forth a son,
    And they shall call his name ⁵ Immanuel ;

which is, being interpreted, God with us [*cp.* 28 20]. **24** And Joseph arose from his sleep, and did as the angel of the Lord commanded him, and took unto him his wife ; **25** and knew her not till she had brought forth a son : and he called his name JESUS.

¹ Or, *generation* : as in ver. 1.   ² Some ancient authorities read *of the Christ.*
³ Or, *Holy Spirit* : and so throughout this book.
⁴ Gr. *begotten.*   ⁵ Gr. *Emmanuel.*

cp. 1 27 ; 2 5.
cp. 1 35.

cp. 1 26, 27.
cp. 1 27 ; 2 4.
cp. 1 35.
cp. 1 31.
cp. 2 11 ; 19 10.

cp. 3 17 ; 4 42 ; 5 34 ; 10 9 ; 12 47.

cp. 2 21.

Matt. 1 23. = Is. 7 14.

§ 4. The Visit of the Magi

Matt. 2 1-12

1 Now when Jesus was born in Bethlehem of Judæa in the days of Herod the king, behold, ¹ wise men from the east came to Jerusalem, **2** saying, ² Where is he that is born King of the Jews [*cp.* 27 11, 29, 37] ? for we saw his star in the east, and are come to worship him. **3** And when Herod the king heard it, he was troubled, and all Jerusalem with him. **4** And gathering together all the chief priests and scribes of the people, he inquired of them where the Christ should be born. **5** And they said unto him, In Bethlehem of Judæa : for thus it is written ³ by the prophet,

  6 And thou Bethlehem, land [*cp.* 2 20, 21 ; 4 15 ; 10 15 ; 11 24] of Judah,
    Art in no wise least among the princes of Judah :
    For out of thee shall come forth a governor,
    Which shall be shepherd of my people Israel.

7 Then Herod privily called the ¹ wise men, and learned of them carefully ⁴ what time the star appeared. **8** And he sent them to Bethlehem, and said, Go and search out carefully concerning the young child ; and when ye have found *him*,

cp. 15 2, 9, 12, 18, 26.

cp. 1 5 ; 2 4-7.
cp. 23 3, 37, 38.

cp. 18 33, 39 ; 19 3, 19, 21.

cp. 7 42.

cp. 3 22.

bring me word, that I also may come and worship him.
9 And they, having heard the king, went their way; and lo,
the star, which they saw in the east, went before them, till it
came and stood over where the young child was.　**10** And
when they saw the star, they rejoiced with exceeding great
joy.　**11** And they came into the house and saw the young
child with Mary his mother; and they fell down [*cp.* 17 14]
and worshipped him [*cp.* 8 2; 9 18; 14 33; 15 25; 20 20;
28 9, 17]; and opening their treasures they offered unto him
gifts [*cp.* 5 23, 24; 8 4], gold and frankincense and myrrh.
12 And being warned *of God* in a dream [*cp.* 1 20; 2 13, 19, 22;
27 19] that they should not return to Herod, they departed
into their own country another way.

	cp. 1 40; 3 11; 5 22, 33; 7 25; 10 17: *also* 5 6.	*cp.* 5 8, 12; 8 28, 41, 47; 17 16: *also* 24 52.	*cp.* 11 32; 18 6: *also* 9 38.

¹ Gr. *Magi.* Compare Esth. 1 13; Dan. 2 12.
² Or, *Where is the King of the Jews that is born?*
³ Or, *through*
⁴ Or, *the time of the star that appeared*

Matt. 2 6=Mic. 5 2: *cp.* II Sam. 5 2; Mic. 5 4.

§ 5. The Flight to Egypt and the Slaughter of the Innocents

Matt. 2 13-18

13 Now when they were departed, behold, an angel of the Lord
appeareth to Joseph in a dream [*cp.* 1 20; 2 12, 19, 22; 27 19],
saying, Arise and take the young child and his mother, and flee
into Egypt, and be thou there until I tell thee: for Herod will
seek the young child to destroy him.　**14** And he arose and took
the young child and his mother by night, and departed into
Egypt; **15** and was there until the death of Herod: that it
might be fulfilled which was spoken by the Lord through the
prophet, saying, Out of Egypt did I call my son.　**16** Then
Herod, when he saw that he was mocked of the ¹ wise men,
was exceeding wroth, and sent forth, and slew all the male
children that were in Bethlehem, and in all the borders thereof,
from two years old and under, according to the time which he
had carefully learned of the ¹ wise men.　**17** Then was fulfilled
that which was spoken ² by Jeremiah the prophet, saying,
18 A voice was heard in Ramah,
　　Weeping and great mourning,
　　Rachel weeping for her children;
　　And she would not be comforted, because they are not.

¹ Gr. *Magi.* Compare Esth. 1 13; Dan. 2 12.　　² Or, *through*

Matt. 2 15=Hos. 11 1.　　　Matt. 2 18=Jer. 31 15.

§ 6. The Return from Egypt and the Settlement at Nazareth

Matt. 2 19-23

19 But when Herod was dead, behold, an angel of the Lord
appeareth in a dream [*cp.* 1 20; 2 12, 13, 22; 27 19] to Joseph
in Egypt, **20** saying, Arise and take the young child and his
mother, and go into the land [*cp.* 2 6, 21; 4 15; 10 15; 11 24]
of Israel: for they are dead that sought the young child's life.
21 And he arose and took the young child and his mother, and
came into the land [*see above*] of Israel.　**22** But when he heard
that Archelaus was reigning over Judæa in the room of his father
Herod, he was afraid to go thither; and being warned *of God* in
a dream [*cp.* 1 20; 2 12, 13, 19; 27 19], he withdrew into the
parts of Galilee, **23** and came and dwelt in a city called Nazareth:
that it might be fulfilled which was spoken ¹ by the prophets,
that he should be called a Nazarene [*cp.* 21 11; 26 71].

			cp. 3 22.
		cp. 2 39.	
	cp. 1 24; 10 47; 14 67; 16 6.	*cp.* 4 34; 18 37; 24 19.	*cp.* 1 45; 18 5, 7; 19 19.

¹ Or, *through*

Matt. 2 23=?

(ii) The Birth and Childhood according to Luke (§§ 7-15)

§ 7. The Announcement of the Birth of John the Baptist

Luke 1 5-25

5 There was in the days of Herod, king of Judæa, a certain priest named Zacharias, of the course of Abijah: and he had a wife of the daughters of Aaron, and her name was Elisabeth. **6** And they were both righteous before God, walking in all the commandments and ordinances of the Lord blameless. **7** And they had no child, because that Elisabeth was barren, and they both were *now* [1] well stricken in years.
8 Now it came to pass, while he executed the priest's office before God in the order of his course, **9** according to the custom of the priest's office, his lot was to enter into the [2] temple of the Lord and burn incense. **10** And the whole multitude of the people were praying without at the hour of incense. **11** And there appeared unto him an angel of the Lord standing on the right side of the altar of incense. **12** And Zacharias was troubled when he saw *him*, and fear fell upon him [*cp.* 1 65; 2 9; 5 26; 7 16; 8 25, 35, 37, 47; 9 34, 45; 24 5, 37]. **13** But the angel said unto him, Fear not, Zacharias: because thy supplication is heard, and thy wife Elisabeth shall bear thee a son, and thou shalt call his name John. **14** And thou shalt have joy and gladness; and many shall rejoice at his birth. **15** For he shall be great in the sight of the Lord, and he shall drink no wine nor [3] strong drink [*cp.* 7 33]; and he shall be filled with the [4] Holy Ghost [*cp.* 1 41, 67; 4 1], even from his mother's womb. **16** And many of the children of Israel shall he turn unto the Lord their God. **17** And he shall [5] go before his face in the spirit and power [*cp.* 1 35; 4 14, 36; 5 17; 6 19; 8 46; 9 1; 24 49] of Elijah [*cp.* 1 76; 3 4; 7 27], to turn the hearts of the fathers to the children, and the disobedient *to walk* in the wisdom of the just; to make ready for the Lord a people prepared *for him*. **18** And Zacharias said unto the angel, Whereby shall I know this? for I am an old man, and my wife [6] well stricken in years. **19** And the angel answering said unto him, I am Gabriel, that stand in the presence of God; and I was sent to speak unto thee, and to bring thee these good tidings [*cp.* 2 10; 3 18; 4 18, 43; 7 22; 8 1; 9 6; 16 16; 20 1]. **20** And behold, thou shalt be silent and not able to speak, until the day that these things shall come to pass, because thou believedst not my words, which shall be fulfilled in their season. **21** And the people were waiting for Zacharias, and they marvelled [7] while he tarried in the [2] temple. **22** And when he came out, he could not speak unto them: and they perceived that he had seen a vision in the [2] temple: and he continued making signs unto them, and remained dumb. **23** And it came to pass, when the days of his ministration were fulfilled, he departed unto his house.
24 And after these days Elisabeth his wife conceived; and she hid herself five months, saying, **25** Thus hath the Lord done unto me in the days wherein he looked upon *me*, to take away my reproach among men.

[1] Gr. *advanced in their days.*   [2] Or, *sanctuary*   [3] Gr. *sikera.*
[4] Or, *Holy Spirit* : and so throughout this book.
[5] Some ancient authorities read *come nigh before his face.*
[6] Gr. *advanced in her days.*   [7] Or, *at his tarrying*

Left margin references:
cp. 2 1.

cp. 9 8; 17 6; 27 54; 28 4, 8.

cp. 11 18.

cp. 3 3, 4; 11 10, 14; 17 10-13.

cp. 11 5.

cp. 4 41; 5 15, 33; 9 6, 32; 10 32; 16 8.

cp. 5 30.
cp. 1 2, 3, 6; 9 11-13.

Right margin references:
cp. 1 21, 23; 3 28.

Luke 1 17: *cp.* Mal. 4 5-6.

§ 8. The Announcement of the Birth of Jesus

Luke 1 26-38

26 Now in the sixth month the angel Gabriel was sent from God unto a city of Galilee, named Nazareth, **27** to a virgin betrothed to a man whose name was Joseph [*cp.* 2 5], of the house of David [*cp.* 2 4]; and the virgin's name was Mary. **28** And he came in unto her, and said, Hail, thou that art

Left margin references:
cp. 1 20.

cp. 1 18.
cp. 1 20.

cp. 1 21.	*cp.* 5 7.	
cp. 1 1; 9 27; 12 23; 15 22; 20 30, 31; 21 9, 15.	*cp.* 10 47, 48.	
cp. 1 18, 20.	*cp.* 5 30. *cp.* 5 7.	
cp. 4 3, 6; 8 29; 14 33; 16 16; 26 63; 27 40, 43, 54: *also* 3 17; 17 5.	*cp.* 1 1; 3 11; 5 7; 15 39: *also* 1 11; 9 7.	*cp.* 1 34; *etc.*

¹ highly favoured, the Lord *is* with thee ². **29** But she was greatly troubled at the saying, and cast in her mind what manner of salutation this might be. **30** And the angel said unto her, Fear not, Mary: for thou hast found ³ favour with God. **31** And behold, thou shalt conceive in thy womb, and bring forth a son, and shalt call his name JESUS. **32** He shall be great, and shall be called the Son of the Most High [*cp.* 1 35, 76; 6 35; 8 28]: and the Lord God shall give unto him the throne of his father David [*cp.* 18 38, 39]: **33** and he shall reign over the house of Jacob ⁴ for ever; and of his kingdom there shall be no end. **34** And Mary said unto the angel, How shall this be, seeing I know not a man? **35** And the angel answered and said unto her, The Holy Ghost shall come upon thee, and the power [*cp.* 1 17; 4 14, 36; 5 17; 6 19; 8 46; 9 1; 24 49] of the Most High [*cp.* 1 32, 76; 6 35; 8 28] shall overshadow thee [*cp.* 24 49]: wherefore also ⁵ that which ⁶ is to be born ⁷ shall be called holy, the Son of God [*cp.* 4 3, 9, 41; 8 28; 22 70: *also* 3 22; 9 35]. **36** And behold, Elisabeth thy kinswoman, she also hath conceived a son in her old age: and this is the sixth month with her that ⁸ was called barren. **37** For no word from God shall be void of power [*cp.* Matt. 19 26: *also* 17 20; Mark 10 27; 14 36: *also* 9 23; Luke 18 27]. **38** And Mary said, Behold, the ⁹ handmaid of the Lord; be it unto me according to thy word. And the angel departed from her.

¹ Or, *endued with grace*
² Many ancient authorities add *blessed* art *thou among women.* See ver. 42.
³ Or, *grace*   ⁴ Gr. *unto the ages.*
⁵ Or, *the holy thing which is to be born shall be called the Son of God.*
⁶ Or, *is begotten*   ⁷ Some ancient authorities insert *of thee.*
⁸ Or, *is*   ⁹ Gr. *bondmaid.*

§ 9. Elizabeth visited by Mary

Luke 1 39-56

		cp. § 18.
cp. 6 9.		
		cp. Luke 1 72-73.

39 And Mary arose in these days and went into the hill country with haste, into a city of Judah; **40** and entered into the house of Zacharias and saluted Elisabeth. **41** And it came to pass, when Elisabeth heard the salutation of Mary, the babe leaped in her womb; and Elisabeth was filled with the Holy Ghost [*cp.* 1 15, 67; 4 1]; **42** and she lifted up her voice with a loud cry, and said, Blessed *art* thou among women, and blessed *is* the fruit of thy womb. **43** And whence is this to me, that the mother of my Lord should come unto me? **44** For behold, when the voice of thy salutation came into mine ears, the babe leaped in my womb for joy. **45** And blessed *is* she that ¹ believed; for there shall be a fulfilment of the things which have been spoken to her from the Lord. **46** And Mary said,
My soul doth magnify the Lord,
47 And my spirit hath rejoiced in God my Saviour.
48 For he hath looked upon the low estate of his ² hand-
maiden:
For behold, from henceforth [*cp.* 5 10; 12 52; 22 18, 69]
all generations shall call me blessed [*cp.* 11 27].
49 For he that is mighty hath done to me great things;
And holy is his name [*cp.* 11 2].
50 And his mercy is unto generations and generations
On them that fear him.
51 He hath shewed strength with his arm;
He hath scattered the proud ³ in the imagination of their
heart.
52 He hath put down princes from *their* thrones,
And hath exalted them of low degree.
53 The hungry he hath filled with good things;
And the rich he hath sent empty away.
54 He hath holpen Israel his servant,
That he might remember mercy
55 (As he spake unto our fathers)
Toward Abraham and his seed for ever.
56 And Mary abode with her about three months, and returned unto her house.

¹ Or, *believed that there shall be*   ² Gr. *bondmaiden.*   ³ Or, *by*

§ 10. The Birth and Childhood of John the Baptist

Luke 1 57-80

57 Now Elisabeth's time was fulfilled that she should be delivered; and she brought forth a son. **58** And her neighbours and her kinsfolk heard that the Lord had magnified his mercy towards her; and they rejoiced with her [*cp.* 15 6, 9]. **59** And it came to pass on the eighth day, that they came to circumcise the child; and they would have called him Zacharias, after the name of his father. **60** And his mother answered and said, Not so; but he shall be called John. **61** And they said unto her, There is none of thy kindred that is called by this name. **62** And they made signs to his father, what he would have him called. **63** And he asked for a writing tablet, and wrote, saying, His name is John. And they marvelled all. **64** And his mouth was opened immediately, and his tongue *loosed*, and he spake, blessing God [*cp.* 2 28; 24 53]. **65** And fear came on all that dwelt round about them [*cp.* 1 12; 2 9; 5 26; 7 16; 8 25, 35, 37, 47; 9 34, 45; 24 5, 37]: and all these sayings were noised abroad throughout all the hill country of Judæa. **66** And all that heard them laid them up in their heart [*cp.* 2 19, 51], saying, What then shall this child be? For the hand of the Lord was with him.

67 And his father Zacharias was filled with the Holy Ghost [*cp.* 1 15, 41; 4 1], and prophesied, saying,

68 Blessed *be* the Lord, the God of Israel;
    For he hath visited [*cp.* 1 78; 7 16] and wrought redemption [*cp.* 2 38; 21 28; 24 21] for his people,

69 And hath raised up a horn of salvation [*cp.* 1 71, 77; 2 30; 3 6; 19 9] for us
    In the house of his servant David

70 (As he spake by the mouth of his holy prophets which have been since the world began),

71 Salvation [*cp.* 1 69, 77; 2 30; 3 6; 19 9] from our enemies, and from the hand of all that hate us [*cp.* 6 22, 27; 21 17];

72 To shew mercy [*cp.* 10 37] towards our fathers,
    And to remember his holy covenant;

73 The oath which he sware unto Abraham our father,

74 To grant unto us that we being delivered out of the hand of our enemies
    Should serve him without fear,

75 In holiness and righteousness before him all our days.

76 Yea and thou, child, shalt be called the prophet [*cp.* 7 26; 20 6] of the Most High [*cp.* 1 32, 35; 6 35; 8 28]:
    For thou shalt go before the face of the Lord to make ready his ways [*cp.* 1 17; 3 4; 7 27];

77 To give knowledge of salvation [*cp.* 1 69, 71; 2 30; 3 6; 19 9] unto his people
    In the remission of their sins [*cp.* 3 3; 24 47],

78 Because of the [1] tender mercy of our God,
    [2] Whereby the dayspring from on high [*cp.* 24 49] [3] shall visit [*cp.* 1 68; 7 16] us,

79 To shine upon them that sit in darkness and the shadow of death;
    To guide our feet into the way of peace [*cp.* 2 14, 29; 10 5, 6; 19 38, 42].

80 And the child grew, and waxed strong [*cp.* 2 40] in spirit, and was in the deserts till the day of his shewing unto Israel.

[1] Or, *heart of mercy*   [2] Or, *Wherein*
[3] Many ancient authorities read *hath visited us.*

Left margin column 1 (cp. references):
- cp. 9 8; 17 6; 27 54; 28 4, 8.
- cp. 10 22; 24 9.
- cp. 11 9; 14 5; 21 26.
- cp. 3 3; 11 10, 14; 17 10-13.
- cp. 26 28.
- cp. 5 9; 10 13.

Left margin column 2 (cp. references):
- cp. 7 35.
- cp. 4 41; 5 15, 33; 9 6, 32; 10 32; 16 8.
- cp. 13 13.
- cp. 11 32.
- cp. 5 7.
- cp. 1 2, 3; 9 11-13.
- cp. 1 4.
- cp. 9 50.

Right margin column 1 (cp. references):
- cp. 4 22.
- cp. 4 22.
- cp. 15 18, 19; 17 14.
- cp. 1 21, 23; 3 28.
- cp. 4 22.
- cp. 14 27; 16 33.

Right margin column 2 (cp. references):
- cp. Luke 54-55

§ 11. The Birth of Jesus

Luke 2 1-7

1 Now it came to pass in those days, there went out a decree from Cæsar Augustus, that all [1] the world should be enrolled.

cp. 2 1.
cp. 1 20.
cp. 1 18.

2 This was the first enrolment made when Quirinius was governor of Syria. **3** And all went to enrol themselves, every one to his own city. **4** And Joseph also went up from Galilee, out of the city of Nazareth, into Judæa, to the city of David [*cp.* 2 11], which is called Bethlehem, because he was of the house and family of David [*cp.* 1 27]; **5** to enrol himself with Mary, who was betrothed to him [*cp.* 1 27], being great with child. **6** And it came to pass, while they were there, the days were fulfilled that she should be delivered. **7** And she brought forth her first-born son; and she wrapped him in swaddling clothes, and laid him in a manger, because there was no room for them in the inn.

cp. 7 42.

[1] Gr. *the inhabited earth.*

§ 12. The Visit of the Shepherds

Luke 2 8-20

cp. 9 8; 17 6; 27 54; 28 4, 8.
cp. 11 5.

cp. 4 41; 5 15, 33; 9 6, 32; 10 32; 16 8.

8 And there were shepherds in the same country abiding in the field, and keeping [1] watch by night over their flock. **9** And an angel of the Lord stood by them, and the glory of the Lord shone round about them: and they were sore afraid [*cp.* 1 12, 65; 5 26; 7 16; 8 25, 35, 37, 47; 9 34, 45; 24 5, 37]. **10** And the angel said unto them, Be not afraid; for behold, I bring you good tidings [*cp.* 1 19; 3 18; 4 18, 43; 7 22; 8 1; 9 6; 16 16; 20 1] of great joy which shall be to all the people:

cp. 1 21.

11 for there is born to you this day in the city of David [*cp.* 2 4] a Saviour [*cp.* 19 10], which is [2] Christ the Lord. **12** And this *is* the sign unto you; Ye shall find a babe wrapped in swaddling clothes, and lying in a manger. **13** And suddenly there was with the angel a multitude of the heavenly host praising God [*cp.* 2 20; 18 43; 19 37], and saying,

cp. 3 17; 4 42; 5 34; 10 9; 12 47.

cp. 5 9; 10 13.
cp. 3 17; 11 26; 12 18; 17 5.

cp. 9 50.
cp. 1 11.

14 Glory to God in the highest [*cp.* 19 38],
    And on earth [3] peace [*cp.* 1 79; 2 29; 10 5, 6; 19 38, 42] among [4] men in whom he is well pleased [*cp.* 3 22; 10 21; 12 32].

cp. 14 27; 16 33.

15 And it came to pass, when the angels went away from them into heaven, the shepherds said one to another, Let us now go even unto Bethlehem, and see this [5] thing that is come to pass, which the Lord hath made known unto us. **16** And they came with haste, and found both Mary and Joseph, and the babe lying in the manger. **17** And when they saw it, they made known concerning the saying which was spoken to them about this child. **18** And all that heard it wondered at the things which were spoken unto them by the shepherds. **19** But Mary kept all these [6] sayings, pondering them in her heart [*cp.* 1 66; 2 51]. **20** And the shepherds returned, glorifying [*cp.* 5 25, 26; 7 16; 13 13; 17 15, 18; 18 43; 23 47] and praising God [*cp.* 2 13; 18 43; 19 37] for all the things that they had heard and seen, even as it was spoken unto them.

cp. 5 16; 9 8; 15 31.

cp. 2 12.

cp. 9 24: *also* 15 8

[1] Or, *night-watches*   [2] Or, *Anointed Lord*
[3] Many ancient authorities read *peace, good pleasure among men.*
[4] Gr. *men of good pleasure.*   [5] Or, *saying*   [6] Or, *things*

§ 13. The Circumcision

Luke 2 21

cp. 1 25.

21 And when eight days were fulfilled for circumcising him, his name was called JESUS, which was so called by the angel before he was conceived in the womb.

§ 14. The Presentation in the Temple and the Return to Nazareth

Luke 2 22-40

22 And when the days of their purification according to the law of Moses were fulfilled, they brought him up to Jerusalem, to present him to the Lord **23** (as it is written in the law of the Lord, Every male that openeth the womb shall be called holy to the Lord), **24** and to offer a sacrifice according to that which is said in the law of the Lord, A pair of turtledoves, or two young pigeons. **25** And behold, there was a man in Jerusalem, whose name was Simeon; and this man was righteous and devout, looking for [*cp.* 2 38; 23 51] the consolation of Israel: and the Holy Spirit was upon him. **26** And it had been revealed unto him by the Holy Spirit, that he should not see death, before he had seen the Lord's Christ. **27** And he came in the Spirit into the temple: and when the parents brought in the child Jesus, that they might do concerning him after the custom of the law, **28** then he received him into his arms, and blessed God [*cp.* 1 64; 24 53], and said,

> **29** Now lettest thou thy [1] servant depart, O [2] Lord,
> According to thy word, in peace [*cp.* 1 79; 2 14; 10 5, 6; 19 38, 42];
> **30** For mine eyes have seen thy salvation [*cp.* 1 69, 71, 77; 3 6; 19 9],
> **31** Which thou hast prepared before the face of all peoples [*cp.* 3 6; 24 47: *also* 13 29; 14 21-24; 20 16];
> **32** A light for [3] revelation to the Gentiles,
> And the glory of thy people Israel.

33 And his father and his mother were marvelling at the things which were spoken concerning him; **34** and Simeon blessed them, and said unto Mary his mother, Behold, this *child* is set for the falling and rising up of many in Israel; and for a sign which is spoken against; **35** yea and a sword shall pierce through thine own soul; that thoughts out of many hearts may be revealed. **36** And there was one Anna, a prophetess, the daughter of Phanuel, of the tribe of Asher (she was [4] of a great age, having lived with a husband seven years from her virginity, **37** and she had been a widow [*cp.* 4 25, 26; 7 12; 18 3; 20 47; 21 2] even for fourscore and four years), which departed not from the temple, worshipping with fastings and supplications [*cp.* 5 33] night and day. **38** And coming up at that very hour she gave thanks unto God, and spake of him to all them that were looking for [*cp.* 2 25; 23 51] the redemption [*cp.* 1 68; 21 28; 24 21] of Jerusalem. **39** And when they had accomplished all things that were according to the law of the Lord, they returned into Galilee, to their own city Nazareth. **40** And the child grew, and waxed strong [*cp.* 1 80], [5] filled with wisdom: and the grace of God was upon him [*cp.* 2 52].

Left margin notes:
cp. 5 9; 10 13.

cp. 10 18; 24 14; 26 13; 28 19: *also* 8 11; 21 31, 41, 43; 22 7-10.

cp. 2 22, 23.

Second column margin notes:
cp. 15 43.

cp. 9 50.

cp. 13 10; 14 9; 16 15: *also* 12 9.

cp. 12 40, 42.

cp. 15 43.

Right margin notes:
cp. 14 27; 16 33.

cp. 4 22.

cp. 10 16; 11 52.

[1] Gr. *bondservant*.   [2] Gr. *Master*.   [3] Or, *the unveiling of the Gentiles*   [4] Gr. *advanced in many days*.   [5] Gr. *becoming full of wisdom*.

Luke 2 22: *cp.* Lev. 12 1-4.   Luke 2 23 = Exod. 13 2, 12.   Luke 2 24 = Lev. 12 8.

§ 15. Jesus in the Temple at the Age of Twelve

Luke 2 41-52

41 And his parents went every year to Jerusalem at the feast of the passover. **42** And when he was twelve years old, they went up after the custom of the feast; **43** and when they had fulfilled the days, as they were returning, the boy Jesus tarried behind in Jerusalem; and his parents knew it not; **44** but supposing him to be in the company, they went a day's journey; and they sought for him among their kinsfolk and acquaintance: **45** and when they found him not, they returned to Jerusalem, seeking for him. **46** And it came to pass, after three days they found him in the temple, sitting in the

cp. 7 28; 13 54; 19 25; 22 22, 33: *also* 8 27; 9 33; 12 23; 15 31; 21 20; 27 14.	*cp.* 1 22, 27; 6 2; 10 24, 26; 11 18; 12 17: *also* 2 12; 5 20, 42; 6 51; 7 37; 10 32; 15 5; 16 8.	midst of the 1 doctors. both hearing them, and asking them questions: **47** and all that heard him were amazed at his understanding and his answers [*cp.* 4 22, 32, 36; 20 26: *also* 5 9, 26; 8 25, 56; 9 43; 11 14; 24 12, 41]. **48** And when they saw him, they were astonished [*see verse* 47 *above*]: and his mother said unto him, 2 Son, why hast thou thus dealt with us? behold, thy father and I sought thee sorrowing. **49** And he said unto them, How is it that ye sought me? wist ye not that I must be 3 in my Father's house? **50** And they understood not the saying which he spake unto them [*cp.* 9 45; 18 34]. **51** And he went down with them, and	*cp.* 7 15, 21, 46.
cp. 15 16; 16 9, 11.	*cp.* 9 32; 4 13; 6 52; 7 18; 8 17, 21; 9 10; 16 14.	came to Nazareth; and he was subject unto them: and his mother kept all *these* 4 sayings in her heart [*cp.* 1 66; 2 19]. **52** And Jesus advanced in wisdom and 5 stature, and in 6 favour with God and men [*cp.* 2 40].	*cp.* 10 6; 12 16: 3 10; 4 33; 8 27, 43; 11 13; 13 7, 28, 36; 14 5-10, 22; 16 17, 18.

1 Or, *teachers*   2 Gr. *Child.*
3 Or, *about my Father's business* Gr. *in the things of my Father.*
4 Or, *things*   5 Or, *age*   6 Or, *grace*

B. The Preparation for the Ministry (§§ 16-22)

(i) The Mission and Message of John the Baptist (§§ 16-19)

§ 16. **The Appearance of John**

Matt. 3 1-6	**Mark 1** 1-6	**Luke 3** 1-6	John 1 6, 23
cp. 4 23; 9 35; 24 14; 26 13.	**1** The beginning of the gospel [*cp.* 1 14, 15; 8 35; 10 29; 13 10; 14 9; 16 15] of Jesus Christ, 1 the Son of God [*cp.* 3 11; 5 7; 15 39: *also* 1 11; 9 7].		
cp. 4 3, 6; 8 29; 14 33; 16 16; 26 63; 27 40, 43, 54; *also* 3 17; 17 5. **1** And in those days		*cp.* 1 35; 4 3, 9, 41; 8 28; 22 70: *also* 3 22; 9 35. **1** Now in the fifteenth year of the reign of Tiberius Cæsar, Pontius Pilate being governor of Judæa, and Herod being tetrarch of Galilee, and his brother Philip tetrarch of the region of Ituræa and Trachonitis, and Lysanias tetrarch of Abilene, **2** in the high-priesthood of Annas and Caiaphas, the word of God came unto	*cp.* 1 34; *etc.*
cp. 26 3, 57. cometh			*cp.* 18 13, 24. *cp.* 11 49; 18 13, 14, 24, 28.
John the Baptist, preaching in the wilderness of Judæa [*cp. vv.* 5, 6],	*verse* 4	John the son of Zacharias in the wilderness. **3** And he came into all the region round about Jordan, preaching the baptism of repentance unto remission of sins [*cp.* 1 77; 24 47];	**1** 6 There came a man, sent from God, whose name was John. *cp.* 1 28; 3 23, 26; 10 40.
cp. 26 28. **2** saying, Repent ye; for the kingdom of heaven is at hand [*cp.* 4 17; 10 7; *also* 12 28]. **3** For this is he that was spoken of 1 by	*cp.* 1 15: *also* 6 12. **2** Even **as it is written** 2 in [*cp.* 12 26]	*cp.* 10 9, 11: *also* 9 2; 11 20; 17 20, 21; 19 11; 21 8. **4** as it is written in the book [*cp.* 4 17; 20 42] of the words of	

Isaiah the prophet, saying,	Isaiah the prophet,	Isaiah the prophet,	
11 10	Behold, I send my messenger before thy face,	7 27	
cp. 3 4; 11 14; 17 10-13.	Who shall prepare thy way [*cp.* 1 6; 9 11-13];	*cp.* 1 17, 76.	*cp.* 1 21; 3 28.
			1 23 He said, I am the voice of one crying in the wilderness,
The voice of one crying in the wilderness, Make ye ready the way of the Lord, Make his paths straight.	3 The voice of one crying in the wilderness, Make ye ready the way of the Lord, Make his paths straight;	The voice of one crying in the wilderness, Make ye ready the way of the Lord, Make his paths straight.	
		5 Every valley shall be filled, And every mountain and hill shall be brought low; And the crooked shall become straight, And the rough ways smooth;	Make straight the way of the Lord, as said Isaiah the prophet.
cp. 10 18; 24 14; 26 13; 28 19: *also* 8 11; 21 31, 41, 43; 22 7-10.	*cp.* 13 10; 14 9; 16 15: *also* 12 9.	6 And all flesh [*cp.* 2 30-32; 24 47: *also* 13 29; 14 21-24; 20 16] shall see the salvation [*cp.* 1 69,71,77; 2 30; 19 9] of God.	*cp.* 10 16; 11 52.
			cp. 4 22.
verse 1	4 John came, who baptized in the wilderness and preached the baptism of repentance unto remission of sins. 5 And there went out unto him all the country of Judæa, and all they of Jerusalem; and they were baptized of him in the river Jordan, confessing their sins [*cp.* 11 32].	*verse* 3	*cp.* 1 28; 3 23, 26; 10 40.
cp. 26 28.		*cp.* 1 77; 24 47.	
verses 5 *and* 6		*cp. verse* 7.	
cp. 14 5; 21 26, 32.		*cp.* 7 29; 20 6.	
4 Now John himself had his raiment of camel's hair, and a leathern girdle about his loins [*cp.* 11 14; 17 10-13]; and his food was locusts and wild honey [*cp.* 11 18]. 5 Then went out unto him Jerusalem, and all Judæa, and all the region round about Jordan; 6 and they were baptized of him in the river Jordan, confessing their sins [*cp.* 14 5; 21 26, 32].	6 And John was clothed with camel's hair, and *had* a leathern girdle about his loins [*cp.* 1 2; 9 11-13], and did eat locusts and wild honey.	*cp.* 1 17, 76.	*cp.* 1 21.
		cp. 7 33.	
	verse 5	*cp. verse* 7.	
	cp. 11 32.	*cp.* 7 29; 20 6.	

[1] Or, *through*

[1] Some ancient authorities omit *the Son of God.*
[2] Some ancient authorities read *in the prophets.*

Mark 1 2 = Exod. 23 20; Mal. 3 1.   Matt. 3 3 ‖ Mark 1 3 ‖ Luke 3 4 ‖ John 1 23 = Is. 40 3.   Luke 3 5-6 = Is. 40 4-5.

§ 17. The Public Preaching of John

Matt. 3 7-10		**Luke 3** 7-14	
7 But when he saw many [*cp.* 5 1; 8 18; 9 36] of the Pharisees and Sadducees coming to his baptism [*cp.* 3 5, 6; 14 5; 21 26, 32], he said unto them, Ye offspring of vipers [*cp.* 12 34; 23 33], who warned you	*cp.* 1 5; 11 32.	7 He said therefore to the multitudes that went out to be baptized of him [*cp.* 7 29; 20 6], Ye offspring of vipers, who warned you	

to flee from the wrath to come?
8 Bring forth therefore fruit worthy
of ¹ repentance: **9** and think not to
say within yourselves, We have
Abraham to our father:

for I say unto you,
that God is able of these stones to
raise up children unto Abraham.
10 And even now is the axe   laid
unto the root of the trees: every tree
therefore that bringeth not forth good
fruit is hewn down, and cast into the
fire [=7 19: cp. 3 12; 5 22, 29, 30; 10
28; 13 42, 50; 18 8, 9; 23 33; 25 41].

¹ Or, *your repentance*

cp. 19 16.   cp. 10 17.

cp. 10 10.   cp. 6 9.
cp. 21 32.

to flee from the wrath to come?
8 Bring forth therefore fruits worthy
of ¹ repentance, and begin not to
say within yourselves, We have
Abraham to our father [cp. 13 16;
16 24, 30; 19 9]: for I say unto you,
that God is able of these stones to
raise up children unto Abraham.
9 And even now is the axe also laid
unto the root of the trees: every tree
therefore that bringeth not forth good
fruit is hewn down, and cast into the
fire [cp. 13 7-9: also 3 17; 12 5]. **10** And
the multitudes [cp. verse 7] asked him,
saying, What then must we do
[cp. 3 12, 14; 10 25; 18 18]? **11** And he answered and said unto
them, He that hath two coats, let him impart to him that hath
none [cp. 9 3]; and he that hath food, let him do likewise.
12 And there came also ²publicans [cp. 7 29] to be baptized,
and they said unto him, ³ Master, what must we do [cp. verse 10
etc., above]? **13** And he said unto them, Extort no more than
that which is appointed you. **14** And ⁴ soldiers also asked
him, saying, And we, what must we do [cp. verse 10, etc., above]?
And he said unto them, Do violence to no man, neither ⁵ exact
anything wrongfully [cp. 19 8]; and be content with your wages.

¹ Or, *your repentance*   ² See footnote on Matt. 5 46.   ³ Or, *Teacher*
⁴ Gr. *soldiers on service.*   ⁵ Or, *accuse* anyone

cp. 9 43, 45, 47.

cp. 8 33, 37, 39, 53.

cp. 15 2, 6.

cp. 6 28.

§18. The Testimony of John concerning his Relationship to the Christ

[Cp. Matt. 3 14; Luke 1 41-44; John 1 15, 29-34, 35-36; 3 26-30: *also* Matt. 11 2-19; 17 10-13; 21 24-32;
Mark 9 11-13; 11 29-33; Luke 7 18-35; 16 16; 20 3-8; John 1 1-8; 5 33-36; 10 41; Acts 1 5; 11 16;
18 25; 19 1-7.]

Matt. 3 11-12	**Mark 1** 7-8	**Luke 3** 15-17	John 1 19-27	Acts 13 25
		15 And as the people were in expectation, and all men reasoned in their hearts concerning John, whether haply he were the Christ;	**19** And this is the witness of John, when the Jews sent unto him from Jerusalem priests and Levites to ask him, Who art thou? **20** And he confessed, and denied not; and he confessed, I am not the Christ. **21** And they asked him, What then? Art thou Elijah? And	**25** And as John was fulfilling his course, he said, What suppose ye that I am? I am not *he.*
cp. 3 4; 11 10, 14; 17 10-13.	cp. 1 2, 6; 9 11-13.	cp. 1 17, 76; 7 27.		
cp. 3 3.	cp. 1 3.	cp. 3 4.	he saith, I am not. Art thou the prophet? And he answered, No. **22** They said therefore unto him, Who art thou? that we may give an answer to them that sent us. What sayest thou of thyself? **23** He said, I am the voice of one crying in the wilderness, Make straight the way of the Lord, as said Isaiah the prophet. **24** ¹And they had been sent from the Pharisees. **25** And they asked him, and said unto him, Why then baptizest thou, if thou art not the Christ, neither Elijah, neither the prophet? **26** John answered them, saying, I baptize ²with water: in the midst of you standeth one whom ye know not, **27** *even* he that cometh [cp. 1 15, 30; 3 31; 6 14; 11 27; 12 13]	
11 I indeed baptize you ¹ with water unto repentance: but he that cometh [cp. 11 3; 21 9; 23 39]	**7** And he preached, saying, *verse 8* There cometh [cp. 11 9]	**16** John answered, saying unto them all, I indeed baptize you with water; but there cometh [cp. 7 19, 20; 13 35; 19 38]		But behold, there cometh

after me is mightier than I, whose shoes I am ²not worthy to bear:	after me he that is mightier than I, the latchet of whose shoes I am not ¹worthy to stoop down and unloose. **8** I baptized you ²with water;	he that is mightier than I, the latchet of whose shoes I am ¹ worthy to unloose:	after me, the latchet of whose shoe I am not worthy to	one after me, the shoes of whose feet I am not worthy to
he shall baptize you ¹with the Ho- ly Ghost and *with* fire: **12** whose fan is in his hand, and he will throughly cleanse his threshing-floor; and he will gather his wheat into the garner [*cp.*13 30: *also* 24 31], but the chaff he will burn up with unquen- chable fire [*cp.* 3 10; 5 22, 29, 30; 7 19; 10 28; 13 42, 50; 18 8, 9; 23 33; 25 41: *also* 13 49; 25 32].	but he shall baptize you ²with the ³Ho- ly Ghost. *cp.* 13 27. *cp.* 9 43, 45, 47, 48.	he shall baptize you ²with the Ho- ly Ghost and *with* fire [*cp.* 12 49, 50]: **17** whose fan is in his hand, throughly to cleanse his threshing-floor, and to gather the wheat into his garner; but the chaff he will burn up with unquen- chable fire [*cp.* 3 9; 12 5].	*cp.* 1 33. *cp.* 15 2, 6.	unloose. *cp.* 11 16: *also* 1 5; 19 6.
¹ Or, *in* ² Gr. *sufficient*.	¹ Gr. *sufficient*. ² Or, *in* ³ Or, *Holy Spirit*: and so throughout this book.	¹ Gr. *sufficient*. ² Or, *in*	¹ Or, *And* certain *had been sent from among the Pharisees*. ² Or, *in*	

§ 19. The Imprisonment of John

Matt. 14 3-4	Mark 6 17-18	Luke 3 18-20
cp. 11 5.		**18** With many other [*cp.* 22 65] exhortations therefore preached he ¹ good tidings [*cp.* 1 19; 2 10; 4 18, 43; 7 22; 8 1; 9 6; 16 16; 20 1] unto the people;
3 For Herod had laid hold on John, and bound him, and put him in prison for the sake of Herodias, his brother Philip's wife. **4** For John said unto him, It is not lawful for thee to have her.	**17** For Herod himself had sent forth and laid hold upon John, and bound him in prison for the sake of Herodias, his brother Philip's wife: for he had married her. **18** For John said unto Herod, It is not lawful for thee to have thy brother's wife.	**19** but Herod the tetrarch, being reproved by him for Herodias his brother's wife, and for all the evil things which Herod had done, **20** added yet this above all, that he shut up John in prison. *cp.* 3 24.
cp. 4 12; 11 2.	*cp.* 1 14.	¹ Or, *the gospel*

(ii) The Preparation of Jesus (§§ 20-22)

§ 20. The Baptism in the Jordan

Matt. 3 13-17	Mark 1 9-11	Luke 3 21-22	John 1 32-34
13 Then cometh Jesus from Galilee to the Jordan unto John, to be baptized	**9** And it came to pass in those days, that Jesus came from Nazareth of Galilee,	**21** Now it came to pass, when all the people were baptized,	

of him. **14** But John would have hindered him, saying, I have need to be baptized of thee, and comest thou to me? **15** But Jesus answering said unto him, Suffer [1] *it* now: for thus it becometh us to fulfil all righteousness [*cp.* 5 6, 10, 20; 6 1, 33; 21 32]. Then he suffereth him. **16** And Jesus, when he was baptized,

cp. 14 23; 19 13; 26 36, 39, 42, 44: *also* 11 25-26.

went up straightway from the water: and lo, the heavens were opened [2] unto him, and he saw the Spirit of God descending

as a dove, and coming upon him; **17** and lo, a voice out of the heavens [*cp.* 17 5], saying, [3] This is my beloved Son [*cp.* 12 18; 17 5: *also* 4 3; *etc.*], in whom I am well pleased [*cp.* 17 5: *also* 11 26; 12 18].

cp. 3 11.

verse 17

[1] Or, me
[2] Some ancient authorities omit *unto him*.
[3] Or, *This is my Son; my beloved in whom I am well pleased*. See ch. 12 18.

---

and was baptized of John [1] in the Jordan. **10** And

cp. 1 35; 6 46; 14 32, 35, 39.

straightway coming up out of the water, he saw the heavens rent asunder, and the Spirit as a dove descending

upon him: **11** and a voice came out of the heavens [*cp.* 9 7], Thou art my beloved Son [*cp.* 9 7; 12 6: *also* 1 1; *etc.*], in thee I am well pleased.

cp. 1 8.

verse 11

[1] Gr. *into*.

---

that, Jesus also having been baptized, and praying [*cp.* 5 16; 6 12; 9 18, 28, 29; 11 1; 22 41, 44: *also* 10 21],

the heaven was opened, **22** and the Holy Ghost descended in a bodily form, as a dove,

upon him, and a voice came out of heaven [*cp.* 9 35], Thou art my beloved Son [*cp.* 9 35; 20 13: *also* 1 35; *etc.*], in thee I am well pleased [*cp.* 2 14; 10 21; 12 32].

cp. 3 16.

verse 22

---

32 And John bare witness, saying,

cp. 11 41-42; 12 27-28; 17 1-26.

I have beheld the Spirit descending as a dove out of heaven; and it abode upon him.

cp. 12 28.

verse 34

cp. 1 14, 18; 3 16, 18: *also* 1 34; *etc.*

33 And I knew him not: but he that sent me to baptize [1] with water, he said unto me, Upon whomsoever thou shalt see the Spirit descending, and abiding upon him, the same is he that baptizeth [1] with the Holy Spirit. **34** And I have seen, and have borne witness that this is the Son of God.

[1] Or, *in*

Matt. 3 17 || Mark 1 11 || Luke 3 22: *cp.* Ps. 2 7; Is. 42 1.

§ 21. The Genealogy of Jesus

Matt. 1 1-17

1 [1] The book of the [2] generation of Jesus Christ, the son of David, the son of Abraham.

cp. 4 17.

cp. 13 55.

2 Abraham begat Isaac; and Isaac begat Jacob; and Jacob begat Judah and his brethren; **3** and Judah begat Perez and Zerah of Tamar; and Perez begat Hezron; and Hezron begat [3] Ram; **4** and [3] Ram begat Amminadab; and Amminadab begat Nahshon; and Nahshon begat Salmon; **5** and Salmon begat Boaz of Rahab; and Boaz begat

Luke 3 23-38

23 And Jesus himself, when he began *to teach*, was about thirty years of age, being the son (as was supposed) of Joseph [*cp.* 4 22], the son of Heli, **24** the *son* of Matthat, the *son* of Levi, the *son* of Melchi, the *son* of Jannai, the *son* of Joseph, **25** the *son* of Mattathias, the *son* of Amos, the *son* of Nahum, the *son* of Esli, the *son* of Naggai, **26** the *son* of Maath, the *son* of Mattathias, the *son* of Semein, the *son* of Josech, the *son* of Joda, **27** the *son* of Joanan, the *son* of Rhesa,

cp. 1 45; 6 42.

Obed of Ruth ; and Obed begat Jesse ;
6 and Jesse begat David the king.

And David begat Solomon of her *that
had been the wife* of Uriah ; 7 and
Solomon begat Rehoboam ; and Rehoboam begat Abijah ; and Abijah begat
⁴ Asa ; 8 and ⁴ Asa begat Jehoshaphat ;
and Jehoshaphat begat Joram ; and
Joram begat Uzziah ; 9 and Uzziah
begat Jotham ; and Jotham begat
Ahaz ; and Ahaz begat Hezekiah ;
10 and Hezekiah begat Manasseh ; and
Manasseh begat ⁵ Amon ; and ⁵ Amon
begat Josiah ; 11 and Josiah begat
Jechoniah and his brethren, at the time
of the ⁶ carrying away to Babylon.

12 And after the ⁶ carrying away
to Babylon, Jechoniah begat ⁷ Shealtiel ; and ⁷ Shealtiel begat Zerubbabel ;
13 and Zerubbabel begat Abiud ; and
Abiud begat Eliakim ; and Eliakim
begat Azor ; 14 and Azor begat Sadoc ;
and Sadoc begat Achim ; and Achim
begat Eliud ; 15 and Eliud begat
Eleazar ; and Eleazar begat Matthan ;
and Matthan begat Jacob ; 16 and
Jacob begat Joseph the husband of
Mary, of whom was born Jesus, who is
called Christ.
17 So all the generations from Abraham
unto David are fourteen generations ;
and from David unto the ⁶ carrying
away to Babylon fourteen generations ;
and from the ⁶ carrying away to Babylon
unto the Christ fourteen generations.

¹ Or, *The genealogy of Jesus Christ*
² Or, *birth* : as in ver. 18.
³ Gr. *Aram.*   ⁴ Gr. *Asaph.*
⁵ Gr. *Amos.*   ⁶ Or, *removal to Babylon.*
⁷ Gr. *Salathiel.*

the *son* of Zerubbabel, the *son* of
¹ Shealtiel, the *son* of Neri, 28 the *son*
of Melchi, the *son* of Addi, the *son* of
Cosam, the *son* of Elmadam, the *son*
of Er, 29 the *son* of Jesus, the *son* of
Eliezer, the *son* of Jorim, the *son* of
Matthat, the *son* of Levi, 30 the *son*
of Symeon, the *son* of Judas, the *son*
of Joseph, the *son* of Jonam, the *son* of
Eliakim, 31 the *son* of Melea, the *son*
of Menna, the *son* of Mattatha, the
son of Nathan, the *son* of David, 32 the
son of Jesse, the *son* of Obed, the *son* of
Boaz, the *son* of ² Salmon, the *son* of
Nahshon, 33 the *son* of Amminadab,
³ the *son* of ⁴ Arni, the *son* of Hezron,
the *son* of Perez, the *son* of Judah,
34 the *son* of Jacob, the *son* of Isaac,
the *son* of Abraham, the *son* of Terah,
the *son* of Nahor, 35 the *son* of Serug,
the *son* of Reu, the *son* of Peleg, the
son of Eber, the *son* of Shelah, 36 the
son of Cainan, the *son* of Arphaxad,
the *son* of Shem, the *son* of Noah, the
son of Lamech, 37 the *son* of Methuselah, the *son* of Enoch, the *son* of
Jared, the *son* of Mahalaleel, the *son*
of Cainan, 38 the *son* of Enos, the *son*
of Seth, the *son* of Adam, the *son*
of God.

¹ Gr. *Salathiel.*
² Some ancient authorities write *Sala.*
³ Many ancient authorities insert *the son of
Admin* : and one writes *Admin* for *Amminadab.*
⁴ Some ancient authorities write *Aram.*

§ 22. The Temptation in the Wilderness

Matt. 4 1-11	Mark 1 12-13	Luke 4 1-13	
1 Then was Jesus	12 And	1 And Jesus, full of the Holy Spirit [*cp.* 1 15, 41, 67], returned from the Jordan,	
led up of the Spirit into the wilderness	straightway the Spirit driveth him forth into the wilderness. 13 And he was in the wilderness forty days tempted of Satan ;	and was led ¹ by the Spirit in the wilderness 2 during forty days, being tempted of the devil. And he did eat nothing in those days :	
to be tempted of the devil. 2 And when he had fasted forty days and forty nights, he afterward hungered.	and he was with the wild beasts ;	and when they were com-pleted, he hungered.	
3 And the tempter came and said unto him, If thou art the Son of God [*cp.* 8 29 ; 14 33 ; 16 16 ; 26 63 ; 27 40, 43, 54 : *also* 3 17 ; 17 5], command that these stones become ¹ bread. 4 But he answered and said, It is written, Man shall not live by bread alone, but by every word that pro-ceedeth out of the mouth of God. 5 Then the devil taketh him into the	*cp.* 1 1 ; 3 11 ; 5 7 ; 15 39 : *also* 1 11 ; 9 7.	3 And the devil said unto him, If thou art the Son of God [*cp.* 1 35 ; 4 41 ; 8 28 ; 22 70 : *also* 3 22 ; 9 35], command this stone that it become ² bread. 4 And Jesus answered unto him, It is written, Man shall not live by bread alone.	*cp.* 1 34 ; *etc.* *cp.* 4 34.
	9 And he led him to		

holy city [*cp.* 27 53]; and he set him on the [2] pinnacle of the temple, **6** and saith unto him, If thou art the Son of God [*see above*], cast thyself down: for it is written,

He shall give his angels charge concerning thee:
And on their hands they shall bear thee up,
Lest haply thou dash thy foot against a stone.

7 Jesus said unto him, Again it is written, Thou shalt not tempt the Lord thy God. **8** Again, the devil taketh him unto an exceeding high mountain, and sheweth him all the kingdoms of the world, and the glory of them;
9 and he said unto him, All these things will I give thee,

if thou wilt fall down and worship me.

10 Then saith Jesus unto him, Get thee hence, Satan [*cp.* 16 23]: for it is written, Thou shalt worship the Lord thy God, and him only shalt thou serve.

5 Then the devil taketh him into the holy city [*cp.* 27 53]; and he set him on the [1]pinnacle of the temple, **6** and saith unto him, If thou art the Son of God [*see above*], cast thyself down: for it is written,

He shall give his angels charge concerning thee:
And on their hands they shall bear thee up,
Lest haply thou dash thy foot against a stone.

7 Jesus said unto him, Again it is written, Thou shalt not tempt the Lord thy God.

11 Then the devil

leaveth him; and behold, angels came and ministered unto him [*cp.* 26 53].

---

see above.

cp. 8 33.

see above.

the angels ministered unto him.

Jerusalem, and set him on the [3] pinnacle of the temple, and said unto him, If thou art the Son of God [*see above*], cast thyself down from hence: **10** for it is written,

He shall give his angels charge concerning thee, to guard thee:
11 and, On their hands they shall bear thee up,
Lest haply thou dash thy foot against a stone.

12 And Jesus answering said unto him, It is said, Thou shalt not tempt the Lord thy God. **5** And he led him up, and shewed him all the kingdoms of [4] the world in a moment of time. **6** And the devil said unto him, To thee will I give all this authority, and the glory of them: for it hath been delivered unto me; and to whomsoever I will I give it. **7** If thou therefore wilt worship before me, it shall all be thine. **8** And Jesus answered and said unto him,

It is written, Thou shalt worship the Lord thy God, and him only shalt thou serve. **9** And he led him to Jerusalem, and set him on the [3] pinnacle of the temple, and said unto him, If thou art the Son of God [*see above*], cast thyself down from hence: **10** for it is written,

He shall give his angels charge concerning thee, to guard thee:
11 and, On their hands they shall bear thee up,
Lest haply thou dash thy foot against a stone.

12 And Jesus answering said unto him, It is said, Thou shalt not tempt the Lord thy God.

13 And when the devil had completed every temptation [*cp.* 8 13; 22 28], he departed from him [5] for a season.

and

cp. 22 43.

---

see above.

see above.

cp. 1 51; 12 29.

---

[1] Gr. *loaves.*   [2] Gr. *wing.*

[1] Or, *in*   [2] Or, *a loaf*
[3] Gr. *wing.*   [4] Gr. *the inhabited earth.*
[5] Or, *until*

Matt. 4 4 || Luke 4 4 = Deut. 8 3.   Matt. 4 6 || Luke 4 10-11 = Ps. 91 11-12.
Matt. 4 7 || Luke 4 12 = Deut. 6 16.   Matt. 4 10 || Luke 4 8 = Deut. 6 13.

C. The Ministry in Galilee and the North (§§ 23-133)

(i) The Beginning of the Ministry (§§ 23-31)

§ 23. **The Good News first proclaimed**

Matt. 4 12-17	Mark 1 14-15	Luke 4 14-15	John 4 1-3, 45
12 Now when he heard	**14** Now after	**14** And	4 1 When therefore the Lord knew how that the Pharisees had heard that Jesus was making and baptizing more disciples than John **2** (although Jesus himself baptized not, but his disciples),
that John	that John		
was delivered up [cp. 11 2; 14 3], he withdrew	was delivered up [cp. 6 17], Jesus came cp. 5 30.	cp. 3 19-20. Jesus returned in the power [cp. 4 36; 5 17; 6 19; 8 46: also 1 17, 35; 9 1; 24 49] of the Spirit into Galilee:	cp. 3 24. 3 he left Judæa, and departed again
into Galilee; **13** and leaving Nazareth, he came and dwelt in Capernaum [cp. 9 1: also 13 54], which is by the sea, in the borders of Zebulun and Naphtali: **14** that it might be fulfilled which was spoken [1] by Isaiah the prophet, saying, **15** The land [cp. 2 6, 20, 21; 10 15; 11 24] of Zebulun and the land of Naphtali, [2] Toward the sea, beyond Jordan, Galilee of the [3] Gentiles, **16** The people which sat in darkness Saw a great light, And to them which sat in the region and shadow of death, To them did light spring up. **17** From that time began Jesus to preach, cp. 4 23; 9 35; 24 14; 26 13. and to say,	into Galilee, cp. 1 21. preaching the gospel [cp. 1 1; 8 35; 10 29; 13 10; 14 9; 16 15] of God, **15** and saying, The time is fulfilled, and the kingdom of God is at	cp. 4 16, 23, 31. cp. 3 23.	into Galilee. cp. 3 22.
Repent ye [cp. 3 2]; for the kingdom of heaven is at hand [cp. 3 2; 10 7: also 12 28].	hand: repent ye [cp. 6 12], and believe in the gospel [see above].	cp. 4 21; 10 9, 11: also 9 2; 11 20; 17 20, 21; 19 11; 21 8. cp. 10 9, 11; etc., above. and a fame went out concerning him through all the region round about [cp. 4 37; 5 15; 7 17]. **15** And he taught in their synagogues [cp. 4 44], being glorified of all.	45 So when he came into Galilee, the Galilaeans received him, having seen all the things that he did in Jerusalem at the feast: for they also went unto the feast.
cp. 4 24: also 9 26.	cp. 1 28.		
cp. 4 23; 9 35.	cp. 1 39.		cp. 18 20.

[1] Or, *through*
[2] Gr. *The way of the sea.*
[3] Gr. *nations*: and so elsewhere.

Matt. 4 15-16 = Is. 9 1-2.

§ 24. **The Rejection at Nazareth**

[*Cp.* Matt. 12 9-14 : Mark 1 21-28; 3 1-6: Luke 4 31-37; 6 6-11; 13 10-17: John 6 59]

Matt. 13 53-58	Mark 6 1-6	**Luke 4** 16-30	John 6 41-42; 4 43-44
53 And it came to pass, when Jesus had finished these parables, he departed thence. 54 And coming into his own country [*cp.* 9 1: *also* 4 13]	1 And he went out from thence; and he cometh into his own country; and his disciples follow him. 2 And when the sabbath was come, he began to teach	16 And he came to Nazareth, where he had been brought up: and he entered, as his custom was [*cp.* 22 39], into the synagogue on the sabbath day, and stood up to read.	*cp.* 1 11.
he taught them in their synagogue,	in the synagogue:		

cp. 12 26. 17 And there was delivered unto him ¹ the book [*cp.* 3 4; 20 42] of the prophet Isaiah. And he opened the ² book, and found the place where it was written,
18 The Spirit of the Lord is upon me,
³Because he anointed me to preach⁴ good tidings [*cp.* 1 19; 2 10; 3 18; 4 43; 7 22; 8 1; 9 6; 16 16; 20 1] to the poor [*cp.* 7 22]:
He hath sent me to proclaim release to the captives,
And recovering of sight to the blind [*cp.* 7 22: *also* 7 21; 18 35-43],
To set at liberty them that are bruised,
19 To proclaim the acceptable year of the Lord.
20 And he closed the ² book, and gave it back to the attendant, and sat down: and the eyes of all in the synagogue were fastened on him. 21 And he began to say unto them, To-day hath this scripture been fulfilled in your ears.

cp. 11 5. cp. 9 27-31; 12 22; 15 30, 31; 20 29-34; 21 14. cp. 8 22-26; 10 46-52. cp. 9 1-7.

		22 And all bare him witness, and wondered [*cp.* 2 47, 48; 4 32, 36; 20 26: *also* 5 9, 26; 8 25, 56; 9 43; 11 14; 24 12, 41] at the words of grace which proceeded out of his mouth: and they said,	6 41 The Jews therefore murmured concerning him,
cp. 4 17. insomuch that they were astonished [*cp.* 7 28; 19 25; 22 22, 33: *also* 8 27; 9 33; 12 23; 15 31; 21 20; 27 14],	*cp.* 1 15. and ¹ many hearing him were astonished [*cp.* 1 22, 27; 10 24, 26; 11 18; 12 17: *also* 2 12; 5 20, 42; 6 51; 7 37; 10 32; 15 5; 16 5, 8],		*cp.* 7 15, 21, 46. because he said, I am the bread which came down out of heaven. 42 And they said,
and said, Whence hath this man *verse* 56. this wisdom, and these ¹ mighty works?	saying, Whence hath this man these things? and, What is the wisdom that is given unto this man, and *what mean* such ² mighty works wrought by his hands? 3 Is not this the carpenter,	Is not this Joseph's son [*cp.* 3 23] ?	Is not this Jesus, the son of Joseph [*cp.* 1 45], whose father and mother we know? how doth he now say, I am come down out of heaven?
55 Is not this the carpenter's son? is not his mother called Mary? and his brethren, James, and Joseph, and Simon, and Judas? 56 And his sisters, are they not all with us? Whence then hath this man all these things? 57 And they were ² offended in him.	the son of Mary, and brother of James, and Joses, and Judas, and Simon? and are not his sisters here with us? *verse* 2 And they were ³ offended in him.		
		23 And he said unto them, Doubtless ye will say unto me this parable, Physician, heal thyself [*cp.* 23 37, 39]: whatsoever we have heard done at Capernaum [*cp.* 4 31], do also here in thine own country. 24 And he said, Verily I say unto you, No prophet [*cp.* 7 16, 39; 13 33; 24 19] is acceptable in his own	
cp. 27 40. *cp.* 4 13.	*cp.* 15 30. *cp.* 1 21.		4 43 And after the two days he went forth from thence into Galilee. 44 For Jesus himself testified, that a prophet [*cp.* 4 19; 6 14; 7 40; 9 17] hath no
But Jesus said unto them, A prophet [*cp.* 21 11, 46] is not without honour, save in his own	4 And Jesus said unto them, A prophet [*cp.* 6 15] is not without honour, save in his own		honour in his own

country, and in his own house.	country, and among his own kin, and in his own house.	country.	country.

cp. 12 40, 42.

25 But of a truth I say unto you, There were many widows [*cp.* 2 37; 7 12; 18 3; 20 47; 21 2] in Israel in the days of Elijah, when the heaven was shut up three years and six months, when there came a great famine over all the land; **26** and unto none of them was Elijah sent, but only to ⁵Zarephath, in the land of Sidon, unto a woman that was a widow. **27** And there were many lepers in Israel in the time of Elisha the prophet; and none of them was cleansed, but only Naaman the Syrian. **28** And they were

58 And he did not many ¹mighty works there

because of their unbelief.

5 And he could there do no ⁴mighty work, save that he laid his hands upon a few sick folk, and healed them. **6** And he marvelled because of their unbelief.

all filled with wrath in the synagogue, as they heard these things; **29** and they rose up, and cast him forth out of the city [*cp.* 20 15], and led him unto the brow of the hill whereon their city was built, that they might throw him down headlong. **30** But he passing through the midst of them went his way.

cp. 1 11.

cp. 8 59; 10 39.

¹ Gr. *powers.*
² Gr. *caused to stumble.*

¹ Some ancient authorities insert *the.* ² Gr. *powers.*
³ Gr. *caused to stumble.*
⁴ Gr. *power.*

¹ Or, *a roll* ² Or, *roll* ³ Or, *Wherefore*
⁴ Or, *the gospel* ⁵ Gr. *Sarepta.*

Luke 4 18-19 = Is. 61 1-2 ; 58 6.

---

§ 25. The Call of the First Disciples (Matt. and Mark)

Matt. 4 18-22	**Mark 1** 16-20	Luke 5 1-11	John 1 35-42
		1 Now it came to pass, while the multitude pressed upon him and heard the word of God, that he was standing by the lake of Gennesaret [*cp.* 5 2; 8 22, 23, 33]; **2** and	
18 And walking by the sea of Galilee [*cp.* 15 29 : also 8 24; *etc.*], he saw two brethren, Simon who is called Peter [*cp.* 10 2; 16 16-18], and Andrew his brother,	**16** And passing along by the sea of Galilee [*cp.* 7 31 : also 2 13; *etc.*], he saw [*cp.* 2 14] Simon *cp.* 3 16. and Andrew the brother of Simon	he saw two *cp.* 6 14. boats standing by the lake : but the fishermen had gone out of them, and were washing their nets.	**35** Again on the morrow John was standing, *cp.* 6 1 ; 21 1 : *also* 6 16, *etc.* and two of his disciples ; *verse* 42 **36** and he looked upon Jesus as he walked, and saith, Behold, the Lamb of God !
casting a net into the sea; for they were fishers. **19** And he saith unto them, Come ye after me [*cp.* 8 22; 9 9; 16 24; 19 21], and I will make you fishers of men. **20** And they straightway left the nets, and followed him [*cp.* 4 22; 9 9; 19 27].	casting a net in the sea : for they were fishers. **17** And Jesus said unto them, Come ye after me [*cp.* 2 14; 8 34; 10 21], and I will make you to become fishers of men. **18** And straightway they left the nets, and followed him [*cp.* 1 20; 2 14; 10 28].	*cp.* 5 27 ; 9 23, 59 ; 18 22. *verse* 10	*cp.* 1 43 ; 12 26 ; 21 19, 22. **37** And the two disciples heard him speak, and they followed Jesus.
		3 And he entered into one of the boats, which was Simon's, and asked him to put out a little from the land. And he sat down and taught the multitudes out of the boat. **4** And when he had left speaking, he said unto Simon, Put out into the deep, and let down your nets for a draught. **5** And Simon answered and said, Master, we toiled all night, and took nothing : but at thy word I will let down the nets. **6** And when they had this done, they inclosed a great multitude of fishes ; and their nets were breaking ; **7** and they beckoned unto their partners in the other boat, that they should come and help them. And they came, and filled both the boats, so that they began to sink. **8** But Simon Peter, when he saw it, fell down at Jesus' knees, saying, Depart from me ; for I am a sinful man, O Lord. **9** For he was amazed, and all that were with him, at the draught of the fishes which they	**38** And Jesus turned, and beheld them following, and saith unto them, What seek ye ? And they said unto him, Rabbi (which is to say, being interpreted, ¹Master), where abidest thou ? **39** He saith unto them, Come, and ye shall see. They came therefore and saw where he abode ; and they abode with him that day : it was about the tenth hour. **40** One of the two that heard John *speak*, and followed him, was Andrew, Simon Peter's [*cp.* 6 8, 68; *etc.*]
cp. 16 16.			
21 And going on from thence he saw other two	**19** And going on a little further, he saw	had taken ; **10** and so were also	brother. **41** He findeth first his own brother Simon, and

brethren, ¹ James the *son* of Zebedee, and John his brother, in the boat with Zebedee their father, mending their nets; and he called them.

verse 19

22 And they straightway left the boat and their father [*cp.* Luke 18 28], and followed him [*cp.* 4 20; 9 9; 19 27].

¹ Or, *Jacob*: and so elsewhere.

James the *son* of Zebedee, and John his brother, who also were in the boat mending the nets. **20** And straightway he called them:

verse 17

and they left their father Zebedee in the boat with the hired servants [*cp.* Luke 18 28], and went after him [*cp.* 1 18; 2 14; 10 28].

James and John, sons of Zebedee,

which were partners with Simon. And Jesus said unto Simon, Fear not; from henceforth thou shalt ¹ catch men. **11** And when they had brought their boats to land, they left all [*cp.* Matt. 19 27: Mark 10 28 : *also* Luke 5 28; 14 33], and followed him [*cp.* 5 28; 18 28].

¹ Gr. *take alive.*

saith unto him, We have found the Messiah (which is, being interpreted, ² Christ). **42** He brought him unto Jesus. Jesus looked upon him, and said, Thou art Simon the son of ³ John: thou shalt be called Cephas (which is by interpretation, ⁴ Peter).
[*cp.* 1 43-51 : Philip and Nathanael]

[*cp. also* 21 1-23]

¹ Or, *Teacher*
² That is, *Anointed.*
³ Gr. *Joanes*: called in Matt. 16. 17, *Jonah.*
⁴ That is, *Rock* or *Stone.*

§ 26. In the Synagogue at Capernaum

[*Cp.* Matt. 12 9-14; 13 53-58 : Mark 3 1-6; 6 1-6: Luke 4 16-30; 6 6-11; 13 10-17: John 6 59]

Matt. 7 28-29

cp. 4 13.

28 And it came to pass, when Jesus ended these words, the multitudes were astonished at his teaching [*cp.* 22 33; 13 54; 19 25; 22 22: *also* 8 27; 9 33; 12 23; 15 31; 21 20; 27 14]: **29** for he taught them as *one* having authority [*cp.* 21 23 *ff.*; 9 6; 28 18], and not as their scribes.

cp. 8 29.

cp. 8 29.
cp. 2 23; 26 71 : *also* 21 11.
cp. similarly 8 29.
cp. 8 26; 17 18.

cp. 17 18.

cp. 7 28 *etc. above.*

Mark 1 21-28

21 And they go into Capernaum; and straightway on the sabbath day he entered into the synagogue and taught. **22** And they were astonished at his teaching [*cp.* 11 18; 1 27; 6 2; 10 24, 26; 12 17: *also* 2 12; 5 20, 42; 6 51; 7 37; 10 32; 15 5; 16 5, 8]: for he taught them as having authority [*cp.* 11 27 *ff.*; 1 27; 2 10], and not as the scribes. **23** And straightway there was in their synagogue a man with an unclean spirit; and he cried out [*cp.* 3 11; 5 7], **24** saying, What have we to do with thee [*cp.* 5 7], thou Jesus of Nazareth [*cp.* 10 47; 14 67; 16 6] ? art thou come to destroy us ? I know thee who thou art, the Holy One of God [*cp. similarly* 3 11; 5 7]. **25** And Jesus rebuked ¹ him [*cp.* 3 12; 4 39; 9 25], saying, Hold thy peace [*cp.* 4 39], and come out [*cp.* 5 8; 9 25] of him. **26** And the unclean spirit, ² tearing him [*cp.* 9 18, 20, 26] and crying with a loud voice [*cp.* 5 7], came out of him [*cp.* 9 26]. **27** And they were all amazed [*cp.* 1 22 *etc. above*], insomuch that they questioned among themselves,

Luke 4 31-37

31 And he came down to Capernaum, a city of Galilee. And he was teaching them on the sabbath day: **32** and they were astonished at his teaching [*cp.* 2 47, 48; 4 22, 36; 20 26: *also* 5 9, 26; 8 25, 56; 9 43; 11 14; 24 12, 41]; for his word was with authority [*cp.* 20 1 *ff.*; 4 36; 5 24]. **33** And in the synagogue there was a man, which had a spirit of an unclean ¹ devil; and he cried out with a loud voice [*cp.* 8 28], **34** ² Ah ! what have we to do with thee [*cp.* 8 28], thou Jesus of Nazareth [*cp.* 18 37; 24 19] ? art thou come to destroy us ? I know thee who thou art, the Holy One of God [*cp. similarly* 4 41; 8 28]. **35** And Jesus rebuked him [*cp.* 4 39, 41; 8 24; 9 42], saying, Hold thy peace, and come out of him. And when the ¹ devil had thrown him down in the midst [*cp.* 9 39, 42], he came out of him, having done him no hurt. **36** And amazement came upon all [*cp.* 4 32 *etc. above*], and they spake together, one with another,

cp. 7 15, 21, 46.

cp. 5 27; 17 2.

cp. 18 5, 7; 19 19: *also* 1 45.
cp. 6 69.

cp. 7 15, 21, 46.

cp. 8 27; 21 10. cp. 7 29 etc. above.	saying, What is this [cp. 2 7; 4 41]? a new teaching! with authority [cp. 1 22 etc. above] cp. 5 30. he commandeth even the unclean spirits, and they	saying, What is ³ this word [cp. 5 21; 7 49; 8 25; 9 9]? for with authority [cp. 4 32 etc. above] and power [cp. 4 14; 5 17; 6 19; 8 46: also 1 17, 35; 9 1; 24 49] he commandeth the unclean spirits, and they	cp. 5 12: also 12 34. cp. 5 27; 17 2.
cp. 8 27.	obey him [cp. 4 41]. **28** And the report of him went out straightway everywhere into all the region of Galilee round about.	come out [cp. 8 25]. **37** And there went forth a rumour concerning him into every place of the region	
cp. 4 24: also 9 26.		round about [cp. 4 14; 5 15; 7 17].	
	¹ Or, it ² Or, convulsing	¹ Gr. demon. ² Or, Let alone ³ Or, this word, that with authority . . . come out?	

§ 27. The Healing of Peter's Wife's Mother

Matt. 8 14-15	Mark 1 29-31	Luke 4 38-39	
14 And when Jesus was come into Peter's house,	**29** And straightway, ¹ when they were come out of the synagogue, they came into the house of Simon and Andrew, with James and John [cp. 5 37; 9 2; 13 3; 14 33].	**38** And he rose up from the synagogue, and entered into the house of Simon.	
cp. 17 1; 26 37. he saw his wife's mother lying sick of a fever.	**30** Now Simon's wife's mother lay sick of a fever; and straightway they tell him of her: **31** and he came and took her by	cp. 8 51; 9 28. And Simon's wife's mother was holden with a great fever; and they besought him for her. **39** And he	
15 And he touched her hand [cp. 9 25; 8 3; 9 18, 29; 14 31; 17 7; 19 13, 15; 20 34: also 9 20; 14 36],	the hand [cp. 5 41; 9 27; 1 41; 5 23; 6 2, 5; 7 33; 8 22, 23, 25; 10 13, 16: also 3 10; 5 27; 6 56], and raised her up;	cp. 8 54; 4 40; 5 13; 7 14; 13 13; 14 4; 18 15; 22 51: also 6 19; 7 39; 8 44.	cp. 9 6: also 20 17.
cp. 8 26; 17 18: also 8 3, 8, 13, 16, 32; 9 6, 22, 29; 12 13; 15 28; 17 7.	cp. 1 25; 3 12; 4 39; 9 25: also 1 41; 2 11; 3 5; 5 8, 13, 34, 41; 7 29, 34; 10 52.	stood over her, and rebuked [cp. 4 35, 41; 8 24; 9 42: also 5 13, 24; 6 10; 7 7, 14; 8 29, 32, 48, 54; 13 12; 17 14; 18 42] the fever;	cp. 4 50; 5 8; 9 7; 11 43.
and the fever left her; and she arose, and ministered unto him.	and the fever left her, and she ministered unto them.	and it left her: and immediately she rose up and ministered unto them.	cp. 4 52.
	¹ Some ancient authorities read when he was come out of the synagogue, he came &c.		

§ 28. Healings in the Evening

Matt. 8 16-17	Mark 1 32-34	Luke 4 40-41	
16 And when even was come, they	**32** And at even, when the sun did set, they	**40** And when the sun was setting, all they that had any sick with divers diseases	
brought unto him many	brought unto him all that were sick, and them that were	brought them unto him;	
¹ possessed with devils:	¹ possessed with devils. **33** And all the city was gathered together at the door.		
cp. 9 18; 19 13, 15: 8 3, 15; 9 25, 29; 14 31; 17 7; 20 34: also 9 20; 14 36. and he cast out the spirits with a word [cp. 8 8: also 8 3, 13, 32; 9 6, 22, 29; 12 13; 15 28; 17 7, 18],	cp. 5 23; 6 5; 8 25; 10 16: 1 31, 41; 5 41; 6 2; 7 33; 9 27; 8 22, 23; 10 13: also 3 10; 5 27; 6 56. cp. 1 25, 41; 2 11; 3 5; 5 8, 13, 34, 41; 7 29, 34; 9 25; 10 52.	and he laid his hands [cp. 13 13: 5 13; 7 14; 8 54; 14 4; 18 15; 22 51: also 6 19; 7 39; 8 44] on every one of them, [cp. 7 7: also 4 35, 39; 5 13, 24; 6 10; 7 14; 8 29, 32, 48, 54; 9 42; 13 12; 17 14; 18 42] and healed them.	cp. 9 6: also 20 17. cp. 4 50; 5 8; 9 7; 11 43.
and healed all [cp. 12 15] that were sick: cp. 4 24.	**34** And he healed many that were sick with divers diseases, and cast out many ² devils;	cp. 6 19. **41** And ¹ devils also	

		3 10 for he had healed many; insomuch that as many as had ³ plagues ⁴ pressed upon him that they might touch him. **11** And the unclean spirits, whensoever they beheld him, fell down before him, and cried, saying, Thou	came out from many,	

cp. 4 3, 6; 8 29; 14 33; 16 16; 26 63; 27 40, 43, 54: *also* 3 17; 17 5.
cp. 8 26; 17 18.

art the Son of God [cp. 1 1; 5 7; 15 39: *also* 1 11; 9 7]. **12** And he charged them much [cp. 1 25; 4 39; 9 25] that they should not make him known.   and he suffered   not the ² devils to speak [cp. 1 25; 3 12: 1 44; 5 43; 7 36; 8 26: *also* 8 30; 9 9], because they knew [cp. 1 24; 3 11; 5 7] him.⁵

crying out, and saying, Thou art the Son of God [cp. 1 35; 4 3, 9; 8 28; 22 70: *also* 3 22; 9 35].   And rebuking them [cp. 4 35, 39; 8 24; 9 42],

he suffered them not to speak [cp. 4 35: 5 14; 8 56: *also* 9 21, 36], because they knew [cp. 4 34; 8 28] that he was the Christ.

cp. 1 34; *etc.*

cp. 8 4; 9 30; 12 16: *also* 16 20; 17 9.
cp. 8 29.

17 that it might be fulfilled which was spoken ² by Isaiah the prophet, saying, Himself took our infirmities, and bare our diseases.

¹ Or, *demoniacs*   ² Or, *through*

¹ Or, *demoniacs*   ² Gr. *demons.*
³ Gr. *scourges.*   ⁴ Gr. *fell.*
⁵ Many ancient authorities add *to be Christ.* See Luke 4 41.

¹ Gr. *demons.*

Matt. 8 17 = Is. 53 4.

§ 29. Departure from Capernaum

Matt. 8 18	Mark 1 35-38	Luke 4 42-43	
18 Now when Jesus saw great multitudes about him, he gave commandment to depart unto the other side.	**35** And in the morning, a great while before day, he rose up and went out, and departed into a desert place [cp. 1 45; 6 31, 32], and there prayed [cp. 6 46; 14 32, 35, 39]. **36** And Simon and they that were with him followed after him; **37** and they found him, and say unto him, All are seeking thee.	**42** And when it was day, he came out and went into a desert place [cp. 5 16; 9 10]:	

cp. 14 13.
cp. 14 23; 19 13; 26 36, 39, 42, 44: *also* 11 25-26.

cp. 3 21; 5 16; 6 12; 9 18, 28, 29; 11 1; 22 41, 44: *also* 10 21.

cp. 11 41-42; 12 27-28; 17 1-26.

and the multitudes sought after him, and came unto him [cp. 5 15], and would have stayed him, that he should not go from them. **43** But he said unto them,

cp. 11 5.

38 And he saith unto them, Let us go elsewhere into the next towns, that I may preach

          I must preach the ¹ good tidings [cp. 1 19; 2 10; 3 18; 4 18; 7 22; 8 1; 9 6; 16 16; 20 1] of the kingdom of God to the other cities also: for therefore was I sent.

there also; for to this end came I forth.

cp. 8 42; 16 28.

¹ Or, *gospel*

§ 30. General Preaching and Healing in Galilee

Matt. 4 23-25	Mark 1 39	Luke 4 44	
23 And ¹ Jesus went about in all Galilee, teaching in their synagogues, and preaching [cp. 9	**39** And he went into their synagogues throughout all Galilee, preaching	**44** And he was preaching in the synagogues [cp. 4 15] of ¹ Galilee.	cp. 18 20.

35; 11 1] the ²gospel of the kingdom [*cp.* 9 35; 24 14: *also* 26 13], and healing all manner of disease and all manner of sickness among the people.

9 35 And Jesus went about all the cities and the villages, teaching in their synagogues, and preaching the gospel of the kingdom, and healing all manner of disease and all manner of sickness.

24 And the report of him went forth [*cp.* 9 26] into all Syria: and they brought unto him all that were sick, holden with divers diseases and torments [*cp.* 8 6], ³ possessed with devils, and epileptic [*cp.* 17 15], and palsied [*cp.* 8 6; 9 2]; and he healed them. **25** And there followed him great multitudes from Galilee and Decapolis and Jerusalem and Judæa

and *from* beyond Jordan.

¹ Some ancient authorities read *he.*
² Or, *good tidings*: and so elsewhere.
³ Or, *demoniacs*

cp. 1 1, 14, 15; 8 35; 10 29; 13 10; 14 9; 16 15.
and casting out ¹ devils.

6 6 And he went round about the villages teaching.

1 28

3 10

3 7 And a great multitude from Galilee followed: [*cp.* 5 20; 7 31] and from Judæa 8 and from Jerusalem, and from Idumæa, and beyond Jordan, and about Tyre and Sidon.

¹ Gr. *demons.*

8 1 And it came to pass soon afterwards, that he went about through cities and villages, preaching and bringing the ² good tidings of the kingdom of God,

and with him the twelve.

4 37: *cp.* 4 14; 5 15; 7 17.

6 18, 19.

6 17 and a great multitude of his disciples, and a great number of the people from all Judæa and Jerusalem,

and the sea coast of Tyre and Sidon.

¹ Very many ancient authorities read *Judæa.*
² Or, *gospel*

§ 31. **The Call of the First Disciples** (Luke)

Matt. 4 18-22	Mark 1 16-20	Luke 5 1-11	John 21 1-11
cp. 13 2.	*cp.* 4 1; 3 9; 5 21.	**1** Now it came to pass, while the multitude pressed upon him and heard the word of God [*cp.* 8 11, 21; 11 28: *also* 1 2; 4 32; 8 12 *ff.*], *himself* on this wise.	**1** After these things Jesus manifested himself again to the disciples at the sea of Tiberias [*cp.* 6 1: *also* 6 16, *etc.*]; and he manifested
cp. 13 19 *ff.*	*cp.* 2 2; 4 14 *ff.*, 33; 16 20.	**2** There were together Simon Peter, and Thomas called ¹ Didymus, and Nathanael of Cana in Galilee, and the *sons* of Zebedee, and two other of his disciples. **3** Simon Peter saith unto them, I go a fishing. They say unto thee. They went forth, and entered	**3** Simon Peter saith unto them, We also come with him into the boat; and that night they took nothing. **4** But when day was now breaking, Jesus stood on the beach: howbeit the disciples knew not that it was Jesus.
		verse 5	
18 And walking by the sea of Galilee [*cp.* 15 29: *also* 8 24; *etc.*], he saw two brethren, Simon who is called Peter [*cp.* 10 2: *also* 16 16-18], and Andrew his brother,	**16** And passing along by the sea of Galilee [*cp.* 7 31: *also* 2 13; *etc.*], he saw Simon *cp.* 3 16. and Andrew the brother of Simon	that he was standing by the lake of Gennesaret [*cp.* 5 2; 8 22, 23, 33]; **2** and he saw two boats standing by the *cp.* 6 14. lake: but the fishermen had gone out of them, and were washing their nets.	*cp.* 1 42.
casting a net into the sea; for they were fishers. **19** And he saith unto them, Come ye after me, and I will make you fishers of men. **20** And they straightway left the nets, and followed him.	casting a net in the sea: for they were fishers. **17** And Jesus said unto them, Come ye after me, and I will make you to become fishers of men. **18** And straightway they left the nets, and followed him.	*verse* 10	**5** Jesus therefore saith unto them, Children, have ye aught to eat? They answered him, No.
		3 And	

cp. 13 1-2.   cp. 4 1; 3 9.

cp. 16 16: also 4 18; 10 2.

cp. 2 11; 17 14; etc.   cp. 1 40; 3 11; etc.

cp. 8 27; 9 33; 12 23; 15 31; 21 20; 27 14: also 7 28; etc.   cp. 2 12; 5 20, 42; 6 51; 7 37; 10 32; 15 5; 16 5, 8: also 1 22; etc.

[Luke]

he entered into one of the boats, which was Simon's, and asked him to put out a little [cp. Mark 1 19] from the land. And he sat down and taught the multitudes out of the boat. **4** And when he had left speaking, he said unto Simon, Put out into the deep, and let down your nets for a draught. **5** And Simon answered and said, Master, we toiled all night, and took nothing: but at thy word I will let down the nets. **6** And when they had this done,

they inclosed a great multitude of fishes;

and their nets were breaking;

7 and they beckoned unto their partners in the other boat, that they should come and help them. And they came, and filled both the boats, so that they began to sink. **8** But Simon Peter,   when he saw it,

fell down at Jesus' knees [cp. 5 12; 8 28, 41, 47; 17 16: also 24 52], saying, Depart from me; for I am a sinful man, O Lord. **9** For he was amazed [cp. 5 26; 8 25, 56; 9 43; 11 14; 24 12, 41: also 2 47, 48; 4 22, 32, 36; 20 26], and all that were with him, at the draught of the fishes which they had taken;

[John]

6 And he said unto them, Cast the net on the right side of the boat, and ye shall find.

verse 3

They cast therefore, and now they were not able to draw it for the multitude of fishes.

verse 11

7 That disciple therefore whom Jesus loved saith unto Peter, It is the Lord. So when Simon Peter [cp. 1 40; etc.] heard that it was the Lord,

cp. 11 32; 18 6: also 9 38.

cp. 7 15, 21, 46.

he girt his coat about him (for he was naked), and cast himself into the sea. **8** But the other disciples came in the little boat (for they were not far from the land, but about two hundred cubits off), dragging the net *full* of fishes. **9** So when they got out upon the land, they see ² a fire of coals there, and ³ fish laid thereon, and ⁴ bread. **10** Jesus saith unto them, Bring of the fish which ye have now taken. **11** Simon Peter therefore went ⁵ up, and drew the net to land, full of great fishes, a hundred and fifty and three: and for all there were so many, the net was not rent.

[Matt.]

21 And going on from thence

he saw other two brethren, ¹ James the *son* of Zebedee, and John his brother,

in the boat with Zebedee their father, mending their nets; and he called them.

[Mark]

verse 6

19 And going on a little [cp. Luke 5 3] further, he saw James the *son* of Zebedee, and John his brother, who also were in the boat

mending the nets. **20** And straightway he called them:

[Luke]

10 and so were also

James and John,

sons of Zebedee,

which were partners with Simon. And Jesus said unto Simon, Fear not; from henceforth [cp. 1 48; 12 52; 22 18, 69] thou shalt ¹ catch men. **11** And when they had brought their boats to land, they left all [cp. Matt. 19 27; Mark 10 28: also Luke 5 28; 14 33],

and followed him [cp. 5 28; 18 28].

[John]

[cp. 21 15-23]

[Matt.]

verse 19

22 And

they straightway left the boat and their father [cp. Luke 18 28],

and followed him [cp. 4 20; 9 9; 19 27].

[Mark]

verse 17

and

they left their father Zebedee in the boat with the hired servants [cp. Luke 18 28], and went after him [cp. 1 18; 2 14; 10 28].

[John]

[cp. also 1 35-51.]

¹ Or, *Jacob*: and so elsewhere.

¹ Gr. *take alive*.

¹ That is, *Twin*.
² Gr. *a fire of charcoal*.
³ Or, *a fish*   ⁴ Or, *a loaf*
⁵ Or, *aboard*

(ii) The Great Sermon (Matt. : §§ 32-51)

§ 32. **The Occasion of the Sermon**

Matt. 5 1-2		Luke 6 20	
			cp. 6 5.
1 And seeing the multitudes [cp. 3 7; 8 18; 9 36], he went up into the mountain [cp. 14 23; 15 29; 17 1; 28 16]: and when he had sat down [cp. 15 29; 24 3], his disciples came unto him [cp. 13 10, 36; 14 15; 15 12, 23; 17 19; 18 1; 24 1, 3; 26 17]: 2 and he opened his mouth and taught them, saying,	cp. 3 13; 6 46; 9 2. cp. 13 3. cp. 6 35.	cp. 6 12 ; 9 28. 20 And he lifted up his eyes on his disciples, cp. 9 12.	cp. 6 3, 15. cp. 6 5.
		and said,	

§ 33. **The Beatitudes**

Matt. 5 3-12		Luke 6 20-26	
3 Blessed are the poor in spirit: for theirs is the kingdom of heaven. 4 ¹ Blessed are they that mourn: for they shall be comforted. 5 Blessed are the meek: for they shall inherit the earth. 6 Blessed are they that hunger and thirst after righteousness [cp. 6 33: also 3 15; 5 10, 20; 6 1; 21 32]: for they shall be filled.		Blessed are ye poor : for yours is the kingdom of God [cp. 16 25]. verse 21 : cp. also verse 25. 21 Blessed are ye that hunger now :	cp. 16 20. cp. 7 37.
verse 4 7 Blessed are the merciful: for they shall obtain mercy. 8 Blessed are the pure in heart: for they shall see God. 9 Blessed are the peacemakers [cp. 10 13]: for they shall be called sons of God [cp. 5 45; 8 12; 13 38]. 10 Blessed are they that have been persecuted for righteousness' [cp. 3 15; 5 6, 20; 6 1, 33; 21 32] sake: for theirs is the kingdom of heaven. 11 Blessed are ye when *men* shall	cp. 9 50.	for ye shall be filled. Blessed are ye that weep now : for ye shall laugh. cp. 6 36. cp. 10 5, 6: also 1 79; 2 14, 29; 19 38, 42. cp. 20 36 : also 6 35 ; 16 8.	cp. 16 20₅ cp. 14 27; 16 33. cp. 12 36: also 1 12; 11 52.
cp. 10 22; 24 9.	cp. 13 13.	22 Blessed are ye, when men shall hate you [cp. 1 71; 6 27; 21 17], and when they shall separate you *from their company*, and reproach you,	cp. 15 18, 19; 17 14.
reproach you, and persecute you, and say all manner of evil against you falsely, for my sake [cp. 10 18, 39; 16 25: also 10 22; 19 29; 24 9]. 12 Rejoice, and be exceeding glad: for great is your reward in heaven: for so persecuted they the prophets [cp. 21 35-36; 22 6; 23 29-34, 37] which were before you.	cp. 8 35; 10 29; 13 9: also 13 13. cp. 12 3-5.	and cast out your name as evil, for the Son of man's sake [cp. 9 24: also 21 12, 17: and 18 29]. 23 Rejoice in that day, and leap for joy: for behold, your reward is great in heaven: for in the same manner did their fathers unto the prophets [cp. 11 47-50; 13 33, 34 ; 20 10-12]. 24 But woe unto you that are rich ! for ye have received your consola-tion [cp. 16 25]. 25 Woe unto	cp. 15 21.
¹ Some ancient authorities transpose ver. 4 and 5.		you, ye that are full now ! for ye shall hunger. Woe *unto you*, ye that laugh now ! for ye shall mourn and weep. 26 Woe *unto you*, when all men shall speak well of you ! for in the same manner did their fathers to the false prophets.	

Matt. 5 5: *cp.* Ps. 37 11.

§ 34. **The Disciples as Salt and Light**

Matt. 5 13-16	Mark 9 50; 4 21	Luke 14 34; 8 16; 11 33	
13 Ye are the salt of the earth: but if the salt have lost its savour, wherewith shall it be salted? it is thenceforth good for nothing, but to be cast out and trodden under foot of men. **14** Ye are the light of the world. A city set on a hill cannot be hid.	**9 50** Salt is good: but if the salt have lost its saltness, wherewith will ye season it?	**14 34** Salt therefore is good: but if even the salt have lost its savour, wherewith shall it be seasoned? **35** It is fit neither for the land nor for the dunghill: *men* cast it out.	*cp.* 8 12: *also* 1 4; 9 5; 12 46.
15 Neither do *men* light a lamp, and put it under the bushel,	**4 21** Is the lamp brought to be put under the bushel, or under the bed, *and* not to be put on the stand?	**8 16** And no man, when he hath lighted a lamp, covereth it with a vessel, or putteth it under a bed; but putteth it on a stand,	**11 33** No man, when he hath lighted a lamp, putteth it in a cellar, neither under the bushel,
but on the stand; and it shineth unto all that are in the house. **16** Even so let your light shine before men, that they may see your good works, and glorify [*cp.* 9 8; 15 31] your Father which is in heaven [*cp.* 5 45; 6 1, 9; 7 11, 21; 10 32, 33; 12 50; 16 17; 18 10, 14, 19: *also* 5 48; 6 14, 26, 32; 15 13; 18 35; 23 9].		but on the stand, that they which enter in may see the light.	
	cp. 2 12.	that they which enter in may see the light.	*cp.* 15 8: *also* 9 24.
	cp. 11 25, 26.	*cp.* 2 20; 5 25, 26; 7 16; 13 13; 17 15, 18; 18 43; 23 47. *cp.* 11 13.	

§ 35. **Jesus, the Disciples, and the Law**

Matt. 5 17-20			
17 Think not that I came to destroy the law or the prophets [*cp.* 7 12; 11 13; 22 40]: I came not to destroy, but to fulfil.		*cp.* 16 16.	
18 For verily I say unto you, Till heaven and earth pass away [*cp.* 24 35], one jot or one tittle shall in no wise pass away from the law, till all things be accomplished. **19** Whosoever therefore shall break one of these least	*cp.* 13 31.	Luke 16 17 But it is easier for heaven and earth to pass away [*cp.* 21 33], than for one tittle of the law to fall.	
commandments, and shall teach men so, shall be called least in the kingdom of heaven [*cp.* 11 11]: but whosoever shall do and teach them, he shall be called great in the kingdom of heaven [*cp.* 11 11; 18 1, 4]. **20** For I say unto you, that except your righteousness [*cp.* 6 1: *also* 3 15; 5 6, 10; 6 33; 21 32] shall exceed *the righteousness* of the scribes and Pharisees ye shall in no wise enter into the kingdom of heaven [*cp.* 7 21; 18 3; 19 23, 24; 21 31; 23 13: *also* 7 13; 18 8, 9; 19 17; 25 21, 23].	*cp.* 9 47; 10 15, 23, 24, 25: *also* 9 43, 45.	*cp.* 7 28. *cp.* 9 48. *cp.* 7 28. *cp.* 18 17, 24, 25: *also* 11 52; 13 24; 24 26.	*cp.* 3 5: *also* 10 1, 2, 9.

§ 36. **Murder, Anger, and the Need for Reconciliation in view of the Coming Judgement**

Matt. 5 21-26		
21 Ye have heard that it was said to them of old time [*cp.* 5 27, 31, 33, 38, 43], Thou shalt not kill; and whosoever shall kill shall be in danger of the judgement: **22** but I say		

unto you, that every one who is angry with his brother [1] shall be in danger of the judgement; and whosoever shall say to his brother, [2] Raca, shall be in danger of the council; and whosoever shall say, [3] Thou fool [cp. 23 17], shall be in danger [4] of the [5] hell of fire [cp. 18 9: also 5 29, 30; 10 28; 23 15, 33: and 3 10, 12; 7 19; 13 42, 50; 18 8; 25 41]. **23** If therefore thou art offering thy gift [cp. 2 11; 8 4] at the altar, and there rememberest that thy brother hath aught against thee, **24** leave there thy gift before the altar, and go thy way, first [cp. 6 33; 7 5; 23 26] be reconciled to thy brother, and then come and offer thy gift.   **25** Agree

	cp. 9 43, 45, 47.	cp. 12 5: also 3 9, 17.	cp. 15 6.
	cp. 11 25. cp. 7 27.	cp. 6 42.	

with thine adversary quickly, whiles thou art with him in the way; lest haply the adversary deliver thee to the judge, and the judge   [6] deliver thee to the officer, and   thou be cast into prison.   **26** Verily I say unto thee, Thou shalt by no means come out thence, till thou have paid the last farthing [cp. 18 34, 35].

Luke 12 58 For as thou art going with thine adversary before the magistrate, on the way give diligence to be quit of him; lest haply he hale thee unto the judge, and the judge shall deliver thee to the [1] officer, and the [1] officer shall cast thee into prison.   59 I say unto thee, Thou shalt by no means come out thence, till thou have paid the very last mite.

[1] Many ancient authorities insert *without cause*.
[2] An expression of contempt.
[3] Or, *Moreh*, a Hebrew expression of condemnation.
[4] Gr. *unto* or *into*.   [5] Gr. *Gehenna of fire*.
[6] Some ancient authorities omit *deliver thee*.

[1] Gr. *exactor*.

Matt. 5 21 = Exod. 20 13; Deut. 5 17.

§ 37. Adultery, the Treatment of Offending Members, and Divorce

Matt. 5 27-32

27 Ye have heard that it was said [cp. 5 21, 31, 33, 38, 43], Thou shalt not commit adultery: **28** but I say unto you, that every one that looketh on a woman to lust after her hath committed adultery with her already in his heart. **29** And if thy right [cp. 5 30, 39; 27 29] eye causeth thee to stumble, pluck it out, and cast it from thee: for it is profitable for thee that one of thy members should perish, and not thy whole body be cast into [1] hell [cp. 5 30; 10 28; 23 15, 33: also 5 22; 18 9].

			cp. 6 6; 22 50.	cp. 18 10.
	verse 9	*verse 47*		
			cp. 12 5.	

30 And if thy right [cp. 5 29, 39; 27 29] hand causeth thee to stumble, cut it off, and cast it from thee: for it is profitable for thee that one of thy members should perish,

and not thy whole body

go into [1] hell [see above].
cp. 3 10, 12: 7 19.

verse 29

Matt. 18 8 And if thy hand or thy foot causeth thee to stumble, cut it off, and cast it from thee: it is good for thee to enter into life maimed or halt, rather than having two hands or two feet to be cast into the eternal fire [cp. 25 41: also 13 42, 50].

Mark 9 43 And if thy hand cause thee to stumble, cut it off: it is good for thee to enter into life maimed, rather than having thy two hands to go into [1] hell, into the unquenchable fire.[2] 45 And if thy foot cause thee to stumble, cut it off: it is good for thee to enter into life halt, rather than having thy two feet to be cast into [1] hell. 47 And if thine eye cause thee

			cp. 6 6; 22 50.	cp. 18 10.
			cp. 12 5.	
			cp. 3 17: also 3 9.	cp. 15 6.
			cp. 12 5.	

9 And if thine eye causeth thee

to stumble, pluck it out, and cast it from thee: it is good for thee to enter into life with one eye, rather than having two eyes to be cast into the [1] hell of fire [cp. 5 22: also 5 29, 30 ; 10 28 ; 23 15, 33].

to stumble, cast it out: it is good for thee to enter into the kingdom of God with one eye, rather than having two eyes to be cast into [1] hell.

cp. 12 5.

31 It was said also [cp. 5 21, 27, 33, 38, 43], Whosoever shall put away his wife, let him give her a writing of divorcement:

32 but I say unto you, that every one that putteth away his wife, saving for the cause of fornication, maketh her an adulteress: and whosoever shall marry her when she is put away committeth adultery.

Matt. 19 7 They say unto him, Why then did Moses command to give a bill of divorcement, and to put *her* away? ... 9 And I say unto you, Whosoever shall put away his wife, [2] except for fornication, and shall marry another, committeth adultery: [3] and he that marrieth her when she is put away committeth adultery.

Mark 10 4 And they said, Moses suffered to write a bill of divorcement, and to put her away. ... 11 And he saith unto them, Whosoever shall put away his wife, and marry another, committeth adultery against her: 12 and if she herself shall put away her husband, and marry another, she committeth adultery.

Luke 16 18 Every one that putteth away his wife, and marrieth another, committeth adultery: and he that marrieth one that is put away from a husband committeth adultery.

[1] Gr. *Gehenna.*

[1] Gr. *Gehenna of fire.*
[2] Some ancient authorities read *saving for the cause of fornication, maketh her an adulteress:* as in ch. 5. 32.
[3] The following words, to the end of the verse, are omitted by some ancient authorities.

[1] Gr. *Gehenna.*
[2] Ver. 44 and 46 (which are identical with ver. 48) are omitted by the best ancient authorities.

Matt. 5 27 = Exod. 20 14 ; Deut. 5 18.   Matt. 5 31 (Matt. 19 7 ‖ Mark 10 4) = Deut. 24 1.

Matt. 5 32 ‖ Matt. 19 9 ‖ Mark 10 11 ‖ Luke 16 18 : *cp.* 1 Cor. 7 10-11, 'But unto the married I give charge, *yea* not I, but the Lord, That the wife depart not from her husband (but and if she depart, let her remain unmarried, or else be reconciled to her husband) ; and that the husband leave not his wife.'

§ 38. **Oaths**

[*Cp.* Matt. 23 16-22]

Matt. 5 33-37

33 Again, ye have heard that it was said to them of old time [*cp.* 5 21, 27, 31, 38, 43], Thou shalt not forswear thyself, but shalt perform unto the Lord thine oaths: **34** but I say unto you, Swear not at all; neither by the heaven, for it is the throne of God [*cp.* 23 22]; **35** nor by the earth, for it is the footstool of his feet; nor [1] by Jerusalem, for it is the city of the great King. **36** Neither shalt thou swear by thy head, for thou canst not make one hair white or black. **37** [2] But let your speech be, Yea, yea; Nay, nay: and whatsoever is more than these is of [3] the evil *one* [*cp.* 5 39; 6 13; 13 19, 38].

cp. 17 15.

[1] Or, *toward*   [2] Some ancient authorities read *But your speech shall be.*
[3] Or, *evil:* as in ver. 39; 6 13.

Matt. 5 33 : *cp.* Lev. 19 12 ; Exod. 20 7 ; Deut. 5 11 ; Numb. 30 2 ; Deut. 23 21 ; Eccl. 5 4 ; Ecclus. 18 22.

§ 39. **Non-resistance**

Matt. 5 38-42		Luke 6 29-30	

Matt. 5 38-42

38 Ye have heard that it was said
[*cp.* 5 21, 27, 31, 33, 43], An eye for an
eye, and a tooth for a tooth: **39** but
I say unto you, Resist not ¹ him that is
evil [*cp.* 5 37; 6 13; 13 19, 38] : but
whosoever smiteth thee on thy right
[*cp.* 5 29, 30; 27 29] cheek, turn to
him the other also. **40** And if any
man would go to law with thee, and
take away thy coat, let him have
thy cloke also. **41** And whosoever shall
² compel thee to go one mile, go with
him twain. **42** Give to him   that
asketh thee, and from him that would
borrow of thee [*cp.* Luke 6 34, 35] turn
not thou away.

¹ Or, *evil*   ² Gr. *impress.*

Luke 6 29-30

29 To
him that smiteth thee on the *one*
[*cp.* 6 6; 22 50] cheek offer
also the other ;   and from
him   that
taketh away thy cloke withhold not
thy coat also.

cp. 17 15.

cp. 18 10.

cp. 19 23.

30. Give to everyone that
asketh thee; and of him that
taketh away thy goods ask them
not again.

Matt. 5 38 = Exod. 21 24 ; Lev. 24 20 ; Deut. 19 21.

§ 40. **The Love that is Perfect**

Matt. 5 43-48

43 Ye have heard that it was said
[*cp.* 5 21, 27, 31, 33, 38], Thou shalt love
thy neighbour, and hate thine enemy :
44 but I say unto you,
Love your enemies, and
            cp. 10 22 ; 24 9.

cp. 13 13.

            pray for them that
persecute   you;
45 that ye may be sons [*cp.* 5 9; 8 12;
13 38] of your Father which is in
heaven [*cp.* 5 16; 6 1, 9; 7 11, 21;
10 32, 33; 12 50; 16 17; 18 10, 14,
19: *also* 5 48; 6 14, 26, 32; 15 13;
18 35; 23 9: Mark 11 25, 26, *and* Luke 11
13] : for he maketh his sun to rise on the
evil and the good, and sendeth rain
on the just and the unjust [*cp.* 13 30].
46 For if ye love them that love you,
what reward [*cp.* Luke 6 35] have ye ?
do not even the ¹ publicans [*cp.* 9 11 ;
11 19; 18 17; 21 31, 32]
        cp. 9 11, 13; 11 19; 26 45.

cp. 2 16.

cp. 2 16, 17;
14 41.

        the same ? **47** And if ye
salute your brethren only,
                    what
do ye more *than others* ? do not even
the ¹ Gentiles [*cp.* 6 7; 18 17: *also* 6 32
and Luke 12 30] the same ?

verse 45

cp. 5 7.

48 Ye therefore shall be

Luke 6 27-28, 32-36

27 But I say unto you which hear,
Love your enemies,   do good to
them that hate you [*cp.* 1 71 ;
6 22 ; 21 17], **28** bless them that
curse you, pray for them that
despitefully use you [*cp.* 23 34].
            verse 35

cp. 15 18, 19;
17 14.

cp. 12 36:
also 1 12;
11 52.

32 And if ye love them that love you,
what thank   have ye ?
for even   [*cp.* 5 30;
7 29, 34; 15 1; 18 10] sinners
[*cp.* 5 8, 30, 32 ; 7 34, 37 ; 15 1, 2 ;
18 13 ; 19 7; 24 7] love those that
love them. **33** And if ye do good
to them that do good to you, what
thank have ye ? for even sinners
[*see above*] do the same. **34** And if ye
lend [*cp.* Matt. 5 42] to them of
whom ye hope to receive, what
thank have ye ? even sinners [*see
above*] lend to sinners, to receive
again as much. **35** But love your
enemies, and do *them* good, and
lend [*cp.* Matt. 5 42], ¹ never despairing ; and your reward [*cp.*
Matt. 5 46] shall be great, and ye
shall be sons [*cp.* 16 8 ; 20 36] of
the Most High [*cp.* 1 32, 35, 76 ;
8 28] : for he is kind toward the
unthankful and evil. **36** Be ye

cp. 9 16, 24,
25, 31.

cp. 12 36: *also*
1 12 ; 11 52.

perfect [cp. 19 21],   as your
heavenly Father [cp. 6 14, 26, 32; 15
13; 18 35; 23 9: also 5 16, 45; 6 1, 9;
7 11, 21; 10 32, 33; 12 50; 16 17; 18
10, 14, 19: Mark 11 25, 26 and Luke
11 13] is perfect.

¹ That is, collectors or renters of Roman taxes: and so
elsewhere.

---

merciful [cp. Matt. 5 7], even as your
Father

is merciful.

¹ Some ancient authorities read despairing
of no man.

Matt. 5 43 = Lev. 19 18.

§ 41. Secrecy the Condition of the Heavenly Reward

Matt. 6 1

1 Take heed that ye do not your righteousness [cp. 5 20: also
3 15; 5 6, 10; 6 33; 21 32] before men, to be seen of them
[cp. 6 2, 5, 16; 23 5, 28]: else ye have no reward with your
Father which is in heaven [cp. 5 16, 45; 6 9; 7 11, 21; 10
32, 33; 12 50; 16 17; 18 10, 14, 19: also 5 48; 6 14, 26,
32; 15 13; 18 35; 23 9].

cp. 11 25, 26.   cp. 11 13.

§ 42. Almsgiving

Matt. 6 2-4

2 When therefore thou doest alms, sound not a trumpet before
thee, as the hypocrites [cp. 6 5, 16; 24 51] do in the synagogues
and in the streets, that they may have glory of men [cp. 6 1,
5, 16; 23 5, 28]. Verily I say unto you, They have received
their reward [cp. 6 5, 16]. **3** But when thou doest alms, let not
thy left hand know what thy right hand doeth: **4** that thine
alms may be in secret: and thy Father which seeth in secret
shall recompense thee [cp. 6 6, 18].

§ 43. Prayer and the Duty of Forgiveness

Matt. 6 5-15

5 And when ye pray [cp. Luke 11 2], ye shall not be as the
hypocrites [cp. 6 2, 16; 24 51]: for they love to stand and
pray in the synagogues and in the corners of the streets, that
they may be seen of men [cp. 6 1, 2, 16; 23 5, 28]. Verily
I say unto you, They have received their reward [cp. 6 2, 16].
6 But thou, when thou prayest, enter into thine inner
chamber, and having shut thy door, pray to thy Father which
is in secret, and thy Father which seeth in secret shall
recompense thee [cp. 6 4, 18]. **7** And in praying use not vain
repetitions, as the Gentiles [cp. 5 47; 18 17: also 6 32] do: for
they think that they shall be heard for their much speaking. **8** Be not therefore like unto them: for ¹ your Father
knoweth [cp. 6 32] what things ye have need of, before
ye ask him. **9** After this manner therefore pray ye:
Our Father [cp. 11 25, 26; 26 39, 42]
which art in heaven [cp. 5 16, 45;
6 1; 7 11, 21; 10 32, 33; 12 50;
16 17; 18 10, 14, 19: also 5 48; 6
14, 26, 32; 15 13; 18 35; 23 9],
Hallowed be thy name.
10 Thy kingdom come. Thy will be
done [cp. 26 39, 42: also 7 21; 12 50;
21 31], as in heaven, so on earth.
11 Give us this day ² our daily
bread. **12** And forgive us our debts,
as we   also have forgiven
our debtors.

cp. 12 40.   cp. 20 47.

cp. 12 30.

Luke 11 2 And he said unto them,
When ye pray [cp. Matt. 6 5], say,
¹ Father [cp. 10 21, 22; 22 42;
23 34, 46],

cp. 11 13.

Hallowed be thy name [cp. 1 49].
Thy kingdom come.²
cp. 22 42.

3 Give us day by day ³ our daily
bread. 4 And forgive us our sins;
for we ourselves also   forgive
every one that is indebted to us.

cp. 14 36.
cp. 11 25, 26.

cp. 14 36:
also 3 35.

cp. 11 41; 12
27, 28; 17
1, 5, 11, 21,
24, 25.

cp. 4 34; 5
30; 6 38;
7 17; 9 31.

13 And bring us not into temptation [*cp*. 26 41], but deliver us from ³ the evil *one* [*cp*. 5 37, 39; 13 19, 38].⁴	*cp*. 14 38.	And bring us not into temptation [*cp*. 22 40, 46].⁴

¹ Many ancient authorities read *Our Father, which art in heaven.* See Matt. 6 9.
¹ Many ancient authorities add *Thy will be done, as in heaven, so on earth.* See Matt. 6 10.
³ Gr. *our bread for the coming day.*
⁴ Many ancient authorities add *but deliver us from the evil one* (or, *from evil*). See Matt. 6 13.

cp. 17 15.

14 For if ye forgive men their trespasses, your heavenly Father [*cp*. 5 48; 6 26, 32; 15 13; 18 35; 23 9: *also* 5 16, 45; 6 1, 9; 7 11, 21; 10 32, 33; 12 50; 16 17; 18 10, 14, 19] will also forgive you. **15** But if ye forgive not men their trespasses, neither will your Father forgive your trespasses [*cp*. 18 21-35].	*cp*. 11 25. *cp*. 11 25, 26. *cp*. 11 26.	*cp*. 17 3-4. *cp*. 11 13.

¹ Some ancient authorities read *God your Father.*
¹ Gr. *our bread for the coming day.*   ³ Or, *evil*
⁴ Many authorities, some ancient, but with variations, add *For thine is the kingdom, and the power, and the glory, for ever. Amen.*

Matt. 6 9 ‖ Luke 11 2 : *cp*. Rom. 8 15 ; Gal. 4 6.

§ 44. **Fasting**

[*Cp*. Matt. 9 14-15 ‖ Mark 2 18-20 ‖ Luke 5 33-35]

Matt. 6 16-18

16 Moreover when ye fast, be not, as the hypocrites [*cp*. 6 2, 5; 24 51], of a sad countenance: for they disfigure their faces, that they may be seen of men [*cp*. 6 1, 2, 5; 23 5, 28] to fast. Verily I say unto you, They have received their reward [*cp*. 6 2, 5]. **17** But thou, when thou fastest, anoint thy head, and wash thy face; **18** that thou be not seen of men to fast, but of thy Father which is in secret: and thy Father, which seeth in secret, shall recompense thee [*cp*. 6 4, 6].		

§ 45. **True Treasure and where it may be found**

Matt. 6 19-34		Luke 11 34-36; 12 22-34; 16 13	
19 Lay not up for yourselves treasures upon the earth, where moth and rust doth consume, and where thieves ¹ break through [*cp*. 24 43] and steal: **20** but lay up for yourselves treasures in heaven [*cp*. 19 21], where neither moth nor rust doth consume, and where thieves do not ¹ break through [*cp*. 24 43] nor steal: **21** for where thy treasure is, there will thy heart be also. **22** The lamp of the body is the eye: if therefore thine eye be single, thy whole body shall be full of light. **23** But if thine eye be evil [*cp*. 20 15], thy whole body shall be full of darkness. If therefore the light that is in thee be darkness, how great is the darkness !	*cp*. 10 21. *cp*. 7 22.	*cp*. 12 39. 12 33 Sell that ye have, and give alms; make for yourselves purses which wax not old, a treasure in the heavens [*cp*. 18 22] that faileth not, where no thief draweth near, neither moth destroyeth. *cp*. 12 39. **34** For where your treasure is, there will your heart be also. 11 34 The lamp of thy body is thine eye : when thine eye is single, thy whole body also is full of light ; but when it is evil, thy body also is full of darkness. **35** Look therefore whether the light that is in thee be not darkness. **36** If therefore thy whole body be full of light, having no part dark, it shall be wholly full	

Matthew

24 No man can serve two masters: for either he will hate the one, and love the other; or else he will hold to one, and despise the other. Ye cannot serve God and mammon.

25 Therefore I say unto you, Be not anxious [cp. 6 31, 34; 10 19] for your life, what ye shall eat, or what ye shall drink; nor yet for your body, what ye shall put on. Is not the life more than the food, and the body than the raiment? 26 Behold the birds of the heaven [cp. 8 20; 13 32: *also* Luke 8 5; 9 58; 13 19], that they sow not, neither do they reap, nor gather into barns; and your heavenly Father [cp. 5 48; 6 14, 32; 15 13; 18 35; 23 9; *and* Luke 11 13: *also* 5 16, 45; 6 1, 9; 7 11, 21; 10 32, 33; 12 50; 16 17; 18 10, 14, 19] feedeth them. Are not ye of much more value than they [cp. 10 31; 12 12]? 27 And which of you by being anxious can add one cubit unto his [2] stature? 28 And why are ye anxious concerning raiment?

Consider the lilies of the field, how they grow; they toil not, neither do they spin: 29 yet I say unto you, that even Solomon in all his glory was not arrayed like one of these. 30 But if God doth so clothe the grass of the field, which to-day is, and to-morrow is cast into the oven, *shall he* not much more *clothe* you, O ye of little faith [cp. 8 26; 14 31; 16 8: *also* 17 20]? 31 Be not therefore anxious, saying, What shall we eat? or, What shall we drink? or, Wherewithal shall we be clothed?

32 For after all these things do the Gentiles [cp. 5 47; 6 7; 18 17] seek; for your heavenly Father [*see references at verse* 26] knoweth [cp. 6 8] that ye have need of all these things. 33 But seek ye first [cp. 5 24; 7 5; 23 26] his kingdom, and his righteousness [cp. 5 6: *also* 3 15; 5 10, 20; 6 1; 21 32]; and all these things shall be added unto you [cp. 19 29]. 34 Be not therefore anxious for the morrow: for the morrow will be anxious for itself. Sufficient [cp. 10 25] unto the day is the evil thereof.

Cross-references (Mark): cp. 13 11. — cp. 4 32. — cp. 11 25, 26. — cp. 4 40; 11 22; 16 14. — cp. 7 27. — cp. 4 24; 10 29-30.

Luke

of light, as when the lamp with its bright shining doth give thee light. 16 13 No [1] servant can serve two masters: for either he will hate the one, and love the other; or else he will hold to one, and despise the other. Ye cannot serve God and mammon. 12 22 And he said unto his disciples, Therefore I say unto you, Be not anxious [cp. 12 11] for *your* [2] life, what ye shall eat; nor yet for your body, what ye shall put on. 23 For the [2] life is more than the food, and the body than the raiment. 24 Consider the ravens, that they sow not, neither reap; which have no store-chamber nor barn; and God feedeth them: of how much more value are ye than the birds [cp. 12 7]! 25 And which of you by being anxious can add a cubit unto his [3] stature? 26 If then ye are not able to do even that which is least, why are ye anxious concerning the rest [cp. 8 10; 18 9, 11; 24 9, 10]? 27 Consider the lilies, how they grow: they toil not, neither do they spin; yet I say unto you, Even Solomon in all his glory was not arrayed like one of these. 28 But if God doth so clothe the grass in the field, which to-day is, and to-morrow is cast into the oven; how much more *shall he* clothe you, O ye of little faith [cp. 8 25; *etc.*]? 29 And seek not ye what ye shall eat, and what ye shall drink, neither be ye of doubtful mind. 30 For all these things do the nations of the world seek after: but your Father knoweth that ye have need of these things. 31 Howbeit seek ye [cp. 6 42] [4] his kingdom, and these things shall be added unto you [cp. 18 29-30].

32 Fear not, little flock; for it is your Father's good pleasure to give you the kingdom.

Cross-references (John): cp. 3 12; 6 64; 14 10; 20 27.

---

[1] Gr. *dig through.* [2] Or, *age*

[1] Gr. *household-servant.* [2] Or, *soul*
[3] Or, *age*
[4] Many ancient authorities read *the kingdom of God.*

§ 46. Judgement of Others

Matt. 7 1-5	Mark 4 24	Luke 6 37-38, 41-42
1 Judge not, that ye be not judged. **2** For with what judgement ye judge, ye shall be judged:		**37** And judge not, and ye shall not be judged:
		and condemn not, and ye shall not be condemned: release, and ye shall be released: **38** give, and it shall be given unto you; good measure, pressed down, shaken together, running over, shall they give into your bosom. For
and with what measure ye mete, it shall be measured unto you.	**24** And he said unto them, Take heed what ye hear: with what measure ye mete it shall be measured unto you: and more shall be given unto you [*cp.* 10 29-30].	with what measure ye mete it shall be measured to you again.
cp. 6 33; 19 29.		*cp.* 12 31; 18 29-30.
3 And why beholdest thou the mote that is in thy brother's eye, but considerest not the beam that is in thine own eye? **4** Or how wilt thou say to thy brother, Let me cast out the mote out of thine eye; and lo, the beam is in thine own eye? **5** Thou hypocrite, cast out first [*cp.* 5 24; 6 33; 23 26] the beam out of thine own eye; and then shalt thou see clearly to cast out the mote out of thy brother's eye.	*cp.* 7 27.	**41** And why beholdest thou the mote that is in thy brother's eye, but considerest not the beam that is in thine own eye? **42** Or how canst thou say to thy brother, Brother, let me cast out the mote that is in thine eye, when thou thyself beholdest not the beam that is in thine own eye? Thou hypocrite, cast out first the beam out of thine own eye, and then shalt thou see clearly to cast out the mote that is in thy brother's eye.

cp. 8 7-9.

§ 47. The Sanctity of Holy Things

Matt. 7 6		
6 Give not that which is holy unto the dogs [*cp.* 15 26], neither cast your pearls before the swine, lest haply they trample them under their feet, and turn and rend you.	*cp.* 7 27.	

§ 48. Answer to Prayer and the Golden Rule

Matt. 7 7-12		Luke 11 9-13; 6 31	John 15 7	John 16 24
7 Ask, and it shall be given you [*cp.* 18 19; 21 22]; seek, and ye shall find; knock, and it shall be opened unto you: **8** for every one that asketh receiveth; and he that seeketh findeth; and to him that knocketh it shall be opened. **9** Or what man is there of you, who, if his son shall ask him for a loaf, will give him a stone; **10** or if he shall ask for a fish, will give him a serpent?	*cp.* 11 24.	**9** And I say unto you, Ask, and it shall be given you; seek, and ye shall find; knock, and it shall be opened unto you. **10** For every one that asketh receiveth; and he that seeketh findeth; and to him that knocketh it shall be opened. **11** And of which of you that is a father shall his son ask a loaf, and he give him a stone? or a fish, and he for a fish give him a serpent? **12** Of if he shall ask an egg, will he give him a scorpion? **13** If ye then, being evil, know how to give good gifts	Ask whatsoever ye will, and it shall be done unto you.	Ask, and ye shall **receive** [*cp.* 14 13; 15 16; 16 23].
11 If ye then, being evil [*cp.* 12 34], know how to give good gifts				

unto your children, how much more shall your Father which is in heaven [*cp.* 5 16, 45; 6 1, 9; 7 21; 10 32, 33; 12 50; 16 17; 18 10, 14, 19: *also* 5 48; 6 14, 26, 32; 15 13; 18 35; 23 9] give good things to them that ask him? **12** All things therefore whatsoever ye would that men should do unto you, even so do ye also unto them:

for this is the law and the prophets [*cp.* 5 17; 11 13; 22 40: *also* Luke 16 16].

cp. 11 25, 26.

unto your children, how much more shall *your* heavenly Father

give the Holy Spirit to them that ask him?
6 31 And as ye would that men should do to you, do ye also to them likewise.

¹ Some ancient authorities omit *a loaf, and he give him a stone? or,*

§ 49. **The Narrow Gate**

Matt. 7 13-14

13 Enter ye in [*cp.* 5 20; 7 21; 18 3, 8, 9; 19 17, 23, 24; 21 31; 23 13; 25 21, 23] by the narrow gate: for wide ¹ is the gate, and broad is the way, that leadeth to destruction, and many be they that enter in thereby. **14** ² For narrow is the gate, and straitened the way, that leadeth unto life, and few [*cp.* Luke 13 23] be they that find it.

¹ Some ancient authorities omit *is the gate.*
² Many ancient authorities read *How narrow is the gate, &c.*

cp. 9 43, 45, 47; 10 15, 23, 24, 25.

Luke 13 23-24

23 And one said unto him, Lord, are they few [*cp.* Matt. 7 14] that be saved? And he said unto them, **24** Strive to enter in [*cp.* 11 52; 18 17, 24, 25; 24 26] by the narrow door:

for many, I say unto you, shall seek to enter in,

and shall not be able.

cp. 10 1, 2, 9; 3 5.

§ 50. **The Criteria of the True Disciple**

Matt. 7 15-27

15 Beware of false prophets [*cp.* 24 11, 24], which come to you in sheep's clothing, but inwardly are ravening wolves. **16** By their fruits ye shall know them. Do *men* gather grapes of thorns, or figs of thistles? **17** Even so every good tree bringeth forth good fruit; but the corrupt tree bringeth forth evil fruit. **18** A good tree cannot bring forth evil fruit, neither can a corrupt tree bring forth good fruit. **19** Every tree that bringeth not forth good fruit is hewn down, and cast into the fire [= 3 10: *cp.* 3 12; 5 22, 29, 30; 10 28; 13 42, 50; 18 8, 9; 23 33; 25 41]. **20** Therefore by their fruits ye shall know them.

verse 16

Matt. 12 33-35

cp. 13 22.

33 Either make the tree good, and its fruit good; or make the tree corrupt, and its fruit corrupt:

cp. 9 43, 45, 47.

for the tree is known by its fruit.

Luke 6 43-49; 13 26-27

6 44

43 For there is no good tree that bringeth forth corrupt fruit; nor again a corrupt tree that bringeth forth good fruit.

3 9: *cp.* 13 7-9: *also* 3 17; 12 5.

44 For each tree is known by its own fruit. For of thorns men do not gather figs, nor of a bramble bush gather they grapes.

cp. 15 2, 6.

34 Ye offspring of vipers, how can ye, being evil, speak good things ?

verse 35

for out of the abundance of the heart the mouth speaketh. **35** The good man out of his good treasure bringeth forth good things : and the evil man out of his evil treasure bringeth forth evil things.

21 Not every one that saith unto me, Lord, Lord, shall enter into the kingdom of heaven [*cp.* 5 20; 18 3; 19 23, 24; 21 31; 23 13: *also* 7 13; 18 8, 9; 19 17; 25 21, 23]; but he that doeth the will [*cp.* 12 50; 21 31: *also* 6 10; 26 39, 42] of my Father which is in heaven [*cp.* 5 16, 45; 6 1, 9; 7 11; 10 32, 33; 12 50; 16 17; 18 10, 14, 19: *also* 5 48; 6 14, 26, 32; 15 13; 18 35; 23 9]. **22** Many will say to me in that day [*cp.* 24 36: *also* 26 29], Lord, Lord, did we not prophesy by thy name, and by thy name cast out ¹ devils, and by thy name do many ² mighty works? **23** And then will I profess unto them [*cp.* 25 34, 41], I never knew you [*cp.* 25 11, 12]: depart from me [*cp.* 25 41], ye that work iniquity. **24** Every one therefore which heareth these words of mine, and doeth them,

shall be likened unto a wise [*cp.* 10 16; 24 45; 25 2 *ff.*] man, which built his house

upon the rock [*cp.* 16 18]: **25** and the rain descended, and the floods came, and the winds blew, and beat upon that house; and it fell not: for it was founded upon the rock. **26** And every one that heareth these words of mine, and doeth them not, shall be likened unto a foolish [*cp.* 25 2 *ff.*] man, which built his house upon the sand:

27 and the rain descended, and the floods came, and the winds blew, and smote upon that house; and it fell: and great was the fall thereof.

¹ Gr. *demons.*   ² Gr. *powers.*

cp. 9 47; 10 15, 23, 24, 25: *also* 9 43, 45. *cp.* 3 35: *also* 14 36. *cp.* 11 25, 26.

cp. 13 32: *also* 14 25.

cp. 9 38.
cp. 9 39.

45 The good man out of the good treasure of his heart bringeth forth that which is good ; and the evil *man* out of the evil *treasure* bringeth forth that which is evil: for out of the abundance of the heart his mouth speaketh.

verse 45

46 And why call ye me, Lord, Lord,
cp. 18 17, 24, 25: *also* 11 52; 13 24; 24 26.
and do not the things which I say ?
cp. 22 42.
cp. 11 13.

13 26 Then shall ye begin to say, [*cp.* 10 12; 17 31; 21 34] We did eat and drink in thy presence, [*cp.* 9 49] and thou didst teach in our streets; **27** and he shall say, I tell you, I know not whence ye are ; depart from me, all ye workers of iniquity. **6 47** Every one that cometh unto me, and heareth my words, and doeth them, I will shew you to whom he is like: **48** he is like a [*cp.* 12 42] man building a house, who digged and went deep, and laid a foundation upon the rock: and when a flood arose, the stream brake against that house, and could not shake it: ¹ because it had been well builded. **49** But he that heareth, and doeth not, is like a man that built a house upon the earth without a foundation ; against which the stream brake, and straightway it fell in ; and the ruin of that house was great.

¹ Many ancient authorities read *for it had been founded upon the rock* : as in Matt. 7 25.

cp. 13 13.
cp. 3 5: *also* 10 1, 2, 9.

cp. 4 34; 5 30; 6 38; 7 17; 9 31.

cp. 14 20; 16 23, 26.

cp. 7 27, 28: 8 14; 9 29, 30.

Matt. **7** 23 || Luke 13 27 = Ps. 6 8.

§ 51. **The Effect of the Sermon**

Matt. 7 28-29	Mark 1 21-22	Luke 7 1; 4 31-32	
28 And it came to pass, when Jesus ended these words [*cp.* 11 1; 13 53; 19 1; 26 1], the multitudes		7 1 After he had ended all his sayings	
cp. 8 5.	**21** And they go into Capernaum; and straightway on the sabbath day he entered into the synagogue and taught. **22** And they were	in the ears of the people, he entered into Capernaum. **4** 31 And he came down to Capernaum, a city of Galilee. And he was teaching them on the sabbath day: **32** and they were	
were astonished at his teaching [*cp.* 22 33; 13 54; 19 25; 22 22: *also* 8 27; 9 33; 12 23; 15 31; 21 20; 27 14]: **29** for he taught them as *one* having authority [*cp.* 21 23 *ff.*; 9 6; 28 18], and not as their scribes.	astonished at his teaching [*cp.* 11 18; 1 27; 6 2; 10 24, 26; 12 17: *also* 2 12; 5 20, 42; 6 51; 7 37; 10 32; 15 5; 16 5, 8]: for he taught them as having authority [*cp.* 11 27 *ff.*; 1 27; 2 10], and not as the scribes.	astonished at his teaching [*cp.* 2 47, 48; 4 22, 36; 20 26: *also* 5 9, 26; 8 25, 56; 9 43; 11 14; 24 12, 41]; for his word was with authority [*cp.* 20 1 *ff.*; 4 36; 5 24].	*cp.* 7 15, 21, 46. *cp.* 5 27; 17 2.

(iii) Events in Galilee I (§§ 52-64)

§ 52. **The Healing of a Leper**

[*Cp.* Luke 17 11-19]

Matt. 8 1-4	**Mark 1** 40-45	**Luke 5** 12-16	
1 And when he was come down from the mountain, great multitudes followed him. **2** And behold, there came to him a leper	**40** And there cometh to him a leper, beseeching him,	**12** And it came to pass, while he was in one of the cities; behold, a man full of leprosy: and when he saw Jesus, he fell on his face [*cp.* 5 8; 8 28, 41, 47; 17 16: *also* 24 52],	*cp.* 9 38; 11 32; 18 6.
and worshipped him [*cp.* 2 11; 9 18; 14 33; 15 25; 20 20; 28 9, 17: *also* 17 14], saying, Lord, if thou wilt, thou canst [*cp.* 9 28] make me clean. **3** And [*cp.* 20 34: *also* 9 36; 14 14; 15 32] he stretched forth his hand, and touched [*cp.* 8 15; 9 20, 29; 14 36; 17 7; 20 34: *also* 9 18, 25; 14 31; 19 13, 15] him, saying, I will; be thou made clean. And straightway his leprosy was cleansed.	1 and kneeling down to him [*cp.* 10 17: *also* 3 11; 5 6, 22, 33; 7 25], and saying unto him, If thou wilt, thou canst [*cp.* 9 22, 23; 6 5] make me clean. **41** And being moved with compassion [*cp.* 6 34; 8 2], he stretched forth his hand, and touched [*cp.* 3 10; 5 27; 6 56; 7 33; 8 22; 10 13: *also* 1 31; 5 23, 41; 6 2, 5; 8 23, 25; 9 27; 10 16] him, and saith unto him, I will; be thou made clean. **42** And straightway the leprosy departed from him, and he was made clean.	and besought him, saying, Lord, if thou wilt, thou canst make me clean. **13** And [*cp.* 7 13: *also* 10 33; 15 20] he stretched forth his hand, and touched [*cp.* 6 19; 7 14, 39; 8 44; 18 15; 22 51: *also* 4 40; 8 54; 13 13; 14 4] him, saying, I will; be thou made clean. And straightway the leprosy departed from him.	*cp.* 9 6; 20 17.
4 And Jesus [*cp.* 9 30] saith unto him, See thou tell no man [*cp.* 9 30; 12 16: *also* 16 20; 17 9]; but go thy way, shew thyself to the priest,	**43** And he 2 strictly charged him, and straightway sent him out, **44** and saith unto him, See thou say nothing to any man [*cp.* 5 43; 7 36; 8 26: *also* 1 25, 34; 3 12; 8 30; 9 9]: but go thy way, shew thyself to the priest,	**14** And he charged him to tell no man [*cp.* 8 56: *also* 4 35, 41; 9 21, 36]: but go thy way, and shew thyself to the priest [*cp.* 17	

and offer the gift [*cp.* 2 11; 5 23, 24] that Moses commanded, for a testimony unto them [*cp.* 10 18; 24 14].	and offer for thy cleansing the things which Moses commanded, for a testimony unto them [*cp.* 6 11; 13 9]. **45** But he went out, and began to publish [*cp.* 7 36] it much, and to spread abroad the ³ matter, *cp.* 1 28.	14], and offer for thy cleansing, according as Moses commanded, for a testimony unto them [*cp.* 9 5; 21 13]. **15** But so much the more went abroad the report concerning him [*cp.* 4 14, 37; 7 17]: and great multitudes came together [*cp.* 4 42] to hear, and to be healed of their infirmities.
cp. 9 31. *cp.* 4 24; 9 26.		
cp. 14 13.	insomuch that ⁴ Jesus could no more openly enter into ⁵ a city, but was without [*cp.* 1 35; 6 31, 32] in desert places: and they came to him from every quarter.	**16** But he withdrew [*cp.* 4 42; 9 10] himself in the deserts,
cp. 14 23; 19 13; 26 36, 39, 42, 44: *also* 11 25-26.	*cp.* 1 35; 5 46; 14 32, 35, 39.	and prayed [*cp.* 3 21; 6 12; 9 18, 28, 29; 11 1; 22 41, 44: *also* 10 21].	*cp.* 11 41-42; 12 27-28; 17 1-26.

¹ Some ancient authorities omit *and kneeling down to him.*
² Or, *sternly*   ³ Gr. *word.*
⁴ Gr. *he.*   ⁵ Or, *the city*

Matt. 8 4 ‖ Mark 1 44 ‖ Luke 5 14: *cp.* Lev. 13 *and* 14.

§ 53. The Centurion at Capernaum

Matt. 8 5-13		Luke 7 1-10; 13 28-30	John 4 46-53
		7 1 After he had ended all his sayings in the ears of the people, he entered into Capernaum.	
5 And when he was entered into Capernaum,		**2** And a certain centurion's ¹servant, who was ²dear unto him, was sick and at the point of death [*cp.* 8 42].	**46** And there was a certain ¹nobleman, whose son was sick at Capernaum.
there came unto him a centurion, beseeching him,		**3** And when he heard concerning Jesus, he sent unto him elders of the Jews, asking him that he would come and save his ¹ servant.	**47** When he heard that Jesus was come out of Judæa into Galilee, he went unto him, and besought *him* that he would come down, and heal his son; for he was at the point of death. **48** Jesus therefore said unto him, Except ye see signs and wonders, ye will in no wise believe. **49** The ¹ nobleman saith unto him, ² Sir, come down ere my child die.
6 and saying, Lord, my ¹servant lieth in the house sick of the palsy [*cp.* 4 24; 9 2 *ff.*], grievously tormented [*cp.* 4 24].	*cp.* 2 3 *ff.*	*cp.* 5 18 *ff.*	
		4 And they, when they came to Jesus, besought him earnestly, saying, He is worthy that thou shouldest do this for him: **5** for he loveth our nation, and himself built us our synagogue.	
7 And he saith unto him, I will come and heal him. **8** And the centurion answered and said, Lord, I am not ²worthy that thou	*cp.* 5 35.	**6** And Jesus went with them. And when he was now not far from the house, the centurion sent friends to him, saying unto him, Lord, trouble [*cp.* 8 49] not thyself: for I am not ³ worthy that thou	

Matthew

shouldest come under my roof:

but only say [3] the word [cp. 8 16: also 8 3, 13, 32; 9 6, 22, 29; 12 13; 15 28; 17 7, 18], and my [1] servant shall be healed. **9** For I also am a man [4] under authority, having under myself soldiers: and I say to this one, Go, and he goeth; and to another, Come, and he cometh; and to my [5] servant, Do this, and he doeth it. **10** And when Jesus heard it, he marvelled, [cp. 9 22; 16 23]

and said to them that followed, Verily I say unto you, [6] I have not found so great faith, no, not in Israel. **11** And I say unto you, that many shall come from the east and the west, and shall [7] sit down [cp. 26 29]

with Abraham, and Isaac, and Jacob, in the kingdom of heaven [cp. 21 31, 41, 43; 22 7-10: also 10 18; 24 14; 26 13; 28 19]: **12** but the sons of the kingdom [cp. 13 38: also 5 9, 45] shall be cast forth into the outer darkness [cp. 22 13; 25 30]: there shall be the weeping and gnashing of teeth [cp. 13 42, 50; 22 13; 24 51; 25 30].

cp. 19 30; 20 16.

13 And Jesus said unto the centurion, Go thy way;

as thou hast believed, so be it done unto thee [cp. 9 29; 15 28].

And the [1] servant was healed in that hour [cp. 9 22; 15 28; 17 18].

cp. 8 15.

Mark references:

cp. 1 25, 41; 2 11; 3 5; 5 8, 34, 41; 7 29, 34; 9 25; 10 52.

cp. 5 30; 8 33.

cp. 14 25.

cp. 12 9; 13 10; 14 9; 16 15.

cp. 10 31.

cp. 7 29.

cp. 7 30.

cp. 1 31.

Luke

shouldest come under my roof: **7** wherefore neither thought I myself worthy to come unto thee: but [4] say the word [cp. 4 35, 39; 5 13, 24; 6 10; 7 14; 8 29, 32, 48, 54; 9 42; 13 12; 17 14; 18 42], and my [5] servant shall be healed. **8** For I also am a man set under authority, having under myself soldiers: and I say to this one, Go, and he goeth; and to another, Come, and he cometh; and to my [1] servant, Do this, and he doeth it. **9** And when Jesus heard these things, he marvelled at him, and turned [cp. 7 44; 9 55; 10 23; 14 25; 22 61; 23 28] and said unto the multitude that followed him, I say unto you, I have not found so great faith, no, not in Israel.

cp. 14 15; 22 16, 18, 30.

13 28 There shall be the weeping and gnashing of teeth, when ye shall see Abraham, and Isaac, and Jacob, and all the prophets, in the kingdom of God [cp. 14 21-24; 20 16: also 2 30-32; 3 6; 24 47], and yourselves cp. 6 35 16 8; 20 36. cast forth without.

29 And they shall come from the east and west, and from the north and south, and shall [6] sit down in the kingdom of God. **30** And behold, there are last which shall be first, and there are first which shall be last.

50 Jesus saith unto him, Go thy way; thy son liveth. The man believed the word that Jesus spake unto him, and he went his way.

7 10 And they that were sent, returning to the house, found the [1] servant whole.

51 And as he was now going down, his [3] servants met him, saying, that his son lived. **52** So he inquired of them the hour when he began to amend. They said therefore unto him, Yesterday at the seventh hour the fever left him. **53** So the father knew that *it was* at that hour in which Jesus said unto him, Thy son liveth: and himself believed, and his whole house.

cp. 4 39.

Luke references:

cp. 4 50; 5 8; 9 7; 11 43.

cp. 1 38.

cp. 10 16; 11 52.

cp. 12 36: also 1 12; 11 52.

---

[1] Or, boy   [2] Gr. sufficient.
[3] Gr. with a word.
[4] Some ancient authorities insert set: as in Luke 7 8.
[5] Gr. bondservant.
[6] Many ancient authorities read With no man in Israel have I found so great faith.
[7] Gr. recline.

[1] Gr. bondservant.
[2] Or, precious to him. Or, honourable with him.
[3] Gr. sufficient.
[4] Gr. say with a word.
[5] Or, boy   [6] Gr. recline.

[1] Or, king's officer   [2] Or, Lord
[3] Gr. bondservants.

§ 54. The Healing of Peter's Wife's Mother

Matt. 8 14-15	Mark 1 29-31	Luke 4 38-39	

14 And   when Jesus
                    was come into Peter's house,
 	
cp. 17 1; 26 37.
he saw his   wife's mother lying sick of a fever.
                    15 And he   touched her hand [*cp.* 9 25; 8 3; 9 18, 29; 14 31; 17 7; 19 13, 15; 20 34: *also* 9 20; 14 36],
 	
cp. 8 26; 17 18: *also* 8 3, 8, 13, 16, 32; 9 6, 22, 29; 12 13; 15 28; 17 7.
 	
and the fever left her; and   she arose, and ministered unto him.
	29 And straightway, [1] when they were come out of the synagogue, they came into the house of Simon and Andrew, with James and John [*cp.* 5 37; 9 2; 13 3; 14 33]. **30** Now Simon's wife's mother lay sick of a fever ; and straightway they tell him of her: **31** and he came and took her by the hand [*cp.* 5 41; 9 27; 1 41; 5 23; 6 2, 5; 7 33; 8 22, 23, 25; 10 13, 16: *also* 3 10; 5 27; 6 56], and raised her up ;
	cp. 1 25; 3 12; 4 39; 9 25; *also* 1 41; 2 11; 3 5; 5 8, 13, 34, 41; 7 29, 34; 10 52.
	and the fever left her, and she ministered unto them.
		38 And he rose up from the synagogue, and entered into the house of Simon.
		
		cp. 8 51; 9 28.
		And Simon's wife's mother was holden with a great fever ; and they besought him for her. **39** And he
		cp. 8 54; 4 40; 5 13; 7 14; 13 13; 14 4; 18 15; 22 51: *also* 6 19; 7 39; 8 44.
		                    stood over her, and rebuked [*cp.* 4 35, 41; 8 24; 9 42: *also* 5 13, 24; 6 10; 7 7, 14; 8 29, 32, 48, 54; 13 12 ; 17 14 ; 18 42] the fever ; and it left her: and immediately she rose up and ministered unto them.
			cp. 9 6: *also* 20 17.
			
			cp. 4 50; 5 8; 9 7; 11 43.
			
			cp. 4 52.

[1] Some ancient authorities read *when he was come out of the synagogue, he came &c.*

§ 55. Healings in the Evening

Matt. 8 16-17	Mark 1 32-34	Luke 4 40-41	

16 And when even was come, they
 	
brought unto him many
[1] possessed with devils :
 	
cp. 9 18; 19 13, 15: 8 3, 15; 9 25, 29; 14 31; 17 7; 20 34: *also* 9 20; 14 36.
  and he cast out the spirits with a word [*cp.* 8 8: *also* 8 3, 13, 32; 9 6, 22, 29; 12 13; 15 28; 17 7, 18],
  and   healed all [*cp.* 12 15] that were sick:
  cp. 4 24.
	32 And at even, when the sun did set, they
	
	brought unto him all that were sick, and them that were [1]possessed with devils. **33** And all the city was gathered together at the door.
	cp. 5 23; 6 5; 8 25; 10 16: 1 31, 41; 5 41; 6 2; 7 33; 9 27; 8 22, 23; 10 13: *also* 3 10; 5 27; 6 56.
	cp. 1 25, 41; 2 11; 3 5; 5 8, 13, 34, 41; 7 29, 34; 9 25; 10 52.
	34 And he healed many that were sick with divers diseases, and cast out many [2] devils ;
	                    3 10 for he had healed many ; insomuch that as many as had [3] plagues [4] pressed upon him that they might touch him. **11** And the unclean spirits, whensoever they beheld him, fell down before him, and cried, saying, Thou art the Son of God [*cp.* 1 1; 5 7; 15 39: *also* 1 11; 9 7]. **12** And he charged them much [*cp.* 1 25 ; 4 39; 9 25] that they should not make him known.
		40 And when the sun was setting, all they that had any sick with divers diseases brought them unto him ;
		
		and he laid his hands [*cp.* 13 13 : 5 13 ; 7 14 ; 8 54 ; 14 4 ; 18 15 ; 22 51: *also* 6 19 ; 7 39 ; 8 44] on every one of them,
		[*cp.* 7 7 : *also* 4 35, 39 ; 5 13, 24 ; 6 10 ; 7 14 ; 8 29, 32, 48, 54 ; 9 42 ; 13 12 ; 17 14 ; 18 42] and healed them.
		cp. 6 19.
		
		                    41 And [1] devils also came out from many,
		
		crying out, and saying, Thou art the Son of God [*cp.* 1 35 ; 4 3, 9 ; 8 28 ; 22 70: *also* 3 22 ; 9 35]. And rebuking them [*cp.* 4 35, 39 ; 8 24 ; 9 42],
			cp. 9 6: *also* 20 17.
			
			cp. 4 50; 5 8; 9 7; 11 43.
			
			cp. 1 34; *etc.*

cp. 4 3, 6; 8 29; 14 33; 16 16; 26 63; 27 40, 43, 54: *also* 3 17; 17 5. *cp.* 8 26; 17 18.			

cp. 8 4; 9 30; 12 16: *also* 16 20; 17 9.
cp. 8 29.

17 that it might be fulfilled which was spoken ² by Isaiah the prophet, saying, Himself took our infirmities, and bare our diseases.

¹ Or, *demoniacs*   ² Or, *through*

---

1 34 and he suffered not the ² devils to speak [cp. 1 25; 3 12; 1 44; 5 43; 7 36; 8 26: *also* 8 30; 9 9], because they knew [cp. 1 24; 3 11; 5 7] him.⁵

¹ Or, *demoniacs*   ² Gr. *demons*.
³ Gr. *scourges*.   ⁴ Gr. *fell*.
⁵ Many ancient authorities add *to be Christ*. See Luke 4 41.

---

he suffered them not to speak [cp. 4 35; 5 14; 8 56: *also* 9 21, 36], because they knew [cp. 4 34; 8 28] that he was the Christ.

¹ Gr. *demons*.

Matt. 8 17 = Is. 53 4.

§ 56. Would-be Disciples

[*Cp.* Matt. 10 37: Luke 14 26]

Matt. 8 18-22

18 Now when Jesus saw great multitudes about him [cp. 3 7; 5 1; 9 36], he gave commandment to depart unto the other side [cp. 14 22]. **19** And there came ¹ a scribe, and said unto him, ² Master, I will follow thee whithersoever thou goest. **20** And Jesus saith unto him, The foxes have holes, and the birds of the heaven *have* ³ nests; but the Son of man hath not where to lay his head. **21** And another of the disciples

verse 22

said unto him, Lord, suffer me first to go and bury my father. **22** But Jesus saith unto him, Follow me [cp. 4 19; 9 9; 16 24; 19 21]; and leave the dead to bury their own dead.

¹ Gr. *one scribe*.   ² Or, *Teacher*
³ Gr. *lodging-places*.

verse 19

---

cp. 4 35; 6 45.

see below.

cp. 1 17; 2 14; 8 34; 10 21.

Luke 9 57-62

cp. 8 22.   **57** And as they went in the way, a certain man said unto him, I will follow thee whithersoever thou goest. **58** And Jesus said unto him, The foxes have holes, and the birds of the heaven *have* ¹ nests; but the Son of man hath not where to lay his head. **59** And he said unto another, Follow me [cp. 5 27; 9 23; 18 22]. But he said, Lord, suffer me first to go and bury my father. **60** But he said unto him,

verse 59

Leave the dead to bury their own dead; but go thou and publish abroad the kingdom of God. **61** And another

---

cp. 6 5.

see below.

cp. 1 43; 12 26; 21 19, 22.

---

also said, I will follow thee [cp. *verse* 57], Lord; but first suffer me [cp. *verse* 59] to bid farewell [cp. 14 33] to them that are at my house. **62** But Jesus said unto him, No man, having put his hand to the plough, and looking back, is fit for the kingdom of God.

¹ Gr. *lodging-places*.

§ 57. The Stilling of a Storm

Matt. 8 23-27

23 And when he was entered into a boat, his disciples followed him.

cp. 8 18; 14 22.

24 And behold, there arose a great tempest in the sea [cp. 4 18; 8 32; *etc.*],

---

Mark 4 35-41

35 And on that day, when even was come, he saith unto them, Let us go over unto the other side [cp. 6 45]. **36** And leaving the multitude, they take him with them, even as he was, in the boat. And other boats were with him. **37** And there ariseth a great storm of wind,

cp. 1 16; 2 13; *etc.*

and the waves beat into the

Luke 8 22-25

22 Now it came to pass on one of those days, that he entered into a boat, himself and his disciples; and he said unto them, Let us go over unto the other side of the lake: and they launched forth.

23 But as they sailed he fell asleep: and there came down a storm of wind on the lake [cp. 5 1, 2; 8 33];

---

cp. 6 1, 16; *etc.*

Matthew

insomuch that the boat was covered with the waves: but he was asleep. **25** And they came to him, and awoke him, saying, Save [*cp.* 14 30], Lord [*cp.* 17 4, 15; 20 30, 33: *and* 7 21; 8 2, 6, 8, 21; *etc.*]; *cp.* 8 19; 12 38; 19 16; 22 16, 24, 36.

we perish. **26** And he saith unto them, Why are ye fearful, O ye of little faith [*cp.* 6 30; 14 31; 16 8: *also* 17 20]? Then he arose, and rebuked [*cp.* 17 18] the winds and the sea;

and there was a great calm.

cp. 17 20; 21 21.
27 And [*cp.* 9 8; 17 6; 27 54; 28 4, 8]

the men marvelled [*cp.* 9 33; 12 23; 15 31; 21 20; 27 14: *also* 7 28; 13 54; 19 25; 22 22, 33], saying, What manner of man is this [*cp.* 21 10], that even the winds and the sea obey him?

Mark

boat, insomuch that the boat was now filling.

38 And he himself was in the stern, asleep on the cushion: and they awake him, and say unto him, *cp.* 7 28.

1 Master [*cp.* 9 17, 38; 10 17, 20, 35; 12 14, 19, 32; 13 1], carest thou not that we perish? **39** And he awoke,

and rebuked [*cp.* 1 25; 3 12; 9 25] the wind, and said unto the sea, Peace, be still [*cp.* 1 25]. And the wind ceased, and there was a great calm. **40** And he said unto them, Why are ye fearful? have ye not yet faith [*cp.* 11 22 16 14]? **41** And they feared exceedingly [*cp.* 5 15, 33; 9 6, 32; 10 32; 16 8], [*cp.* 2 12; 5 20, 42; 6 51; 7 37; 10 32; 15 5; 16 5, 8: *also* 1 22, 27; 6 2; 10 24, 26; 11 18; 12 17] and said one to another, Who then is this [*cp.* 1 27; 2 7], that even the wind and the sea obey him [*cp.* 1 27]?

1 Or, *Teacher*

Luke

and they were filling *with water*, and were in jeopardy.

24 And they came to him, and awoke him, saying, [*cp.* 18 41: *and* 5 8, 12; 6 46; 7 6; *etc.*] [*cp.* 7 40; 9 38; 10 25; 11 45; 12 13; 18 18; 19 39; 20 21, 28, 39; 21 7] Master, master [*cp.* 9 33, 49: *and* 5 5; 8 45; 17 13], we perish. And he awoke,

cp. 12 28.

and rebuked [*cp.* 4 35, 39, 41; 9 42] the wind and the raging of the water: [*cp.* 4 35] and they ceased, and there was a calm. **25** And he said unto them, Where is your faith [*cp.* 17 5, 6; 22 32; 24 25, 38]? And being afraid [*cp.* 1 12, 65; 2 9; 5 26; 7 16; 8 35, 37, 47; 9 34, 45; 24 5, 37] they marvelled [*cp.* 5 9, 26; 8 56; 9 43; 11 14; 24 12, 41: *also* 2 47, 48; 4 22, 32, 36; 20 26], saying one to another, Who then is this [*cp.* 4 36; 5 21; 7 49; 9 9], that he commandeth even the winds and the water, and they obey him [*cp.* 4 36]?

Right margin cross-references:

cp. 4 11, 15, 19, 49; 5 7; *etc.*
cp. 1 38; 20 16.

cp. 3 12; 6 64; 14 10; 20 27.

cp. 7 15, 21, 46.

cp. 5 12: *also* 12 34.

§ 58. The Gadarene Swine

Matt. 8 28-34   Mark 5 1-20   Luke 8 26-39

Matthew

28 And when he was come to the other side into the country of the Gadarenes,

there met him two [*cp.* 9 27; 20 30] 1 possessed with devils, coming forth out of the tombs,

exceeding fierce, so that no man could pass by that way.

Mark

1 And they came to the other side of the sea, into the country of the Gerasenes.

2 And when he was come out of the boat, straightway there met him out of the tombs a man with an unclean spirit, **3** who had his dwelling in the tombs: and no man could any more bind him, no, not with a chain; **4** because that he had been often bound with fetters and chains, and the chains had been rent asunder by him, and the fetters broken in pieces: and no man had strength to tame him. **5** And always,

Luke

26 And they arrived at the country of the 1 Gerasenes, which is over against Galilee. **27** And when he was come forth upon the land, there met him a certain man out of the city, who had 2 devils; and for a long time he had worn no clothes, and abode not in *any* house, but in the tombs.

verse 29

Matthew

cp. 2 11; 8 2; 9 18; 14 33; 15 25; 17 14; 20 20; 28 9, 17.

29 And behold, they cried out,

saying, What have we to do with thee, thou Son [cp. 4 3, 6; 14 33; 16 16; 26 63; 27 40, 43, 54] of God? cp. 26 63.
art thou come hither to torment us before the time?

30 Now there was afar off from them a herd of many swine feeding. **31** And the [2] devils besought him, saying, If thou cast us out, send us away into the herd of swine.

32 And he said unto them, Go. And they came out, and went into the swine: and behold, the whole herd rushed down the steep into the sea [cp. 4 18; 8 24; etc.], and perished in the waters. **33** And they that fed them

fled, and went away into the city, and told everything, and what was befallen to them that were [1] possessed with devils. **34** And behold, all the city came out to

meet Jesus: and when they saw him,

Mark

night and day, in the tombs and in the mountains, he was crying out, and cutting himself with stones. 6 And when he saw Jesus from afar, he ran and worshipped him [cp. 1 40; 3 11; 5 22, 33; 7 25; 10 17]; 7 and

crying out

with a loud voice [cp. 1 26], he saith, What have I to do with thee [cp. 1 24], Jesus, thou Son [cp. 1 1; 3 11; 15 39] of the Most High God [cp. similarly 1 24; 3 11]? I adjure thee cp. 1 24. by God, torment me not. 8 For he said unto him, Come forth [cp. 1 25; 9 25], thou unclean spirit, out of the man.

verses 4 and 5

9 And he asked him, What is thy name? And he saith unto him, My name is Legion; for we are many.

10 And he besought him much that he would not send them away out of the country. 11 Now there was there on the mountain side a great herd of swine feeding. 12 And they besought him, saying, Send us into the swine, that we may enter into them. 13 And he gave them leave. And the unclean spirits came out, and entered into the swine: and the herd rushed down the steep into the sea [cp. 1 16; 2 13; etc.], *in number* about two thousand; and they were choked in the sea. 14 And they that fed them

fled, and told it in the city, and in the country.

verse 16
And they came to see what it was that had come to pass. 15 And they come to Jesus, and behold [1] him

Luke

28 And when he saw Jesus, he cried out, and fell down [cp. 5 8, 12; 8 41, 47; 17 16; 24 52] before him, and with a loud voice [cp. 4 33] said, What have I to do with thee [cp. 4 34], Jesus, thou Son [cp. 1 35; 4 3, 9, 41; 22 70] of the Most High [cp. 1 32, 35, 76; 6 35] God [cp. similarly 4 34, 41]? I beseech thee, cp. 4 34. torment me not. 29 For he cp. 4 35. commanded the unclean spirit to come out from the man. For [3] oftentimes it had seized him: and he was kept under guard, and bound with chains and fetters; and breaking the bands asunder, he was driven of the [4] devil into the deserts. 30 And Jesus asked him, What is thy name? And he said, Legion; for many [2] devils were entered into him. 31 And they intreated him that he would not command them to depart into the abyss. 32 Now there was there a herd of many swine feeding on the mountain: and they intreated him

that he would give them leave to enter into them. And he gave them leave. 33 And the [2] devils came out from the man, and entered into the swine: and the herd rushed down the steep into the lake [cp. 5 1, 2; 8 22, 23], and were choked. 34 And when they that fed them saw what had come to pass, they fled, and told it in the city and in the country.

35 And they went out to see what had come to pass; and they came to Jesus, and found the

Right margin cross-references:

cp. 9 38; 11 32; 18 6.

cp. 1 34; etc.

cp. 6 1, 16; etc.

	that was possessed with devils sitting, clothed and in his right mind,	man, from whom the [2] devils were gone out, sitting, clothed and in his right mind, at the feet of Jesus [*cp.* 7 38 ; 10 39]:
cp. 9 8; 17 6; 27 54; 28 4, 8.	*even* him that had the legion : and they were afraid [*cp.* 4 41 ; 5 33 ; 9 6, 32 ; 10 32 ; 16 8].	and they were afraid [*cp.* 1 12, 65 ; 2 9 ; 5 26 ; 7 16 ; 8 25, 37, 47 ; 9 34, 45 ; 24 5, 37].
verse 33	16 And they that saw it declared unto them how it befell [1] him that was possessed with devils, and concerning the swine. 17 And they	36 And they that saw it told them how he that was possessed with [2] devils was [5] made whole.
they	began to beseech him to depart from their borders.	37 And all the people of the country of the Gerasenes round about asked him to depart from them ; for
besought *him* that he would depart from their borders.	18 And as he was entering into the boat, he that had been possessed with [2] devils besought him that he might be with him. 19 And he suffered him not, but saith unto him, Go to thy house unto thy friends, and tell them how great things the Lord hath done for thee, and *how* he had mercy on thee. 20 And he went his way, and began to	they were holden with great fear [*cp. verse* 35 *above*] : and he entered into a boat, and returned. 38 But the man from whom the [2] devils were gone out prayed him that he might be with him : but he sent him away, saying, 39 Return to thy house, and declare how great things God hath done for thee.
cp. 4 25.	publish in Decapolis [*cp.* 7 31] how great things Jesus had done for him : and	And he went his way, publishing throughout the whole city how great things Jesus had done for him.
cp. 8 27; 9 33; 12 23; 15 31; 21 20; 27 14: *also* 7 28; 13 54; 19 25; 22 22, 33.	all men did marvel [*cp.* 2 12 ; 5 42 ; 6 51 ; 7 37 ; 10 32 ; 15 5 ; 16 5, 8 : *also* 1 22, 27 ; 6 2 ; 10 24, 26 ; 11 18 ; 12 17].	*cp.* 5 9, 26 ; 8 25, 56 ; 9 43 ; 11 14 ; 24 12, 41 : *also* 2 47, 48 ; 4 22, 32, 36 ; 20 26.	*cp.* 7 15, 21, 46.

[1] Or, *demoniacs*   [2] Gr. *demons.*   [1] Or, *the demoniac*   [2] Gr. *demons.*

[1] Many ancient authorities read *Gergesenes*; others, *Gadarenes*: and so in ver. 37.
[2] Gr. *demons.*   [3] Or, *of a long time*
[4] Gr. *demon.*   [5] Or, *saved*

§ 59. The Healing of a Paralytic

Matt. 9 1-8	**Mark 2** 1-12	**Luke 5** 17-26	
1 And he entered into a boat, and crossed over, and came into his own city [*cp.* 4 13 : *also* 13 54].	1 And when he entered again into Capernaum after some days, it was noised that he was [1] in the house. 2 And many were gathered together, so that there was no longer room *for them*, no, not even about the door: and he spake the	17 And it came to pass on one of those days, that he was teaching;	
cp. 13 19 *ff.*	word [*cp.* 4 33 : *also* 4 14 *ff.*; 16 20] unto them.	*cp.* 1 2; 8 12 *ff.*: *also* 4 32: *and* 5 1; 8 11, 21; 11 28. and there were Pharisees and doctors of the law sitting by, which were come out of every village of Galilee and Judæa	*cp.* 4 41; 5 24, 38; *etc.*
cp. 15 1.	*verse* 6 *cp.* 3 22; 7 1. *cp.* 5 30.	and Jerusalem : and the power [*cp.* 4 14, 36; 6 19; 8 46: *also* 1 17, 35; 9 1; 24 49] of the Lord was with him [1] to heal.	*cp.* 1 19.
2 And behold,	3 And	18 And behold,	

Matthew (col. 1)

they　　brought to him
a man sick of the palsy,
lying on a bed:

　　　　　　　and Jesus
seeing their faith　said unto
the sick of the palsy, [1] Son,
be of good cheer [*cp.* 9 22;
14 27]; thy sins are forgiven.
　　　　3 And behold,
certain of the scribes

said within themselves,
cp. 8 27; 21 10.

This man
blasphemeth [*cp.* 26 65].

　　　4 And
Jesus [2] knowing
　　their thoughts [*cp.* 12
25; 16 8]
　　　　said,
Wherefore　think ye evil in
your hearts? 5 For whether is
easier, to say,
　　Thy sins are forgiven;
or to say, Arise,
　　　and walk? 6 But that
ye may know that the Son of
man hath [3] power [*cp.* 7 29;
21 23 *ff.*; 28 18] on earth to
forgive sins
(then saith he to the
sick of the palsy),
　　　Arise,
　　　and take
up thy bed, and go
unto thy house.
　　　7 And
he arose,

and departed
to his house.

8 But when the multitudes
saw it, they were afraid
[*cp.* 17 6; 27 54; 28 4, 8],

cp. 8 27; 9 33; 12 23; 15 31;
21 20; 27 14: *also* 7 28;
13 54; 19 25; 22 22, 33.
　　　　　and
glorified God [*cp.* 5 16;
15 31],
　　which had given such
[3] power unto men [*cp.* 11 27;
28 18: *also verse* 6 *above*].
　　see above.

Mark (col. 2)

they come, bringing unto him
a man sick of the palsy,
　　　borne of four.

4 And when they could not
[2] come nigh unto him
　　　　for the crowd
[*cp.* 3 9],　　　they
uncovered the roof where he
was: and when they had broken
it up, they let　down
　　　the bed whereon
the sick of the palsy lay.
　　　5 And Jesus
seeing their faith saith unto
the sick of the palsy, [3] Son,
cp. 6 50; 10 49.
thy sins are forgiven.
　　6 But
there were certain of the scribes
　　　sitting there,
and reasoning in their hearts,
cp. 4 41: *also* 1 27.
　　　7 Why doth
this man thus speak? he
blasphemeth [*cp.* 14 64]:
who can forgive sins but one,
even God? 8 And straightway
Jesus, perceiving in his spirit
that they so reasoned within
themselves [*cp.* 8 17],
　　　saith unto them,
Why reason ye these things in
your hearts? 9 Whether is
easier, to say to the sick of the
palsy, Thy sins are forgiven;
or to say, Arise, and take up
thy bed, and walk? 10 But that
ye may know that the Son of
man hath [4] power [*cp.* 1 22,
27; 11 28 *ff.*] on earth to
forgive sins
　　(he saith to the
sick of the palsy), 11 I
say unto thee, Arise [*cp.* 3
3; 5 41; 10 49],　　take
up thy bed, and go
unto thy house.
　　　12 And
　　he arose,
　and straightway took
up the bed,
and went forth,
　　before them all;

cp. 4 41; 5 15, 33; 9 6, 32;
10 32; 16 8.
insomuch that they were all
amazed [*cp.* 5 20, 42; 6 51;
7 37; 10 32; 15 5; 16 5, 8:
also 1 22, 27; 6 2; 10 24,
26; 11 18; 12 17], and
glorified God,

Luke (col. 3)

men　　　bring　　　on
a bed a man that was palsied:

and they sought to bring him
in, and to lay him before him.
19 And not finding by what
way they might bring him
in because of the multitude
[*cp.* 8 19; 19 3], they went up
to the housetop,

　and let him down through
the tiles with his couch
　　　into the
midst before Jesus. 20 And
seeing their faith, he said,
　　　　Man,

　　thy sins are forgiven
thee [*cp.* 7 48]. 21 And
　　　the scribes
and the Pharisees [*cp. verse* 17]
began to reason, saying,
Who is this [*cp.* 7 49; 8 25;
9 9: *also* 4 36]
　　　that speaketh
blasphemies?
Who can forgive sins, but
God alone? 22 But
Jesus perceiving
　their reasonings [*cp.* 6 8;
9 47; 11 17],　　　an-
swered and said unto them,
[2] What reason ye　　in
your hearts? 23 Whether is
easier, to say,
　Thy sins are forgiven thee;
or to say, Arise
　　　and walk? 24 But that
ye may know that the Son of
man hath [3] power [*cp.* 4 32,
36; 20 2 *ff.*] on earth to
forgive sins
　　　(he said unto
him that was palsied), I
say unto thee, Arise [*cp.* 6
8; 7 14; 8 54], and take
up thy couch, and go
unto thy house.
　　25 And
immediately he rose up
before them, and　took
up that whereon he lay,
　and departed
to his house,
glorifying God [*cp. verse* 26].

　　see below.

　　　26 And
amazement took hold on all
[*cp.* 5 9; 8 25, 56; 9 43; 11
14; 24 12, 41: *also* 2 47, 48;
4 22, 32, 36; 20 26], and
they glorified God [*cp.* 2 20;
7 16; 13 13; 17 15, 18; 18
43; 23 47];
　　cp. 10 22.
　　　and they
were filled with fear [*cp.* 1 12,
65; 2 9; 7 16; 8 25, 35, 37,

References (col. 4)

cp. 16 33.

cp. 5 12: *also*
12 34.

cp. 10 33, 36.

cp. 1 48; 2
24, 25; 4
19, 29; 5
6, 42; 6
61; 11 14;
13 18; 16
19, 30; 18
4; 21 17.
cp. 5 8.

cp. 5 27;
17 2.

John 5 8 Jesus saith unto
him,

　　Arise,

　　take
up thy bed, and walk
[*cp.* Matt. 9 5; Mark 2 9;
Luke 5 23]. 9 And
straightway the man was
made whole, and　took
up his bed

and walked.

cp. 7 15, 21,
46.

cp. 9 24.

cp. 3 35; 5
27; 13 3;
17 2.

## Left margin

Matt.
5 7-8;
Mark 8
5-17.

	saying, We never saw it on this fashion.	47; 9 34, 45; 24 5, 37], saying, We have seen strange things to-day.

¹ Gr. *Child.*
² Many ancient authorities read *seeing.*
³ Or, *authority*

¹ Or, *at home*
² Many ancient authorities read *bring him unto him.*
³ Gr. *Child.*   ⁴ Or, *authority*

¹ Gr. *that he should heal.* Many ancient authorities read *that he should heal them.*   ² Or, *Why*
³ Or, *authority*

§ 60. The Call of Levi (Matthew)

Matt. 9 9-13	**Mark 2** 13-17	**Luke 5** 27-32

13 And   he went forth again by the sea side [*cp.* 1 16]; and all the multitude resorted unto him, and he taught them. **14** And as he passed by,

27 And after these things he went forth,

9 And as Jesus passed by from thence [*cp.* 9 27], he saw a man, called Matthew [*cp.* 10 3: Mark 3 18: Luke 6 15], sitting at the place of toll: and he saith unto him, Follow me [*cp.* 4 19; 8 22; 16 24; 19 21]. And he   [*cp.* 19 27] arose, and followed him [*cp.* 4 20, 22; 19 27]. **10** And it came to pass, as he ¹ sat at meat in the house,   behold,   many publicans and sinners came and sat down   with Jesus and his disciples.

he saw [*cp.* 1 16] Levi the *son* of Alphæus   sitting at the place of toll, and he saith unto him, Follow me [*cp.* 1 17; 8 34; 10 21]. And he   [*cp.* 10 28]   arose and followed him [*cp.* 1 18, 20; 10 28]. **15** And it came to pass, that he was sitting at meat in his house, and   many ¹ publicans and sinners   sat down   with Jesus and his disciples: for there were many, and they followed him. **16** And the scribes ² of the Pharisees,   when they saw that he was eating with the sinners and publicans,   said unto his disciples,   ³ He eateth ⁴ and drinketh with publicans and sinners.

and beheld a publican, named Levi,   sitting at the place of toll, and   said unto him, Follow me [*cp.* 9 23, 59; 18 22]. **28** And he forsook all [*cp.* 5 11; 14 33], and rose up and followed him [*cp.* 5 11; 18 28]. **29** And Levi made him a great feast in his house: and there was a great multitude of publicans and of others that were sitting at meat with them.

11 And when the Pharisees   saw it,   they said unto his disciples,   Why eateth your ² Master   with the publicans and sinners [*cp.* 11 19]? **12** But when he heard it, he said, They that are ³ whole have no need of a physician, but they that are sick. **13** But go ye and learn what *this* meaneth, I desire mercy, and not sacrifice [*cp.* 12 7: *also* 23 23]: for I came not to call the righteous, but sinners [*cp.* 21 31].

17 And when Jesus heard it, he saith unto them, They that are ⁵ whole have no need of a physician, but they that are sick:

30 And ¹ the Pharisees and their scribes   murmured against his disciples, saying, Why do ye eat and drink with the publicans and sinners [*cp.* 7 34, 39; 15 2; 19 7]? **31** And Jesus answering said unto them, They that are whole have no need of a physician; but they that are sick.

cp. 12 33.
I came not to call the righteous, but sinners.

32 I am not come to call the righteous but sinners [*cp.* 19 10: *also* 7 29-30, 47; 18 14] to repentance [*cp.* 15 7, 10].

cp. 1 43; 12 26; 21 19, 22.

¹ Gr. *reclined:* and so always.
² Or, *Teacher*   ³ Gr. *strong.*

¹ See marginal note on Matt. 5 46.
² Some ancient authorities read *and the Pharisees.*
³ Or, How is it *that he eateth . . . sinners?*
⁴ Some ancient authorities omit *and drinketh.*   ⁵ Gr. *strong.*

¹ Or, *the Pharisees and the scribes among them*

Matt. 9 13 = Hos. 6 6

§ 61. A Question about Fasting

[*Cp.* Matt. 12 1-8; 15 1-20: Mark 2 23-28; 7 1-23: Luke 6 1-5; 11 37-41]

Matt. 9 14-17	**Mark 2** 18-22	**Luke 5** 33-39	
14 Then come to him the disciples of John [*cp.* 11 2; 14 12], saying, Why do we and the Pharisees fast [1] oft,	**18** And John's disciples and the Pharisees were fasting: and they come and say unto him, Why do John's disciples [*cp.* 6 29] and the disciples of the Pharisees fast,	**33** And they said unto him, The disciples of John [*cp.* 7 18, 19; 11 1] fast often, and make supplications [*cp.* 2 37: *also* 11 1]; likewise also the *disciples* of the Pharisees; but thine eat and drink [*cp.* 6 2].	*cp.* 1 35, 37; 3 25; 4 1.
but thy disciples fast not [*cp.* 12 2; 15 2]? **15** And Jesus said unto them, Can the sons of the bride-chamber mourn, as long as the bridegroom is with them?	but thy disciples fast not [*cp.* 2 24; 7 5]? **19** And Jesus said unto them, Can the sons of the bride-chamber fast, while the bridegroom is with them? as long as they have the bridegroom with them, they cannot fast. **20** But the days will come,	**34** And Jesus said unto them, Can ye make the sons of the bride-chamber fast, while the bridegroom is with them?	*cp.* 3 29.
but the days will come,		**35** But the days will come [*cp.* 17 22; 21 6: *also* 19 43; 23 29]; and	
when the bridegroom shall be taken away from them, and then will they fast. **16** And	when the bridegroom shall be taken away from them, and then will they fast in that day.	when the bridegroom shall be taken away from them, then will they fast in those days. **36** And he spake also a parable unto them; No man rendeth a piece from a new garment and putteth it	*cp.* 16 19, 20.
no man	**21** No man		
putteth a piece of undressed cloth upon an old garment; for that which should fill it up taketh from the garment, and a worse rent is made. **17** Neither do *men* put new wine into old [2] wine-skins: else the skins burst, and the wine is spilled, and the skins perish: but they put new wine into fresh wine-skins, and both are preserved.	seweth a piece of undressed cloth on an old garment: else that which should fill it up taketh from it, the new from the old, and a worse rent is made. **22** And no man putteth new wine into old [1] wine-skins: else the wine will burst the skins, and the wine perisheth, and the skins: but *they put* new wine into fresh wine-skins.	upon an old garment; else he will rend the new, and also the piece from the new will not agree with the old. **37** And no man putteth new wine into old [1] wine-skins; else the new wine will burst the skins, and itself will be spilled, and the skins will perish. **38** But new wine must be put into fresh wine-skins. **39** And no man having drunk old *wine* desireth new: for he saith, The old is [2] good.	*cp.* 2 10.

[1] Some ancient authorities omit *oft.*
[2] That is, *skins used as bottles.*

[1] That is, *skins used as bottles.*

[1] That is, *skins used as bottles.*
[2] Many ancient authorities read *better.*

§ 62. A Ruler's Daughter and a Woman with an Issue of Blood

[*Cp.* Luke 7 11-17 ; John 11 1-46]

Matt. 9 18-26	Mark 5 21-43	Luke 8 40-56	
18 While he spake these things unto them,			
	21 And when Jesus had crossed over again in the boat unto the other side, a great multitude was gathered unto him : and he was by the sea [*cp.* 3 7 ; 4 1].	**40** And as Jesus returned, the multitude welcomed him ; [*cp.* 5 1] for they were all waiting for him. **41** And	
cp. 13 1.			
behold, there came [1] a	**22** And there cometh one of the	behold, there came a man	

ruler,

and worshipped [*cp.* 2 11; 8 2; 14 33; 15 25; 20 20; 28 9, 17: *also* 17 14] him,	rulers of the synagogue, Jaïrus by name ; and seeing him, he falleth at his feet [*cp.* 3 11; 5 33; 7 25: *also* 1 40; 5 6; 10 17], **23** and beseecheth him much,	named Jaïrus, and he was a ruler of the synagogue [*cp.* 13 14] : and he fell down [*cp.* 5 8, 12; 8 28, 47; 17 16: *also* 24 52] at Jesus' feet, and besought him to come into his house ; **42** for he had an only [*cp.* 7 12; 9 38] daughter, about twelve years of age, and she lay a dying [*cp.* 7 2].	*cp.* 11 32; 18 6: *also* 9 38.

verse 42

saying, My daughter is even now dead : but come and lay thy hand [*cp.* 19 13, 15: *also* 8 3, 15; 9 20, 25, 29; 14 31, 36; 17 7; 20 34] upon her, and she shall live. **19** And Jesus arose, and followed him, and *so did* his disciples.	saying, My little daughter is at the point of death : *I pray thee*, that thou come and lay thy hands [*cp.* 6 5; 8 25; 10 16: *also* 1 31, 41; 3 10; 5 27, 41; 6 2, 56; 7 33; 8 22, 23; 9 27; 10 13] on her, that she may be [1]made whole, and live. **24** And he went with him ;		*cp.* 4 47.

		cp. 4 40; 13 13 : *also* 5 13; 6 19; 7 14, 39; 8 44, 54; 14 4; 18 15; 22 51.	*cp.* 9 6; 20 17.

20 And behold, a woman, who had an issue of blood twelve years,	and a great multitude followed him, and they thronged him. **25** And a woman, which had an issue of blood twelve years, **26** and had suffered many things of many physicians, and had spent all that she had, and was nothing bettered, but rather grew worse, **27** having heard the things concerning Jesus,	But as he went the multitudes thronged him. **43** And a woman having an issue of blood twelve years [*cp.* 13 11], which [1] had spent all her living upon physicians, and could not be healed of any,	

came behind him, and touched [*cp.* 8 3, 15; 9 29; 14 36; 17 7; 20 34: *also* 9 18, 25; 14 31; 19 13, 15] the border [*cp.* 14 36] of his garment : **21** for she said within herself, If I do but touch his garment, I shall be [2]made whole.	came in the crowd behind, and touched [*cp.* 1 41; 3 10; 6 56; 7 33; 8 22; 10 13: *also* 1 31; 5 23, 41; 6 2, 5; 8 23, 25; 9 27; 10 16] [*cp.* 6 56] his garment. **28** For she said, If I touch but his garments, I shall be [1]made whole. **29** And	came behind him, and touched [*cp.* 5 13; 6 19; 7 14, 39; 18 15; 22 51: *also* 4 40; 8 54; 13 13; 14 4] the border of his garment :	*cp.* 20 17; 9 6.

	straightway the fountain of her blood was dried up ; and she felt in her body that she was healed of her [1]plague. **30** And straightway Jesus, perceiving in himself that the power *proceeding* from him had gone forth, turned him about [*cp.* 8 33] in the crowd, and said, Who touched my garments? **31** And his disciples said unto him,	and immediately the issue of her blood stanched. **45** And Jesus	

verse 46

cp. 9 22; 16 23.		*cp.* 7 9, 44; 9 55; 10 23; 14 25; 22 61; 23 28. said, Who is it that touched me? And when all denied, Peter said, [1] and they that were with him, Master, the multitudes press thee and crush *thee*.	*cp.* 1 38.

	Thou seest the multitude thronging thee, and sayest thou, Who touched me? **32** And he looked round about [*cp.* 3 5, 34; 9 8; 10 23; 11 11] to see her that had done this thing.	*cp.* 6 10.	

verse 30

cp. 9 8; 17 6; 27 54; 28 4, 8.	**33** But the woman fearing and trembling [*cp.* 4 41; 5 15; 9 6, 32; 10 32; 16 8], knowing what had been done to her, came and fell down [*cp. verse 22 above*] before him, and told him all the truth.	**46** But Jesus said, Some one did touch me : for I perceived that power [*cp.* 4 14, 36; 5 17; 6 19: *also* 1 17, 35; 9 1; 24 49] had gone forth from me. **47** And when the woman saw that she wa not hid, she came trembling [*cp.* 1 12, 65; 2 9; 5 26; 7 16; 8 25, 35, 37; 9 34, 45; 24 5, 37], and falling down [*cp. verse 41 above*] before him declared	*cp.* 11 32; 18 6: *also* 9 38.

22 But Jesus turning [*cp.* 16 23]

and seeing her said,
Daughter, be of good cheer
[*cp.* 9 2; 14 27]; thy faith
hath ³ made thee whole.

And the woman was
² made whole from that hour
[*cp.* 8 13; 15 28; 17 18].

cp. 17 1; 26 37.
23 And when Jesus came into
the ruler's house,

cp. 17 1; 26 37.

and saw the flute-players, and
the crowd making a tumult,

24 he said,
Give place:

for the damsel is not dead, but
sleepeth. And they laughed
him to scorn.
25 But when the crowd
was put forth,

he entered in,
and took
her   by the hand [*cp.* 8
15; 8 3; 9 18, 29; 14 31; 17 7;
19 13, 15; 20 34: *also* 9 20;
14 36];

cp. 9 6.
and
the damsel
arose.

cp. 8 27; 9 33; 12 23; 15 31;
21 20; 27 14: *also* 7 28;
13 54; 19 25; 22 22, 33.

---

34 And he [*cp.* 5 30; 8 33]

said unto her,
Daughter,
[*cp.* 6 50; 10 49] thy faith
hath ³ made thee whole [*cp.*
10 52];   go
in peace, and be whole of thy
¹ plague.

35 While he yet spake, they come
from the ruler of the synagogue's
house, saying, Thy daughter is dead:
why troublest thou the ⁴ Master any
further? **36** But Jesus, ⁵ not heeding
the word spoken, saith unto the
ruler of the synagogue, Fear not,
only believe.
37 And he suffered no man to
follow with him, save Peter, and
James, and John the brother of James
[*cp.* 1 29; 9 2; 13 3; 14 33].
38 And   they come to
the house of the ruler of the
synagogue;

verse 37

verse 40
and he beholdeth
a tumult,
and *many* weeping and wailing greatly. **39** And when he
was entered in, he saith unto
them,   Why make
ye a tumult, and weep?

the child is not dead, but
sleepeth. **40** And they laughed
him to scorn.
But he, having put
them all forth, taketh the
father of the child and her
mother and them that were
with him, and goeth in where
the child was. **41** And taking
the child by the hand [*cp.* 1
31; 9 27; 1 41; 5 23; 6 2,
5; 7 33; 8 22, 23, 25; 10
13, 16: *also* 3 10; 5 27;
6 56], he saith unto her,
Talitha cumi; which is,
being interpreted, Damsel, I
say unto thee, Arise [*cp.* 2 11;
3 3; 10 49]. **42** And straightway   the damsel
rose up,   and walked;
for she was twelve years old.

verse 43
And they   were
amazed straightway with a
great amazement [*cp.* 2 12; 5
20; 6 51; 7 37; 10 32; 15 5;
16 5, 8: *also* 1 22, 27; 6 2;
10 24, 26; 11 18; 12 17].
43 And he charged them

---

in the presence of all the people for
what cause she touched him, and
how she was healed immediately.
48 And he [*cp.* 7 9, 44; 9 55;
10 23; 14 25; 22 61; 23 28]
said unto her,
Daughter,
thy faith
hath ³ made thee whole [*cp.*
7 50; 17 19; 18 42]; go
in peace [*cp.* 7 50].

49 While he yet spake, there cometh
one from the ruler of the synagogue's
house, saying, Thy daughter is dead;
trouble [*cp.* 7 6] not the ⁴ Master.
50 But Jesus   hearing
it,   answered
him,   Fear not:
only believe, and she shall be ⁵ made
whole.

verse 51

51 And when he came to
the house,
he suffered not any man
to enter in with him, save
Peter, and John, and James
[*cp.* 9 28], and the father of
the maiden and her mother.
52 And

all were weeping, and bewailing her:

but he said,

Weep
not [*cp.* 7 13; 23 28];
for she   is not dead, but
sleepeth. **53** And they laughed
him to scorn, knowing that
she was dead. **54** But he,

verse 51

taking
her   by the hand [*cp.* 4
40; 5 13; 7 14; 13 13;
14 4; 18 15; 22 51: *also* 6
19; 7 39; 8 44],
called, saying,

Maiden,
arise [*cp.* 5 24;
6 8; 7 14]. **55** And
her spirit returned, and she
rose up immediately: ·
verse 42
and he commanded that
something be given her to eat.
56 And her parents were
amazed [*cp.* 5 9, 26; 8 25;
9 43; 11 14; 24 12, 41: *also*
2 47, 48; 4 22, 32, 36; 20 26]:

but he charged them

---

cp. 1 38.

cp. 16 33.

cp. 4 53.

cp. 20 13, 15.

cp. 11 11.

cp. 9 6: *also*
20 17.

cp. 5 8.

cp. 7 15, 21,
46.

cp. 8 4; 9 30; 12 16: *also* 16 20; 17 9.	much that no man should know this [*cp.* 1 44; 7 36; 8 26: *also* 1 25, 34; 3 12; 8 30; 9 9]: and he commanded that *something* should be given her to eat.	to tell no man what had been done [*cp.* 5 14: *also* 4 35, 41; 9 21, 36].
26 And [4] the fame hereof went forth into all that land [*cp.* 4 24].	*cp.* 1 28.	*verse* 55 *cp.* 4 14, 37; 5 15; 7 17.

¹ Gr. *one ruler.*   ² Or, *saved*
³ Or, *saved thee*   ⁴ Gr. *this fame.*

¹ Or, *saved*   ³ Gr. *scourge.*
³ Or, *saved thee*   ⁴ Or, *Teacher*
⁵ Or, *overhearing*

¹ Some ancient authorities omit *had spent all her living upon physicians, and.*
² Some ancient authorities omit *and they that were with him.*
³ Or, *saved thee*   ⁴ Or, *Teacher*
⁵ Or, *saved*

§ 63. The Healing of Two Blind Men

[*Cp.* Matt. 12 22; 15 30-31; 20 29-34; 21 14: Mark 8 22-26; 10 46-52: Luke 7 21; 18 35-43: John 9 1-7]

Matt. 9 27-31

27 And as Jesus passed by from thence [*cp.* 9 9], two [*cp.* 8 28; 20 30] blind men followed him, crying out, and saying, Have mercy on us, thou son of David [*cp.* 15 22; 20 30, 31: *also* 17 15: *and* 1 1; 12 23; 21 9, 15]. **28** And when he was come into the house, the blind men came to him: and Jesus saith unto them, Believe ye that I am able [*cp.* 8 2] to do this? They say unto him, Yea, Lord. **29** Then touched [*cp.* 8 3, 15; 9 18, 25; 14 31; 17 7; 20 34: *also* 9 20; 14 36; 19 13, 15] he their eyes, saying, According to your faith be it done unto you [*cp.* 8 13; 15 28]. **30** And their eyes were opened. And Jesus ¹ strictly charged them, saying, See that no man know it [*cp.* 8 4; 12 16: *also* 16 20; 17 9]. **31** But they went forth, and spread abroad his fame in all that land.	*cp.* 10 47, 48. *cp.* 1 40; 9 22, 23: *also* 6 5. *cp.* 1 41; *etc.* *cp.* 1 43. *cp.* 1 44; *etc.* *cp.* 1 45; 7 36.	*cp.* 18 38, 39: *also* 17 13: *and* 1 32. *cp.* 5 12. *cp.* 4 40; *etc.* *cp.* 5 14; *etc.* *cp.* 5 15.	*cp.* 9 6; 20 17.

¹ Or, *sternly*

§ 64. The Healing of a Dumb Demoniac

[*Cp.* Matt. 15 29-31: Mark 7 31-37; 9 25]

Matt. 9 32-34	Matt. 12 22-24	Mark 3 22	Luke 11 14-15	
32 And as they went forth, behold, there was brought to him a dumb man possessed with a ¹ devil. **33** And when the ¹ devil was cast out, the dumb man spake: and the multitudes marvelled [*cp.* 8 27; 15 31; 21 20; 27 14: *also* 7 28; 13 54; 19 25; 22 22, 33], saying, It was never so seen in Israel. **34** But the Pharisees *cp.* 15 1.	**22** Then was brought unto him ¹ one possessed with a devil, blind [*cp.* 9 27] and dumb: and he healed him, insomuch that the dumb man spake and saw. **23** And all the multitudes were amazed. and said, Is this the son of David [*cp.* 1 1; 9 27; 15 22; 20 30, 31; 21 9, 15]? **24** But when the Pharisees heard it, they	*cp.* 2 12; 5 20, 42; 6 51; 7 37; 10 32; 15 5; 16 5, 8: *also* 1 22, 27; 6 2; 10 24, 26; 11 18; 12 17. *cp.* 10 47, 48. **22** And the scribes which came down from Jerusalem [*cp.* 7 1]	**14** And he was casting out a ¹ devil *which was* dumb. And it came to pass, when the ¹ devil was gone out, the dumb man spake; and the multitudes marvelled [*cp.* 5 9, 26; 8 25, 56; 9 43; 24 12, 41: *also* 2 47, 48; 4 22, 32, 36: 20 26]. *cp.* 1 32; 18 38, 39. **15** But some of them *cp.* 5 17.	*cp.* 7 15, 21, 46. *cp.* 1 19.

said,	said,	said, He hath Beelze-	said,
	This man doth not	bub,	
[2] By	cast out [1] devils, but	and,	
the prince of the	[2] by Beelzebub [cp. 10	[1] By	[1] By Beelzebub	cp. 7 20; 8
[3] devils casteth he out	25] the prince of the	the prince of the	the prince of the	48, 52; 10
[3] devils.	[1] devils.	[2] devils casteth he out	devils casteth he out	20.
		the [3] devils.	[3] devils.	
[1] Gr. demon. [2] Or, In	[1] Or, a demoniac	[1] Or, In [2] Gr. demons.	[1] Gr. demon. [2] Or, In	
[3] Gr. demons.	[2] Gr. demons. [3] Or, in		[3] Gr. demons.	

Matt. 9 33 : *cp.* Judges 19 30.

(iv) The Mission of the Twelve (Matt. : §§ 65–72).

§ 65. **The Occasion of the Mission**

Matt. 9 35-**10** 1	Mark 6 6b, 34, 7	Luke 8 1; 10 2; 9 1	
		8 1 And it came to pass soon afterwards, that he went	
35 And Jesus went about all the cities and the villages, teaching in their synagogues, and preaching [cp. 4 23; 11 1] the [1] gospel	6 6 And he went round about the villages teaching.	about through cities and villages [cp. 13 22], preaching and bringing the [1] good tidings [cp. 1 19;	
cp. 11 5. of the kingdom [cp. 4 23; 24 14 : also 26 13], and healing all manner of disease and all manner of sickness.	cp. 1 1, 14, 15 ; 8 35 ; 10 29 ; 13 10 ; 14 9 ; 16 15.	2 10 ; 3 18 ; 4 18, 43 ; 7 22 ; 9 6 ; 16 16 ; 20 1] of the kingdom of God,	
4 23 And Jesus went about in all Galilee, teaching in their synagogues, and preaching the [1] gospel of the kingdom, and healing all manner of disease and all manner of sickness among the people.	1 39 And he went into their synagogues throughout all Galilee, preaching and casting out [1] devils.	and with him the twelve. 4 44 And he was preaching in the synagogues [cp. 4 15] of [2] Galilee.	cp. 18 20.
36 But when he saw the multitudes [cp. 3 7; 5 1; 8 18], he was moved with compassion [cp. 14 14; 15 32 : also 20 34] for them, because they were distressed and scattered, as sheep not having a shepherd [cp. 10 6; 15 24 : also 26 31]. **37** Then saith he unto his disciples, The harvest truly is plenteous, but the labourers are few.	6 34 And he came forth and saw a great multitude, and he had compassion [cp. 8 2 : also 1 41] on them, because they were as sheep not having a shepherd [cp. 14 27].	cp. 7 13.	cp. 6 5.
38 Pray ye therefore the Lord of the harvest, that he send forth labourers into his harvest. **10 1** And he called unto him his twelve disciples,		10 2 And he said unto them, The harvest is plenteous, but the labourers are few : pray ye therefore the Lord of the harvest, that he send forth labourers into his harvest. 9 1 And he called	cp. 10 11-16. cp. 4 35-38.
and gave them authority over unclean spirits [cp. 10 8; 17 16], to cast them out, and to heal all manner of disease and all manner of sickness.	6 7 And he called unto him the twelve [cp. 3 13-14], and began to send them forth by two and two; and he gave them authority over the unclean spirits [cp. 3 15 : also 6 12-13 ; 9 18].	the twelve [cp. 6 13] together, [cp. 10 1] and gave them power and authority over all [3] devils [cp. 10 9 : also 9 6, 40 ; 10 17], and to cure diseases.	
[1] Or, good tidings	[1] Gr. demons.	[1] Or, gospel [2] Very many ancient authorities read *Judæa*. [3] Gr. demons.	

§ 66. The Names of the Twelve

Matt. 10 2-4	Mark 3 13-19a	Luke 6 12-16		Acts 1 13
	13 And he goeth up into the mountain,	12 And it came to pass in these days, that he went out into the mountain to pray; and he continued all night in prayer to God. 13 And when it was day, he called his disciples :		
1 And he called unto him	and calleth unto him whom he himself would : and they went unto him. 14 And he appointed twelve, 1 that they might be with him, and that he might send them forth to preach, 15 and to have authority	and he chose from them		
his twelve disciples,				
and gave them authority over unclean spirits, to cast them out [cp. 10 8 ; 17 16], and to heal all manner of disease and all manner of sickness. 2 Now the names of the twelve	to cast out 2 devils [cp. 6 7: also 6 12-13; 9 18]:	cp. 9 1, 2 ; 10 1, 9 : also 9 6, 40 ; 10 17.		
apostles	cp. 6 30.	twelve, whom also he named apostles [cp. 9 10 ; 17 5 ; 22 14 ; 24 10] ;		13 And when they were come in, they went up into the upper chamber, where they were abiding ; both Peter
are these : The first, Simon, who is called Peter [cp. 4 18 : also 16 16-18], and Andrew his brother;	16 3 and Simon he surnamed Peter ;	14 Simon, whom he also named Peter [cp. 5 8], and Andrew his brother, and James	cp. 1 42 : also 1 40 ; 6 8 ; etc.	
James the son of Zebedee, and John his brother ;	17 and James the son of Zebedee, and John the brother of James ; and them he surnamed Boanerges, which is, Sons of thunder : 18 and Andrew, and Philip,	and John,		and John and James
3 Philip, and Bartholomew; Thomas, and Matthew the publican [cp. 9 9]; James the son of Alphæus, and Thaddæus ; 4 Simon the 1 Cananæan,	and Bartholomew, and Matthew, and Thomas, and James the son of Alphæus, and Thaddæus, and Simon the 4 Cananæan,	and Philip and Bartholomew, 15 and Matthew and Thomas, and James the son of Alphæus, and Simon which was called the Zealot, 16 and Judas the 1 son of James, and	cp. 14 22.	and Andrew, Philip and Thomas, Bartholomew and Matthew, James the son of Alphæus, and Simon the Zealot, and Judas the son of James.
and Judas Iscariot, who also 2 betrayed him.	19 and Judas Iscariot, which also betrayed him.	Judas Iscariot, which was the traitor.		
1 Or, Zealot. See Luke 6 15; Acts 1 13. 2 Or, delivered him up : and so always.	1 Some ancient authorities add whom also he named apostles. See Luke 6 13. 2 Gr. demons. 3 Some ancient authorities insert and he appointed twelve. 4 Or, Zealot. See Luke 6 15; Acts 1 13.	1 Or, brother. See Jude 1.		Or, brother. See Jude 1.

§ 67. The Mission Charge (i)

Matt. 10 5-15	Mark 6 7-11	Luke 9 1-5	Luke 10 1-2, 4-12	
	7 And he called unto	**1** And he called	**1** Now after these things the Lord appointed seventy [1] others, and	
5 These twelve	him the twelve,	the twelve together, and gave them power and authority over all [1] devils, and to cure diseases. **2** And		
Jesus sent forth,	and began to send them forth by two and two ; and he gave them authority over the unclean spirits ;	he sent them forth	sent them two and two before his face into every city and place, whither he himself was about to come.	
		to preach the kingdom of God, and to heal [2] the sick.	*cp. verse 9.*	
and charged them, saying, Go not into *any* way of the Gentiles, and enter not into any city of the Samaritans : **6** but go rather to the lost sheep of the house of Israel [*cp.* 15 24 : *also* 9 36].	**8** and he charged them	**3** And he said unto them,	**2** And he said unto them. . . . *cp. 9 52.*	*cp. 4 9.*
7 And as ye go, preach, saying, The kingdom of heaven is at hand [*cp.* 3 2 ; 4 17 : *also* 12 28]. **8** Heal the sick, raise the dead, cleanse the lepers, cast out [1] devils : freely ye received, freely give.	*cp.* 6 34. *cp.* 1 15 : *also* 6 12. *cp.* 6 13.	*cp. verse 2 : also* 9 6. *cp.* 9 6.	*verses 9 and 11* *verse 9*	*cp.* 10 16.
9 Get you	that they should take nothing for *their* journey, save a staff only ; no bread, no wallet,	Take nothing for your journey, neither staff, nor wallet, nor bread,	**4** Carry	
no gold, nor silver, nor brass in your [2] purses ; **10** no wallet for *your* journey, neither two coats, nor shoes, nor staff :	no [1] money in their [2] purse ; **9** but *to go* shod with sandals : and, *said he,* put not on two coats.	nor money ; neither have two coats [*cp.* 3 11].	no purse, no wallet, no shoes [*cp.* 22 35] : and salute no man on the way.	
for the labourer is worthy of his food.			*verse 7*	*cp.* 4 36.
11 And into whatsoever city or village ye shall enter, search out who in it is worthy ; and there abide till ye go forth. **12** And as ye enter into the house, salute it.	**10** And he said unto them, Wheresoever ye enter into a house, there abide till ye depart thence.	**4** And into whatsoever house ye enter, there abide, and thence depart.	**5** And into whatsoever house ye shall [2] enter, *verse 7* first say, Peace *be* to this house.	
13 And if the house be worthy, let your peace come upon it [*cp.* 5 9] : but if it be not worthy, let your peace return to you.	*cp.* 9 50.	*cp.* 1 79 ; 2 14, 29 ; 19 38.	**6** And if a son of peace be there, your peace shall rest upon [3] him : but if not, it shall turn to you again. **7** And in that	*cp.* 14 27 ; 16 33.

verse 11

verse 10

verses 7 and 8

cp. verse 2.

same house remain, eating and drinking such things as they give : for the labourer is worthy of his hire. Go not from house to house. 8 And into whatsoever city ye enter, and they receive you, eat such things as are set before you : 9 and heal the sick that are therein, and say unto them, The kingdom of God is come nigh unto you [*cp.* 11 20 ; 17 20, 21 ; 19 11 ; 21 8]. 10 But into whatsoever city ye shall enter, and they receive you not [*cp.* 9 53],

14 And whosoever shall not receive you, nor hear your words, as ye go forth out of that house or that city, shake off the dust of your feet.

11 And whatsoever place shall not recieve you, and they hear you not, as ye go forth thence, shake off the dust that is under your feet for a testimony unto them [*cp.* 1 44 ; 13 9].

5 And as many as receive you not, when ye depart from that city, shake off the dust from your feet for a testimony against them [*cp.* 5 14; 21 13].

go out into the streets thereof and say, 11 Even the dust from your city, that cleaveth to our feet, we do wipe off against you : howbeit know this, [*cp.* 12 39], that the kingdom of God is come nigh [*cp. verse* 9]. 12 I say unto you, It shall be more tolerable in that day [*cp.* 17 31 ; 21 34] for

Sodom,

than

for that city.

cp. 8 4; 10 18; 24 14.

cp. 24 43.

15 Verily I say unto you, It shall be more tolerable [*cp.* 7 22; 24 36: also 26 29] for the land [*cp.* 2 6, 20, 21; 4 15; 11 24] of Sodom and Gomorrah in the day of judgement [*cp.* 11 22, 24; 12 36], than for that city [*cp.* 11 24].

cp. 13 32 : also 14 25.

cp. 14 20; 16 23, 26. *cp.* 3 22.

¹ Gr. *demons.*   ² Gr. *girdles.*

¹ Gr. *brass.*   ² Gr. *girdle.*

¹ Gr. *demons.*   ² Some ancient authorities omit *the sick.*

¹ Many ancient authorities add *and two*: and so in ver. 17.   ² Or, *enter first, say*   ³ Or, *it*

§ 68. **The Mission Charge** (ii)

Matt. 10 16-23	Matt. 24 9, 13	Mark 13 9-13	Luke 21 12-19	Luke 10 3; 12 11-12
				10 3 Go your ways: behold, I send you forth as lambs in the midst of wolves.
16 Behold, I send you forth as sheep in the midst of wolves: be ye therefore wise [*cp.* 7 24; 24 45; 25 2 *ff.*] as serpents, and ¹ harmless as doves. **17** But beware of men :			*cp.* 12 42.	
for they will	9 Then shall they	9 But take ye heed to yourselves : for they shall	12 But before all these things, they shall lay their hands on you,	

Matthew

deliver you up to councils, and in their synagogues they will scourge you;

18 yea and before governors and kings shall ye be brought for my sake [cp. 5 11; 10 39; 16 25: also 10 22; 19 29; 24 9],

for a testimony to them [cp. 8 4; 24 14]

and to the Gentiles [cp. 24 14: also 8 11; 21 31,41,43; 22 7-10; 26 13; 28 19]. **19** But when they

deliver you up,

be not anxious [cp. 6 25, 31, 34] how or

what ye shall speak: for it shall be given you in that hour what ye shall speak. **20** For it is not ye that speak, but the Spirit of your Father that speaketh in you.

21 And brother shall deliver up brother to death, and the father his child: and children shall rise up against parents, and ² cause them to be put to death [cp. 10 35, 36]. **22** And ye shall be hated of all men for my name's sake [cp. 19 29: also 5 11; 10 18, 39; 16 25]:

Mark (2 22)

deliver you up unto tribulation,

cp. 23 34.

Mark (2 23)

deliver you up to councils; and in synagogues shall ye be beaten;

and before governors and kings shall ye stand for my sake [cp. 8 35; 10 29: also 13 13],

for a testimony unto them [cp. 1 44; 6 11]. **10** And the gospel must first be preached unto all the nations [cp. 12 9; 14 9; 16 15].

11 And when they lead you to judgement, and

deliver you up,

be not anxious beforehand

what ye shall speak: but whatsoever shall be given you in that hour, that speak ye: For it is not ye that speak, but the Holy Ghost.

12 And brother shall deliver up brother to death, and the father his child; and children shall rise up against parents, and ¹ cause them to be put to death.

13 And ye shall be hated of all men for my name's sake [cp. 8 35; 10 29; 13 9]:

Luke (6 1)

and shall persecute you, delivering you up to the synagogues and prisons,¹ bringing you before kings and governors for my name's sake [cp. 21 17: also 6 22; 9 24; 18 29].

13 It shall turn unto you for a testimony [cp. 5 14; 9 5].

cp. 2 30-32; 3 6; 13 29; 14 21-24; 20 16; 24 47.

verse 12

14 Settle it therefore in your hearts, not to meditate beforehand how to answer:

15 for I will give you a mouth and wisdom,

which all your adversaries shall not be able to withstand or to gainsay. **16** But ye shall be delivered up even by parents, and brethren, and kinsfolk, and friends; and some of you ² shall they cause to be put to death [cp. 12 53]. **17** And ye shall be hated of all men for my name's sake [cp. 21 12: also 6 22; 9 24; 18 29]. **18** And not

Luke (5 39)

cp. 12 11 below.

12 11 And when they bring you before the synagogues, and the rulers, and the authorities,

be not anxious [cp. 12 22] how or what ye shall say: **12** for the Holy Spirit shall teach you in that very hour what ye ought to say.

cp. 1 71; 6 22, 27.

Cross-references

cp. 15 21.

cp. 10 16; 11 52.

cp. 14 26.

cp. 16 2.

cp. 15 18-21; 17 14.

			cp. 10 30.	*cp.* 12 7.
			a hair of your head shall per- ish. **19** In your patience [*cp.* 8 15] ye shall win your ³ souls.	

but he that endureth to the end, the same shall be saved. **23** But when they perse- cute you in this city, flee into the next: for verily I say unto you, Ye shall not have gone through the cities of Israel, till the Son of man be come.

13 But he that endureth to the end, the same shall be saved.

cp. 23 34.

but he that endureth to the end, the same shall be saved.

cp. 16 28: *also* 23 36; 24 34.

cp. 9 1: *also* 13 30.

cp. 9 27: *also* 11 51; 21 32.

¹ Or, *simple*
² Or, *put them to death*

¹ Or, *put them to death*

¹ Gr. you *being brought*.
² Or, *shall they put to death*
³ Or, *lives*

§ 69. **The Mission Charge** (iii)

Matt. 10 24-33	Luke 6 40	John 13 16	John 15 20
		16 Verily, verily, I say unto you,	**20** Remember the word that I said unto you,

24 A disciple is not above his ¹ master, nor a ² servant above his lord.

40 The disciple is not above his ¹ master:

A ¹ servant is not greater than his lord; neither ² one that is sent greater than he that sent him.

A ¹ servant is not greater than his lord.

25 It is enough [*cp.* 6 34] for the disciple that he be as his ¹ master, and the ² servant as his lord. If they have called the master of the house ³ Beelzebub [*cp.* 9 34; 12 24], how much more *shall they call* them of his house- hold [*cp.* 10 36]!

but every one when he is perfected shall be as his ¹master.

cp. 3 22.

cp. 11 15, 18.

cp. 7 20; 8 48, 52; 10 20.

If they persecuted me, they will also persecute you; if they kept my word, they will keep yours also.

¹ Or, *teacher* ² Gr. *bondservant*.
³ Gr. *Beelzebul*.

¹ Or, *teacher*

¹ Gr. *bondservant*.
² Gr. *an apostle*.

¹ Gr. *bondservant*.

26 Fear them not therefore: for there is nothing covered, that shall not be re- vealed; and hid,

Mark 4 22 For there is nothing

Luke 8 17 For nothing is

Luke 12 2 But there is nothing covered up, that shall not be re- vealed: and hid,

hid, save that it should be manifested; neither was *anything* made secret, but that it should come to light.

hid, that shall not be made manifest; nor *anything* secret, that shall not be known and come to light.

that shall not be known.

that shall not be known.

27 What I tell you in the darkness, speak ye in the light: and what ye hear in the ear, proclaim upon the housetops. **28** And be not afraid of them which kill the body, but are not able to kill the soul:

but rather

3 Where- fore whatsoever ye have said in the darkness shall be heard in the light; and what ye have spoken in the ear in the inner chambers shall be proclaimed upon the housetops. **4** And I say unto you my friends, Be not afraid of them which kill the body, and after that have no more that they can do. **5** But I will warn you whom ye shall fear:

fear him which
            is able to destroy
both soul and body in ¹ hell [*cp.* 5 22,
29, 30; 18 9; 23 15, 33: *also* 3 10, 12;
7 19; 13 42, 50; 18 8; 25 41].
29 Are not two sparrows sold for
a farthing? and not one of them
shall fall on the ground without your
Father: **30** but the very hairs of your
head are all numbered. **31** Fear
not therefore; ye are of more value
than many sparrows [*cp.* 6 26: *also*
12 12]. **32** Every one therefore who
shall confess ² me before men, ³ him
will   I also confess
before my Father which is in
heaven [*cp.* 5 16, 45; 6 1, 9; 7 11, 21;
12 50; 16 17; 18 10, 14, 19: *also* 5 48;
6 14, 26, 32; 15 13; 18 35; 23 9].
33 But
whosoever shall deny me before
men, him will I also deny before
my Father which is in heaven [*see above*].

Gr. *Gehenna.*   ² Gr. *in me.*   ³ Gr. *in him.*

cp. 9 43, 45,
47.

cp. 11 25, 26.

Fear him, which after he hath killed
hath ¹ power to cast
            into ² hell [*cp.* 3 9,
17]; yea, I say unto you, Fear him.

6 Are not five sparrows sold for
two farthings? and not one of them
is forgotten   in the sight of
God. **7** But the very hairs of your
head are all numbered [*cp.* 21 18]. Fear
not: ye are of more value
than many sparrows [*cp.* 12 24]. **8** And
I say unto you, Every one   who
shall confess ³ me before men, ⁴ him
shall the Son of man also confess
before

cp. 11 13.

the angels of God [*cp.* 15 10]: **9** but
he that denieth me in the presence of
men shall be denied in the presence of

the angels of God [*see above*].

¹ Or, *authority*   ² Gr. *Gehenna.*
³ Gr. *in me.*   ⁴ Gr. *in him.*

cp. 15 6.

                Matt. 16 **27** For
the Son of man
            shall come
            in the
glory   of his
Father with his   angels;
and then shall he render
unto every man according
to his ¹ deeds.

¹ Gr. *doing.*

Mark 8 **38** For whosoever shall
be ashamed of me and of my
words in this adulterous and
sinful generation,
the Son of man also shall be
ashamed of him,
when he cometh in the
glory   of his
Father with the holy angels.

Luke 9 **26** For whosoever shall
be ashamed of me and of my
words,
        of him shall
the Son of man   be
ashamed,
when he cometh in his own
glory, and *the glory* of the
Father, and of the holy angels.

---

§ 70. **The Mission Charge** (iv)

Matt. 10 34-39

cp. 3 11.

            34 Think not that I
came to ¹ send peace on the earth:
I came not to ¹ send peace, but
a sword.

35 For I came to set a man at variance
against his father,

        and the daughter against
her mother,
        and the daughter
in law against her mother in law:
36 and a man's foes *shall be* they of his
own household [*cp.* 10 25: *also* 10 21].

37 He that loveth   father
or mother   more

cp. 10 38, 39.

cp. 13 12.

Luke 12 49-53; 14 26-27; 17 33

12 **49** I came to cast fire upon the
earth [*cp.* 3 16]; and what will I, if
it is already kindled? **50** But I have a
baptism to be baptized with; and
how am I straitened till it be accomplished! **51** Think ye that I
am come to give peace in the earth?
I tell you, Nay;   but rather
division: **52** for there shall be from
henceforth five in one house divided,
three against two, and two against
three. **53** They shall be divided,

        father against son, and
son against father; mother against
daughter, and   daughter against
her mother; mother in law against her
daughter in law, and   daughter
in law against her mother in law.

cp. 21 16.

14 **26** If any man cometh unto
me, and hateth not his own father,
and mother, and wife [*cp.* 18 29],

cp. 12 27.

than me is not worthy of me; and he that loveth son or daughter *cp.* 19 27-29.

more

cp. 8 18-22.

38 And he that doth not take his cross and follow after me, is not worthy of me.

39 He that [2] findeth his [3] life shall lose it ; and he that [4] loseth his [3] life for my sake [*see below*]   shall find it.

Matt. 16 **24** If any man would come after me, let him deny himself, and take up his cross, and follow me [*cp.* 4 19 ; 8 22 ; 9 9 ; 19 21].	Mark 8 **34** If any man would come after me, let him deny himself, and take up his cross, and follow me [*cp.* 1 17 ; 2 14 ; 10 21].
25 For whosoever would save his [3] life shall lose it : and whosoever shall lose his [3] life for my sake [*cp.* 5 11 ; 10 18 : *also* 10 22 ; 19 29 ; 24 9] shall find it.	**35** For whosoever would save his [1] life shall lose it ; and whosoever shall lose his [1] life for my sake [*cp.* 10 29 ; 13 9 : *also* 13 13] and the gospel's [*cp.* 10 29] shall save it.
[1] Gr. *cast.* [2] Or, *found* [3] Or, *soul* [4] Or, *lost*	[1] Or, *soul*

cp. 10 28-30.

Luke 17 **33** Whosoever shall seek to gain his [1] life shall lose it : but whosoever shall lose *his* [1] *life*   shall [2] preserve it.

Luke 9 **23** If any man would come after me, let him deny himself, and take up his cross daily, and follow me [*cp.* 5 27 ; 9 59 ; 18 22].	
24 For whosoever would save his [1] life shall lose it ; but whosoever shall lose his [1] life for my sake [*cp.* 6 22 ; 18 29 ; 21 12, 17], the same shall save it.	
[1] Or, *soul* [2] Gr. *save it alive.*	

    and children, and brethren, and sisters [*cp.* 18 28-30], yea, and his own life also,

    he cannot be my disciple [*cp.* 9 57-62].

27 Whosoever doth not bear his own cross, and come after me,   cannot be my disciple.

John 12 **25** He that loveth his [1] life loseth it ; and he that hateth his [1] life   in this world shall keep it unto life eternal.

26 If any man serve me,   let him

    follow me [*cp.* 1 43 ; 21 19, 22] ; and where I am, there shall also my servant be : if any man . . .

cp. 15 21.

[1] Or, *soul*

Matt. 10 **35-36** ‖ Luke 12 **52-53** : Mic. 7 6 ; *cp.* Is. 19 **2**.

§ 71. **The Mission Charge** (v)

Matt. 10 40-42		Luke 10 16	John 13 20
		16 He that heareth you heareth me ; and he that rejecteth you rejecteth me ; and he that rejecteth me rejecteth him that sent me.	**20** Verily, verily, I say unto you, He that receiveth whomsoever I send receiveth me ; and he that receiveth me receiveth him that sent me [*cp.* 12 44-48].

40 He that receiveth you receiveth me, and he that receiveth me receiveth him that sent me.

Matt. 18 **5** And whoso shall receive one such little child in my name receiveth me.	Mark 9 **37** Whosoever shall receive one of such little children in my name, receiveth me: and whosoever receiveth me, receiveth not me, but him that sent me.	Luke 9 **48** Whosoever shall receive this little child in my name receiveth me: and whosoever shall receive me receiveth him that sent me.

41 He that receiveth a prophet in the name of a prophet shall receive a prophet's reward ; and he that receiveth a righteous man in the name of a righteous man shall receive a righteous man's reward.   **42** And whosoever shall give   to drink unto one of these little ones [*cp.* 18 6, 10, 14] a cup of cold water only, in the name of a disciple,   verily I say unto you, he shall in no wise lose his reward [*cp.* 25 34-40].

Mark 9 **41** For whosoever shall give you a cup of water to drink, *cp.* 9 42.

[1] because ye are Christ's, verily I say unto you, he shall in no wise lose his reward.

[1] Gr. *in name that ye are.*

cp. 17 2.

§ 72. The Conclusion of the Charge

Matt. 11 1

1 And it came to pass, when Jesus had made an end [*cp.* 7 28; 13 53; 19 1; 26 1] of commanding his twelve disciples, he departed thence to teach and preach [*cp.* 4 23; 9 35] in their cities.

cp. 7 1.

(v) Events in Galilee II (§§ 73–80)

§ 73. The Question of John the Baptist and the Testimony of Jesus concerning him

Matt. 11 2-19		Luke 7 18-35; 16 16	
2 Now when John heard in the prison [*cp.* 4 12; 14 3] the works of the Christ [*cp.* 1 17], he sent by his disciples [*cp.* 9 14; 14 12],	*cp.* 1 14; 6 17. *cp.* 2 18; 6 29. *cp.* 16 19, 20.	**7 18** And the disciples of John told him of all these things. **19** And John	*cp.* 3 24.
		cp. 3 20.	
3 and said unto him, Art thou he that cometh [*cp.* 3 11; 21 9; 23 39], or look we for another ? *cp.* 18 1; 26 55.	*cp.* 11 9.	calling unto him ¹ two of his disciples [*cp.* 5 33; 11 1] sent them to the Lord [*cp.* 7 13; 10 1, 39, 41; 11 39; 12 42; 13 15; 17 5, 6; 18 6; 19 8; 22 61; 24 34: *also* 24 3], saying, Art thou he that cometh, or look we for another ? **20** And when the men were come unto him, they said, John the Baptist hath sent us unto thee, saying, Art thou he that cometh [*cp.* 13 35; 19 38], or look we for another ? **21** In that hour [*cp.* 10 21; 13 31] he cured many of diseases and ² plagues and evil spirits ; and on many that were blind he bestowed sight. **22** And	*cp.* 1 35, 37; 3 25; 4 1. *cp.* 4 1; 6 23; 11 2; 20 2, 18, 20, 25; 21 7, 12. *cp.* 1 15, 27; 3 31; 6 14; 11 27; 12 13.
4 And Jesus answered and said unto them, Go your way and tell John the things which ye do hear and see : **5** the blind receive their sight, and the lame walk, the lepers are cleansed, and the deaf hear [*cp.* 15 31], and the dead are raised up, and the poor have ¹ good tidings preached to them. **6** And blessed is he, whosoever shall find none occasion of stumbling [*cp.* 13 57; 15 12; 26 31, 33: *also* 13 21; 24 10] in me. **7** And as these went their way, Jesus began to say unto the multitudes concerning John, What went ye out into the wilderness to behold ? a reed shaken with the wind ? **8** But what went ye out for to see ? a man clothed in soft *raiment* ? Behold, they that wear soft *raiment* are in kings' houses. **9** ² But wherefore went ye out ? to see a prophet [*cp.* 14 5; 21 26] ? Yea, I say unto you, and much more than a prophet. **10** This is he, of whom it is written,	*cp.* 6 3; 14 27, 29: *also* 4 17. *cp.* 11 32.	he answered and said unto them, Go your way, and tell John what things ye have seen and heard ; the blind receive their sight, the lame walk, the lepers are cleansed, and the deaf hear, the dead are raised up, the poor have ³ good tidings preached [*cp.* 1 19; 2 10; 3 18; 4 18, 43; 8 1; 9 6; 16 16; 20 1] to them [*cp.* 4 18]. **23** And blessed is he, whosoever shall find none occasion of stumbling in me. **24** And when the messengers of John were departed, he began to say unto the multitudes concerning John, What went ye out into the wilderness to behold ? a reed shaken with the wind ? **25** But what went ye out to see ? a man clothed in soft raiment ? Behold, they which are gorgeously apparelled, and live delicately, are in kings' courts. **26** But what went ye out to see ? a prophet [*cp.* 1 76; 20 6] ? Yea, I say unto you, and much more than a prophet. **27** This is he of whom it is written,	*cp.* 6 61 : *also* 16 1.
Behold, I send my messenger before thy face, Who shall prepare thy way before thee.	1 2	Behold, I send my messenger before thy face, Who shall prepare thy way before thee [*cp.* 1 17, 76].	*cp.* 1 21, 23; 3 28.
11 Verily I say unto you, Among them		**28** I say unto you, Among them	

that are born of women there hath not arisen a greater than John the Baptist: yet he that is [3] but little   in the kingdom of heaven is greater [*cp.* 5 19; 18 1, 4] than he.

cp. 21 32.

cp. 21 25, 32: *also* 3 7.

cp. 9 13; 21 31.
      12 And from the days of John the Baptist until now the kingdom of heaven suffereth violence, and men of violence take it by force. **13** For all the prophets and the law [*cp.* 5 17; 7 12; 22 40]   prophesied until John.

      14 And if ye are willing to receive [4] *it*, this is Elijah, which is to come [*cp.* 17 12, 13: *also* 3 3, 4]. **15** He that hath ears [5] to hear, let him hear [*cp.* 13 9, 43: *also* 19 12]. **16** But whereunto   shall I liken this generation?
      It is like unto children sitting in the market-places, which call unto their fellows, **17** and say, We piped unto you, and ye did not dance; we wailed, and ye did not [6] mourn. **18** For John   came neither eating [*cp.* 3 4]   nor drinking, and they say, He hath a [7] devil. **19** The Son of man   came eating   and drinking, and they say, Behold, a gluttonous man, and a wine-bibber, a friend of publicans and sinners [*cp.* 9 11]!
      And wisdom [8] is justified by   her   [9] works.

---

[1] Or, *the gospel*
[2] Many ancient authorities read *But what went ye out to see? a prophet?*
[3] Gr. *lesser.*   [4] Or, *him*
[5] Some ancient authorities omit *to hear.*
[6] Gr. *beat the breast.*   [7] Gr. *demon.*
[8] Or, *was*
[9] Many ancient authorities read *children:* as in Luke 7 35.

---

cp. 11 31.

cp. 2 17.

cp. 9 13: *also* 1 2-3, 6.

cp. 4 9, 23; 7 16.

cp. 1 6.

cp. 2 16.

---

that are born of women there is none greater than John: yet he that is [4] but little [*cp.* 9 48] in the kingdom of God is greater
      than he. **29** And all the people [*cp.* 3 10] when they heard, and the publicans [*cp.* 3 12], justified God, [5] being baptized with the baptism of John. **30** But the Pharisees and the lawyers rejected for themselves [*cp.* 20 5] the counsel of God, [6] being not baptized of him [*cp.* 5 32; 7 47; 15 7, 10; 18 14; 19 10].

16 16 The law and the prophets

were until John: from that time the gospel of the kingdom of God is preached [*cp.* 1 19; 2 10; 3 18; 4 18, 43; 7 22; 8 1; 9 6; 20 1], and every man entereth violently into it.

      cp. 1 17.

      cp. 8 8; 14 35.
7 31 Whereunto then shall I liken the men of this generation, and to what are they like? **32** They are like unto children that sit in the market-place, and call one to another; which say, We piped unto you, and ye did not dance; we wailed, and ye did not weep. **33** For John the Baptist is come   eating no bread nor drinking wine [*cp.* 1 15]; and ye say, He hath a [7] devil. **34** The Son of man is come eating [*cp.* 7 36] and drinking; and ye say, Behold, a gluttonous man, and a wine-bibber, a friend of publicans and sinners [*cp.* 5 30: *also* 7 37, 39; 15 2; 19 7]! **35** And wisdom [*cp.* 11 49] [8] is justified of all her children.

---

[1] Gr. *certain two.*   [2] Gr. *scourges.*
[3] Or, *the gospel*   [4] Gr. *lesser.*
[5] Or, *having been*   [6] Or, *not having been*
[7] Gr. *demon.*   [8] Or, *was*

---

cp. 1 21.

cp. 6 60.

Matt. 11 5 ‖ Luke 7 22: *cp.* Is. 29 18-19; 35 5-6; 61 1.
Matt. 11 10 ‖ Luke 7 27 = Exod. 23 20; Mal. 3 1.   Matt. 11 14: *cp.* Mal. 4 5.

§ 74. The Upbraiding of the Cities

Matt. 11 20-24

20 Then began he to upbraid the cities wherein most of his [1] mighty works were done, because they repented not.
      cp. 7 22; 24 36: *also* 26 29.
      verse 24
      21 Woe unto thee, Chorazin! woe unto thee, Bethsaida! for if the [1] mighty works had been done in Tyre and Sidon

cp. 13 32: *also* 14 25.

Luke 10 12-15

      12 I say unto you, It shall be more tolerable in that day [*cp.* 17 31; 21 34] for Sodom, than for that city. **13** Woe unto thee, Chorazin! woe unto thee, Bethsaida! for if the [1] mighty works had been done in Tyre and Sidon,

cp. 14 20; 16 23, 26.

which were done in you, they would have repented long ago   in sackcloth and ashes. **22** Howbeit I say unto you, it shall be more tolerable for Tyre and Sidon in the day of judgement [*cp.* 10 15; 11 24; 12 36], than for you. **23** And thou, Capernaum, shalt thou be exalted unto heaven? thou shalt ² go   down unto Hades: for if the ¹ mighty works had been done in Sodom which were done in thee, it would have remained until this day [*cp.* 27 8; 28 15]. **24** Howbeit I say unto you, that it shall be more tolerable for the land [*cp.* 2 6, 20, 21; 4 15; 10 15] of Sodom in the day of judgement [*cp. above*], than for thee [*cp.* 10 15].

¹ Gr. *powers*.
² Many ancient authorities read *be brought down*.

which were done in you, they would have repented long ago, sitting in sackcloth and ashes. **14** Howbeit   it shall be more tolerable for Tyre and Sidon in the   judgement,   than for you. **15** And thou, Capernaum, shalt thou be exalted unto heaven? thou shalt be brought down unto Hades.

verse 12

¹ Gr. *powers*.

cp. 3 22.

Matt. 11 23 ‖ Luke 10 15 : *cp.* Is. 14 13-15.

§ 75. **The Thanksgiving of Jesus and His Invitation to the Weary**

Matt. 11 25-30

25 At that season [*cp.* 12 1; 14 1: *also* 18 1; 26 55] Jesus answered   and said, I ¹ thank thee, O Father [*cp.* 26 39, 42: *also* 6 9], Lord of heaven and earth, that thou didst hide these things from the wise and understanding, and didst reveal them unto babes [*cp.* 16 17]: **26** yea, Father [*see above*], ² for so it was well-pleasing [*cp.* 3 17; 12 18; 17 5] in thy sight. **27** All things have been delivered unto me of my Father [*cp.* 9 8; 28 18]: and no one knoweth   the Son,   save the Father; neither doth any know the Father,   save the Son, and he to whomsoever the Son willeth to reveal *him*. **28** Come unto me, all ye that labour and are heavy laden, and I will give you rest. **29** Take my yoke upon you, and learn of me; for I am meek and lowly in heart: and ye shall find rest unto your souls. **30** For my yoke is easy, and my burden is light.
cp. 9 22; 16 23.

cp. 17 1, 19; 20 17; 24 3. **13 16** But blessed are your eyes, for they see;   and your ears, for they hear. **17** For verily I say unto you, that many prophets and righteous men desired to see the things which ye see, and saw them not; and to hear the things which ye hear, and heard them not.

¹ Or, *praise*   ² Or, *that*

cp. 14 36.

cp. 1 11.

cp. 5 30; 8 33.
cp. 4 10, 34; 6 31, 32; 9 2, 28; 13 3.

Luke 10 21-24

21 In that same hour [*cp.* 7 21; 13 31] he rejoiced ¹ in the Holy Spirit, and said, I ² thank thee, O Father [*cp.* 2 42; 23 34, 46: *also* 11 2], Lord of heaven and earth, that thou didst hide these things from the wise and understanding, and didst reveal them unto babes: yea, Father [*see above*]; ³ for so it was well-pleasing [*cp.* 2 14; 3 22; 12 32] in thy sight. **22** All things have been delivered unto me of my Father: and no one knoweth who the Son is, save the Father; and   who the Father is, save the Son, and he to whomsoever the Son willeth to reveal *him*.

23 And turning [*cp.* 7 9, 44; 9 55; 14 25; 22 61; 23 28] to the disciples, he said privately [*cp.* 9 10], Blessed *are* the eyes which see the things that ye see: **24** for   I say unto you, that many prophets and kings   desired to see the things which ye see, and saw them not; and to hear the things which ye hear, and heard them not.

¹ Or, *by*   ² Or, *praise*   ³ Or, *that*

cp. 11 41; 12 27, 28; 17 1, 5, 11, 21, 24, 25.

see above.

cp. 3 35; 5 27; 13 3; 17 2.
cp. 1 18; 6 46; 7 29; 8 19; 10 15; 17 25-26.
cp. 6 37; 7 37.

cp. 1 38.

Matt. 11 28–30 : *cp.* Ecclus. 51 23-27 ; Jer. 6 16 ; Zech. 9 9.

§ 76. A Controversy in the Cornfields on the Sabbath

[*Cp.* Matt. 12 9-14; Mark 3 1-6; Luke 6 6-11; 13 10-17; 14 1-6; John 5 2-18; 7 21-24; 9 1-34]

Matt. 12 1-8	Mark 2 23-28	Luke 6 1-5
1 At that season [*cp.* 11 25; 14 1] Jesus went on the sabbath day through the cornfields; and his disciples were an hungred, and began to pluck ears of corn, and to eat. **2** But the Pharisees, when they saw it, said unto him, Behold, thy disciples do that which it is not lawful to do upon the sabbath [*cp.* 9 14; 15 2]. **3** But he said unto them, Have ye not read [*cp.* 12 5; 19 4; 21 16, 42; 22 31] what David did, when he was an hungred, and they that were with him; **4** how he entered into the house of God, and [1] did eat the shewbread, which it was not lawful for him to eat, neither for them that were with him, but only for the priests?	**23** And it came to pass, that he was going on the sabbath day through the cornfields; and his disciples [1] began, as they went, to pluck the ears of corn. **24** And the Pharisees said unto him, Behold, why do they on the sabbath day that which is not lawful [*cp.* 2 18; 7 5]? **25** And he said unto them, Did ye never read [12 10, 26] what David did, when he had need, and was an hungred, he, and they that were with him? **26** How he entered into the house of God [2] when Abiathar was high priest, and did eat the shewbread, which it was not lawful to eat	**1** Now it came to pass on a [1] sabbath, that he was going through the cornfields; and his disciples plucked the ears of corn, and did eat, rubbing them in their hands. **2** But certain of the Pharisees said, Why do ye that which it is not lawful to do on the sabbath day [*cp.* 5 33]? **3** And Jesus answering them said, Have ye not read [*cp.* 10 26] even this, what David did, when he was an hungred, he, and they that were with him; **4** how he entered into the house of God, and did take and eat the shewbread, and gave also to them that were with him; which it is not lawful to eat
	save for the priests, and gave also to them that were with him?	save for the priests alone?
5 Or have ye not read [*see verse* 3 *above*] in the law, how that on the sabbath day the priests in the temple profane the sabbath, and are guiltless? **6** But I say unto you, that [2] one greater than the temple is here [*cp.* 12 41, 42]. **7** But if ye had known what this meaneth, I desire mercy, and not sacrifice [*cp.* 9 13 : *also* 23 23], ye would not have condemned the guiltless.		*cp.* 7 22-23.
		cp. 11 31, 32.
	cp. 12 33.	
	27 And he said unto them, The sabbath was made for man, and not man for the sabbath : **28** so that the Son of man is lord even of the sabbath.	**5** And he said unto them, The Son of man is lord of the sabbath.
8 For the Son of man is lord of the sabbath.		

[1] Some ancient authorities read *they did eat.* [2] Gr. *a greater thing.*	[1] Gr. *began to make* their *way plucking.* [2] Some ancient authorities read *in the days of Abiathar the high priest.*	[1] Many ancient authorities insert *second-first.*

Matt. 12 3-4 ‖ Mark 2 25-26 ‖ Luke 6 3-4 : *cp.* I Sam. 21 1-6.   Matt. 12 4b ‖ Mark 2 26b ‖ Luke 6 4b : *cp.* Lev. 24 5-9.
Matt. 12 5 : *cp.* Num. 28 9-10.   Matt. 12 7 = Hos. 6 6.

§ 77. The Healing of a Man with a Withered Hand

[*Cp.* Matt. 12 1-8; Mark 2 23-28; Luke 6 1-5; 13 10-17; John 5 2-18; 7 21-24; 9 1-34]

Matt. 12 9-14	**Mark 3** 1-6	**Luke 6** 6-11	Luke 14 1-6	
9 And he departed thence, and went into their synagogue [*cp.* 13 54: *also* 4 23; 9 35]: **10** and behold, a man having [*cp.* 5 29, 30, 39; 27 29] a withered hand.	**1** And he entered again into the synagogue [*cp.* 1 21; 6 2: *also* 1 39]; and there was a man there which had his hand withered.	**6** And it came to pass on another sabbath, that he entered into the synagogue [*cp.* 4 16, 33; 13 10: *also* 4 15, 44] and taught: and there was a man there, and his right [*cp.* 22 50] hand was withered. **7** And the scribes and the Pharisees	**1** And it came to pass, when he went into the house of one of the rulers of the Pharisees on a sabbath to eat bread [*cp.* 7 36; 11 37], that they were watching him [*cp.* 20 20].	*cp.* 6 59; 18 20.
verse 14	*verse* 6			*cp.* 18 10.
see below.	**2** And they watched him, whether he would heal him on the sabbath day; that they might accuse him [*cp.* 12 13].	watched him, whether he would heal on the sabbath; that they might find how to accuse him [*cp.* 11 53-54; 20 20].	**2** And behold, there was before him a certain man which had the dropsy.	*cp.* 8 6.
cp. 9 4; 12 25; 16 8.	*cp.* 2 8; 8 17. **3** And he saith unto the man that had his hand withered, ¹ Stand forth [*cp.* 2 11; 5 41; 10 49].	**8** But he knew their thoughts [*cp.* 5 22; 9 47; 11 17]; and he said to the man that had his hand withered, Rise up, and stand forth [*cp.* 5 24; 7 14; 8 54] in the midst. And he arose and stood forth. **9** And Jesus said unto them,		*cp.* 1 48: 2 24, 25; 4 19, 29; 5 6, 42; *etc.*
cp. 9 6.				*cp.* 5 8.
And they asked him, saying, Is it lawful [*cp.* 19 3; 22 17] to heal on the sabbath day? that they might accuse him [*cp.* 22 15].	**4** And he saith unto them, Is it lawful [*cp.* 10 2; 12 14] on the sabbath day *verse* 2 to do good, or to do harm? to save a life, or to kill? But they held their peace.	I ask you, Is it lawful [*cp.* 20 22] on the sabbath *verse* 7 to do good, or to do harm? to save a life, or to destroy it?	**3** And Jesus answering spake unto the lawyers and Pharisees, saying, Is it lawful to heal on the sabbath, or not?	
			4 But they held their peace. And he took him, and healed [*cp.* 6 19; 9 2, 11, 42; 22 51] him, and let him go. **5** And he said unto them, Which of you shall have ¹ an ass or an ox fallen into a well, and will not straightway draw him up on a sabbath day?	
11 And he said unto them, What man shall there be of you, that shall have one sheep, and if this fall into a pit on the sabbath day, will he not lay hold on it, and lift it out? **12** How much then is a man of more value		*cp.* 13 15-16.		

				cp. 12 7, 24.
than a sheep [*cp.* 6 26; 10 31]! Wherefore it is lawful to do good on the sabbath day. **13** Then	**5** And when he had looked round about [*cp.* 3 34; 5 32; 9 8; 10 23; 11 11] on them with anger, being grieved at the hardening of their heart [*cp.* 10 5: *also* 6 52; 8 17; 16 14],	**10** And he looked round about on them all,		*cp.* 7 23.
cp. 19 8.				*cp.* 12 40.
saith he to the man, Stretch forth thy hand. And he stretched it forth; and it was restored whole, as the other. **14** But the Pharisees went out, and	he saith to the man, Stretch forth thy hand. And he stretched it forth: and his hand was restored. **6** And the Pharisees went out, and straightway with the Herodians [*cp.* 12 13]	and said unto him, Stretch forth thy hand. And he did *so*: and his hand was restored. *verse* 7		
cp. 22 16.				
took counsel [*cp.* 22 15; 27 1, 7; 28 12] against him, how they might destroy him [*cp.* 21 46; 26 4].	took counsel [*cp.* 15 1] against him, how they might destroy him [*cp.* 11 18; 12 12; 14 1].	**11** But they were filled with [1] madness; and communed one with another what they might do to Jesus [*cp.* 19 47; 20 19, 20; 22 2].		*cp.* 5 16, 18; 7 30, 32; 11 53.
cp. 22 46.				
			6 And they could not answer again unto these things.	
	[1] Gr. *Arise into the midst.*	[1] Or, *foolishness*	[1] Many ancient authorities read *a son.* See ch. 13 15.	

§ 78. The Choice of the Twelve (Luke)

Matt. 10 1-4	Mark 3 13-19a	**Luke 6** 12-16		Acts 1 13
		12 And it came to pass in these days, that he went out into the mountain [*cp.* 9 28] to pray [*cp.* 3 21; 5 16; 9 18, 28, 29; 11 1; 22 41, 44: *also* 10 21]; and he continued all night in prayer to God. **13** And when it was day, he called his disciples:		
cp. 5 1; 14 23; 15 29; 17 1; 28 16. *cp.* 14 23; 19 13; 26 36, 39, 42, 44: *also* 11 25-26.	**13** And he goeth up into the mountain [*cp.* 6 46; 9 2], *cp.* 1 35; 6 46; 14 32, 35, 39.		*cp.* 6 3, 15. *cp.* 11 41-42; 12 27-28; 17 1-26.	
1 And he called unto him	and calleth unto him whom he himself would: and they went unto him. **14** And he appointed twelve, [1] that they might be with him, and that he might send them forth to preach, **15** and to have authority to cast out [2] devils [*cp.* 6 7: *also* 6 12-13; 9 18]:	and he chose from them twelve,	*cp.* 6 70; 13 18; 15 16, 19.	
his twelve disciples,				
and gave them authority over unclean spirits, to cast them out [*cp.* 10 8; 17 16], and to heal all manner of disease and all manner of sickness. **2** Now the names of the twelve		*cp.* 9 1, 2; 10 1, 9: *also* 9 6, 40; 10 17.		
		whom also		**13** And when

apostles

are these:
The first, Simon, who is
called Peter [*cp.* 4 18:
also 16 16-18], and
Andrew his brother;
James the *son*
of Zebedee, and John
his brother;

3 Philip,
and   Bartholomew;
Thomas, and Matthew
the publican [*cp.* 9 9];
James the *son* of
Alphæus,   and   Thad-
dæus;   **4** Simon the
[1] Cananæan,

and
Judas Iscariot, who
also [2] betrayed him.

[1] Or, *Zealot.* See Luke
6 15; Acts 1 13.
[2] Or, *delivered him up*: and
so always.

---

cp. 6 30.

16 [3] and Simon he
surnamed Peter;

17 and James the *son*
of Zebedee, and John
the brother of James;
and them he sur-
named Boanerges,
which is, Sons of thun-
der: **18** and Andrew,
and Philip,
and Bartholomew,
and Matthew,
and Thomas,
and James the *son* of
Alphæus, and Thad-
dæus, and Simon the
[4] Cananæan,

19 and
Judas Iscariot, which
also betrayed him.

[1] Some ancient authori-
ties add *whom also he
named apostles.* See
Luke 6 13.
[2] Gr. *demons.*
[3] Some ancient authori-
ties insert *and he
appointed twelve.*
[4] Or, *Zealot.* See Luke
6 15; Acts 1 13.

---

he named apostles
[*cp.* 9 10; 17 5; 22
14; 24 10];
14 Simon, whom he
also named Peter [*cp.*
5 8],   and
Andrew his brother,
and James
and John,

and Philip
and Bartholomew,
15 and Matthew
and Thomas,
and James *the son* of
Alphæus,
and Simon which
was called the Zealot,
16 and Judas *the*
[1] *son* of James, and
Judas Iscariot, which
was the traitor;

[1] Or, *brother.* See Jude 1.

---

cp. 1 42: *also*
1 40; 6 8;
etc.

cp. 14 22.

---

they were come in,
they went up into the
upper chamber, where
they were abiding;
both   Peter

and John
and James

and Andrew,
Philip and Thomas,
Bartholomew
and Matthew,

James *the son* of
Alphæus,
and Simon
the Zealot,
and Judas *the*
[1] *son* of James.

[1] Or, *brother.* See Jude 1.

---

§ 79. Healings of the Multitude

Matt. 12 15-21	**Mark 3** 7-12	**Luke 6** 17-19	
15 And Jesus perceiving *it* [*cp.* 16 8; 22 18; 26 10]	**7** And Jesus *cp.* 8 17.	**17** and he came down with them, and stood on a level place, and a great multitude of his disciples, [*cp.* 5 1] and a great number of the people	*cp.* 5 6; 6 15.

withdrew
from thence   [*cp.* 13 1]: and
many
followed him;
4 24 And the report of him went
forth into all Syria: and they
brought unto him all that were
sick, holden with divers diseases
and torments, [1] possessed with
devils, and epileptic, and palsied;
and he healed them. **25** And there
followed him great multitudes from
Galilee   and Decapolis
and
Jerusalem and Judæa
and *from*
beyond Jordan.

---

with his disciples withdrew
to the sea [*cp.* 4 1; 5 21]: and
a great multitude

from
Galilee followed:
and from   Judæa, **8** and
from Jerusalem,   and
from Idumæa, and
beyond Jordan, and about
Tyre and Sidon,
a great multitude, hearing
[1] what great things he did,
came unto him.

9 And he
spake to his disciples, that

---

from all Judæa and
Jerusalem,

and the
sea coast of Tyre and Sidon,

which
came to hear him, and to
be healed of their diseases;
18 and they that were
troubled with unclean spirits
were healed.

cp. 13 2.

a little boat [*cp.* 4 1] should wait on him because of the crowd [*cp.* 2 4], lest they should throng him: **10** for he had healed many; insomuch that as many as had ² plagues ³ pressed upon him that they might touch him [*cp.* 5 27; 6 56: *also* 1 31, 41; *etc.*].

cp. 5 3.

    19 And all the multitude [*cp.* 5 19; 8 19; 19 3]

cp. 9 20; 14 36: *also* 8 3, 15; *etc.*

cp. 5 30.

sought to touch him [*cp.* 7 39; 8 44: *also* 5 13; *etc.*]: for power came forth

and he healed

them all [*cp.* 8 16],

from him [*cp.* 4 14, 36; 5 17; 8 46: *also* 1 17, 35; 9 1; 24 49], and healed [*cp.* 9 2, 11, 42; 14 4; 22 51] *them* all [*cp.* 4 40]. **4 41** And ¹ devils also came out from many,

[*cp.* 2 11; 8 2; 9 18; 14 33; 15 25; 17 14; 20 20; 28 9, 17] *cp.* 8 29.
[*cp.* 4 3, 6; 8 29; 14 33; 16 16; 26 63; 27 40, 43, 54: *also* 3 17; 17 5] **16** and charged them that they should not make him known [*cp.* 8 4; 9 30: *also* 16 20; 17 9]:

     11 And the unclean spirits, whensoever they beheld him, fell down before him [*cp.* 5 6: *also* 1 40; 5 22, 33; 7 25; 10 17], and cried, saying [*cp.* 1 24; 5 7], Thou art the Son of God [*cp.* 1 1; 5 7; 15 39: *also* 1 11; 9 7]. **12** And he charged them much that they should not make him known [*cp.* 1 25, 34, 44; 5 43; 7 36; 8 26: *also* 8 30; 9 9: *and* 7 24; 9 30].

[*cp.* 8 28: *also* 5 8, 12; 8 41; 47; 17 16; 24 52] crying out, and saying [*cp.* 4 33; 8 28], Thou art the Son of God [*cp.* 1 35; 4 3, 9; 8 28; 22 70: *also* 3 22; 9 35]. And rebuking them, he suffered them not to speak [*cp.* 4 35; 5 14; 8 56: *also* 9 21, 36], because they knew that he was the Christ.

cp. 9 38; 11 32; 18 6.

cp. 1 34; *etc.*

17 that it might be fulfilled which was spoken ² by Isaiah the prophet, saying, **18** Behold, my servant whom I have chosen;
My beloved in whom my soul is well pleased [*cp.* 3 17; 11 26; 17 5]:
I will put my Spirit upon him,
And he shall declare judgement to the Gentiles.
19 He shall not strive, nor cry aloud;
Neither shall any one hear his voice in the streets.
20 A bruised reed shall he not break,
And smoking flax shall he not quench,
Till he send forth judgement unto victory.
21 And in his name shall the Gentiles hope.

¹ Or, *all the things that he did*
² Gr. *scourges.*   ³ Gr. *fell.*

¹ Gr. *demons.*

cp. 1 11.

cp. 2 14; 3 22; 10 21; 12 32.

¹ Or, *demoniacs*   ² Or, *through*

Matt. 12 18-21 = Is. 42 1-4.

§ 80. **The Appointment of the Twelve** (Mark)

Matt. 10 1-4	**Mark 3** 13-19a	Luke 6 12-16		Acts 1 13
cp. 5 1; 14 23; 15 29; 17 1; 28 16. *cp.* 14 23; 19 13; 26 36, 39, 42, 44: *also* 11 25-26.	**13** And he goeth up into the mountain [*cp.* 6 46; 9 2], *cp.* 1 35; 6 46; 14 32, 35, 39.	**12** And it came to pass in these days, that he went out into the mountain [*cp.* 9 28] to pray [*cp.* 3 21; 5 16; 9 18, 28, 29; 11 1; 22 41, 44: *also* 10 21]; and he continued all night in prayer to God. **13** And when it was day, he called his disciples:	*cp.* 6 3, 15. *cp.* 11 41-42; 12 27-28; 17 1-26.	
1 And he called unto him his twelve disciples,	and calleth unto him whom he himself would: and they went unto him. **14** And he appointed twelve, ¹ that they might be with him, and that he might send them forth to	and he chose from them twelve,	*cp.* 6 70; 13 18; 15 16, 19.	

Matt.

and gave them authority over unclean spirits, to cast them out [cp. 10 8; 17 16], and to heal all manner of disease and all manner of sickness.

2 Now the names of the twelve apostles are these:

The first, Simon, who is called Peter [cp. 4 18: also 16 16 - 18], and Andrew his brother; James the son of Zebedee, and John his brother

3 Philip, and Bartholomew; Thomas, and Matthew the publican [cp. 9 9]; James the son of Alphæus, and Thaddæus; 4 Simon the ¹ Cananæan,

and Judas Iscariot, who also ² betrayed him.

¹ Or, *Zealot*. See Luke 6 15; Acts 1 13.
² Or, *delivered him up*: and so always.

Mark.

preach, 15 and to have authority to cast out ² devils [cp. 6 7: also 6 12-13; 9 18]:

cp. 6 30.

16 ³ and Simon he surnamed Peter;

17 and James the son of Zebedee, and John the brother of James; and them he surnamed Boanerges, which is, Sons of thunder: 18 and Andrew, and Philip, and Bartholomew, and Matthew, and Thomas, and James the son of Alphæus, and Thaddæus, and Simon the ⁴ Cananæan,

19 and Judas Iscariot, which also betrayed him.

¹ Some ancient authorities add *whom also he named apostles*. See Luke 6 13.
² Gr. *demons*.
³ Some ancient authorities insert *and he appointed twelve*.
⁴ Or, *Zealot*. See Luke 6 15; Acts 1 13.

cp. 9 1, 2; 10 1, 9: also 9 6, 40; 10 17.

Luke.

whom also he named apostles [cp. 9 10; 17 5; 22 14; 24 10]; 14 Simon, whom he also named Peter [cp. 5 8], and Andrew his brother, and James

and John,

and Philip and Bartholomew, 15 and Matthew and Thomas, and James the son of Alphæus,

and Simon which was called the Zealot, 16 and Judas the ¹ son of James, and Judas Iscariot, which was the traitor.

¹ Or, *brother*. See Jude 1.

cp. 1 42: also 1 40; 6 8; etc.

cp. 14 22.

Acts.

13 And when they were come in, they went up into the upper chamber, where they were abiding; both Peter

and John and James

and Andrew, Philip and Thomas, Bartholomew and Matthew,

James the son of Alphæus, and Simon the Zealot, and Judas the ¹ son of James.

¹ Or, *brother*. See Jude 1.

(vi) The Great Sermon (Luke: §§ 81–84)

§ 81. The Beatitudes and the Woes

Matt. 5 1-12   **Luke 6 20-26**

Matt.

1 And seeing the multitudes [cp. 3 7; 8 18; 9 36], he went up into the mountain [cp. 14 23; 15 29; 17 1; 28 16]: and when he had sat down [cp. 15 29; 24 3], his disciples came unto him [cp. 13 10, 36; 14 15; 15 12, 23; 17 19; 18 1; 24 1, 3; 26 17]: 2 and he opened his mouth and taught them, saying, 3 Blessed are the poor in spirit: for theirs is the kingdom of heaven.

4 ¹ Blessed are they that mourn: for they shall be comforted. 5 Blessed are the meek: for they shall inherit the earth. 6 Blessed are they that hunger and thirst after righteousness [cp. 6 33: also 3 15; 5 10, 20; 6 1; 21 32]: for they shall be filled.

verse 4

cp. 3 13; 6 46; 9 2.
cp. 13 3.
cp. 6 35.

Luke.

cp. 6 5.

cp. 6 12; 9 28.   cp. 6 3: also 6 15.

20 And he lifted up his eyes on his disciples, cp. 9 12.   cp. 6 5.

and

said, Blessed *are* ye poor: for yours is the kingdom of God [cp. 16 25].

verse 21: cp. also *verse* 25.   cp. 16 20.

21 Blessed *are* ye that hunger now: cp. 7 37.

for ye shall be filled. Blessed *are* ye that weep now: for ye shall laugh.   cp. 16 20.

7 Blessed are the merciful: for they shall obtain mercy. 8 Blessed are the pure in heart: for they shall see God. 9 Blessed are the peacemakers [*cp.* 10 13]: for they shall be called sons of God [*cp.* 5 45; 8 12; 13 38]. 10 Blessed are they that have been persecuted for righteousness'¹ [*cp.* 3 15; 5 6, 20; 6 1, 33; 21 32] sake: for theirs is the kingdom of heaven. 11 Blessed are ye when *men* shall [*cp.* 10 22; 24 9]

cp. 9 50.

cp. 13 13.

cp. 6 36.

cp. 10 5, 6: *also* 1 79; 2 14, 29; 19 38.
cp. 20 36: *also* 6 35; 16 8.

cp. 14 27; 16 33.
cp. 12 36: *also* 1 12; 11 52.

22 Blessed are ye, when men shall hate you [*cp.* 1 71; 6 27; 21 17], and when they shall separate you *from their company*, and reproach you,

cp. 15 18, 19; 17 14.

reproach you, and persecute you, and say all manner of evil against you falsely, for my sake [*cp.* 10 18, 39; 16 25: *also* 10 22; 19 29; 24 9]. 12 Rejoice, and be exceeding glad: for great is your reward in heaven: for so persecuted they the prophets [*cp.* 21 35-36; 22 6; 23 29-34, 37] which were before you.

cp. 8 35; 10 29; 13 9: *also* 13 13.

cp. 12 3-5.

and cast out your name as evil, for the Son of man's sake [*cp.* 9 24: *also* 21 12, 17: *and* 18 29]. 23 Rejoice in that day, and leap *for joy*: for behold, your reward is great in heaven: for in the same manner did their fathers unto the prophets [*cp.* 11 47-50; 13 33, 34; 20 10-12]. 24 But woe unto you that are rich! for ye have received your consolation [*cp.* 16 25]. 25 Woe unto you, ye that are full now! for ye shall hunger. Woe *unto you*, ye that laugh now! for ye shall mourn and weep. 26 Woe *unto you*, when all men shall speak well of you! for in the same manner did their fathers to the false prophets.

cp. 15 21.

¹ Some ancient authorities transpose ver. 4 and 5.

Matt, 5 5: *cp.* Ps. 37 11.

§ 82. Love of Enemies and Judgement of Others

Matt. 5 44, 39-42; 7 12; 5 46-47, 45, 48; 7 1-2

Luke 6 27-38

5 44 But I say unto you, Love your enemies, *cp.* 10 22; 24 9.

cp. 13 13.

27 But I say unto you which hear, Love your enemies, do good to them that hate you [*cp.* 1 71; 6 22; 21 17], 28 bless them that curse you, pray for them that despitefully use you [*cp.* 23 34].

cp. 15 18, 19; 17 14.

and pray for them that persecute you; 39 but I say unto you, Resist not ¹ him that is evil: but whosoever smiteth thee on thy right [*cp.* 5 29, 30; 27 29] cheek, turn to him the other also. 40 And if any man would go to law with thee, and take away thy coat, let him have thy cloke also. 41 And whosoever shall ² compel thee to go one mile, go with him twain. 42 Give to him that asketh thee, and from him that would borrow [*cp.* Luke 6 35] of thee turn not thou away. 7 12 All things therefore whatsoever ye would that men should do unto you, even so do ye also unto them: for this is the law and the prophets [*cp.* 5 17; 11 13; 22 40]. 5 46 For if ye love them that love you, what reward [*cp.* Luke 6 35] have ye? do not even the *cp.* 9 11, 13; 11 19; 26 45.

29 To him that smiteth thee on the [*cp.* 6 6; 22 50] *one* cheek offer also the other; and from him that taketh away thy cloke withhold not thy coat also.

cp. 18 10.

cp. 19 23.

30 Give to every one that asketh thee; and of him that taketh away thy goods ask them not again. 31 And as ye would that men should do to you, do ye also to them likewise.
cp. 16 16.
32 And if ye love them that love you, what thank have ye? for even sinners [*cp.* 5 8, 30, 32; 7 34, 37, 39; 15 1, 2; 18 13; 19 7; 24 7] *cp.* 5 30; 7 29, 34; 15 1; 18 13. love those that love them. 33 And if ye do good to them that do good to you, what thank have ye? for even sinners do the same.

cp. 2 16, 17; 14 41.
cp. 2 16.

cp. 9 16, 24, 25, 31.

³ publicans [*cp.* 9 11; 11 19; 18 17; 21 31, 32]

the same?

47 And if ye salute your brethren only, what do ye more *than others*? do not even the Gentiles [*cp.* 6 7; 18 17: *also* 6 32 *and* Luke 12 30] the same?

cp. 5 42.

45 that ye may be sons [*cp.* 5 9; 8 12; 13 38] of your Father which is in heaven [*cp.* 5 16; 6 1, 9; 7 11, 21; 10 32, 33; 12 50; 16 17; 18 10, 14, 19: *also* 5 48; 6 14, 26, 32; 15 13; 18 35; 23 9]: for he maketh his sun to rise on the evil and the good, and sendeth rain on the just and the unjust [*cp.* 13 30]. 48 Ye therefore shall be perfect [*cp.* 19 21], as your heavenly Father [*cp.* 6 14, 26, 32; 15 13; 18 35; 23 9: *also* 5 16, 45; 6 1, 9; 7 11, 21; 10 32, 33; 12 50; 16 17; 18 10, 14, 19] is perfect. 7 1 Judge not, that ye be not judged. 2 For with what judgement ye judge, ye shall be judged:

and with what measure ye mete, it shall be measured unto you.

cp. 6 33.

[1] Or, *evil*   [2] Gr. *impress.*
[2] That is, *collectors or renters of Roman taxes*: and so elsewhere.

cp. 5 7.

cp. 11 25, 26.

cp. 11 25, 26.

Mark 4 24 And he said unto them, Take heed what ye hear: with what measure ye mete it shall be measured unto you: and more shall be given unto you.

34 And if ye lend to them of whom ye hope to receive, what thank have ye? even sinners lend to sinners, to receive again as much.

35 But love your enemies, and do *them* good, and lend, [1] never despairing; and your reward [*cp.* Matt. 5 46] shall be great, and ye shall be sons [*cp.* 16 8; 20 36] of the Most High [*cp.* 1 32, 35, 76; 8 28]: *cp.* 11 13.

for he is kind toward the unthankful and evil.

36 Be ye merciful [*cp.* Matt. 5 7], even as your Father *cp.* 11 13. is merciful.

37 And judge not, and ye shall not be judged: and condemn not, and ye shall not be condemned: release, and ye shall be released: 38 give, and it shall be given unto you; good measure, pressed down, shaken together, running over, shall they give into your bosom.

For with what measure ye mete it shall be measured to you again.

cp. 12 31.

[1] Some ancient authorities read *despairing of no man.*

cp. 12 36: *also* 1 12; 11 52.

§ 83. **The Criteria of the True Disciple** (i)

Matt. 15 14; 10 24-25; 7 3-5, 16-18; 12 33-35

Luke 6 39-45

15 14 And if the blind guide the blind [*cp.* 23 16, 17, 19, 24, 26], both shall fall into a pit. 10 24 A disciple is not above his [1] master, nor a [2] servant above his lord. 25 It is enough for the disciple that he be as his [1] master, and the [2] servant as his lord. 7 3 And why beholdest thou the mote that is in thy brother's eye, but considerest not the beam that is in thine own eye? 4 Or how wilt thou say to thy brother, Let me cast out the mote out of thine eye; and lo, the beam is in thine own eye? 5 Thou hypocrite, cast out first [*cp.* 5 24; 6 33; 23 26] the beam out of thine own eye; and then shalt thou see clearly to cast out the mote out of thy brother's eye.

cp. 7 27.

39 And he spake also a parable unto them, Can the blind guide the blind? shall they not both fall into a pit? 40 The disciple is not above his [1] master: but every one when he is perfected shall be as his [1] master. 41 And why beholdest thou the mote that is in thy brother's eye, but considerest not the beam that is in thine own eye? 42 Or how canst thou say to thy brother, Brother, let me cast out the mote that is in thine eye, when thou thyself beholdest not the beam that is in thine own eye? Thou hypocrite, cast out first the beam out of thine own eye, and then shalt thou see clearly to cast out the mote that is in thy brother's eye.

cp. 9 39-41.

cp. 13 16; 15 20.

cp. 8 7-9.

7 **16** By their fruits ye shall know them. Do *men* gather grapes of thorns, or figs of thistles? **17** Even so every good tree bringeth forth good fruit; but the corrupt tree bringeth forth evil fruit. **18** A good tree cannot bring forth evil fruit, neither can a corrupt tree bring forth good fruit.

cp. verse 16 above.

cp. verse 33 below.

12 **33** Either make the tree good, and its fruit good; or make the tree corrupt, and its fruit corrupt:

for the tree is known by its fruit.

34 Ye offspring of vipers [*cp.* 3 7; 23 33], how can ye, being evil [*cp.* 7 11], speak good things? for out of the abundance of the heart the mouth speaketh [*cp.* 15 18, 19]. **35** The good man out of his good treasure [*cp.* 13 52] bringeth forth good things: and the evil man out of his evil treasure bringeth forth evil things.

verse 34

cp. verse 44.

verse 44

43 For there is no good tree that bringeth forth corrupt fruit; nor again a corrupt tree that bringeth forth good fruit. **44** For each tree is known by its own fruit. For of thorns men do not gather figs, nor of a bramble bush gather they grapes.

cp. 3 7.
cp. 11 13.

verse 45

45 The good man out of the good treasure of his heart bringeth forth that which is good; and the evil *man* out of the evil *treasure* bringeth forth that which is evil: for out of the abundance of the heart his mouth speaketh.

Or, *teacher*　² Gr. *bondservant*.

¹ Or, *teacher*

§ 84. The Criteria of the True Disciple (ii)

Matt. 7 21-27

21 Not every one that saith unto me, Lord, Lord, shall enter into the kingdom of heaven [*cp.* 5 20; 18 3; 19 23, 24; 21 31; 23 13: *also* 7 13; 18 8, 9; 19 17; 25 21, 23]; but he that doeth the will [*cp.* 12 50; 21 31: *also* 6 10; 26 39, 42] of my Father which is in heaven [*cp.* 5 16, 45; 6 1, 9; 7 11; 10 32, 33; 12 50; 16 17; 18 10, 14, 19: *also* 5 48; 6 14, 26, 32; 15 13; 18 35; 23 9]. **22** Many will say to me in that day, Lord, Lord, did we not prophesy by thy name, and by thy name cast out ¹ devils, and by thy name do many ² mighty works? **23** And then will I profess unto them [*cp.* 25 34, 41], I never knew you [*cp.* 25 11, 12]: depart from me [*cp.* 25 41], ye that work iniquity. **24** Every one therefore which heareth these words of mine, and doeth them, shall be likened unto a wise [*cp.* 10 16; 24 45; 25 2 *ff.*] man, which built his house

cp. 9 47; 10 15, 23, 24, 25: *also* 9 43, 45.
cp. 3 35: *also* 14 36.
cp. 11 25, 26.

cp. 9 38.
cp. 9 39.

Luke 6 46-49

46 And why call ye me, Lord, Lord,
cp. 18 17, 24, 25: *also* 11 52; 13 24; 24 26.
and do not the things which I say?
cp. 22 42.
cp. 11 13.

13 **26** then shall ye begin to say,
We did eat and drink in thy presence,
cp. 9 49.
and thou didst teach in our streets;
27 and he shall say,
I tell you, I know not whence ye are; depart from me, all ye workers of iniquity.
47 Every one that cometh unto me, and heareth my words, and doeth them, I will shew you to whom he is like: **48** he is like a [*cp.* 12 42] man building a house, who digged and went deep, and laid a foundation

cp. 13 13.
cp. 3 5: *also* 10 1, 2, 9.

cp. 4 34; 5 30; 6 38; 7 17; 9 31.

upon the rock [*cp.* 16 18] : **25** and the rain descended, and the floods came, and the winds blew, and   beat upon that house ; and it fell not :
for it was founded upon the rock.
26 And every one that heareth these words of mine, and doeth them not, shall be likened unto a foolish [*cp.* 25 2 *ff.*] man, which built his house upon the sand :
          27 and the rain descended, and the floods came, and the winds blew, and   smote upon that house ; and   it fell :
and
great was the fall thereof.

          [1] Gr. *demons.*   [2] Gr. *powers.*

upon the rock :   and when
          a flood arose,
          the stream brake against that house, and could not shake it :
[1] because it had been well builded.
49 But he   that heareth,
          and doeth
          not,   is like   a
          man that built
a house upon the earth without a foundation ;

against which the stream brake,
          and straightway it fell in ;
and the ruin of that house was great.

[1] Many ancient authorities read *for it had been founded upon the rock* : as in Matt. 7 25.

Matt. 7 23 ‖ Luke 13 27 = Ps. 6 8.

(vii) Events in Galilee III (§§ 85-92)

§ 85. The Centurion at Capernaum

Matt. 7 28; 8 5-13	Luke 7 1-10	John 4 46-53

7 28 And it came to pass, when Jesus ended these words [*cp.* 11 1 ; 13 53 ; 19 1 ; 26 1],
the multitudes were astonished at his teaching.

          8 5 And when he was entered into Capernaum,

1 After he had ended all his sayings in the ears of the people,

          he entered into Capernaum.
2 And a certain centurion's [1] servant, who was [2] dear unto him, was sick and at the point of death [*cp.* 8 42]. **3** And when he heard concerning Jesus,
          he sent unto him elders of the Jews,   asking him that he would come   and save his [1] servant.

46 And there was a certain [1] nobleman, whose son was sick
          at Capernaum.

47 When he heard that Jesus was come out of Judæa into Galilee, he went unto him,
          and besought *him* that he would come down, and heal his son ;   for he was at the point of death. **48** Jesus therefore said unto him, Except ye see signs and wonders, ye will in no wise believe.
49 The [1] nobleman saith unto him, [2] Sir, come down ere my child die.

          there came
unto him
a centurion, beseeching him,

          6 and
          saying,
          Lord.   my
[1] servant   lieth in the house sick of the palsy [*cp.* 4 24; 9 2 *ff.*], grievously tormented [*cp.* 4 24].

cp. 2 3 *ff.*

cp. 5 18 *ff.*

4 And they, when they came to Jesus, besought him earnestly, saying, He is worthy that thou shouldest do this for him : **5** for he loveth our nation, and himself built us our synagogue.

6 And Jesus went with them. And when he was now not far from the house, the centurion sent friends to him, saying unto him, Lord, trouble [*cp.* 8 49] not thyself : for I am not [3] worthy that thou

7 And he saith unto him, I will come and heal him.
          8 And   the centurion
answered and said,
Lord,
          I am not [2] worthy that thou

cp. 5 35.

[Matthew]

shouldest come under my roof:

but only say [3] the word [cp. 8 16: also 8 3, 13, 32; 9 6, 22, 29; 12 13; 15 28; 17 7, 18], and my [1] servant shall be healed. 9 For I also am a man [4] under authority, having under myself soldiers: and I say to this one, Go, and he goeth; and to another, Come, and he cometh; and to my [5] servant, Do this, and he doeth it. 10 And when Jesus heard it, he marvelled, [cp. 9 22; 16 23]

and said to them that followed, Verily I say unto you, [6] I have not found so great faith, no, not in Israel. 11 And I say unto you that many shall come from the east and the west, and shall [7] sit down [cp. 26 29]

with Abraham, and Isaac, and Jacob, in the kingdom of heaven [cp. 21 31, 41, 43; 22 7-10: also 10 18; 24 14; 26 13; 28 19]: 12 but the sons of the kingdom [cp. 13 38: also 5 9, 45] shall be cast forth into the outer darkness [cp. 22 13; 25 30]: there shall be the weeping and gnashing of teeth [cp. 13 42, 50; 22 13; 24 51; 25 30].

cp. 19 30; 20 16.

13 And Jesus said unto the centurion, Go thy way; as thou hast believed, so be it done unto thee [cp. 9 29; 15 28].

And the [1] servant was healed in that hour [cp. 9 22 15 28; 17 18].

cp. 8 15.

[Mark references]

cp. 1 25, 41; 2 11; 3 5; 5 8, 34 41; 7 29, 34; 9 25; 10 52.

cp. 5 30; 8 33.

cp. 14 25.

cp. 12 9; 13 10; 14 9; 16 15.

cp. 10 31.

cp. 7 29.

cp. 7 30.

cp. 1 31.

[Luke 7]

shouldest come under my roof: 7 wherefore neither thought I myself worthy to come unto thee: but [4] say the word [cp. 4 35, 39; 5 13, 24; 6 10; 7 14; 8 29, 32, 48, 54; 9 42; 13 12; 17 14; 18 42], and my [5] servant shall be healed. 8 For I also am a man set under authority, having under myself soldiers: and I say to this one, Go, and he goeth; and to another, Come, and he cometh; and to my [1] servant, Do this, and he doeth it. 9 And when Jesus heard these things, he marvelled at him, and turned [cp. 7 44; 9 55; 10 23; 14 25; 22 61; 23 28] and said unto the multitude that followed him, I say unto you, I have not found so great faith, no, not in Israel.

cp. 14 15; 22 16, 18, 30.

13 28 There shall be the weeping and gnashing of teeth, when ye shall see Abraham, and Isaac, and Jacob, and all the prophets, in the kingdom of God [cp. 14 21-24; 20 16: also 2 30-32; 3 6; 24 47], and yourselves cp. 6 35; 16 8; 20 36. cast forth without.

29 And they shall come from the east and west, and from the north and south, and shall [6] sit down in the kingdom of God. 30 And behold, there are last which shall be first, and there are first which shall be last.

10 And they that were sent, returning to the house, found the [1] servant whole.

cp. 4 39.

[John references]

cp. 4 50; 5 8; 9 7; 11 43.

cp. 1 38.

cp. 10 16; 11 52.

cp. 12 36: also 1 12; 11 52.

[John]

50 Jesus saith unto him, Go thy way; thy son liveth. The man believed the word that Jesus spake unto him, and he went his way.

51 And as he was now going down, his [3] servants met him, saying, that his son lived.

52 So he inquired of them the hour when he began to amend. They said therefore unto him, Yesterday at the seventh hour the fever left him. 53 So the father knew that it was at that hour in which Jesus said unto him, Thy son liveth: and himself believed, and his whole house.

---

[1] Or, boy   [2] Gr. sufficient.
[3] Gr. with a word.
[4] Some ancient authorities insert set: as in Luke 7 8.
[5] Gr. bondservant.
[6] Many ancient authorities read With no man in Israel have I found so great faith.   [7] Gr. recline.

[1] Gr. bondservant.
[2] Or, precious to him   Or, honourable with him.
[3] Gr. sufficient.
[4] Gr. say with a word.   [5] Or, boy
[6] Gr. recline.

[1] Or, king's officer   [2] Or, Lord
[3] Gr. bondservants.

§ 86. The Widow's Son at Nain

[*Cp.* Matt. 9 18-26 ‖ Mark 5 21-43 ‖ Luke 8 40-56: John 11 1-46]

Luke 7 11-17

	cp. 5 35; 9 26. *cp.* 12 40, 42. *cp.* 16 19, 20.	**11** And it came to pass [1] soon afterwards, that he went to a city called Nain; and his disciples went with him, and a great multitude. **12** Now when he drew near to the gate of the city, behold, there was carried out one that was dead [*cp.* 8 49], the only [*cp.* 8 42; 9 38] son of his mother, and she was a widow [*cp.* 2 37; 4 25, 26; 18 3; 20 47; 21 2]: and much people of the city was with her. **13** And when the Lord [*cp.* 7	*cp.* 4 1; 6 23; 11 2; 20 2, 18; *etc.*
cp. 9 36; *etc.* *cp.* 8 3, 15; *etc.*	*cp.* 1 41; *etc.* *cp.* 5 39. *cp.* 1 41; 3 10; *etc.*	19; 10 1, 39, 41; 11 39; 12 42; 13 15; 17 5, 6; 18 6; 19 8; 22 61; 24 3, 34] saw her, he had compassion [*cp.* 10 33; 15 20] on her, and said unto her, Weep not [*cp.* 8 52; 23 28]. **14** And he came nigh and touched [*cp.* 5 13; 6 19; 7 39; 8	*cp.* 20 13, 15.
cp. 9 6.	*cp.* 2 11; 3 3; 5 41.	44; 18 15; 22 51: *also* 4 40; 8 54; 13 13; 14 4] the bier: and the bearers stood still. And he said, Young man, I say unto thee, Arise [*cp.* 5 24; 6 8; 8 54]. **15** And he that was	*cp.* 5 8.
cp. 9 8; 17 6; *etc.* *cp.* 9 8; *etc.* *cp.* 13 57; 21 11, 46.	*cp.* 4 41; 5 15, 33; *etc.* *cp.* 2 12. *cp.* 6 4, 15.	dead sat up, and began to speak. And he gave him to his mother [*cp.* 9 42]. **16** And fear [*cp.* 1 12, 65; 2 9; 5 26; 8 25, 35, 37, 47; 9 34, 45; 24 5, 37] took hold on all: and they glorified God [*cp.* 2 20; 5 25, 26; 13 13; 17 15, 18; 18 43; 23 47], saying, A great prophet [*cp.* 4 24; 7 39; 13 33; 24 19] is arisen among us: and, God hath visited [*cp.* 1 68, 78] his people. **17** And this report went forth concern-	*cp.* 9 24. *cp.* 4 19, 44; 6 14; 7 40; 9 17.
cp. 4 24; 9 26.	*cp.* 1 28.	ing him in the whole of Judæa, and all the region round about [*cp.* 4 14, 37; 5 15].	

[1] Many ancient authorities read *on the next day.*

Luke 7 15: *cp.* I Kings 17 23.

§ 87. The Question of John the Baptist and the Testimony of Jesus concerning him

Matt. 11 2-19		Luke 7 18-35	
2 Now when John heard in the prison [*cp.* 4 12; 14 3] the works of the Christ [*cp.* 1 17], he sent by his disciples [*cp.* 9 14; 14 12],	*cp.* 1 14; 6 17. *cp.* 2 18; 6 29. *cp.* 16 19, 20.	**18** And the disciples of John told him of all these things. **19** And John *cp.* 3 20. calling unto him [1] two of his disciples [*cp.* 5 33; 11 1] sent them to the Lord [*cp.* 7 13; 10 1, 39, 41; 11 39; 12 42; 13 15; 17 5, 6; 18 6; 19 8; 22 61; 24 34; *also* 24 3], saying, Art thou he that cometh, or look we for another? **20** And when the men were come unto him, they said, John the Baptist hath sent us	*cp.* 3 24. *cp.* 1 35, 37; 3 25; 4 1. *cp.* 4 1; 6 23; 11 2; 20 2; 18, 20, 25; 21 7, 12.
3 and said unto him, Art thou he that cometh [*cp.* 3 11; 21 9; 23 39], or look we for another? *cp.* 18 1; 26 55.	*cp.* 11 9.	unto thee, saying, Art thou he that cometh [*cp.* 13 35; 19 38], or look we for another? **21** In that hour [*cp.* 10 21; 13 31] he cured many of diseases and [2] plagues and evil spirits; and on many that were blind he bestowed sight. **22** And	*cp.* 1 15, 27; 3 31; 6 14; 11 27; 12 13.
4 And Jesus answered and said unto them, Go your way and tell John the things which ye do hear and see: **5** the blind receive their sight, and the lame walk, the lepers are cleansed, and the deaf hear [*cp.* 15 31], and the dead are raised up, and the poor have [1] good tidings preached to them.		he answered and said unto them, Go your way, and tell John what things ye have seen and heard; the blind receive their sight, the lame walk, the lepers are cleansed, and the deaf hear, the dead are raised up, the poor have [3] good tidings preached [*cp.* 1 19; 2 10; 3 18; 4 18, 43; 8 1; 9 6; 16 16; 20 1] to them [*cp.* 4 18]. **23** And blessed is he, whoso-	
6 And blessed is he, whoso- ever shall find none occasion of stumbling [*cp.* 13 57; 15 12; 26 31, 33: *also* 13 21; 24 10] in me. **7** And as these went their way, Jesus began to	*cp.* 6 3; 14 27, 29: *also* 4 17.	ever shall find none occasion of stumbling in me. **24** And when the messengers of John were departed, he began to	*cp.* 6 61: *also* 16 1.

say unto the multitudes concerning John, What went ye out into the wilderness to behold? a reed shaken with the wind? **8** But what went ye out for to see? a man clothed in soft *raiment*? Behold, they that wear soft *raiment*

are in kings' houses. **9** [2] But wherefore went ye out? to see a prophet [*cp.* 14 5; 21 26]? Yea, I say unto you, and much more than a prophet. **10** This is he, of whom it is written,

Behold, I send my messenger before thy face,
Who shall prepare thy way before thee.

11 Verily I say unto you, Among them that are born of women there hath not arisen a greater than John the Baptist: yet he that is [3] but little   in the kingdom of heaven is greater [*cp.* 5 19; 18 1, 4] than he.

cp. 21 32.

cp. 21 25, 32: *also* 3 7.

cp. 9 13; 21 31.

12 And from the days of John the Baptist until now the kingdom of heaven suffereth violence, and men of violence take it by force. **13** For all the prophets and the law [*cp.* 5 17; 7 12   22 40] prophesied until John.

14 And if ye are willing to receive [4] *it*, this is Elijah, which is to come [*cp.* 17 12, 13: *also* 3 3, 4]. **15** He that hath ears [5] to hear, let him hear [*cp.* 13 9, 43: *also* 19 12]. **16** But whereunto   shall I liken this generation?

It is like unto children sitting in the marketplaces, which call unto their fellows, **17** and say, We piped unto you, and ye did not dance; we wailed, and ye did not [6] mourn. **18** For John   came neither eating [*cp.* 3 4]   nor drinking, and they say, He hath a [7] devil. **19** The Son of man   came eating and drinking, and they say, Behold, a gluttonous man, and a wine-bibber, a friend of publicans and sinners [*cp.* 9 11]!

And wisdom
[8] is justified by   her   [9] works.

---

cp. 11 32.

1 2

cp. 11 31.

cp. 2 17.

cp. 9 13: *also* 1 2-3, 6.
cp. 4 9, 23; 7 16.

cp. 1 6.

cp. 2 16.

---

say unto the multitudes concerning John, What went ye out into the wilderness to behold? a reed shaken with the wind? **25** But what went ye out   to see? a man clothed in soft raiment? Behold, they which are gorgeously apparelled, and live delicately, are in king's courts. **26** But what went ye out to see? a prophet [*cp.* 1 76; 20 6]? Yea, I say unto you, and much more than a prophet. **27** This is he of whom it is written,

Behold, I send my messenger before thy face,
Who shall prepare thy way before thee [*cp.* 1 17, 76].

28 I say unto you, Among them that are born of women there is none greater than John: yet he that is [4] but little [*cp.* 9 48] in the kingdom of God is greater

than he. **29** And all the people [*cp.* 3 10] when they heard, and the publicans [*cp.* 3 12], justified God, [5] being baptized with the baptism of John. **30** But the Pharisees and the lawyers rejected for themselves [*cp.* 20 5] the counsel of God, [6] being not baptized of him [*cp.* 5 32; 7 47; 15 7, 10; 18 14; 19 10].

16 16 The law and the prophets

were until John: from that time the gospel of the kingdom of God is preached [*cp.* 1 19; 2 10; 3 18; 4 18, 43; 7 22; 8 1; 9 6; 20 1], and every man entereth violently into it.

cp. 1 17.

cp. 8 8; 14 35.

31 Whereunto then shall I liken the men of this generation, and to what are they like? **32** They are like unto children that sit in the marketplace, and call one to another; which say, We piped unto you, and ye did not dance; we wailed, and ye did not weep. **33** For John the Baptist is come   eating no bread nor drinking wine [*cp.* 1 15]; and ye say, He hath a [7] devil. **34** The Son of man is come eating [*cp.* 7 36] and drinking; and ye say, Behold, a gluttonous man, and a wine-bibber, a friend of publicans and sinners [*cp.* 5 30: *also* 7 37, 39; 15 2; 19 7]! **35** And wisdom [*cp.* 11 49] [8] is justified of all her children.

---

cp. 1 21, 23; 3 28.

cp. 1 21.

cp. 6 60.

---

[1] Or, *the gospel*
[2] Many ancient authorities read *But what went ye out to see? a prophet?*
[3] Gr. *lesser*.   [4] Or, *him*
[5] Some ancient authorities omit *to hear*.
[6] Gr. *beat the breast*.   [7] Gr. *demon*.
[8] Or, *was*
[9] Many ancient authorities read *children*: as in Luke 7 35.

[1] Gr. *certain two*.   [2] Gr. *scourges*.
[3] Or, *the gospel*   [4] Gr. *lesser*.
[5] Or, *having been*   [6] Or, *not having been*
[7] Gr. *demon*.   [8] Or, *was*

Matt. 11 5 ‖ Luke 7 22: *cp.* Is. 29 18-19; 35 5-6; 61 1.
Matt. 11 10 ‖ Luke 7 27 = Exod. 23 20; Mal. 3 1.   Matt. 11 14: *cp.* Mal. 4 5.

§ 88. The Anointing in Galilee

Matt. 26 6-13	Mark 14 3-9	**Luke 7** 36-50	John 12 1-8
		36 And one of the Pharisees desired him that he would eat [cp. 7 34] with him. And he entered into the Pharisee's house,	
6 Now when Jesus was in Bethany, in the house of Simon the leper,	3 And while he was in Bethany in the house of Simon the leper,	cp. 7 40, 43, 44. cp. 10 40.	1 Jesus therefore six days before the passover came to Bethany, where Lazarus was, whom Jesus raised from the dead. 2 So they made him a supper there: and Martha served; but Lazarus was one of them that sat at meat with him.
7 there came unto him a woman	as he sat at meat, there came a woman	and sat down to meat [cp 11 37; 14 1]. **37** And behold, a woman which was in the city, a sinner [cp. 7 34]; and when she knew that he was sitting at meat in the Pharisee's house, she brought ¹ an alabaster cruse of ointment,	3 Mary therefore
having ¹ an alabaster cruse of exceeding precious ointment, and she poured it upon his head, as he sat at meat.	having ¹ an alabaster cruse of ointment of ² spikenard very costly *and* she brake the cruse, and poured it over his head.		took a pound of ointment of ¹ spikenard, very precious,
		38 and standing behind at his feet [cp. 8 35; 10 39], weeping, she began to wet his feet with her tears, and wiped them with the hair of her head, and ² kissed his feet, and anointed them	and anointed the feet of Jesus, and wiped his feet with her hair: and the house was filled with the odour of the ointment.
		with the ointment. **39** Now when the Pharisee which had bidden him	4 But Judas Iscariot, one of his disciples, which should betray him,
8 But when the disciples saw it, they had indignation, saying, To what purpose is this waste?	4 But there were some that had indignation among themselves, *saying,* To what purpose hath this waste of the ointment been made? 5 For this	saw it, he spake within himself [cp. 11 38], saying,	saith,
9 For this *ointment* might have been sold for much, and given to the poor.	ointment might have been sold for above three hundred ³ pence, and given to the poor. And they murmured against her [cp. 10 13].		5 Why was not this ointment sold for three hundred ² pence, and given to the poor?
cp. 15 23; 19 13.		cp. 18 15.	6 Now this he said, not because he cared for the poor; but because he was a thief, and having the ³ bag [cp. 13 29] ⁴ took away what was
10 But Jesus perceiving it [cp. 12 15; 16 8; 22 18] said unto them, Why trouble ye the woman? for she hath wrought a good work upon me. cp. 19 14.	6 But Jesus cp. 8 17. said, Let her alone; why trouble ye her? she hath wrought a good work on me. cp. 10 14.	cp. 18 16.	put therein. 7 Jesus therefore cp. 5 6; 6 15. said,
			5 Suffer her to keep it against

[Matthew]

11 For ye have the poor always with you; but me ye have not always. 12 For in that she ² poured this ointment upon my body, she did it to prepare me for burial. 13 Verily I say unto you, Wheresoever ³ this gospel [cp. 4 23; 9 35; 24 14] shall be preached in the whole world [cp. 24 14: also 8 11; 10 18; 21 31, 41, 43; 22 7-10; 28 19], that also which this woman hath done shall be spoken of for a memorial of her.

¹ Or, a flask   ² Gr. cast.
³ Or, these good tidings

[Mark]

7 For ye have the poor always with you, and whensoever ye will ye can do them good: but me ye have not always. 8 She hath done what she could: she hath anointed my body aforehand for the burying. 9 And verily I say unto you, Wheresoever the gospel [cp. 1 1, 14, 15; 8 35; 10 29; 13 10; 16 15] shall be preached throughout the whole world [cp. 13 10: also 12 9; 16 15], that also which this woman hath done shall be spoken of for a memorial of her.

¹ Or, a flask
² Gr. pistic nard, pistic being perhaps a local name. Others take it to mean genuine; others, liquid.
³ See marginal note on Matt. 18 28.

cp. 2 30-32; 3 6; etc.

[Luke]

the day of my burying. 8 For the poor ye have always with you; but me ye have not always.

cp. 10 16; 11 52.

¹ See marginal note on Mark 14 3.
² See marginal note on Matt. 18 28.
³ Or, box
⁴ Or, carried what was put therein
⁵ Or, Let her alone: it was that she might keep it

---

cp. 13 57; 21 11, 46.   cp. 6 4, 15.

cp. 9 11; 11 19.   cp. 2 16.

cp. 26 6.   cp. 14 3.

cp. 18 23-34.

cp. 18 25.

cp. 9 22; 16 23.   cp. 5 30; 8 33.

cp. 9 13; 21 31.   cp. 2 17.

cp. 9 2.   cp. 2 5.

cp. 8 27; 21 10.   cp. 1 27; 2 7; 4 41.

cp. 9 22.   cp. 5 34; 10 52.

[Luke]

This man, if he were ³ a prophet [cp. 4 24; 7 16; 13 33; 24 19], would have perceived who and what manner of woman this is which toucheth [cp. 6 19; 8 44: Matt. 9 20; 14 36: Mark 3 10; 5 27; 6 56: John 20 17] him, that she is a sinner [cp. 5 30; 15 2; 19 7]. 40 And Jesus answering said unto him, Simon, I have somewhat to say unto thee. And he saith, ⁴ Master, say on. 41 A certain lender had two debtors: the one owed five hundred ⁵ pence, and the other fifty. 42 When they had not *wherewith* to pay, he forgave them both. Which of them therefore will love him most? 43 Simon answered and said, He, I suppose, to whom he forgave the most. And he said unto him, Thou hast rightly judged [cp. 10 28]. 44 And turning [cp. 7 9; 9 55; 10 23; 14 25; 23 28] to the woman, he said unto Simon, Seest thou this woman? I entered into thine house, thou gavest me no water for my feet: but she hath wetted my feet with her tears, and wiped them with her hair. 45 Thou gavest me no kiss: but she, since the time I came in, hath not ceased to ⁶ kiss my feet. 46 My head with oil thou didst not anoint: but she hath anointed my feet with ointment. 47 Wherefore I say unto thee, Her sins, which are many, are forgiven; for she loved much: but to whom little is forgiven, *the same* loveth little [cp. 5 32; 7 29, 30; 15 7, 10; 18 14; 19 10]. 48 And he said unto her, Thy sins are forgiven [cp. 5 20]. 49 And they that sat at meat with him began to say ⁷ within themselves, Who is this [cp. 5 21: also 4 36; 8 25; 9 9] that even forgiveth sins? 50 And he said unto the woman, Thy faith hath saved thee [cp. 8 48; 17 19; 18 42]; go in peace [cp. 8 48].

cp. 4 19, 44; 6 14; 7 40; 9 17.

cp. 1 38.

cp. 5 12: also 12 34.

¹ Or, a flask   ² Gr. kissed much.
³ Some ancient authorities read the prophet. See John 1 21, 25.
⁴ Or, Teacher   ⁵ See footnote on Matt. 18 28.
⁶ Gr. kiss much.   ⁷ Or, among

---

§ 89. A Controversy about Casting out Devils

Matt. 12 22-37	Matt. 9 32-34; 7 16-18	Mark 3 19b-30	Luke 11 14-23; 12 10; 6 43-45
		And he cometh ¹ into a house. 20 And the multitude cometh together again, so that they could not so much as eat bread [cp. 6 31]. 21 And when his friends	

cp. 13 57-58.

9 **32** And as they went forth, behold, there was brought to him a dumb man possessed with a ¹ devil.

22 Then was brought unto him ¹ one possessed with a devil, blind [*cp.* 9 27] and dumb: and
he healed him, insomuch that the dumb man spake and saw.

heard it, they went out to lay hold on him [*cp.* 3 31] : for they said, He is beside himself [*cp.* 6 3-6].

cp. 7 5.

11 **14** And he was casting out a ¹ devil *which was* dumb. And it came to pass, when the ¹ devil was gone out, the dumb man spake ;

33 And when the ¹ devil was cast out, the dumb man spake : and the multitudes marvelled [*cp.* 8 27 ; 15 31 ; 21 20 ; 27 14 : *also* 7 28 ; 13 54 ; 19 25 ; 22 22, 33], saying, It was never so seen in Israel.

23 And all the multitudes were amazed,

cp. 2 12 ; 5 20, 42 ; 6 51 ; 7 37 ; 10 32 ; 15 5 ; 16 5, 8 : *also* 1 22, 27 ; 6 2 ; 10 24, 26 ; 11 18 ; 12 17.

and the multitudes marvelled [*cp.* 5 9, 26 ; 8 25, 56 ; 9 43 ; 24 12, 41 : *also* 2 47,48 ; 4 22,32,36 20 26].

cp. 7 15, 21, 46.

and said,

Is this the son of David [*cp.* 1 1 ; 9 27 ; 15 22 ; 20 30, 31 ; 21 9, 15]?

cp. 10 47, 48.

cp. 1 32 ; 18 38, 39.

24 But when the Pharisees

34 But the Pharisees

22 And the scribes which came down from Jerusalem [*cp.* 7 1] said, He hath Beelzebub, and,

15 But some of them

cp. 5 17.

cp. 1 19.

cp. 15 1.

heard it, they said,

said,

said,

cp. 7 20 ; 8 48, 52 ; 10 20.

This man doth not cast out ² devils, but ³ by Beelzebub [*cp.* 10 25] the prince of the ² devils.

² By the prince of the ³ devils casteth he out ³ devils.

² By the prince of the ³ devils casteth he out the ³ devils.

² By Beelzebub the prince of the ³ devils casteth he out ³ devils.

¹ Gr. *demon.*   ² Or, *In*
³ Gr. *demons.*

16 And others, tempting *him* [*cp.* 10 25], sought of him a sign from heaven.   **17** But he, knowing their thoughts [*cp.* 5 22 ; 6 8 ; 9 47], said unto them,

cp. 8 6.
cp. 2 18 ; 6 30.

cp. 16 1 : *also* 19 3 ; 22 18, 35 : *and* 12 38.

cp. 8 11 : *also* 10 2 ; 12 15.

25 And knowing their thoughts [*cp.* 9 4 ; 16 8] he said unto them,

23 And he
cp. 2 8 ; 8 17.
called them unto him, and said unto them in parables, How can Satan cast out Satan?

cp. 1 48 ; 2 24, 25 ; 4 19, 29 ; 5 6, 42 ; 6 61 ; 11 14 ; 13 18 ; 16 19, 30 ; 18 4 ; 21 17.

Every kingdom divided against itself is brought to desolation ; and every city or house divided against itself shall not stand :

24 And if a kingdom be divided against itself, that kingdom cannot stand.

Every kingdom divided against itself is brought to desolation ; ⁴ and a house *divided* against a house falleth.

26 And if Satan casteth out Satan, he is divided against himself ; how then shall his kingdom stand ?

25 And if a house be divided against itself, that house will not be able to stand.
26 And if Satan hath risen up against himself, and is divided, he cannot stand, but hath an end.

18 And if Satan also is divided against himself, how shall his kingdom stand ? because ye say that I cast out ³ devils ² by Beelzebub.   **19** And if I ² by Beelzebub cast out ³ devils, by whom do your sons cast them out ? therefore shall they be your judges.   **20** But if I by the finger of God cast out ³ devils, then is the kingdom of God come upon you [*cp.* 9 2 ; 10 9, 11 ; 17 20, 21 ; 19 11 ; 21 8].

27 And if I ³ by Beelzebub cast out ² devils, ³ by whom do your sons cast them out ? therefore shall they be your judges.   **28** But if I ³ by the Spirit of God cast out ² devils, then is the kingdom of God come upon you [*cp.* 3 2 ; 4 17 ; 10 7].
29 Or how can one enter

cp. 1 15 ; 6 12.

27 But no one can enter

into the house of the strong *man*,

    and spoil his goods,
        except he first
bind the strong *man*? and then

he
will spoil his house. **30** He that is not with me is against me; and he that gathereth not with me scattereth.
31 Therefore I say unto you, Every sin and blasphemy shall be forgiven [4] unto men;

    but the blasphemy against the Spirit shall not be forgiven. **32** And whosoever shall speak a word against the Son of man, it shall be forgiven him; but whosoever shall speak against the Holy Spirit, it shall not be forgiven him, neither in this [5] world, nor in that which is to come.
cp. 18 8; 25 41, 46.

cp. verse 33 below.

33 Either make the tree good, and its   fruit good; or make the tree corrupt, and its fruit corrupt:

        for the tree is known by its   fruit.

34 Ye offspring of vipers [*cp.* 3 7; 23 33], how can ye, being evil [*cp.* 7 11], speak good things? for out of the abundance of the heart the mouth speaketh [*cp.* 15 18, 19]. **35** The good man out of his good treasure [*cp.* 13 52] bringeth forth   good things: and the evil man out of his evil treasure bringeth forth   evil things.
verse 34

36 And I say unto you, that every idle word that men shall speak, they shall give account thereof in the day of judgement [*cp.* 10 15; 11 22, 24]. **37** For by thy words thou shalt be justified, and by thy words thou shalt be condemned.

[1] Or, *a demoniac* [2] Gr. *demons.* [3] Or, *in*
[4] Some ancient authorities read *unto you men.*
[5] Or, *age*

---

into the house of the strong *man*,

    and spoil his goods,
        except he first
bind the strong *man*; and then

he
will spoil his house.

cp. 9 40.
28 Verily I say unto you, All their sins shall be forgiven unto the sons of men, and their blasphemies wherewith soever they shall blaspheme:

29 but whosoever shall blaspheme against the Holy Spirit hath never forgiveness,

cp. 10 30.
but is guilty of an eternal sin: **30** because they said, He hath an unclean spirit.
[1] Or, *home* [2] Or, *In* [3] Gr. *demons.*

7 16 By their fruits ye shall know them. Do *men* gather grapes of thorns, or figs of thistles? **17** Even so every good tree bringeth forth good fruit; but the corrupt tree bringeth forth evil fruit. **18** A good tree cannot bring forth evil fruit, neither can a corrupt tree bring forth good fruit.
cp. verse 16 *above.*

verse 16 *above*

---

21 When the strong *man* fully armed guardeth his own court,   his goods are in peace: **22** but when a stronger than he shall come upon him, and overcome him, he taketh from him his whole armour wherein he trusted, and divideth his spoils. **23** He that is not with me is against me; and he that gathereth not with me scattereth [*cp.* 9 50].

12 10 And everyone who shall speak a word against the Son of man, it shall be forgiven him: but unto him that blasphemeth against the Holy Spirit it shall not be forgiven.

cp. 18 30.

6 44

6 43 For there is no good tree that bringeth forth corrupt fruit; nor again a corrupt tree that bringeth forth good fruit. **44** For each tree is known by its own fruit. For of thorns men do not gather figs, nor of a bramble bush gather they grapes.
cp. 3 7.
cp. 11 13.

verse 45
45 The good man out of the good treasure of his heart bringeth forth that which is good; and the evil *man* out of the evil *treasure* bringeth forth that which is evil: for out of the abundance of the heart his mouth speaketh.

[1] Gr. *demon.* [2] Or, *In* [3] Gr. *demons.*
[4] Or, *and house falleth upon house*

§ 90. A Request for a Sign refused

Matt. 12 38-45	Matt. 16 1-2, 4	Mark 8 11-13	Luke 11 29-32, 24-26	
38 Then certain of the scribes and Pharisees	1 And the Pharisees and Sadducees came, and tempting him [*cp.* 19 3; 22 35: *also* 22 18]	11 And the Pharisees came forth, and began to question with him [*cp* 9 14, 16; 12 28],	29 And when the multitudes were gathering together unto him, *cp.* 10 25 ; 11 16.	*cp.* 8 6.
answered him, saying, 1 Master, we would see a sign from thee.	asked him to shew them a sign from heaven.	seeking of him a sign from heaven, tempting him [*cp.* 10 2 : *also* 12 15].	11 16 *cp.* 10 25 ; 11 16.	*cp.* 2 18; 6 30. *cp.* 8 6.
39 But he answered and said unto them,	2 But he answered and said unto them, . . .	12 And he sighed deeply [*cp.* 7 34] in his spirit, and saith, Why doth this generation	he began to say, This generation is an evil generation	
An evil and adulterous generation [*cp.* 12 45] seeketh after a sign;	4 An evil and adulterous generation [*cp.* 17 17] seeketh after a sign ;	*cp.* 8 38 ; 9 19. seek a sign? verily I say unto you,	[*cp.* 9 41] : it seeketh after a sign;	
and there shall no sign be given to it but the sign of Jonah the prophet :	and there shall no sign be given unto it, but the sign of Jonah. And he left them, and departed.	There shall no sign be given unto this generation. 13 And he left them, and again entering into *the boat* departed to the other side.	and there shall no sign be given to it but the sign of Jonah.	

40 for as Jonah was three days and three nights in the belly of the 2 whale; so shall the Son of man be three days and three nights in the heart of the earth [*cp.* 16 21; 17 23; 20 19; 26 61; 27 40, 63, 64].	*cp.* 8 31; 9 31; 10 34; 14 58; 15 29.	even as Jonah became a sign unto the Ninevites, so shall also the Son of man be to this generation. *cp.* 9 22 ; 13 32 ; 18 33 ; 24 7, 21, 46.	30 For	*cp.* 2 19-22.
41 The men of Nineveh shall stand up in the judgement with this generation, and shall condemn it: for they repented at the preaching of Jonah; and behold, 3 a greater than Jonah is here [*cp.* 12 6]. **42** The queen of the south shall rise up in the judgement with this generation, and shall condemn it: for she came from the ends of the earth to hear the wisdom of Solomon; and behold, 3 a greater than Solomon is here [*cp.* 12 6].		*verse 32*	31 The queen of the south shall rise up in the judgement with the men of this generation, and shall condemn them : for she came from the ends of the earth to hear the wisdom of Solomon ; and behold, 1 a greater than Solomon is here. 32 The men of Nineveh shall stand up in the judgement with this generation, and shall condemn it: for they repented at the preaching of Jonah ; and behold, 1 a greater than Jonah is here.	
verse 41			24 The unclean spirit when 2 he is gone out of the man, passeth through waterless places, seeking rest ; and finding none,	
43 But the unclean spirit, when 4 he is gone out of the man, passeth through waterless places, seeking rest, and findeth it not. **44** Then 4 he saith, I will return into my house whence I came out; and when 4 he is come, 4 he findeth it empty, swept, and garnished. **45** Then goeth 4 he, and taketh with 5 himself seven other spirits more evil than 5 himself, and they enter in and dwell there : and the last state of that			2 he saith, I will turn back unto my house whence I came out. 25 And when 2 he is come, 2 he findeth it swept and garnished. 26 Then goeth 2 he, and taketh *to him* seven other spirits more evil than 3 himself ; and they enter in and dwell there : and the last state of that	

man becometh worse than the first. Even so shall it be also unto this evil generation [*cp. verse* 39].	man becometh worse than the first.
¹ Or, *Teacher*　³ Gr. *sea-monster.*　³ Gr. *more than.* ⁴ Or, *it*　⁵ Or, *itself*	¹ Gr. *more than.*　² Or, *it*　³ Or, *itself*

Matt. 12 39 ; 16 4 ‖ Luke 11 29 : *cp.* Jonah 3 4.　　Matt. 12 40 : *cp.* Jonah 1 17.　　Matt. 12 41 ‖ Luke 11 32 : *cp.* Jonah 3 5.
Matt. 12 42 ‖ Luke 11 31 : *cp.* I Kings 10 1 *ff.*

§ 91. The True Brethren of Jesus
[*Cp.* Luke 11 27-28]

Matt. 12 46-50	**Mark 3** 31-35	Luke 8 19-21	
46 While he was yet speaking [*cp.* 17 5 ; 26 47] to the multitudes,	*cp.* 5 35 ; 14 43.	*cp.* 8 49 ; 22 47, 60.	
behold, his mother and his brethren	**31** And there come his mother and his brethren [*cp.* 3 21] ;	**19** And there came to him his mother and brethren, and they could not come at him for the crowd [*cp.* 5 19 ; 19 3].	
stood without,	*cp.* 2 4 ; 3 9. and, standing without, they sent unto him, calling him. **32** And a multitude was sitting about		
seeking to speak to him.	him ; and they say unto him, Behold, thy mother and thy	**20** And it was told him, Thy mother and thy brethren stand without, de-	
47 ¹ And one said unto him, Behold, thy mother and thy brethren stand without, seeking to speak to thee. **48** But he answered and said unto him that told him, Who is my mother ? and who are my brethren ? **49** And	brethren without seek for thee. **33** And **he** answereth them, and saith, Who is my mother and my brethren ? **34** And looking round [*cp.* 3 5 ; 5 32 ; 9 8 ; 10 23 ; 11 11] on them which sat round about him,	siring to see thee. **21** But he answered and said unto them, *cp.* 6 10.	
he stretched forth his hand towards his disciples, and said, Behold, my mother and my brethren ! **50** For whosoever *cp.* 13 19-23.	he saith, Behold, my mother and my brethren ! **35** For whosoever *cp.* 2 2 ; 4 14-20, 33 ; 16 20.	My mother and my brethren are these which hear the word of God [*cp.* 5 1 ; 8 11 ; 11 28 : *also* 1 2 ; 8 12-15 ; *and* 4 32], and do it. *cp.* 22 42.	*cp.* 4 41 ; 5 24, 38 ; *etc.*
shall do the will [*cp.* 7 21 ; 21 31 : *also* 6 10 ; 26 39, 42] of my Father which is in heaven [*cp.* 5 16, 45 ; 6 1, 9 ; 7 11, 21 ; 10 32, 33 ; 16 17 ; 18 10, 14, 19 : *also* 5 48 ; 6 14, 26, 32 ; 15 13 ; 18 35 ; 23 9], he is my brother, and sister, and mother.	shall do the will [*cp.* 14 36] of God, *cp.* 11 25, 26. the same is my brother, and sister, and mother.	*cp.* 11 13.	*cp.* 4 34 ; 5 30 ; 6 38 ; 7 17 ; 9 31.

¹ Some ancient authorities omit ver. 47.

§ 92. General Preaching with the Twelve and the Ministering Women

Matt. 9 35	Mark 6 6b	**Luke 8** 1-3
35 And Jesus went about all the cities and the villages, teaching in their synagogues, and preaching [*cp.* 4 23 ; 11 1] the ¹ gospel *cp.* 11 5. of the kingdom [*cp.* 4 23 ; 24 14 : *also* 26 13], and healing all manner	**6** And he went round about the villages teaching. *cp.* 1 1, 14, 15 ; 8 35 ; 10 29 ; 13 10 ; 14 9 ; 16 15.	**1** And it came to pass soon afterwards, that he went about through cities and villages [*cp.* 13 22], preaching and bringing the ¹ good tidings [*cp.* 1 19 ; 2 10 ; 3 18 ; 4 18, 43 ; 7 22 ; 9 6 ; 16 16 ; 20 1] of the kingdom of God,

Matt.	Mark	Luke	
of disease and all manner of sickness.		and with him the twelve,	
cp. 10 1.	*cp.* 6 7.	4 44 And he was	
4 23 And Jesus went about in all Galilee, teaching in their synagogues,	1 39 And he went into their synagogues throughout all Galilee, preaching	preaching in the synagogues [*cp.* 4 15] of ⁴ Galilee.	*cp.* 18 20.
and preaching the ¹ gospel of the kingdom, and healing all manner of disease and all manner of sickness among the people.	and casting out ¹ devils.		
cp. 27 55.	*cp.* 15 40.	2 and certain women [*cp.* 23 49, 55; 24 1, 10, 22, 24] which had been healed of evil spirits and infirmities, Mary that was called Magdalene [*cp.* 24 10],	
cp. 27 56, 61 ; 28 1.	*cp.* 15 40, 47 ; 16 1, 9.	from whom seven ² devils had gone out, 3 and Joanna [*cp.* 24 10] the wife of Chuza Herod's steward, and Susanna, and many others,	*cp.* 19 25; 20 1, 18.
cp. 27 55.	*cp.* 15 41.	which ministered unto ³them of their substance.	
¹ Or, *good tidings*	¹ Gr. *demons.*	¹ Or, *gospel* ² Gr. *demons.* ³ Many ancient authorities read *him.* ⁴ Very many ancient authorities read *Judæa.*	

(viii) Teaching by Parables (§§ 93-104)

§ 93. **The Sower**

Matt. 13 1-9	Mark 4 1-9	Luke 8 4-8	
1 On that day went Jesus out of the house, and sat by the sea side.	1 And again he began to teach by the sea side [*cp.* 3 7; 5 21].		
2 And there were gathered unto him great multitudes,	And there is gathered unto him a very great multitude,	*cp.* 5 1. 4 And when a great multitude came together, and they of every city resorted unto him,	
so that he entered into a boat, and sat; and all the multitude stood on the beach. 3 And he spake to them many things in parables, saying,	so that he entered into a boat, and sat in the sea [*cp.* 3 9]; and all the multitude were by the sea on the land. 2 And he taught them many things in parables, and said unto them in his teaching [*cp.* 12 38], 3 Hearken: Behold, the sower went forth to sow:	*cp.* 5 3. he spake by a parable:	*cp.* 16 25.
Behold, the sower went forth to sow; 4 and as he sowed, some *seeds* fell by the way side,		5 The sower went forth to sow his seed: and as he sowed, some fell by the way side; and it was trodden under foot, and the birds of the heaven [*cp.* 9 58; 13 19] devoured it.	
cp. 6 26; 8 20; 13 32.	4 and it came to pass, as he sowed, some *seed* fell by the way side,		
came and devoured them: 5 and others fell upon the rocky places, where they had not much earth: and straightway they sprang up, because they had no deepness of earth: 6 and when the sun was risen, they were scorched; and because they had no root, they withered away.	*cp.* 4 32. and the birds came and devoured it. 5 And other fell on the rocky *ground*, where it had not much earth; and straightway it sprang up, because it had no deepness of earth: 6 and when the sun was risen, it was scorched; and because it had no root, it withered away.	6 And other fell on the rock; and as soon as it grew, it withered away, because it had no moisture. 7 And other	
7 And others fell upon the thorns; and the thorns grew up, and choked them:	7 And other fell among the thorns, and the thorns grew up, and choked it, and it yielded no	fell amidst the thorns; and the thorns grew with it, and choked it.	

8 and others fell upon the good ground, and yielded fruit,

some a hundredfold, some sixty, some thirty.

9 He that hath ears[1],   let him hear [cp. 11 15; 13 43: also 19 12].

[1] Some ancient authorities add here, and in ver. 43, to hear: as in Mark 4 9: Luke 8 8.

fruit. **8** And others fell into the good ground, and yielded fruit, growing up and increasing; and brought forth, thirtyfold, and sixtyfold, and a hundredfold.

9 And he said, Who hath ears to hear, let him hear [cp. 4 23; 7 16].

8 And other fell into the good ground, and grew, and brought forth fruit a hundredfold.

As he said these things, he cried, He that hath ears to hear, let him hear [cp. 14 35].

cp. 6 60.

§ 94. The Interpretation of the Sower

Matt. 13 10-23	**Mark 4** 10-20	**Luke 8** 9-15	
10 And cp. 17 1, 19; 20 17; 24 3.	**10** And when he was alone [cp. 4 34; 6 31, 32; 9 2, 28; 13 3], they that were about him with the twelve cp. 6 35.	**9** And cp. 9 10; 10 23.	
the disciples came [cp. 5 1; 13 36; 14 15; 15 12, 23; 17 19; 18 1; 24 1, 3; 26 17], and said unto him, Why speakest thou unto them in parables [cp. 13 36; 15 15]? **11** And he answered and said unto them, Unto you it is given to know the mysteries of the kingdom of heaven [cp. 13 51], but to them it is not given [cp. 19 11].	asked of him the parables [cp. 7 17]. **11** And he said unto them, Unto you is given the mystery of the kingdom of God: but unto them that are without, all things are done	his disciples cp. 9 12. asked him what this parable might be. **10** And he said, Unto you it is given to know the mysteries of the kingdom of God: but to the rest [cp. 12 26; 18 9, 11; 24 9, 10]	
12 For whosoever hath, to him shall be given, and he shall have abundance: but whosoever hath not, from him shall be taken away even that which he hath.	4 25 For he that hath, to him shall be given: and he that hath not, from him shall be taken away even that which he hath.	8 18 For whosoever hath, to him shall be given; and whosoever hath not, from him shall be taken away even that which he [1] thinketh he hath.	
25 29 For unto every one that hath shall be given, and he shall have abundance: but from him that hath not, even that which he hath shall be taken away.		19 26 I say unto you, that unto every one that hath shall be given; but from him that hath not, even that which he hath shall be taken away from him.	
13 Therefore speak I to them in parables; because seeing they see not, and hearing they hear not, neither do they understand.	in parables: **12** that seeing they may see, and not perceive; and hearing they may hear, and not understand [cp. 8 18]; lest haply they should turn again, and it should be forgiven them.	in parables; that seeing they may not see, and hearing they may not understand.	cp. 9 39.
14 And unto them is fulfilled the prophecy of Isaiah, which saith, By hearing ye shall hear, and shall in no wise understand; And seeing ye shall see, and shall in no wise perceive: **15** For this people's heart is waxed gross, And their ears are dull of hearing, And their eyes they have closed; Lest haply they should perceive with their eyes, And hear with their ears, And understand with their heart, And should turn again, And I should heal them.			cp. 12 39-40.
cp. 9 22; 16 23.	cp. 5 30; 8 33.	10 23 And turning [cp. 7 9, 44; 9 55; 14 25; 22 61; 23 28] to the disciples, he said privately [cp. 9 10], Blessed are the eyes which see the things that ye see:	cp. 1 38.
cp. 17 1, 19; 20 17; 24 3. **16** But blessed are your eyes, for they see; and your ears, for they hear. **17** For verily I say unto you,	cp. 4 10, 34; 6 31, 32; 9 2, 28; 13 3.	**24** for I say unto you,	

that many prophets and righteous men desired to see the things which ye see, and saw them not; and to hear the things which ye hear, and heard them not.

cp. 15 16; 16 8-12.

18 Hear then ye the parable of the sower [*cp.* 13 37].

19 When any one heareth the word of the kingdom, and understandeth it not, *then* cometh the evil *one* [*cp.* 5 37, 39; 6 13; 13 38], and snatcheth away that which hath been sown in his heart.

This is he that was sown by the way side. **20** And he that was sown upon the rocky places, this is he that heareth the word, and straightway with joy receiveth it; **21** yet hath he not root in himself, but endureth for a while; and when tribulation or persecution ariseth because of the word, straightway he stumbleth [*cp.* 24 10: *also* 11 6; 13 57; 15 12; 26 31, 33]. **22** And he that was sown among the thorns, this is he that heareth the word; and the care of the [1] world, and the deceitfulness of riches, choke the word, and he becometh unfruitful. **23** And he that was sown upon the good ground, this is he that heareth the word, and understandeth it; who verily beareth fruit, and bringeth forth, some a hundredfold, some sixty, some thirty.

[1] Or, *age*

---

that many prophets and kings desired to see the things which ye see, and saw them not; and to hear the things which ye hear, and heard them not.

13 And he saith unto them, Know ye not this parable [*cp.* 6 52; 7 18; 8 17-21; 9 10, 32; 16 14]? and how shall ye know all the parables? **14** The sower soweth the word [*cp.* 2 2; 4 33; 16 20]. **15** And these are they by the way side, where the word is sown; and when they have heard, straightway cometh Satan, and taketh away the word which hath been sown in them.

16 And these in like manner are they that are sown upon the rocky *places*, who, when they have heard the word, straightway receive it with joy; **17** and they have no root in themselves, but endure for a while; then, when tribulation or persecution ariseth because of the word, straightway they stumble [*cp.* 6 3; 14 27, 29]. **18** And others are they that are sown among the thorns; these are they that have heard the word, **19** and the cares of the [1] world, and the deceitfulness of riches, and the lusts of other things entering in, choke the word, and it becometh unfruitful. **20** And those are they that were sown upon the good ground; such as hear the word, and accept it, and bear fruit, thirtyfold, and sixtyfold, and a hundredfold.

[1] Or, *age*

---

cp. 2 50; 9 45; 18 34.

11 Now the parable is this: The seed is the word of God [*cp.* 5 1; 8 21; 11 28: *also* 1 2 *and* 4 32]. **12** And those by the way side are they that have heard; then cometh the devil, and taketh away the word from their heart, that they may not believe and be saved.

13 And those on the rock *are* they which, when they have heard, receive the word with joy; and these have no root, which for a while believe, and in time of temptation [*cp.* 4 13; 22 28]

cp. 7 23.

fall away. **14** And that which fell among the thorns, these are they that have heard, and as they go on their way they are choked with cares [*cp.* 21 34] and riches and pleasures of *this* life [*cp.* 21 34], and bring no fruit to perfection. **15** And that in the good ground, these are such as in an honest and good heart, having heard the word, hold it fast, and bring forth fruit

with patience [*cp.* 21 19].

[1] Or, *seemeth to have*

---

cp. 3 10; 4 33; 8 27, 43; *etc.*

cp. 17 15.

cp. 6 61; 16 1.

cp. 15 4, 8, 16.

Matt. 13 13 || Mark 4 12 || Luke 8 10 : *cp.* Is. 6 9-10.   Matt. 13 14-15 = Is. 6 9-10.

---

§ 95. Miscellaneous Sayings

Matt. 5 15; 10 26-27; 7 2; 13 12; 25 29	**Mark 4** 21-25	Luke 8 16-18	Luke 11 33; 12 2-3; 6 38; 19 26
5 15 Neither do *men* light	**21** And he said unto them, Is	**16** And no man, when he hath lighted	**11** 33 No man, when he hath lighted

a lamp,

and put it, under the bushel, but on the stand; and it shineth unto all that are in the house.

10 26 For there is nothing covered, that shall not be revealed; and hid,

that shall not be known. **27** What I tell you in the darkness, speak ye in the light: and what ye hear in the ear, proclaim upon the house-tops.

cp. 11 15; 13 9, 43: also 19 12.

7 2 And with what measure ye mete, it shall be measured unto you.

cp. 6 33: also 19 28-29. **13 12** For whosoever hath, to him shall be given, and he shall have abundance: but whosoever hath not, from him shall be taken away even that which he hath.

25 29 For unto every one that hath shall be given, and he shall have abundance: but from him that hath not, even that which he hath shall be taken away.

the lamp brought to be put under the bushel, or under the bed, *and* not to be put on the stand?

22 For there is nothing hid, save that it should be manifested; neither was *anything* made secret, but that it should

come to light.

23 If any man hath ears to hear, let him hear [*cp.* 4 9; 7 16]. **24** And he said unto them, Take heed what ye hear: with what measure ye mete it shall be measured unto you: and more shall be given unto you [*cp.* 10 29-30]. **25** For he that hath, to him shall be given: and he that hath not, from him shall be taken away even that which he hath.

a lamp, covereth it with a vessel, or putteth it under a bed; but putteth it on a stand,

that they which enter in may see the light. **17** For nothing is hid, that shall not be made manifest; nor *anything* secret, that shall not be known

and come to light.

cp. 8 8; 14 35.

18 Take heed therefore how ye hear:

cp. 12 31: also 18 29-30. for whosoever hath, to him shall be given; and whosoever hath not, from him shall be taken away even that which he [1] thinketh he hath.

a lamp, putteth it in a cellar, neither under the bushel, but on the stand,

that they which enter in may see the light. **12 2** But there is nothing covered up, that shall not be revealed: and hid,

that shall not be known. **3** Wherefore whatsoever ye have said in the darkness shall be heard in the light; and what ye have spoken in the ear in the inner chambers shall be proclaimed upon the house-tops.

cp. 6 60.

6 38 For with what measure ye mete it shall be measured to you again.

19 26 I say unto you, that unto every one that hath shall be given;

but from him that hath not, even that which he hath shall be taken away from him.

[1] Or, *seemeth to have*

---

§ 96. The Tares (Matt.): The Seed Growing Secretly (Mark)

Matt. 13 24-30   **Mark 4** 26-29

24 Another parable set he before them, saying, The kingdom of heaven is likened unto a man that sowed good seed in his field: **25** but while men slept, his enemy came and sowed

26 And he said, So is the kingdom of God, as if a man should cast seed upon the earth; **27** and should sleep and rise night and day,

¹ tares also among the wheat, and
went away. **26** But when the blade
       sprang up, and

brought forth fruit,

       then appeared the
tares also. **27** And the ² servants
of the householder [*cp.* 13 52; 20 1;
21 33] came and said unto him,
Sir, didst thou not sow good seed in
thy field ? whence then hath it tares ?
28 And he said unto them, ³ An
enemy hath done this. And the
² servants say unto him, Wilt thou
then that we go and gather them
up ? **29** But he saith, Nay; lest
haply while ye gather up the tares,
ye root up [*cp.* 15 13] the wheat with
them. **30** Let both grow together
until the harvest [*cp.* 5 45: *also* 13
47 *ff.*; 22 10; 25 32] :

and in the time of the harvest
    I will say to the reapers, Gather
up first the tares, and bind them in
bundles to burn them : but gather the
wheat into my barn [*cp.* 3 12: *also* 24 31].

¹ Or, *darnel*   ² Gr. *bondservants.*
    ³ Gr. *A man that is an enemy.*

and
the seed should spring up and grow,
he knoweth not how. **28** The earth
¹ beareth   fruit of herself; first
the blade, then the ear, then the full
corn in the ear.

               29 But when the
fruit ² is ripe, straightway he
³ putteth forth the sickle, because
             the harvest is
come.

cp. 13 27.

¹ Or, *yieldeth*   ² Or, *alloweth*
    ³ Or, *sendeth forth*

cp. 14 21.

cp. 6 35.

cp. 3 17.

§ 97. The Mustard Seed

Matt. 13 31-32	Mark 4 30-32	Luke 13 18-19
31 Another parable set he before them, saying, The kingdom of heaven is like unto a grain of mustard seed [*cp.* 17 20], which a man took, and sowed in his field : **32** which indeed is less than all seeds ; but when it is grown, it is greater than the herbs, and becometh a tree, so that the birds of the heaven come and lodge in the branches thereof.	**30** And he said, How shall we liken the kingdom of God ? or in what parable shall we set it forth ? **31** ¹ It is like a grain of mustard seed, which, when it is sown upon the earth, though it be less than all the seeds that are upon the earth, **32** yet when it is sown, groweth up, and becometh greater than all the herbs, and putteth out great branches; so that the birds of the heaven can lodge under the shadow thereof.	**18** He said therefore, Unto what is the kingdom of God like ? and whereunto shall I liken it ? **19** It is like unto a grain of mustard seed [*cp.* 17 6], which a man took, and cast into his own garden ; and it grew, and became a tree ; and the birds of the heaven lodged in the branches thereof.

¹ Gr. *As unto.*

§ 98. The Leaven

Matt. 13 33	Luke 13 20-21
33 Another parable spake he unto them ; The kingdom of heaven is like unto leaven, which a woman took, and hid in three ¹ measures of meal, till it was all leavened.	**20** And again he said, Whereunto shall I liken the kingdom of God ? **21** It is like unto leaven, which a woman took and hid in three ¹ measures of meal, till it was all leavened.

¹ The word in the Greek denotes the Hebrew
seah, a measure containing nearly a peck and
a half.

¹ See footnote on Matt. 13 33.

§ 99. The Parabolic Method

Matt. 13 34-35	**Mark 4** 33-34		
34 All these things spake Jesus [*cp.* 13 19 *ff.*] in parables unto the multitudes; and without a parable spake he nothing unto them: *cp.* 17 1, 19; 20 17; 24 3.	**33** And with many such parables spake he the word [*cp.* 2 2; 4 14 *ff.*; 16 20] unto them, as they were able to hear it: **34** and without a parable spake he not unto them: but privately [*cp.* 4 10; 6 31,32; 9 2,28; 13 3] to his own disciples he expounded all things.	*cp.* 5 1; 8 11 *ff.*, 21; 11 28: *also* 1 2 *and* 4 32. *cp.* 9 10; 10 23.	*cp.* 6 60; 16 12, 25.
35 that it might be fulfilled which was spoken [1] by the prophet, saying, I will open my mouth in parables; I will utter things hidden from the foundation [2] of the world [*cp.* 25 34].			
[1] Or, *through* [2] Many ancient authorities omit *of the world*.		*cp.* 11 50.	*cp.* 17 24.

Matt. 13 35 = Ps. 78 2.

§ 100. The Interpretation of the Tares

Matt. 13 36-43			
36 Then he left the multitudes, and went into the house [*cp.* 17 25]: and his disciples came unto him [*cp.* 5 1; 13 10; 14 15; 15 12, 23; 17 19; 18 1; 24 1, 3; 26 17: *also* Mark 6 35; *and* Luke 9 12], saying, Explain unto us the parable [*cp.* 15 15] of the tares of the field. **37** And he answered and said, He that soweth [*cp.* 13 18, 24: *also* Mark 4 14] the good seed is the Son of man; **38** and the field is the world; and the good seed, these are the sons of the kingdom [*cp.* 8 12: *also* 5 9, 45]; and the tares are the sons of the evil one [*cp.* 5 37, 39; 6 13; 13 19: *also* John 17 15]; **39** and the enemy that sowed them is the devil: and the harvest is [1] the end of the world [*cp.* 13 40, 49; 24 3; 28 20]; and the reapers are angels. **40** As therefore the tares are gathered up and burned with fire; so shall it be in [1] the end of the world [*cp. verse* 39 *above*]. **41** The Son of man shall send forth his angels [*cp.* 24 31: *also* 13 49; 16 27; 25 31], and they shall gather out of his kingdom all things that cause stumbling, and them that do iniquity, **42** and shall cast them into the furnace of fire [*cp.* 13 50: *also* 3 10, 12; 5 22, 29, 30; 7 19; 10 28; 18 8, 9; 23 33; 25 41]: there shall be the weeping and gnashing of teeth [*cp.* 8 12; 13 50; 22 13; 24 51; 25 30]. **43** Then shall the righteous shine forth as the sun in the kingdom of their Father [*cp.* 26 29]. He that hath ears, let him hear [*cp.* 11 15; 13 9: *also* 19 12].	*cp.* 7 17; 9 28, 33; 10 10. *cp.* 4 10, 13; 7 17. *cp.* 13 27: *also* 8 38. *cp.* 9 43, 45, 47. *cp.* 4 9, 23; 7 16.	*cp.* 8 9. *cp.* 6 35; 16 8; 20 36. *cp.* 10 19. *cp.* 9 26; 12 8, 9. *cp.* 3 9, 17; 12 5. *cp.* 13 28. *cp.* 8 8; 14 35.	*cp.* 12 36: *also* 1 12; 11 52. *cp.* 15 6. *cp.* 6 60.
[1] Or, *the consummation of the age*			

Matt. 13 43 : *cp.* Dan. 12 3.

§ 101. The Hidden Treasure

Matt. 13 44		
44 The kingdom of heaven is like unto a treasure hidden in the field; which a man found, and hid; and [1] in his joy he goeth and selleth all that he hath, and buyeth that field.		
[1] Or, *for joy thereof*		

§ 102. The Pearl of Great Price

Matt. 13 45-46		
45 Again, the kingdom of heaven is like unto a man that is a merchant seeking goodly pearls: **46** and having found one pearl of great price, he went and sold all that he had, and bought it.		

§ 103. **The Drag-Net**

Matt. **13** 47-50

47 Again, the kingdom of heaven is like unto a ¹ net, that was cast into the sea, and gathered of every kind [*cp.* 13 30; 22 10; 25 32]: **48** which, when it was filled, they drew up on the beach; and they sat down, and gathered the good into vessels, but the bad they cast away. **49** So shall it be in ² the end of the world [*cp.* 13 39, 40; 24 3; 28 20]: the angels shall come forth [*cp.* 13 41; 16 27; 24 31; 25 31], and sever the wicked from among the righteous [*cp.* 25 32: *also* 3 12], **50** and shall cast them into the furnace of fire [*cp.* 13 42: *also* 3 10, 12; 5 22, 29, 30; 7 19; 10 28; 18 8, 9; 23 33; 25 41]: there shall be the weeping and gnashing of teeth [*cp.* 8 12; 13 42; 22 13; 24 51; 25 30].

cp. 8 38; 13 27.

cp. 9 43, 45, 47.

cp. 9 26; 12 8, 9.
cp. 3 17.
cp. 3 9, 17; 12 5.
cp. 13 28.

cp. 15 6.

¹ Gr. *drag-net*.   ² Or, *the consummation of the age*

§ 104. **The Householder and his Treasure**

Matt. **13** 51-52

51 Have ye understood all these things? They say unto him, Yea [*cp.* 13 11]. **52** And he said unto them, Therefore every scribe who hath been made a disciple [*cp.* 27 57; 28 19] to the kingdom of heaven is like unto a man that is a householder [*cp.* 20 1; 21 33: *also* 13 27], which bringeth forth out of his treasure [*cp.* 12 35] things new and old.

cp. 4 11.

cp. 8 10.

cp. 14 21.
cp. 6 45.

(ix) Events in Galilee IV (§§ 105-113).

§ 105. **The True Brethren of Jesus**

[*Cp.* Luke 11 27-28]

Matt. 12 46-50	Mark 3 31-35	Luke 8 19-21	
46 While he was yet speaking [*cp.* 17 5; 26 47] to the multitudes, behold, his mother and his brethren	*cp.* 5 35; 14 43. **31** And there come his mother and his brethren [*cp.* 3 21];	*cp.* 8 49; 22 47, 60. **19** And there came to him his mother and brethren, and they could not come at him for the crowd [*cp.* 5 19; 19 3].	
stood without, seeking to speak to him.	*cp.* 2 4; 3 9. and, standing without, they sent unto him, calling him. **32** And a multitude was sitting about him; and they say unto him,		
47 ¹ And one said unto him, Behold, thy mother and thy brethren stand without, seeking to speak to thee. **48** But he answered and said unto him that told him, Who is my mother? and who are my brethren? **49** And	Behold, thy mother and thy brethren without seek for thee. **33** And he answereth them, and saith, Who is my mother and my brethren? **34** And looking round [*cp.* 3 5; 5 32; 9 8; 10 32; 11 11] on them which sat round about him,	**20** And it was told him, Thy mother and thy brethren stand without, desiring to see thee. **21** But he answered and said unto them,	
he stretched forth his hand towards his disciples, and said, Behold, my mother and my brethren! **50** For whosoever *cp.* 13 19-23.	he saith, Behold, my mother and my brethren! **35** For whosoever *cp.* 2 2; 4 14-20, 33; 16 20.	*cp.* 6 10. My mother and my brethren are these which hear the word of God [*cp.* 5 1; 8 11; 11 28: *also* 1 2; 8 12-15; *and* 4 32], and do it *cp.* 22 42.	*cp.* 4 41; 5 24, 38; *etc.*
shall do the will [*cp.* 7 21; 21 31: *also* 6 10; 26 39, 42] of my Father which is in heaven	shall do the will [*cp.* 14 36] of God,		*cp.* 4 34; 5 30; 6 38; 7 17; 9 31.

[*cp.* 5 16, 45; 6 1, 9; 7 11, 21; 10 32, 33; 16 17; 18 10, 14, 19: *also* 5 48; 6 14, 26, 32; 15 13; 18 35; 23 9],
  he is my brother, and sister, and mother.

¹ Some ancient authorities omit ver. 47.

cp. 11 25, 26.

  the same is my brother, and sister, and mother.

cp. 11 13.

§ 106. The Stilling of a Storm

Matt. 8 23-27

3 And
  when
  he was entered into a boat, his disciples followed him.

  cp. 8 18; 14 22.

24 And behold, there arose a great tempest in the sea [*cp.* 4 18; 8 32; *etc.*],

  insomuch that the boat was covered with the waves:
  but he
  was
asleep.   25 And they came to him, and awoke him, saying,   Save [*cp.* 14 30], Lord [*cp.* 17 4, 15; 20 30, 33: *and* 7 21; 8 2, 6, 8, 21; *etc.*];
  cp. 8 19; 12 38; 19 16; 22 16, 24, 36.

  we perish.
  26 And he saith unto them, Why are ye fearful, O ye of little faith [*cp.* 6 30; 14 31; 16 8: *also* 17 20]? Then he arose, and rebuked [*cp.* 17 18] the winds and   the sea;

and there was a great calm.

  cp. 17 20; 21 21.
  27 And
[*cp.* 9 8; 17 6; 27 54; 28 4, 8]

the men marvelled [*cp.* 9 33; 12 23; 15 31; 21 20; 27 14: *also* 7 28; 13 54; 19 25; 22 22, 33],
  saying,
What manner of man is this [*cp.* 21 10],
that   even the winds and the sea obey him?

Mark 4 35-41

35 And   on that day, when even was come,

  he saith unto them, Let us go over unto the other side [*cp.* 6 45].   36 And leaving the multitude, they take him with them, even as he was, in the boat. And other boats were with him.
  37 And   there ariseth a great storm of wind, *cp.* 1 16; 2 13; *etc.* and the waves beat into the boat, insomuch that the boat was now filling.
  38 And he himself was in the stern, asleep on the cushion: and they   awake him, and say unto him, *cp.* 7 28.

  ¹ Master [*cp.* 9 17, 38; 10 17, 20, 35; 12 14, 19, 32; 13 1],
  carest thou not that we perish? 39 And he awoke,

  and rebuked [*cp.* 1 25; 3 12; 9 25] the wind, and said unto the sea, Peace, be still [*cp.* 1 25]. And the wind ceased, and there was a great calm. 40 And he said unto them, Why are ye fearful? have ye not yet faith [*cp.* 11 22; 16 14]?   41 And they feared exceedingly [*cp.* 5 15, 33; 9 6, 32; 10 32; 16 8],   [*cp.* 2 12; 5 20, 42; 6 51; 7 37; 10 32; 15 5; 16 5, 8: *also* 1 22, 27; 6 2; 10 24, 26; 11 18; 12 17] and said one to another, Who then   is this [*cp.* 1 27; 2 7], that   even the wind and the sea obey him [*cp.* 1 27]?

¹ Or, *Teacher*

Luke 8 22-25

22 Now it came to pass on one of those days,   that he entered into a boat, himself and his disciples; and he said unto them, Let us go over unto the other side of the lake: and   they launched forth.

  23 But as they sailed he fell asleep: and   there came down a   storm of wind on the lake [*cp.* 5 1, 2; 8 33];

  and they were filling *with water*, and were in jeopardy.

  24 And they came to him, and awoke him, saying,
  [*cp.* 18 41: *and* 5 8, 12; 6 46; 7 6; *etc.*] [*cp.* 7 40; 9 38; 10 25; 11 45; 12 13; 18 18; 19 39; 20 21, 28, 39; 21 7] Master, master [*cp.* 9 33, 49: *and* 5 5; 8 45; 17 13], we perish. And he awoke,

  cp. 12 28.

  and rebuked [*cp.* 4 35, 39, 41; 9 42] the wind and the raging of the water: [*cp.* 4 35] and they   ceased, and there was a   calm. 25 And he said unto them, Where is your faith [*cp.* 17 5, 6; 22 32; 24 25, 38]? And being afraid [*cp.* 1 12, 65; 2 9; 5 26; 7 16; 8 35, 37, 47; 9 34, 45; 24 5, 37] they marvelled [*cp.* 5 9, 26; 8 56; 9 43; 11 14; 24 12, 41: *also* 2 47, 48; 4 22, 32, 36; 20 26], saying one to another, Who then   is this [*cp.* 4 36; 5 21; 7 49; 9 9], that he commandeth even the winds and the water, and they obey him [*cp.* 4 36]?

cp. 6 1, 16; *etc.*

cp. 4 11, 15, 19, 49; 5 7; *etc.*
cp. 1 38; 20 16.

cp. 3 12; 6 64; 14 10; 20 27.

cp. 7 15, 21, 46.

cp. 5 12: *also* 12 34.

§ 107. The Gerasene Demoniac

Matt. 8 28-34	Mark 5 1-20	Luke 8 26-39	
28 And when he was come to the other side into the country of the Gadarenes,	**1** And they came to the other side of the sea, into the country of the Gerasenes.	**26** And they arrived at the country of the [1] Gerasenes, which is over against Galilee.	
	2 And when he was come out of the boat, straightway there met him	**27** And when he was come forth upon the land, there met him a certain man	
there met him two [cp. 9 27; 20 30] [1] possessed with devils, coming forth out of the tombs,	out of the tombs a man with an unclean spirit,	out of the city, who had [2] devils; and for a long time he had worn no clothes, and abode not in *any* house, but in the tombs.	
	3 who had his dwelling in the tombs: and no man could any more bind him, no, not with a chain; **4** because that he had been often bound with fetters and chains, and the chains had been rent asunder by him, and the fetters broken in pieces: and no man had strength to tame him. **5** And always, night and day, in the tombs and in the mountains, he was crying out, and cutting himself with stones. **6** And when he saw Jesus from afar, he ran and worshipped him [cp. 1 40; 3 11; 5 22, 33; 7 25; 10 17]; **7** and	*verse 29*	
exceeding fierce, so that no man could pass by that way.			
cp. 2 11; 8 2; 9 18; 14 33; 15 25; 17 14; 20 20; 28 9, 17. **29** And behold, they cried out,	crying out	**28** And when he saw Jesus, he cried out, and fell down [cp. 5 8, 12; 8 41, 47; 17 16; 24 52] before him, and with a	cp. 9 38; 11 32; 18 6.
saying, What have we to do with thee, thou Son [cp. 4 3, 6; 14 33; 16 16; 26 63; 27 40, 43, 54] of	with a loud voice [cp. 1 26], he saith, What have I to do with thee [cp. 1 24], Jesus, thou Son [cp. 1 1; 3 11; 15 39] of	loud voice [cp. 4 33] said, What have I to do with thee [cp. 4 34], Jesus, thou Son [cp. 1 35; 4 3, 9, 41; 22 70] of	cp. 1 34; etc.
God? cp. 26 63. art thou come hither to torment us before the time?	the Most High God [cp. similarly 1 24; 3 11]? I adjure thee cp. 1 24. by God, torment me not. **8** For he said unto him, Come forth [cp. 1 25; 9 25], thou unclean spirit, out of the man.	the Most High [cp. 1 32, 35, 76; 6 35] God [cp. similarly 4 34, 41]? I beseech thee, cp. 4 34. torment me not. **29** For he cp. 4 35. commanded the unclean spirit to come out from the man. For [3] oftentimes it had seized him: and he was kept under guard, and bound with chains and fetters; and breaking the bands asunder, he was driven of the [4] devil into the deserts.	
	verses 4 and 5		
	9 And he asked him, What is thy name? And he saith unto him, My name is Legion; for we are many.	**30** And Jesus asked him, What is thy name? And he said, Legion; for many [2] devils were entered into him.	
	10 And he besought him much that he would not send them away out of the country. **11** Now there was there on the mountain side a great herd of swine feeding.	**31** And they intreated him that he would not command them to depart into the abyss. **32** Now there was there	
30 Now there was afar off from them a herd of many swine feeding.		a herd of many swine feeding	

31 And the [2] devils besought him, saying, If thou cast us out, send us away into the herd of swine.

32 And he said unto them, Go. And they came out,
and went into the swine: and behold, the whole herd rushed down the steep into the sea [*cp.* 4 18; 8 24; *etc.*],
    and
perished in the waters. **33** And they that fed them

fled, and went away into the city, and told everything, and
what was befallen to them that were [1] possessed with devils. **34** And behold, all the city came out to

        meet Jesus:
and when they saw him,

cp. 9 8; 17 6; 27 54; 28 4, 8.

verse 33

    they

besought *him* that he would depart from their borders.

cp. 4 25.

cp. 8 27; 9 33; 12 23; 15 31; 21 20; 27 14: *also* 7 28; 13 54; 19 25; 22 22, 33.

[1] Or, *demoniacs*   [2] Gr. *demons*.

---

12 And they besought him, saying,
    Send us
into the   swine, that we may enter into them. **13** And he gave them leave. And the unclean spirits came out,
and entered into the swine: and   the herd rushed down the steep into the sea [*cp.* 1 16; 2 13; *etc.*], *in number about two thousand*; and they were choked in the sea.   **14** And they that fed them

fled,
    and told it in the city, and in the country.

verse 16
    And
they came   to see what it was that had come to pass. **15** And they come to Jesus, and   behold [1] him that was possessed with devils   sitting, clothed and in his right mind,

even him that had the legion: and they were afraid [*cp.* 4 41; 5 33; 9 6, 32; 10 32; 16 8].   **16** And they that saw it declared unto them how it befell [1] him that was possessed with devils,
    and concerning the swine. **17** And they

began to beseech him   to depart from their borders.

18 And as he was entering into the boat,   he that had been possessed with [2] devils   besought him that he might be with him. **19** And he suffered him not, but saith unto him, Go to thy house unto thy friends, and tell them how great things the Lord hath done for thee, and *how* he had mercy on thee. **20** And he went his way, and began to publish in Decapolis [*cp.* 7 31] how great things Jesus had done for him: and all men did marvel [*cp.* 2 12; 5 42; 6 51; 7 37; 10 32; 15 5; 16 5, 8: *also* 1 22, 27; 6 2; 10 24, 26; 11 18; 12 17].

[1] Or, *the demoniac*   [2] Gr. *demons*.

---

on the mountain: and they intreated him

that he would give them leave to enter into them. And he gave them leave. **33** And the [2] devils came out from the man, and entered into the swine: and   the herd rushed down the steep into the lake [*cp.* 5 1, 2; 8 22, 23],
    and   were choked.   **34** And when they that fed them saw what had come to pass, they fled,
    and told it in the city and in the country.

35 And they went out to see what had come to pass; and they came to Jesus, and   found the man, from whom the [2] devils were gone out, sitting, clothed and in his right mind, at the feet of Jesus [*cp.* 7 38; 10 39]:
    and they were afraid [*cp.* 1 12, 65; 2 9; 5 26; 7 16; 8 25, 37, 47; 9 34, 45; 24 5, 37]. **36** And they that saw it told them how   he that was possessed with [2] devils was [5] made whole.

37 And all the people of the country of the Gerasenes round about asked him   to depart from them;   for they were holden with great fear [*cp. verse* 35 *above*]: and he   entered into a boat, and returned. **38** But the man from whom the [2] devils were gone out prayed him that he might be with him: but he sent him away,   saying,   **39** Return to thy house, and declare   how great things   God hath done for thee.
    And he went his way, publishing throughout the whole city how great things Jesus had done for him.
cp. 5 9, 26; 8 25, 56; 9 43; 11 14; 24 12, 41: *also* 2 47, 48; 4 22, 32, 36; 20 26.

[1] Many ancient authorities read *Gergesenes*: others, *Gadarenes*: and so in ver. 37.
[2] Gr. *demons*.   [3] Or, *of a long time*
[4] Gr. *demon*.   [5] Or, *saved*

---

cp. 6 1, 16; *etc.*

cp. 7 15, 21, 46.

§ 108. Jaïrus's Daughter and a Woman with an Issue of Blood

[*Cp.* Luke 7 11-17; John 11 1-46]

Matt. 9 18-26	Mark 5 21-43	Luke 8 40-56	
18 While he spake these things unto them,	21 And when Jesus had crossed over again in the boat unto the other side, a great multitude was gathered unto him: and he was by the sea [*cp.* 3 7; 4 1].	40 And as Jesus returned, the multitude welcomed him; [*cp.* 5 1] for they were all waiting for him. 41 And behold, there came a man	
cp. 13 1. behold, there came ¹a ruler,	22 And there cometh one of the rulers of the synagogue, Jaïrus by name;	named Jaïrus, and he was a ruler of the synagogue [*cp.* 13 14]: and	
and worshipped [*cp.* 2 11; 8 2; 14 33; 15 25; 20 20; 28 9, 17: *also* 17 14] him,	and seeing him, he falleth at his feet [*cp.* 3 11; 5 33; 7 25: *also* 1 40; 5 6; 10 17], 23 and beseecheth him much,	he fell down [*cp.* 5 8, 12; 8 28, 47; 17 16: *also* 24 52] at Jesus' feet, and besought him to come into his house; 42 for he had an only [*cp.* 7 12; 9 38] daughter, about twelve years of age, and she lay a dying [*cp.* 7 2].	*cp.* 11 32; 18 6: *also* 9 38. *cp.* 4 47.
saying, My daughter is even now dead: but come and lay thy hand [*cp.* 19 13, 15: *also* 8 3, 15; 9 20, 25, 29; 14 31, 36; 17 7; 20 34] upon her, and she shall live. 19 And Jesus arose, and followed him, and so *did* his disciples.	*verse 42* saying, My little daughter is at the point of death: *I pray thee*, that thou come and lay thy hands [*cp.* 6 5; 8 25; 10 16: *also* 1 31, 41; 3 10; 5 27, 41; 6 2, 56; 7 33; 8 22, 23; 9 27; 10 13] on her, that she may be ¹made whole, and live. 24 And he went with him;	*cp.* 4 40; 13 13: *also* 5 13; 6 19; 7 14, 39; 8 44, 54; 14 4; 18 15; 22 51.	*cp.* 9 6; 20 17.
20 And behold, a woman, who had an issue of blood twelve years,	and a great multitude followed him, and they thronged him. 25 And a woman, which had an issue of blood twelve years, 26 and had suffered many things of many physicians, and had spent all that she had, and was nothing bettered, but rather grew worse, 27 having heard the things concerning Jesus,	But as he went the multitudes thronged him. 43 And a woman having an issue of blood twelve years [*cp.* 13 11], which ¹ had spent all her living upon physicians, and could not be healed of any,	
came behind him, and touched [*cp.* 8 3, 15; 9 29; 14 36; 17 7; 20 34: *also* 9 18, 25; 14 31; 19 13, 15] the border [*cp.* 14 36] of his garment: 21 for she said within herself, If I do but touch his garment, I shall be ²made whole.	came in the crowd behind, and touched [*cp.* 1 41; 3 10; 6 56; 7 33; 8 22; 10 13: *also* 1 31; 5 23, 41; 6 2, 5; 8 23, 25; 9 27; 10 16] [*cp.* 6 56] his garment. 28 For she said, If I touch but his garments, I shall be ¹made whole. 29 And	44 came behind him, and touched [*cp.* 5 13; 6 19; 7 14, 39; 18 15; 22 51: *also* 4 40; 8 54; 13 13; 14 4] the border of his garment:	*cp.* 20 17; 9 6.
cp. 9 22; 16 23.	straightway the fountain of her blood was dried up; and she felt in her body that she was healed of her ²plague. 30 And straightway Jesus, perceiving in himself that the power *proceeding* from him had gone forth, turned him about [*cp.* 8 33] in the crowd, and said, Who touched my garments? 31 And his disciples	and immediately the issue of her blood stanched. 45 And Jesus *verse 46* said, Who is it that touched me? And when all denied,	*cp.* 7 9, 44; 9 55; 10 23; 14 25; 22 61; 23 28. *cp.* 1 38.

(line) *cp.* 7 9, 44; 9 55; 10 23; 14 25; 22 61; 23 28.

And when Peter

cp. 14 28; 15 15; 16 22; 17 4; 18 21; 19 27; 26 33: also 16 16; 17 24.

[cp. 8 32; 9 5; 10 28; 11 21; 14 29: also 8 29] said unto him,
Thou seest the multitude thronging thee, and sayest thou, Who touched me? 32 And he looked round about [cp. 3 5, 34; 9 8; 10 23; 11 11] to see her that had done this thing.

[cp. 9 33; 12 41; 18 28: also 5 8; 9 20] said,
2 and they that were with him, Master, the multitudes press thee and crush *thee*.

cp. 13 36, 37; 21 21: also 6 68.

verse 30

cp. 6 10.

33 But the woman fearing and trembling [cp. 4 41; 5 15; 9 6, 32; 10 32; 16 8], knowing what had been done to her, came and fell down [cp. verse 22 above] before him, and told him all the truth.

cp. 9 8; 17 6; 27 54; 28 4, 8.

46 But Jesus said, Some one did touch me: for I perceived that power [cp. 4 14, 36; 5 17; 6 19: also 1 17, 35; 9 1; 24 49] had gone forth from me. 47 And when the woman saw that she was not hid, she came trembling [cp. 1 12, 65; 2 9; 5 26; 7 16; 8 25, 35, 37; 9 34, 45; 24 5, 37], and falling down [cp. verse 41 above] before him declared in the presence of all the people for what cause she touched him, and how she was healed immediately.

cp. 11 32; 18 6: also 9 38.

22 But Jesus turning [cp. 16 23] and seeing her said, Daughter, be of good cheer [cp. 9 2; 14 27]; thy faith hath 3 made thee whole.

34 And he [cp. 5 30; 8 33] said unto her, Daughter, [cp. 6 50; 10 49] thy faith hath 3 made thee whole [cp. 10 52]; go in peace, and be whole of thy 2 plague.

48 And he [cp. 7 9, 44; 9 55: 10 23; 14 25; 22 61; 23 28] said unto her, Daughter, thy faith hath 3 made thee whole [cp. 7 50; 17 19; 18 42]; go in peace [cp. 7 50].

cp. 1 38.

cp. 16 33.

And the woman was 2 made whole from that hour [cp. 8 13; 15 28; 17 18].

cp. 4 53.

35 While he yet spake, they come from the ruler of the synagogue's *house*, saying, Thy daughter is dead [cp. 9 26]: why troublest thou the 4 Master any further? 36 But Jesus, 5 not heeding the word spoken, saith unto the ruler of the synagogue, Fear not, only believe.
37 And he suffered no man to follow with him, save Peter, and James, and John the brother of James [cp. 1 29; 9 2; 13 3; 14 33].

49 While he yet spake, there cometh one from the ruler of the synagogue's *house*, saying, Thy daughter is dead [cp. 7 12]; trouble [cp. 7 6] not the 4 Master. 50 But Jesus hearing it, answered him, Fear not: only believe, and she shall be 5 made whole.

verse 51

cp. 17 1; 26 37.

23 And when Jesus came into the ruler's house,

38 And they come to the house of the ruler of the synagogue;

51 And when he came to the house, he suffered not any man to enter in with him, save Peter, and John, and James [cp. 9 28], and the father of the maiden and her mother. 52 And all were weeping, and bewailing her: but he said,

cp 17 1; 26 37.

verse 37

verse 40

and saw the flute-players, and the crowd making a tumult,

and he beholdeth a tumult, and *many* weeping and wailing greatly. 39 And when he was entered in, he saith unto them, Why make ye a tumult, and weep?

Weep not [cp. 7 13; 23 28]; for she is not dead, but sleepeth. 53 And they laughed him to scorn, knowing that she was dead. 54 But he,

cp. 20 13, 15.

24 he said, Give place:

cp. 11 11.

for the damsel is not dead, but sleepeth. And they laughed him to scorn. 25 But when the crowd was put forth,

the child is not dead, but sleepeth. 40 And they laughed him to scorn. But he, having put them all forth, taketh the father of the child and her mother and them that were with him, and goeth in where the child was. 41 And taking the child by the hand [cp. 1 31; 9 27; 1 41; 5 23; 6 2, 5; 7 33; 8 22, 23, 25; 10

verse 51

he entered in, and took her by the hand [cp. 8 15; 8 3; 9 18, 29; 14 31; 17 7; 19 13, 15; 20 34: also 9 20;

taking her by the hand [cp. 4 40; 5 13; 7 14; 13 13; 14 4; 18 15; 22 51: also 6

cp. 9 6: also 20 17.

14 36];

cp. 9 6.

and

the damsel

arose.

13, 16: *also* 3 10; 5 27; 6 56], he saith unto her, Talitha cumi; which is, being interpreted, Damsel, I say unto thee, Arise [cp. 2 11; 3 3; 10 49]. **42** And straight-way   the damsel rose up,   and walked; for she was twelve years old.

verse 43

And they   were amazed straightway with a great amazement [cp. 2 12; 5 20; 6 51; 7 37; 10 32; 15 5; 16 5, 8: *also* 1 22, 27; 6 2; 10 24, 26; 11 18; 12 17]. **43** And he charged them much that no man should know this [cp. 1 44; 7 36; 8 26: *also* 1 25, 34; 3 12; 8 30; 9 9]: and he com-manded that *something* should be given her to eat.

cp. 1 28.

19; 7 39; 8 44], called, saying,

Maiden, arise [cp. 5 24; 6 8; 7 14]. **55** And her spirit returned, and she rose up immediately:

verse 42

and he commanded that *something* be given her to eat. **56** And her parents were amazed [cp. 5 9, 26; 8 25; 9 43; 11 14; 24 12, 41: *also* 2 47, 48; 4 22, 32, 36; 20 26]:

but he charged them to tell no man what had been done [cp. 5 14: *also* 4 35, 41; 9 21, 36].

verse 55

cp. 4 14, 37; 5 15; 7 17.

cp. 8 27; 9 33; 12 23; 15 31; 21 20; 27 14: *also* 7 28; 13 54; 19 25   22 22, 33.

cp. 8 4; 9 30; 12 16: *also* 16 20; 17 9.

26 And [4] the fame hereof went forth into all that land [cp. 4 24].

cp. 5 8.

cp. 7 15, 21, 46.

[1] Gr. *one ruler.* [2] Or, *saved*
[3] Or, *saved thee* [4] Gr. *this fame.*

[1] Or, *saved* [2] Gr. *scourge.*
[3] Or, *saved thee* [4] Or, *Teacher*
[5] Or, *overhearing*

[1] Some ancient authorities omit *had spent all her living upon physi-cians, and.*
[2] Some ancient authorities omit *and they that were with him.*
[3] Or, *saved thee* [4] Or, *Teacher*
[5] Or, *saved*

§ 109. The Rejection in the Synagogue

[*Cp.* Matt. 12 9-14: Mark 1 21-28; 3 1-6: Luke 4 31-37; 6 6-11; 13 10-17: John 6 59]

Matt. 13 53-58	**Mark 6** 1-6a	Luke 4 16-30	John 6 41-42; 4 43-44
53 And it came to pass, when Jesus had finished [cp. 7 28; 11 1; 19 1; 26 1] these parables, he depar-ted thence. **54** And coming into his own country [cp. 9 1: *also* 4 13]	**1** And		
	he went out from thence; and he cometh into his own country; and his disciples follow him. **2** And when the sabbath was come, he began to teach in the synagogue:	cp. 7 1.	
he taught them in their synagogue,		16 And he came to Nazareth, where he had been brought up: and he entered, as his custom was, into the synagogue on the sabbath day, and stood up to read. . . . 21 And he began to say unto them, To-day hath this scripture been fulfilled in your ears. **22** And	cp. 1 11.
cp. 4 17.	cp. 1 15.		
insomuch that they were astonished [cp. 7 28; 19 25; 22 22, 33: *also* 8 27; 9 33; 12 23; 15 31; 21 20; 27 14],	and [1] many hearing him were astonished [cp. 1 22, 27; 10 24, 26; 11 18; 12 17: *also* 2 12; 5 20, 42; 6 51; 7 37; 10 32; 15 5; 16 8],	all bare him witness, and wondered [cp. 2 47, 48; 4 32, 36; 20 26: *also* 5 9, 26; 8 25, 56; 9 43; 11 14; 24 12, 41] at the words of grace which pro-ceeded out of his mouth: and they said,	6 41 The Jews therefore murmured concerning him, cp. 7 15, 21, 46. because he said, I am the bread which came down out of heaven. **42** And they said,
and said, Whence hath this man [cp. *verse* 56] this wisdom, and these [1] mighty works?	saying, Whence hath this man these things? and, What is the wisdom that is given unto this man, and *what mean* such [2] mighty works wrought		

cp. 8 3, 15; 9 18, 25, 29; 20 34: *also* 14 31; 17 7; 19 13, 15.	by his hands [*cp.* 1 31, 41; 5 23, 41; 6 5; 7 33; 8 22, 23, 25; 9 27: *also* 10 13, 16]?	cp. 4 40; 5 13; 7 14; 8 54; 13 13; 14 4; 22 51: *also* 18 15.	cp. 9 6.
55 Is not this the carpenter's son? is not his mother called Mary? and his brethren, James, and Joseph, and Simon, and Judas? **56** And his sisters, are they not all with us? Whence then hath this man all these things? **57** And they were [2] offended [*cp.* 11 6; 15 12; 26 31, 33: *also* 13 21; 24 10] in him.	**3** Is not this the carpenter, the son of Mary, and brother of James, and Joses, and Judas, and Simon? and are not his sisters here with us? *verse 2* And they were [3] offended [*cp.* 14 27, 29: *also* 4 17] in him.	Is not this Joseph's son [*cp.* 3 23]?	Is not this Jesus, the son of Joseph [*cp.* 1 45], whose father and mother we know? how doth he now say, I am come down out of heaven?
cp. 27 40.	cp. 15 30.	cp. 7 23.	cp. 6 61: *also* 16 1.
cp. 4 13.	cp. 1 21.	**23** And he said unto them, Doubtless ye will say unto me this parable, Physician, heal thyself [*cp.* 23 37, 39]: whatsoever we have heard done at Capernaum [*cp.* 4 31], do also here in thine own country. **24** And he said, Verily I say unto you, No prophet [*cp.* 7 16, 39; 13 33; 24 19] is acceptable in his own country	
But Jesus said unto them, A prophet [*cp.* 21 11, 46] is not without honour, save in his own country, and in his own house. **58** And he cp. 9 28: *also* 8 2. did not many [1] mighty works there cp. 8 3, 15; *etc.* because of their unbelief.	**4** And Jesus said unto them, A prophet [*cp.* 6 15] is not without honour, save in his own country, and among his own kin, and in his own house. **5** And he could [*cp.* 9 22, 23: *also* 1 40] there do no [4] mighty work, save that he laid his hands [*cp.* 1 31, 41; *etc.*] upon a few sick folk, and healed them. **6** And he marvelled because of their unbelief [*cp.* 16 14].	cp. 5 12. cp. 4 40; 5 13; *etc.*	**4 43** And after the two days he went forth from thence into Galilee. **44** For Jesus himself testified, that a prophet [*cp.* 4 19; 6 14; 7 40; 9 17] hath no honour in his own country.
		28 And they were all filled with wrath in the synagogue, as they heard these things; **29** and they rose up, and cast him forth out of the city [*cp.* 20 15], and led him unto the brow of the hill whereon their city was built, that they might throw him down headlong. **30** But he passing through the midst of them went his way.	cp. 7 5. cp. 1 11. cp. 8 59; 10 39.

[2] Gr. *powers.*
[2] Gr. *caused to stumble.*

[1] Some ancient authorities insert *the.*   [2] Gr. *powers.*
[3] Gr. *caused to stumble.*
[4] Gr. *power.*

Luke 4 18-19 = Is. 61 1-2; 58 6.

§ 110. General Teaching

Matt. 9 35	Mark 6 6b	Luke 8 1	
35 And Jesus went about all the cities and the villages, teaching in their synagogues, and preaching [*cp.* 4 23; 11 1] the [1] gospel cp. 11 5. of the kingdom [*cp.* 4 23; 24 14: *also* 26 13], and healing all manner	**6** And he went round about the villages teaching. cp. 1 1, 14, 15; 8 35; 10 29; 13 10; 14 9; 16 15.	**1** And it came to pass soon afterwards, that he went about through cities and villages [*cp.* 13 22], preaching and bringing the [1] good tidings [*cp.* 1 19; 2 10; 3 18; 4 18, 43; 7 22; 9 6; 16 16; 20 1] of the kingdom of God,	

of disease and all manner of sickness. *cp.* 10 1.		and with him the twelve.	
	cp. 6 7.		
4 23 And Jesus went about in all Galilee, teaching in their synagogues,	1 39 And he went	4 44 And he was	
	into	preaching in	
and preaching	their synagogues throughout all Galilee, preaching	the synagogues [*cp.* 4 15]	*cp.* 18 20.
the 1 gospel of the kingdom, and		of 2 Galilee.	
healing all manner of disease and all manner of sickness among the people.	and casting out 1 devils.		
1 Or, *good tidings*	1 Gr. *demons.*	1 Or, *gospel* 2 Very many ancient authorities read *Judæa.*	

§ 111. The Mission of the Twelve

Matt. 10 1, 5-8; 9 37-38; 10 16, 9-15	**Mark 6** 7-13	**Luke 9** 1-6	Luke 10 1-12	
1 And	7 And	1 And	1 Now after these things the Lord [*cp.* 7 13, 19; 10 39, 41; 11 39; 12 42; 13 15; 17 5, 6; 18 6; 19 8; 22 61; 24 3, 34]	*cp.* 4 1; 6 23; 11 2; 20 2, 18, 20, 25; 21 7, 12.
he	he *cp.* 16 19, 20.	he		
called unto him his twelve disciples,	called unto him the twelve [*cp.* 3 13, 14],	called the twelve [*cp.* 6 13] together,	appointed seventy 1 others,	
and gave them	*cp.* 5 30.	and gave them power [*cp.* 1 17, 35; 4 14, 36; 5 17; 6 19; 8 46; 24 49] and authority over all 1 devils [*cp.* 9 6, 40; 10 9, 17], and to cure diseases.		
authority over unclean spirits [*cp.* 10 8; 17 16], to cast them out, and to heal all manner of disease and all manner of sickness. 5 These twelve Jesus sent forth, *cp.* 21 1.	and began to send them forth by two and two [*cp.* 11 1; 14 13]; and he gave them authority over the unclean spirits [*cp.* 3 15: *also* 6 12, 13; 9 18];	2 And he sent them forth *cp.* 19 29; 22 8.	and sent them two and two	
verses 7 and 8		to preach the kingdom of God, and to heal [*cp.* 6 19; 9 11, 42; 14 4; 22 51] 2 the sick.	*verses 9 and* 11 before his face into every city and place, whither he himself was about to come [*cp.* 9 52]. 2 And he said unto them,	
and charged them, saying, Go not into *any* way of the Gentiles, and enter not into any city of the Samaritans: 6 but go rather to the lost sheep of the house of Israel [*cp.* 15 24: *also* 9 36]. 7 And as ye go, preach, saying, The kingdom of heaven is at hand [*cp.* 3 2; 4 17: *also* 12 28]. 8 Heal the sick, raise the dead, cleanse the lepers, cast out	8 and he charged them	3 And he said unto them, *cp.* 9 52. *cp.* 6 34. *cp.* verse 2: *also* 9 6.	*cp.* 4 9. *cp.* 10 16. *verses 9 and* 11	

¹ devils: freely ye received, freely give. 9 37 The harvest truly is plenteous, but the labourers are few. 38 Pray ye therefore the Lord of the harvest, that he send forth labourers into his harvest.

10 16 Behold, I send you forth as sheep in the midst of wolves:

9 Get you

no gold, nor silver, nor brass in your ² purses; 10 no wallet for *your* journey, neither two coats, nor shoes, nor staff:

for the labourer is worthy of his food. 11 And into whatsoever city or village ye shall enter, search out who in it is worthy; and there abide till ye go forth. 12 And as ye enter into the house, salute it.

13 And if the house be worthy, let your peace come upon it [cp. 5 9]: but if it be not worthy, let your peace return to you.

verse 11

verse 10

verses 7 and 8

14 And whosoever

shall not receive you, nor hear your words, as ye go forth out of that house or that city, shake off

cp. verse 13.

that they should take nothing for *their* journey, save a staff only; no bread, no wallet, no ¹ money in their ² purse;

9 but *to go* shod with sandals: and, *said he*, put not on two coats.

10 And he said unto them, Wheresoever ye enter into a house,

there abide till ye depart thence.

cp. 9 50.

11 And whatsoever place

shall not receive you, and they hear you not, as ye go forth thence, shake off

Take nothing for your journey, neither staff, nor wallet, nor bread, nor money;

neither have two coats [cp. 3 11].

4 And into whatsoever house ye enter,

there abide, and thence depart.

cp. 1 79; 2 14, 29; 19 38.

verse 2

5 And as many as receive you not,

when ye depart from that city, shake off

The harvest is plenteous, but the labourers are few: pray ye therefore the Lord of the harvest, that he send forth labourers into his harvest. 3 Go your ways: behold, I send you forth as lambs in the midst of wolves.   *cp. 4 35-38.*

4 Carry

no purse, no wallet,

no shoes [cp. 22 35]:

and salute no man on the way. *verse 7*   *cp. 4 36.*

5 And into whatsoever house ye shall ² enter,

verse 7

first say, Peace *be* to this house. 6 And if a son of peace be there, your peace shall rest upon ³ him: but if not, it shall turn to you again. 7 And in that same house remain, eating and drinking such things as they give: for the labourer is worthy of his hire. Go not from house to house. 8 And into whatsoever city ye enter, and they receive you, eat such things as are set before you: 9 and heal the sick that are therein, and say unto them, The kingdom of God is come nigh unto you [cp. 11 20; 17 20, 21; 19 11; 21 8]. 10 But into whatsoever city ye shall enter, and they receive you not [cp. 9 53], go out into the streets thereof and say, 11 Even

   cp. 14 27; 16 33.

   cp. 4 36.

the dust of your feet. cp. 8 4; 10 18; 24 14. cp. 24 43. **15** Verily I say unto you, It shall be more tolerable [cp. 7 22; 24 36: *also* 26 29] for the land [cp. 2 6, 20, 21; 4 15; 11 24] of Sodom and Gomorrah in the day of judgement [cp. 11 22, 24; 12 36], than for that city [cp. 11 24]. cp. 11 5. cp. 3 2; 4 17. cp. verse 8.	the dust that is under your feet for a testimony unto them [cp. 1 44; 13 9]. cp. 13 32: *also* 14 25. **12** And they went out, and preached that *men* should repent [cp. 1 15]. **13** And they cast out many ³ devils, and anointed with oil many that were sick, and healed them.	the dust from your feet for a testimony against them [cp. 5 14; 21 13]. **6** And they departed, and went throughout the villages, preaching the gospel [cp. 1 19; 2 10; 3 18; 4 18, 43; 7 22; 8 1; 16 16; 20 1], and healing everywhere.	the dust from your city, that cleaveth to our feet, we do wipe off against you: howbeit know this [cp. 12 39], that the kingdom of God is come nigh [cp. *verse* 9]. **12** I say unto you, It shall be more tolerable in that day [cp. 17 31; 21 34] for Sodom, than for that city. cp. 13 3, 5.	cp. 14 20; 16 23, 26. cp. 3 22.
¹ Gr. *demons*. ² Gr. *girdles*.	¹ Gr. *brass*. ² Gr. *girdle*. ³ Gr. *demons*.	¹ Gr. *demons*. ² Some ancient authorities omit *the sick*.	¹ Many ancient authorities add *and two*: and so in ver. 17. ² Or, *enter first, say* ³ Or, *it*	

§ 112. Herod's Opinion on Jesus and the Death of John the Baptist

Matt. 14 1-12	**Mark 6** 14-29	**Luke 9** 7-9	
1 At that season [cp. 11 25; 12 1] Herod the tetrach heard the report concerning Jesus, **2** and said [cp. 16 14] unto his servants, This is John the Baptist; he is risen from the dead; and therefore do these powers work in him. cp. 13 57; 21 11, 46. cp. 8 27; 21 10.	**14** And king Herod heard *thereof*; for his name had become known: and *verse* 20 ¹ he said [8 28], John ² the Baptist is risen from the dead, and therefore do these powers work in him. **15** But others said, It is Elijah. And others said, *It is* a prophet [cp. 6 4], *even* as one of the prophets. **16** But Herod, when he heard *thereof*, said, John, whom I beheaded, he is risen. cp. 1 27; 2 7; 4 41.	**7** Now Herod the tetrach heard of all that was done [cp. 23 8]: and he was much perplexed, because that it was said by some [cp. 9 19], that John was risen from the dead; **8** and by some, that Elijah had appeared; and by others, [cp. 4 24; 7 16, 39; 13 33; 24 19] that one of the old prophets was risen again. **9** And Herod said, John I beheaded: but who is this [cp. 4 36; 5 21; 7 49; 8 25], about whom I hear such things? And he sought to see him [cp. 23 8: *also* 19 3].	cp. 4 19, 44; 6 14; 7 40; 9 17. cp. 5 12: *also* 12 34.
3 For Herod had laid hold on John, and bound him, and put him in prison [cp. 4 12; 11 2] for the sake of	**17** For Herod himself had sent forth and laid hold upon John, and bound him in prison [cp. 1 14] for the sake of	**3 19** But Herod the tetrach, being reproved by him for	cp. 3 24.

Herodias, his brother Philip's wife.

4 For John said unto him, It is not lawful for thee to have her.

     5 And when he would have put him to death,

he feared   the multitude [*cp.* 21 26: *also* 21 46; 26 5], because they counted him as a prophet [*cp.* 21 26 *and* 46: *also* 11 9].

6 But when   Herod's   birthday came,

         the daughter of Herodias danced in the midst, and   pleased Herod.

     7 Whereupon he promised with an oath to give her whatsoever she should ask.

     8 And she, being put forward by her mother,

        saith, Give me here in a charger the head of John the Baptist. **9** And the king was grieved; but for the sake of his oaths, and of them which sat at meat with him, he commanded it to be given; **10** and he sent,

        and beheaded John in the prison. **11** And his head was brought   in a charger, and given to the damsel: and she brought it to her mother. **12** And   his disciples [*cp.* 9 14; 11 2] came, and took up the corpse, and buried him; and they went and told Jesus.

Herodias, his brother Philip's wife: for he had married her. **18** For John said unto Herod, It is not lawful for thee to have thy brother's wife. **19** And Herodias set herself against him, and desired to kill him; and she could not; **20** for Herod feared John,

   cp. 11 32: *also* 11 18;   12 12; 14 2.

    cp. 11 32.   knowing that he was a righteous man and a holy, and kept him safe. And when he heard him, he [3] was much perplexed; and he heard him gladly [*cp.* 12 37].

21 And when a convenient day was come, that Herod on his birthday made a supper to his lords, and the [4] high captains, and the chief men of Galilee; **22** and when [5] the daughter of Herodias herself came in and danced,   [6] she pleased Herod and them that sat at meat with him; and the king said unto the damsel, Ask of me whatsoever thou wilt, and I will give it thee. **23** And he sware unto her,   Whatsoever thou shalt ask of me, I will give it thee, unto the half of my kingdom. **24** And she went out, and said unto her mother, What shall I ask? And she said, The head of John [2] the Baptist. **25** And she came in straightway with haste unto the king, and asked, saying, I will that thou forthwith give me   in a charger the head of John the Baptist. **26** And the king was exceeding sorry; but for the sake of his oaths, and of them that sat at meat,   he would not reject her. **27** And straightway the king sent forth a soldier of his guard, and commanded to bring his head: and he went and beheaded him in the prison, **28** and   brought his head in a charger, and gave it to the damsel; and the damsel gave it to her mother. **29** And when his disciples [*cp.* 2 18] heard *thereof*, they came and took up his corpse, and laid it in a tomb.

      cp. 6 30.

---

[1] Some ancient authorities read *they*.
[2] Gr. *the Baptizer*.
[3] Many ancient authorities read *did many things*.
[4] Or, *military tribunes* Gr. *chiliarchs*.
[5] Some ancient authorities read *his daughter Herodias.*   [6] Or, *it*

Herodias his brother's wife, and for all the evil things which Herod had done, **20** added yet this above all, that he shut up John in prison.

   cp. 20 6: *also* 20 19; 22 2.

   cp. 20 6: *also* 1 76; 7 26.

     verse 7

---

cp. 5 33; 7 18; 11 1.

cp. 1 35, 37; 3 25; 4 1.

Matt. 14 4 ‖ Mark 6 18: *cp.* Lev. 18 16; 20 21.

§ 113. The Return of the Twelve and the Feeding of the Five Thousand

[*Cp*. Matt. 15 32-39: Mark 8 1-10]

Matt. 14 13-21	Mark 6 30-44	Luke 9 10-17	John 6 1-14
cp. 10 2.	**30** And the apostles	**10** And the apostles [*cp.* 6 13; 17 5; 22 14; 24 10], when they were returned [*cp.* 10 17],	
13 Now when Jesus *cp.* 14 12.	gather themselves together unto Jesus; and they told him all things, whatsoever they had done, and whatsoever they had taught.	declared unto him what things they had done.	**1** After these things Jesus
heard *it*, *cp.* 17 1, 19; 20 17; 24 3.	**31** And he saith unto them, Come ye yourselves apart [*cp.* 4 10, 34; 9 2, 28; 13 3] into a desert place, and rest a while. For there were many coming and going, and they had no leisure so much as to eat [*cp.* 3 20].	And he took them, *cp.* 10 23.	
he withdrew [*cp.* 8 18] from thence in a boat, to a desert place apart [*see above*]:	**32** And they went away [*cp.* 1 35, 45] in the boat to a desert place apart [*see above*]. *cp.* 6 45; 8 22.	and withdrew [*cp.* 4 42; 5 16] apart [*see above*] to a city called Bethsaida.	went away to the other side of the sea of Galilee, which is *the sea* of Tiberias. **2** And a great multitude
and when the multitudes heard thereof, they followed him [1] on foot from the cities.	**33** And *the people* saw them going, and many knew *them*, and they ran there together [1] on foot from all the cities, and outwent them.	**11** But the multitudes perceiving it followed him:	followed him,
14 And he came forth, and saw a great multitude, and he had compassion on them [*cp.* 9 36; 15 32: *also* 20 34],	**34** And he came forth and saw a great multitude, and he had compassion on them [*cp.* 8 2: *also* 1 41], because they were as sheep not having a shepherd [*cp.* 14 27]: and he began to teach them many things.	and he welcomed them [*cp.* 7 13: *and* 10 33; 15 20],	*cp.* 10 11-16.
cp. 9 36: *also* 10 6; 15 24; 26 31.		and spake to them of the kingdom of God, and them that had need of healing he healed [*cp.* 6 19; 9 2, 42; 14 4; 22 51].	
and healed their sick.			because they beheld the signs which he did on them that were sick. **3** And Jesus went up into the mountain [*cp.* 6 15], and there he sat with his disciples. **4** Now the passover, the feast of the Jews, was at hand. **5** Jesus therefore lifting up his eyes, and seeing that a great multitude cometh unto him, saith unto Philip,
cp. 5 1; 14 23; 15 29; 17 1; 28 16. *cp.* 15 29: *also* 5 1; 24 3.	*cp.* 3 13; 6 46; 9 2. *cp.* 13 3.	*cp.* 6 12; 9 28. *cp.* 6 20.	
cp. 3 7; 5 1; 8 18; 9 36.			
15 And when even was come, the disciples came to him, saying, The place is desert, and the time is already past; send the multitudes away [*cp.* 15 23], that they may go into the villages,	**35** And when the day was now far spent, his disciples came unto him, and said, The place is desert, and the day is now far spent: **36** send them away, that they may go into the country and villages round about,	**12** And the day began to wear away; and the twelve came, and said unto him, Send the multitude away, that they may go into the villages and country round about, and lodge, and get victuals:	Whence are we to buy [1] bread, that these
and buy themselves food.	and buy themselves some-		

[Matthew]

16 But Jesus said unto them, They have no need to go away; give ye them to eat. 17 And they say unto him,

cp. 15 34.

We have here but five loaves, and two fishes.

verse 21
18 And he said, Bring them hither to me [*cp.* 17 17]. 19 And he commanded the multitudes to ² sit down

on the grass;

verse 21
and he took the five loaves, and the two fishes, and looking up to heaven, he blessed [*cp.* 26 26: *also* 15 36; 26 27], and brake and gave the loaves to the disciples, and the disciples to the multitudes.

20 And they did all eat, and were filled :

and they took up

that which remained over of the broken pieces, twelve baskets full. 21 And they that did eat were about five thousand men, beside women and children [*cp.*

[Mark]

what to eat.

37 But he answered and said unto them,

Give ye them to eat. And they say unto him, Shall we go and buy two hundred ² pennyworth of bread, and give them to eat ? 38 And he saith unto them, How many loaves have ye [*cp.* 8 5] ? go *and* see. And when they knew,

they say,

Five, and two fishes.

verse 44
39 And he commanded them that all should ³ sit down by companies upon the green grass. 40 And they

sat down in ranks, by hundreds, and by fifties.

verse 44
41 And he took the five loaves and the two fishes, and looking up to heaven [*cp.* 7 34], he blessed [*cp.* 8 7; 14 22: *also* 8 6; 14 23], and brake the loaves; and he gave to the disciples to set before them; and the two fishes divided he among them all. 42 And they did all eat, and were filled.

43 And they took up

broken pieces, twelve basketfuls, and also of the fishes. 44 And they that ate the loaves were five thousand men.

[Luke]

for we are here in a desert place. 13 But he said unto them,

Give ye them to eat. And they said,

We have no more than five loaves and two fishes; except we should go and buy food for all this people. 14 For they were about five thousand men. And he said unto his disciples,

Make them ¹ sit down in companies, about fifty each. 15 And they did so, and made them all ¹ sit down.

verse 14
16 And he took the five loaves and the two fishes, and looking up to heaven, he blessed [*cp.* 24 30; *also* 22 17, 19] them, and brake; and gave to the disciples to set before the multitude.

17 And they did eat, and were all filled :

and there was taken up

that which remained over to them of broken pieces, twelve baskets.

verse 14

[John]

may eat ? 6 And this he said to prove him : for he himself knew what he would do.

7 Philip answered him, Two hundred ² pennyworth of ¹ bread is not sufficient for them, that every one may take a little.

8 One of his disciples, Andrew, Simon Peter's brother, saith unto him, 9 There is a lad here, which hath five barley loaves, and two fishes : but what are these among so many ?

verse 10
10 Jesus said,

Make the people sit down. Now there was much grass in the place. So the men sat down, in number about five thousand. 11 Jesus therefore took the loaves; and *cp.* 11 41 ; 17 1.

having given thanks,

he distributed to them that were set down ; likewise also of the fishes as much as they would. 12 And when they were filled, he saith unto his disciples, Gather up the broken pieces which remain over, that nothing be lost. 13 So they gathered them up, and filled twelve baskets with broken pieces from the five barley loaves, which remained over unto them

that had eaten.

verse 10

15 38].

cp. 12 23; 14 2; 21 11; 27 54: *also* 8 27; 21 10.	*cp.* 6 15; 15 39: *also* 2 7; 4 41, *and* 1 27.	*cp.* 23 47: *also* 5 21; 7 49; 8 25; 9 9, *and* 4 36.	14 When therefore the people saw the ³ sign which he did, they said, This is [*cp.* 1 34; 4 29, 42; 7 41]
cp. 13 57; 21 11, 46.	*cp.* 6 4, 15.	*cp.* 4 24; 7 16, 39; 13 33; 24 19.	of a truth the prophet [*cp.* 4 19, 44; 7 40; 9 17]
cp. 3 11; 11 3: 21 9; 23 39.	*cp.* 11 9.	*cp.* 7 19, 20; 13 35; 19 38.	that cometh [*cp.* 1 15, 27; 3 31; 11 27; 12 13] into the world.

¹ Or, *by land* ² Gr. *recline.*	¹ Or, *by land* ² See marginal note on Matt. 18 28. ³ Gr. *recline.*	¹ Gr. *recline.*	¹ Gr. *oaves.* ² See marginal note on Matt. 18 28. ³ Some ancient authorities read *signs.*

(x) Journeying in the North (Matt. and Mark: in Galilee, Luke: §§ 114-128).

§ 114. Jesus walks on the Water

[*Cp.* Matt. 8 23-27: Mark 4 35-41: Luke 8 22-25]

Matt. 14 22-33	**Mark 6** 45-52		John 6 15-21
cp. 12 15; 16 8; 22 18; 26 10.	*cp.* 8 17.		15 Jesus therefore perceiving [*cp.* 5 6] that they were about to come and take him by force, to make him king,
22 And straightway he constrained the disciples to enter into the boat, and to go before him unto the other side [*cp.* 8 18],	45 And straightway he constrained his disciples to enter into the boat, and to go before *him* unto the other side [*cp.* 4 35] to Bethsaida [*cp.* 8 22], while he himself sendeth the multitude away. 46 And after he had taken leave of them,	*cp.* 8 22. *cp.* 9 10.	
till he should send the multitudes away. 23 And after he had sent the multitudes away, he went up into the mountain [*cp.* 5 1; 15 29; 17 1; 28 16] apart to pray [*cp.* 19 13; 26 36, 39, 42, 44; *and* 11 25]: and when even was come,	he departed into the mountain [*cp.* 3 13; 9 2] to pray [*cp.* 1 35; 14 32, 35, 39]. 47 And when even was come,	*cp.* 6 12; 9 28: *also* 3 21; 5 16; 9 18, 29; 11 1; 22 41, 44; *and* 10 21.	withdrew again into the mountain [*cp.* 6 3] himself alone. *cp.* 11 41; 12 27-28; 17 1 *ff.* 16 And when evening came, his disciples went down unto the sea; 17 and they entered into a boat, and were going over the sea unto Capernaum.
he was there alone. 24 But the boat ¹ was now in the midst of the sea,	the boat was in the midst of the sea, and he alone on the land.		And it was now dark, and Jesus had not yet come to them. 18 And the sea was rising by reason of a great wind that blew. 19 When therefore they had rowed about five and twenty or thirty furlongs,
distressed by the waves; for the wind was contrary. 25 And	48 And seeing them distressed in rowing, for the wind was contrary unto them,		
in the fourth watch of the night he came unto them, walking upon the sea.	about the fourth watch of the night he cometh unto them, walking on the sea; and he would have passed by them: 49 but they, when they saw him walking on the sea,		they behold Jesus walking on the sea, and drawing nigh unto the boat:
26 And when the disciples saw him walking on the sea, they were troubled, saying, It is an apparition; and they cried out for fear. 27 But straightway Jesus spake unto them, saying, Be of good cheer [*cp.* 9 2, 22]; it is I; be not afraid [*cp.* 17 7; 28 10]. 28 And Peter [*cp.* 15 15; 16 22; 17 4; 18 21;	supposed that it was an apparition, and cried out: 50 for they all saw him, and were troubled. But straightway spake with them, and saith unto them, Be of good cheer [*cp.* 10 49]: it is I; be not afraid. *cp.* 8 32; 9 5; 10 28; 11 21; 14 29: *also* 8 29.	*cp.* 24 37. *cp.* 8 45; 9 33; 12 41;	and they were afraid. 20 But he saith unto them, *cp.* 16 33. It is I; be not afraid. *cp.* 13 36, 37; 21 21: *also* 6 68.

19 27; 26 33: *also* 16 16; 17 24] answered him and said, Lord, if it be thou, bid me come unto thee upon the waters. **29** And he said, Come. And Peter went down from the boat, and walked upon the waters, [2] to come to Jesus. **30** But when he saw the [3] wind, he was afraid; and beginning to sink, he cried out, saying, Lord, save me [*cp.* 8 25]. **31** And immediately Jesus stretched forth his hand, and took hold of him [*cp.* 8 3; 9 25: *also* 8 15; 9 18, 29; 17 7; 19 13, 15; 20 34], and saith unto him, O thou of little faith [*cp.* 6 30; 8 26; 16 8: *also* 17 20], wherefore didst thou doubt [*cp.* 21 21; 28 17]? **32** And when they were

gone up   into the boat,   the wind ceased.

cp. 14 34.

33 And they that were in the boat worshipped him [*cp.* 28 9, 17: *also* 2 11; *and* 8 2; 9 18; 15 25; 17 14; 20 20], saying, Of a truth thou art the Son of God [*cp.* 4 3, 6; 8 29; 16 16; 26 63; 27 40, 43, 54: *also* 3 17; 17 5].

cp. 8 27; 21 20: *also* 9 33; 12 23; 15 31; 27 14: *and* 7 28; 13 54; 19 25; 22 22, 33.

cp. 16 8-12: *also* 15 16.

cp. 19 8.

---

cp. 1 31, 41; 5 41; 8 23; 9 27: *also* 5 23; 6 2, 5; 7 33; 8 22, 25; 10 13, 16.

cp. 4 40; 11 22; 16 14.

cp. 11 23; 16 14.   **51** And he went up unto them into the boat; and   the wind ceased [*cp.* 4 39]:

cp. 6 53.
and they   were

cp. 3 11; 5 33; *and* 1 40; 5 6, 22; 7 25; 10 17.

cp. 1 1; 3 11; 5 7; 15 39: *also* 1 11; 9 7.

sore amazed in themselves [*cp.* 10 32; 16 5, 8: *also* 2 12; 5 20, 42; 7 37; 15 5: *and* 1 22, 27; 6 2; 10 24, 26; 11 18; 12 17]; **52** for they understood not concerning the loaves [*cp.* 8 17-21: *also* 4 13; 7 18; 9 10, 32], but their heart was hardened [*cp.* 8 17; 16 14: *also* 3 5; 10 5].

---

18 28: *also* 5 8; 9 20.

cp. 5 13; 8 54: *also* 4 40; *etc.*

cp. 12 28: *also* 8 25; 17 5, 6; 22 32; 24 25, 38.

cp. 5 8; 24 52: *also* 8 47; 17 16; *etc.*

cp. 1 35; 4 3, 9, 41; 8 28; *etc.*

cp. 5 9; 8 25; 24 12, 41: *also* 5 26; *etc.*

cp. 2 50; 9 45; 18 34.

---

cp. 21 7.

cp. 3 12; 6 64; 14 10; 20 27.

21 They were willing therefore to receive   him into the boat: and straightway   the boat was at the land whither they were going.

cp. 9 38; 18 6; *and* 11 32.

cp. 1 34; *etc.*

cp. 7 15, 21, 46.

cp. 4 33: *also* 3 10; 8 27, 43 10 6; *etc.*
cp. 12 40.

---

[1] Some ancient authorities read *was many furlongs distant from the land.*
[2] Some ancient authorities read *and came.*
[3] Many ancient authorities add *strong.*

§ 115. Healings in Gennesaret

Matt. 14 34-36	**Mark 6** 53-56		
34 And when they had crossed over, they came to the land, unto Gennesaret. **35** And when the men of that place knew him, they sent into all that region round about, and brought unto him [*cp.* 9 2] all that were sick;	**53** And when they had [1] crossed over, they came to the land unto Gennesaret, and moored to the shore. **54** And when they were come out of the boat, straightway *the people* knew him, **55** and ran round about that whole region, and began to carry about on their beds [*cp.* 2 4] those that were sick, where they heard he was. **56** And wheresoever he entered, into villages, or into cities, or into the country, they laid the sick in the marketplaces, and besought him that they	*cp.* 6 21. *cp.* 5 18	 *cp.* 5 3-6.
36 and they besought him that they might only touch [*cp.* 9 20: *also* 8 3, *etc.*] the	might touch [*cp.* 3 10; 5 27: *also* 1 31, 41; *etc.*] if it were but the	*cp.* 6 19; 7 39; 8 44; *etc.*	

Matt.	Mark		
border [*cp.* 9 20] of his garment : and as many as touched were made whole.	border of his garment : and as many as touched ² him were made whole.	*cp.* 8 44.	

¹ Or, *crossed over to the land, they came unto Gennesaret*
² Or, *it*

§ 116. A Question about the Tradition of the Elders

[*Cp.* Luke 11 38-41 : *also* Matt. 9 14-17; Mark 2 18-22; Luke 5 33-39]

Matt. 15 1-20	**Mark 7** 1-23		
1 Then there come to Jesus from Jerusalem Pharisees and scribes,	**1** And there are gathered together unto him the Pharisees, and certain of the scribes, which had come from Jerusalem [*cp.* 3 22], **2** and had seen that some of his disciples ate their bread with ¹ defiled, that is, unwashen, hands. **3** For the Pharisees, and all the Jews, except they wash their hands ² diligently, eat not, holding the tradition of the elders : **4** and *when they come* from the marketplace, except they ³ wash themselves, they eat not : and many other things there be, which they have received to hold, ⁴ washings of cups, and pots, and brasen vessels.⁵	*cp.* 5 17.	*cp.* 1 19.
cp. verse 20.			
cp. 23 25.			
saying, **2** Why do thy disciples transgress [*cp.* 9 14; 12 2] the tradition of the elders ? for they wash not their hands when they eat bread.	**5** And the Pharisees and the scribes ask him, Why walk not thy disciples [*cp.* 2 18, 24] according to the tradition of the elders, but eat their bread with ¹ defiled hands ? **6** And he said unto them, Well did Isaiah prophesy of you hypocrites [*cp.* 12 15], as it is written,	*cp.* 11 39. *cp.* 5 33; 6 2. *cp.* 11 38.	
	This people honoureth me with their lips, But their heart is far from me. **7** But in vain do they worship me, Teaching *as their* doctrines the precepts of men. **8** Ye leave the commandment of God, and hold fast the tradition of men. **9** And he said unto them, Full well do ye reject the commandment of God, that ye may keep your tradition.	*cp.* 12 56; 13 15: *also* 12 1.	
verses 7-9			
3 And he answered and said unto them, Why do ye also transgress the commandment of God because of your tradition ? **4** For God said, Honour thy father and thy mother : and, He that speaketh evil of father or mother, let him ¹ die the death. **5** But ye say, Whosoever shall say to his father or his mother, That wherewith thou mightest have been profited by me is given *to God*; **6** he shall not honour his father.² And ye have made void the ³ word of God because of your tradition.	**10** For Moses said, Honour thy father and thy mother; and, He that speaketh evil of father or mother, let him ⁶ die the death : **11** but ye say, If a man shall say to his father or his mother, That wherewith thou mightest have been profited by me is Corban, that is to say, Given *to God*; **12** ye no longer suffer him to do aught for his father or his mother; **13** making void the word of God by your tradition, which ye have delivered : and many such like things ye do.		
7 Ye hypocrites [*cp.* 22 18; 23 13, 15, 23, 25, 27 29: *also* 6 2, 5, 16; 24 51: *and* 23 28], well did Isaiah prophesy of you, saying, **8** This people honoureth me with their lips; But their heart is far from me. **9** But in vain do they worship me,		*cp.* 12 56; 13 15: *also* 12 1.	
	verses 6-7		

Teaching *as their* doctrines the precepts of men.

10 And he called to him the multitude, and said unto them, Hear, and understand: **11** Not that which entereth into the mouth defileth the man; but that which proceedeth out of the mouth, this defileth the man.

cp. 11 15; 13 9, 43: *also* 19 12.

cp. 13 36; 17 25.

12 Then came the disciples [cp. 5 1; 13 10, 36; 14 15; 15 23; 17 19; 18 1; 24 1, 3; 26 17], and said unto him, Knowest thou that the Pharisees were 4 offended [cp. 11 6; 13 57; 26 31, 33: *also* 13 21; 24 10], when they heard this saying? **13** But he answered and said, Every 5 plant which my heavenly Father [cp. 5 48; 6 14, 26, 32; 18 35; 23 9: *also* 5 16, 45; 6 1; *etc.*] planted not, shall be rooted up [cp. 13 29]. **14** Let them alone: they are blind guides [cp. 23 16, 17, 19, 24, 26]. And if the blind guide the blind, both shall fall into a pit. **15** And Peter [cp. 14 28; 16 22; 17 4; 18 21; 19 27; 26 33: *also* 16 16; 17 24] answered and said unto him, Declare unto us the parable [cp. 13 36]. **16** And he said, Are ye also even yet without understanding [cp. 16 8-12]? **17** Perceive ye not, that whatsoever goeth into the mouth passeth into the belly, and is cast out into the draught? cp. 23 26. **18** But the things which proceed out of the mouth come forth out of the heart [cp. 12 34]; and they defile the man. **19** For [cp. 23 25, 26, 28] out of the heart come forth evil thoughts, murders, adulteries, fornications, thefts, [cp. 6 23; 20 15] false witness, railings: **20** these are the things which defile the man: but to eat with unwashen hands defileth not the man.

1 Or, *surely die*
2 Some ancient authorities add *or his mother.*
3 Some ancient authorities read *law.*
4 Gr. *caused to stumble.*   5 Gr. *planting.*

14 And he called to him the multitude again, and said unto them, Hear me all of you, and understand: **15** there is nothing from without the man, that going into him can defile him: but the things which proceed out of the man are those that defile the man. 7 [cp. 4 9, 23]. **17** And when he was entered into the house [cp. 9 28, 33; 10 10] from the multitude, his disciples [cp. 6 35]

cp. 6 3; 14 27, 29: *also* 4 17.

cp. 11 25, 26.

Luke 6 39 And he spake also a parable unto them. Can the blind guide the blind? shall they not both fall into a pit? cp. 8 45; 9 33; 12 41; 18 28: *also* 5 8; 9 20.

cp. 8 32; 9 5; 10 28; 11 21; 14 29: *also* 8 29.

asked of him the parable [cp. 4 10]. **18** And he saith unto them, Are ye so without understanding also [cp. 4 13; 8 17-21: *also* 6 52; 9 10, 32; 16 14]? Perceive ye not, that whatsoever from without goeth into the man, *it* cannot defile him; **19** because it goeth not into his heart, but into his belly, and goeth out into the draught? *This he said,* making all meats clean. **20** And he said, That which proceedeth out of the man, that defileth the man. **21** For from within, out of the heart of men, 8 evil thoughts proceed, fornications, **22** thefts, murders, adulteries, covetings, wickednesses, deceit, lasciviousness, an evil eye, railing, pride, foolishness: **23** all these evil things proceed from within, and defile the man.

cp. *verse* 2.

1 Or, *common*
2 Or, *up to the elbow* Gr. *with the fist.*
3 Gr. *baptize.* Some ancient authorities read *sprinkle themselves.*
4 Gr. *baptizings.*
5 Many ancient authorities add *and couches.*
6 Or, *surely die*
7 Many ancient authorities insert ver. 16, *If any man hath ears to hear, let him hear.*
8 Gr. *thoughts that are evil.*

cp. 8 8; 14 35.

cp. 9 12.

cp. 7 23.

cp. 11 13.

cp. 8 9.

cp. 2 50; 9 45; 18 34.

cp. 11 41.

cp. 6 45.

cp. 11 39, 41.

cp. 11 34.

cp. 6 60.

cp. 6 61: *also* 16 1.

cp. 9 39-41.

cp. 13 36, 37; 21 21: *also* 6 68.

cp. 3 10; 4 33; 8 27, 43; *etc.*

Matt. 15 4 || Mark 7 10: Exod. 20 12; 21 17; Lev. 20 9; Deut. 5 16.   Matt. 15 8-9 || Mark 7 6-7: Is. 29 13.

§ 117. **The Syrophœnician Woman**

Matt. 15 21-28	**Mark 7** 24-30		
21 And Jesus went out thence, and withdrew into the parts of Tyre and Sidon.	**24** And from thence he arose, and went away into the borders of Tyre ¹ and Sidon. And he entered into a house, and would have no man know it [*cp.* 9 30: *also* 1 25; *etc.*]: and he could not be hid. **25** But straightway a woman,	*cp.* 4 35; *etc.*	
cp. 8 4; *etc.*			
22 And behold, a Canaanitish woman came out from those borders, and cried, saying,	whose little daughter had an unclean spirit, having heard of him, came and fell down at his feet [*cp.* 3 11; 5 22, 33: *also* 1 40; 10 17]. **26** Now the woman was a ² Greek, a Syrophœnician by race. And she besought him that he would cast forth the ³ devil out of her daughter.	*cp.* 5 8, 12; 8 28, 41, 47; 17 16.	*cp.* 11 32; 18 6.
cp. 2 11: *also* 17 14.			
Have mercy on me [*cp.* 9 27; 17 15; 20 30, 31], O Lord, thou son of David [*cp.* 9 27; 20 30, 31: *also* 1 1; 12 23; 21 9, 15]; my daughter is grievously vexed with a ¹ devil.	*cp.* 10 47, 48.	*cp.* 17 13; 18 38, 39.	
	cp. 10 47, 48.	*cp.* 18 38, 39: *also* 1 32.	
23 But he answered her not a word [*cp.* 26 63; 27 12, 14]. And his disciples came [*cp.* 5 1; 13 10, 36; 14 15; 15 12; 17 19; 18 1; 24 1, 3; 26 17] and besought him, saying, Send her away [*cp.* 14 15: *also* 19 13; 26 8-9]; for she crieth after us.	*cp.* 14 61; 15 5.	*cp.* 23 9.	*cp.* 19 9.
	cp. 6 35.	*cp.* 9 12.	
	cp. 6 36: *also* 10 13; 14 4-5.	*cp.* 9 12: *also* 18 15.	*cp.* 12 5.
24 But he answered and said, I was not sent but unto the lost sheep of the house of Israel [*cp.* 10 6: *also* 9 36; 26 31]. **25** But she came and worshipped [*cp.* 2 11; 8 2; 9 18; 14 33; 20 20; 28 9, 17] him, saying, Lord, help me. **26** And he answered and said,	*cp.* 6 34; 14 27.		*cp.* 10 11-16.
	cp. 5 6.	*cp.* 24 52.	*cp.* 9 38.
[*cp.* 5 24; 6 33; 7 5; 23 26] It is not meet to take the children's ² bread and cast it to the dogs [*cp.* 7 6]. **27** But she said, Yea, Lord: for even the dogs eat of the crumbs which fall from their masters' table.	*cp.* 9 22. **27** And he said unto her, Let the children first be filled: for it is not meet to take the children's ⁴ bread and cast it to the dogs. **28** But she answered and saith unto him, Yea, Lord: even the dogs under the table eat of the children's crumbs.	*cp.* 6 42.	
28 Then Jesus answered and said unto her, O woman, great is thy faith: be it done unto thee even as thou wilt [*cp.* 8 13; 9 29].	**29** And he said unto her,	*cp.* 16 21.	
cp. 8 13. And her daughter was healed from that hour [*cp.* 8 13; 9 22; 17 18].	For this saying go thy way; the ³ devil is gone out of thy daughter. **30** And she went away unto her house, and found the child laid upon the bed, and the ³ devil gone out.	*cp.* 7 10.	*cp.* 4 50. *cp.* 4 53.

¹ Gr. *demon*.   ² Or, *loaf*

¹ Some ancient authorities omit *and Sidon*.
² Or, *Gentile*   ³ Gr. *demon*.   ⁴ Or, *loaf*

§ 118. **Healings by the Sea of Galilee** (Matt.): **The Healing of a Deaf-Mute** (Mark)

[*Cp.* Matt. 9 32-34; 12 22: Mark 9 17, 25: Luke 11 14: *also* Matt. 11 5 *and* Luke 7 22]

Matt. 15 29-31	**Mark 7** 31-37	
29 And Jesus departed thence, and came nigh unto the sea of Galilee;	**31** And again he went out from the borders of Tyre, and came through Sidon unto the sea of Galilee, through the midst of the borders of Decapolis [*cp.* 5 20].	*cp.* 6 1.
cp. 4 25. and he		

Matt.	Mark	Luke	John
went up into the mountain [*cp.* 5 1; 14 23; 17 1; 28 16], and sat there [*cp.* 5 1; 24 3]. **30** And there came unto him great multitudes, having with them the lame, blind, dumb, maimed, and many others, and they cast them down at his feet;	*cp.* 3 13; 6 46; 9 2. *cp.* 13 3. **32** And they bring unto him one that was deaf, and had an impediment in his speech;	*cp.* 6 12; 9 28.	*cp.* 6 3, 15.
	and they beseech him to lay his hand upon him [*cp.* 8 22]. **33** And he took him aside from the multitude privately [*cp.* 8 23], and put his fingers into his ears, and he spat [*cp.* 8 23], and touched [*cp.* 1 41; 8 22; 10 13: *also* 1 31; 5 41; 8 23, 25; 9 27; 10 16: *and* 5 23; 6 2, 5] his tongue; **34** and looking up to heaven [*cp.* 6 41], he sighed [*cp.* 8 12], and saith unto him, Ephphatha, that is, Be opened. **35** And his ears were opened, and the bond of his tongue was loosed, and he spake plain [*cp.* 8 25].		*cp.* 9 6.
cp. 8 3, 15; 9 29; 17 7; 20 34: *also* 9 25; 14 31; 19 13, 15: *and* 9 18. *cp.* 14 19.		*cp.* 5 13; 7 14; 18 15; 22 51; *etc.* *cp.* 9 16.	*cp.* 11 41; 17 1.
and he healed them:		*cp.* 1 64.	
cp. 8 4; 9 30; 12 16: *also* 16 20; 17 9. *cp.* 9 31.	**36** And he charged them that they should tell no man [*cp.* 1 44; 5 43; 8 26: *also* 1 25, 34; 3 12: *and* 8 30; 9 9]: but the more he charged them, so much the more a great deal they published it [*cp.* 1 45].	*cp.* 5 14; 8 56: *also* 4 35; *etc.* *cp.* 5 15.	
31 insomuch that the multitude wondered [*cp.* 9 33; 12 23; 27 14: *also* 8 27; 21 20: *and* 7 28; 13 54; 19 25; 22 22, 33], when they saw	**37** And they were beyond measure astonished [*cp.* 2 12; 5 20, 42; 15 5: *also* 6 51; 10 32; 16 5, 8: *and* 1 22, 27; 6 2; 10 24, 26; 11 18; 12 17], saying, He hath done all things well: he maketh even the deaf to hear, and the dumb to speak.	*cp.* 5 26; 8 56; 9 43; 11 14; *etc.*	*cp.* 7 15, 21, 46.
the dumb speaking, the maimed whole, and the lame walking, and the blind seeing [*cp.* 11 5]: and they glorified the God [*cp.* 9 8: *also* 5 16] of Israel.	*cp.* 2 12.	*cp.* 7 22. *cp.* 5 25, 26: *also* 2 20; 7 16; 13 13; 17 15, 18; 18 43; 23 47.	*cp.* 9 24.

§ 119. The Feeding of the Four Thousand

[*Cp.* Matt. 14 13-21: Mark 6 30-44: Luke 9 10-17: John 6 1-14]

Matt. 15 32-39	**Mark 8** 1-10	
32 And Jesus called unto him his disciples, and said, I have compassion [*cp.* 9 36; 14 14: *also* 20 34] on the multitude, because they continue with me now three days and have nothing to eat: and I would not send them away fasting, lest haply they faint in the way. **33** And the disciples say unto him, Whence should we have so many loaves in a desert place, as to fill so great a multitude?	**1** In those days, when there was again a great multitude, and they had nothing to eat, he called unto him his disciples, and saith unto them, **2** I have compassion [*cp.* 6 34: *also* 1 41] on the multitude, because they continue with me now three days, and have nothing to eat: **3** and if I send them away fasting to their home, they will faint in the way; and some of them are come from far. **4** And his disciples answered him, Whence shall one be able to fill these men with ¹ bread here in a desert place?	*cp.* 7 13: *and* 10 33; 15 20.
34 And Jesus saith unto them, How many loaves have ye? And they said, Seven, and a few small fishes. **35** And he commanded the multitude to sit down on the ground; **36** and	**5** And he asked them, How many loaves have ye [*cp.* 6 38]? And they said, Seven. **6** And he commandeth the multitude to sit down on the ground: and	

he took the seven loaves and the fishes; and he gave thanks [cp. 26 27] and brake, and gave to the disciples. and the disciples to the multitudes.

cp. 14 19; 26 26.

37 And they did all eat, and were filled: and they took up that which remained over of the broken pieces, seven baskets full. 38 And they that did eat were four thousand men, beside women and children [cp. 14 21]. 39 And he sent away the multitudes, and entered into the boat, and came into the borders of Magadan. | he took the seven loaves, and having given thanks [cp. 14 23], he brake, and gave to his disciples, to set before them; and they set them before the multitude. 7 And they had a few small fishes: and having blessed [cp. 6 41; 14 22] them, he commanded to set these also before them. 8 And they did eat, and were filled: and they took up, of broken pieces that remained over, seven baskets. 9 And they were about four thousand:

and he sent them away. 10 And straightway he entered into the boat with his disciples, and came into the parts of Dalmanutha. | cp. 22 17, 19.

cp. 9 16; 24 30. | cp. 6 11. |

¹ Gr. *loaves*.

§ 120. A Request for a Sign refused

Matt. 12 38-39	**Matt. 16** 1-4	**Mark 8** 11-13	Luke 12 54-56; 11 29		
38 Then certain of the scribes and Pharisees	1 And the Pharisees and Sadducees came, and tempting him [cp. 19 3; 22 35: *also* 22 18]	11 And the Pharisees came forth, and

began to question with him [cp. 9 14, 16; 12 28], | | | |
| answered him, saying, ¹ Master, we would see a sign from thee. | asked him to shew them a sign from heaven. | seeking of him a sign from heaven, tempting him [cp. 10 2: *also* 12 15]. | 11 16

cp. 10 25; 11 16. | cp. 2 18; 6 30.

cp. 8 6. | |
| 39 But he

answered and said unto them, | 2 But he

answered and said unto them, ¹ When it is evening, ye say, *It will be* fair weather: for the heaven is red. 3 And in the morning, *It will be* foul weather to-day: for the heaven is red and lowring. | 12 And he sighed deeply [cp. 7 34] in his spirit, and saith, | 12 54 And he said to the multitudes also, When ye see a cloud rising in the west, straightway ye say, There cometh a shower; and so it cometh to pass. 55 And when *ye see* a south wind blowing, ye say, There will be a ¹ scorching heat; and it cometh to pass. | | |
| cp. 15 7; 22 18; 23 13, *etc.*: *also* 6 2, 5, 16; 24 51: *and* 23 28. | Ye know how to discern the face of the heaven; but ye cannot *discern* the signs of the times [cp. 24 32-33]. | cp. 7 6: *also* 12 15.

cp. 13 28-29. | 56 Ye hypocrites [cp. 13 15: *also* 12 1], ye know how to ² interpret the face of the earth and the heaven; but how is it that ye know not how to ² interpret this time [cp. 21 29-31]? 11 29 And when the multitudes were gathering together unto him, he began to say, | | |
| An | 4 An | Why doth this generation | This generation is an | | |

evil and adulterous generation [*cp.* 12 45] seeketh after a sign ;	evil and adulterous generation [*cp.* 17 17] seeketh after a sign;	*cp.* 8 38; 9 19. seek a sign ? verily I say unto you, There shall no sign	evil generation [*cp.* 9 41] : it seeketh after a sign ;
and there shall no sign be given to it but the sign of Jonah the prophet. *cp.* 21 17.	and there shall no sign be given unto it, but the sign of Jonah. And he left them, and	be given unto this generation. **13** And he left them, and again entering into *the boat* departed to the other side [*cp.* Matt. 16 5].	and there shall no sign be given to it but the sign of Jonah.
	departed.		
¹ Or, *Teacher*.	¹ The following words, to the end of ver. 3, are omitted by some of the most ancient and other important authorities.		¹ Or, *hot wind* ² Gr. *prove*.

§ 121. **The Leaven of the Pharisees and Sadducees** (Matt.: **Herod,** Mark)

Matt. 16 5-12	**Mark 8** 14-21	Luke 12 1
5 And the disciples came to the other side [*cp.* Mark 8 13] and forgot to take ¹ bread.	**14** And they forgot to take bread; and they had not in the boat with them more than one loaf. **15** And he charged them, saying, Take heed, beware [*cp.* 12 38] of the leaven of the Pharisees and the leaven of Herod. *cp.* 12 15 : *also* 7 6.	**1** In the mean time, when ¹ the many thousands of the multitude were gathered together, insomuch that they trode one upon another, he began to ² say unto his disciples first of all, Beware [*cp.* 20 46: *also* 17 3 ; 21 34] ye of the leaven of the Pharisees, which is hypocrisy [*cp.* 12 56 ; 13 15].
6 And Jesus said unto them, Take heed and beware of the leaven of the Pharisees and Sadducees. *cp.* 23 28: *also* 6 2, 5, 16; 15 7; 22 18; 23 13, *etc*; 24 51.		
		¹ Gr. *the myriads of.* ² Or, *say unto his disciples, First of all beware ye*

cp. Matt. 9 3-4; Mark 2 6-8; Luke 5 21-22.	**7** And they reasoned among themselves, saying, ² We took no ¹ bread. **8** And Jesus perceiving it [*cp.* 12 15 ; 22 18 ; 26 10] said, O ye of little faith [*cp.* 6 30; 8 26; 14 31: *also* 17 20: 21 21; 28 17], why reason ye among yourselves, because ye have no ¹ bread ? **9** Do ye not yet perceive, neither *cp.* 19 8.	**16** And they reasoned one with another, ¹ saying, ² We have no bread. **17** And Jesus perceiving it saith unto them, *cp.* 4 40; 11 22; 16 14. Why reason ye, because ye have no bread ? do ye not yet perceive, neither understand ? have ye your heart hardened [*cp.* 6 52; 16 14: *also* 3 5; 10 5]? **18** Having eyes, see ye not ? and having ears, hear ye not			
			cp. 12 28: *also* 8 25; 17 5, 6; 22 32; 24 25, 38.	*cp.* 5 6; 6 15; *etc.* *cp.* 3 12; 6 64; 14 10; 20 27.	
				cp. 12 40.	
	cp. 13 13 : *also* 15 16; 16 11. remember the five loaves of the five thousand, and how many ³ baskets ye took up ?	[*cp.* 4 12: *also* 4 13; 6 52; 7 18; 8 21; 9 10, 32; 16 14]? and do ye not remember ? **19** When I brake the five loaves among the five thousand, how many ³ baskets full of broken pieces took ye up ? They say unto him, Twelve. **20** And when the seven among the four thousand,	*cp.* 8 10 : *also* 2 50; 9 45; 18 34.	*cp.* 3 10; 4 33; 8 27, 43; *etc.*	
	10 Neither the seven loaves of the four thousand, and how many ³ baskets ye took up ?	how many ³ basketfuls of broken pieces took ye up ? And they say unto him, Seven. **21** And he said unto them,			
	11 How is it that ye do not [*see verse* 9 *above*] perceive that I spake not to you concerning ¹ bread ? But beware of the leaven of the Pharisees and Sadducees. **12** Then understood they [*cp.* 17 13] how that he bade them not	Do ye not yet understand [*see verse* 18 *above*] ?	see above.	see above.	

beware of the leaven of [1] bread, but of the teaching of the Pharisees and Sadducees.

[1] Gr. *loaves*.
[2] Or, It is *because we took no bread*.
[3] *Basket* in ver. 9 and 10 represents different Greek words.

[1] Some ancient authorities read *because they had no bread*.
[2] Or, It is *because we have no bread*.
[3] *Basket* in ver. 19 and 20 represents different Greek words.

Mark 8 17-18 : *cp.* Ps. 115 5-6 ; 135 16-17 ; Is. 6 9-10 ; 43 8 ; Jer. 5 21 ; Ezek. 12 2.

§ 122. **The Healing of a Blind Man at Bethsaida**

[*Cp.* Matt. 9 27-31 ; 12 22 ; 15 30-31 ; 20 29-34 ; 21 14 : Mark 10 46-52 : Luke 7 21 ; 18 35-43 : John 9 1-7]

Mark 8 22-26

22 And they come unto Bethsaida [*cp.* 6 45]. And they bring to him a blind man, and beseech him to touch him [*cp.* 7 32]. **23** And he took hold of the blind man by the hand, and brought him out of the village [*cp.* 7 33] ; and when he had spit [*cp.* 7 33] on his eyes, and laid his hands [*cp.* 8 25 ; 10 16 : *also* 1 31, 41 ; 5 41 ; 7 33 ; 8 22 ; 9 27 ; 10 13 ; *and* 5 23 ; 6 2, 5] upon him, he asked him, Seest thou aught ? **24** And he looked up, and said, I see men ; for I behold *them* as trees, walking. **25** Then again he laid his hands [*see above*] upon his eyes ; and he looked stedfastly, and was restored, and saw all things clearly [*cp.* 7 35]. **26** And he sent him away to his home, saying, Do not even enter into the village [*cp.* 1 44 ; 5 43 ; 7 36 : *also* 1 25, 34 ; 3 12 ; *and* 7 24 ; 8 30 ; 9 9, 30].

cp. 19 13, 15 : *also* 8 3, 15 ; 9 25, 29 ; 14 31 ; 17 7 ; 20 34 ; *and* 9 18.

cp. 8 4 ; 9 30 ; 12 16 : *also* 16 20 ; 17 9.

cp. 9 10.

cp. 4 40 ; 13 13 : *also* 5 13 ; 7 14 ; 8 54 ; 14 4 ; 18 15 ; 22 51.

cp. 5 14 ; 8 56 : *also* 4 35, 41 ; *and* 9 21, 36.

cp. 9 6.
cp. 9 6.

§ 123. **Peter's Confession**

Matt. 16 13-20	**Mark 8** 27-30	**Luke 9** 18-21	**John** 6 66-69 ; 1 41-42 ; 20 22-23
13 Now when Jesus came into the parts of Cæsarea Philippi,	**27** And Jesus went forth, and his disciples, into the villages of Cæsarea Philippi : and in the way		6 **66** Upon this many of his disciples went back, and walked no more with him.
cp. 14 23 ; 19 13 ; 26 36, 39, 42, 44 : *also* 11 25.	*cp.* 1 35 ; 6 46, 47 ; 14 32, 35, 39.	**18** And it came to pass, as he was praying [*cp.* 3 21 ; 5 16 ; 6 12 ; 9 28, 29 ; 11 1 ; 22 41, 44 : *also* 10 21] alone, the disciples were with him : and he	*cp.* 11 41 ; 12 27-28 ; 17 1-26.
he asked his disciples, saying, Who do men say [1] that the Son of man is ? **14** And they said [*cp.* 14 2], Some *say* John the Baptist ; some, Elijah : and others, Jeremiah, or one of the prophets.	he asked his disciples, saying unto them, Who do men say that I am ? **28** And they told him, saying [*cp.* 6 14, 15], John the Baptist : and others, Elijah ; but others, One of the prophets.	asked them, saying, Who do the multitudes say that I am ? **19** And they answering said [*cp.* 9 7, 8], John the Baptist ; but others *say*, Elijah ; and others, that one of the old prophets is risen again.	**67** Jesus said therefore unto the twelve, Would ye also go away ?
15 He saith unto them, But who say ye that I am ? **16** And Simon [*cp.* 4 18 ; 10 2] Peter answered and said,	**29** And he asked them, But who say ye that I am ? Peter answereth and saith unto him,	**20** And he said unto them, But who say ye that I am ? *cp.* 5 8. Peter answering said,	**68** Simon [*cp.* 1 40 ; 6 8 ; 13 6; *etc.*] Peter answered him, Lord, to whom shall we go ? thou [1] hast the words of eternal life. **69** And we have believed and know that thou art
Thou art	**Thou art**		

Matt.	Mark	Luke	John
the Christ [*cp.* 26 63: *also* 26 68; 27 17, 22],	the Christ [*cp.* 14 61; *also* 15 32].	The Christ [*cp.* 22 67: *also* 23 2, 35, 39]	[*cp.* 1 41; 4 25, 26, 29; 7 26, 41; 9 22; 10 24; 11 27] the Holy One
	cp. 1 24.	*cp.* 4 34.	*cp.* 1 34; *etc.*
the Son [*cp.* 4 3, 6; 8 29; 14 33; 26 63; 27 40, 43, 54: *also* 3 17; 17 5] of the living [*cp.* 26 63] God.	*cp.* 1 1; 3 11; 5 7; 15 39: *also* 1 11; 9 7.	*cp.* 1 35; 4 3, 9, 41; 8 28; 22 70: *also* 3 22; 9 35. of God [*cp.* 23 35].	of God. **1 41** He findeth first his own brother Simon, and saith unto him, We have found the Messiah (which is, being interpreted, ² Christ). **42** He brought him unto Jesus. Jesus looked upon him, and said,
17 And Jesus answered and said unto him, Blessed art thou, Simon [*cp.* 17 25] Bar-Jonah:	*cp.* 14 37.	*cp.* 22 31.	Thou art Simon [*cp.* 21 15, 16, 17] the son of ³ John [*cp.* 21 15, 16, 17]:
for flesh and blood hath not revealed it unto thee [*cp.* 11 25], but		*cp.* 10 21.	
my Father which is in heaven [*cp.* 5 16, 45; 6 1, 9; 7 11, 21; 10 32, 33; 12 50; 18 10, 14, 19: *also* 5 48; 6 14, 26, 32; 15 13; 18 35; 23 9]. **18** And I also say unto thee, that thou art	*cp.* 11 25, 26.	*cp.* 11 13.	
	cp. 3 16.	*cp.* 6 14.	thou shalt be called Cephas (which is by interpretation, ⁴ Peter).
² Peter, and upon this ³ rock [*cp.* 7 24] I will build my church; and the gates of Hades shall not prevail against it. **19** I will give unto thee the keys of the kingdom of heaven [*cp.* 23 13]: and whatsoever thou shalt bind on earth shall be bound in heaven: and whatsoever thou shalt loose on earth shall be loosed in heaven.	*cp.* 18 17. Matt. 18 18 Verily I say unto you, What things soever ye shall bind on earth shall be bound in heaven: and what things soever ye shall loose on earth shall be loosed in heaven.	*cp.* 6 48. *cp.* 22 32.	*cp.* 21 15-17. **20 22** And when he had said this, he breathed on them, and saith unto them, Receive ye the ⁵ Holy Ghost: **23** whose soever sins ye forgive, they are forgiven unto them; whose soever *sins* ye retain, they are retained.
20 Then charged he the disciples that they should tell no man [*cp.* 17 9: *also* 8 4; 9 30; 12 16] that he was the Christ.	**30** And he charged them that they should tell no man [*cp.* 9 9: *also* 1 25, 34, 44; 3 12; 5 43; 7 36; 8 26] of him.	**21** But he charged them, and commanded *them* to tell this to no man [*cp.* 9 36: *also* 4 35, 41; 5 41; 8 56];	

¹ Many ancient authorities read *that I the Son of man am.* See Mark 8 27; Luke 9 18.
² Gr. *Petros.*   ³ Gr. *petra.*

¹ Or, *hast words*
² That is, *Anointed.*
³ Gr. *Joanes*: called in Matt. 16 17, *Jonah.*
⁴ That is, *Rock* or *Stone.*
⁵ Or, *Holy Spirit*

Matt. 16 19: *cp.* Is. 22 22.

§ 124. The First Prediction of the Passion and Resurrection

[*Cp.* Matt. 17 22-23 ‖ Mark 9 30-32 ‖ Luke 9 43b-45; Matt. 20 17-19 ‖ Mark 10 32-34 ‖ Luke 18 31-34: *also* Matt. 17 9, 12; 20 28; 26 2, 12, 18, 24, 32, 45: Mark 9 9, 12; 10 45; 14 8, 21, 28, 41: Luke 13 32-33; 17 25; 22 22; 24 7, *and* 26, 44, 46: John 2 19-22; 3 14; 12 32-33]

Matt. 16 21-23	Mark 8 31-33	Luke 9 22
21 From that time began ¹ Jesus to shew unto his disciples, how that he must go unto Jerusalem [*cp.* 20 18], and suffer many things	**31** And he began to teach them, *cp.* 10 33. that the Son of man must suffer many things, and be	**22** saying, *cp.* 9 31, 51; 13 33; 18 31. The Son of man must suffer many things, and be

of the elders and chief priests and scribes, and be killed, *cp.* 27 63.

and the third day [*cp.* 17 23; 20 19; *also* 12 40; 26 61; 27 40, 64] *cp.* 17 9. be raised up [*cp.* 17 23; 20 19; 26 32; 27 63, 64; 28 6, 7].

22 And Peter [*cp.* 14 28; 15 15; 17 4; 18 21; 19 27; 26 33: *also* 16 16; 17 24] took him, and began to rebuke him, saying, [2] Be it far from thee, Lord: this shall never be unto thee. **23** But he turned [*cp.* 9 22],

and said unto Peter, Get thee behind me, Satan [*cp.* 4 10]: thou art a stumbling block unto me: for thou mindest not the things of God, but the things of men.

rejected by the elders, and the chief priests, and the scribes, and be killed, and after three days [*cp.* 9 31; 10 34: *also* 14 58; 15 29]

rise again [*cp.* 9 9, 31; 10 34; 16 9]. *cp.* 14 28; 16 6, 14.

32 And he spake the saying openly. And Peter [*cp.* 9 5; 10 28; 11 21; 14 29: *also* 8 29] took him, and began to rebuke him.

33 But he turning about [*cp.* 5 30], and seeing his disciples, rebuked Peter, and saith, Get thee behind me, Satan:

for thou mindest not the things of God, but the things of men.

rejected [*cp.* 17 25] of the elders and chief priests and scribes, and be killed,

and the third day [*cp.* 13 32; 18 33; 24 7, 46: *also* 24 21] be raised up [*cp.* 24 6, 34].

cp. 8 45; 9 33; 12 41; 18 28: *also* 5 8; 9 20.

cp. 7 9, 44; 9 55; 10 23; 14 25; 22 61; 23 28.

cp. 2 19.

cp. 20 9. *cp.* 2 19-22; 21 14. *cp.* 7 4, 13, 26; 10 24. *cp.* 13 36, 37; 21 21: *also* 6 68.

cp. 1 38.

[1] Some ancient authorities read *Jesus Christ.*
[2] Or, God *have mercy on thee*

§ 125. The Cost and Rewards of Discipleship

[*Cp.* Matt. 10 16-42; 19 27-30; 24 9: Mark 10 28-31; 13 9-13: Luke 12 8-12; 14 25-35; 18 28-30; 21 12-19; 22 28-30: John 14 2-3; 15 18-21; 16 2-3, 33]

Matt. 16 24-28	**Mark 8** 34-9 1	**Luke 9** 23-27	John 12 26, 25
24 Then	**34** And he called unto him the multitude with his disciples, and said unto them,	**23** And he	
said Jesus unto his disciples, If any man would come after me, let him deny himself, and take up his cross, and follow me [*cp.* 4 19; 8 22; 9 9; 19 21].	If any man would come after me, let him deny himself, and take up his cross, and follow me [*cp.* 1 17; 2 14; 10 21].	said unto all, If any man would come after me, let him deny himself, and take up his cross daily, and follow me [*cp.* 5 27; 9 59; 18 22].	**26** If any man serve me, let him follow me [*cp.* 1 43; 21 19, 22]; and where I am, there shall also my servant be: if any man serve me, him will the Father honour. **25** He that loveth his [1] life loseth it; and he that hateth his [1] life
25 For whosoever would save his [1] life shall lose it: and whosoever shall lose his [1] life for my sake [*cp.* 5 11; 10 18, 39: *also* 10 22; 19 29; 24 9] *cp.* 4 23; 9 35; 24 14; 26 13.	**35** For whosoever would save his [1] life shall lose it; and whosoever shall lose his [1] life for my sake [*cp.* 10 29; 13 9: *also* 13 13] and the gospel's [*cp.* 10 29: *also* 1 1, 14, 15; 13 10; 14 9; 16 15]	**24** For whosoever would save his [1] life shall lose it; but whosoever shall lose his [1] life for my sake [*cp.* 6 22; 18 29; 21 12, 17],	*cp.* 15 21.
shall find it.	shall save it.	the same shall save it.	in this world shall keep it unto life eternal.

Matt. 10 **37** He that loveth father or mother more than me is not worthy of me; and he that loveth son or daughter more

Luke 14 **26** If any man cometh unto me, and hateth not his own father, and mother, and wife, and children, and brethren, and sisters, yea, and his own life also,

than me is not worthy of me [*cp.* 19 27-29]. **38** And he that doth not take his cross and follow after me, is not worthy of me. **39** He that ² findeth his ¹ life shall lose it; and he that ³ loseth his ¹ life for my sake [*see above*] shall find it.	*cp.* 10 28-30.	he cannot be my disciple [*cp.* 18 28-30]. **27** Whosoever doth not bear his own cross, and come after me, cannot be my disciple. **17 33** Whosoever shall seek to gain his ¹ life shall lose it: but whosoever shall lose *his* ¹ *life* shall ² preserve it.
26 For what shall a man be profited, if he shall gain the whole world, and forfeit his ¹ life? or what shall a man give in exchange for his ¹ life? **27** For	**36** For what doth it profit a man, to gain the whole world, and forfeit his ¹ life? **37** For what should a man give in exchange for his ¹ life? **38** For whosoever shall be ashamed of me and of my words in this adulterous and sinful generation [*cp.* 9 19], the Son of man also shall be ashamed of him, when he cometh in *cp.* 10 37. the glory of his Father with the holy angels [*cp.* 13 26, 27; 14 62].	**25** For what is a man profited, if he gain the whole world, and lose or forfeit his own self? **26** For whosoever shall be ashamed of me and of my words, *cp.* 9 41; 11 29. of him shall the Son of man be ashamed, when he cometh in his own glory [*cp.* 9 32; 24 26], and *the glory* of the Father, and of the holy angels [*cp.* 21 27].

cp. 12 39, 45; 16 4; 17 17. the Son of man shall come in *cp.* 19 28; 25 31. the glory of his Father with his angels [*cp.* 24 30, 31; 25 31; 26 64: *also* 13 41, 49]; and then shall he render unto every man according to his ⁴ deeds [25 31-46].		

Matt. 10 **32** Every one therefore who shall confess ⁵ me before men, ⁶ him will I also confess before my Father which is in heaven [*cp.* 5 16, 45; 6 1, 9; 7 11, 21; 12 50; 16 17; 18 10, 14, 19: *also* 5 48; 6 14, 26, 32; 15 13; 18 35; 23 9]. **33** But whosoever shall deny me before men, him will I also deny before my Father which is in heaven [*see above*].	*cp.* 11 25, 26.	Luke 12 **8** Every one who shall confess ³ me before men, ⁴ him shall the Son of man also confess before *cp.* 11 13. the angels of God [*cp.* 15 10]: **9** but he that denieth me in the presence of men shall be denied in the presence of the angels of God [*see above*].

28 Verily I say unto you, There be some of them that stand here [*cp.* 27 47; *also* 26 73], which shall in no wise taste of death, till they see [*cp.* 26 64: *also* 10 23; 23 36; 24 34] the Son of man coming in his [*cp.* 20 21] kingdom [*see verse* 27].	**9 1** And he said unto them, Verily I say unto you, There be some here of them that stand by [*cp.* 11 5; 14 47; 15 35: *also* 14 69, 70; 15 39], which shall in no wise taste of death, till they see [*cp.* 14 62: *also* 13 30] the kingdom of God come with power.	**27** But I tell you of a truth [*cp.* 12 44; 21 3], There be some of them that stand here [*cp.* 19 24], which shall in no wise taste of death, till they see *cp.* 11 51; 21 32. the kingdom of God. *cp.* 22 29-30; 23 42.	*cp.* 12 29. *cp.* 8 51, 52. *cp.* 1 51. *cp.* 18 36.

¹ Or, *soul* ² Or, *found* ³ Or, *lost* ⁴ Gr. *doing.* ⁵ Gr. *in me.* ⁶ Gr. *in him.*	¹ Or, *soul*	¹ Or, *soul* ² Gr. *save it alive.* ³ Gr. *in me.* ⁴ Gr. *in him.* ¹ Or, *soul*

§ 126. The Transfiguration

Matt. 17 1-8	Mark 9 2-8	Luke 9 28-36	
1 And after six days Jesus taketh with him Peter, and James, and John his brother, and bringeth them up into a high mountain [*cp.* 5 1; 14 23; 15 29; 28 16] apart [*cp.* 17 19; 20 17; 24 3]:	**2** And after six days Jesus taketh with him Peter, and James, and John, and bringeth them up into a high mountain [*cp.* 3 13; 6 46] apart [*cp.* 4 10, 34; 6 31, 32; 9 28; 13 3] by themselves:	**28** And it came to pass about eight [*cp.* 1 59; 2 21] days after these sayings, he took with him Peter and John and James, and went up into the mountain [*cp.* 6 12] *cp.* 9 10; 10 23.	*cp.* 20 26. *cp.* Mat 37: M 29; 5 3 3; 14 Luke 8 *cp.* 6 3, 15.

cp. 14 23; 19 13; 26 36, 39, 42, 44: *also* 11 25-26.

2 and he was transfigured before them: and his face   did shine as the sun, and his garments became white [*cp.* 28 3] as the light.

3 And behold, there appeared unto them   Moses and Elijah talking with him.

cp. 16 21; 20 18.

cp. 26 40, 43.

cp. 19 28; 25 31

4 And

Peter [*cp.* 14 28; 15 15; 16 22; 18 21; 19 27; 26 33: *also* 16 16; 17 24] answered, and said unto Jesus, Lord [*cp.* 8 25; 17 15; 20 30, 33: *and* 7 21; 8 2, 6, 8, 21; *etc.*], *cp.* 26 25, 49: *also* 23 7, 8.

it is good for us to be here: if thou wilt, I will make here three ¹ tabernacles; one for thee, and one for Moses, and one for Elijah.

verse 6

5 While he was yet speaking [*cp.* 12 46; 26 47], behold, a bright cloud overshadowed them: *verse 6*

and behold,   a voice   out of the cloud [*cp.* 3 17], saying, This is my beloved Son [*cp.* 3 17; 12 18: *also* 4 3; *etc.*], in whom I am well pleased [*cp.* 3 17: *also* 11 26; 12 18]; hear ye him. **6** And when the disciples heard it, they fell on their face, and were sore afraid [*cp.* 9 8; 27 54; 28 4, 8]. **7** And Jesus came and touched them [*cp.* 8 3, 15; 9 18, 25, 29; 14 31; 19 13, 15; 20 34: *also* 9 20; 14 36] and said, Arise [*cp.* 9 5, 6; 26 46], and

---

cp. 1 35; 6 46; 14 32, 35, 39.

and he was transfigured before them:

3 and his garments became glistering, exceeding white [*cp.* 16 5];   so as no fuller on earth can whiten them. **4** And   there appeared unto them Elijah with Moses: and they were talking with Jesus.

cp. 10 33.

cp. 14 37, 40.

cp. 10 37.

5 And

Peter [*cp.* 8 32; 10 28; 11 21; 14 29: *also* 8 29]   answereth and saith to Jesus, *cp.* 7 28.

Rabbi [*cp.* 11 21; 14 45: *and* 10 51],

it is good for us to be here: and   let us make   three ¹ tabernacles; one for thee, and one for Moses, and one for Elijah. **6** For he wist not what to answer [*cp.* 14 40]; for they became sore afraid [*cp.* 4 41; 9 32; 10 32: *also* 5 15, 33; 16 8]. **7** And *cp.* 5 35; 14 43. there came a cloud overshadowing them: *verse 6*

and   there came a voice   out of the cloud [*cp.* 1 11],   This is my beloved Son [*cp.* 1 11; 12 6: *also* 1 1; *etc.*]:

cp. 1 11. hear ye him.

verse 6

cp. 1 31, 41; 5 23, 41; 6 2, 5; 7 33; 8 22, 23, 25; 9 27; 10 13, 16: *also* 3 10; 5 27; 6 56. *cp.* 2 9, 11; 3 3; 5 41; 14 42.

---

to pray [*cp.* 5 16; 6 12; 22 41, 44: *also* 10 21]. **29** And as he was praying [*cp.* 3 21; 9 18; 11 1],   the fashion of his countenance was altered,   and his raiment *became* white *and* dazzling [*cp.* 24 4].

30 And behold, there

talked with him two men, which were Moses and Elijah; **31** who appeared in glory, and spake of his ¹ decease which he was about to accomplish at Jerusalem [*cp.* 9 51; 13 33; 18 31]. **32** Now Peter and they that were with him were heavy with sleep [*cp.* 22 45]: but ² when they were fully awake, they saw his glory [*cp.* 9 26; 24 26], and the two men that stood with him. **33** And it came to pass, as they were parting from him, Peter [*cp.* 8 45; 12 41; 18 28: *also* 5 8; 9 20]   said unto Jesus, *cp.* 18 41: *and* 5 8, 12; 6 46; 7 6; 9 54, 59, 61; *etc.*   Master [*cp.* 8 24; 9 49: *and* 5 5; 8 45; 17 13], it is good for us to be here: and   let us make   three ³ tabernacles; one for thee, and one for Moses, and one for Elijah: not knowing what he said.

verse 34

34 And while he said these things [*cp.* 8 49; 22 47, 60], there came a cloud and overshadowed them: and they feared [*cp.* 8 25; 9 45; 24 5, 37: *also* 1 12, 65; 2 9; 5 26; 7 16; 8 35, 37, 47] as they entered into the cloud. **35** And   a voice came out of the cloud [*cp.* 3 22], saying, This is ⁴ my   Son [*cp.* 3 22; 20 13: *also* 1 35; *etc.*], my chosen [*cp.* 23 35]: *cp.* 3 22: *also* 2 14; 10 21; 12 32.   hear ye him.

verse 34

cp. 4 40; 5 13; 7 14; 8 54; 13 13; 14 4; 18 15; 22 51: *also* 6 19; 7 39; 8 44. *cp.* 5 23, 24; 6 8; 7 14; 8 54.

---

cp. 11 41; 12 27-28; 17 1-26.

cp. 20 12.

cp. 1 14; 2 11; 12 41; 17 5, 22, 24. *cp.* 13 36, 37; 21 21: *also* 6 68. *cp.* 4 11, 15, 19, 49; 5 7; *etc.* *cp.* 1 38, 49; 3 2; *etc.*: *and* 20 16.

cp. 12 28. *cp.* 1 14, 18, 34; *etc.*

cp. 9 6; 20 17.

cp. 5 8; 14 31.

be not afraid [*cp.* 14 27; 28 10]. **8** And lifting up their eyes,	*cp.* 6 50. **8** And suddenly looking round about [*cp.* 3 5, 34; 5 32; 10 23; 11 11],	**36** And	*cp.* 6 20.
		cp. 6 10. when the voice **5** came,	
they saw no one, save Jesus only.	they saw no one any more, save Jesus only with themselves.	Jesus was found alone. And they held their peace, and told no man in those days any of the things which they had seen.	
cp. 17 9.	*cp.* 9 9.		
[1] Or, *booths*	Or, *booths*	[1] Or, *departure* [2] Or, *having remained awake* [3] Or, *booths* [4] Many ancient authorities read *my beloved Son.* See Matt. 17 5; Mark 9 7. [5] Or, *was past*	

Matt. 17 5 ‖ Mark 9 7 ‖ Luke 9 35: *cp.* Ps. 2 7; Is. 42 1; Deut. 18 15.

§ 127. A Question about Elijah

Matt. 17 9-13	**Mark 9** 9-13		
9 And as they were coming down from the mountain, Jesus commanded them, saying, Tell the vision to no man [*cp.* 16 20: *also* 8 4; 9 30; 12 16], until the Son of man be risen from the dead [*cp.* 16 21; 17 23; 20 19; 26 32; 27 63, 64; 28 6].	**9** And as they were coming down from the mountain, he charged them that they should tell no man [*cp.* 8 30: *also* 1 25, 34, 44; 3 12; 5 43; 7 36; 8 26] what things they had seen, save when the Son of man should have risen again from the dead [*cp.* 8 31; 9 31; 10 34; 14 28]. **10** And they	**9** 37 *cp.* 9 36 *and* 9 21: *also* 4 35, 41; 5 14; 8 56.	
cp. 15 16; 16 8-12.	kept the saying, questioning among themselves [*cp.* 4 13; 6 52; 7 18; 8 17-21; 9 32: *also* 16 14] what the rising again from the dead should mean.	*cp.* 9 22; 13 32; 18 33; 24 7, 26, 46.	*cp.* 2 19-22.
10 And his disciples asked him, saying, Why then say the scribes that Elijah must first come? **11** And he answered and said, Elijah indeed cometh, and shall restore all things:	**11** And they asked him, saying, [1] The scribes [*cp.* 12 35] say that Elijah must first [*cp.* 13 10] come. **12** And he said unto them, Elijah indeed cometh first,	*cp.* 2 50; 9 45; 18 34.	*cp.* 3 10; 4 33; 8 27, 43; 10 6; 11 13; 12 16; *etc.*
cp. 21 42; 26 24, 31, 54, 56.	and restoreth all things: and how is it written [*cp.* 12 10; 14 21, 27, 49] of the Son of man, that he should	*cp.* 17 25; 21 9.	
verse 12 **12** but I say unto you, that Elijah is come already, and they knew him not, but did unto him whatsoever they listed. Even so shall the Son of man also suffer of them [*cp.* 16 21-23; *etc.*]. **13** Then understood the disciples [*cp.* 16 12] that he spake unto them of John the Baptist [*cp.* 11 10, 14: *also* 3 3, 4].	suffer many things and be set at nought [*cp.* 8 31-33; *etc.*]? **13** But I say unto you, that Elijah is come, and they have also done unto him whatsoever they listed, even as it is written of him. *verse* 12	*cp.* 18 31; 20 17; 22 37; 24 25-27, 44-46. *cp.* 9 22; *etc.*: *also* 23 11.	*cp.* 5 39; 13 18; 15 25; 17 12. *cp.* 2 19-22; 3 14; 12 32-33.
	cp. 1 2-3, 6.	*cp.* 1 17, 76; 7 27.	*cp.* 1 21, 23; 3 28.
	[1] Or, How is it *that the scribes say . . . come?*		

Matt. 17 10, 11 ‖ Mark 9 11 12: *cp.* Mal. 4 5.

§ 128. The Healing of an Epileptic Boy

Matt. 17 14-20 (21)	**Mark 9** 14-29	**Luke 9** 37-43a	
		37 And it came to pass, on the next day, when they were come down from the mountain,	
17 9 **14** And when they were come to the multitude,	9 9 **14** And when they came to the disciples, they saw a great multitude about them,	a great multitude	

there came to him a man,
kneeling
to him [cp. 8 2; 9 18; 14 33;
15 25; 20 20], and saying,
15 Lord [cp. 8 25; 17 4;
20 30, 33: and 7 21; 8 2, 6, 8,
21; 9 28; etc.],
cp. 8 19; 12 38; 19 16; 22
16, 24, 36.
have mercy
[cp. 9 27; 15 22; 20 30, 31]
on my son: for he is

epileptic [cp. 4 24], and
suffereth grievously:
cp. 9 32-34; 12 22; 15 30-31:
also 11 5.

for oft-
times he falleth into the fire,
and oft-times into the water.

16 And I brought him to thy
disciples,
cp. 10 1, 8.
and they could not cure him.
17 And Jesus answered
and said, O faithless and
perverse generation [cp. 12 39,
45; 16 4], how long shall I be
with you? how long shall I
bear with you? bring him
hither   to me
[cp. 14 18].

verse 15

cp. 15 25.

cp. 8 2; 9 28.
verse 20

and scribes questioning with
them [cp. 8 11; 9 16; 12 28].
15 And straightway all the
multitude, when they saw
him, were greatly amazed,
and running to him saluted
him. **16** And he asked them,
What question ye with them
[see above]? **17** And
                one of the
multitude
[cp. 1 40; 3 11; 5 6, 22,
33; 7 25; 10 17] answered
him,
        cp. 7 28.
          1 Master [cp. 4
38; 9 38; 10 17, 20, 35;
12 14, 19, 32; 13 1],
    I brought unto thee
        cp. 10 47, 48.
    my son,

which hath a dumb [cp. 7
32-37] spirit; **18** and wheresoever it taketh him,
                        it
2 dasheth   him down:
    verse 22

and he foameth, and grindeth
his teeth, and pineth away:

and I spake   to thy
disciples that they should cast
it out [cp. 3 15; 6 7, 13];
and they were not able.
19 And he answereth them
and saith, O faithless
    generation [cp. 8 38],
        how long shall I be
with you? how long shall I
bear with you? bring him
            unto me.
    20 And
        they brought
him unto him: and when he
saw him, straightway the
spirit
    3 tare him grievously
[cp. 1 26]; and he fell on the
ground, and wallowed foam-
ing. **21** And he asked his
father, How long time is it
since this hath come unto
him? And he said, From a
child. **22** And oft-times it
hath cast him both into the
fire and into the waters, to
destroy him: but if thou
canst do anything, have compassion on us, and help us.
23 And Jesus said unto him,
If thou canst [cp. 1 40; 6 5-6]!
All things are possible [cp. 10
27; 14 36] to him that
believeth. **24** Straightway
the father of the child cried
out, and said 4, I believe;
help thou mine unbelief.

met   him.

38 And behold,
        a man
from the multitude
    [cp. 5 8, 12; 8 28,
41, 47; 17 16] cried, saying,
        [cp. 18 41: and
5 8, 12; 6 46; 7 6; 9 54, 59,
61; etc.] 1 Master [cp. 7
40; 10 25; 11 45; 12 13;
18 18; 19 39; 20 21, 28, 39;
21 7], I beseech thee to look
    cp. 17 13; 18 38, 39.
upon my son; for he is mine
only [cp. 7 12; 8 42] child:

39 and behold,
    a [cp. 11 14: also
7 22] spirit
        taketh him, and he
suddenly crieth out; and it
2 teareth him

that he foameth,

and it hardly departeth from
him, bruising him sorely.
40 And I besought   thy
disciples   to cast
it out [cp. 9 1, 6; 10 9, 17];
and they could not.
41 And Jesus answered
and said, O faithless and
perverse generation [cp. 11 29],
        how long shall I be
with you, and
bear with you? bring
hither thy son.
    42 And as he was
yet a coming,
            the
3 devil 4 dashed him down,
and 5 tare him grievously
[cp. 4 35].

cp. 5 12.
cp. 1 37; 18 27.

cp. 4 11, 15,
19, 49; 5
7; etc.
cp. 1 38;
20 16.

cp. 14 9.

Matthew

18 And Jesus rebuked [cp. 8 26] him;

and the ¹ devil went out from him:

cp. 28 4.

cp. 9 25; 14 31: also 8 3, 15; 9 18, 29; 17 7; 19 13, 15; 20 34.
and the boy was cured from that hour [cp. 8 13; 9 22; 15 28].

cp. 8 27; 9 33; 12 23; 15 31; 21 20; 27 14: and 7 28; etc.

cp. 13 36; 17 25.
19 Then came the disciples to Jesus [cp. 5 1; 13 10, 36; 14 15; 15 12, 23; 18 1; 24 1, 3; 26 17] apart [cp. 17 1; 20 17; 24 3], and said, Why could not we cast it out? 20 And he saith unto them, Because of your little faith [cp. 6 30; 8 26; 14 31; 16 8]: for verily I say unto you, If ye have faith as a grain of mustard seed [cp. 13 31], ye shall say unto this mountain, Remove hence to yonder place; and it shall remove; and nothing shall be impossible unto you [cp. 19 26].²

21 21 And Jesus answered and said unto them,
Verily I say unto you, If ye have faith, and doubt not, ye shall not only do what is done to the fig tree, but even if ye shall say unto this mountain, Be thou taken up and cast into the sea,

it shall be done.

22 And all things, whatsoever

Mark

25 And when Jesus saw that a multitude came running together, he rebuked [cp. 1 25; 3 12; 4 39] the unclean spirit, saying unto him, Thou dumb and deaf spirit [see verse 17], I command thee, come out of him [cp. 1 25; 5 8], and enter no more into him. 26 And having cried out, and ³ torn him much, he came out [cp. 1 26]: and the child became as one dead; insomuch that the more part said, He is dead [cp. 5 35]. 27 But Jesus took him by the hand, and raised him up [cp. 1 31; 5 41: also 1 41; 5 23; 6 2, 5; 7 33; 8 22, 23, 25; 10 13, 16]; and he arose.

cp. 2 12; 5 20, 42; 6 51; 7 37; 10 32; 15 5; 16 5, 8: and 1 22; etc.
28 And when he was come into the house [cp. 7 17; 9 33; 10 10], his disciples
cp. 6 35.

asked him privately [cp. 4 10, 34; 6 31, 32; 9 2; 13 3], ⁵ saying, We could not cast it out. 29 And he said unto them,

cp. 4 40.

cp. 4 31.

verse 23
This kind can come out by nothing, save by prayer ⁶.

11 22 And Jesus answering saith unto them, Have faith in God. 23 Verily I say unto you,

Whosoever shall say unto this mountain, Be thou taken up and cast into the sea; and shall not doubt in his heart, but shall believe that what he saith cometh to pass; he shall have it.
24 Therefore I say unto you, All things whatsoever

Luke

But Jesus rebuked [cp. 4 35, 39, 41; 8 24] the unclean spirit,

cp. 4 35.

cp. 4 35.

cp. 7 12; 8 49.

cp. 8 54: also 4 40; 5 13; 7 14; 13 13; 14 4; 18 15; 22 51.
and healed [cp. 6 19; 9 2, 11; 14 4; 22 51] the boy,

and gave him back to his father [cp. 7 15]. 43 And they were all astonished [cp. 5 9, 26; 8 25, 56; 11 14; 24 12, 41: and 2 47, 48; 4 22; etc.] at the majesty of God.

cp. 9 12.

cp. 9 10; 10 23.

17 6 And the Lord said,
cp. 12 28: and 8 25; 17 5; 22 32.
If ye have faith as a grain of mustard seed [cp. 13 19], ye would say unto this sycamine tree,

cp. 1 37; 18 27.

Be thou rooted up, and be thou planted in the sea; and

it would have obeyed you.

(right margin cross-references)
cp. 9 6.
cp. 4 53.
cp. 7 15, 21, 46.
cp. 3 12; 6 64; 14 10.

ye shall ask [*cp.* 7 7; 18 19] in prayer, believing, ye shall receive.	ye pray and ask for, believe that ye have received them, and ye shall have them.	*cp.* 11 9.	*cp.* 14 13, 14; 15 7, 16; 16 23, 24.

[1] Gr. *demon.* [3] Many authorities, some ancient, insert verse 21 *But this kind goeth not out save by prayer and fasting.* See Mark 9 29.	[1] Or, *Teacher* [2] Or, *rendeth him* [3] Or, *convulsed* [4] Many ancient authorities add *with tears.* [5] Or, *How is it that we could not cast it out?* [6] Many ancient authorities add *and fasting.*	[1] Or, *Teacher* [3] Gr. *demon.* [5] Or, *convulsed*	[2] Or, *convulseth* [4] Or, *rent him*

Matt. 17 17 || Mark 9 19 || Luke 9 41 : *cp.* Deut. 32 5.

(xi) Events in Galilee V (§§ 129-133)

§ 129. **The Second Prediction of the Passion and Resurrection**

[*Cp.* Matt. 16 21-23 || Mark 8 31-33 || Luke 9 22; Matt. 20 17-19 || Mark 10 32-34 || Luke 18 31-34: *also* Matt. 17 9, 12; 20 28; 26 2, 12, 18, 24, 32, 45: Mark 9 9, 12; 10 45; 14 8, 21, 28, 41: Luke 13 32-33; 17 25; 22 22; 24 7, *and* 26, 44, 46: John 2 19-22; 3 14; 12 32-33]

Matt. 17 22-23	Mark 9 30-32	Luke 9 43b-45	
22 And while they [1] abode in Galilee,	**30** And they went forth from thence, and passed through Galilee; and he would not that any man should know it [*cp.* 7 24: *also* 1 25; *etc.*].		
cp. 8 4; *etc.*	**31** For	*cp.* 24 6-7.	
cp. 8 27; 9 33; 12 23; 15 31; 21 20; 27 14: *also* 7 28; 13 54; 19 25; 22 22, 33.	*cp.* 2 12; 5 20, 42; 6 51; 7 37; 10 32; 15 5; 16 5, 8: *also* 1 22, 27; 6 2; 10 24, 26; 11 18; 12 17.	*cp.* 4 35; *etc.* But while all were marvelling [*cp.* 5 9, 26; 8 25, 56; 11 14; 24 12, 41: *also* 2 47, 48; 4 22, 32, 36; 20 26] at all the things which he did, he	*cp.* 7 15, 21, 46.
Jesus said unto them,	he taught his disciples, and said unto them,	said unto his disciples, **44** Let these words sink into your ears: for the Son of man	
The Son of man shall be delivered up into the hands of men; **23** and they shall kill him, and	The Son of man is delivered up into the hands of men, and they shall kill him; and when he	shall be delivered up into the hands of men.	
cp. 27 63.	is killed, after three days [*cp.* 8 31; 10 34: *also* 14 58; 15 29]		*cp.* 2 19.
the third day [*cp.* 16 21; 20 19: *also* 12 40; 26 61; 27 40, 64] he shall	he shall rise again	*cp.* 9 22; 13 32; 18 33; 24 7, 46: *also* 24 21.	
cp. 17 9.	[*cp.* 8 31; 9 9; 10 34; 16 9].	*cp.* 18 33; 24 7, 46.	*cp.* 20 9.
be raised up [*cp.* 16 21; 20 19; 26 32; 27 63, 64; 28 6, 7].	*cp.* 14 28; 16 6, 14.	*cp.* 9 22; 24 6, 34.	*cp.* 2 19-22; 21 14.
And they *cp.* 15 16; 16 8-12.	**32** But they understood not the saying [*cp.* 4 13; 6 52; 7 18; 8 17-21; 9 10],	**45** But they understood not this saying [*cp.* 2 50; 18 34], and it was concealed from them, that they should not perceive it: and they were	*cp.* 10 6; 12 16: *also* 3 10; 4 33; 8 27, 43; 11 13; 13 7, 28, 36; 14 5-10, 22; 16 17-18.
cp. 17 6: *also* 9 8; 27 54; 28 4, 8.	and were afraid [*cp.* 4 41; 9 6; 10 32: *also* 5 15, 33; 16 8] to ask him.	afraid [*cp.* 8 25; 9 34; 24 5, 37: *also* 1 12, 65; 2 9; 5 26; 7 16; 8 35, 37, 47] to ask him about this saying.	*cp.* 16 6, 20, 22.
were exceeding sorry [*cp.* 18 31: *also* 26 22 *and* 37].	*cp.* 14 19.	*cp.* 22 45.	

[1] Some ancient authorities read *were gathering themselves together.*

§ 130. **A Question about Payment of the Temple-Tax**

Matt. 17 24-27	
24 And when they were come to Capernaum, they that received the [1] half-shekel came to Peter, and said, Doth not your [2] master pay the [1] half-shekel? **25** He saith, Yea. And	9 33

when he came into the house [cp. 13 36], Jesus spake first to him, saying, What thinkest thou [cp. 18 12; 21 28; 22 17, 42; 26 66], Simon [cp. 16 17]? the kings of the earth, from whom do they receive toll or tribute? from their sons, or from strangers? **26** And when he said, From strangers, Jesus said unto him, Therefore the sons are free. **27** But, lest we cause them to stumble, go thou to the sea, and cast a hook, and take up the fish that first cometh up; and when thou hast opened his mouth, thou shalt find a ³ shekel: that take, and give unto them for me and thee.	9 33: cp. 7 17; 9 28; 10 10. cp. 14 37.	cp. 22 31.	cp. 11 56. cp. 1 42; 21 15, 16, 17.

¹ Gr. didrachma.   ² Or, teacher   ³ Gr stater.

Matt. 17 24: cp. Exod. 30 13; 38 26.

§ 131. **Rivalry among the Disciples and Sayings of Rebuke** (Mark and Luke)
A Question about Who is the Greatest and Sayings about Little Ones (Matt.)

[Cp. Matt. 20 20-28; Mark 10 35-45; Luke 22 24-27]

Matt. 18 1-14	**Mark 9** 33-50	**Luke 9** 46-50	
17 24	**33** And they came to Capernaum: and when he was in the house [cp. 7 17; 9 28; 10 10] he asked them, What were ye reasoning in the way? **34** But they held their peace: for they had disputed one with another in the way,	**46** And there arose a reasoning among them,	
17 25: cp. 13 36.		cp. 7 21; 10 21; 13 31. cp. 9 12.	
1 In that hour [cp. 26 55] came the disciples unto Jesus [cp. 5 1; 13 10, 36; 14 15; 15 12, 23; 17 19; 24 1,3; 26 17], saying, Who then is ¹ greatest in the kingdom of heaven [cp. 5 19; 18 4: also 11 11]? **2** And he called	cp. 6 35. who was the ¹ greatest.	which of them should be ¹ greatest [cp. 22 24].	
	35 And he sat down, and called the twelve; and he saith unto them, If any man would be first, he shall be last of all, and minister of all. **10 43** But whosoever would become great among you, shall be your ² minister: **44** and whosoever would be first among you, shall be ³ servant of all.	cp. 7 28. verse 48	
20 26 But whosoever would become great among you shall be your ² minister; **27** and whosoever would be first among you shall be your ³ servant. **23 11** But he that is ¹ greatest among you shall be your ⁴ servant.		**22 26** But he that is the greater among you, let him become as the younger; and he that is chief, as he that doth serve.	cp. 13 2 ff.
cp. 9 4; 12 25; 16 8.	**36** And	**47** But when Jesus saw the reasoning of their heart [cp. 5 22; 6 8; 11 17], he took a little child, and set him by his side, **48** and	cp. 1 48; 2 24, 25; 4 19, 29; 5 6, 42; etc.
to him a little child, and set him in the midst of them, **3** and said,	cp. 2 8; 8 17. he took a little child, and set him in the midst of them: and taking him in his arms [cp. 10 16], he said unto them,	said unto them,	
Verily I say unto you, Except ye turn, and become as little children,	**10 15** Verily I say unto you, Whosoever shall not receive the kingdom of God as a little child,	**18 17** Verily I say unto you, Whosoever shall not receive the kingdom of God as a little child,	**3 3** Verily, verily, I say unto thee, Except a man be born ¹ anew, he cannot see the kingdom of God. . . . **5** Verily, verily, I say unto thee, Except a man be born of water and the Spirit, he cannot
ye shall in no wise enter [cp. 5 20; 7 21; 19 23, 24; 21 31; 23 13:	he shall in no wise enter [cp. 9 47; 10 23, 24, 25: also 9 43,	he shall in no wise enter [cp. 18 24, 25: also 11 52; 13 24; 24 26]	enter [cp. 10 1, 2, 9]

also 7 13; 18 8, 9; 19 17; 25 21, 23] into the kingdom of heaven. **4** Whosoever therefore shall humble himself [*cp.* 23 12] as this little child, the same is the ¹ greatest in the kingdom of heaven [*cp.* 5 19; 18 1: *also* 11 11]. **5** And whoso shall receive one such little child in my name [*cp.* 18 20; 24 5: *also* 7 22] receiveth me:

10 **40** He that receiveth you receiveth me, and he that receiveth me receiveth him that sent me.

cp. 11 11.

cp. 8 19; 12 38; 19 16; 22 16, 24, 36.

cp. 7 22.

cp. 19 14.

cp. 7 22.

cp. 12 30.   10 **42** And whosoever shall give to drink unto one of these little ones a cup of cold water only, in the name of a disciple, verily I say unto you, he shall in no wise lose his reward [*cp.* 25 34-40].

verse 7

6 but whoso shall cause one of these little ones which believe on me to stumble, it is profitable for him that ⁵ a great millstone should be hanged about his neck, and *that* he should be sunk in the depth of the sea.

7 Woe unto the world because of occasions of stumbling ! for it must needs

---

45] therein.

37 Whosoever shall receive one of such little children in my name [*cp.* 9 38, 39; 13 6; 16 17], receiveth me: and whosoever receiveth me, receiveth not me, but him that sent me.

verse 35

38 John said unto him, ⁴ Master [*cp.* 4 38; 9 17: *also* 10 17, 20, 35; 12 14, 19, 32; 13 1],

we saw one casting out ⁵ devils in thy name [*see above*]: and we forbade him, because he followed not us. **39** But Jesus said, Forbid him not [*cp.* 10 14]: for there is no man which shall do a ⁶ mighty work in my name [*see above*], and be able quickly to speak evil of me. **40** For he that is not against us is for us. **41** For whosoever shall give you a cup of water to drink,

⁷ because ye are Christ's, verily I say unto you, he shall in no wise lose his reward.

cp. 14 21.

42 And whosoever shall cause one of these little ones that believe ⁸ on me to stumble, it were better for him if ⁹ a great millstone were hanged about his neck, and he were cast into the sea.

---

therein.

cp. 14 11; 18 14.

cp. 7 28.

Whosoever shall receive this little child in my name [*cp.* 9 49; 10 17; 21 8; 24 47] receiveth me: and whosoever shall receive me receiveth him that sent me:

10 **16** He that heareth you heareth me; and he that rejecteth you rejecteth me; and he that rejecteth me rejecteth him that sent me.

for he that is ² least [*cp.* 7 28] among you all, the same is great.

49 And John answered and said, [*cp.* 7 40; 9 38; 10 25; 11 45; 12 13; 18 18; 19 39; 20 21, 28, 39; 21 7] Master [*cp.* 8 24; 9 33: *also* 5 5; 8 45; 17 13], we saw one casting out ³ devils in thy name [*see above*]; and we forbade him, because he followeth not with us. **50** But Jesus said unto him, Forbid *him* not [*cp.* 18 16]:

for he that is not against you is for you [*cp.* 11 23].

17 **1** And he said unto his disciples, It is impossible but that occasions of stumbling should come: but woe unto him [*cp.* 22 22: *also* 11 42 *ff.*], through whom they come !

² It were well for him if a millstone were hanged about his neck, and he were thrown into the sea, rather than that he should cause one of these little ones to stumble.

---

into the kingdom of God.

cp. 14 13, 14, 26; 15 16; 16 23, 24, 26.

12 **44** He that believeth on me, believeth not on me, but on him that sent me.

13 **20** He that receiveth whomsoever I send receiveth me; and he that receiveth me receiveth him that sent me.

¹ Or, *from above*

cp. 1 38; 20 16.

cp. 14 13, 14, 26; 15 16; 16 23, 24, 26.

cp. 14 13, 14, 26; 15 16; 16 23, 24, 26.

be that the occasions come; but woe to that man [cp. 26 24: also 23 13 ff.] through whom the occasion cometh!

8 And if thy hand or thy foot causeth thee to stumble, cut it off, and cast it from thee: it is good for thee to enter [see verse 3 above] into life maimed or halt,

rather than having two hands or two feet to be cast

into the eternal [cp. 25 41: also 13 42, 50] fire.

9 And if thine eye causeth thee to stumble, pluck it out, and cast it from thee: it is good for thee to enter [see verse 3 above] into life with one eye,

rather than having two eyes to be cast into the 6 hell of fire [cp. 5 22: also 5 29, 30; 10 28; 23 15, 33].

10 See that ye despise not one of these little ones; for I say unto you, that in heaven their angels do always behold the face of my Father which is in heaven [cp. 5 16, 45; 6 1, 9; etc.].7

12 How think ye [cp. 17 25; 21 28; 22 17, 42; 26 66]? if any man have a hundred sheep, and one of them be gone astray, doth he not leave the ninety and nine, and go unto the mountains, and seek that which goeth astray?

13 And if so be that he find it, verily I say unto you, he rejoiceth over it

more than over the ninety and nine which have not gone astray.

cp. 14 21.

Matt. **5** 30 And if thy right [cp. 5 29, 39; 27 29] hand causeth thee to stumble, cut it off, and cast it from thee: for it is profitable for thee

that one of thy members should perish, and not thy whole body

go into 6 hell [cp. 5 29; 10 28; 23 15, 33: also 5 22; 18 9]. cp. 3 12.

29 And if thy right [see above] eye causeth thee to stumble, pluck it out, and cast it from thee: for it is profitable for thee

that one of thy members should perish, and not thy whole body

be cast into 6 hell [see above].

cp. 11 25, 26.

17 1

43 And if thy hand cause thee to stumble, cut it off: it is good for thee to enter [cp. 9 45, 47; 10 15, 23, 24, 25] into life maimed, rather than having thy two hands to go into 10 hell,

into the unquenchable fire.11 **45** And if thy foot cause thee to stumble, cut it off: it is good for thee to enter [see verse 43 above] into life halt, rather than having thy two feet to be cast into 10 hell. **47** And if thine eye cause thee to stumble, cast it out: it is good for thee to enter [see verse 43 above] into the kingdom of God with one eye,

rather than having two eyes to be cast into 10 hell; **48** where their worm dieth not, and the fire is not quenched.

cp. 11 13.

Luke **15** 3 And he spake unto them this parable, saying,

4 What man of you, having a hundred sheep, and having lost one of them, doth not leave the ninety and nine in the wilderness, and go after that which is lost, until he find it [cp. 15 8: also 19 10]? 5 And when he hath found it, he layeth it on his shoulders, rejoicing.

6 And when he cometh home, he calleth together his friends and his neighbours, saying unto them, Rejoice with me [cp. 15 9: also 1 58], for I have found my sheep which was lost [cp. 15 9, 24, 32]. 7 I say unto you, that even so there shall be joy in heaven over one sinner that repenteth [cp. 15 10], more than over ninety and nine righteous persons, which need no repentance [cp. 5 32].

Reference columns (Mark parallels)

cp. 6 6; 22 50.

cp. 18 17, 24, 25: also 11 52; 13 24; 24 26.

cp. 12 5.

cp. 3 17.

cp. 18 17, etc., above.

cp. 12 5.

cp. 6 6; 22 50.

cp. 18 17, etc., above.

cp. 12 5.

Far right reference column (Luke)

cp. 18 10.

cp. 3 5: also 10 1, 2, 9.

cp. 3 5: also 10 1, 2, 9.

cp. 18 10.

cp. 3 5: also 10 1, 2, 9.

cp. 11 56.

cp. 10 1 ff.

cp. 6 39.

14 Even so it is not [8] the will of [9] your Father which is in heaven [*cp.* 5 16, 45; 6 1, 9; *etc.*], that one of these little ones should perish.

cp. 11 25, 26.

cp. 11 13.

Matt. 5 **13** Ye are the salt of the earth : but if the salt have lost its savour, wherewith shall it be salted ? it is thenceforth good for nothing,
but to be cast out and trodden under foot of men.
cp. 5 9 ; 10 13.

49 For every one shall be salted with fire [12].   **50** Salt is good : but if the salt have lost its saltness, wherewith will ye season it ?

Have salt in yourselves, and be at peace one with another.

Luke 14 **34** Salt therefore is good : but if even the salt have lost its savour, wherewith shall it be seasoned ? **35** It is fit neither for the land nor for the dunghill : *men* cast it out.
cp. 10 5, 6 : *also* 1 79 ; 2 14, 29 ; 19 38.

cp. 14 27 ; 16 33.

[1] Gr. *greater.*   [2] Or, *servant*
[3] Gr. *bondservant.*   [4] Or, *minister*
[5] Gr. *a millstone turned by an ass.*
[6] Gr. *Gehenna.*
[7] Many authorities, some ancient, insert ver. **11** *For the Son of man came to save that which was lost.* See Luke 19 10.
[8] Gr. *a thing willed before your Father.*
[9] Some ancient authorities read *my.*

[1] Gr. *greater.*   [2] Or, *servant*
[3] Gr. *bondservant.*   [4] Or, *Teacher*
[5] Gr. *demons.*   [6] Gr. *power.*
[7] Gr. *in name that ye are.*
[8] Many ancient authorities omit *on me.*
[9] Gr. *a millstone turned by an ass.*
[10] Gr. *Gehenna.*
[11] Ver. 44 and 46 (which are identical with ver. 48) are omitted by the best ancient authorities.
[12] Many ancient authorities add *and every sacrifice shall be salted with salt.* See Lev. 2 13.

[1] Gr. *greater.*   [2] Gr. *lesser.*
[3] Gr. *demons.*

Mark 9 48 : Is. 66 24. Mark 9 49 : *cp.* Lev. 2 13.

§ 132. The Treatment of a Brother's Fault and the Authority of the Church

Matt. 18 15-20

Luke 17 3-4

15 And if thy brother sin [1] against thee, go, shew him his fault between thee and him alone : if he hear thee, thou hast gained thy brother.

3 Take heed to yourselves : if thy brother sin, rebuke him ;

and if he repent, forgive him [*cp.* 11 4]. **4** And if he sin against thee seven times in the day, and seven times turn again to thee, saying, I repent ; thou shalt forgive him.

cp. 11 25.

18 21

16 But if he hear *thee* not, take with thee one or two more, that at the mouth of two witnesses or three every word may be established. **17** And if he refuse to hear them, tell it unto the [2] church [*cp.* 16 18] : and if he refuse to hear the [2] church also, let him be unto thee as the Gentile [*cp.* 5 47 ; 6 7, 32] and the publican [*cp.* 5 46 ; 9 11 ; 11 19 ; 21 31, 32].

cp. 8 17.

18 Verily I say unto you,

Matt. 16 **19** I will give unto thee the keys of the kingdom of heaven : and whatsoever thou shalt bind on earth shall be bound in heaven : and whatsoever thou shalt loose on earth shall be loosed in heaven.

John 20 **22** And when he had said this, he breathed on them, and saith unto them, Receive ye the [1] Holy Ghost : **23** whose soever sins ye forgive, they are forgiven unto them ; whose soever *sins* ye retain, they are retained.

cp. 2 16.

cp. 12 30: *and* 5 30; 7 34; 15 1; 18 10.

What things soever ye shall bind on earth shall be bound in heaven : and what things soever ye shall loose on earth shall be loosed in heaven.

[1] Or, *Holy Spirit*

19 Again I say unto you, that if two of you shall agree on earth as touching anything that they shall ask, it shall be done for them [*cp.* 7 7 ; 21 22] of my Father which is in heaven [*cp.* 5 16, 45 ; 6 1, 9 ; 7 11, 21 ; 10 32, 33 ; 12 50 ; 16 17 ; 18 10, 14 : *also* 5 48 ; 6 14, 26, 32 ; 15 13 ; 18 35 ; 23 9]. **20** For where two or three are gathered together in my name [*cp.* 18 5 ; 24 5 : *also* 7 22], there am I in the midst of them [*cp.* 28 20].

cp. 11 24.
cp. 11 25, 26.

cp. 9 37, 39 ; 13 6 ; 16 17: *also* 9 38.

cp. 11 9.
cp. 11 13.

cp. 9 48 ; 21 8 : *also* 9 49 ; 10 17 ; 24 47.

cp. 14 13, 14 ; 15 7, 16 ; 16 23, 24.

cp. 14 13, 14, 26 ; 15 16 ; 16 23, 24, 26.

[1] Some ancient authorities omit *against thee.*

[2] Or, *congregation*

Matt. 18 16 : *cp.* Deut. 19 15 ; *also* Num. 35 30.

§ 133. The Obligation to Forgive a Brother and the Parable of the Two Debtors

[Cp. Luke 7 40-48]

Matt. 18 21-35			Luke 17 3-4	
			3 Take heed to yourselves: if thy brother sin, rebuke him; and if he repent, forgive him [cp. 11 4].	
18 15				
21 Then came Peter [cp. 14 28; 15 15; 16 22; 17 4; 19 27; 26 33: also 16 16; 17 24], and said to him, Lord, how oft shall my brother sin against me, and I forgive him [cp. 6 12, 14, 15]? until seven times?	cp. 8 32; 9 5; 10 28; 11 21; 14 29: also 8 29. cp. 11 25.	cp. 8 45; 9 33; 12 41; 18 28: also 5 8; 9 20. he sin against thee seven times in the day, and seven times turn again to thee, saying, I repent; thou shalt forgive him.	**4** And if	cp. 13 36, 37; 21 21: also 6 68.
22 Jesus saith unto him, I say not unto thee, Until seven times; but, Until [1] seventy times seven. **23** Therefore is the kingdom of heaven likened unto a certain king [cp. 22 2 ff.: also 25 34, 40], which would make a reckoning [cp. 25 19] with his [2] servants [cp. 25 14]. **24** And when he had begun to reckon, one was brought unto him, which owed him ten thousand [3] talents [cp. 25 15, etc.]. **25** But forasmuch as he had not wherewith to pay, his lord [cp. 25 18, etc.] commanded him to be sold, and his wife, and children, and all that he had, and payment to be made. **26** The [4] servant therefore fell down and worshipped him, saying, Lord, have patience with me, and I will pay thee all. **27** And the lord of that [4] servant [cp. 24 50; 25 19], being moved with compassion, released him, and forgave him the [5] debt. **28** But that [4] servant went out, and found one of his fellow-servants [cp. 24 49], which owed him a hundred [6] pence: and he laid hold on him, and took him by the throat, saying, Pay what thou owest. **29** So his fellow-servant fell down and besought him, saying, Have patience with me, and I will pay thee. **30** And he would not: but went and cast him into prison, till he should pay that which was due. **31** So when his fellow-servants saw what was done, they were exceeding sorry [cp. 17 23; 26 22], and came and told unto their lord all that was done. **32** Then his lord called him unto him, and saith to him, Thou wicked [4] servant [cp. 25 26: also 24 48], I forgave thee all that debt, because thou besoughtest me: **33** shouldest not thou also have had mercy on thy fellow-servant, even as I had mercy on thee? **34** And his lord was wroth [cp. 22 7], and delivered him to the tormentors, till he should pay all that was due [cp. 5 25, 26]. **35** So shall also my heavenly Father [cp. 5 48; 6 14, 26, 32; 15 13; 23 9: also 5 16, 45; etc.] do unto you, if ye forgive not every one his brother from your hearts [cp. 6 15].	cp. 11 25, 26.	cp. 19 12, 15, 27. cp. 7 42. cp. 12 46. cp. 19 22. cp. 14 21. cp. 12 58, 59. cp. 11 13.		

[1] Or, seventy times and seven
[2] Gr. bondservants.
[3] This talent was probably worth about £240.
[4] Gr. bondservant.
[5] Gr. loan.
[6] The word in the Greek denotes a coin worth about eight pence halfpenny.

D. The Journey to Jerusalem (§§ 134-193)

(i) Events on the Journey I (§§ 134-146)

§ 134. The Start of the Journey and Rejection in a Samaritan Village

[Cp. § 183]

Matt. 19 1	Mark 10 1	Luke 9 51-56
1 And it came to pass when Jesus had finished these words [cp. 7 28; 11 1; 13 53; 26 1],	**1** And	**51** And it came to pass, when cp. 7 1. the days [1] were well-nigh come that he should be received up, he stedfastly set his face to go to Jerusalem

cp. 16 21; 20 17, 18.	*cp.* 10 32, 33.	[*cp.* 9 53; 13 22; 17 11; 19 11, 41: *also* 9 31; 13 33; 18 31],	

he departed from Galilee, and came into the borders of Judæa beyond Jordan;

cp. 10 5.

cp. 10 14.

cp. 20 20.

cp. 9 22; 16 23.

he arose from thence, and cometh into the borders of Judæa and beyond Jordan:

cp. 6 11.

cp. 10 35.

cp. 5 30; 8 33.

52 and sent messengers before his face [*cp.* 10 1]: and they went, and entered into a village [*cp.* 9 56; 10 38; 17 12] of the Samaritans [*cp.* 17 11: *also* 10 33; 17 16], to make ready for him. **53** And they did not receive him [*cp.* 10 10: *also* 9 5], because his face was *as though he were* going to Jerusalem [*see above*]. **54** And when his disciples James and John saw *this*, they said, Lord, wilt thou that we bid fire to come down from heaven, and consume them [2]? **55** But he turned [*cp.* 7 9, 44; 10 23; 14 25; 22 61; 23 28], and rebuked them [3]. **56** And they went to another village [*see verse* 52].

cp. 10 40.

cp. 4 4, 5, 39, 40.

cp. 4 9.

cp. 1 38.

[1] Gr. *were being fulfilled.*   [2] Many ancient authorities add *even as Elijah did.*
[3] Some ancient authorities add *and said, Ye know not what manner of spirit ye are of.* Some, but fewer, add also *For the Son of man came not to destroy men's lives, but to save them.*

Luke 9 54 : *cp.* II Kings 1 10, 12.

§ 135. **Would-be Disciples**

[*Cp.* Matt. 10 37; Luke 14 26]

Matt. 8 18-22		Luke 9 57-62	

18 Now when Jesus saw great multitudes about him [*cp.* 3 7; 5 1; 9 36], he gave commandment to depart unto the other side. **19** And there came [1] a scribe, and said unto him, [2] Master, I will follow thee whithersoever thou goest. **20** And Jesus saith unto him, The foxes have holes, and the birds of the heaven *have* [3] nests ; but the Son of man hath not where to lay his head. **21** And another of the disciples

verse 22

said unto him, Lord, suffer me first   to go and bury my father. **22** But Jesus saith unto him, Follow me [*cp.* 4 19 ; 9 9 ; 16 24 ; 19 21]; and leave the dead to bury their own dead.

[1] Gr. *one scribe.*   [2] Or, *Teacher*
[3] Gr. *lodging-places.*

verse 19

57 And as they went in the way,

cp. 6 5.

a certain man said unto him,   I will follow thee [*cp. verse* 61] whithersoever thou goest. **58** And Jesus said unto him, The foxes have holes, and the birds of the heaven *have* [1] nests ; but the Son of man hath not where to lay his head. **59** And he said unto another, Follow me [*cp.* 5 27; 9 23; 18 22]. But he said,   Lord, suffer me first [*cp. verse* 61] to go and bury my father. **60** But he said unto him,

verse 59

Leave the dead to bury their own dead ; but go thou and publish abroad the kingdom of God. **61** And another

cp. 1 17; 2 14; 8 34; 10 21.

see above.

cp. 1 43; 12 26; 21 19, 22.

see above.

also said, I will follow thee [*cp. verse* 57], Lord ; but first suffer me [*cp. verse* 59] to bid farewell [*cp.* 14 33] to them that are at my house. **62** But Jesus said unto him, No man, having put his hand to the plough, and looking back, is fit for the kingdom of God.

[1] Gr. *lodging-places.*

§ 136. **The Mission of the Seventy**

Matt. 10 1, 5-8; 9 37-38; 10 16, 9-15; 11 21-24	Mark 6 7-11	Luke 9 1-5	Luke 10 1-16	
1 And	**7** And	**1** And	**1** Now after these things the Lord [*cp.* 7 13, 19; 10 39, 41; 11 39; 12 42; 13 15; 17 5, 6; 18 6; 19 8; 22 61; 24 3, 34]	*cp.* 4 1; 6 23; 11 2; 20 2, 18, 20, 25; 21 7, 12.
he	he	he		
	cp. 16 19, 20.			
called unto him his twelve disciples,	called unto him the twelve [*cp.* 3 13, 14],	called the twelve [*cp.* 6 13] together,	appointed seventy [1] others,	
and		and		
gave them	*cp.* 5 30.	gave them power [*cp.*		

[Column 1 — Matthew]

authority over unclean spirits [cp. 10 8 ; 17 16], to cast them out, and to heal all manner of disease and all manner of sickness. **5** These twelve Jesus sent forth, cp. 21 1.

verses 7 and 8

and charged them, saying, Go not into *any* way of the Gentiles, and enter not into any city of the Samaritans : **6** but go rather to the lost sheep of the house of Israel [cp. 15 24 : *also* 9 36]. **7** And as ye go, preach, saying, The kingdom of heaven is at hand [cp. 3 2; 4 17: *also* 12 28]. **8** Heal the sick, raise the dead, cleanse the lepers, cast out [1] devils : freely ye received, freely give. **9 37** The harvest truly is plenteous, but the labourers are few. **38** Pray ye therefore the Lord of the harvest, that he send forth labourers into his harvest. **10 16** Behold, I send you forth as sheep in the midst of wolves: **9** Get you

no gold, nor silver, nor brass in your [2] purses ; **10** no wallet for *your* journey, neither two coats, nor shoes, nor staff :

for the labourer is worthy of his food. **11** And into whatsoever city or village ye shall

[Column 2 — Mark]

and began to send them forth by two and two [cp. 11 1 ; 14 13] ; and he gave them authority over the unclean spirits [cp. 3 15 : *also* 6 12, 13 ; 9 18] ;

8 and he charged them

cp. 6 34.

cp. 1 15 : *also* 6 12.

cp. *verse* 13.

that they should take nothing for *their* journey, save a staff only ; no bread, no wallet,

no [1] money in their [2] purse ;

9 but *to go* shod with sandals : and, *said he,* put not on two coats.

10 And he said unto them, Wheresoever

ye

[Column 3 — Mark]

1 17, 35 ; 4 14, 36; 5 17 ; 6 19 ; 8 46; 24 49] and authority over all [1] devils [cp. 9 6, 40 ; 10 9, 17], and to cure diseases.

2 And he sent them forth cp. 19 29 ; 22 8.

to preach the kingdom of God, and to heal [cp. 6 19 ; 9 11, 42 ; 14 4 ; 22 51] [2] the sick.

3 And he said unto them,

cp. 9 52.

cp. *verse* 2 : *also* 9 6.

Take nothing for your journey, neither staff, nor wallet, nor bread,

nor money ;

neither have two coats [cp. 3 11].

4 And into whatsoever house ye

[Column 4 — Luke]

and sent them two and two

verses 9 and 11

before his face into every city and place, whither he himself was about to come [cp. 9 52]. **2** And he said unto them,

cp. 4 9.
cp. 10 16.

verses 9 and 11

The harvest is plenteous, but the labourers are few : pray ye therefore the Lord of the harvest, that he send forth labourers into his harvest. **3** Go your ways: behold, I send you forth as lambs in the midst of wolves. **4** Carry

no purse, no wallet,

no shoes [cp. 22 35]:

and salute no men on the way. *verse* 7

5 And into whatsoever house ye shall

[Right margin references]

cp. 4 35-38.

cp. 4 36.

enter,
search out who in it is worthy; and there abide till ye go forth. 12 And as ye enter into the house, salute it.

13 And if the house be worthy, let your peace come upon it [cp. 5 9]: but if it be not worthy, let your peace return to you.

verse 11

verse 10

verses 7 and 8

14 And whosoever

shall not receive you, nor hear your words, as ye go forth out of that house or that city, shake off the dust

of your feet.

cp. 8 4; 10 18; 24 14.

cp. 24 43.

15 Verily I say unto you, It shall be more tolerable [cp. 7 22; 24 36: *also* 26 29] for the land [cp. 2 6, 20, 21; 4 15; 11 24] of Sodom and Gomorrah in the day of judgement [cp. 11 22, 24; 12 36], than for that city [cp. 11 24].

---

enter into a house,

there abide till ye depart thence.

cp. 9 50.

11 And whatsoever place

shall not receive you, and they hear you not, as ye go forth thence, shake off the dust that is under your feet for a testimony unto them [cp. 1 44; 13 9].

cp. 13 32: *also* 14 25.

1 Gr. *brass*. 2 Gr. *girdle*.

---

enter,

there abide,   and thence depart.

cp. 1 79; 2 14, 29; 19 38.

verse 2

5 And as many as receive you not,

when ye depart from that city, shake off the dust from your feet for a testimony against them [cp. 5 14; 21 13].

1 Gr. *demons*.
2 Some ancient authorities omit *the sick*.

---

2 enter,

verse 7

first say, Peace *be* to this house. 6 And if a son of peace be there, your peace shall rest upon 3 him: but if not, it shall turn to you again. 7 And in that same house remain, eating and drinking such things as they give: for the labourer is worthy of his hire. Go not from house to house. 8 And into whatsoever city ye enter, and they receive you, eat such things as are set before you: 9 and heal the sick that are therein, and say unto them, The kingdom of God is come nigh unto you [cp. 11 20; 17 20, 21; 19 11; 21 8]. 10 But into whatsoever city ye shall enter, and they receive you not [cp. 9 53], go out into the streets thereof and say, 11 Even the dust from your city, that cleaveth to our feet, we do wipe off against you: howbeit know this [cp. 12 39], that the kingdom of God is come nigh [cp. v. 9]. 12 I say unto you, It shall be more tolerable in that day [cp. 17 31; 21 34] for

Sodom,

than

---

cp. 14 27; 16 33.

cp. 4 36.

cp. 14 20; 16 23, 26.
cp. 3 22.

Matthew (lower span):
11 21 Woe unto thee, Chorazin! woe unto thee, Bethsaida! for if the 3 mighty works had been done in Tyre and Sidon which were done in you, they would have repented long ago in sackcloth and ashes. 22 Howbeit I say unto you, it shall be more tolerable for Tyre and Sidon in the day of judgement [cp. 10 15; 11 24; 12 36], than for you. 23 And thou, Capernaum, shalt thou be exalted unto heaven? thou shalt 4 go   down unto

Luke (lower span):
for that city.   13 Woe unto thee, Chorazin! woe unto thee, Bethsaida! for if the 4 mighty works had been done in Tyre and Sidon, which were done in you, they would have repented long ago, sitting in sackcloth and ashes. 14 Howbeit it shall be more tolerable for Tyre and Sidon in the   judgement,   than for you. 15 And thou, Capernaum, shalt thou be exalted unto heaven? thou shalt be brought down unto

Hades: for if the [3] mighty works had been done in Sodom which were done in thee, it would have remained until this day [*cp.* 27 8; 28 15]. **24** Howbeit I say unto you, that it shall be more tolerable for the land [*cp.* 2 6, 20, 21; 4 15; 10 15] of Sodom in the day of judgement, than for thee [*cp.* 10 15].

Hades.

verse 12

cp. 3 22.

16 He that heareth you heareth me; and he that rejecteth you rejecteth me;

     and he that rejecteth me rejecteth him that sent me.

John 12 **48** He that rejecteth me, and receiveth not my sayings ...

Matt. 10 40 He that receiveth you

     receiveth me, and he that receiveth me receiveth him that sent me. **18 5** And whoso shall receive one   such little child in my name receiveth me.

Mark 9 37 Whosoever shall receive one of such little children in my name, receiveth me: and whosoever receiveth me, receiveth not me, but him that sent me.

Luke 9 48 Whosoever shall receive this little child   in my name receiveth me: and whosoever shall receive me receiveth   him that sent me.

13 20 He that receiveth whomsoever I send receiveth me; and he that receiveth me receiveth him that sent me [*cp.* 12 44, 45].

[1] Gr. *demons.*   [2] Gr. *girdles.*
[3] Gr. *powers.*
[4] Many ancient authorities read *be brought down.*

[1] Many ancient authorities add *and two*: and so in ver. 17.
[2] Or, *enter first, say*
[3] Or, *it*   [4] Gr. *powers.*

Matt. 11 23 ‖ Luke 10 15: *cp.* Is. 14 13-15.

§ 137. The Return of the Seventy

[*Cp.* Mark 6 30: Luke 9 10]

         Mark 16 17-18

Luke 10 17-20

cp. 7 22: *also* 18 5, 20; 24 5.

17 And these signs shall follow them that believe:
     in my name [*cp.* 9 38, 39: *also* 9 37; 13 6] shall they cast out [1] devils; they shall speak with [2] new tongues; **18** they shall

17 And the seventy returned with joy, saying,
     Lord, even the [1] devils are subject unto us in thy name [*cp.* 9 49: *also* 9 48; 21 8; 24 47].

cp. 14 13, 14, 26; 15 16; 16 23, 24, 26. *cp.* 12 31; 16 11.

cp. 10 1, 8: *also* 17 16. *cp.* 13 39.

[*cp.* 3 15; 6 7: *also* 6 13; 9 18] take up serpents,

     and if they drink any deadly thing, it shall in no wise hurt them; they shall lay hands on the sick, and they shall recover.

18 And he said unto them, I beheld Satan fallen as lightning from heaven. **19** Behold, I have given you authority [*cp.* 10 9; 9 1: *also* 9 6, 40] to tread upon serpents and scorpions, and over all the power of the enemy: and   nothing shall in any wise hurt you.

20 Howbeit in this rejoice not, that the spirits are subject unto you; but rejoice that your names are written in heaven.

[1] Gr. *demons.*
[2] Some ancient authorities omit *new.*

[1] Gr. *demons.*

Luke 10 20: *cp.* Dan. 12 1.

§ 138. The Thanksgiving of Jesus and the Blessedness of His Disciples

     Matt. 11 25-30; 13 16-17

Luke 10 21-24

25 At that season [*cp.* 12 1; 14 1: *also* 18 1; 26 55] Jesus answered   and said, I [1] thank thee, O Father [*cp.* 26 39, 42: *also* 6 9], Lord of heaven and

cp. 14 36.

21 In that same hour [*cp.* 7 21; 13 31] he rejoiced [1] in the Holy Spirit, and said, I [2] thank thee, O Father [*cp.* 22 42; 23 34, 46: *also* 11 2], Lord of heaven and

cp. 11 41; 12 27, 28;

earth, that thou didst hide these things from the wise and understanding, and didst reveal them unto babes [*cp.* 16 17]: **26** yea, Father [*see above*], [2] for so it was well-pleasing [*cp.* 3 17; 12 18; 17 5] in thy sight. **27** All things have been delivered unto me of my Father [*cp.* 9 8; 28 18]: and no one knoweth the Son, save the Father; neither doth any know the Father, save the Son, and he to whomsoever the Son willeth to reveal *him*. **28** Come unto me, all ye that labour and are heavy laden, and I will give you rest. **29** Take my yoke upon you, and learn of me; for I am meek and lowly in heart: and ye shall find rest unto your souls. **30** For my yoke is easy, and my burden is light.

cp. 9 22; 16 23.

cp. 17 1, 19; 20 17; 24 3.   **13 16** But blessed are your eyes, for they see; and your ears, for they hear. **17** For verily I say unto you, that many prophets and righteous men desired to see the things which ye see, and saw them not; and to hear the things which ye hear, and heard them not.

[1] Or, *praise*   [2] Or, *that*

---

cp. 1 11.

cp. 5 30; 8 33.

cp. 4 10, 34; 6 31, 32; 9 2, 28; 13 3.

---

earth, that thou didst hide these things from the wise and understanding, and didst reveal them unto babes: yea, Father [*see above*]; [3] for so it was well-pleasing [*cp.* 2 14; 3 22; 12 32] in thy sight. **22** All things have been delivered unto me of my Father: and no one knoweth who the Son is, save the Father; and who the Father is, save the Son, and he to whomsoever the Son willeth to reveal *him*.

23 And turning [*cp.* 7 9, 44; 9 55; 14 25; 22 61; 23 28] to the disciples, he said privately [*cp.* 9 10], Blessed *are* the eyes which see the things that ye see: **24** for I say unto you, that many prophets and kings desired to see the things which ye see, and saw them not; and to hear the things which ye hear, and heard them not.

[1] Or, *by*   [2] Or, *praise*   [3] Or, *that*

---

17 1, 5, 11, 21, 24, 25.

see above.

cp. 3 35; 5 27; 13 3; 17 2.

cp. 1 18; 6 46; 7 29; 8 19; 10 15; 17 25-26.

cp. 6 37; 7 37.

cp. 1 38.

Matt. 11 28-30: *cp.* Ecclus. 51 23-27; Jer. 6 16; Zech. 9 9.

§ 139. A Lawyer's Question and the Parable of the Good Samaritan

[*Cp.* Matt. 19 16-22 ‖ Mark 10 17-22 ‖ Luke 18 18-23]

Matt. 22 34-40	Mark 12 28-31	Luke 10 25-37	
34 But the Pharisees, when they heard that he had put the Sadducees to silence, gathered themselves together. **35** And one of them, a lawyer,	**28** And one of the scribes came, and heard them questioning together [*cp.* 8 11; 9 14, 16], and knowing that he had answered them well, asked him,	**25** And behold, a certain lawyer stood up and	
asked him a question, tempting [*cp.* 16 1; 19 3: *also* 22 18] him, **36** [1] Master,	*cp.* 8 11; 10 2: *also* 12 15.	tempted [*cp.* 11 16] him, saying, [1] Master, what shall I do [*cp.* 3 10, 12, 14] to inherit eternal life [*cp.* 18 18, 30]?	*cp.* 8 6. *cp.* 6 28. *cp.* 3 15; *etc.*
cp. 19 16, 29; 25 46. which is the great commandment in the law? **37** And he said unto him,	*cp.* 10 17, 30. What commandment is the first of all? **29** Jesus	**26** And he said unto him, What is written in the law? how readest thou [*cp.* 6 3]? **27** And he answering said,	
cp. 12 3, 5; 19 4; 21 16, 42; 22 31.	*cp.* 2 25; 12 10, 26. answered, The first is, Hear, O Israel; [1] The Lord our God, the Lord is one: **30** and thou shalt love the Lord thy God [2] with all thy heart, and [2] with all thy soul, and [2] with all thy mind, and [2] with all thy strength.		
Thou shalt love the Lord thy God with all thy heart, and with all thy soul, and with all thy mind.		Thou shalt love the Lord thy God [2] with all thy heart, and with all thy soul, and with all thy strength, and with all thy mind;	
38 This is the great and first com-			

mandment.   39   [2] And a second like *unto it* is this, Thou shalt love thy neighbour as thyself [*cp.* 19 19].

40 On these two commandments hangeth the whole law, and the prophets [*cp.* 5 17; 7 12; 11 13].

[1] Or, *Teacher*
[2] Or, *And a second is like unto it, Thou shalt love &c.*

31 The second   is this, Thou shalt love thy neighbour as thyself. There is none other commandment greater than these.

[1] Or, *The Lord is our God; the Lord is one*   [2] Gr. *from.*

and

thy neighbour as thyself.

cp. 16 16.

28 And he said unto him, Thou hast answered right [*cp.* 7 43]: this do, and thou shalt live.

29 But he, desiring to justify himself [*cp.* 16 15], said unto Jesus, And who is my neighbour? 30 Jesus made answer and said, A certain man was going down from Jerusalem to Jericho; and he fell among robbers, which both stripped him and beat him, and departed, leaving him half dead.   31 And by chance a certain priest was going down that way: and when he saw him, he passed by on the other side. 32 And in like manner a Levite also, when he came to the place, and saw him, passed by on the other side. 33 But a certain Samaritan [*cp.* 17 16: *also* 9 52; 17 11], as he journeyed, came where he was: and when he saw him, he was moved with compassion [*cp.* 15 20: *also* 7 13], 34 and came to him, and bound up his wounds, pouring on *them* oil and wine; and he set him on his own beast, and brought him to an inn, and took care of him.   35 And on the morrow he took out two [3] pence, and gave them to the host, and said, Take care of him; and whatsoever thou spendest more, I, when I come back again, will repay thee.   36 Which of these three, thinkest thou, proved neighbour unto him that fell among the robbers? 37 And he said, He that shewed mercy [*cp.* 1 72] on him. And Jesus said unto him, Go, and do thou likewise.

[1] Or, *Teacher*   [2] Gr. *from.*   [3] See footnote on Matt. 18 28.

cp. 4 9: *also* 4 39, 40.

Mark 12 29 = Deut. 6 4.

Matt. 22 39 ‖ Mark 12 31 ‖ Luke 10 27 = Lev. 19 18.

Matt. 22 37 ‖ Mark 12 30 ‖ Luke 10 27 = Deut. 6 5.

Luke 10 28 : *cp.* Lev. 18 5.

§ 140. **In the House of Martha and Mary**

Luke 10 38-42

38 Now as they went on their way, he entered into a certain village [*cp.* 9 52, 56; 17 12]: and a certain woman named Martha received him into her house.   39 And she had a sister called Mary, which also sat at the Lord's [*see below*] feet [*cp.* 7 38; 8 35], and heard his word. 40 But Martha was [1] cumbered about much serving; and she came up to him, and said, Lord, dost thou not care that my sister did leave me to serve alone? bid her therefore that she help me. 41 But the Lord [*cp.* 7 13, 19; 10 1, 39; 11 39; 12 42; 13 15; 17 5, 6; 18 6; 19 8; 22 61; 24 3, 34] answered and said unto her, [2] Martha, Martha, thou art anxious and troubled about many things: 42 [3] but one thing is needful: for Mary hath chosen the good part, which shall not be taken away from her.

cp. 16 19, 20.

cp. 11 1.

cp. 12 2.

cp. 4 1; 6 23; 11 2; 20 2, 18, 20, 25; 21 7, 12.

[1] Gr. *distracted.*
[2] A few ancient authorities read *Martha, Martha, thou art troubled: Mary hath chosen &c.*
[3] Many ancient authorities read *but few things are needful, or one.*

§ 141. **The Lord's Prayer**

Matt. 6 9-13

cp. 14 23; 19 13; 26 36, 39, 42, 44: *also* 11 25.

Luke 11 1-4

1 And it came to pass, as he was praying [*cp.* 3 21; 5 16; 6 12; 9 18, 28, 29; 22 41, 44: *also* 10 21] in a certain place, that when he ceased, one of his disciples said unto him,

cp. 1 35; 6 46; 14 32, 35, 39.

cp. 11 41-42; 12 27-28; 17 1-26.

cp. 9 14; 11 2; 14 12.

9 After this manner therefore pray ye: Our Father [*cp.* 11 25, 26; 26 39, 42] which art in heaven [*cp.* 5 16, 45; 6 1; 7 11, 21; 10 32, 33; 12 50; 16 17; 18 10, 14, 19: *also* 5 48; 6 14, 26, 32; 15 13; 18 35; 23 9], Hallowed be thy name. **10** Thy kingdom come. Thy will be done [*cp.* 26 39, 42: *also* 7 21; 12 50; 21 31], as in heaven, so on earth. **11** Give us this day ¹ our daily bread. **12** And forgive us our debts, as we also have forgiven our debtors [*cp.* 6 14, 15; 18 21-35]. **13** And bring us not into temptation [*cp.* 26 41], but deliver us from ² the evil one [*cp.* 5 37, 39; 13 19, 38].³

¹ Gr. *our bread for the coming day.*
² Or, *evil*
³ Many authorities, some ancient, but with variations, add *For thine is the kingdom, and the power, and the glory, for ever. Amen.*

cp. 2 18; 6 29.

cp. 14 36.
cp. 11 25, 26.

cp. 14 36:
also 3 35.

cp. 11 25.

cp. 14 38.

Lord, teach us to pray, even as John also taught his disciples [*cp.* 5 33: *also* 7 18]. **2** And he said unto them, When ye pray [*cp.* Matt. 6 5], say, ¹ Father [*cp.* 10 21, 22; 22 42; 23 34, 46], *cp.* 11 13.

Hallowed be thy name [*cp.* 1 49]. Thy kingdom come.²
cp. 22 42.
3 Give us day by day ³ our daily bread. **4** And forgive us our sins; for we ourselves also forgive every one that is indebted to us [*cp.* 17 3-4]. And bring us not into temptation [*cp.* 22 40, 46].⁴

¹ Many ancient authorities read *Our Father, which art in heaven.* See Matt. 6 9.
² Many ancient authorities add *Thy will be done, as in heaven, so on earth.* See Matt. 6 10.
³ Gr. *our bread for the coming day.*
⁴ Many ancient authorities add *but deliver us from the evil one* (or, *from evil*). See Matt. 6 13.

cp. 1 35, 37; 3 25; 4 1.

cp. 11 41; 12 27, 28; 17 1, 5, 11, 21, 24, 25.

cp. 4 34; 5 30; 6 38; 7 17; 9 31.

cp. 17 15.

§ 142. Teaching about Prayer

Luke 11 5-13

5 And he said unto them, Which of you shall have a friend, and shall go unto him at midnight, and say to him, Friend [*cp.* 14 10], lend me three loaves; **6** for a friend of mine is come to me from a journey, and I have nothing to set before him; **7** and he from within shall answer and say, Trouble me [*cp.* 18 5] not: the door is now shut, and my children are with me in bed; I cannot rise and give thee? **8** I say unto you, Though he will not rise and give him, because he is his friend, yet because of his importunity [*cp.* 18 4, 5] he will arise and give him ¹ as many as he needeth. **9** And I say unto you,

cp. 26 10.   *cp.* 14 6.

Matt. 7 7-11

Ask, and it shall be given you [*cp.* 18 19; 21 22]; seek, and ye shall

cp. 11 24.

Ask, and it shall be given you; seek, and ye shall

John 15 7

Ask whatsoever ye will, and it shall be done unto you.

John 16 24

Ask, and ye shall receive [*cp.* 14 13; 15 16; 16 23].

find; knock, and it shall be opened unto you: **8** for every one that asketh receiveth; and he that seeketh findeth; and to him that knocketh it shall be opened. **9** Or what man is there of you, who, if his son shall ask him for a loaf, will give him a stone; **10** or if he shall ask for a fish, will give him a serpent?

11 If ye then, being evil [*cp.* 12 34], know how to give good gifts unto your children, how much more shall your Father which is in heaven [*cp.* 5 16, 45; 6 1; 9; 7 21; 10 32, 33; 12 50; 16 17; 18 10, 14, 19: *also* 5 48; 6 14, 26, 32; 15 13; 18 35; 23 9] give good things to them that ask him?

find; knock, and it shall be opened unto you. **10** For every one that asketh receiveth; and he that seeketh findeth; and to him that knocketh it shall be opened. **11** And of which of you that is a father shall his son ask ² a loaf, and he give him a stone? or a fish, and he for a fish give him a serpent? **12** Of if he shall ask an egg, will he give him a scorpion? **13** If ye then, being evil, know how to give good gifts unto your children, how much more shall *your* heavenly Father

cp. 11 25, 26.

give the Holy Spirit to them that ask him?

¹ Or, *whatsoever things*
² Some ancient authorities omit *a loaf, and he give him a stone? or,*

§ 143. A Controversy about Casting out Devils

Matt. 12 22-30, 43-45	Matt. 9 32-34	Mark 3 22-27	Luke 11 14-26	
22 Then was brought unto him ¹ one possessed with a devil, blind [*cp.* 9 27] and dumb: and he healed him, insomuch that the dumb man spake and saw. **23** And all the multitudes were amazed,	**32** And as they went forth, behold, there was brought to him a dumb man possessed with a ¹ devil. **33** And when the ¹ devil was cast out, the dumb man spake: and the multitudes marvelled [*cp.* 8 27; 15 31; 21 20; 27 14: *also* 7 28; 13 54; 19 25; 22 22, 33], saying, It was never so seen in Israel.		**14** And he was casting out a ¹ devil *which was* dumb. And it came to pass, when the ¹ devil was gone out, the dumb man spake; and the multitudes marvelled [*cp.* 5 9, 26; 8 25, 56; 9 43; 24 12, 41: *also* 2 47, 48; 4 22, 32, 36; 20 26].	
		cp. 2 12; 5 20, 42; 6 51; 7 37; 10 32; 15 5; 16 5, 8: *also* 1 22, 27; 6 2; 10 24, 26; 11 18; 12 17.		*cp.* 7 15, 21, 46.
and said, Is this the son of David [*cp.* 1 1; 9 27; 15 22; 20 30, 31; 21 9, 15]? **24** But when the Pharisees	**34** But the Pharisees	*cp.* 10 47, 48.	*cp.* 1 32; 18 38, 39.	
	cp. 15 1.	**22** And the scribes which came down from Jerusalem [*cp.* 7 1] said, He hath Beelzebub, and,	**15** But some of them	
heard it, they said,	said,		*cp.* 5 17. said,	*cp.* 1 19.
This man doth not cast out ² devils, but ³ by Beelzebub [*cp.* 10 25] the prince of the ² devils.	² By the prince of the ³ devils casteth he out ³ devils. ¹ Gr. *demon.* ² Or, *In* ³ Gr. *demons.*	¹ By the prince of the ² devils casteth he out the ² devils.	² By Beelzebub the prince of the ³ devils casteth he out ³ devils.	*cp.* 7 20; 8 48, 52; 10 20.
cp. 16 1: *also* 19 3; 22 18, 35: *and* 12 38.	*cp.* 8 11: *also* 10 2; 12 15.	**16** And others, tempting *him* [*cp.* 10 25], sought of him a sign from heaven. **17** But he, knowing their thoughts [*cp.* 5 22; 6 8; 9 47], said unto them,		*cp.* 8 6. *cp.* 2 18; 6 30.
25 And knowing their thoughts [*cp.* 9 4; 16 8] he said unto them,	**23** And he *cp.* 2 8; 8 17. called them unto him, and said unto them in parables, How can Satan cast out Satan? **24** And if a kingdom be divided against itself, that kingdom cannot stand.			*cp.* 1 48; 2 24, 25; 4 19, 29; 5 6, 42; 6 61; 11 14; 13 18; 16 19, 30; 18 4; 21 17.
Every kingdom divided against itself is brought to desolation; and every city or house divided against itself shall not stand: **26** and if Satan casteth out Satan, he is divided against himself; how then shall his kingdom stand?	**25** And if a house be divided against itself, that house will not be able to stand. **26** And if Satan hath risen up against himself, and is divided, he cannot stand, but hath an end.		Every kingdom divided against itself is brought to desolation; ⁴ and a house *divided* against a house falleth. **18** And if Satan also is divided against himself, how shall his kingdom stand? because ye say that I cast out ³ devils ² by Beelzebub.	
27 And if I ³ by Beelzebub cast out ² devils, ³ by whom do your sons cast them out? therefore shall they be your judges. **28** But if I ³ by the Spirit of God cast out ² devils, then is the kingdom of God come upon you [*cp.* 3 2; 4 17; 10 7].			**19** And if I ² by Beelzebub cast out ³ devils, by whom do your sons cast them out? therefore shall they be your judges. **20** But if I by the finger of God cast out ³ devils, then is the kingdom of God come upon you [*cp.* 9 2; 10 9, 11; 17 20, 21; 19 11; 21 8].	
29 Or how can one enter into the house of the strong *man,*	*cp.* 1 15; 6 12. **27** But no one can enter into the house of the strong *man,*		**21** When the strong *man* fully armed guardeth his	

and spoil his goods, except he first bind the strong *man* ? and then	and spoil his goods, except he first bind the strong *man*; and then	own court, his goods are in peace :

he will spoil his house. **30** He that is not with me is against me ; and he that gathereth not with me scattereth. . . . . **43** But the unclean spirit, when ⁴ he is gone out of the man, passeth through waterless places, seeking rest, and findeth it not. **44** Then ⁴ he saith, I will return into my house whence I came out ; and when ⁴ he is come, ⁴ he findeth it empty, swept, and garnished. **45** Then goeth ⁴ he, and taketh with ⁵ himself seven other spirits more evil than ⁵ himself, and they enter in and dwell there : and the last state of that man becometh worse than the first. Even so shall it be also unto this evil generation [*cp.* 12 39; 16 4; 17 17].	he will spoil his house. *cp.* 9 40. *cp.* 8 38 ; 9 19.	**22** but when a stronger than he shall come upon him, and overcome him, he taketh from him his whole armour wherein he trusted, and divideth his spoils. **23** He that is not with me is against me ; and he that gathereth not with me scattereth [*cp.* 9 50]. **24** The unclean spirit when ⁵ he is gone out of the man, passeth through waterless places, seeking rest ; and finding none, ⁵ he saith, I will turn back unto my house whence I came out. **25** And when ⁵he is come, ⁵ he findeth it swept and garnished. **26** Then goeth ⁵ he, and taketh *to him* seven other spirits more evil than ⁶ himself ; and they enter in and dwell there : and the last state of that man becometh worse than the first. *cp.* 9 41 ; 11 29.

¹ Or, *a demoniac* ² Gr. *demons.* ³ Or, *in* ⁴ Or, *it* ⁵ Or, *itself*	¹ Or, *In* ² Gr. *demons.*	¹ Gr. *demon.* ² Or, *In* ³ Gr. *demons.* ⁴ Or, *and house falleth upon house.* ⁵ Or, *it* ⁶ Or, *itself*

§ 144. The Truly Blessed

[*Cp.* Matt. 12 46-50; Mark 3 31-35; Luke 8 19-21]

Luke 11 27-28

		27 And it came to pass, as he said these things, a certain woman out of the multitude lifted up her voice [*cp.* 17 13], and said unto him, Blessed is the womb that bare thee, and the breasts which thou didst suck [*cp.* 1 48]. **28** But he said, Yea rather, blessed are they that hear the word of God [*cp.* 5 1 ; 8 11, 21 : *also* 1 2 ; 8 12-15 : *and* 4 32], and keep it.		
cp. 13 19-23.	*cp.* 2 2 ; 4 14-20, 33 ; 16 20.		*cp.* 4 41 ; 5 24, 38 ; *etc.*	

§ 145. A Sign refused

Matt. 12 38-42	Matt. 16 1-2, 4	Mark 8 11-13	Luke 11 29-32	
38 Then certain of the scribes and Pharisees	**1** And the Pharisees and Sadducees came, and tempting him [*cp.* 19 3 ; 22 35 : *also* 22 18]	**11** And the Pharisees came forth, and began to question with him [*cp.* 9 14, 16 ; 12 28],	**29** And when the multitudes were gathering together unto him, *cp.* 10 25 ; 11 16.	*cp.* 8 6.
answered him, saying, ¹ Master, we would see a sign from thee.	asked him to shew them a sign from heaven.	seeking of him a sign from heaven, tempting him [*cp.* 10 2 : *also* 12 15].	11 16 *cp.* 10 25 ; 11 16.	*cp.* 2 18 ; 6 30. *cp.* 8 6.
39 But he answered and said unto them,	**2** But he . . . answered and said unto them,	**12** And he sighed deeply [*cp.* 7 34] in his spirit, and saith, Why doth this generation	he began to say, This generation is an evil	
An evil and	**4** An evil and			

adulterous generation [*cp.* 12 45] seeketh after a sign;

and there shall no sign be given to it
but the sign of Jonah the prophet:

40 for as Jonah
was three days and three nights in the belly of the [2] whale; so shall the Son of man
be three days and three nights in the heart of the earth [*cp.* 16 21; 17 23; 20 19; 26 61; 27 40, 63, 64]. **41** The men of Nineveh shall stand up in the judgement with this generation, and shall condemn it: for they repented at the preaching of Jonah; and behold, [3] a greater than Jonah is here [*cp.* 12 6]. **42** The queen of the south shall rise up in the judgement with this generation, and shall condemn it: for she came from the ends of the earth to hear the wisdom of Solomon; and behold, [3] a greater than Solomon is here [*cp.* 12 6].

verse 41

[1] Or, *Teacher*   [2] Gr. *sea-monster.*
[3] Gr. *more than.*

---

adulterous generation [*cp.* 17 17] seeketh after a sign;

and there shall no sign be given unto it,
but the sign of Jonah.
And he left them, and
departed.

cp. 8 31; 9 31; 10 34; 14 58; 15 29.

---

cp. 8 38; 9 19. seek   a sign? verily I say unto you, There shall no sign be given unto this generation.

13 And he left them, and again entering into *the boat* departed to the other side.

cp. 7 22.

---

generation [*cp.* 9 41]: it seeketh after a sign;

and there shall no sign be given to it
but the sign of Jonah.

30 For even as Jonah became a sign unto the Ninevites,
so shall also the Son of man be to this generation.

cp. 9 22; 13 32; 18 33; 24 7, 21, 46.

verse 32

31 The queen of the south shall rise up in the judgement with the men of this generation, and shall condemn them: for she came from the ends of the earth to hear the wisdom of Solomon; and behold, [1] a greater than Solomon is here.

32 The men of Nineveh shall stand up in the judgement with this generation, and shall condemn it: for they repented at the preaching of Jonah; and behold, [1] a greater than Jonah is here.

[1] Gr. *more than.*

---

cp. 2 19-22.

Luke 11 29 ‖ Matt. 12 39; 16 4: *cp.* Jonah 3 4.
Luke 11 31 ‖ Matt. 12 42: *cp.* I Kings 10 1 *ff.*

Matt. 12 40: *cp.* Jonah 1 17.
Luke 11 32 ‖ Matt. 12 41: *cp.* Jonah 3 5.

---

§ 146. Sayings about Light

Matt. 5 15; 6 22-23

5 15 Neither do   *men*

light   a lamp,
and put it

under the bushel,

but   on the stand; and it shineth unto all that are in the house.

6 22 The lamp of the body is the eye: if therefore thine eye be single, thy whole body shall be full of light. **23** But if thine eye be evil [*cp.* 20 15], thy whole body shall be full of darkness. If therefore the light that is in thee be   darkness, how great is the darkness!

Mark 4 21

21 Is the lamp brought
to be put

under the bushel, or under the bed, *and* not to be   put   on the stand?

cp. 7 22.

Luke 8 16

16 And no man, when he hath lighted   a lamp, covereth it with a vessel, or putteth it

under a bed;
but putteth it on a stand,

that they which enter in may see the light.

Luke 11 33-36

33 No man, when he hath lighted   a lamp,

putteth it in a cellar, neither under the bushel,

but   on the stand,

that they which enter in may see the light. **34** The lamp of thy body is thine eye: when thine eye is single, thy whole body also is full of light; but when   it is evil, thy   body also is full of darkness. **35** Look therefore whether the light that is in thee be not darkness. **36** If therefore thy whole body be full of light, having no part dark, it shall be wholly full of light, as when the lamp with its bright shining doth give thee light.

(ii) Jesus a Guest in the House of a Pharisee (§§ 147-150)

§ 147. **Ritual Washing and Moral Cleanliness**

[*Cp.* Matt. 15 1-20; Mark 7 1-23: *also* Matt. 9 14-17; Mark 2 18-22; Luke 5 33-39]

Matt. 23 25-26		Luke 11 37-41	
		37 Now as he spake, a Pharisee asketh him to ¹ dine with him: and he went in, and sat down to meat [*cp.* 7 36; 14 1]. **38** And when the Pharisee saw it, he marvelled [*cp.* 7 39] that he had not first washed before	
cp. 15 2.	*cp.* 7 5. *cp.* 16 19, 20.	¹dinner. **39** And the Lord [*cp.* 7 13, 19; 10 1, 39, 41; 12 42; 13 15; 17 5, 6; 18 6; 19 8; 22 61; 24 3, 34] said unto him,	*cp.* 4 1; 6 23; 11 2; 20 2, 18, 20, 25; 21 7, 12.
25 Woe unto you [*cp.* 23 13, *etc.*: *also* 18 7; 26 24], scribes and Pharisees, hypocrites [*cp.* 15 7; 22 18; 23 13, *etc.*: *also* 6 2, 5, 16; 23 28; 24 51]! for ye cleanse the outside of the cup and of the platter, but within [*cp.* 15 19; 23 28] they are full from extortion and	*cp.* 14 21. *cp.* 7 6: also 12 15. *cp.* 7 4. *cp.* 7 21-23. *cp.* 12 40.	*cp.* 11 42, *etc.*: *also* 17 1; 22 22. *cp.* 12 56; 13 15: *also* 12 1. Now do ye Pharisees cleanse the outside of the cup and of the platter; but your inward part is full of extortion [*cp.* 16 14; 20 47] and	
excess. *cp.* 22 18. *cp.* 23 17. **26** Thou blind [*cp.* 15 14; 23 16, 17, 19, 24] Pharisee,		wickedness. **40** Ye foolish ones [*cp.* 12 20], *cp.* 6 39. did not he that made the outside make the inside also? **41** Howbeit give for alms	*cp.* 9 39, 40, 41.
cleanse first [*cp.* 5 24; 6 33; 7 5] the inside of the cup and of the platter, that the outside thereof may	*cp.* 7 27.	[*cp.* 12 33] *cp.* 6 42. those things which ² are within;	
become clean also.	*cp.* 7 19.	and behold, all things are clean unto you.	

¹ Gr. *breakfast*.   ² Or, *ye can*

§ 148. **Woes against Pharisees**

Matt. 23 23-24, 6-7, 27-28		Luke 11 42-44	
23 Woe unto you [*cp.* 23 13, *etc.*: *also* 18 7; 26 24], scribes and Pharisees, hypocrites [*cp.* 15 7; 22 18; 23 13, *etc.*: *also* 6 2, 5, 16; 23 28; 24 51]! for ye tithe mint and ¹ anise and cummin,	*cp.* 14 21. *cp.* 7 6: also 12 15.	**42** But woe unto you [*cp.* 11 43, 44, 46, 47, 52: *also* 17 1; 22 22] Pharisees! *cp.* 12 56; 13 15: *also* 12 1. for ye tithe mint and rue and every herb, and pass over judgement and the love of	
cp. 22 37. and have left undone the weightier matters of the law, judgement, and mercy [*cp.* 9 13; 12 7], and faith: but these ye ought to have done, and not to have left the other undone. **24** Ye blind guides [*cp.* 15 14; 23 16, 17, 19, 26], which strain out the gnat, and swallow the camel.	*cp.* 12 30, 33.	God [*cp.* 10 27]: but these ought ye to have done, and not to leave the other undone. *cp.* 6 39. **43** Woe unto you [*see above*] Pharisees! for ye *cp.* 12 1.	*cp.* 5 42. *cp.* 9 39, 40, 41.

cp. 16 6.		Mark 12 **38** Beware of [*cp.* 8 15] the scribes, which desire to walk in long robes, and *to have*	Luke 20 **46** Beware of the scribes, which desire to walk in long robes, and love	
6 and love the chief place at feasts, and the chief seats in the synagogues, **7** and the salutations in the marketplaces,		salutations in the marketplaces, **39** and chief seats in the synagogues, and chief places at feasts.	salutations in the marketplaces, and chief seats in the synagogues, and chief places at feasts.	love the chief seats in the synagogues, and the salutations in the marketplaces.

27 Woe unto you [*see above*], scribes and Pharisees, hypocrites [*see above*] ! for ye are like unto whited sepulchres, which outwardly appear   beautiful, but inwardly are full of dead men's bones, and of all uncleanness.

28 Even so ye also outwardly appear [*cp.* 6 1, 2, 5, 16 ; 23 5] righteous unto men, but inwardly [*cp.* 15 19 ; 23 25, 26] ye are full of hypocrisy [*see verse 23 above*] and iniquity.

[1] Or, *dill*

---

44 Woe unto you [*see above*] !

                                for ye are as   the tombs which   appear not,

                                and the men that walk over *them* know it not.

cp. 7 21-23.   *cp.* 11 39-41.
cp. 12 15 :
also 7 6.   *cp.* 12 1 : *also* 12 56 ; 13 15.

---

§ 149. Woes against Lawyers

Matt. 23 4, 29-36, 13

Luke 11 45-52

cp. 23 13, *etc.* : *also* 18 7 ; 26 24.   *cp.* 14 21.

4 Yea, they bind   heavy burdens [1] and grievous to be borne, and lay them on men's shoulders ; but they themselves will not move them   with   their finger. **29** Woe unto you [*see above*], scribes and Pharisees, hypocrites [*cp.* 15 7 ; 22 18 ; 23 13, *etc.* : *also* 6 2, 5, 16 ; 23 28 ; 24 51] ! for ye build the sepulchres of the prophets, and garnish the tombs of the righteous, **30** and say, If we had been in the days of our fathers, we should not have been partakers with them in the blood of the prophets. **31** Wherefore ye   witness to yourselves,

                that ye are sons of them that slew the prophets [*cp.* 5 12 ; 21 35-36 ; 22 6 ; 23 37]. **32** Fill ye up then the measure of your fathers. **33** Ye serpents, ye offspring of vipers [*cp.* 3 7 ; 12 34], how shall ye escape the judgement of [2] hell [*cp.* 5 29, 30 ; 10 28 ; 23 15 : *also* 5 22 ; 18 9] ? **34** Therefore,
cp. 11 19.   behold, I send unto you prophets, and wise men, and scribes :
                cp. 10 2.
some of them   shall ye kill and crucify [*cp.* 20 19 ; 27 26] ; and some of them shall ye scourge in your synagogues [*cp.* 10 17], and persecute from city to city [*cp.* 10 23] : **35** that upon you may come all the righteous blood
                shed on the earth,
                cp. 13 35 ; 25 34.

        from the blood of Abel the righteous unto the blood of Zachariah son of Barachiah, whom ye slew between the sanctuary and the altar. **36** Verily I say unto you, All these things shall come upon   this generation [*cp.* 24 34 : *also* 10 23 ; 16 28]. **13** But woe unto you [*see above*], scribes and Pharisees, hypocrites [*see above*] ! because ye shut the kingdom of heaven [3] against men :

---

45 And one of the lawyers answering saith unto him, [1] Master, in saying this thou reproachest us also. **46** And he said, Woe unto you [*cp.* 11 42, 43, 44, 47, 52 : *also* 17 1 ; 22 22] lawyers also ! for ye lade men with burdens   grievous to be borne, and ye yourselves   touch not the burdens with one of your fingers. **47** Woe unto you [*see above*] !
        cp. 12 56 ; 13 15 : *also* 12 1.

for ye build the tombs of the prophets, and

your fathers   killed them.

                48 So ye are witnesses   and consent unto the works of your fathers: for they   killed them [*cp.* 6 23 ; 13 33, 34 ; 20 10-12], and ye build *their tombs*.

                        cp. 3 7.

                        cp. 12 5.
                49 Therefore also said the wisdom [*cp.* 7 35] of God,   I will send unto them prophets   and apostles [*cp.* 6 13 ; 9 10 ; 17 5 ; 22 14 ; 24 10] ; and *some* of them they shall   kill

                and persecute ;
                50 that   the   blood of all the prophets, which was shed from the foundation of the world, may be required of this generation [*see below*] ; **51** from the blood of Abel   unto the blood of Zachariah,   who perished between   the altar and the [2] sanctuary : yea, I say unto you, it   shall   be required of this generation [*cp.* 21 32 : *also* 9 27].   **52** Woe unto you [*see above*] lawyers !
        for ye
                took away the

---

cp. 7 6 :
also 12 15.

cp. 12 3-5.

cp. 9 43, 45, 47.

cp. 6 30.
cp. 15 15.
cp. 13 9.

cp. 13 30.
also 9 1.

cp. 13 16.

cp. 17 24.

cp. 16 19. for ye enter [cp. 5 20 ; 7 13, 21 ; 18 3, 8, 9 ; 19 17, 23, 24 ; 25 21, 23] not in yourselves [cp. 21 31], neither suffer ye them that are entering in to enter.	cp. 9 43, 45, 47; 10 15, 23, 24, 25.	key of knowledge: ye entered [cp. 13 24; 18 17, 24, 25 : also 24 26] not in yourselves, and them that were entering in ye hindered.	cp. 3 5; 10 1, 2, 9.

[1] Many ancient authorities omit *and grievous to be borne.*   [2] Gr. *Gehenna.*   [3] Gr. *before.*

Luke 11 50-51 ‖ Matt. 23 35 : cp. Gen. 4 8 ; II Chron. 24 20-22.

§ 150. The Increasing Hostility of the Scribes and Pharisees

Luke 11 53-54

cp. 12 10; 22 15.	cp. 3 2; 12 13.	53 And when he was come out from thence, the scribes and the Pharisees began to [1] press upon *him* vehemently, and to provoke him to speak of [2] many things ; 54 laying wait for him, to catch something out of his mouth [cp. 6 7; 20 20].	cp. 8 6.

[1] Or, *set themselves vehemently against* him   [2] Or, *more*

(iii) A Sermon to the Disciples in the Presence of the Multitude (§§ 151-159).

§ 151. Miscellaneous Teaching

Luke 12 1-12

Matthew	Mark	Luke	
Matt. 16 5 And the disciples came to the other side and forgot to take [1] bread.

6 And Jesus said unto them, Take heed and beware of the leaven of the Pharisees and Sadducees.

cp. 23 28 : *also* 6 2, 5, 16 ; 15 7 ; 22 18 ; 23 13, *etc.* ; 24 51. | Mark 8 14 And they forgot to take bread; and they had not in the boat with them more than one loaf. 15 And he charged them, saying, Take heed, beware [cp. 12 38] of the leaven of the Pharisees and the leaven of Herod. cp. 12 15 : *also* 7 6. | 1 In the mean time, when [1] the many thousands of the multitude were gathered together, insomuch that they trode one upon another, he began to [2] say unto his disciples first of all, Beware [cp. 20 46] ye [cp. 17 3; 21 34] of the leaven of the Pharisees, which is hypocrisy [cp. 12 56; 13 15]. | |
Matt. 10 26 For there is nothing covered, that shall not be revealed ; and hid,	Mark 4 22 For there is nothing	Luke 8 17 For nothing is	2 But there is nothing covered up, that shall not be revealed : and hid,
	hid, save that it should be manifested ; neither was *anything* made secret, but that it should come to light.	hid, that shall not be made manifest ; nor *anything* secret, that shall not be known and come to light.	
that shall not be known.			that shall not be known. 3 Wherefore whatsoever ye have said in the darkness shall be heard in the light ; and what ye have spoken in the ear in the inner chambers shall be proclaimed upon the housetops. 4 And I say unto you my friends, Be not afraid of them which kill the body,
27 What I tell you in the darkness, speak ye in the light : and what ye hear in the ear, proclaim upon the housetops. 28 And be not afraid of them which kill the body, but are not able to kill the soul : but rather fear him which is able to destroy both soul and body in [2] hell [cp. 5 22, 29, 30 ; 18 9 ; 23 15, 33 : *also* 3 10, 12 ; 7 19 ; 13 42, 50 ; 18 8 ; 25 41]. 29 Are not two sparrows sold for a farthing ? and not one of them shall fall on the ground without your Father : 30 but the very hairs of your head are all numbered. 31 Fear not therefore ; ye are of more value than many		and after that have no more that they can do. 5 But I will warn you whom ye shall fear : Fear him, which after he hath killed hath [3] power to cast into [4] hell [cp. 3 9, 17] ; yea, I say unto you, Fear him. 6 Are not five sparrows sold for two farthings ? and not one of them is forgotten in the sight of God. 7 But the very hairs of your head are all numbered [cp. 21 18]. Fear not : ye are of more value than many	cp. 15 14, 15.

cp. 15 6. |

cp. 9 43, 45, 47.

Matthew

sparrows [cp. 6 26: also 12 12].

32 Every one therefore who shall confess [3]me before men, [4]him will I also confess before my Father which is in heaven [cp. 5 16, 45; 6 1, 9; 7 11, 21; 12 50; 16 17; 18 10, 14, 19: also 5 48; 6 14, 26, 32; 15 13; 18 35; 23 9]. **33** But whosoever shall deny me before men, him will I also deny before my Father which is in heaven [see above].

Matt. 16 **27** For the Son of man shall come in the glory of his Father with his angels; and then shall he render unto every man according to his [5]deeds. 12 **31** Therefore I say unto you, Every sin and blasphemy shall be forgiven [6]unto men;

but the blasphemy against the Spirit shall not be forgiven. **32** And whosoever shall speak a word against the Son of man, it shall be forgiven him; but whosoever shall speak against the Holy Spirit, it shall not be forgiven him, neither in this [7]world, nor in that which is to come.

cp. 18 8; 25 41, 46.

Matt. 10 **17** For they will deliver you up to councils, and in their synagogues [cp. 23 34] they will scourge you; **18** yea and before governors and kings shall ye be brought for my sake [cp. 5 11; 10 39; 16 25: also 10 22; 19 29; 24 9], for a testimony to them [cp. 8 4; 24 14] and to the Gentiles [cp. 24 14: also 8 11; 21 31, 41, 43; 22 7-10; 26 13; 28 19]. **19** But when they deliver you up, be not anxious [cp. 6 25, 31, 34] how or

Mark

cp. 11 25, 26.

Mark 8 **38** For whosoever shall be ashamed of me and of my words in this adulterous and sinful generation, the Son of man also shall be ashamed of him, when he cometh in the glory of his Father with the holy angels.

Mark 3 **28** Verily I say unto you, All their sins shall be forgiven unto the sons of men, and their blasphemies wherewith soever they shall blaspheme: **29** but whosoever shall blaspheme against the Holy Spirit hath never forgiveness, but is guilty of an eternal sin.

Mark 13 **9** For they shall deliver you up to councils; and in synagogues shall ye be beaten; and before governors and kings shall ye stand for my sake [cp. 8 35; 10 29: also 13 13], for a testimony unto them [cp. 1 44; 6 11]. **10** And the gospel must first be preached unto all the nations [cp. 12 9; 14 9; 16 15]. **11** And when they lead you to *judgement*, and deliver you up, be not anxious beforehand

Luke

sparrows [cp. 12 24]. **8** And I say unto you, Every one who shall confess [5]me before men, [6]him shall the Son of man also confess before cp. 11 13.

the angels of God [cp. 15 10]: **9** but he that denieth me in the presence of men shall be denied in the presence of the angels of God [see above].

Luke 9 **26** For whosoever shall be ashamed of me and of my words, of him shall the Son of man be ashamed, when he cometh in his own glory, and *the glory* of the Father, and of the holy angels.

10 And every one who shall speak a word against the Son of man, it shall be forgiven him: but unto him that blasphemeth against the Holy Spirit it shall not be forgiven.

Luke 21 **12** But before all these things, they shall lay their hands on you, and shall persecute you, delivering you up to the synagogues and prisons, [7]bringing you before kings and governors for my name's sake. **13** It shall turn unto you for a testimony.

cp. 2 30-32; 3 6; 13 29; 14 21-24; 20 16; 24 47.

14 Settle it therefore in your hearts, not to meditate beforehand how to answer:

11 And when they bring you before the synagogues, and the rulers, and the authorities [cp. 20 20],

cp. 21 17: also 6 22; 9 24; 18 29.

cp. 5 14; 9 5.

be not anxious [cp. 12 22] how or what ye shall answer,

cp. 15 21.

cp. 10 16; 11 52.

what ye shall speak: for it shall be given you in that hour what ye shall speak. **20** For it is not ye that speak, but the Spirit of your Father that speaketh in you.	what ye shall speak: but whatsoever shall be given you in that hour, that speak ye: for it is not ye that speak, but the Holy Ghost.	**15** for I will give you a mouth and wisdom, which all your adversaries shall not be able to withstand or to gainsay.	or what ye shall say: **12** for the Holy Spirit shall teach you in that very hour what ye ought to say.

cp. 14 26.

[1] Gr. *loaves.* [2] Gr. *Gehenna.*
[3] Gr. *in me.* [4] Gr. *in him.*
[5] Gr. *doing.*
[6] Some ancient authorities read *unto you men.*
[7] Or, *age*

[1] Gr. *the myriads of.*
[2] Or, *say unto his disciples. First of all beware ye*
[3] Or, *authority* [4] Gr. *Gehenna.* [5] Gr. *in me.*
[6] Gr. *in him.* [7] Gr. *you being brought.*

§ 152. A Request to Divide an Inheritance and the Parable of the Rich Fool

Luke 12 13-21

13 And one out of the multitude said unto him, [1] Master, bid my brother divide the inheritance with me. **14** But he said unto him, Man, who made me a judge or a divider over you? **15** And he said unto them, Take heed, and keep yourselves from all covetousness: [2] for a man's life consisteth not in the abundance of the things which he possesseth. **16** And he spake a parable unto them, saying, The ground of a certain rich man [*cp.* 16 1, 19] brought forth plentifully: **17** and he reasoned within himself, saying, What shall I do [*cp.* 16 3; 20 13], because I have not where to bestow my fruits? **18** And he said, This will I do: I will pull down my barns [*cp.* 12 24], and build greater; and there will I bestow all my corn and my goods. **19** And I will say to my [3] soul [*cp.* 12 22], [3] Soul, thou hast much goods laid up for many years; take thine ease, eat [*cp.* 12 22], drink [*cp.* 12 22], be merry [*cp.* 15 23]. **20** But God said unto him, Thou foolish one [*cp.* 11 40], this night [4] is thy [3] soul required of thee; and the things which thou hast prepared, whose shall they be? **21** So is he that layeth up treasure for himself, and is not rich toward God [*cp.* 12 33-34; 18 22].

cp. 6 19-21; 19 21.

cp. 10 21.

[1] Or, *Teacher*
[3] Or, *life* [4] Gr. *they require thy soul.*
[2] Gr. *for not in a man's abundance consisteth his life, from the things which he possesseth.*

Luke 12 19: cp. Eccl. 2 24; Is. 22 13.

§ 153. True Treasure and where it may be found

Matt. 6 25-34, 19-21		Luke 12 22-34
25 Therefore I say unto you, Be not anxious [*cp.* 6 31, 34; 10 19] for your life, what ye shall eat, or what ye shall drink; nor yet for your body, what ye shall put on. Is not the life more than the food, and the body than the raiment? **26** Behold the birds of the heaven [*cp.* 8 20; 13 32], that they sow not, neither do they reap, nor gather into barns; and your heavenly Father [*cp.* 5 48; 6 14, 32; 15 13; 18 35; 23 9: *also* 5 16, 45, *etc.*] feedeth them. Are not ye of much more value than they [*cp.* 10 31; 12 12]? **27** And which of you by being anxious can add one cubit unto his [1] stature? **28** And why are ye anxious concerning raiment? Consider the	cp. 13 11. cp. 4 32. cp. 11 25, 26. cp. 4 19.	**22** And he said unto his disciples, Therefore I say unto you, Be not anxious [*cp.* 12 11] for *your* [1] life [*cp.* 12 19], what ye shall eat [*cp.* 12 19]; [*cp.* 12 19] nor yet for your body, what ye shall put on. **23** For the [1] life is more than the food, and the body than the raiment. **24** Consider the ravens [*cp.* 8 5; 9 58; 13 19], that they sow not, neither reap; which have no store chamber nor barn [*cp.* 12 18]; and God feedeth them: of how much more value are ye than the birds [*cp.* 12 7]! **25** And which of you by being anxious can add a cubit unto his [2] stature? **26** If then ye are not able to do even that which is least [*cp.* 16 10; 19 17], why are ye anxious concerning the rest [*cp.* 8 10; 18 9, 11; 24 9, 10]? **27** Consider the

Matthew (left column)

lilies of the field, how they grow ; they toil not, neither do they spin : **29** yet I say unto you, that even Solomon in all his glory was not arrayed like one of these. **30** But if God doth so clothe the grass of the field, which to-day is, and to-morrow is cast into the oven, *shall he* not much more *clothe* you, O ye of little faith [*cp.* 8 26 ; 14 31 ; 16 8 : *also* 17 20] ? **31** Be not therefore anxious, saying, What shall we eat ? or, What shall we drink ? or, Wherewithal shall we be clothed ? **32** For after all these things do the Gentiles [*cp.* 5 47 ; 6 7 ; 18 17] seek ; for your heavenly Father [*see verse* 26] knoweth [*cp.* 6 8] that ye have need of all these things. **33** But seek ye first [*cp.* 5 24 ; 7 5 ; 23 26] his kingdom, and his righteousness [*cp.* 5 6 : *also* 3 15 ; 5 10, 20 ; 6 1 ; 21 32] ; and all these things shall be added unto you. **34** Be not therefore anxious for the morrow : for the morrow will be anxious for itself. Sufficient [*cp.* 10 25] unto the day is the evil thereof.

cp. 26 31.

cp. 3 17 ; 11 26 ; 12 18 ; 17 5.

19 Lay not up for yourselves treasures upon the earth, where moth and rust doth consume, and where thieves [2] break through [*cp.* 24 43] and steal : **20** but lay up [*cp.* 19 21] for yourselves treasures in heaven [*cp.* 19 21], where neither moth nor rust doth consume, and where thieves do not [2] break through [*cp.* 24 43] nor steal : **21** for where thy treasure is, there will thy heart be also.

[1] Or, *age*   [2] Gr. *dig through.*

cp. 4 40 ; 11 22 ; 16 14.
cp. 7 27.
cp. 4 24 ; *also* 10 29-30.
cp. 14 27.
cp. 1 11.
cp. 10 21.
cp. 10 21.

Luke (right column)

lilies, how they grow : they toil not, neither do they spin ; yet I say unto you, Even Solomon in all his glory was not arrayed like one of these. **28** But if God doth so clothe the grass in the field, which to-day is, and to-morrow is cast into the oven ; how much more *shall he clothe* you, O ye of little faith [*cp.* 8 25 ; 17 5, 6 ; 22 32 ; 24 25, 38] ? **29** And seek not ye what ye shall eat, and what ye shall drink, neither be ye of doubtful mind. **30** For all these things do the nations of the world seek after : but your Father knoweth that ye have need of these things. **31** Howbeit seek ye [*cp.* 6 42] [3] his kingdom, and these things shall be added unto you.

32 Fear not, little flock ; for it is your Father's good pleasure [*cp.* 2 14 ; 3 22 ; 10 21] to give you the kingdom.

cp. 12 39.
33 Sell [*cp.* 18 22 : *also* 22 36] that ye have, and give alms [*cp.* 11 41] ; make for yourselves [*cp.* 16 9] purses which wax not old, a treasure in the heavens [*cp.* 18 22 : *also* 12 21] that faileth not, where no thief draweth near, neither moth destroyeth.
cp. 12 39.
34 For where your treasure is, there will your heart be also.

[1] Or, *soul*   [2] Or, *age*   [3] Many ancient authorities read *the kingdom of God.*

Luke right-margin references:
cp. 3 12 ; 6 64 ; 14 10 ; 20 27.
cp. 10 1 *ff.*

§ 154. Injunctions to be Ready for the End

Matt. 25 13 ; 24 42-44

cp. 25 1-13.

25 13 Watch [*cp.* 24 42 ; 26 38, 41] therefore, [*cp.* 26 41] for ye know not the day nor the hour.

cp. 25 14-15.

Mark 13 33-36

13 33 Take ye heed, watch [*cp.* 13 35, 37 : 14 34, 38] [1] and pray [*cp.* 14 38] : for ye know not when the time is.

34 *It is* as *when* a· man, sojourning in another country, having left his house, and given

Luke 12 35-40

35 Let your loins be girded about [*cp.* 12 37 ; 17 8], and your lamps burning ; **36** and be ye yourselves like unto men looking for their lord, when he shall return from the marriage feast ; that, when he cometh and knocketh, they may straightway open unto him.

21 36 But watch [*cp.* 12 37] ye at every season, making supplication [*cp.* 22 40, 46], that ye may prevail to escape all these things that shall come to pass, and to stand before the Son of man.

cp. 19 12-13.

authority to his
² servants,

37 Blessed are
those ¹ servants, whom the
lord when he cometh shall
find [*cp.* 12 38, 43]   *cp.* 13 17.

cp. 24 46.

to each one
his work, commanded also the
porter to watch. **35** Watch [*see
verse* 33] therefore: for
ye know not when
the lord of the house cometh,

watching [*cp.* 21 36]:

24 42 Watch [*cp.*
25 13 : 26 38, 41] therefore: for
ye know not   on what day
your Lord   cometh.

verily I say unto you, that he
shall gird himself [*cp.* 12 35;   *cp.* 13 4.
17 8], and make them sit down
to meat, and shall come and
serve them [*cp.* 22 27: *also*   *cp.* 13 5.
17 8]. **38** And if he shall come
in the second watch, and if in
the third,

whether at even, or at
midnight, or at cockcrowing,
or in the morning; **36** lest
coming suddenly he find you
sleeping [*cp.* 14 37, 40].

and find
[*cp.* 22 45] *them* so,
blessed are those *servants* [*cp.*   *cp.* 13 17.
12 37, 43]. **39** ² But know this
[*cp.* 10 11], that if the master of
the house had known in what
hour the thief was coming, he
would have watched, and
not have left his house to be
³ broken through.

cp. 25 5; 26 40, 43.

43 ¹ But know this,
that if the master of
the house had known in what
watch the thief was coming, he
would have watched, and would
not have suffered his house to be
² broken through [*cp.* 6 19, 20].
44 Therefore be ye also ready
[*cp.* 25 10]:   for in
an hour that ye think not [*cp.*
24 36, 42, 50; 25 13] the Son of
man cometh.

40 Be ye also ready
[*cp.* 12 47: *also* 17 8]: for in
an hour that ye think not [*cp.*
12   46] the Son   of
man cometh.

cp. 13 32, 33, 35.

¹ Or, *But this ye know.*
² Gr. *digged through.*

¹ Some ancient authorities omit
and pray.   ² Gr. *bondservants.*

¹ Gr. *bondservants.*
² Or, *But this ye know*
³ Gr. *digged through.*

§ 155. ⸿The Obligations of Stewards in the Interim

[*Cp.* Matt. 25 14-30; Luke 19 11-27]

Matt. 24 45-51	Mark 13 37	Luke 12 41-48	
cp. 14 28; 15 15; 16 22; 17 4; 18 21; 19 27; 26 33: *also* 16 16; 17 24.	**37** And [*cp.* 8 32; 9 5; 10 28; 11 21; 14 29: *also* 8 29] what I say unto you I say unto all, Watch [*see* 13 33]. *cp.* 16 19, 20.	**41** And Peter [*cp.* 8 45; 9 33; 18 28: *also* 5 8; 9 20] said, Lord, speakest thou this parable unto us, or even unto all ? **42** And the Lord [*cp.* 7 13, 19; 10 1, 39, 41; 11 39; 13 15; 17 5, 6; 18 6; 19 8; 22 61; 24 3, 34] said, Who then is	*cp.* 13 36, 37; 21 21: *also* 6 68. *cp.* 4 1; 6 23; 11 2; 20 2, 18, 20, 25; 21 7, 12.

45 Who then is
the faithful [*cp.* 25 21, 23]
and wise [*cp.* 7 24; 10 16; 25 2 *ff.*]
¹ servant, whom his lord hath
set over [*cp.* 24 47; 25 21, 23] his
household, to give them their
food in due season? **46** Blessed is
that ¹ servant, whom his lord when
he cometh shall find   so
doing. **47** Verily
I say unto you, that he will set him
over [*cp.* 25 21, 23: *also* 24 45] all that
he hath. **48** But if that evil [*cp.* 18 32;
25 26] ¹ servant shall say in his heart,
My lord tarrieth [*cp.* 25 5];   **49** and
shall begin to beat his fellow-servants
[*cp.* 18 28, 29, 31, 33],
and shall eat and drink with
the drunken;   **50** the lord of
that ¹ servant [*cp.* 18 27; 25 19] shall
come in a day when he expecteth not,

¹ the faithful [*cp.* 16 10, 11, 12; 19 17]
and wise [*cp.* 16 8]   steward
[*cp.* 16 1 *ff.*],   whom his lord shall
set over [*cp. verse* 44]   his
household, to give them their portion
of food in due season? **43** Blessed is
that ² servant, whom his lord when
he cometh shall find [*cp.* 12 37, 38] so
doing. **44** Of a truth [*cp.* 9 27; 21 3]
I say unto you, that he will set him
over [*cp. verse* 42: *also* 19 17,19] all that   *cp.* 13 17.
he hath. **45** But if that   [*cp.* 19 22]
² servant shall say in his heart,
My lord delayeth his coming; and
shall begin to beat the menservants
and the maid-
servants, and to eat and drink, and to
be drunken [*cp.* 21 34]; **46** the lord of
that ² servant   shall
come in a day when he expecteth not,

and in an hour when he knoweth not [*cp.* 24 36, 42, 44 ; 25 13], 51 and shall [2] cut him asunder, and appoint his portion with the hypocrites [*cp.* 6 2, 5, 16 : *also* 15 7 ; 22 18 ; 23 13 *ff.*] : there shall be the weeping and gnashing of teeth [*cp.* 8 12 ; 13 42, 50 ; 22 13 ; 25 30].	*cp.* 13 32, 33, 35. *cp.* 7 6 ; 12 15.	and in an hour when he knoweth not [*cp.* 12 40], and shall [3] cut him asunder, and appoint his portion with the [*cp.* 12 1, 56 ; 13 15] unfaithful.

¹ Gr. *bondservant.*   ² Or, *severely scourge him*

		cp. 13 28.
		47 And that [2] servant, which knew his lord's will, and made not ready [*cp.* 12 40 : *also* 17 8], nor did according to his will, shall be beaten with many *stripes* ; **48** but he that knew not, and did things worthy of stripes, shall be beaten with few *stripes*. And to whomsoever much is given, of him shall much be required : and to whom they commit much, of him will they ask the more [*cp.* 19 11-27].
cp. 25 14-30.		

¹ Or, *the faithful steward, the wise* man *whom &c.*   ² Gr. *bondservant.*
³ Or, *severely scourge him*

§ 156. Divisions within Families

Matt. 10 34-36		Luke 12 49-53	
cp. 3 11.		**49** I came to cast fire upon the earth [*cp.* 3 16] ; and what will I, if it is already kindled ? **50** But I have a baptism to be baptized with ; and how am I straitened till it be accomplished [*cp.* 18 31 ; 22 37 : *also* 13 32] ! **51** Think ye that I am come to give peace in the earth ? I tell you, Nay ; but rather division : **52** for there shall be from henceforth [*cp.* 1 48 ; 5 10 ; 22 18, 69] five in one house divided, three against two, and two against three. **53** They shall be divided, father against son, and son against father ; mother against daughter, and daughter against her mother ; mother in law against her daughter in law, and daughter in law against her mother in law.	*cp.* 12 27. *cp.* 19 28, 30 : *also* 4 34 ; 5 36 ; 17 4.
	cp. 10 38, 39.		
34 Think not that I came to [1] send peace on the earth : I came not to [1] send peace, but a sword.			
35 For I came to set a man at variance against his father, and the daughter against her mother, and the daughter in law against her mother in law : **36** and a man's foes *shall be* they of his own household [*cp.* 10 25 : *also* 10 21].	*cp.* 13 12.	*cp.* 21 16.	

¹ Gr. *cast.*

Luke 12 52-53 ‖ Matt. 10 35-36 : Mic. 7 6 ; *cp.* Is. 19 2.

§ 157. The Signs of the Times and the Need for Reconciliation in view of the Coming Judgement

Matt. 16 2-3 ; 5 25-26		Luke 12 54-59
16 **2** But he answered and said unto them, [1] When it is [*cp.* 24 15, 33] evening, ye say, *It will be* fair weather : for the heaven is red. **3** And in the morning, [*cp.* 24 15, 33] *It will be* foul weather to-day : for the heaven is red and lowring. *cp.* 15 7 ; 22 18 ; 23 13, *etc.* : *also* 6 2, 5, 16 ; 24 51 : *and* 23 28. Ye know how to discern the face of the heaven ; but ye cannot *discern* the signs of the times [*cp.* 24 32-33].	*cp.* 13 14, 29. *cp.* 13 14, 29. *cp.* 7 6 : *also* 12 15. *cp.* 13 28-29.	**54** And he said to the multitudes also, When ye see [*cp.* 12 55 ; 21 20, 31] a cloud rising in the west, straightway ye say, There cometh a shower ; and so it cometh to pass. **55** And when *ye see* [*cp.* 12 54 ; 21 20, 31] a south wind blowing, ye say, There will be a [1] scorching heat ; and it cometh to pass. **56** Ye hypocrites [*cp.* 13 15 : *also* 12 1], ye know how to [2] interpret the face of the earth and the heaven ; but how is it that ye know not how to [2] interpret this time [*cp.* 21 29-31] ?

5 **25** Agree with thine adversary quickly, whiles thou art with him in the way; lest haply the adversary deliver thee to the judge, and the judge [2] deliver thee to the officer, and thou be cast into prison. **26** Verily I say unto thee, Thou shalt by no means come out thence, till thou have paid the last farthing [*cp.* 18 34, 35].

57 And why even of yourselves [*cp.* 21 30] judge ye not what is right? **58** For as thou art going with thine adversary before the magistrate, on the way give diligence to be quit of him; lest haply he hale thee unto the judge, and the judge shall deliver thee to the [3] officer, and the [3] officer shall cast thee into prison. **59** I say unto thee, Thou shalt by no means come out thence, till thou have paid the very last mite.

cp. 7 24.

[1] The following words, to the end of ver. 3, are omitted by some of the most ancient and other important authorities.
[2] Some ancient authorities omit *deliver thee*.

[1] Or, *hot wind*   [2] Gr. *prove*.   [3] Gr. *exactor*.

§ 158. An Exhortation to Repentance

[*Cp.* John 9 1-12]

Luke 13 1-5

cp. 3 2; 4 17: *also* 11 20.

cp. 1 15; 6 12.

1 Now there were some present at that very season which told him of the Galilæans, whose blood Pilate had mingled with their sacrifices. **2** And he answered and said unto them, Think ye that these Galilæans were sinners above all the Galilæans, because they have suffered these things? **3** I tell you, Nay: but, except ye repent, ye shall all in like manner perish. **4** Or those eighteen [*cp.* 13 11, 16], upon whom the tower in Siloam fell, and killed them, think ye that they were [1] offenders above all the men that dwell in Jerusalem? **5** I tell you, Nay: but, except ye repent, ye shall all likewise perish.

cp. 9 7, 11.

[1] Gr. *debtors*.

§ 159. The Parable of the Fig Tree

[*Cp.* Matt. 24 32-33 ‖ Mark 13 28-29 ‖ Luke 21 29-31: *also* Matt 21 18-20 ‖ Mark 11 12-14, 20-21]

Luke 13 6-9

cp. 20 1; 21 28, 33.
cp. 21 19.
cp. 3 10; 7 19.

cp. 12 1.

cp. 11 13.

6 And he spake this parable; A certain man had a fig tree planted in his vineyard [*cp.* 20 9]; and he came seeking fruit thereon, and found none. **7** And he said unto the vinedresser, Behold, these three years I come seeking fruit on this fig tree, and find none: cut it down [*cp.* 3 9]; why doth it also cumber the ground? **8** And he answering saith unto him, Lord, let it alone this year also, till I shall dig about it, and dung it: **9** and if it bear fruit thenceforth, *well*; but if not, thou shalt cut it down.

cp. 15 2, 6.

(iv) Events on the Journey II (§§ 160-163)

§ 160. The Healing of a Woman with a Spirit of Infirmity

[*Cp.* Matt. 12 9-14 ‖ Mark 3 1-6 ‖ Luke 6 6-11; Luke 14 1-6; John 5 2-18, 7 21-24, 9 1-34: *also* Matt. 12 1-8 ‖ Mark 2 23-28 ‖ Luke 6 1-5]

Luke 13 10-17

cp. 12 9; 13 54: *also* 4 23; 9 35.

cp. 9 20.

cp. 1 21; 3 1; 6 2: *also* 1 39.

cp. 5 25-26.

10 And he was teaching in one of the synagogues [*cp.* 4 16, 31-33; 6 6: *also* 4 15, 44] on the sabbath day. **11** And behold, a woman which had a spirit of infirmity eighteen [*cp.* 13 4] years; and she was bowed together, and could in no wise lift herself up [*cp.* 8 43]. **12** And when Jesus saw her, he called her, and said to her, Woman, thou art loosed from thine

cp. 6 59: *also* 18 20.

cp. 9 18; 19 13, 15; etc.
cp. 9 8; 15 31: also 5 16.

cp. 5 23; 6 5; 8 23, 25; etc.
cp. 2 12.
cp. 5 22.

infirmity. **13** And he laid his hands [cp. 4 40: also 5 13; 7 14; 8 54; 14 4; 18 15; 22 51] upon her: and immediately she was made straight, and glorified God [cp. 2 20; 5 25, 26; 7 16; 17 15, 18; 18 43; 23 47]. **14** And the ruler of the synagogue [cp. 8 41], being moved with indignation because Jesus had healed on the sabbath, answered and said to the multitude, There are six days in which men ought to work: in them therefore come and be healed, and not on the day of the sabbath.

cp. 9 6; 20 17.
cp. 9 24.

12 11 And he

cp. 16 19, 20.

15 But the Lord [cp. 7 13, 19; 10 1, 39, 41; 11 39; 12 42; 17 5, 6; 18 6; 19 8; 22 61; 24 3, 34] answered him, and said, Ye hypocrites [cp. 12 56: also 12 1], doth not each one of you on the sabbath loose his ox or his ass from the 1 stall, and lead him away to watering?

Luke 14 **5** And he

cp. 4 1; 6 23; 11 2; 20 2, 18, 20, 25; 21 7, 12.

said unto them,
cp. 15 7; 22 18; 23 13 ff.: also 6 2, 5, 16; 24 51.
What man shall there be of you, that shall have
one
sheep,
and if this fall into a pit on the sabbath day,

will he not
lay hold on it, and lift it out?
12 How much then is a man of more value [cp. 6 26; 10 31] than a sheep!
cp. 3 9.

cp. 7 6: also 12 15.

said unto them,

Which
of you   shall have
1 an ass or an ox
fallen into a well,
and
will   not straightway draw him
up on a sabbath day?

1 Many ancient authorities read *a son.* See ch. 13 15.

16 And ought not this woman,
cp. 12 7, 24.
being a daughter of Abraham [cp. 19 9: also 3 8; 16 24, 30], whom Satan had bound, lo, *these* eighteen years [*see above*], to have been loosed from this bond on the day of the sabbath?

cp. 8 33, 37, 39, 53.

Wherefore it is lawful to do good on the sabbath day.

cp. 3 4.

cp. 6 9.

cp. 7 23.

17 And as he said these things, all his adversaries were put to shame: and all the multitude rejoiced for all the glorious things that were done by him.

1 Gr. *manger.*

Luke 13 **14**: cp. Exod. 20 9-10; Deut. 5 13-14.

§ 161. The Parables of the Mustard Seed and the Leaven

Matt. 13 31-33	Mark 4 30-32	Luke 13 18-21
	30 And he said, How shall we liken the kingdom of God? or in what parable shall we set it forth?	**18** He said therefore, Unto what is the kingdom of God like? and
31 Another parable set he before them,		whereunto shall I liken it?
saying, The kingdom of heaven is like unto a grain of mustard seed [cp. 17 20], which a man took, and sowed in his field: **32** which indeed is less than all seeds;	**31** 1 It is like a grain of mustard seed, which, when it is sown upon the earth, though it be less than all the seeds that are upon the earth, **32** yet	**19** It is like unto a grain of mustard seed [cp. 17 6], which a man took, and cast into his own garden;
but when it is grown, it is greater than the herbs,	when it is sown, groweth up, and becometh greater than all the herbs, and putteth out great branches;	and it grew,
and becometh a tree, so that the birds of the heaven come and lodge in the branches thereof.	so that the birds of the heaven can lodge under the shadow thereof.	and became a tree; and the birds of the heaven lodged in the branches thereof.

33 Another parable spake he unto them ;
The kingdom
of heaven   is like unto leaven,
which a woman took, and hid in three
¹ measures of meal, till it was all
leavened.

¹ The word in the Greek denotes the Hebrew
seah, a measure containing nearly a peck and
a half.

¹ Gr. As unto.

20 And again he said,
Whereunto shall I liken the kingdom
of God ? 21 It is like unto leaven,
which a woman took and hid in three
¹ measures of meal, till it was all
leavened.

¹ See footnote on Matt. 13 33.

§ 162. A Question about Salvation

Matt. 7 13-14; 25 10-12; 7 22-23;
8 11-12.

Luke 13 22-30

cp. 9 35.

cp. 16 21 ; 20 17, 18.

cp. 6 6.

cp. 10 32, 33.

22 And he went on his way through
cities and villages [cp. 8 1], teaching,
and journeying on unto Jerusalem
[cp. 9 51, 53 ; 17 11 ; 19 11, 41 : also
9 31 ; 13 33 ; 18 31]. 23 And one
said unto him, Lord, are they few
[cp. Matt. 7 14] that be saved ? And
he said unto them, 24 Strive to enter
in [cp. 11 52 ; 18 17, 24, 25 ; 24 26]
by
the narrow door :

7 13 Enter
ye in [cp. 5 20 ; 7 21 ; 18 3, 8, 9 ; 19
17, 23, 24 ; 21 31 ; 23 13 ; 25 21, 23] by
the narrow gate : for wide ¹ is the gate,
and broad is the way, that leadeth to
destruction, and many
be they that enter in thereby. 14 ² For
narrow is the gate, and straitened the way,
that leadeth unto life, and few [cp. Luke
13 23] be they that find it.

cp. 9 43, 45,
47 ; 10 15,
23, 24, 25.

for many, I say unto you,
shall seek to enter in,

and shall not be ¹ able.

cp. 10 1, 2,
9 ; 3 5.

25 10 And while they went away to buy,
the bridegroom came ; and they that
were ready went in with him to the
marriage feast :
and
the door was shut. 11 Afterward come
also the other virgins,

25 When once the master
of the house is risen up, and hath shut
to the door,
and ye begin to
stand without, and to knock at the
door, saying, Lord,   open to us ;
and he shall answer and say to you,
I know you not

cp. 7 27, 28 ;
etc. below.
cp. 14 20 ;
16 23, 26.

saying, Lord, Lord, open to us.
12 But he answered and said,
Verily I say unto you, I know you not.
7 22 Many
will say to me in that day [cp. 24 36 : also
26 29], Lord, Lord, did we not prophesy
by thy name, and by thy name cast out
³ devils, and by thy name do many
⁴ mighty works ?

cp. 13 32 :
also 14 25.

cp. 9 38, 39.

whence ye are ; 26 then shall ye begin
to say,   [cp. 10 12 ; 17
31 ; 21 34] We did

cp. 9 49.
eat and drink in
thy presence, and thou didst teach in
our streets ; 27 and   he shall say,
I tell you, I
know not whence ye are ; depart from
me,   all ye workers of
iniquity.

23 And then will I profess
unto them [cp. 25 34, 41],   I
never knew   you : depart from
me [cp. 25 41], ye that work
iniquity. 8 11 And I say unto you, that
many shall come from the east and the
west, and shall ⁵ sit down with

Abraham, and
Isaac, and Jacob,
in the kingdom of heaven :
12 but the sons of the kingdom [cp. 13 38 :
also 5 9, 45] shall be cast forth into the
outer darkness [cp. 22 13 ; 25 30] : there
shall be the weeping and gnashing of
teeth [cp. 13 42, 50 ; 22 13 ; 24 51 ; 25 30].

cp. 7 27, 28 ;
8 14 ; 9
29, 30.

28 There
shall be the weeping and gnashing of
teeth, when ye shall see Abraham, and
Isaac, and Jacob, and all the prophets,
in the kingdom of God, and yourselves   [cp. 6 35 ;
16 8 ; 20 36]   cast forth
without.

cp. 12 36.

cp. 26 29.

cp. 14 25.

29 And they shall come from the east
and west, and from the north and
south, and shall ² sit down [cp. 14 15 ;
22 16, 18, 30] in the kingdom of God

cp. 21 31, 41, 43 ; 22 7-10: *also* 10 18 ; 24 14 ; 26 13 ; 28 19.	*cp.* 12 9: *also* 13 10; 14 9; 16 15.	[*cp.* 14 21-24; 20 16: *also* 2 30-32; 3 6; 24 47]. **30** And behold, there are last which shall be first, and there are first which shall be last.	*cp.* 10 16; 11 52.
cp. 19 30 ; 20 16.	*cp.* 10 31.		

¹ Some ancient authorities omit *is the gate.*
² Many ancient authorities read *How narrow is the gate, &c.*
³ Gr. *demons.*   ⁴ Gr. *powers.*   ⁵ Gr. *recline.*

¹ Or, *able, when once*   ² Gr. *recline.*

Luke 13 27 ‖ Matt. 7 23 = Ps. 6 8.   Luke 13 29 ‖ Matt. 8 11 : *cp.* Ps. 107 3 *and* Is. 49 12.

§ 163. **Advice from the Pharisees and a Lament over Jerusalem**

[*Cp.* Luke 19 41-44: *also* 23 27-31 *and* 21 20]

Luke 13 31-35

cp. 18 1; 26 55.		**31** In that very hour [*cp.* 7 21 ; 10 21] there came certain Pharisees, saying to him, Get thee out, and go hence: for Herod would fain kill thee. **32** And he said unto them, Go and say to that fox, Behold, I cast out ¹ devils and perform cures to-day and to-morrow, and the third *day* [*cp.* 9 22 ; 18 33 ; 24 7, 21, 46] I am perfected [*cp.* 12 50 ; 18 31 ; 22 37: John 19 28, 30: *also* John 4 34 ; 5 36 ; 17 4]. **33** Howbeit I must go on my way to-day and to-morrow and the *day* following: for it cannot be that a prophet [*cp.* 4 24 ; 7 16, 39 ; 24 19] perish out of Jerusalem [*cp.* 9 31, 51 ; 18 31]. **34** O Jerusalem, Jerusalem, which killeth the prophets [*cp.* 6 23 ; 11 47-50; 20 10-12], and stoneth them that are sent unto her ! how often would I have gathered thy children [*cp.* 19 44] together, even as a hen *gathereth* her own brood under her wings, and ye would not ! **35** Behold, your house is left unto you *desolate* [*cp.* 21 20: *also* 19 43-44; 23 29-31]: and I say unto you, Ye shall not see me, until ye shall say, Blessed *is* he that cometh [*cp.* 7 19, 20: *also* 3 16] in the name of the Lord [= 19 38 *and* John 12 13].	*cp.* 2 19.
cp. 12 40; 16 21 ; *etc.* *cp.* 8 31 ; *etc.*			
cp. 13 57 ; 21 11, 46. *cp.* 16 21 ; 20 17, 18. Matt. 23 **37** O Jerusalem, Jerusalem, which killeth the prophets [*cp.* 5 12 ; 21 35-36; 22 6 ; 23 29-34], and stoneth [*cp.* 21 35] them that are sent unto her ! how often would I have gathered thy children together, even as a hen gathereth her chickens under her wings, and ye would not ! **38** Behold, your house is left unto you ¹ desolate.	*cp.* 6 4, 15. *cp.* 10 32, 33. *cp.* 12 3-5.	*cp.* 4 19, 44 ; 6 14 ; 7 40 ; 9 17.	
39 For I say unto you, Ye shall not see me henceforth [*cp.* 26 29, 64], till ye shall say, Blessed *is* he that cometh [*cp.* 3 11 ; 11 3] in the name of the Lord [= 21 9 *and* John 12 13].	*cp.* 1 7. 11 9.		*cp.* 13 19; 14 7. *cp.* 1 15, 27; 3 31 ; 6 14; 11 27: *also* 1 30.

¹ Some ancient authorities omit *desolate.*

¹ Gr. *demons.*

Luke 13 35 ‖ Matt. 23 39 = Ps. 118 26.

(v) Jesus a Guest in the House of a Ruler of the Pharisees on the Sabbath (§§ 164-167)

§ 164. **The Healing of a Man with the Dropsy**

[*Cp.* Matt. 12 1-8; Mark 2 23-28; Luke 6 1-5; 13 10-17; John 5 2-18; 7 21-24; 9 1-34]

Matt. 12 9-14	Mark 3 1-6	Luke 6 6-11	**Luke 14** 1-6	
9 And he departed thence, and went into their synagogue [*cp.* 13 54: *also* 4 23; 9 35]: **10** and behold, a man having [*cp.* 5 29, 30, 39 ; 27 29] a withered hand.	**1** And he entered again into the synagogue [*cp.* 1 21 ; 6 2: *also* 1 39]; and there was a man there which had his hand withered.	**6** And it came to pass on another sabbath, that he entered into the synagogue [*cp.* 4 16, 33 ; 13 10: *also* 4 15, 44] and taught : and there was a man there, and his right [*cp.* 22 50] hand was withered. **7** And the scribes and the Pharisees	**1** And it came to pass, when he went into the house of one of the rulers of the Pharisees on a sab-bath to eat bread [*cp.* 7 36 ; 11 37], that they were watching	*cp.* 6 59; 18 20. *cp* 18 10.
verse 14	*verse 6* **2** And they watched	watched		

Matthew	Mark	Mark	Luke
	him, whether he would heal him on the sabbath day; that they might accuse him [cp. 12 13].	him, whether he would heal on the sabbath; that they might find how to accuse him [cp. 11 53-54; 20 20].	him [cp. 20 20].
see below.			**2** And behold, there was before him a certain man which had the dropsy.
			cp. 8 6.
cp. 9 4; 12 25; 16 8.	*cp. 2 8; 8 17.*	**8** But he knew their thoughts [cp. 5 22; 9 47; 11 17]; and he said to the man that had his hand withered, Rise up, and stand forth [cp. 5 24; 7 14; 8 54] in the midst. And he arose and stood forth. **9** And Jesus said unto them,	*cp. 1 48; 2 24, 25; 4 19, 29; 5 6, 42; etc.*
	3 And he saith unto the man that had his hand withered, 1 Stand forth [cp. 2 11; 5 41; 10 49].		
cp. 9 6.			*cp. 5 8.*
And they asked him, saying, Is it lawful [cp. 19 3; 22 17] to heal on the sabbath day? that they might accuse him [cp. 22 15].	**4** And he saith unto them, Is it lawful [cp. 10 2; 12 14] on the sabbath day *verse 2* to do good, or to do harm? to save a life, or to kill? But they held their peace.	I ask you, Is it lawful on the sabbath *verse 7* to do good, or to do harm? to save a life, or to destroy it?	**3** And Jesus answering spake unto the lawyers and Pharisees, saying, Is it lawful [cp. 20 22] to heal on the sabbath, or not?
11 And he said unto them, What man shall there be of you, that shall have one sheep, and if this fall into a pit on the sabbath day, will he not lay hold on it, and lift it out?			**4** But they held their peace. And he took him, and healed [cp. 6 19; 9 2, 11, 42; 22 51] him, and let him go. **5** And he said unto them, Which of you shall have 1 an ass or an ox fallen into a well, and will not straightway draw him up on a sabbath day?
		cp. 13 15-16.	
12 How much then is a man of more value than a sheep [cp. 6 26; 10 31]! Wherefore it is lawful to do good on the sabbath day. **13** Then			*cp. 12 7, 24.*
			cp. 7 23.
	5 And when he had looked round about [cp. 3 34; 5 32; 9 8; 10 23; 11 11] on them with anger, being grieved at the hardening of their heart [cp. 10 5: *also* 6 52; 8 17; 16 14],	**10** And he looked round about on them all,	
cp. 19 8.			*cp. 12 40.*
saith he to the man, Stretch forth thy hand. And he stretched it forth; and it was restored whole, as the other. **14** But the Pharisees went out, and	he saith unto the man, Stretch forth thy hand. And he stretched it forth: and his hand was restored. **6** And the Pharisees went out, and straightway with	and said unto him, Stretch forth thy hand. And he did *so*: and his hand was restored. *verse 7*	

cp. 22 16.

the Herodians [cp. 12 13]

took counsel [cp. 22 15; 27 1, 7; 28 12] against him, how they might destroy him [cp. 21 46; 26 4]. cp. 22 46.

took counsel [cp. 15 1] against him, how they might destroy him [cp. 11 18; 12 12; 14 1].

11 But they were filled with ¹ madness; and communed one with another what they 19 47; 20 19, 20; 22 might do to Jesus [cp. 2].

6 And they could not answer again unto these things.

cp. 5 16, 18; 7 30, 32; 11 53.

¹ Gr. *Arise into the midst.*   Or, *foolishness*   ¹ Many ancient authorities read *a son.* See ch. 13 15.

§ 165. Advice to Guests

Luke 14 7-11

cp. 23 6.   cp. 12 39.

cp. 22 2 *ff.*

7 And he spake a parable unto those which were bidden, when he marked how they chose out the chief seats [cp. 20 46: *also* 11 43]; saying unto them, 8 When thou art bidden of any man to a marriage feast, ¹ sit not down in the chief seat; lest haply a more honourable man than thou be bidden of him, 9 and he that bade thee and him shall come and say to thee, Give this man place; and then thou shalt begin with shame to take the lowest place. 10 But when thou art bidden, go and sit down in the lowest place; that when he that hath bidden thee cometh, he may say to thee, Friend [cp. 11 5], go up higher: then shalt thou have glory in the presence of all that sit at meat with thee. 11 For every one

Matt. 23 12 And whosoever shall exalt himself shall be humbled; and whosoever shall humble himself [cp. 18 4] shall be exalted.

that exalteth himself shall be humbled; and he that humbleth himself shall be exalted.

Luke 18 14 For every one that exalteth himself shall be humbled; but he that humbleth himself shall be exalted.

¹ Gr. *recline not.*

§ 166. Advice to Hosts

Luke 14 12-14

12 And he said to him also that had bidden him, When thou makest a dinner or a supper, call not thy friends, nor thy brethren, nor thy kinsmen, nor rich neighbours; lest haply they also bid thee again, and a recompense be made thee. 13 But when thou makest a feast, bid the poor, the maimed, the lame, the blind [cp. 14 21]: 14 and thou shalt be blessed; because they have not *wherewith* to recompense thee: for thou shalt be recompensed in the resurrection of the just.

§ 167. The Parable of the Great Supper

[*Cp.* Matt. 8 11; 21 31, 41-43: *also* 10 18; 24 14; 26 13; 28 19: Mark 12 9-11: *also* 13 10; 14 9; 16 15: Luke 13 29; 20 16-17: *also* 2 30-32; 3 6; 24 47: John 10 16; 11 52]

Matt. 22 1-14

Luke 14 15-24

15 And when one of them that sat at meat with him heard these things, he said unto him, Blessed is he that shall eat bread in the kingdom of God [cp. 13 29; 22 16, 18, 30]. 16 But he

cp. 8 11; 26 29.

1 And Jesus answered and spake again in parables unto them, saying, 2 The kingdom of heaven is likened unto a certain king [cp. 18 23 : *also* 25 34, 40], which made a marriage feast for his son,

cp. 14 25.

said unto him,

A certain   [cp. 19 12, 15, 27] man made   [cp. 14 8] a great supper; and he bade many:

3 and   sent forth his ¹ servants [cp. 21 34]   to call them that

cp. 12 2.

17 and he sent forth his ¹ servant [cp. 20 10] at supper time to say to them that

were bidden to the marriage feast: and they would not come. **4** Again he sent forth other [1] servants [*cp.* 21 36], saying, Tell them that are bidden, Behold, I have made ready my dinner: my oxen and my fatlings are killed, and all things are ready: come to the marriage feast. **5** But they made light of it, and went their ways, one to his own farm,

another to his merchandise:

6 and the rest laid hold on his [1] servants, and entreated them shamefully, and killed them [*cp.* 21 35, 36: *also* 5 12; 23 29-34, 37].

cp. 13 27, 52; 20 1; 21 33.
7 But the king was wroth [*cp.* 18 34]; and he sent his armies, and destroyed those murderers [*cp.* 21 41], and burned their city. **8** Then saith he to his [1] servants, The wedding is ready, but they that were bidden were not worthy. **9** Go ye therefore unto

the partings of the highways, and as many as ye shall find, bid to the marriage feast.

10 And those [1] servants went out into the highways, and gathered together all as many as they found, both bad and good [*cp.* 13 30, 47; 25 32]: and the wedding was filled with guests. **11** But when the king came in to behold the guests, he saw there a man which had not on a wedding-garment: **12** and he saith unto him, Friend [*cp.* 20 13; 26 50], how camest thou in hither not having a wedding-garment? And he was speechless. **13** Then the king said to the [2] servants, Bind him hand and foot, and cast him out into the outer darkness [*cp.* 8 12; 25 30]; there shall be the weeping and gnashing of teeth [*cp.* 8 12; 13 42, 50; 24 51; 25 30]. **14** For many are called, but few chosen.

[1] Gr. *bondservants.*   [2] Or, *ministers*

cp. 12 4-5.

cp. 12 3, 4, 5.

cp. 12 9.

were bidden,

cp. 20 11-12.

Come; for *all* things are now ready. **18** And they all with one *consent* began to make excuse. The first said unto him, I have bought a field, and I must needs go out and see it: I pray thee have me excused. **19** And another said, I have bought five yoke of oxen, and I go to prove them: I pray thee have me excused. **20** And another said, I have married a wife, and therefore I cannot come.

cp. 20 10, 11, 12; *also* 6 23; 11 47-50; 13 33, 34.
21 And the [1] servant came, and told his lord these things. Then the master of the house being angry

cp. 20 16.
said to his [1] servant,
Go out quickly into the streets and lanes of the city, and bring in hither the poor and maimed and blind and lame [*cp.* 14 13]. **22** And the [1] servant said, Lord, what thou didst command is done, and yet there is room. **23** And the lord said unto the [1] servant, Go out into the highways and hedges, and constrain *them* to come in, that my house may be filled. **24** For I say unto you, that none of those men which were bidden shall taste of my supper.

[1] Gr. *bondservant.*

cp. 13 28.

(vi) An Address to the Multitudes (§ 168)

§ 168. **The Cost of Discipleship**

Luke 14 25-35

cp. 9 22; 16 23.

Matt. 10 **37** He that loveth

cp. 5 30; 8 33.

25 Now there went with him great multitudes: and he turned [*cp.* 7 9, 44; 9 55; 10 23; 22 61; 23 28], and said unto them, **26** If any man cometh unto me, and hateth not his own

cp. 1 38.

cp. 12 25.

father or mother
more than me is not worthy of me;
and he that loveth son or daughter

cp. 19 29.

cp. 10 39 ; 16 25-26.
more than me is not worthy of me.

cp. 8 18-22.

38 And he that
doth not take his cross and follow
after me, is not worthy of me.

cp. 10 29.
cp. 8 35-37.

father, and mother, and wife [*cp.* 18 29],
and children, and
brethren, and sisters [*cp.* 18 29], yea,
and his own life [*cp.* 9 24 ; 17 33] also,
he
cannot be my disciple [*cp. verses* 27 *and* 33: *also* 9 57-62]. **27** Whosoever
doth not bear his own cross, and come
after me, cannot
be my disciple [*cp. verses* 26 *and* 33].

cp. 12 25.

Matt. 16 **24** If any man
would come after
me, let him deny him-
self, and take up his
cross, and follow
me [*cp.* 4 19 ; 8 22 ; 9
9 ; 19 21].

Mark 8 **34** If any man
would come after
me, let him deny him-
self, and take up his
cross, and follow
me [*cp.* 1 17 ; 2 14 ;
10 21].

Luke 9 **23** If any man
would come after
me, let him deny him-
self, and take up his
cross daily, and follow
me [*cp.* 5 27 ; 9 59 ;
18 22].

John 12 **26** If any man
serve
me, let him

follow
me [*cp.* 1 43 ; 21 19,
22] ; and where I am,
there shall also my ser-
vant be.

28 For which of you, desiring to build a tower, doth not first
sit down and count the cost, whether he have *wherewith* to complete it ? **29** Lest haply, when he hath laid a foundation, and
is not able to finish, all that behold begin to mock him, **30** saying, This man began to build, and was not able to finish. **31** Or
what king, as he goeth to encounter another king in war, will
not sit down first and take counsel whether he is able with ten
thousand to meet him that cometh against him with twenty
thousand ? **32** Or else, while the other is yet a great way off,
he sendeth an ambassage [*cp.* 19 14], and asketh conditions of
peace. **33** So therefore whosoever he be of you that renounceth
[*cp.* 9 61] not all that he hath [*cp.* 5 11, 28], he cannot be my
disciple [*cp. verses* 26 *and* 27].

cp. 19 27.
cp. 10 28.

Matt. 5 **13** Ye are the salt of the
earth : but if the salt
have lost its savour, wherewith
shall it be salted ? it
is thenceforth good for nothing,
but to
be cast out and trodden under
foot of men.

Mark 9 **50** Salt is
good : but if the salt
have lost its saltness, wherewith
will ye season it ?

34 Salt therefore is
good : but if even the salt
have lost its savour, wherewith
shall it be seasoned ? **35** It
is fit neither for the
land nor for the dunghill:
men cast it out.

He that hath
ears to hear, let him hear
[*cp.* 8 8].

cp. 11 15 ; 13 9, 43 : *also* 19 12.
cp. 4 9, 23 ; 7 16.
cp. 6 60.

(vii) Three Parables on Things Lost and Found (§§ 169-172)

§ 169. **The Occasion of the Parables**

Luke 15 1-2

1 Now all the publicans and sinners were drawing near unto
him for to hear him. **2** And both the Pharisees and the scribes
murmured, saying, This man receiveth sinners, and eateth
with them [*cp.* 5 30 ; 7 34, 39 ; 19 7].

cp. 9 11 ; 11 19.
cp. 2 16.

§ 170. **The Lost Sheep**

Matt. 18 12-13

Luke 15 3-7

12 How think ye
[*cp.* 17 25 ; 21 28 ; 22 17, 42 ; 26 66] ?
if any man have a hundred
sheep, and one of them
be gone astray, doth he not leave the
ninety and nine, and
go unto the mountains, and seek that
which goeth astray ?

3 And he spake unto them this
parable, saying,

4 What man of you, having a hundred
sheep, and having lost one of them,
doth not leave the
ninety and nine in the wilderness, and
go after that
which is lost, until he find it [*cp.* 15 8:

cp. 11 56.
cp. 10 1 *ff.*

13 And if so be that he
find it,
verily I say unto you, he rejoiceth
over it

more than over the
ninety and nine
which have not gone astray.

also 19 10]? **5** And when he hath
found it, he layeth it on his shoulders,
rejoicing.
6 And when he cometh home,
he calleth together his friends and his
neighbours, saying unto them, Rejoice
with me [*cp.* 15 9: *also* 1 58], for I
have found my sheep which was lost
[*cp.* 15 9, 24, 32]. **7** I say unto you,
that even so there shall be joy in
heaven over one sinner that repenteth
[*cp.* 15 10, 32], *more* than over
ninety and nine righteous persons,
which need no repentance [*cp.* 5 32].

cp. 6 39.

§ 171. The Lost Coin

Luke 15 8-10

8 Or what woman having ten ¹ pieces of silver, if she lose one
piece, doth not light a lamp, and sweep the house, and seek
diligently until she find it [*cp.* 15 4: *also* 19 10] ? **9** And when
she hath found it, she calleth together her friends and neighbours, saying, Rejoice with me [*cp.* 15 6: *also* 1 58], for I have
found the piece which I had lost [*cp.* 15 6, 24, 32]. **10** Even so,
I say unto you, there is joy in the presence of the angels of God
[*cp.* 12 8, 9] over one sinner that repenteth [*cp.* 15 7, 32: *also*
5 32].

¹ Gr. *drachma*, a coin worth about eight pence.

§ 172. The Lost Son

[*Cp.* Matt. 21 28-32]

Luke 15 11-32

cp. 21 28.

11 And he said, A certain man had two sons: **12** and the
younger of them said to his father, Father, give me the portion
of ¹ *thy* substance that falleth to me. And he divided unto
them his living. **13** And not many days after the younger son
gathered all together, and took his journey into a far country
[*cp.* 19 12]; and there he wasted his substance with riotous
living. **14** And when he had spent all, there arose a mighty
famine in that country; and he began to be in want. **15** And
he went and joined himself to one of the citizens of that country;
and he sent him into his fields to feed swine. **16** And he would
fain have been filled with ² the husks that the swine did eat:
and no man gave unto him. **17** But when he came to himself
he said, How many hired servants of my father's have bread
enough and to spare, and I perish here with hunger ! **18** I will
arise and go to my father, and will say unto him, Father, I
have sinned against heaven, and in thy sight: **19** I am no more
worthy to be called thy son: make me as one of thy hired servants. **20** And he arose, and came to his father. But while he
was yet afar off, his father saw him, and was moved with compassion [*cp.* 10 33: *also* 7 13], and ran, and fell on his neck, and
³ kissed him. **21** And the son said unto him, Father, I have
sinned against heaven, and in thy sight: I am no more worthy
to be called thy son.⁴ **22** But the father said to his ⁵ servants,
Bring forth quickly the best robe, and put it on him; and put
a ring on his hand, and shoes on his feet: **23** and bring the
fatted calf, *and* kill it, and let us eat, and make merry: **24** for
this my son was dead, and is alive again; he was lost, and is
found [*cp. verse* 32: *also* 15 6, 9]. And they began to be merry.
25 Now his elder son was in the field: and as he came and
drew nigh to the house, he heard music and dancing. **26** And
he called to him one of the servants, and inquired what these
things might be. **27** And he said unto him, Thy brother is
come; and thy father hath killed the fatted calf, because he

hath received him safe and sound. **28** But he was angry, and would not go in: and his father came out, and intreated him. **29** But he answered and said to his father, Lo, these many years do I serve thee, and I never transgressed a commandment of thine: and *yet* thou never gavest me a kid, that I might make merry with my friends: **30** but when this thy son came, which hath devoured thy living with harlots, thou killedst for him the fatted calf. **31** And he said unto him, [6] Son, thou art ever with me, and all that is mine is thine. **32** But it was meet to make merry, and be glad: for this thy brother was dead, and is alive *again*; and *was* lost, and is found [*cp. verse* 24: *also* 15 6, 9].

[1] Gr. *the*.   [2] Gr. *the pods of the carob tree*.   [3] Gr. *kissed him much*.
[4] Some ancient authorities add *make me as one of thy hired servants*. See ver. 19.
[5] Gr. *bondservants*.   [6] Gr. *Child*.

(viii) A Discourse mainly on Money, its Uses, and its Effects (§§ 173-175)

[*Cp.* Matt. 19 16-24 || Mark 10 17-25 || Luke 18 18-25]

§ 173. **The Parable of the Unrighteous Steward**

Luke 16 1-13

1 And he said also unto the disciples, There was a certain rich man [*cp.* 12 16; 16 19], which had a steward [*cp.* 12 42]; and the same was accused unto him that he was wasting his goods. **2** And he called him, and said unto him, What is this that I hear of thee? render the account of thy stewardship; for thou canst be no longer steward. **3** And the steward said within himself, What shall I do [*cp.* 12 17; 20 13], seeing that my lord taketh away the stewardship from me? I have not strength to dig; to beg I am ashamed. **4** I am resolved what to do, that, when I am put out of the stewardship, they may receive me into their houses. **5** And calling to him each one of his lord's debtors, he said to the first, How much owest thou unto my lord? **6** And he said, A hundred [1] measures of oil. And he said unto him, Take thy [2] bond, and sit down quickly and write fifty. **7** Then said he to another, And how much owest thou? And he said, A hundred [3] measures of wheat. He saith unto him, Take thy [2] bond, and write fourscore. **8** And his lord commended [4] the unrighteous steward [*cp.* 18 6; *also* 13 27] because he had done wisely: for the sons of this [5] world [*cp.* 20 34] are for their own generation wiser [*cp.* 12 42] than the sons of the light [*cp.* 6 35; 20 36: Matt. 5 9, 45; 8 12; 13 38]. **9** And I say unto you, Make to yourselves [*cp.* 12 33] friends [6] by means of the mammon of unrighteousness [*cp.* 18 6; *also* 13 27]; that, when it shall fail, they may receive you into the eternal tabernacles. **10** He that is faithful [*cp.* 12 42; 19 17] in a very little [*cp.* 19 17: *also* 12 26] is faithful also in much: and he that is unrighteous in a very little is unrighteous also in much. **11** If therefore ye have not been faithful in the unrighteous mammon, who will commit to your trust the true *riches* [*cp.* 19 15-26]? **12** And if ye have not been faithful in that which is another's, who will give you that which is [7] your

cp. 7 24; 10 16; 24 45; 25 2 *ff.*

cp. 24 45; 25 21, 23.

cp. 25 19-30.

cp. 12 36: *also* 1 12; 11 52.

Matt. 6 **24** No man can serve two masters: for either he will hate the one, and love the other; or else he will hold to one, and despise the other. Ye cannot serve God and mammon.

own? **13** No [8] servant can serve two masters: for either he will hate the one, and love the other; or else he will hold to one, and despise the other. Ye cannot serve God and mammon.

[1] Gr. *baths*, the bath being a Hebrew measure. See Ezek. 45 10, 11, 14.   [2] Gr. *writings*.
[3] Gr. *cors*, the cor being a Hebrew measure. See Ezek. 45 14.
[4] Gr. *the steward of unrighteousness*.
[5] Or, *age*   [6] Gr. *out of*.
[7] Some ancient authorities read *our own*.
[8] Gr. *household-servant*.

§ 174. The Pharisees rebuked and Three Detached Sayings

Luke 16 14-18

cp. 23 25.

14 And the Pharisees, who were lovers of money [*cp.* 11 39; 20 47], heard all these things; and they scoffed [*cp.* 23 35] at him. **15** And he said unto them, Ye are they that justify yourselves [*cp.* 10 29] in the sight of men; but God knoweth your hearts: for that which is exalted among men is an abomination in the sight of God. **16** The law and the prophets *were* until

Matt. 11 **12** And from the days of John the Baptist until now the kingdom of heaven

*cp.*11 5.

suffereth violence, and
men   of violence take it by force. **13** For all the prophets and the law [*cp.* 5 17; 7 12; 22 40] prophesied until John.

John: from that time
          the gospel of the kingdom of God is preached [*cp.* 1 19; 2 10; 3 18; 4 18, 43; 7 22; 8 1; 9 6; 20 1],   and every man entereth violently into it.

Matt. 5 **18** For verily I say unto you, Till heaven and earth   pass away [*cp.* 24 35],   one jot or one tittle shall in no wise pass away from the law,   till all things be accomplished.

cp. 13 31.

17 But it is easier for   heaven and earth to pass away [*cp.* 21 33], than for   one tittle   of the law to fall.

Matt. 5 **32** But I say unto you, that every one that putteth away his wife, saving for the cause of fornication,

Matt. 19 **9** And I say unto you, Whosoever shall put away his wife, [1] except for   fornication, and shall marry another, committeth adultery:

Mark 10 **11** And he saith unto them, Whosoever shall put away his wife,

          and   marry another, committeth adultery against her:

18 Every one that putteth away his wife,

          and marrieth another, committeth adultery:

maketh her an adulteress: and whosoever shall marry her when she is put away   committeth adultery.

[2] and he that marrieth her when she is put away   committeth adultery.

          and he that marrieth one that is put away from a husband committeth adultery.

12 and if she herself shall put away her husband, and marry another, she committeth adultery.

[1] Some ancient authorities read *saving for the cause of fornication, maketh her an adulteress*: as in ch. 5 32.
[2] The following words, to the end of the verse, are omitted by some ancient authorities.

§ 175. The Parable of the Rich Man and Lazarus

Luke 16 19-31

19 Now there was a certain rich man [*cp.* 12 16; 16 1], and he was clothed in purple and fine linen, [1] faring sumptuously every day: **20** and a certain beggar named Lazarus was laid at his gate, full of sores, **21** and desiring to be fed with the *crumbs* that fell from the rich man's table; yea, even the dogs came and licked his sores. **22** And it came to pass, that the beggar died, and that he was carried away by the angels into Abraham's bosom: and the rich man also died, and was buried. **23** And in Hades he lifted up his eyes, being in torments, and seeth Abraham afar off, and Lazarus in his bosom. **24** And he cried and said, Father Abraham [*cp. verse* 30: *also* 3 8; 13 16; 19 9], have mercy on me, and send Lazarus, that he may dip the tip of his finger in water, and cool my tongue; for I am in anguish in this flame. **25** But Abraham said, [2] Son, remember that thou in thy lifetime receivedst thy good things, and Lazarus in like manner evil things: but now here he is comforted, and thou art in anguish [*cp.* 6 20, 24]. **26** And [3] beside all this, between

cp. 15 27.   *cp.* 7 28.

cp. 3 9.

cp. 8 33, 37, 39, 53.

‖

| | | us and you there is a great gulf fixed, that they which would pass from hence to you may not be able, and that none may cross over from thence to us. **27** And he said, I pray thee therefore, father, that thou wouldest send him to my father's house; **28** for I have five brethren; that he may testify unto them, lest they also come into this place of torment. **29** But Abraham saith, They have Moses and the prophets [*cp. verse* 31 *and* 24 27]; let them hear them. **30** And he said, Nay, father Abraham [*cp. verse* 24: *also* 3 8; 13 16; 19 9]: but if one go to them from the dead, they will repent. **31** And he said unto him, If they hear not Moses and the prophets [*see above*], neither will they be persuaded, if one rise from the dead. | *cp.* 1 45.

cp. 8 33, 37, 39, 53.
cp. 1 45.
cp. 12 9. |
| *cp.* 3 9. | | | |

¹ Or, *living in mirth and splendour every day*
² Gr. *Child.*   ³ Or, *in all these things*

(ix) Events on the Journey III (§§ 176-182)

§ 176. Sayings about Occasions of Stumbling, the Treatment of a Brother's Fault, and the Obligation to Forgive him

Matt. 18 7, 6, 15, 21-22	Mark 9 42	Luke 17 1-4	
7 Woe unto the world [*cp.* 26 24: *also* 23 13 *ff.*] because of occasions of stumbling! for it must needs be that the occasions come; but woe to that man [*cp.* 26 24: *also* 23 13 *ff.*] through whom the occasion cometh! **6** But whoso shall cause one of these little ones [*cp.* 10 42; 18 10, 14] which believe on me to stumble, it is profitable for him that ¹ a great millstone should be hanged about his neck, and *that* he should be sunk in the depth of the sea.	*cp.* 14 21. *cp.* 14 21. **42** And whosoever shall cause one of these little ones that believe ¹ on me to stumble, it were better for him if ² a great millstone were hanged about his neck, and he were cast into the sea. ¹ Many ancient authorities omit *on me.* ² Gr. *a millstone turned by an ass.*	**1** And he said unto his disciples, It is impossible but that occasions of stumbling should come: but woe unto him [*cp.* 22 22: *also* 11 42 *ff.*], through whom they come! **2** It were well for him if a millstone were hanged about his neck, and he were thrown into the sea, rather than that he should cause one of these little ones to stumble. **3** Take heed to yourselves [*cp.* 12 1; 21 34]: if thy brother sin, rebuke him; and if he repent,	
15 And if thy brother sin ² against thee, go, shew him his fault between thee and him alone: if he hear thee, thou hast gained thy brother. . . . **21** Then came Peter, and said to him, Lord, how oft shall my brother sin against me, and I forgive him [*cp.* 6 12, 14, 15]? until seven times? **22** Jesus saith unto him, I say not unto thee, Until seven times; but, Until ³ seventy times seven. ¹ Gr. *a millstone turned by an ass.* ² Some ancient authorities omit *against thee.* ³ Or, *seventy times and seven*	*cp.* 11 25.	forgive him [*cp.* 11 4]. **4** And if he sin against thee seven times in the day, and seven times turn again to thee, saying, I repent; thou shalt forgive him.	

§ 177. Sayings about Faith and the Obligations of Servants

Matt. 17 19-20; 21 21-22	Mark 9 28-29; 11 22-24	Luke 17 5-10	
cp. 10 2.	*cp.* 6 30. *cp.* 16 19, 20.	**5** And the apostles [*cp.* 6 13; 9 10; 22 14; 24 10] said unto the Lord [*cp.* 7 13, 19; 10 1, 39, 41; 11 39; 12 42; 13 15; 18 6; 19 8; 22 61; 24 3, 34], Increase our faith.	*cp.* 4 1; 6 23; 11 2; 20 2, 18, 20, 25; 21 7, 12.
17 19 Then	**9 28** And when he was		

came   the dis-
ciples to Jesus
apart, and said, Why could
not we cast it out ? **20** And he
            saith unto
them, Because of your little
faith [*cp.* 6 30; 8 26; 14 31;
16 8]:

for verily I say unto you, If ye
have faith as a grain of mustard seed [*cp.* 13 31], ye shall
say unto this
mountain, Remove hence to
yonder place ; and it shall remove ; and nothing shall be
impossible unto you [*cp.* 19 26].[1]
21 21 And Jesus answered and
said unto them,
            Verily I say unto
you, If ye have faith, and doubt
not, ye shall not only do what
is done to the fig tree, but
even if ye shall say unto this
mountain, Be thou taken up
and   cast into the
sea,

            it shall be
done.
            22 And all things,
whatsoever ye   shall
ask [*cp.* 7 7 ; 18 19] in prayer,
believing,
            ye shall receive.

[1] Many authorities, some ancient,
insert ver. 21 *But this kind goeth not
out save by prayer and fasting.*
See Mark 9 29.

cp. 25 30.

come into the house, his disciples   asked him
privately, [1] *saying,* We could
not cast it out. **29** And he
            said unto
them,
        cp. 4 40 ; 16 14.
            This kind can come out
by nothing, save by prayer.[2]

        cp. 4 31.

        cp. 9 23 ; 10 27 ; 14 36.
11 22 And Jesus answering
saith unto them, Have faith
in God. **23** Verily I say unto
you,

Whosoever shall say unto this
mountain, Be thou taken up
and   cast into the
sea ; and shall not doubt in
his heart, but shall believe
that what he saith cometh to
pass ;   he shall have
it.   **24** Therefore I
say unto you,   All things
whatsoever ye pray and
ask for,
believe that ye have received
them, and ye shall have them.

[1] Or, How is it *that we could not cast
it out ?*
[2] Many ancient authorities add
and fasting.

6 And the
Lord [*see above*] said,

cp. 12 28: *also* 8 25; 22 32;
        24 25, 38.

            If ye
have faith as a grain of mustard seed [*cp.* 13 19], ye would
say unto this sycamine tree,

        cp. 1 37; 18 27.

            Be thou rooted up,
and be thou planted   in the
sea;

            and it would have
obeyed you.

        cp. 11 9.

7 But who is there of you,
having a [1] servant plowing or
keeping sheep, that will say
unto him, when he is come in

cp. 3 12; 6
64; 14 10;
20 27.

cp. 14 13,
14; 15 7,
16; 16 23,
24.

from the field, Come straightway and sit down to meat; **8** and
will not rather say unto him, Make ready [*cp.* 12 47] wherewith
I may sup, and gird thyself [*cp.* 12 35, 37], and serve me
[*cp.* 12 37; 22 27], till I have eaten and drunken; and afterward thou shalt eat and drink ? **9** Doth he thank the [1] servant
because he did the things that were commanded ? **10** Even so
ye also, when ye shall have done all the things that are commanded you, say, We are unprofitable [2] servants; we have done
that which it was our duty to do.

        [1] Gr. *bondservant.*   [2] Gr. *bondservants.*

cp. 13 4-5.

§ 178. **The Healing of Ten Lepers**

[*Cp.* Matt. 8 1-4 ‖ Mark 1 40-45 ‖ Luke 5 12-16]

Luke 17 11-19

cp. 16 21;
20 17, 18.

cp. 10 32, 33.

11 And it came to pass, [1] as they were on the way to Jerusalem [*cp.* 9 51, 53; 13 22; 19 11, 41: *also* 9 31; 13 33; 18 31],
that he was passing [2] through the midst of Samaria [*cp.* 9 52]
and Galilee. **12** And as he entered into a certain village [*cp.* 9
52, 56; 10 38], there met him ten men that were lepers, which
stood afar off: **13** and they lifted up their voices [*cp.* 11 27],
saying, Jesus, Master, have mercy on us [*cp.* 18 38, 39]. **14** And
when he saw them, he said unto them, Go and shew yourselves
unto the priests [*cp.* 5 14]. And it came to pass, as they went,
they were cleansed. **15** And one of them, when he saw that he
was healed, turned back, with a loud voice glorifying God
[*cp.* 2 20; 5 25, 26; 7 16; 13 13; 18 43; 23 47]; **16** and he

cp. 4 4.
cp. 4 5.

cp. 9 27; 15
22; *etc.*

cp. 10 47, 48.

cp. 8 4.

cp. 1 44.

cp. 9 8; 15 31.

cp. 2 12.

cp. 9 24.

cp. 2 11: also 8 2; 9 18; etc.	cp. 3 11; 5 22, 33; 7 25: also 1 40; 5 6; 10 17.	fell upon his face [cp. 5 8, 12; 8 28, 41, 47: also 24 52] at his feet, giving him thanks: and he was a Samaritan [cp. 10 33]. 17 And Jesus answering said, Were not the ten cleansed? but where are the nine? 18 ³ Were there none found that returned to give glory to God [see verse 15], save this ⁴ stranger? 19 And he said unto him, Arise, and go thy way: thy faith hath ⁵ made thee whole [cp. 7 50; 8 48; 18 42].	cp. 11 32; etc. cp. 4 39-42.
cp. 9 22.	cp. 5 34; 10 52.		

¹ Or, as he was   ² Or, between   ³ Or, There were none found . . . save this stranger.
⁴ Or, alien   ⁵ Or, saved thee

Luke 7 12: cp. Lev. 13 45-46.   Luke 17 14: cp. Lev. 13 49; 14 2.

§ 179. A Question and Answer about the Coming of the Kingdom

Luke 17 20-21

20 And being asked by the Pharisees, when the kingdom of God cometh [cp. 19 11], he answered them and said, The kingdom of God cometh not with observation: 21 neither shall they say, Lo, here! or, There [cp. 17 23]! for lo, the kingdom of God is ¹ within you [cp. 9 2; 10 9, 11; 11 20: also 19 11; 21 8].

cp. 24 23, 26. cp. 3 2; 4 17; 10 7; 12 28.	cp. 13 21. cp. 1 15; 6 12.

¹ Or, in the midst of you

§ 180. A Description of the Day of the Son of Man

Matt. 24 23, 26-27, 37-39, 17-18; 10 39; 24 40-41, 28.	Mark 13 21, 15-16	Luke 17 22-37	
cp. 9 15.	cp. 2 20.	22 And he said unto the disciples, The days will come [cp. 5 35; 19 43; 21 6; 23 29], when ye shall desire to see one of the days of the Son of man, and ye shall not see it. 23 And they shall say to you, Lo, there! Lo, here [cp. 17 21]!	
24 23 Then if any man shall say unto you, Lo, here is the Christ [cp. 24 5], or, Here; believe ¹ it not. 26 If therefore they shall say unto you, Behold, he is in the wilderness; go not forth: Behold, he is in the inner chambers; believe ² it not. 27 For as the lightning cometh forth from the east, and is seen even unto the west; so shall be the ³ coming [cp. 24 3, 37, 39] of the Son of man.	21 And then if any man shall say unto you, Lo, here is the Christ [cp. 13 6]; or, Lo, there; believe ¹ it not. ¹ Or, him	go not away, nor follow after them [cp. 21 8]: 24 for as the lightning, when it lighteneth out of the one part under the heaven, shineth unto the other part under heaven; so shall the Son of man be ¹ in his day.	
cp. 17 10. cp. 16 21-23; 17 12, 22-23; 20 17-19, 28; 26 2, 12, 18, 24, 45.	cp. 9 11, 12; 13 10. cp. 8 31-33; 9 12, 30-32; 10 32-34, 45; 14 8, 21, 41. cp. 8 31.	25 But first [cp. 21 9] must he suffer [cp. 9 22, 43-45; 13 32, 33; 18 31-34; 22 22; 24 7, 26, 44, 46] many things and be rejected [cp. 9 22] of this generation. 26 And as it came to pass in the days of Noah, even so shall it be also in the days of the Son of man.	cp. 2 19, 22; 3 14; 12 32-33.
24 37 And as were the days of Noah, so shall be the ³ coming cp. 24 3, 27, 39] of the Son of man. 38 For as in those days which were before the flood they were eating and drinking, marrying and giving in marriage, until the day that Noah entered into the ark, 39 and they knew not until the flood came, and took them all away;		27 They ate, they drank, they married, they were given in marriage, until the day that Noah entered into the ark, and the flood came, and destroyed them all. 28 Likewise even as it came to	

so shall   be
the ³ coming [cp. 24 3, 27, 37]
of the Son of man.

cp. 7 22; 24 36: also 26 29.

24 **17** Let him that
is on the housetop

not go down   to
take out the things that are in
his house: **18** and let him that
is in the field   not
return back to take his cloke.

10 39 He that
⁴ findeth his ⁵ life shall lose it;
and he that   ⁶ loseth his
⁵ life for my sake [see below] shall
find it.

Matt. **16 25** For whosoever
would save his ⁵ life shall
lose it: and whosoever
shall lose his ⁵ life for my
sake [cp. 5 11; 10 18, 39:
also 10 22; 19 29; 24 9]
cp. 4 23; 9 35; 24 14; 26
13.

                shall
find it.

24 **40** Then shall   two men
be in the field;   one
is taken, and   one
is left:
41 two women *shall* be grinding
at the mill;   one   is
taken, and   one   is
left.

28 Wheresoever the carcase is,
there will the ⁷ eagles
be gathered together.

¹ Or, *him*   ² Or, *them*
³ Gr. *presence.*   ⁴ Or, *found*
⁵ Or, *soul*   ⁶ Or, *lost*
⁷ Or, *vultures*

---

cp. 13 32: also 14 25.
15 And let him that
is on the housetop

not go down, nor enter in, to
take anything out   of
his house: **16** and let him that
is in the field   not
return back to take his cloke.

Mark **8 35** For whosoever
would save his ¹ life shall
lose it; and whosoever
shall lose his ¹ life for my
sake [cp. 10 29; 13 9:
also 13 13]
and the gospel's [cp. 10
29: also 1 1, 14, 15; 13
10; 14 9; 16 15]

                shall
save it.

¹ Or, *soul*

---

pass in the days of Lot; they
ate, they drank, they bought,
they sold, they planted, they
builded; **29** but in the day
that Lot went out from Sodom
it rained fire and brimstone
from heaven, and destroyed
them all: **30** after the same
manner shall it be in the day
that
the Son of man is revealed.
31 In that day [cp. 10 12; 21
34],   he which shall
be on the housetop, and his
goods in the house, let him
not go down   to
take them away:
            and let him that
is in the field likewise not
return back [cp. 21 21].
32 Remember Lot's wife.
33 Whosoever shall seek to
gain his ² life shall lose it:
but whosoever shall lose *his*
² *life*   shall
³ preserve it.

Luke **9 24** For whosoever
would save his ² life shall
lose it; but whosoever
shall lose his ² life for my
sake [cp. 6 22; 18 29;
21 12, 17],

the same shall

save it.

34 I say unto you, In that
night there shall be two men
on one bed; the one shall
be taken, and the other shall
be left. **35** There shall be
two women   grinding
together; the one shall be
taken, and the other shall be
left.⁴ **37** And they answering
say unto him, Where, Lord?
And he said unto them,
Where   the body *is*,
thither will the ⁵ eagles also
be gathered together.

¹ Some ancient authorities omit *in his
day.*
² Or, *soul*   ³ Gr. *save it alive.*
⁴ Some ancient authorities add ver. 36,
*There shall be two men in the field; the
one shall be taken, and the other shall
be left.*   ⁵ Or, *vultures*

---

cp. 14 20; 16
23, 26.

John **12 25** He
that loveth his ¹ life
loseth it; and he
that hateth his ¹ life
cp. 15 21.

in this
world   shall
keep it unto life eternal.

¹ Or. *soul*

Luke 17 26-27 ‖ Matt. 24 37-39: Gen. 6 11-13; 7 7, 21-23. Luke 17 28-29: Gen. 18 20 ff.; 19 16, 24-25. Luke 17 32:
Gen. 19 26.

§ 181. The Parable of the Unrighteous Judge

Luke 18 1-8

cp. 12 40, 42.

1 And he spake a parable unto them to the end that they
ought always to pray, and not to faint; **2** saying, There was
in a city a judge, which feared not God, and regarded not man:
3 and there was a widow [cp. 2 37; 4 25, 26; 7 12; 20 47;
21 2] in that city; and she came oft unto him, saying, ¹ Avenge

cp. 26 10.	*cp.* 14 6.	me of mine adversary. **4** And he would not for a while: but afterward he said within himself, Though I fear not God, nor regard man; **5** yet because this widow troubleth me [*cp.* 11 7], I will avenge her, lest she ² wear me out by her continual coming [*cp.* 11 8]. **6** And the Lord [*cp.* 7 13, 19; 10 1, 39, 41; 11 39; 12 42; 13 15; 17 5, 6; 19 8; 22 61; 24 3, 34] said, Hear what ³ the unrighteous judge [*cp.* 16 8, 9: *also* 13 27] saith. **7** And shall not God avenge [*cp.* 21 22] his elect, which cry to him day and night, and he is longsuffering over them ? **8** I say unto you, that he will avenge them speedily. Howbeit when the Son of man cometh, shall he find ⁴ faith on the earth ?	*cp.* 4 1; 6 23; 11 2; 20 2, 18, 20, 25; 21 7, 12.
	cp. 16 19, 20.		
cp. 24 22, 24, 31.	*cp.* 13 20, 22, 27.		

¹ Or, Do me justice of: and so in ver. 5, 7, 8.
² Gr. <i>bruise.</i>   ³ Gr. <i>the judge of unrighteousness.</i>   ⁴ Or, <i>the faith</i>

§ 182. The Parable of the Pharisee and the Publican

[Cp. Matt. 9 13; 21 31: Mark 2 17: Luke 5 32; 7 29-30, 47; 15 7, 10; 19 10]

Luke 18 9-14

9 And he spake also this parable unto certain which trusted in themselves that they were righteous, and set ¹ all others at nought: **10** Two men went up into the temple to pray; the one a Pharisee, and the other a publican. **11** The Pharisee stood and prayed thus with himself, God, I thank thee, that I am not as the rest of men, extortioners, unjust, adulterers, or even as this publican. **12** I fast twice in the week; I give tithes of all that I get. **13** But the publican, standing afar off, would not lift up so much as his eyes unto heaven, but smote his breast [*cp.* 23 48], saying, God, ² be merciful to me ³ a sinner. **14** I say unto you, This man went down to his house justified

Matt. 23 12 And whosoever shall exalt himself shall be humbled ; and whosoever shall humble himself [*cp.* 18 4] shall be exalted.	Luke 14 11 For every one that exalteth himself shall be humbled ; and he that humbleth himself shall be exalted.	rather than the other : for every one that exalteth himself shall be humbled ; but he that humbleth himself shall be exalted.

¹ Gr. the rest.
² Or, <i>be propitiated</i>
³ Or, <i>the sinner</i>

(x) In ' the Borders of Judæa and beyond Jordan ' (§§ 183-189)

§ 183. General Teaching (Mark) and Healing (Matt.)

[Cp. § 134]

Matt. 19 1-2	Mark 10 1	Luke 9 51	
1 And it came to pass when Jesus had finished these words [*cp.* 7 28; 11 1; 13 53; 26 1],	1 And	51 And it came to pass, when	
		cp. 7 1.	
		the days ¹ were well-nigh come that he should be received up, he stedfastly set his face to go to Jerusalem [*cp.* 9 53; 13 22; 17 11; 19 11, 41: *also* 9 31; 13 33; 18 31],	
cp. 16 21; 20 17, 18.	*cp.* 10 32, 33.		
			cp. 10 40.
he departed from Galilee, and came into the borders of Judæa beyond Jordan ; **2** and great multitudes followed him ; and he healed them there.	he arose from thence, and cometh into the borders of Judæa and beyond Jordan : and multitudes come together unto him again ; and, as he was wont, he taught them again.		

¹ Gr. were being fulfilled.

§ 184. A Question about Divorce

Matt. 19 3-12

3 And there came unto him [1] Pharisees, tempting [*cp.* 16 1; 22 35: *also* 22 18] him, and saying, Is it lawful [*cp.* 12 10; 22 17] *for a man* to put away his wife for every cause ?
4 And he answered and said,

verses 7 and 8

Have ye not read [*cp.* 12 3, 5; 21 16, 42; 22 31], that he which [2] made *them* from the beginning made them male and female, **5** and said, For this cause shall a man leave his father and mother, and shall cleave to his wife; and the twain shall become one flesh ? **6** So that they are no more twain, but one flesh. What therefore God hath joined together, let not man put asunder. **7** They say unto him, Why then did Moses command to give a bill of divorcement, and to put *her* away [*cp.* 5 31]? **8** He saith unto them, Moses for your hardness of heart suffered you to put away your wives: but from the beginning it hath not been so.
cp. 13 36; 17 25.

9 And I say unto you, Whosoever shall put away his wife, [3] except for fornication, and shall marry another, committeth adultery:

[4] and he that marrieth her when she is put away committeth adultery.

10 The disciples say unto him, If the case of the man is so with his wife, it is not expedient to marry. **11** But he said unto them, All men cannot receive this saying [*cp. verse* 12], but they to whom it is given [*cp.* 13 11]. **12** For there are eunuchs, which were so born from their mother's womb: and there are eunuchs, which were made eunuchs by men: and there are eunuchs, which made themselves eunuchs for the kingdom of heaven's

Matt. 5 32 But I say unto you, that every one that putteth away his wife, saving for the cause of fornication

maketh her an adulteress: and whosoever shall marry her when she is put away committeth adultery.

Mark 10 2-12

2 And there came unto him Pharisees, and asked him, Is it lawful [*cp.* 3 4; 12 14] for a man to put away *his* wife ? tempting [*cp.* 8 11: *also* 12 15] him. **3** And he answered and said unto them, What did Moses command you ? **4** And they said, Moses suffered to write a bill of divorcement, and to put her away. **5** But Jesus said unto them, For your hardness of heart [*cp.* 3 5: *also* 6 52; 8 17; 16 14] he wrote you this commandment. **6** But *cp.* 2 25; 12 10, 26.
from the beginning of the creation [*cp.* 13 19; 16 15], Male and female made he them. **7** For this cause shall a man leave his father and mother, [1] and shall cleave to his wife; **8** and the twain shall become one flesh: so that they are no more twain, but one flesh. **9** What therefore God hath joined together, let not man put asunder.

verses 3-5

10 And in the house [*cp.* 7 17; 9 28, 33] the disciples asked him again of this matter. **11** And he saith unto them, Whosoever shall put away his wife,

and marry another, committeth adultery against her:

12 and if she herself shall put away her husband, and marry another, she committeth adultery.

¹ Some ancient authorities omit *and shall cleave to his wife.*

Luke 16 18

Every one that putteth away his wife,

and marrieth another, committeth adultery:

and he that marrieth one that is put away from a husband committeth adultery.

cp. 10 25; 11 16.

cp. 6 9; 14 3; 20 22.

cp. 10 25; 11 16.

cp. 6 3; 10 26.

cp. 4 11.

cp. 8 6.

cp. 8 6.

cp. 12 40.

cp. 8 10.

cp. 8 37.

sake. He that is able to receive it, let him receive it [*cp. verse* 11: *also* 11 15; 13 9, 43].   *cp.* **4** 9, 23; **7** 16.   *cp.* **8** 8; **14** 35.   *cp.* **8** 37: *also* **6** 60.

[1] Many authorities, some ancient, insert *the*.
[2] Some ancient authorities read *created*.
[3] Some ancient authorities read *saving for the cause of fornication, maketh her an adulteress*: as in ch. 5 32.
[4] The following words, to the end of the verse, are omitted by some ancient authorities.

Matt. 19 4 ‖ Mark 10 6 = Gen. 1 27; 5 2.   Matt. 19 5 ‖ Mark 10 7-8 = Gen. 2 24.
Matt. 19 7 ‖ Mark 10 4 : Deut. 24 1.

§ 185. The Blessing of Little Children

Matt. 19 13-15	**Mark 10** 13-16	**Luke 18** 15-17	John 3 3, 5
13 Then were there brought unto him little children, that he should lay his hands on them [*cp.* 8 3, 15; 9 18, 25, 29; 14 31; 17 7; 20 34: *also* 9 20; 14 36], and pray: and the disciples rebuked them [*cp.* 15 23; 26 8-9]. **14** But Jesus	**13** And they brought unto him little children, that he should touch them [*cp.* 1 31, 41; 5 23, 41; 6 2, 5; 7 33; 8 22, 23, 25; 9 27: *also* 3 10; 5 27; 6 56]: and the disciples rebuked them [*cp.* 14 4-5]. **14** But when Jesus saw it, he was moved with indignation, and	**15** And they brought unto him also their babes, that he should touch them [*cp.* 4 40; 5 13; 7 14; 8 54; 13 13; 14 4; 22 51: *also* 6 19; 7 39; 8 44]: but when the disciples saw it, they rebuked them. **16** But Jesus	*cp.* 9 6: *also* 20 17. *cp.* 12 5.
said, Suffer [*cp.* 26 10] the little children, and forbid them not, to come unto me: for of such is the kingdom of heaven.	said unto them, Suffer [*cp.* 14 6] the little children to come unto me; forbid them not [*cp.* 9 39]: for of such is the kingdom of God.	called them unto him, saying, Suffer the little children to come unto me, and forbid them not [*cp.* 9 50]: for of such is the kingdom of God.	*cp.* 12 7.
18 3 Verily I say unto you, Except ye turn, and become as little children, ◄	**15** Verily I say unto you, Whosoever shall not receive the kingdom of God as a little child,	**17** Verily I say unto you, Whosoever shall not receive the kingdom of God as a little child,	3 3 Verily, verily, I say unto thee, Except a man be born [1] anew, he cannot see the kingdom of God. ....5 Verily, verily, I say unto thee, Except a man be born of water and the Spirit, he cannot enter [*cp.* 10 1, 2, 9]
ye shall in no wise enter [*cp.* 5 20; 7 21; 19 23, 24; 21 31; 23 13: *also* 7 13; 18 8, 9; 19 17; 25 21, 23] into the kingdom of heaven. **15** And he laid his hands on them [*cp. verse* 13], and departed thence.	he shall in no wise enter [*cp.* 9 47; 10 23, 24, 25: *also* 9 43, 45] therein. **16** And he took them in his arms [*cp.* 9 36], and blessed them, laying his hands upon them [*cp. verse* 13].	he shall in no wise enter [*cp.* 18 24, 25: *also* 11 52; 13 24; 24 26] therein. *cp. verse* 15.	into the kingdom of God.

[1] Or, *from above*

§ 186. A Question about Inheriting Eternal Life

Matt. 19 16-22	**Mark 10** 17-22	**Luke 18** 18-23	
16 And behold, one came to him and *cp.* 17 14: *and* 2 11; 8 2; *etc.* said, [1, 2] Master, what good thing shall I do,	**17** And as he was going forth [1] into the way, there ran one to him, and kneeled to him [*cp.* 1 40: *and* 3 11; *etc.*], and asked him, Good [2] Master, what shall I do	**18** And a certain ruler *cp.* 5 8, 12; *etc.* asked him, saying, Good [1] Master, what shall I do [*cp.* 3 10, 12, 14;	*cp.* 9 38; 11 32; 18 6. *cp.* 6 28.

that I may have eternal life [*cp.* 19 29: *also* 25 46]? **17** And he said unto him, ³ Why askest thou me concerning that which is good?	that I may inherit eternal life [*cp.* 10 30]? **18** And Jesus said unto him, Why callest thou me	10 25] to inherit eternal life [*cp.* 18 30: *also* 10 25]? **19** And Jesus said unto him, Why callest thou me	*cp.* 3 15; *etc.*
One there is who is good: but if thou wouldest enter into life [*cp.* 18 8, 9: *also* 5 20; 7 21; 18 3; 19 23, 24; 21 31; 23 13: *and* 7 13; 25 21, 23], keep the commandments. **18** He saith unto him, Which? And Jesus said, Thou shalt not kill, Thou shalt not commit adultery, Thou shalt not steal, Thou shalt not bear false witness, **19** Honour thy father and thy mother: and, Thou shalt love thy neighbour as thyself [*cp.* 22 39]. **20** The young man saith unto him, All these things have I observed: what lack I yet?	good? none is good, save one, *even* God. **19** Thou knowest [*cp.* 9 43, 45: *also* 9 47; 10 15, 23, 24, 25] the commandments,	good? none is good, save one, *even* God. **20** Thou knowest [*cp.* 18 17, 24, 25: *also* 11 52; 13 24: *and* 24 26] the commandments,	*cp.* 3 5: *also* 10 1, 2, 9.
	Do not kill, Do not commit adultery, Do not steal, Do not bear false witness, Do not defraud, Honour thy father and mother. *cp.* 12 31.	Do not commit adultery, Do not kill, Do not steal, Do not bear false witness, Honour thy father and mother. *cp.* 10 27.	
21 Jesus said unto him, If thou wouldest be perfect [*cp.* 5 48], go, sell that thou hast,	**20** And he said unto him, ² Master, all these things have I observed from my youth. **21** And Jesus looking upon him loved him [*cp.* 12 34], and said unto him, One thing thou lackest: go, sell whatsoever thou hast,	**21** And he said, All these things have I observed from my youth up. **22** And when Jesus heard it, he said unto him, One thing thou lackest yet: sell all that thou hast [*cp.* 12 33: *also* 22 36],	
and give to the poor, and thou shalt have treasure in heaven [*cp.* 6 19-21]: and come, follow me [*cp.* 4 19; 8 22; 9 9; 16 24]. **22** But when the young man heard the saying, he went away sorrowful: for he was one that had great possessions.	and give to the poor, and thou shalt have treasure in heaven: and come, follow me [*cp.* 1 17; 2 14; 8 34]. **22** But his countenance fell at the saying, and he went away sorrowful: for he was one that had great possessions.	and distribute unto the poor, and thou shalt have treasure in heaven [*cp.* 12 33, 34: *also* 12 21]: and come, follow me [*cp.* 5 27; 9 23, 59]. **23** But when he heard these things, he became exceeding sorrowful; for he was very rich.	*cp.* 1 43; 12 26; 21 19, 22.

¹ Or, *Teacher*
² Some ancient authorities read *Good Master.* See Mark 10 17; Luke 18 18.
³ Some ancient authorities read *Why callest thou me good? None is good save one,* even *God.* See Mark 10 18; Luke 18 19.

¹ Or, *on his way*   ² Or, *Teacher*

¹ Or, *Teacher*

Matt. 19 18, 19a ‖ Mark 10 19 ‖ Luke 18 20 : Exod. 20 12-16 ; Deut. 5 16-20.   Matt. 19 19b : Lev. 19 18.

§ 187. Sayings on the Danger of Riches and the Rewards of Discipleship.
The Parable of the Labourers in the Vineyard

[*Cp.* Luke 16 1-31]

[*Cp.* Matt. 10 16-42 ; 16 24-28 : Mark 8 34-9 1 ; 13 9-13 : Luke 9 23-27 ; 21 12-19 ; 22 28-30 : John 14 2-3]

Matt. 19 23-20 16	**Mark 10** 23-31	**Luke 18** 24-30	
23 And Jesus said unto his disciples, Verily I say unto you, It is hard for a rich man to enter into the kingdom of heaven [*cp.* 5 20; 7 21; 18 3; 19 24; 21 31; 23 13: *also* 18 8, 9; 19 17: *and*	**23** And Jesus looked round about [*cp.* 3 5, 34; 5 32; 9 8; 11 11], and saith unto his disciples, How hardly shall they that have riches enter into the kingdom of God [*cp.* 9 47; 10 15, 24, 25: *also* 9 43, 45] !	**24** And Jesus seeing him *cp.* 6 10. said, How hardly shall they that have riches enter into the kingdom of God [*cp.* 18 17, 25: *also* 11 52; 13 24: *and* 24 26]!	*cp.* 3 5: *also* 10 1, 2, 9.

[Matthew]

1 73; 25 21, 23]. **24** And

cp. 7 28; 13 54; 19 25; 22 22, 33: also 8 27; etc.

again　　I say unto you,

It is easier for a camel to go through a needle's eye, than for a rich man to enter into the kingdom of God [see verse 23]. **25** And when the disciples heard it, they were astonished exceedingly [see verse 24], saying, Who then can be saved? **26** And Jesus looking upon them said to them,

With men this is impossible; but with God all things are possible [cp. 17 20].
27 Then answered Peter [cp. 14 28; 15 15; 16 22; 17 4; 18 21; 26 33: also 16 16; 17 24]　　and said unto him, Lo, we have left all, and followed thee [cp. 4 20, 22; 9 9]; what then shall we have? **28** And Jesus said unto them, Verily I say unto you, that ye　　which have followed　　me,

in the regeneration when the Son of man shall sit on the throne of his glory [cp. 25 31: also 16 27],

cp. 8 11; 26 29.

[cp. 16 28; 20 21]　　ye also shall sit upon twelve thrones, judging the twelve tribes of Israel. **29** And every one　　that hath left houses,
　　or brethren, or sisters,
　　or father, or mother, ¹ or children [cp. 10 37], or lands, for my name's sake [cp. 10 22; 24 9: also 5 11; 10 18, 39; 16 25],
cp. 4 23; 9 35; 24 14; 26 13.

shall receive² a hundredfold [cp. 13 8, 23: and 6 33],

cp. 13 21.
and [cp. 12 32] shall inherit eternal life [cp. 19 16: also 25 46]. **30** But many shall be last that are first; and

[Mark]

24 And the disciples were amazed at his words [cp. 1 22, 27; 6 2; 10 26; 11 18; 12 17: also 2 12; etc.]. But Jesus answereth again, and saith unto them, Children, how hard is it ¹ for them that trust in riches to enter into the kingdom of God [see verse 23] ! **25** It is easier for a camel to go through a needle's eye, than for a rich man to enter into the kingdom of God [see verse 23]. **26** And　　they were astonished exceedingly [see verse 24], saying ² unto him, Then who can be saved? **27** Jesus looking upon them saith,

With men it is impossible, but not with God: for all things are possible with God [cp. 14 36: also 9 23].
28 Peter [cp. 8 32; 9 5; 11 21; 14 29: also 8 29] began to say unto him, Lo, we have left all, and have followed thee [cp. 1 18, 20; 2 14].
29 Jesus said, Verily I say unto you,

cp. 10 37: also 8 38.

cp. 14 25.

There is no man that hath left house, or brethren, or sisters, or mother, or father, or children, or lands, for my　　sake [cp. 8 35; 13 9: also 13 13], and for the gospel's sake [cp. 8 35: also 1 1, 14, 15; 13 10; 14 9; 16 15],

30 but he shall receive a hundredfold [cp. 4 8, 20, and 24] now in this time, houses, and brethren, and sisters, and mothers, and children, and lands, with persecutions [cp. 4 17]; and in the ³ world to come eternal life [cp. 10 17]. **31** But many that are first shall be last;　　and

[Luke]

cp. 2 47, 48; 4 22, 32, 36; 20 26: also 5 9; etc.

25 For it is easier for a camel to enter in through a needle's eye, than for a rich man to enter into the kingdom of God [see verse 24]. **26** And　　they that heard it
see above.
said,　　Then who can be saved? **27** But he　　said, The things which are impossible with men

are possible with God [cp. 1 37]. **28** And　　Peter [cp. 8 45; 9 33; 12 41: also 5 8; 9 20]　　said, Lo, we have left [cp. 5 11, 28; 14 33] ¹ our own, and followed thee [cp. 5 11, 28].

29 And he said unto them, Verily I say unto you, 22 **28** But ye are they which have continued with me in my temptations [cp. 4 13; 8 13];

[cp. 9 26, 32; 24 26] **29** and ² I appoint unto you a kingdom, even as my Father appointed unto me, **30** that ye may eat and drink at my table [cp. 13 29; 14 15; 22 16, 18] in my kingdom [cp. 23 42]; and ye shall sit on thrones judging the twelve tribes of Israel.
There is no man that hath left house, or wife [cp. 14 26], or brethren, or parents, or children [cp. 14 26],

cp. 6 22; 9 24; 21 12, 17.

for the kingdom of God's sake, **30** who shall not receive [cp. 8 8] manifold more [cp. 12 31] in this time,

and in the ³ world to come eternal life [cp. 18 18: also 10 25].

13 **30** And

[John references]

cp. 7 15, 21, 46.

see above.

see above.

cp. 13 36, 37; 21 21: also 6 68.

cp. Joh 13 36-14

cp. 1 14; 2 11; 12 41; 17 5, 22, 24.

cp. 18 36.

cp. 15 21.

cp. 3 15; etc.

	the last first.	behold, there are last which shall be first, and there are first which shall be last.

first *that are* last [*cp.* 20 8, 16].
20 1 For the kingdom of heaven is like unto a man that is a householder [*cp.* 13 52; 21 33: *also* 13 27 *and* Luke 14 21], which went out early in the morning to hire labourers into his vineyard [*cp.* 21 28, 33]. **2** And when he had agreed with the labourers for a ³ penny a day, he sent them into his vineyard. **3** And he went out about the third hour, and saw others standing in the marketplace idle; **4** and to them he said, Go ye also into the vineyard [*cp.* 21 28], and whatsoever is right I will give you. And they went their way. **5** Again he went out about the sixth and the ninth hour, and did likewise. **6** And about the eleventh *hour* he went out, and found others standing; and he saith unto them, Why stand ye here all the day idle? **7** They say unto him, Because no man hath hired us. He saith unto them, Go ye also into the vineyard [*cp.* 21 28]. **8** And when even was come, the lord of the vineyard [*cp.* 21 40] saith unto his steward, Call the labourers, and pay them their hire, beginning from the last unto the first [*cp.* 19 30; 20 16]. **9** And when they came that *were hired* about the eleventh hour, they received every man a ³ penny. **10** And when the first came, they supposed that they would receive more; and they likewise received every man a ³ penny. **11** And when they received it, they murmured against the householder, **12** saying, These last have spent *but* one hour, and thou hast made them equal unto us, which have borne the burden of the day and the ⁴ scorching heat. **13** But he answered and said to one of them, Friend [*cp.* 22 12; 26 50], I do thee no wrong: didst not thou agree with me for a ³ penny? **14** Take up that which is thine, and go thy way; it is my will to give unto this last, even as unto thee. **15** Is it not lawful for me to do what I will with mine own? or is thine eye evil [*cp.* 6 23], because I am good? **16** So the last shall be first, and the first last [*cp.* 19 30; 20 8].

¹ Some ancient authorities omit *for them that trust in riches.*
² Many ancient authorities read *among themselves.*
³ Or, *age*

¹ Or, *our own homes*
² Or, *I appoint unto you, even as my Father appointed unto me a kingdom, that ye may eat and drink &c.*
³ Or, *age*

cp. 12 1.   *cp.* 13 6; 20 9.

cp. 12 9.   *cp.* 20 13, 15.

cp. 7 22.   *cp.* 11 34.

¹ Many ancient authorities add *or wife*: as in Luke 18 29.
² Some ancient authorities read *manifold.*   ³ See marginal note on ch. 18 28.
⁴ Or, *hot wind*

§ 188. The Third Prediction of the Passion and Resurrection

[*Cp.* Matt. 16 21-23 ‖ Mark 8 31-33 ‖ Luke 9 22; Matt. 17 22-23 ‖ Mark 9 30-32 ‖ Luke 9 43b-45: *also* Matt. 17 9, 12; 20 28; 26 2, 12, 18, 24, 32, 45; Mark 9 9, 12; 10 45; 14 8, 21, 28, 41: Luke 13 32-33; 17 25; 22 22; 24 7, *and* 26, 44, 46: John 2 19-22; 3 14; 12 32-33]

Matt. 20 17-19	**Mark 10** 32-34	**Luke 18** 31-34	
17 And as Jesus was going up to Jerusalem,	**32** And they were in the way, going up to Jerusalem; and Jesus was going before them: and they were amazed [*cp.* 2 12; 5 20, 42; 6 51; 7 37; 15 5; 16 5, 8: *also* 1 22, 27; 6 2; 10 24, 26; 11 18; 12 17]; ¹ and they that followed were afraid [*cp.* 4 41; 9 6, 32: *also* 5 15, 33; 16 8]. And he took again the twelve, [*cp.* 4 10, 34; 6 31, 32; 9 2, 28; 13 3] and began to tell them the things that were to happen unto him, **33** *saying,* Behold, we go up to Jerusalem; and	*cp.* 19 28: *also* 9 51, 53; 13 22; 17 11.	*cp.* 7 15, 21, 46.
cp. 8 27; 9 33; 12 23; 15 31; 21 20; 27 14: *also* 7 28; 13 54; 19 25; 22 22, 33.		*cp.* 5 9, 26; 8 25, 56; 9 43; 11 14; 24 12, 41: *also* 2 47, 48; 4 22, 32, 36; 20 26.	
cp. 17 6: *also* 9 8; 27 54; 28 4, 8.		*cp.* 8 25; 9 34, 45; 24 5, 37: *also* 1 12, 65; 2 9; 5 26; 7 16; 8 35, 37, 47.	
he took the twelve disciples apart [*cp.* 17 1, 19; 24 3], and in the way he said unto them, **18** Behold, we go up to Jerusalem [*cp.* 16 21]; and		**31** And he took unto him the twelve, [*cp.* 9 10; 10 23] and said unto them, Behold, we go up to Jerusalem [*cp.* 9 31, 51; 13 33], and all	

cp. 21 42; 26 24, 31, 54, 56.	*cp.* 9 12; 12 10; 14 21, 27, 49.	the things that are written ¹ by the prophets [*cp.* 20 17; 22 37; 24 25-27, 44-46] shall be accomplished [*cp.* 12 50; 22 37: *also* 13 32] unto the Son of man. **32** For he shall be delivered up	*cp.* 5 39; 13 18; 15 25; 17 12. *cp.* 4 34; 5 36; 17 4; 19 28, 30.

the Son of man   shall be delivered   unto the chief priests and   scribes; and they shall condemn him to death, **19** and shall deliver him unto the Gentiles   to mock [*cp.* 27 27-31: *also* 27 41],

      cp. 27 30: *also* 26 67.
      and   to scourge [*cp.* 27 26],
      and to crucify [*cp.* Luke 24 7: *also* Matt. 23 34]:
      cp. 27 63.
      and the third day [*cp.* 16 21; 17 23: *also* 12 40; 26 61; 27 40, 64] he shall   [*cp.* 17 9] be raised up [*cp.* 16 21; 17 23; 26 32; 27 63, 64; 28 6, 7].

      cp. 15 16; 16 8-12.

the Son of man   shall be delivered   unto the chief priests and the scribes; and they shall condemn him to death, and shall deliver him unto the Gentiles: **34** and they shall   mock [*cp.* 15 16-20: *also* 15 31] him, and shall spit upon [*cp.* 15 19: *also* 14 65] him, and   shall scourge [*cp.* 15 15] him, and shall kill him;

      and after three days [*cp.* 8 31; 9 31: *also* 14 58; 15 29]

he shall rise again [*cp.* 8 31; 9 9, 31; 16 9].
      cp. 14 28; 16 6, 14.

cp. 4 13; 6 52; 7 18; 8 17-21; 9 10, 32.

unto the Gentiles,   and   shall be mocked [*cp.* 23 36: *also* 22 63; 23 11, 35], and shamefully entreated, and   spit upon: **33** and they shall scourge   and kill him:

      and the third day [*cp.* 9 22; 13 32; 24 7, 46: *also* 24 21] he shall rise again [*cp.* 24 7, 46].
      cp. 9 22; 24 6, 34.
      34 And they understood none of these things [*cp.* 2 50; 9 45]; and this saying was hid from them, and they perceived not the things that were said.

cp. 19 2-3.

cp. 19 1.

cp. 2 19.

cp. 20 9.

cp. 2 19-22; 21 14.

cp. 10 6; 12 16: *also* 3 10; 4 33; 8 27, 43; 11 13; 13 7, 28, 36; 14 5-10; 16 17, 18.

¹ Or, *but some as they followed were afraid*

¹ Or, *through*

---

§ 189. **Rivalry among the Disciples and Sayings of Rebuke**

[*Cp.* Matt. 18 1–14; Mark 9 33-50; Luke 9 46-50]

Matt. 20 20-28	**Mark 10** 35-45		
20 Then came to him the mother [*cp.* 27 56] of the sons of Zebedee with her sons, worshipping *him* [*cp.* 2 11; 8 2; 9 18; 14 33; 15 25; 28 9, 17: *also* 17 14], and	**35** And there come near unto him James and John, the sons of Zebedee,		
	cp. 5 6: *also* 1 40; 3 11; 5 22, 33; 7 25; 10 17.	*cp.* 9 54.	*cp.* 9 38; 11 32; 18 6.
asking a certain thing of him. **21** And he said unto her, What wouldest thou [*cp.* 20 32]? She saith unto him, Command that these my two sons may sit, one on thy right hand, and one on thy left hand, in thy [*cp.* 19 28; 25 31: *also* 16 27] kingdom [*cp.* 16 28]. **22** But Jesus answered and said, Ye know not what ye ask. Are ye able to drink the cup [*cp.* 26 39] that I am about to drink?	saying unto him, ¹ Master, we would that thou shouldest do for us whatsoever we shall ask of thee. **36** And he said unto them, What would ye that I should do for you [*cp.* 10 51]? **37** And they said unto him, Grant unto us that we may sit, one on thy right hand, and one on *thy* left hand, in thy glory [*cp.* 8 38].	*cp.* 24 52: *also* 5 8, 12; *etc.* *cp.* 18 41. *cp.* 9 26, 32; 24 26: *and* 22 29, 30; 23 42.	*cp.* 1 14; 2 11; 12 41; 17 5, 22, 24; *and* 18 36. *cp.* 18 11.
	38 But Jesus said unto them, Ye know not what ye ask. Are ye able to drink the cup [*cp.* 14 36] that I drink? or to be baptized with the baptism that I am baptized with?	*cp.* 22 42.	
They say unto him, We are able. **23** He saith unto them, My cup indeed ye shall drink:	**39** And they said unto him, We are able. And Jesus said unto them, The cup that I drink ye shall drink; and with the baptism that I am baptized withal shall ye be baptized:	*cp.* 12 50.	
but to sit on my right hand, and on	**40** but to sit on my right hand or on		

my left hand, is not mine to give, but *it is for them* for whom it hath been prepared [*cp.* 25 34] of my Father.	*my* left hand is not mine to give: but *it is for them* for whom it hath been prepared.	
24 And when the ten heard it, they were moved with indignation concerning the two brethren.	**41** And when the ten heard it, they began to be moved with indignation concerning James and John.	

cp. 18 1.	*cp.* 9 33-34.	

25 But Jesus called them unto him, and said, Ye know that the rulers of the Gentiles lord it over them, and their great ones exercise authority over them.	**42** And Jesus called them to him, and saith unto them, Ye know that they which are accounted to rule over the Gentiles lord it over them; and their great ones exercise authority over them.	Luke 22 **24** And there arose also a contention among them [*cp.* 9 46], which of them is accounted to be [1] greatest. **25** And he said unto them,
26 Not so shall it be among you: but whosoever would become great among you shall be your [1] minister;	**43** But it is not so among you: but whosoever would become great among you, shall be your [2] minister:	The kings of the Gentiles have lordship over them; and they that have authority over them are called Benefactors. **26** But ye *shall* not *be* so: but he that is the greater
27 and whosoever would be first among you shall be your [2] servant:	**44** and whosoever would be first among you, shall be [3] servant of all.	among you, let him become as the younger; and he that is chief, as he that doth serve.
23 11 But he that is [3] greatest among you shall be your [4] servant.	9 **35** If any man would be first, he shall be last of all, and minister of all.	9 **48** For he that is [2] least among you all, the same is great. 22 **27** For whether is greater, he that [3] sitteth at meat, or he that serveth? is not he that [3] sitteth at meat [*cp.* 17 7-8]? but I am in the midst [*cp.* 9 55 ; 19 10] of you as he that serveth [*cp.* 12 37].
28 even as the Son of man came [*cp.* 18 11] not to be ministered unto, but to minister, and to give his life a ransom for many [*cp.* 26 28].	**45** For verily the Son of man came not to be ministered unto, but to minister, and to give his life a ransom for many [*cp.* 14 24].	

[1] Or, *servant* [2] Gr. *bondservant.* [3] Gr. *greater.* [4] Or, *minister*	[1] Or, *Teacher* [2] Or, *servant* [3] Gr. *bondservant.*	[1] Gr. *greater.* [2] Gr. *lesser.* [3] Gr. *reclineth.*

cp. John 13 2-17.

cp. 10 11, 15, 17; 11 51, 52.

Matt. 20 28 ‖ Mark 10 45 : *cp.* Is. 52 15 ; 53 4-6, 8, 11, 12.

(xi) At Jericho (§§ 190-193)

§ 190. **The Healing of a Blind Man** (Mark and Luke: **of Two Blind Men,** Matt.)

[*Cp.* Matt. 9 27-31 ; 12 22 ; 15 30-31 ; 21 14: Mark 8 22-26: Luke 7 21: John 9 1-7]

Matt. 20 29-34	**Mark 10** 46-52	**Luke 18** 35-43	
	46 And they come to Jericho: and as he went out from Jericho, with his disciples and a great multitude,	**35** And it came to pass, as he drew nigh unto Jericho,	
29 And as they went out from Jericho, a great multitude followed him. **30** And behold, two [*cp.* 8 28; 9 27] blind men sitting by the way side,	the son of Timæus, Bartimæus, a blind beggar, was sitting by the way side.	a certain blind man sat by the way side begging: **36** and hearing a multitude going by, he inquired what this meant.	*cp.* 9 8.
when they heard that Jesus [*cp.* 2 23; 21 11; 26 71] was passing by, cried out, saying, Lord [*cp.* 8 25; 17 4, 15; 20 33: *and* 7 21; 8 2; *etc.*], have mercy on us	**47** And when he heard that it was Jesus of Nazareth [*cp.* 1 24; 14 67; 16 6], he began to cry out, and say, Jesus, [*cp.* 7 28]	**37** And they told him, that Jesus of Nazareth [*cp.* 4 34; 24 19] passeth by. **38** And he cried, saying, Jesus, [*cp.* 18 41: *and* 5 8, 12; *etc.*]	*cp.* 1 45; 18 5, 7; 19 19. *cp.* 4 11, 15; *etc.*

[cp. 9 27; 15 22; 17 15; 20 31], thou son of David [cp. 1 1; 9 27; 12 23; 15 22; 20 31; 21 9, 15].
31 And the multitude [cp. 21 9] rebuked them, that they should hold their peace: but they cried out the more, saying, Lord, have mercy on us thou son of David.
32 And Jesus stood still, and called them,

cp. 9 2, 22; 14 27.

and said,
What will ye [cp. 20 21] that I should do unto you?
33 They say unto him, Lord [cp. 8 25; 17 4, 15; 20 30: and 7 21; 8 2; etc.], cp. 26 25, 49: also 23 7, 8.
that our eyes may be opened. **34** And Jesus, being moved with compassion [cp. 9 36; 14 14; 15 32], touched [cp. 8 3, 15; 9 18, 25, 29; 14 31; 17 7; 19 13, 15: also 9 20; 14 36] their eyes:
cp. 8 3, 8, 13, 16, 32; 9 6, 22, 29; 12 13; 15 28; 17 7, 18.

cp. 9 22.

and straightway they received their sight, and followed him.
cp. 9 8; 15 31: also 5 16.

---

thou son of David,

have mercy on me.
48 And many [cp. 11 9] rebuked him, that he should hold his peace: but he cried out the more a great deal,
Thou son of David, have mercy on me.
49 And Jesus stood still, and said, Call ye him.
And they call the blind man, saying unto him, Be of good cheer [cp. 6 50]: rise, he calleth thee. **50** And he, casting away his garment, sprang up, and came to Jesus. **51** And Jesus answered him, and said, What wilt thou [cp. 10 36] that I should do unto thee? And the blind man said unto him, [cp. 7 28]

Rabboni [cp. 9 5; 11 21; 14 45], that I may receive my sight. **52** And Jesus
cp. 1 41; 6 34; 8 2.
cp. 1 31, 41; 5 23, 41; 6 2, 5; 7 33; 8 22, 23, 25; 9 27; 10 13, 16: also 3 10; 5 27; 6 56.
said [cp. 1 25, 41; 2 11; 3 5; 5 8, 13, 34, 41; 7 29, 34; 9 25]
unto him,
Go thy way; thy faith hath [1] made thee whole [cp. 5 34]. And straightway he received his sight, and followed him in the way. cp. 2 12.

---

thou son of David [cp. 1 32],

have mercy on me [cp. 17 13]. **39** And they that went before rebuked [cp. 19 39] him, that he should hold his peace [cp. 19 40]: but he cried out [cp. 19 40] the more a great deal,
Thou son of David, have mercy on me.
40 And Jesus stood, and commanded him to be brought unto him:

and when he

was come near, he asked him,
41 What wilt thou that I should do unto thee? And he said,
Lord [cp. 5 8, 12; etc.],

that I may receive my sight. **42** And Jesus
cp. 7 13: also 10 33; 15 20.
cp. 4 40; 5 13; 7 14; 8 54; 13 13; 14 4; 18 15; 22 51: also 6 19; 7 39; 8 44.

said [cp. 4 35, 39; 5 13, 24; 6 10; 7 7, 14; 8 29, 32, 48, 54; 9 42; 13 12; 17 14] unto him, Receive thy sight: thy faith hath [1] made thee whole [cp. 7 50; 8 48; 17 19]. **43** And immediately he received his sight, and followed him, glorifying God [cp. 2 20; 5 25, 26; 7 16; 13 13; 17 15; 23 47]: and all the people, when they saw it, gave praise [cp. 2 13, 20; 19 37] unto God.

---

cp. 16 33.

cp. 4 11, 15; etc.
cp. 20 16: also 1 38; etc.

cp. 9 6; 20 17.

cp. 4 50; 5 8; 9 7; 11 43.

cp. 9 24.

---

[1] Or, *saved thee*   [1] Or, *saved thee*

---

§ 191. Zacchæus

[*Cp*. Matt. 9 13; 21 31: Mark 2 17: Luke 5 32; 7 29-30, 47; 15 7, 10; 18 14]

Luke 19 1-10

1 And he entered and was passing through Jericho. **2** And behold, a man called by name Zacchæus; and he was a chief publican, and he was rich. **3** And he sought to see Jesus who he was; and could not for the crowd [cp. 5 19; 8 19], because he was little of stature. **4** And he ran on before, and climbed up into a sycomore tree to see him: for he was to pass that way. **5** And when Jesus came to the place, he looked up, and said unto him, Zacchæus, make haste, and come down; for to-day I must abide at thy house. **6** And he made haste, and came down, and received him joyfully. **7** And when they saw it, they all murmured, saying, He is gone in to lodge with a man that is a sinner [cp. 5 30; 7 34, 39; 15 2]. **8** And Zacchæus

cp. 2 4; 3 9.

cp. 9 11; 11   cp. 2 16.

| 19: *also* 21 31. | *cp.* 16 19, 20. | stood, and said unto the Lord [*cp.* 7 13, 19; 10 1, 39, 41; 11 39; 12 42; 13 15; 17 5, 6; 18 6; 22 61; 23, 3, 34], Behold, Lord, the half of my goods I give to the poor; and if I have wrongfully exacted aught [*cp.* 3 14] of any man, I restore four-fold. **9** And Jesus said unto him, To-day is salvation [*cp.* 1 69, 71, 77; 2 30; 3 6] come to this house, forasmuch as he also is a son of Abraham [*cp.* 3 8; 13 16; 16 24, 30]. **10** For the Son of man came [*cp.* 9 55] to seek and to save [*cp.* 2 11] that which was lost [*cp.* 15 4, 8]. | *cp* 4 1; 6 23; 11 2; 20 2, 18, 20, 25; 21 7, 12. *cp.* 4 22. |
| *cp.* 3 9. *cp.* 18 11: *also* 20 28: *and* 1 21. | *cp.* 10 45. | | *cp.* 8 33 *ff.* *cp.* 3 17; 4 42; 5 34; 10 9; 12 47. |

§ 192. **The Parable of the Pounds**

[*Cp.* Matt. 24 45-51: Luke 12 41-48; 16 10-12]

Matt. 25 14-30		Luke 19 11-27	
cp. 16 21; 20 17, 18.	*cp.* 10 32, 33.	**11** And as they heard these things, he added and spake a parable, because he was nigh to Jerusalem [*cp.* 19 41: *also* 9 51, 53; 13 22; 17 11: *and* 9 31; 13 33; 18 31], and *because* they supposed that the kingdom of God was immediately to appear [*cp.* 9 2; 10 9, 11; 11 20; 17 20, 21; 21 8]. **12** He said therefore, A certain nobleman went into a far [*cp.* 15 13] country [*cp.* 20 9], to receive for himself a kingdom, and to return.	
cp. 3 2; 4 17; 10 7; 12 28.	*cp.* 1 15; 6 12.	**13** And he called ten ¹ servants of his,	
14 For *it is* as *when* a man, going into another country [*cp.* 21 33], *cp.* 18 23; 22 2 *ff.*; 25 34, 40.	Mark 13 **34** *It is* as *when* a man, sojourning in another country [*cp.* 12 1],	and gave them ten ² pounds,	
called his own ¹ servants,	hav-ing left his house, and given authority to his ¹ servants, to each one his work, commanded also the porter to watch.	and said unto them, trade ye *herewith* till I come. *cp.* 20 9.	*cp.* 21 22, 23.
and delivered unto them his goods. **15** And unto one he gave five talents [*cp.* 18 24], to another two, to another one; to each according to his several ability;	¹ Gr. *bondservants.*	**14** But his citizens hated him, and sent an ambassage [*cp.* 14 32] after him, saying, We will not that this man reign over us.	
and he went on his journey [*cp.* 21 33].	*cp.* 12 1.		
16 Straightway he that received the five talents went and traded with them, and made other five talents. **17** In like manner he also that *received* the two gained other two. **18** But he that received the one went away and digged in the earth, and hid his lord's [*cp.* 18 25, *etc.*] money. **19** Now after a long time the lord of those ¹ servants [*cp.* 18 27; 24 50] cometh,		**15** And it came to pass, when he [*cp.* 12 46] was come back again, having received the kingdom, that he commanded these ¹ servants, unto whom he had given the money, to be called to him, that he might know what they had gained by trading. **16** And the first came before him,	
and maketh a reckoning with them [*cp.* 18 23]. **20** And he that received the five talents came and brought other five talents, saying, Lord, thou deliveredst unto me five talents: lo, I have gained other five talents. **21** His lord said unto him, Well done, good and faith-		saying, Lord, thy pound hath made ten pounds more. **17** And he said unto him, Well done, thou good	

ful [cp. 24 45] ² servant : thou hast been faithful over a few things, I will set thee over [cp. 24 47 and 45] many things : enter [cp. 7 13 ; etc.] thou into the joy of thy lord. **22** And he also that *received* the two talents came and said, Lord, thou deliveredst unto me two talents : lo, I have gained other two talents. **23** His lord said unto him, Well done, good and faithful [cp. 24 45] ² servant ; thou hast been faithful over a few things, I will set thee over [cp. 24 47 and 45] many things : enter [cp. 7 13 ; etc.] thou into the joy of thy lord. **24** And he also that had received the one talent came and said, Lord,

I knew thee that thou art a hard man,

reaping where thou didst not sow, and gathering where thou didst not scatter : **25** and I was afraid, and went away and hid thy talent in the earth : lo, thou hast thine own. **26** But his lord answered and said unto him,

Thou wicked [cp. 18 32 : *also* 24 48] and slothful ² servant, thou knewest that I

reap where I sowed not, and gather where I did not scatter ; **27** thou oughtest therefore to have put my money to the bankers, and at my coming I should have received back mine own with interest.

cp. 16 28 ; 26 73 ; 27 47.

28 Take ye away therefore the talent from him, and give it unto him that hath the ten talents [cp. 21 43].

cp. 9 43 ; etc.

cp. 9 43 ; etc.

cp. 9 1 ; 11 5 ; 14 47, 69, 70 ; 15 35, 39.

[cp. 12 42] ³ servant : because thou wast found faithful in a very little [cp. 16 10 : *also* 12 26], have thou authority over [cp. 12 44 and 42] ten cities. cp. 13 24 ; etc.

18 And the second came, saying, Thy pound, Lord, hath made five pounds. **19** And he said unto him also, cp. 12 42. cp. 16 10 : *also* 12 26. Be thou also over [cp. 12 44 and 42] five cities. cp. 13 24 ; etc.

20 And ⁴ another came, saying, Lord, behold, *here is* thy pound, which I kept laid up in a napkin : **21** for I feared thee, because thou art an austere man : thou takest up that thou layedst not down, and reapest that thou didst not sow.

22 He saith unto him, Out of thine own mouth will I judge thee, thou wicked ³ servant. Thou knewest that I am an austere man, taking up that I laid not down, and reaping that I did not sow ; **23** then wherefore gavest thou not my money into the bank, and ⁵ I at my coming should have required it with interest ? **24** And he said unto them that stood by [cp. 9 27], Take away from him the pound, and give it unto him that hath the ten pounds. **25** And they said unto him, Lord, he hath ten pounds. **26** I say unto you, that unto every one that hath shall be given ; but from him that hath not, even that which he hath shall be taken away from him.

cp. 3 5 ; 10 1, 2, 9 : *and* 15 11 ; 17 13.

cp. 3 5 ; 10 1, 2, 9 : *and* 15 11 ; 17 13.

cp. 12 29.

29 For unto every one that hath shall be given, and he shall have abundance : but from him that hath not, even that which he hath shall be taken away.

Matt. 13 12 For whosoever hath, to him shall be given, and he shall have abundance : but whosoever hath not, from him shall be taken away even that which he hath.

Mark 4 25 For he that hath, to him shall be given : and he that hath not, from him shall be taken away even that which he hath.

Luke 8 18 For whosoever hath, to him shall be given ; and whosoever hath not, from him shall be taken away even that which he ⁶ thinketh he hath. cp. 17 10.

30 And cast ye out the unprofitable ² servant into the outer darkness [cp. 8 12 ; 22 13] :

there shall be the weeping and gnashing of teeth [cp. 8 12 ; 13 42, 50 ; 22 13 ; 24 51].

27 Howbeit these mine enemies, which would not that I should reign over them, bring hither, and slay them before me.

cp. 13 28.

¹ Gr. *bondservants*. ² Gr. *bondservant*.

¹ Gr. *bondservants*.
² *Mina*, here translated a pound, is equal to one hundred drachmas. See ch. 15 8.
³ Gr. *bondservant*. ⁴ Gr. *the other*.
⁵ Or, *I should have gone and required*
⁶ Or, *seemeth to have*

§ 193. **Departure from Jericho**

Luke 19 28

cp. 20 17: *also* 16 21; 20 18.	*cp.* 10 32: *also* 10 33.	**28** And when he had thus spoken, he went on before, going up to Jerusalem [*cp.* 9 51, 53; 13 22; 17 11: *also* 9 31; 13 33; 18 31; 19 11, 41].

E. The Ministry in Jerusalem (§§ 194-224)

(i) Arrival and Initial Activity (§§ 194-200)

§ 194. **The Triumphal Entry**

Matt. 21 1-11	**Mark 11** 1-10	**Luke 19** 29-40	John 12 12-19
1 And when they drew nigh unto Jerusalem, and came unto Bethphage, unto the mount of Olives, then Jesus sent two disciples, **2** saying unto them, Go into the village that is over against you, and straightway ye shall find an ass tied, and a colt with her:	**1** And when they draw nigh unto Jerusalem, unto Bethphage and Bethany, at the mount of Olives, he sendeth two [*cp.* 14 13: *also* 6 7] of his disciples, **2** and saith unto them, Go your way into the village that is over against you: and straightway as ye enter into it, ye shall find a colt tied,	**29** And it came to pass, when he drew nigh unto Bethphage and Bethany, at the mount that is called *the mount* of Olives, he sent two [*cp.* 22 8: *also* 10 1] of the disciples, **30** saying, Go your way into the village over against *you*; in the which as ye enter ye shall find a colt tied,	*cp.* 12 1.
loose *them*, and bring *them* unto me. **3** And if any one say aught unto you, ye shall say, The Lord hath need of them; and straightway he will send them. **4** Now this is come to pass, that it might be fulfilled which was spoken ¹ by the prophet, saying, **5** Tell ye the daughter of Zion, Behold, thy King cometh unto thee, Meek, and riding upon an ass, And upon a colt the foal of an ass.	whereon no man ever yet sat; loose him, and bring him. **3** And if any one say unto you, Why do ye this? say ye, The Lord hath need of him; and straightway he ¹ will send him ² back hither.	whereon no man ever yet sat [*cp.* 23 53]: loose him, and bring him. **31** And if any one ask you, Why do ye loose him? thus shall ye say, The Lord hath need of him.	*cp.* 19 41. *verse* 15
6 And the disciples went, and did *cp.* 16 28: 27 47: *also* 26 73. even as Jesus appointed them [*cp.* 26 19],	**4** And they went away, and found a colt tied at the door without in the open street; and they loose him. **5** And certain of them that stood there [*cp.* 9 1; 14 47; 15 35: *also* 14 69, 70; 15 39] said unto them, What do ye, loosing the colt? **6** And they said unto them even as Jesus had said: and they let them go.	**32** And they that were sent went away, and found even as he had said unto them [*cp.* 22 13]. **33** And as they were loosing the colt, *cp.* 9 27: *also* 19 24. the owners thereof said unto them, Why loose ye the colt? **34** And they said, The Lord hath need of him.	*cp.* 12 29.

7 and   brought the ass, and the colt,
     and   put on them   their   garments; and he sat thereon. **8** And the most   part   of the multitude

     spread their garments in the way; and others cut branches from the trees,
     and spread them in the way. **9** And

the   multitudes
     that went before   him, and that followed, cried,

     saying, Hosanna [*cp*. 21 15] to the son of David [*cp*. 1 1; 9 27; 12 23; 15 22; 20 30, 31; 21 15]: Blessed *is* he   [*cp*. 2 2; 21 5; 25 34, 40; 27 11, 29, 37, 42]
     that cometh [*cp*. 3 11; 11 3]
     in the name of the Lord [=23 39];

cp. 5 9; 10 13.
     Hosanna in the highest.

verse 7

verses 4 *and* 5

cp. 15 16; 16 8-12.

cp. 26 75.

---

7 And they bring   the colt unto Jesus, and   cast on him their   garments; and he sat upon him. **8** And

many

     spread their garments upon the way; and others ³ branches,
     which they had cut from the fields.

     9 And

they
     that went before,   and they that followed, cried,

Hosanna;
     cp. 10 47, 48.

     Blessed *is* he   [*cp*. 15 2, 9, 12, 18, 26, 32]

     that cometh [*cp*. 1 7]

     in the name of the Lord:
     10 Blessed *is* the kingdom that cometh, *the kingdom* of our father David:
cp. 9 50.
     Hosanna in the highest.

verse 7

cp. 4 13; 6 52; 7 18; 8 17-21; 9 10, 32: *also* 16 14.

---

35 And they brought   him   to Jesus: and they threw   their garments upon the colt, and   set Jesus thereon. **36** And

     as he went,   they spread their garments in the way.

     37 And as he was now drawing nigh, *even* at the descent of the mount of Olives, the whole multitude of the disciples
     cp. 18 39.
     began to rejoice and praise God [*cp*. 2 13, 20; 18 43] with a loud voice for all the ¹ mighty works which they had seen; **38** saying,

cp. 18 38, 39: *also* 1 32.

     Blessed *is* the King [*cp*. 23 2, 3, 37, 38: *also* 1 33]
     that cometh [*cp*. 7 19, 20: *also* 3 16]
     in the name of the Lord [=13 35]:

     peace [*cp*. 2 14: *also* 1 79; 2 29; 19 42] in heaven, and glory in the highest [*cp*. 2 14].

verse 35

cp. 9 45; 18 34: *also* 2 50.

cp. 24 6, 8.

verse 37

---

verse 14

12 On the morrow ¹ a great multitude that had come to the feast, when they heard that Jesus was coming to Jerusalem,

     13 took the branches of the palm trees,

     and

     went forth to meet him, and   cried out,

verses 17 *and* 18

Hosanna:

     Blessed *is* he   [*cp*. 1 49; 12 15; 18 33, 37, 39; 19 3, 12, 14, 15, 19, 21: *also* 6 15] that cometh [*cp*. 1 15, 27; 3 31; 6 14; 11 27: *also* 1 30] in the name of the Lord, even the King of Israel.

cp. 14 27; 16 33.

     14 And Jesus, having found a young ass, sat thereon; as it is written, **15** Fear not, daughter of Zion: behold, thy King cometh, sitting on an ass's colt. **16** These things understood not his disciples [*cp*. 4 33; 11 13; 13 7, 28, 36; 14 5-10; 16 17-18: *also* 3 10; 8 27, 43; 10 6] at the first: but when Jesus was glorified, then [*cp*. 13 7] remembered they that these things were written of him, and that they had done these things unto him [*cp*. 2 22]. **17** The multitude therefore that was with him when he called Lazarus out of the tomb, and raised him from the dead, bare witness. **18** For this cause also the multitude went

			and met him, for that they heard that he had done this sign.
		39 And some of the Pharisees from the multitude said unto him, ² Master, rebuke [*cp.* 18 39] thy disciples. **40** And he answered and said, I tell you that, if these shall hold their peace [*cp.* 18 39], the stones will cry out [*cp.* 18 39].	**19** The Pharisees therefore said
cp. 21 15-16.			among themselves, ² Behold how ye prevail nothing : lo, the world is gone after him.
10 And when he was come into Jerusalem, all the city was stirred, saying, Who is this [*cp.* 8 27]? **11** And the multitudes said, This is the prophet [*cp.* 13 57; 21 46], Jesus, from Nazareth [*cp.* 2 23; 26 71] of Galilee.	**11** And ¹ he entered into Jerusalem ...		
	cp. 4 41: *also* 1 27.	*cp.* 5 21; 7 49; 8 25; 9 9: *also* 4 36.	*cp.* 5 12: *also* 12 34.
	cp. 6 4, 15.	*cp.* 4 24; 7 16, 39; 13 33; 24 19.	*cp.* 4 19, 44; 6 14; 7 40; 9 17.
	cp. 1 24; 10 47; 14 67; 16 6.	*cp.* 4 34; 18 37; 24 19.	*cp.* 1 45; 18 5, 7; 19 19.
¹ Or, *through*	¹ Gr. *sendeth.* ² Or, *again* ³ Gr. *layers of leaves.*	¹ Gr. *powers.* ² Or, *Teacher*	¹ Some ancient authorities read *the common people.* ² Or, *Ye behold*

Matt. 21 5 = Is. 62 11.   Matt. 21 5 || John 12 15 = Zech. 9 9.   Matt. 21 9 || Mark 11 9 || Luke 19 38 || John 12 13 : *cp.* Ps. 118 25-26.

§ 195. A Lament over Jerusalem

[*Cp.* Matt. 23 37-39 || Luke 13 34-35 : *also* Luke 23 27-31 *and* 21 20]

		Luke 19 41-44	
cp. 16 21; 20 17, 18.	*cp.* 10 32, 33.	**41** And when he drew nigh, he saw the city [*cp.* 9 51, 53; 13 22; 17 11; 19 11: *also* 9 31; 13 33; 18 31] and wept over it [*cp.* 23 28], **42** saying, ¹ If thou hadst known in this day, even thou, the things which belong unto peace [*cp.* 1 79; 2 14, 29; 19 38] ! but now they are hid from thine eyes. **43** For the days shall come [*cp.* 5 35; 17 22; 21 6; 23 29] upon thee, when thine enemies shall cast up a ² bank about thee, and compass thee round [*cp.* 21 20], and keep thee in on every side, **44** and shall dash thee to the ground, and thy children [*cp.* 13 34] within thee; and they shall not leave in thee one stone upon another [*cp.* 21 6]; because thou knewest not the time of thy visitation.	*cp.* 14 27; 16 33.
cp. 5 9; 10 13.	*cp.* 9 50.		
cp. 9 15.	*cp.* 2 20.		
cp. 23 37.			
cp. 24 2.	*cp.* 13 2.		
		¹ Or, *O that thou hadst known* ² Gr. *palisade.*	

Luke 19 44 : *cp.* Ps. 137 9.

§ 196. A Visit to the Temple (Mark); The Cleansing of the Temple (Matt.)
Retirement to Bethany

[*Cp.* Mal. 3 1 : Zech. 14 21]

Matt. 21 (10-11) 12-17	**Mark 11** 11 (15-17)	Luke 19 45-46	John 2 13-17
			13 And the passover of the Jews was at hand, and Jesus went up to Jerusalem.
10 And when he was come into Jerusalem, all the city was stirred, saying, Who is this [*cp.* 8 27]? **11** And the multitudes said, This is the prophet [*cp.* 13 57; 21 46], Jesus, from Nazareth	**11** And ¹ he entered into Jerusalem, into the temple;		
	cp. 4 41: *also* 1 27.	*cp.* 5 21; 7 49; 8 25; 9 9: *also* 4 36.	*cp.* 5 12: *also* 12 34.
	cp. 6 4, 15.	*cp.* 4 24; 7 16, 39; 13 33; 24 19.	*cp.* 4 19, 44; 6 14; 7 40; 9 17.

[*cp.* 2 23 ; 26 71] of Galilee.	*cp.* 1 24; 10 47; 14 67; 16 6.	*cp.* 4 34; 18 37; 24 19.	*cp.* 1 45; 18 5, 7; 19 19.

Matthew — **12** And Jesus entered into the temple ¹ of God,

and cast out all them that sold and bought in the temple,

and overthrew the tables of the money-changers, and the seats of them that sold the doves;

13 and he saith unto them, It is written, My house shall be called a house of prayer: but ye make it a den of robbers.

14 And the blind and the lame came to him in the temple: and he healed them. **15** But when the chief priests and the scribes saw the wonderful things that he did, and the children that were crying in the temple and saying, Hosanna [*cp.* 21 9] to the son of David [*cp.* 1 1; 9 27; 12 23; 15 22; 20 30, 31; 21 9]; they were moved with indignation, **16** and said unto him, Hearest thou what these are saying? And Jesus saith unto them, Yea: did ye never read [*cp.* 12 3, 5; 19 4; 21 42; 22 31], Out of the mouth of babes and sucklings thou hast perfected praise? **17** And

he left them [*cp.* 16 4], and went forth out [*cp.* 26 30] of the city to Bethany, and lodged there.

Mark — **15** And they come to Jerusalem: and he entered into the temple,

and began to cast out them that sold and them that bought in the temple,

and overthrew the tables of the money-changers, and the seats of them that sold the doves; **16** and he would not suffer that any man should carry a vessel through the temple. **17** And he taught, and said unto them, Is it not written, My house shall be called a house of prayer for all the nations? but ye have made it a den of robbers.

cp. 11 18.

cp. 11 9, 10.
cp. 10 47, 48.

cp. 2 25; 12 10, 26.

and when he **had** looked round about [*cp.* 3 5, 34; 5 32; 9 8; 10 23] upon all things, it being now eventide, he [*cp.* 8 13] went out [*cp.* 11 19; 14 26] unto Bethany with the twelve.

Luke — **45** And he entered into the temple,

and began to cast out them that sold,

46 saying unto them, It is written, And my house shall be a house of prayer: but ye have made it a den of robbers.

cp. 19 47.

cp. 18 38, 39: also 1 32.

cp. 19 39-40.

cp. 6 3: also 10 26.

cp. 6 10.

cp. 21 37; 22 39.

John — **14** And he found in the temple those that sold oxen and sheep and doves, and the changers of money sitting : **15** and he made a scourge of cords, and cast all out of the temple, both the sheep and the oxen ; and he poured out the changers' money, and overthrew their tables ; **16** and to them that sold the doves he said, Take these things hence ; make not my Father's house a house of merchandise. **17** His disciples remembered that it was written, The zeal of thine house shall eat me up.

cp. 2 18.

cp. 12 13.

cp. 12 19.

cp. 18 1-2: also 8 1.

¹ Many ancient authorities omit *of God.*

Mark 11 16 : *cp.* Zech. 14 21.   Matt. 21 13 ‖ Mark 11 17 ‖ Luke 19 46 = Is. 56 7: *cp.* Jer. 7 11.   Matt. 21 16 = Ps. 8 2.   John 2 17 = Ps. 69 9.

§ 197. The Cursing of a Fig Tree

[*Cp.* Matt. 24 32-33 ‖ Mark 13 28-29 ‖ Luke 21 29-31; Luke 13 6-9]

Matt. 21 18-19	Mark 11 12-14	
18 Now in the morning as he returned to the city, he hungered. **19** And seeing ¹ a fig tree by the way side, he came to it, and found nothing thereon, but leaves only; and he saith unto it, Let there be no fruit from thee henceforward for ever. And immediately the fig tree withered away. ¹ Or, *a single*	**12** And on the morrow, when they were come out from Bethany, he hungered. **13** And seeing a fig tree afar off having leaves, he came, if haply he might find anything thereon: and when he came to it, he found nothing but leaves; for it was not the season of figs. **14** And he answered and said unto it, No man eat fruit from thee henceforward for ever. And his disciples heard it.	*cp.* 13 6.

§ 198. The Cleansing of the Temple

[*Cp.* Mal. 3 1: Zech. 14 21]

Matt 21 12-13	Mark 11 15-18	Luke 19 45-48	John 2 13-17
12 And Jesus entered into the temple ¹ of God, and cast out all them that sold and bought in the temple, and overthrew the tables of the money-changers, and the seats of them that sold the doves; **13** and he saith unto them, It is written, My house shall be called a house of prayer: but ye make it a den of robbers.	**15** And they come to Jerusalem: and he entered into the temple, and began to cast out them that sold and them that bought in the temple, and overthrew the tables of the money-changers, and the seats of them that sold the doves; **16** and he would not suffer that any man should carry a vessel through the temple. **17** And he taught, and said unto them, Is it not written, My house shall be called a house of prayer for all the nations? but ye have made it a den of robbers.	**45** And he entered into the temple, and began to cast out them that sold, **46** saying unto them, It is written, And my house shall be a house of prayer: but ye have made it a den of robbers. **47** And he was teaching daily in the temple [*cp.* 21 37; 22 53: *also* 20 1]. But the chief priests and the scribes and the principal men of the	**13** And the passover of the Jews was at hand, and Jesus went up to Jerusalem. **14** And he found in the temple those that sold oxen and sheep and doves, and the changers of money sitting: **15** and he made a scourge of cords, and cast all out of the temple, both the sheep and the oxen; and he poured out the changers' money, and overthrew their tables; **16** and to them that sold the doves he said, Take these things hence; make not my Father's house a house of merchandise. **17** His disciples remembered that it was written, The zeal of thine house shall eat me up.
cp. 26 55: *also* 21 23. *cp.* 21 15.	*cp.* 14 49: *also* 12 35. **18** And the chief priests and the scribes		*cp.* 18 20: *also* 7 28; 8 20. *cp.* 2 18.

cp. 12 14; 21 46; 26 4. *cp.* 21 46; 26 5: *also* 14 5; 21 26.	heard it, and sought how they might destroy him [*cp.* 3 6; 12 12; 14 1]: for they feared [*cp.* 12 12; 14 2: *also* 11 32] him,	people sought to destroy him [*cp.* 6 11; 20 19; 22 2]: **48** and they [*cp.* 20 19; 22 2: *also* 20 6] could not find what they might do; for the people all	*cp.* 5 16, 18; 7 30, 32; 11 53, 57.
cp. 7 28; 13 54; 19 25; 22 22, 33: *also* 8 27; 9 33; *etc.*	for all the multitude was astonished [*cp.* 1 22, 27; 6 2; 10 24, 26; 12 17: *also* 2 12; 5 20; *etc.*] at his teaching. *cp.* 12 37.	*cp.* 2 47, 48; 4 22, 32, 36; 20 26: *also* 5 9, 26; *etc.* hung upon him, listening [*cp.* 21 38].	*cp.* 7 15, 21, 46.

¹ Many ancient authorities omit *of God.*

Mark 11 16: *cp.* Zech. 14 21.   Matt. 21 13 ‖ Mark 11 17 ‖ Luke 19 46=Is. 56 7: *cp.* Jer. 7 11.   John 2 17=Ps. 69 9.

§ 199. Retirement in the Evenings

	Mark 11 19	**Luke 21** 37-38	
cp. 26 55: *also* 21 23. *cp.* 21 17; 26 30. *cp.* 24 3; 26 30.	*cp.* 14 49: *also* 12 35. **19** And ¹ every evening ² he went forth out [*cp.* 11 11; 14 26] of the city. *cp.* 13 3; 14 26. *cp.* 12 37.	37 And every day he was teaching in the temple [*cp.* 19 47; 22 53: *also* 20 1]; and every night he went out [*cp.* 22 39], and lodged in the mount that is called *the mount* of Olives [*cp.* 22 39]. 38 And all the people came early in the morning to him in the temple, to hear him [*cp.* 19 48].	*cp.* 18 20: *also* 7 28; 8 20. *cp.* 18 1-2. *cp.* 8 1. *cp.* 8 2.

¹ Gr. *whenever evening came.*
² Some ancient authorities read *they.*

§ 200. The Fig Tree withered and Sayings about Faith

Matt. 21 20-22	**Mark 11** 20-25 (26)	**Luke 17** 6	
20 And when the disciples saw it,	**20** And as they passed by in the morning, they saw the fig tree withered away from the roots. **21** And Peter [*cp.* 8 32; 9 5; 10 28; 14 29: *also* 8 29] calling to remembrance [*cp.* 6 51; 10 32; 16 8; *etc.*: *also* 10 24, 26; *etc.*] saith unto him, Rabbi [*cp.* 9 5; 14 45: *also* 10 51], behold, the fig tree which thou cursedst is withered away.		*cp.* 13 36, 37; 21 21: *also* 6 68.
cp. 14 28; 15 15; 16 22; 17 4; 18 21; 19 27; 26 33: *also* 16 16; 17 24. they marvelled [*cp.* 8 27; *etc.*: *also* 19 25; *etc.*], saying, *cp.* 26 25, 49. How did the fig tree immediately wither away?		*cp.* 8 45; 9 33; 12 41; 18 28: *also* 5 8; 9 20. *cp.* 5 9; 8 25; 24 12, 41; *etc.*	
17 19 Then came the disciples to Jesus apart, and said, Why could not we cast it out? **20** And he saith unto them, Because of your little faith [*cp.* 6 30; 8 26; 14 31; 16 8]:	9 28 And when he was come into the house, his disciples asked him privately, ¹ *saying,* We could not cast it out. 29 And he said unto them, *cp.* 4 40; 16 14. This kind can come out by nothing, save by prayer.²	6 And the Lord said, *cp.* 12 28: *also* 8 25; 17 5; 22 32; 24 25, 38.	*cp.* 1 38, 49; *etc.*: *also* 20 16. *cp.* 3 12; 6 64; 14 10; 20 27.
for verily I say unto you, If ye have faith as a grain of mustard seed [*cp.* 13 31], ye shall say unto this mountain, Remove hence to yonder place; and it shall remove; and nothing shall be impossible unto you [*cp.* 19 26].¹	*cp.* 4 31. *cp.* 9 23; 10 27; 14 36.	If ye have faith as a grain of mustard seed [*cp.* 13 19], ye would say unto this sycamine tree, *cp.* 1 37; 18 27.	

21 And Jesus answered and said unto them,
Verily I say unto you, If ye have faith, and doubt not, ye shall not only do what is done to the fig tree, but even if ye shall say unto this mountain, Be thou taken up and cast into the sea,

it shall be done.

22 And all things, whatsoever ye shall ask in prayer, believing,

ye shall receive.

cp. 18 19.

Matt. 7 7 Ask,

and it shall be given you ; seek, and ye shall find ; knock, and it shall be opened unto you.

cp. 5 23.

cp. 6 14-15 : *also* 6 12 ; 18 21-35.

Many authorities, some ancient, insert ver. 21 *But this kind goeth not out save by prayer and fasting.* See Mark 9 29.

---

22 And Jesus answering saith unto them, Have faith in God. **23** Verily I say unto you,

Whosoever shall say unto this mountain, Be thou taken up and cast into the sea ; and shall not doubt in his heart, but shall believe that what he saith cometh to pass ; he shall have it.

24 Therefore I say unto you, All things whatsoever ye

pray and ask for, believe that ye have received them, and ye shall have them.

25 And whensoever ye stand praying, forgive, if ye have aught against any one ; that your Father also which is in heaven may forgive you your trespasses.[3]

[1] Or, How is it *that we could not cast it out ?*
[2] Many ancient authorities add *and fasting.*
[3] Many ancient authorities add ver. 26 *But if ye do not forgive, neither will your Father which is in heaven forgive your trespasses.*

Be thou rooted up, and be thou planted in the sea ; and

it would have obeyed you.

John 14 13
And whatsoever ye shall ask

in my name,

that will I do. . . .
14 If ye shall ask [1] me anything

in my name, that will I do.

John 15 7 Ask whatsoever ye will, and it shall be done unto you.

[1] Many ancient authorities omit *me.*

John 15 16
. . . that whatsoever ye shall ask of the Father

in my name,

he may give it you.
16 23 If ye shall ask anything of the Father, he will give it you in my name.
24 Hitherto have ye asked nothing in my name : ask,

and ye shall receive.

cp. 11 4 ; 17 3-4.

(ii) Debate and Teaching in the Temple (§§ 201-212)

§ 201. **A Question about Authority**

Matt. 21 23-32

23 And when he was come into the temple, *cp.* 11 5.

the chief priests and the elders of the people came unto him as he was teaching [*cp.* 26 55], and said,

---

Mark 11 27-33

27 And they come again to Jerusalem : and as he was walking [*cp.* 12 35 ; 14 49] in the temple,

there come to him the chief priests, and the scribes, and the elders ;

cp. 12 35 ; 14 49.
28 and they said unto

Luke 20 1-8

1 And it came to pass, on one of the days, as he was teaching [*cp.* 19 47 ; 21 37 ; 22 53] the people in the temple, and preaching the gospel [*cp.* 1 19 ; 2 10 ; 3 18 ; 4 18, 43 ; 7 22 ; 8 1 ; 9 6 ; 16 16], there came upon him the chief priests and the scribes with the elders ;

2 and they spake, saying unto

cp. 18 20 ; *also* 7 28 ; 8 20.

cp. 18 20 : *also* 7 28 ; 8 20.

By what authority [cp. 7 29; 9 6; 28 18] doest thou these things? and who gave thee this authority? **24** And Jesus answered and said unto them, I also will ask you one ¹ question, which if ye tell me, I likewise will tell you by what authority I do these things. **25** The baptism of John, whence was it? from heaven or from men?

And they reasoned with themselves, saying, If we shall say, From heaven; he will say unto us, Why then did ye not believe him [cp. verse 32]? **26** But if we shall say, From men; we fear the multitude [cp. 14 5: also 21 46; 26 5]; for all hold John as a prophet [cp. 14 5: also 11 9: and 21 46]. **27** And they answered Jesus, and said, We know not.

He also said unto them, Neither tell I you by what authority I do these things. **28** But what think ye [cp. 17 25; 18 12; 22 17, 42; 26 66]? A man had two sons; and he came to the first, and said, ² Son, go work to-day in the vineyard [cp. 20 1, 2, 4, 7: also 21 33; Mark 12 1; Luke 20 9 and 13 6]. **29** And he answered and said, I will not: but afterward he repented himself, and went. **30** And he came to the second, and said likewise. And he answered and said, I go, sir: and went not. **31** Whether of the twain did the will [cp. 7 21; 12 50: also 6 10; 26 39, 42] of his father? They say, The first. Jesus saith unto them, Verily I say unto you, that the publicans and the harlots go into the kingdom of God [cp. 5 20; 7 21; 18 3; 19 23, 24; 23 13: also 7 13; 18 8, 9; 19 17; 25 21, 23] before you [cp. 9 13: Mark 2 17: Luke 5 32; 7 29, 30, 47; 15 7, 10; 18 14; 19 10]. **32** For John came unto you in the way of righteousness [cp. 3 15; 5 6, 10, 20; 6 1, 33], and ye believed him not [cp. verse 25: Mark 11 31: Luke 20 5]: but the publicans and the harlots believed him: and ye, when ye saw it, did not even repent yourselves afterward, that ye might believe him.

¹ Gr. word.
² Gr. Child.

---

him, By what authority [cp. 1 22, 27; 2 10] doest thou these things? or who gave thee this authority to do these things? **29** And Jesus said unto them, I will ask of you one ¹ question, and answer me, and I will tell you by what authority I do these things. **30** The baptism of John, was it from heaven, or from men? answer me. **31** And they reasoned with themselves, saying, If we shall say, From heaven; he will say, Why then did ye not believe him? **32** ² But should we say, From men—they feared the people [cp. 11 18; 12 12; 14 2]: ³ for all verily held John to be a prophet.

33 And they answered Jesus and say, We know not. And Jesus saith unto them, Neither tell I you by what authority I do these things.

¹ Gr. word.
² Or, But shall we say, From men?
³ Or, for all held John to be a prophet indeed.

---

him, Tell us: By what authority [cp. 4 32, 36; 5 24] doest thou these things? or who is he that gave thee this authority? **3** And he answered and said unto them, I also will ask you a ¹ question; and tell me:

4 The baptism of John, was it from heaven, or from men? **5** And they reasoned with themselves, saying, If we shall say, From heaven; he will say, Why did ye not believe him [cp. 7 30]? **6** But if we shall say, From men; all the people [cp. 20 19; 22 2] will stone us: for they be persuaded that John was a prophet [cp. 1 76; 7 26]. **7** And they answered, that they knew not whence it was. **8** And Jesus said unto them, Neither tell I you by what authority I do these things.

cp. 15 11-32.

¹ Gr. word.

---

cp. 2 18: also 5 27; 17 2.

cp. 3 27.

cp. 11 56.

---

cp. 3 35: also 14 36.	cp. 22 42.	cp. 4 34; 5 30; 6 38; 7 17; 9 31.
cp. 9 47; 10 15, 23-25: also 9 43, 45.	cp. 18 17, 24, 25: also 11 52; 13 24; 24 26.	cp. 3 5: also 10 1, 2, 9.
	cp. 7 30. cp. 3 12; 7 29.	

---

§ 202. **The Parable of the Wicked Husbandmen**

Matt. 21 33-46	**Mark 12** 1-12	**Luke 20** 9-19
33 Hear another parable: There was a man that was a householder [cp. 13 52; 20 1: also 13 27], which planted a vineyard [cp. 20 1; 21 28], and set a hedge about it, and digged a winepress in it, and built a tower, and let it out to husbandmen, and went into another country	**1** And he began to speak unto them in parables. A man planted a vineyard, and set a hedge about it, and digged a pit for the winepress, and built a tower, and let it out to husbandmen, and went into another country	**9** And he began to speak unto the people this parable: A man cp. 14 21. planted a vineyard [cp. 13 6], and let it out to husbandmen, and went into another country

[cp. 25 14, 15].
34 And when the season of the fruits drew near, he sent his ¹ servants [cp. 22 3] to the husbandmen,
to receive
² his
fruits.   **35** And the husbandmen took his ¹ servants, and beat one, and killed another, and stoned [cp. 23 37] another.

36 Again, he sent
other ¹ servants [cp. 22 4] more than the first: and

they

[cp. 22 6: also 5 12; 23 29-34, 37] did unto them in like manner. **37** But

cp. 3 17; 12 18; 17 5.
afterward he sent
unto them his son, saying,

cp. 3 17; 12 18; 17 5.
They will reverence my son.
38 But   the husbandmen, when they saw the son, said among themselves,
This is the heir; come, let us kill him, and take his inheritance.
39 And they took him, and cast him forth out of the vineyard, and killed him. **40** When therefore   the lord of the vineyard [cp. 20 8] shall come, what will he do unto those husbandmen? **41** They say unto him, He will miserably destroy those miserable men [cp. 22 7], and will let out the vineyard unto other

husbandmen [cp. 8 11; 21 31; 22 7-10: also 10 18; 24 14; 26 13; 28 19], which shall render him the fruits in their seasons [cp. verse 43].

42 Jesus saith
unto them, Did ye never read [cp. 12 3, 5; 19 4; 21 16; 22 31] in the scriptures,

The stone which the builders rejected,
The same was made the head of the corner [cp. 26 24, 31, 54, 56]:

[cp. 13 34].
2 And at the season
he sent
to the
husbandmen a ¹ servant,
that he might receive from the husbandmen of the fruits of the vineyard. **3** And they   took him, and beat him,

and sent
him away empty. **4** And again he sent unto them another ¹ servant;
and him
they wounded in the head,   and handled shamefully.
5 And he sent another; and him they killed:
and many others; beating some, and killing some.

6 He
had yet one,
a beloved son [cp. 1 11; 9 7]: he sent him last unto them,   saying,

They will reverence my son.
7 But   those husbandmen
said among themselves,
This is the heir; come, let us kill him, and   the inheritance shall be ours.
8 And they took him, and killed him, and cast him forth out of the vineyard.
9 What therefore will the lord of the vineyard
do?

he will come and destroy the husbandmen,   and will give the vineyard unto others [cp. 13 10; 14 9; 16 15].

10 Have ye not read [cp. 2 25; 12 26]
even this scripture;

The stone which the builders rejected,
The same was made the head of the corner [cp. 9 12; 14 21, 27, 49]:

[cp. 19 12] for a long time.
10 And at the season
he sent
unto the
husbandmen a ¹ servant [cp. 14 17], that they should give him   of the fruit of the vineyard: but the husbandmen
beat him,
cp. 13 34.
and sent
him away empty. **11** And he sent
yet another ¹ servant:
and him
also they
beat, and handled him shamefully, and sent him away empty. **12** And he sent yet a third: and him also they wounded,   and cast him forth.
cp. 6 23; 11 47-50; 13 33, 34.

13 And the lord of the vineyard

said, What shall I do [cp. 12 17; 16 3]? I will send my beloved son [cp. 3 22; 9 35]: it may be they will reverence him.
14 But when the husbandmen saw him,   they reasoned one with another, saying, This is the heir: let us kill him, that   the inheritance may be ours.
15 And they
cast him forth out of the vineyard [cp. 4 29], and killed him. What therefore will the lord of the vineyard
do unto them?

16 He will come and destroy these husbandmen,   and will give the vineyard unto others [cp. 13 29; 14 21-24: also 2 30-32; 3 6; 24 47].

And
when they heard it, they said, ² God forbid. **17** But he looked upon them, and said,

cp. 6 3; 10 26.

What then is this that is written,
The stone which the builders rejected,
The same was made the head of the corner [cp. 18 31; 22 37; 24 25-27,

---

cp. 1 11.

cp. 10 16; 11 52.

cp. 5 39; 13 18; 15 25; 17 12.

This was from the Lord, And it is marvellous in our eyes?	**11** This was from the Lord, And it is marvellous in our eyes?	44-46] ?
43 Therefore say I unto you, The kingdom of God shall be taken away from you, and shall be given to a nation bringing forth the fruits thereof [*cp.* 25 28: *also verse* 41 *above*]. **44** [3] And he that falleth on this stone shall be broken to pieces: but on whomsoever it shall fall, it will scatter him as dust. **45** And when the chief priests and the Pharisees heard his parables, they perceived that he spake of them. **46** And when they sought to lay hold on him [*cp.* 12 14; 26 4], *cp.* 18 1; 26 55. they feared the multitudes [*cp.* 26 5: *also* 14 5; 21 26], because they took him for a prophet [*cp.* 14 5; 21 26: *also* 13 57; 21 11]. *cp.* 22 22.	*cp. verse 9 above.* ... **12** And they sought to lay hold on him [*cp.* 3 6; 11 18; 14 1]; and they feared the multitude [*cp.* 11 18; 14 2: *also* 11 32]; for they perceived that he spake the parable against them: *cp.* 11 32: *also* 6 4, 15. and they left him, and went away.	*cp.* 19 24: *also verse 16 above.* **18** Every one that falleth on that stone shall be broken to pieces; but on whomsoever it shall fall, it will scatter him as dust. **19** And the scribes and the chief priests sought to lay hands on him [*cp.* 6 11; 19 47; 22 2] in that very hour [*cp.* 7 21; 10 21; 13 31]; and they feared the people [*cp.* 22 2: *also* 20 6]: for they perceived that he spake this parable against them. *cp.* 20 6: *also* 4 24; 7 16, 39; 13 33; 24 19.

cp. 5 16, 18; 7 30, 32; 11 53, 57.

cp. 4 19, 44; 6 14; 7 40; 9 17.

[1] Gr. *bondservants.*
[2] Or, *the fruits of it*
[3] Some ancient authorities omit ver. 44.

[1] Gr. *bondservant.*

[1] Gr. *bondservant.*
[2] Gr. *Be it not so.*

Matt. 21 33-34 ‖ Mark 12 1-2 ‖ Luke 20 9-10: *cp.* Is. 5 1-2.   Matt. 21 42 ‖ Mark 12 10-11 ‖ Luke 20 17 = Ps. 118 22-23.
Matt. 21 44 ‖ Luke 20 18: *cp.* Is. 8 14-15.

§ 203. The Parable of the Marriage Feast

[*Cp.* Matt. 8 11; 21 31, 41-43: *also* 10 18; 24 14; 26 13; 28 19: Mark 12 9-11: *also* 13 10; 14 9;
16 15: Luke 13 29; 20 16-17: *also* 2 30-32; 3 6; 24 47: John 10 16; 11 52]

Matt. 22 1-14		**Luke 14** 15-24
		15 And when one of them that sat at meat with him heard these things, he said unto him, Blessed is he that shall eat bread in the kingdom of God [*cp.* 13 29; 22 16, 18, 30]. **16** But he
cp. 8 11; 26 29. **1** And Jesus answered and spake again in parables unto them, saying, **2** The kingdom of heaven is likened unto a certain king [*cp.* 18 23: *also* 25 34, 40], which made a marriage feast for his son, **3** and sent forth his [1] servants [*cp.* 21 34] to call them that were bidden to the marriage feast: and they would not come. **4** Again he sent forth other [1] servants [*cp.* 21 36], saying, Tell them that are bidden, Behold, I have made ready my dinner: my oxen and my fatlings are killed, and all things are ready: come to the marriage feast. **5** But they made light of it, and went their ways, one to his own	*cp.* 14 25. ... *cp.* 12 2. ... *cp.* 12 4-5.	said unto him, A certain [*cp.* 19 12, 15, 27] man made [*cp.* 14 8] a great supper; and he bade many: **17** and he sent forth his [1] servant [*cp.* 20 10] at supper time to say to them that were bidden, *cp.* 20 11-12. Come; for *all* things are now ready. **18** And they all with one *consent* began to make excuse. The first said unto him, I have bought a

farm,

another   to his merchandise :

6 and the rest laid hold on his ¹servants,
and entreated them shamefully, and
killed them [*cp.* 21 35, 36: *also* 5 12;
23 29-34, 37].

    cp. 13 27, 52; 20 1; 21 33.
       7 But the king was wroth
[*cp.* 18 34]; and he sent his armies,
and destroyed those murderers [*cp.*
21 41], and burned their city. **8** Then
saith he to his ¹ servants, The wedding
is ready, but they that were bidden
were not worthy. **9** Go ye therefore
unto

                 the
partings of the highways,
and as many as ye shall find, bid to the
marriage feast.

10 And those ¹ servants went out into
the highways, and gathered together
all as many as they found, both bad
and good [*cp.* 13 30, 47; 25 32]:
and the wedding was filled with guests.
11 But when the king came in to behold the guests, he saw
there a man which had not on a wedding-garment : **12** and he
saith unto him, Friend [*cp.* 20 13; 26 50], how camest thou in
hither not having a wedding-garment ? And he was speechless.
13 Then the king said to the ² servants, Bind him hand and
foot, and cast him out into the outer darkness [*cp.* 8 12; 25 30];
there shall be the weeping and gnashing of teeth [*cp.* 8 12;
13 42, 50; 24 51; 25 30]. **14** For many are called, but few
chosen.

¹ Gr. *bondservants.*   ¹ Or, *ministers*

cp. 12 3, 4, 5.

cp. 12 9.

field, and I must needs go out and see
it : I pray thee have me excused.
19 And another said, I have bought
five yoke of oxen, and I go to prove
them : I pray thee have me excused.
20 And another said, I have married
a wife, and therefore I cannot come.

cp. 20 10, 11, 12: *also* 6 23; 11 47-50;
      13 33, 34.
      21 And the ¹ servant
came, and told his lord these things.
Then the master of the house being
angry

        cp. 20 16.

said   to his ¹ servant,

              Go out quickly
into the streets and lanes of the city,
and bring in hither the poor and
maimed and blind and lame [*cp.* 14 13].
22 And the ¹ servant said, Lord, what
thou didst command is done, and yet
there is room. **23** And the lord said
unto the ¹ servant, Go out into the
            highways and hedges,
and   constrain *them*
      to come in, that my
house may be filled. **24** For I say unto
you, that none of those men which
were bidden shall taste of my supper.

      ¹ Gr. *bondservant.*

cp. 13 28.

---

§ 204. A Question about Tribute

Matt. 22 15-22	Mark 12 13-17	Luke 20 20-26	
	13 And they [*cp.* 3 2] send	**20** And they watched him [*cp.* 6 7; 14 1], and sent forth spies, which feigned themselves to be righteous,	
15 Then went the Pharisees, and took counsel [*cp.* 12 14; 27 1, 7; 28 12] how they might ensnare him in *his* talk [*cp.* 12 10].	unto him certain of the Pharisees and of the Herodians [*cp.* 3 6], *cp.* 3 6; 15 1. that they might catch him in talk [*cp.* 3 2].	that they might take hold of his speech [*cp.* 6 7; 11 53, 54], so as to deliver him up [*cp.* 23 2] to the rule and to the authority [*cp.* 12 11] of the governor. **21** And	*cp.* 8 6.
cp. 27 2, *etc.*; 28 14. **16** And they send to him their disciples, with the Herodians,	**14** And when they were come, they	they	

saying,

1 Master, we know that thou art true,

and teachest the way of God in truth, and carest not for any one: for thou regardest not the person of men.

17 Tell us therefore, What thinkest thou [*cp.* 17 25; 18 12; 21 28; 22 42; 26 66]? Is it lawful [*cp.* 12 10; 19 3] to give tribute unto Cæsar, or not?

18 But Jesus perceived [*cp.* 12 15; 16 8; 26 10] their wickedness [*cp.* Luke 11 39], and said, Why tempt ye me [*cp.* 16 1; 19 3; 22 35], ye hypocrites [*cp.* 15 7; 23 13, (14,) 15, *etc.*: *also* 6 2, 5, 16; 24 51]? **19** Shew me the tribute money. And they brought unto him a 2 penny.

20 And he saith unto them, Whose is this image and superscription? **21** They say unto him, Cæsar's. Then saith he unto them, Render therefore unto Cæsar the things that are Cæsar's; and unto God the things that are God's.

22 And when they heard it, they marvelled [*cp.* 7 28; 13 54; 19 25; 22 33: *also* 8 27; 9 33; 12 23; 15 31; 21 20; 27 14],

and left him, and went their way.

1 Or, *Teacher*
2 See marginal note on ch. 18 28.

say unto him,

1 Master, we know that thou art true,

and carest not for any one: for thou regardest not the person of men, but of a truth teachest the way of God:

Is it lawful [*cp.* 3 4; 10 2] to give tribute unto Cæsar, or not? **15** Shall we give, or shall we not give? But he, knowing [*cp.* 8 17] their hypocrisy [*cp.* Matt. 23 28; Luke 12 1], said unto them, Why tempt ye me [*cp.* 8 11; 10 2]? *cp.* 7 6.

bring me a 2 penny, that I may see it. **16** And they brought it. And he saith unto them, Whose is this image and superscription? And they said unto him, Cæsar's. **17** And Jesus said unto them, Render unto Cæsar the things that are Cæsar's, and unto God the things that are God's.

And they marvelled [*cp.* 1 22, 27; 6 2; 10 24, 26; 11 18: *also* 2 12; 5 20, 42; 6 51; 7 37; 10 32; 15 5; 16 5, 8] greatly at him.

cp. 12 12.

1 Or, *Teacher*
2 See marginal note on Matt. 18 28.

asked him, saying,

1 Master, we know that thou sayest and teachest rightly,

and

acceptest not the person *of any*, but of a truth teachest the way of God:

22 Is it lawful [*cp.* 6 9; 14 3] for us to give tribute unto Cæsar, or not?

23 But he perceived their craftiness, and said unto them,
cp. 10 25; 11 16.
cp. 12 56; 13 15.

24 Shew me

a 2 penny.

Whose image and superscription hath it? And they said, Cæsar's. **25** And he said unto them, Then render unto Cæsar the things that are Cæsar's, and unto God the things that are God's. **26** And they were not able to take hold of the saying before the people: and they marvelled [*cp.* 2 47, 48; 4 22, 32, 36: *also* 5 9, 26; 8 25, 56; 9 43; 11 14; 24 12, 41] at his answer, and held their peace.

1 Or, *Teacher*
2 See marginal note on Matt. 18 28.

cp. 3 2.

cp. 11 56.

cp. 5 6; 6 15.

cp. 8 6.

cp. 7 15, 21, 46.

§ 205. **A Question about Resurrection**

Matt. 22 23-33	**Mark 12** 18-27	**Luke 20** 27-40
23 On that day there came to him Sadducees, 1 which say that there is no resurrection: and they asked him, **24** saying, 2 Master, Moses said, If a man die, having no children, his brother 3 shall marry his wife, and raise up seed unto his brother. **25** Now there were with us seven brethren: and the first married and deceased, and having no seed left his wife unto his brother; **26** in like	**18** And there come unto him Sadducees, which say that there is no resurrection; and they asked him, saying, **19** 1 Master, Moses wrote unto us, If a man's brother die, and leave a wife behind him, and leave no child, that his brother should take his wife, and raise up seed unto his brother. **20** There were seven brethren: and the first took a wife, and dying left no seed;	**27** And there came to him certain of the Sadducees, they which say that there is no resurrection; and they asked him, **28** saying, 1 Master, Moses wrote unto us, that if a man's brother die, having a wife, and he be childless, his brother should take the wife, and raise up seed unto his brother. **29** There were therefore seven brethren: and the first took a wife, and died childless;

Matt.

manner the second also,

and the third,
unto the
4 seventh.
27 And after them all the woman   died. **28** In the resurrection therefore whose wife   shall she be of the seven? for they all   had her.   **29** But Jesus answered and said unto them,
Ye do err,   not knowing   the scriptures, nor the power of God.

30 For in
the
resurrection
they neither marry, nor are given in marriage,

but   are as
angels 5 in heaven.
cp. 5 9: also 5 45; 8 12; 13 38.
31 But as touching the resurrection of the dead,
have ye not read [cp. 12 3, 5; 19 4; 21 16, 42]
that which was spoken unto you by God, saying, **32** I am the God of Abraham, and the God of Isaac, and the God of Jacob?
God is not the God of the dead, but of the living.

33 And when the multitudes heard it, they were astonished at his teaching [cp. 7 28; 13 54; 19 25; 22 22: also 8 27; etc.].

22 46

1 Gr. saying.   2 Or, Teacher
3 Gr. shall perform the duty of a husband's brother to his wife. Compare Deut. 25 5.   4 Gr. seven.
5 Many ancient authorities add of God.

Mark

21 and the second took her, and died, leaving no seed behind him; and the third likewise: **22** and   the seven   left no seed.
Last of all the woman also died. **23** In the resurrection   whose wife   shall she be of them? for the seven had her to wife.
24 Jesus   said unto them, Is it not for this cause that ye   err, that ye know   not the scriptures, nor the power of God?

25 For when they
shall rise from the dead, they neither marry, nor are given in marriage;

but   are as
angels in heaven.

26 But as touching
the dead, that they are raised; have ye not read [2 25; 12 10] in the book of Moses,   in the place concerning the Bush, how God spake unto him,
saying, I am the God of Abraham, and the God of Isaac, and the God of Jacob?
27 He is not the God of the dead, but of the living: ye do greatly err.

cp. 1 22, 27; 6 2; 10 24, 26; 11 18; 12 17: also 2 12; etc.

12 28, 32.

12 34

1 Or, Teacher

Luke

30 and the second;

31 and the third took her; and likewise the seven also left no children, and died.   **32** Afterward the woman also died.
33 In the resurrection therefore whose wife of them shall she be?   for the seven had her to wife. **34** And Jesus   said unto them,

The sons of this 2 world [cp. 16 8] marry, and are given in marriage: **35** but   they that are accounted worthy to attain to that 2 world, and the resurrection from the dead,   neither marry, nor are given in marriage: **36** for neither can they die any more: for they are equal unto the angels;
and are sons of God [cp. 6 35; 16 8], being sons of the resurrection.   **37** But that
the dead   are raised,
cp. 6 3; 10 26.
[cp. 3 4; 4 17; 20 42] even Moses shewed in the place concerning the Bush, when he calleth   the Lord the God of Abraham, and the God of Isaac, and the God of Jacob. **38** Now he is not the God of the dead, but of the living: for all live unto him.

cp. 2 47, 48; 4 22, 32, 36; 20 26: also 5 9; etc.
39 And certain of the scribes answering said, 1 Master, thou hast well said.   **40** For they durst not any more ask him any question.

1 Or, Teacher   2 Or, age

cp. 1 12; 11 52; 12 36.

cp. 7 15, 21, 46.

Matt. 22 24 || Mark 12 19 || Luke 20 28: cp. Deut. 25 5.   Matt. 22 32 || Mark 12 26 || Luke 20 37 = Exod. 3 6, 15.

§ 206. A Question about the 'First' Commandment

Matt. 22 34-40

34 But the Pharisees, when they heard that he had put the Sadducees to silence, gathered themselves together. **35** And one of them,   a lawyer,

Mark 12 28-34

28 And one of the scribes came, and heard them questioning together [cp. 8

Luke 10 25-28; 20 39-40

25 And behold, a certain lawyer

asked him a question, tempting [cp. 16 1; 19 3: also 22 18] him, **36** ¹ Master,

cp. 19 16, 29; 25 46.
which is the great commandment in the law? **37** And he said unto him,

cp. 12 3, 5; 19 4; 21 16, 42; 22 31.

Thou shalt love the Lord thy God with all thy heart, and with all thy soul, and with all thy mind.

38 This is the great and first commandment. **39** ² And a second like unto it is this, Thou shalt love thy neighbour as thyself [cp. 19 19].

40 On these two commandments hangeth the whole law, and the prophets [cp. 5 17; 7 12; 11 13].

cp. 9 13; 12 7; 23 23.

22 46 And no one was able to answer him a word, neither durst any man from that day forth ask him any more questions.

¹ Or, *Teacher*
² Or, *And a second is like unto it, Thou shalt love &c.*

11; 9 14, 16], and knowing that he had answered them well [cp. verse 32], asked him, cp. 8 11; 10 2: also 12 15.

cp. 10 17, 30.
What commandment is the first of all? **29** Jesus

cp. 2 25; 12 10, 26.
answered, The first is, Hear, O Israel; ¹ The Lord our God, the Lord is one: **30** and thou shalt love the Lord thy God ² with all thy heart, and ² with all thy soul, and ² with all thy mind, and ² with all thy strength.

31 The second is this, Thou shalt love thy neighbour as thyself. There is none other commandment greater than these.

32 And the scribe said unto him, Of a truth, ³ Master, thou hast well said [cp. verse 28] that he is one; and there is none other but he: **33** and to love him with all the heart, and with all the understanding, and with all the strength, and to love his neighbour as himself, is much more than all whole burnt offerings and sacrifices. **34** And when Jesus saw that he answered discreetly, he said unto him, Thou art not far from the kingdom of God [cp. 10 21]. And no man after that durst ask him any question.

¹ Or, *The Lord is our God; the Lord is one*
² Gr. *from.*
³ Or, *Teacher*

[cp. 20 39] stood up and tempted [cp. 11 16] him, saying, ¹ Master, what shall I do [cp. 3 10, 12, 14] to inherit eternal life [cp. 18 18, 30]?

26 And he said unto him, What is written in the law? how readest thou [cp. 6 3]? **27** And he answering said,

Thou shalt love the Lord thy God ² with all thy heart, and with all thy soul, and with all thy strength, and with all thy mind;

and thy neighbour as thyself.

cp. 16 16.
28 And he said unto him, Thou hast answered right [cp. 7 43]: this do, and thou shalt live. 20 **39** And certain of the scribes answering said, ¹ Master, thou hast well said.

40 For they cp. 14 6. durst not any more ask him any question.

¹ Or, *Teacher*　　² Gr. *from.*

---

cp. 8 6.

cp. 6 28.
cp. 3 15; etc.

Mark 12 29 = Deut. 6 4.　Matt. 22 37 || Mark 12 30 || Luke 10 27 = Deut. 6 5.
Matt. 22 39 || Mark 12 31 || Luke 10 27 = Lev. 19 18.　Luke 10 28: cp. Lev. 18 5.
Mark 12 33: cp. I Sam. 15 22.

§ 207. A Question about the Christ as Son of David

Matt. 22 41-46	**Mark 12** 35-37	**Luke 20** 41-44	
41 Now while the Pharisees were gathered together, Jesus asked them a question, **42** saying, *cp.* 21 23; 26 55. *cp.* 17 10. What think ye [*cp.* 17 25; 18 12; 21 28; 22 17; 26 66] of the Christ? whose son is he? They say unto him, *The son of David.* **43** He saith unto them, How then doth David in the Spirit call him Lord, saying,	**35** And Jesus answered and said, as he taught in the temple [*cp.* 14 49], How say the scribes [*cp.* 9 11] that the Christ is the son of David?	**41** And he said unto them, *cp.* 19 47; 20 1; 21 37; 22 53. How say they that the Christ is David's son?	*cp.* 18 20: *also* 7 28; 8 20. *cp.* 11 56.
44 The Lord said unto my Lord, Sit thou on my right hand, Till I put thine enemies underneath thy feet? **45** If David then calleth him Lord, how is he his son?	**36** David himself said in the Holy Spirit, [*cp.* 12 26] The Lord said unto my Lord, Sit thou on my right hand, Till I make thine enemies ¹ the footstool of thy feet. **37** David himself calleth him Lord; and whence is he his son? And ² the common people heard him gladly [*cp.* 6 20].	**42** For David himself saith in the book [*cp.* 3 4; 4 17] of Psalms [*cp.* 24 44], The Lord said unto my Lord, Sit thou on my right hand, **43** Till I make thine enemies the footstool of thy feet. **44** David therefore calleth him Lord, and how is he his son?	
46 And no one was able to answer him a word, neither durst any man from that day forth ask him any more questions.	12 34	*cp.* 19 48; 21 38. *cp.* 14 6. 20 40	

¹ Some ancient authorities read *underneath thy feet.*
² Or, *the great multitude*

Matt. 22 44 ‖ Mark 12 36 ‖ Luke 20 42-43 = Ps. 110 1.

§ 208. A Warning against Scribes (Mark and Luke) and Pharisees (Matt.)

Matt. 23 1-12	**Mark 12** 38-40	**Luke 20** 45-47	
1 Then spake Jesus to the multitudes and to his disciples, **2** saying, The scribes and the Pharisees sit on Moses' seat: **3** all things therefore whatsoever they bid you, *these* do and observe: but do not ye after their works; for they say, and do not [*cp.* 7 21].	**38** And in his teaching [*cp.* 4 2] he said,	**45** And in the hearing of all the people he said unto his disciples,	
4 Yea, they bind heavy burdens ¹ and grievous to be borne, and lay them on men's shoulders; but they themselves will not move them with their finger. **5** But all their works they do for to be seen of men [*cp.* 6 1, 2, 5, 16; 23 28]: for they make broad their phylacteries, and enlarge the borders *of their* garments, *cp.* 16 6.		11 **46** And he said, Woe unto you lawyers also! for ye lade men with burdens grievous to be borne, and ye yourselves touch not the burdens with one of your fingers.	
	Beware of [*cp.* 8 15] the scribes, which desire to walk	Luke 11 43 Woe unto you Pharisees!	**46** Beware of [*cp.* 12 1] the scribes, which desire to walk

6 and love the chief place at feasts, and the chief seats in the synagogues, **7** and the salutations in the market places,

cp. 23 25.

cp. 6 5.

and to be called of men, Rabbi. **8** But be not ye called Rabbi: for one is your teacher [*cp.* 26 18, 25, 49: *also* 10 24, 25], and all ye are brethren. **9** And call no man your father on the earth: for one is your Father, ² which is in heaven [*cp.* 5 48; 6 14, 26, 32; 15 13; 18 35: *also* 5 16, 45; 6 1, 9; 7 11, 21; 10 32, 33; 12 50; 16 17; 18 10, 14, 19]. **10** Neither be ye called masters: for one is your master, *even* the Christ.

11 But he that is ³ greatest among you shall be your ⁴ servant.

20 26 But whosoever would become great among you shall be your ⁵ minister; **27** and whosoever would be first among you shall be your ⁶ servant.

12 And whosoever shall exalt himself shall be humbled; and whosoever shall humble himself [*cp.* 18 4] shall be exalted.

¹ Many ancient authorities omit *and grievous to be borne.*
⁴ Gr. *the heavenly.* ³ Gr. *greater.*
Or, *minister* ⁵ Or, *servant*
⁶ Gr. *bondservant.*

---

in long robes, and *to have*

salutations in the market places, **39** and chief seats in the synagogues, and chief places at feasts:

40 they which devour widows' [*cp.* 12 42] houses, ¹ and for a pretence make long prayers; these shall receive greater condemnation.

cp. 4 38; 9 5, 38; 10 35; 11 21; 13 1; 14 14, 45.

cp. 11 25, 26.

9 35 If any man would be first, he shall be last of all, and minister of all.
10 43 But whosoever would become great among you, shall be your ² minister: **44** and whosoever would be first among you, shall be ³ servant of all.

—

¹ Or, *even while for a pretence they make*
² Or, *servant* ³ Gr. *bondservant.*

---

for ye love the chief seats in the synagogues, and the salutations in the market places.

cp. 14 7-11.

47 which devour [*cp.* 11 39; 16 14] widows' [*cp.* 21 2: *also* 2 37; 4 25-26; 7 12; 18 3] houses, and for a pretence make long prayers: these shall receive greater condemnation.

cp. 11 13.

9 48 For he that is ¹ least among you all, the same is great.
22 26 But he that is the greater among you, let him become as the younger; and he that is chief, as he that doth serve.
14 11 *and* **18 14** For every one that exalteth himself shall be humbled; and [but] he that humbleth himself shall be exalted.

¹ Gr. *lesser.*

---

cp. 1 38, 49; 4 31; 9 2; 11 8, 28; 13 13, 14; 20 16.

cp. 13 2-17.

---

§ 209. Woes against Scribes and Pharisees

Matt. 23 13-36

13 But woe unto you [*cp. verses* 15, 16, 23, 25, 27, 29: *also* 18 7; 26 24], scribes and Pharisees, hypocrites [*cp.* 15 7; 22 18; 23 15, 23, 25, 27, 29: *also* 6 2, 5, 16; 23 28; 24 51]! because ye shut the kingdom of heaven ¹ against men:
cp. 16 19.
for ye enter [*cp.* 5 20; 7 13, 21; 18 3, 8, 9; 19 17, 23, 24; 25 21, 23] not in yourselves [*cp.* 21 31], neither suffer ye them that are entering in to enter.²
15 Woe unto you,

cp. 14 21.

cp. 7 6: *also* 12 15.

cp. 9 43, 45, 47; 10 15, 23, 24, 25.

Luke 11 52, 42, 39-41, 44, 47-51

52 Woe unto you [*cp.* 11 42, 43, 44, 46, 47: *also* 17 1; 22 22] lawyers!
cp. 12 56; 13 15: *also* 12 1.
for ye took away the key of knowledge: ye entered [*cp.* 13 24; 18 17, 24, 25: *also* 24 26] not in yourselves, and them that were entering in ye hindered.

cp. 3 5; 10 1, 2, 9.

scribes and Pharisees, hypocrites [*see above*] ! for ye compass
sea and land to make one proselyte; and when he is become
so, ye make him twofold more a son of ³ hell [*cp.* 5 29, 30;
10 28; 23 33: *also* 5 22; 18 9] than yourselves. **16** Woe unto
you [*see above*], ye blind guides [*cp.* 15 14; 23 17, 19, 24, 26],
which say, Whosoever shall swear by the ⁴ temple, it is nothing;
but whosoever shall swear by the gold of the ⁴ temple, he is
⁵ a debtor. **17** Ye fools [*cp.* 5 22] and blind [*cp. verse* 16]: for
whether is greater, the gold, or the ⁴ temple that hath sanctified
the gold? **18** And, Whosoever shall swear by the altar, it is
nothing; but whosoever shall swear by the gift that is upon
it, he is ⁵ a debtor. **19** Ye blind [*cp. verse* 16]: for whether is
greater, the gift, or the altar that sanctifieth the gift? **20** He
therefore that sweareth by the altar, sweareth by it, and by all
things thereon. **21** And he that sweareth by the ⁴ temple,
sweareth by it, and by him that dwelleth therein. **22** And he
that sweareth by the heaven, sweareth by the throne of God [*cp.* 5 34],
and by him that sitteth thereon.

cp. 9 43, 45, 47.   *cp.* 12 5.
    cp. 6 39.   *cp.* 9 39, 40, 41.
cp. 11 40.

23 Woe unto you, scribes and
Pharisees, hypocrites [*see above*]! for
ye tithe mint and ⁶ anise and cummin,
and
cp. 22 37.
have left undone the weightier mat-
ters of the law, judgement, and mercy
[*cp.* 9 13; 12 7], and faith: but these
ye ought   to have done, and not to
have left the other undone. **24** Ye
blind guides [*cp.* 15 14; 23 16, *etc.*],
which strain out the gnat, and swallow
the camel. **25** Woe unto you,
scribes and Pharisees, hypocrites [*see
above*]! for ye cleanse the outside of
the cup and of the platter, but within
[*cp.* 15 19; 23 28] they are full from
extortion   and excess.
cp. 22 18. **26** Thou blind [*cp. verse* 16]
Pharisee,   *cp. verse* 17.

cp. 12 30, 33.

42 But
woe unto you [*see above*]
Pharisees !   for
ye tithe mint and
rue and every herb, and pass over judgement and the love of God [*cp.* 10 27]:

cp. 5 42.

but these
ought ye to have done, and not to
leave the other undone.
cp. 6 39.

cp. 9 39, 40, 41.

39 Now do ye
Pharisees
cleanse the outside of
the cup and of the platter; but your
inward part   is full of
extortion [*cp.* 16 14; 20 47] and
wickedness.   *cp.* 6 39.
40 Ye foolish ones [*cp.* 12 20],
did not he that made the outside make
the inside also? **41** Howbeit
[*cp.* 6 42]   give for
alms [*cp.* 12 33] those things which
¹ are within;

cp. 7 4.
cp. 7 21-23.
cp. 12 40.

cp. 9 39, 40, 41.

cleanse
first [*cp.* 5 24; 6 33; 7 5]
the inside of the cup and of the
platter, that the outside thereof
    may become clean
also.   **27** Woe unto you,
    scribes and Pharisees, hypo-
crites [*see above*] ! for ye are like unto
whited sepulchres, which outwardly
appear   beautiful, but inwardly are
full of dead men's bones, and of all
uncleanness.
    28 Even so
ye also outwardly appear [*cp.* 6 1, 2, 5,
16; 23 5] righteous unto men, but
inwardly [*cp.* 15 19; 23 25, 26] ye
are full of hypocrisy [*cp. verse* 13] and
iniquity. **29** Woe unto you,
scribes and Pharisees, hypocrites [*see
above*] ! for ye build the sepulchres
of the prophets, and garnish the tombs
of the righteous, **30** and say, If we had
been in the days of our fathers, we
should not have been partakers with
them in the blood of the prophets.
31 Wherefore ye   witness to yourselves,
    that ye are sons of
them that slew the prophets [*cp.* 5 12;
21 35-36; 22 6; 23 37].
    32 Fill ye up then the
measure of your fathers. **33** Ye ser-

cp. 7 27.

cp. 7 19.

cp. 7 21-23.
cp. 12 15:
also 7 6.

cp. 12 3-5.

and
behold, all things are   clean
unto you. **44** Woe unto you [*see
above*] !
    for ye are as
the tombs which
appear not,
    and the men that walk
over *them* know it not.

cp. 11 39-41.
cp. 12 1: *also* 12 56; 13 15.
47 Woe unto you [*see above*]!

for ye build the tombs
of the prophets, and

your fathers
    killed
them.
48 So ye are witnesses
and consent unto the works of
your fathers: for
they   killed them [*cp.* 6 23; 13 33,
34; 20 10-12],   and ye build
their tombs.

pents, ye offspring of vipers [*cp.* 3 7; 12 34], how shall ye escape the judgement of ³ hell [*cp.* 5 29, 30; 10 28; 23 15: *also* 5 22; 18 9]? **34** Therefore, *cp.* 11 19.
behold, I   send unto you prophets, and wise men, and scribes:
cp. 10 2.
        some of them   shall ye kill and crucify [*cp.* 20 19; 27 26]; and some of them shall ye scourge in your synagogues [*cp.* 10 17], and persecute from city to city [*cp.* 10 23]: **35** that upon you may come all the righteous blood
        shed on the earth,
cp. 13 35; 25 34.

from the blood of Abel the righteous unto the blood of Zachariah son of Barachiah, whom ye slew between the sanctuary and the altar.   **36** Verily I say unto you, All these things shall come upon
        this generation [*cp.* 24 34: *also* 10 23; 16 28].

¹ Gr. *before*.
² Some ancient authorities insert here, or after ver. 12, ver. 14 *Woe unto you, scribes and Pharisees, hypocrites! for ye devour widows' houses, even while for a pretence ye make long prayers: therefore ye shall receive greater condemnation.* See Mark 12 40; Luke 20 47.   ³ Gr. *Gehenna*.
Or, *sanctuary:* as in ver. 35.
⁵ Or, *bound* by his oath   ⁶ Or, *dill*

cp. 9 43, 45, 47.

cp. 6 30.

cp. 15 15.

cp. 13 9.

cp. 13 30: *also* 9 1.

cp. 3 7.

cp. 12 5.
        49 Therefore also said the wisdom [*cp.* 7 35] of God, I will send unto them prophets
            and
apostles [*cp.* 6 13; 9 10; 17 5; 22 14; 24 10]; and *some* of them they shall kill

        and
persecute;
50 that   the
        blood of all the prophets, which was shed   from the foundation of the world, may be required of this generation [*see below*]; **51** from the blood of Abel unto the blood of Zachariah,
        who perished between
        the altar and the
² sanctuary: yea, I say unto you, it   shall   be required of this generation [*cp.* 21 32: *also* 9 27].

¹ Or, *ye can*   ² Gr. *house*.

cp. 13 16.

cp. 17 24.

Matt. 23 35 ‖ Luke 11 50-51: *cp.* Gen. 4 8; II Chron. 24 20-22.

§ 210. A Lament over Jerusalem

[*Cp.* Luke 19 41-44: *also* 23 27-31 *and* 21 20]

Matt. 23 37-39

37 O Jerusalem, Jerusalem, which killeth the prophets [*cp.* 5 12; 21 35, 36; 22 6; 23 29-34], and stoneth [*cp.* 21 35] them that are sent unto her! how often would I have gathered thy children   together, even as a hen gathereth her chickens under her wings, and ye would not! **38** Behold, your house is left unto you ¹ desolate.
    39 For I say unto you, Ye shall not see me henceforth [*cp.* 26 29, 64], till ye shall say, Blessed *is* he that cometh [*cp.* 3 11; 11 3] in the name of the Lord [=21 9 *and* John 12 13].

¹ Some ancient authorities omit *desolate*.

cp. 12 3-5.

cp. 1 7. 11 9.

Luke 13 34-5

34 O Jerusalem, Jerusalem, which killeth the prophets [*cp.* 6 23; 11 47-50; 20 10-12], and stoneth
        them that are sent unto her! how often would I have gathered thy children [*cp.* 19 44] together, even as a hen *gathereth* her own brood under her wings, and ye would not! **35** Behold, your house is left unto you *desolate* [*cp.* 21 20: *also* 19 43-44; 23 29-31]: and I say unto you, Ye shall not see me,
        until ye shall say, Blessed *is* he that cometh [*cp.* 7 19, 20: *also* 3 16] in the name of the Lord [= 19 38 *and* John 12 13].

cp. 13 19; 14 7.

cp. 1 15, 27; 3 31; 6 14; 11 27: *also* 1 30.

Matt. 23 39 ‖ Luke 13 35 = Ps. 118 26.

§ 211. A Widow's Mites

Mark 12 41-44

41 And he sat down over against the treasury,   and beheld how the multitude cast ¹ money into the treasury: and many that were

Luke 21 1-4

1 And he
        looked up, ¹ and saw
        the

rich   cast
in   much. **42** And
there came   ² a   poor
widow [*cp.* 12 40],
 	
              and she cast   in
two mites, which make a
farthing. **43** And he called unto him
his disciples, and said unto them,
Verily   I say unto
you, This poor widow cast in more
than all they which are casting into
the treasury: **44** for they all did cast
in of their superfluity;
              but she of her want did
cast in all that she had, *even* all her
living.
	rich men that were casting their gifts
	into the treasury. **2** And
	he saw a certain poor
	widow [*cp.* 20 47: *also* 2 37; 4 25,
	26; 7 12; 18 3] casting in
	thither two mites.
	
	          3 And he
	              said,
	Of a truth [*cp.* 9 27; 12 44] I say unto
	you, This poor widow cast in more
	than they all :
	          4 for all these did
	of their superfluity cast in unto
	the gifts : but she of her want did
	cast in all the
	living that she had.

¹ Gr. *brass*. ² Gr. *one*.	¹ Or, *and saw them that . . . treasury, and they were rich.*

§ 212. A Prophecy of the Destruction of the Temple

Matt. 24 1-2	**Mark 13** 1-2	**Luke 21** 5-6

1 And   Jesus went   out
from the temple, and
was going on his way ; and
      his disciples came to
him [*cp.* 5 1; 13 10, 36; 14
15; 15 12, 23; 17 19; 18 1;
24 3; 26 17] to shew him
 	
      the buildings of the
temple. **2** But he answered
and said unto them,
              See ye
not all these things ?
verily I say unto you,
      cp. 9 15.
 	
There shall not be left here
one stone upon another,
that shall not be thrown
down.
	1 And as he went forth out
	of the temple,
	
	one of his disciples
	      cp. 6 35.
	
	              saith unto him,
	¹ Master, behold, what man-
	ner of stones and
	what manner of buildings !
	      2 And Jesus
	      said unto him,
	              Seest thou
	these great buildings ?
	
	      cp. 2 20.
	
	there shall not be left here
	one stone upon another,
	      which shall not be thrown
	down.
		5 And as
		some spake of the temple,
		
		      cp. 9 12.
		
		              how it was adorned
		with goodly stones and
		offerings,
		              he
		      said, **6** As for
		these things which ye behold,
		
		              the days
		will come [*cp.* 5 35; 17 22:
		also 19 43; 23 29], in which
		there shall not be left here
		one stone upon another [*cp.* 19
		44], that shall not be thrown
		down.

	¹ Or, *Teacher*	

(iii) The Great Apocalyptic Discourse (§§ 213-223)

§ 213. The Occasion of the Discourse

False Christs ; Wars among Nations ; Disturbances in Nature

Matt. 24 3-8	**Mark 13** 3-8	**Luke 21** 7-11	

3 And as he sat on the mount
of Olives [*cp.* 26 30],
      the disciples
      cp. 17 1; 26 37.
 	
      came unto him [*cp.* 5 1;
13 10, 36; 14 15; 15 12, 23;
17 19; 18 1; 24 1; 26 17]
      privately [*cp.* 17 1,
19; 20 17],   saying,
      Tell us, when
shall these things be ?
and what *shall be* the sign
[*cp.* 24 30]
 	
      of thy ¹ coming [*cp.*
	3 And as he sat on the mount
	of Olives [*cp.* 14 26] over
	against the temple, Peter and
	James and John [*cp.* 1 29;
	5 37; 9 2; 14 33] and
	Andrew
	      cp. 6 35.
	
	asked him privately [*cp.* 4 10,
	34; 6 31, 32; 9 2, 28],
	      4 Tell us, when
	shall these things be ?
	and what *shall be* the sign
	              when these things
	are all about to be accom-
	plished ?
		7 And
		      cp. 21 37; 22 39.
		              they
		      cp. 8 51; 9 28.
		
		      cp. 9 12.
		
		asked him, [*cp.* 9 10;
		10 23] saying,
		¹ Master, when there-
		fore shall these things be ?
		and what *shall be* the sign
		[*cp.* 21 25] when these things
		are about to come to
		pass ?
			cp. 8 1.

24 27, 37, 39], and of ² the end of the world [*cp.* 13 39, 40, 49; 28 20] ? **4** And Jesus answered and said unto them, Take heed

that no man lead you astray. **5** For many shall come in my name [*cp.* 7 22; 18 5, 20], saying, I am the Christ;

cp. 3 2; 4 17; 10 7. *cp.* 24 26.

and shall lead many astray [*cp.* 24 11, 24]. **6** And ye shall hear of wars and rumours of wars: see that ye be not troubled: for *these things* must needs come to pass; [*cp.* 17 10] but the end is not yet.

7 For nation shall rise against nation, and kingdom against kingdom: and there shall be famines and earthquakes in divers places.

cp. 16 1: *also* 24 29. **8** But all these things are the beginning of travail.

¹ Gr. *presence.*
² Or, *the consummation of the age*

---

5 And Jesus began to say unto them, Take heed [*cp.* 13 9, 23, 33] that no man lead you astray. **6** Many shall come in my name [*cp.* 9 37, 38, 39; 16 17], saying, I am *he* [*cp.* 14 62];

cp. 1 15.

and shall lead many astray [*cp.* 13 22]. **7** And when ye shall hear of wars and rumours of wars, be not troubled: *these things* must needs come to pass; [*cp.* 9 11, 12; 13 10] but the end is not yet.

8 For nation shall rise against nation, and kingdom against kingdom: there shall be earthquakes in divers places; there shall be famines:

cp. 8 11: *also* 13 24, 25. these things are the beginning of travail.

---

8 And he said,

Take heed that ye be not led astray: for many shall come in my name [*cp.* 9 48, 49: *also* 10 17; 24 47], saying, I am *he* [*cp.* 22 70]; and, The time is at hand [*cp.* 10 9, 11]: go ye not after them [*cp.* 17 23]. *cp.* 17 21, 23.

9 And when ye shall hear of wars and tumults, be not terrified: for these things must needs come to pass first [*cp.* 17 25]; but the end is not immediately. **10** Then said he unto them, Nation shall rise against nation, and kingdom against kingdom: **11** and there shall be great earthquakes, and in divers places famines and pestilences; and there shall be terrors and great signs from heaven [*cp.* 11 16: *also* 21 25, 26].

¹ Or, *Teacher*

---

cp. 14 13, 14, 26; 15 16; 16 23, 24, 26: *also* 8 24, 28; 13 19.

---

§ 214. Persecution of Disciples

Matt. 24 9-14	Matt. 10 17-22	**Mark 13** 9-13	**Luke 21** 12-19	
	17 But beware of men: for they will	**9** But take ye heed [*cp.* 13 5, 23, 33] to yourselves: for they shall	**12** But before all these things, they shall lay their hands on you, and shall persecute you, delivering you up to	
9 Then shall they deliver you up unto tribulation, *cp.* 23 34.	deliver you up to councils, and in their synagogues they will scourge you; **18** yea and before governors and kings shall ye be brought for my sake [*cp.* 5 11; 10 39; 16 25: *also* 10 22; 19 29; 24 9], for a testimony to them [*cp.* 8 4; 24 14]	deliver you up to councils; and in synagogues shall ye be beaten; and before governors and kings shall ye stand for my sake [*cp.* 8 35; 10 29: *also* 13 13], for a testimony unto them [*cp.* 1 44; 6 11]. **10** And the gospel [*cp.* 1 1, 14, 15; 8 35; 10 29; 14 9; 16 15]	the synagogues and prisons, ¹ bringing you before kings and governors for my name's sake [*cp.* 21 17: *also* 6 22; 9 24; 18 29]. **13** It shall turn unto you for a testimony. *cp.* 5 14; 9 5.	*cp.* 15 21.
verse 14	*cp.* 17 10. and to the Gentiles [*cp.* 8 11; 21 31, 41, 43; 22 7-10; 26 13; 28 19].	must first [*cp.* 9 11, 12] be preached unto all the nations [*cp.* 12 9; 14 9; 16 15].	*cp.* 17 25; 21 9. *cp.* 2 30-32; 3 6; 13 29; 14 21-24; 20 16; 24 47.	*cp.* 10 16; 11 52.
	19 But when they	**11** And when they lead you to *judgement,*	Luke 12 11 And when they bring you before the	

and shall

kill you:
and ye shall be hated
of all the nations
for my name's sake
[cp. 19 29: also 5 11;
10 18, 39; 16 25].

verse 10

10 And then shall many stumble [cp. 13 21: also 11 6; 13 57; 15 12; 26 31, 33], and shall deliver up one another, and shall hate one another. **11** And many false prophets [cp. 24 24: also 7 15] shall arise, and shall lead many astray [cp. 24 5, 24]. **12** And because iniquity shall be multiplied, the love of the many shall wax cold. **13** But he that endureth to the end, the same shall be saved. **14** And ¹ this gospel of the kingdom [cp. 4 23; 9 35: also 26 13] shall be preached in the whole ² world [cp. 26 13] for a testimony [cp. 8 4; 10 18] unto

and
deliver you up,

be not anxious
[cp. 6 25, 31, 34]
how or what
ye shall

speak: for it shall be
given you in that
hour what ye shall
speak.
20 For it is not ye that speak, but the Spirit of your Father that speaketh in you.

21 And brother shall deliver up brother to death, and the father his child: and children shall rise up against parents, and ¹ cause them to be put to death [cp. 10 35, 36]. **22** And ye shall be hated of all men for my name's sake:

cp. 10 30.

verse 21

but he that endureth to the end, the same shall be saved.

cp. 1 44; 6 11; 13 9.

deliver you up,

be not anxious before-
hand what ye shall

speak: but whatsoever shall be given you in that hour, that speak ye: for it is not ye that speak, but the Holy Ghost.

12 And brother shall deliver up brother to death, and the father his child; and children shall rise up against parents, and ¹ cause them to be put to death. **13** And ye shall be hated of all men for my name's sake [cp. 8 35; 10 29; 13 9]:

cp. 4 17: also 6 3;
14 27, 29.
verse 12

cp. 13 22.

cp. 13 6, 22.

but he that endureth to the end, the same shall be saved.

verse 10
cp. 14 9.

synagogues, and the rulers, and the authorities,

be not anxious [cp. 12 22] how or what ye shall answer, or what ye shall say: **12** for the Holy Spirit shall teach you in that very hour what ye ought to say.

14 Settle it therefore in your hearts, not to meditate beforehand how to answer: **15** for I will give you a mouth and wisdom,

which all your adversaries shall not be able to withstand or to gainsay. **16** But ye shall be delivered up even by parents, and brethren, and kinsfolk, and friends; and *some* of you ² shall they cause to be put to death [cp. 12 53]. **17** And ye shall be hated [cp. 1 71; 6 22, 27] of all men for my name's sake [cp. 21 12: also 6 22; 9 24; 18 29]. **18** And not a hair of your head [cp. 12 7] shall perish.

cp. 7 23.

verse 16

19 In your patience [cp. 8 15] ye shall win your ³ souls.

cp. 5 14; 9 5; 21 13.

cp. 14 26; 15 26.

cp. 16 2.

cp. 15 18-21; 17 14.

cp. 16 1: also 6 61.

all the nations [*cp.* 8 11; 10 18; 21 31, 41, 43; 22 7-10; 26 13; 28 19]; and then shall the end come.	*cp.* 12 9; 13 10; 14 9; 16 15.	*cp.* 2 30-32; 3 6; 13 29; 14 21-24; 20 16; 24 47.	*cp.* 10 16; 11 52.
¹ Or, *these good tidings* ² Gr. *inhabited earth.*	¹ Or, *put them to death*	¹ Or, *put them to death*	¹ Gr. *you being brought.* ² Or, *shall they put to death* ³ Or, *lives*

§ 215. **Desolation and Tribulation in Judæa: The Lure of False Teachers**

Matt. 24 15-28	**Mark 13** 14-23	**Luke 21** 20-24
15 When therefore ye see [*cp.* 24 33] the abomination of desolation [*cp.* 23 38], which was spoken of ¹ by Daniel the prophet, standing in ² the holy place (let him that readeth understand), **16** then let them that are in Judæa flee unto the mountains :	**14** But when ye see [*cp.* 13 29] the abomination of desolation standing where he ought not (let him that readeth understand), then let them that are in Judæa flee unto the mountains :	**20** But when ye see [*cp.* 12 54, 55; 21 31] Jerusalem compassed with armies [*cp.* 19 43], then know that her desolation [*cp.* 13 35: *also* 19 43-44; 23 29-31] is at hand.
17 let him that is on the housetop not go down to take out the things that are in his house : **18** and let him that is in the field not return back to take his cloke.	**15** and let him that is on the housetop not go down, nor enter in, to take anything out of his house : **16** and let him that is in the field not return back to take his cloke.	**21** Then let them that are in Judæa flee unto the mountains; and let them that are in the midst of her depart out; 17 31 In that day, he which shall be on the housetop, and his goods in the house, let him not go down to take them away : and let him that is in the field likewise not return back.
		and let not them that are in the country enter therein. **22** For these are days of vengeance [*cp.* 18 7, 8], that all things which are written may be fulfilled. **23** Woe unto them that are with child and to them that give suck in those days !
19 But woe unto them that are with child and to them that give suck in those days ! **20** And pray ye that your flight be not in the winter, neither on a sabbath : **21** for then shall be great tribulation,	**17** But woe unto them that are with child and to them that give suck in those days ! **18** And pray ye that it be not in the winter. **19** For those days shall be tribulation,	
		for there shall be great distress upon the ¹ land, and wrath unto this people. **24** And they shall fall by the edge of the sword, and shall be led captive into all the nations : and Jerusalem shall be trodden down of the Gentiles, until the times of the Gentiles be fulfilled.
such as hath not been from the beginning of the world until now, no nor ever shall be. **22** And except those days had been shortened, no flesh would have been saved : but for the elect's [*cp.* 24 24, 31] sake those days shall be shortened. **23** Then if any man shall say unto you, Lo,	such as there hath not been the like from the beginning of the creation [*cp.* 10 6; 16 15] which God created until now, and never shall be. **20** And except the Lord had shortened the days, no flesh would have been saved : but for the elect's [*cp.* 13 22, 27] sake, whom he chose, he shortened the days. **21** And then if any man shall say unto you, Lo,	*cp.* 18 7. 17 23 And they shall say to you, Lo,

here is the Christ [*cp.* 24 5], or,   Here; believe [3] *it* not. **24** For there shall arise false Christs, and false prophets [*cp.* 24 11: *also* 7 15], and shall shew great signs and wonders;   so as to lead astray [*cp.* 24 5, 11], if possible, even the elect [*cp.* 24 22, 31].

25 Behold, I have told you beforehand. **26** If therefore they shall say unto you, Behold, he is in the wilderness; go not forth:

Behold, he is in the inner chambers; believe [4] *it* not. **27** For as the lightning cometh forth from the

east, and is seen even unto the west; so shall be the [5] coming [*cp.* 24 3, 37, 39] of the Son of man.

28 Wheresoever the carcase is, there will the [6] eagles be gathered together.

[1] Or, *through*   [2] Or, *a holy place*
[3] Or, him   [4] Or, *them*
[5] Gr. *presence.* [6] Or, *vultures*

---

here is the Christ [*cp.* 13 6]; or, Lo, there; believe [1] *it* not: **22** for there shall arise false Christs and false prophets,   and shall shew signs and wonders, that they may lead astray [*cp.* 13 6], if possible,   the elect [*cp.* 13 20, 27]. **23** But take ye heed [*cp.* 13 5, 9, 33]: behold, I have told you all things beforehand.

[1] Or, him

---

there !   *cp.* 21 8.
  Lo, here [*cp.* 17 21]!

cp. 18 7.

go not *away*, nor follow after *them* [*cp.* 21 8]:

24 for as the lightning, when it lighteneth out of the one part under the heaven, shineth unto the other part under heaven; so shall

the Son of man be [2] in his day . . . . . **37** And they answering say unto him, Where, Lord? And he said unto them, Where the body *is*, thither will the [3] eagles also be gathered together.

[1] Or, *earth*
[2] Some ancient authorities omit *in his day.*   [3] Or, *vultures*

---

cp. 13 19; 14 29; 16 4.

Matt. 24 15 || Mark 13 14: *cp.* Dan. 9 27; 11 31; 12 11.

§ 216. Signs in Heaven and the Coming of the Son of Man

Matt. 24 29-31	**Mark 13** 24-27	**Luke 21** 25-28

29 But immediately, after the tribulation of those days, *cp.* 24 3, 30.
    the sun shall be darkened, and the moon shall not give her light, and the stars shall   fall   from heaven,

and the powers of the heavens shall be shaken: **30** and then shall appear the sign [*cp.* 24 3] of the Son of man in heaven: and then shall all the tribes of the earth mourn, and   they shall see the Son of man coming on the clouds of heaven with   power and great glory [*cp.* 16 27; 25 31; 26 64]. **31** And   he shall send forth his angels [*cp.* 13 41: *also* 13 49; 16 27; 25 31]

---

24 But in those days, after that tribulation, *cp.* 13 4.
    the sun shall be darkened, and the moon shall not give her light, **25** and the stars shall be falling from heaven,

and the powers that are in the heavens shall be shaken.

cp. 13 4.

26 And then shall they see the Son of man coming in clouds   with great power and   glory [*cp.* 8 38; 14 62]. **27** And then shall he send forth the angels [*cp.* 8 38],

---

25 And there shall be signs [*cp.* 21 7, 11] in sun   and   moon   and stars;   and upon the earth distress of nations, in perplexity for the roaring of the sea and the billows; **26** men [1] fainting for fear, and for expectation of the things which are coming on [2] the world: for the powers of the heavens shall be shaken.

cp. 21 7, 11, 25.

27 And then shall they see the Son of man coming in a cloud   with power and great glory [*cp.* 9 26].

cp. 9 26; 12 8, 9.

[1] with [2] a great sound of a trumpet, and they shall gather together his elect [cp. 24 22, 24: also 3 12; 13 30] from the four winds, from one end of heaven to the other.	and shall gather together his elect [cp. 13 20, 22] from the four winds, from the uttermost part of the earth to the uttermost part of heaven.	cp. 18 7: also 3 17.
		28 But when these things begin to come to pass, look up, and lift up your heads; because your redemption [cp. 1 68; 2 38; 24 21] draweth nigh.

[1] Many ancient authorities read *with a great trumpet, and they shall gather &c.*
[2] Or, *a trumpet of great sound*

[1] Or, *expiring*
[2] Gr. *the inhabited earth.*

Matt. 24 30 ‖ Mark 13 26 ‖ Luke 21 27: *cp.* Dan. 7 13-14.

§ 217. The Parable of the Fig Tree and the Date of the Coming

[*Cp.* Luke 13 6-9: *also* Matt. 21 18-20 ‖ Mark 11 12-14, 20-21; *and* Matt. 16 2-3 ‖ Luke 12 54-56]

Matt. 24 32-36	Mark 13 28-32	Luke 21 29-33	
32 Now from the fig tree learn her parable: when her branch is now become tender, and putteth forth its leaves, ye know that the summer is nigh; **33** even so ye also, when ye see [cp. 24 15] all these things, know ye that [1] he is nigh, *even* at the doors. **34** Verily I say unto you, This generation shall not pass away, till all these things be accomplished [cp. 23 36: *also* 10 23; 16 28]. **35** Heaven and earth shall pass away [cp. 5 18], but my words shall not pass away. **36** But of that day [cp. 7 22: *also* 26 29] and hour knoweth no one [cp. 24 42, 44, 50; 25 13], not even the angels of heaven, [2] neither the Son, but the Father only.	**28** Now from the fig tree learn her parable: when her branch is now become tender, and putteth forth its leaves, ye know that the summer is nigh; **29** even so ye also, when ye see [cp. 13 14] these things coming to pass, know ye that [1] he is nigh, *even* at the doors. **30** Verily I say unto you, This generation shall not pass away, until all these things be accomplished [cp. 9 1]. **31** Heaven and earth shall pass away: but my words shall not pass away. **32** But of that day [cp. 14 25] or that hour knoweth no one [cp. 13 33, 35], not even the angels in heaven, neither the Son, but the Father.	**29** And he spake to them a parable: Behold the fig tree, and all the trees: **30** when they now shoot forth, ye see it and know of your own selves [cp. 12 57] that the summer is now nigh. **31** Even so ye also, when ye see [cp. 12 54, 55; 21 20] these things coming to pass, know ye that the kingdom of God is nigh. **32** Verily I say unto you, This generation shall not pass away, till all things be accomplished [cp. 11 51: *also* 9 27]. **33** Heaven and earth shall pass away [cp. 16 17]: but my words shall not pass away. cp. 10 12; 17 31; 21 34. cp. 12 40, 46.	cp. 14 20; 16 23, 26.

[1] Or, *it*   [2] Many authorities, some ancient, omit *neither the Son.*

[1] Or, *it*

§ 218. A Description of the Coming

Matt. 24 37-41	Luke 17 26-30, 34-35	
37 And as *were* the days of Noah, so shall be the [1] coming [cp. 24 3, 27, 39] of the Son of man. **38** For as in those days which were before the flood they were eating and drinking, marrying and giving in marriage, until the day that Noah entered into the ark, **39** and they knew not until the flood came, and took them all away;	**26** And as it came to pass in the days of Noah, even so shall it be also in the days of the Son of man. **27** They ate, they drank, they married, they were given in marriage, until the day that Noah entered into the ark, and the flood came, and destroyed them all. **28** Likewise	

so shall be the ¹ coming [*cp.* 24 3, 27, 37] of the Son of man. **40** Then shall two men be in the field; one is taken, and one is left: **41** two women *shall* be grinding at the mill; one is taken, and one is left.	even as it came to pass in the days of Lot; they ate, they drank, they bought, they sold, they planted, they builded; **29** but in the day that Lot went out from Sodom it rained fire and brimstone from heaven, and destroyed them all: **30** after the same manner shall it be in the day that the Son of man is revealed. . . . **34** I say unto you, In that night there shall be two men on one bed; the one shall be taken, and the other shall be left. **35** There shall be two women grinding together; the one shall be taken, and the other shall be left.¹
¹ Gr. *presence*.	¹ Some ancient authorities add ver. 36 *There shall be two men in the field; the one shall be taken, and the other shall be left.*

Matt. 24 37-39 ‖ Luke 17 26-27 : Gen. 6 11-13 ; 7 7, 21-23.   Luke 17 28-29 : Gen. 18 20 *ff*.; 19 16, 24-25.

§ 219. Injunctions to Watch

Matt. 24 42-44	**Mark 13** 33-37	**Luke 21** 34-36	
	33 Take ye heed [*cp.* 13 5, 9, 23],	**34** But take heed to yourselves [*cp.* 12 1; 17 3], lest haply your hearts be overcharged with surfeiting, and drunkenness [*cp.* 12 45], and cares of this life [*cp.* 8 14], and that day [*cp.* 10 12; 17 31] come on you suddenly as a snare: **35** for *so* shall it come upon all them that dwell on the face of all the earth. **36** But watch [*cp.* 12 37] ye at every season, making supplication [*cp.* 22 40, 46], that ye may prevail to escape all these things that shall come to pass, and to stand before the Son of man.	*cp.* 14 20; 16 23, 26.
cp. 13 22.	*cp.* 4 19.		
cp. 7 22 ; 24 36: *also* 26 29.	*cp.* 13 32: *also* 14 25.		
25 13 Watch [*cp.* 24 42; 26 38, 41] therefore, *cp.* 26 41.	watch [*cp.* 13 35, 37; 14 34, 38] ¹ and pray [*cp.* 14 38]:		
for ye know not [*cp.* 24 36, 42, 44, 50] the day nor the hour. **14** For *it is* as *when* a man, going into another country [*cp.* 21 33],	for ye know not [*cp.* 13 32, 35] when the time is. **34** *It is* as *when* a man, sojourning in another country [*cp.* 12 1],	*cp.* 12 40, 46.	
called his own ¹ servants, and delivered unto them his goods.	having left his house, and given authority to his ² servants,	**19** 12 A certain nobleman went into a far [*cp.* 15 13] country [*cp.* 20 9], to receive for himself a kingdom, and to return. **13** And he called ten ¹ servants of his, and gave them ten ² pounds. 12 **37** Blessed are those ¹ servants, whom the lord when he cometh shall find [*cp.* 12 38, 43]	*cp.* 13 17.
	to each one his work, commanded also the porter to watch. **35** Watch therefore: for ye know not [*cp.* 13 32, 33] when the lord of the house cometh,	watching [*cp.* 21 36]: *cp.* 12 40, 46.	
42 Watch [*cp.* 25 13; 26 38, 41] therefore: for ye know not [*cp.* 24 36, 44, 50; 25 13] on what day your Lord cometh.		verily I say unto you, that he shall gird himself [*cp.* 12 35; 17 8], and make them sit down to meat, and shall come and serve them [*cp.* 22 27:	*cp.* 13 4. *cp.* 13 5.

cp. 25 6.

cp. 25 5; 26 40, 43.

whether at even, or at midnight, or at cockcrowing, or in the morning; **36** lest coming suddenly he find you sleeping [cp. 14 37, 40].

also 17 8]. **38** And if he shall come in the second watch, and if in the third,

43 ² But know this, that if the master of the house had known in what watch the thief was coming, he would have watched, and would not have suffered his house to be ³ broken through [cp. 6 19, 20]. **44** Therefore be ye also ready [cp. 25 10]: for in an hour that ye think not [cp. 24 36, 42, 50; 25 13] the Son of man cometh.

and find [cp. 22 45] *them* so, blessed are those *servants* [cp. 12 37, 43]. **39** ³ But know this [cp. 10 11], that if the master of the house had known in what hour the thief was coming, he would have watched, and not have left his house to be ⁴ broken through. **40** Be ye also ready [cp. 12 47: *also* 17 8]: for in an hour that ye think not [cp. 12 46] the Son of man cometh. **41** And Peter [cp. 8 45; 9 33; 18 28: *also* 5 8; 9 20] said, Lord, speakest thou this parable unto us, or even unto all?

cp. 13 17.

cp. 14 28; 15 15; 16 22; 17 4; 18 21; 19 27; 26 33: *also* 16 16; 17 24.

cp. 13 32, 33, 35.

37 And [cp. 8 32; 9 5; 10 28; 11 21; 14 29: *also* 8 29] what I say unto you I say unto all, Watch [*see verse* 33].

cp. 13 36, 37; 21 21: *also* 6 68.

¹ Gr. *bondservants.*
² Or, *But this ye know*
³ Gr. *digged through.*

¹ Some ancient authorities omit *and pray.* ² Gr. *bondservants.*

¹ Gr. *bondservants.*
² *Mina,* here translated a pound, is equal to one hundred drachmas. See ch. 15 8. ³ Or, *But this ye know*
⁴ Gr. *digged through.*

§ 220. The Obligations of Servants in the Interim

[*Cp.* Matt. 25 14-30; Luke 19 11-27]

Matt. 24 45-51

45 Who then is the faithful [cp. 25 21, 23] and wise [cp. 7 24; 10 16; 25 2 *ff.*] ¹ servant, whom his lord hath set over [cp. 24 47; 25 21, 23] his household, to give them their food in due season? **46** Blessed is that ¹ servant, whom his lord when he cometh shall find so doing. **47** Verily I say unto you, that he will set him over [cp. 25 21, 23: *also* 24 45] all that he hath. **48** But if that evil [cp. 18 32; 25 26] ¹ servant shall say in his heart, My lord tarrieth [cp. 25 5]; **49** and shall begin to beat his fellow-servants [cp. 18 28, 29, 31, 33], and shall eat and drink with the drunken; **50** the lord of that ¹ servant [cp. 18 27; 25 19] shall come in a day when he expecteth not, and in an hour when he knoweth not [cp. 24 36, 42, 44; 25 13], **51** and shall ² cut his portion asunder, and appoint his portion with the hypocrites [cp. 6 2, 5, 16: *also* 15 7; 22 18; 23 13 *ff.*]: there shall be the weeping and gnashing of teeth [cp. 8 12; 13 42, 50; 22 13; 25 30].

cp. 13 32, 33, 35.
cp. 7 6; 12 15.

Luke 12 42-46

42 And the Lord said, Who then is ¹ the faithful [cp. 16 10, 11, 12; 19 17] and wise [cp. 16 8] steward [cp. 16 1 *ff.*], whom his lord shall set over [cp. *verse* 44] his household, to give them their portion of food in due season? **43** Blessed is that ² servant, whom his lord when he cometh shall find [cp. 12 37, 38] so doing. **44** Of a truth [cp. 9 27; 21 3] I say unto you, that he will set him over [cp. *verse* 42: *also* 19 17, 19] all that he hath. **45** But if that [cp. 19 22] ² servant shall say in his heart, My lord delayeth his coming; and shall begin to beat the menservants and the maidservants, and to eat and drink, and to be drunken [cp. 21 34]; **46** the lord of that ² servant shall come in a day when he expecteth not, and in an hour when he knoweth not [cp. 12 40], and shall ³ cut him asunder, and appoint his portion with the [cp. 12 1, 56; 13 15] unfaithful.

cp. 13 28.

cp. 13 17.

¹ Gr. *bondservant.* ² Or, *severely scourge him*

¹ Or, *the faithful steward, the wise* man *whom &c.*
² Gr. *bondservant.*
³ Or, *severely scourge him*

§ 221. The Parable of the Ten Virgins

[*Cp.* Luke 12 35-36]

Matt. 25 1-13

1 Then shall the kingdom of heaven be likened unto ten virgins, which took their [1] lamps, and went forth to meet the bridegroom. **2** And five of them were foolish [*cp.* 7 26], and five were wise [*cp.* 7 24; 10 16; 24 45]. **3** For the foolish, when they took their [1] lamps, took no oil with them: **4** but the wise took oil in their vessels with their [1] lamps. **5** Now while the bridegroom tarried [*cp.* 24 48], they all slumbered and slept [*cp.* 26 40, 43]. **6** But at midnight [*cp.* Mark 13 35] there is a cry, Behold, the bridegroom ! Come ye forth to meet him. **7** Then all those virgins arose, and trimmed their [1] lamps. **8** And the foolish said unto the wise, Give us of your oil; for our [1] lamps are going out. **9** But the wise answered, saying, Peradventure there will not be enough for us and you: go ye rather to them that sell, and buy for yourselves. **10** And while they went away to buy, the bridegroom came; and they that were ready [*cp.* 24 44] went in with him to the marriage feast:

and
the door was shut.

11 Afterward come also the other virgins, saying, Lord, Lord, open to us. **12** But he answered and said, Verily I say unto you, I know you not [*cp.* 7 23].

13 Watch [*cp.* 26 38, 41] therefore,
cp. 26 41.
for ye know not [*cp.* 24 36, 44, 50] the day nor the hour.

24 **42** Watch therefore : for ye know not on what day your Lord cometh.

[1] Or, *torches*

---

cp. 13 36; 14 37, 40.

Mark 13 **33** Take ye heed, watch [*cp.* 13 37; 14 34, 38]

[1] and pray [*cp.* 14 38]:
for ye know not [*cp.* 13 32]
when the time is.
35 Watch therefore : for ye know not when the lord of the house cometh.

[1] Some ancient authorities omit *and pray*.

---

cp. 12 42.

cp. 22 45.

cp. 12 40, 47.

Luke 13 **25** When once the master of the house is risen up, and hath shut to the door, and ye begin to stand without, and to knock at the door,

saying, Lord, open to us; and he shall answer and say to you, I know you not [*cp.* 13 27] whence ye are.   21 **36** But watch [*cp.* 12 37]
ye at every season, making supplication [*cp.* 22 40, 46].
cp. 12 40, 46.

---

cp. 7 27, 28; 8 14; 9 29, 30.

§ 222. The Parable of the Talents

[*Cp.* Matt. 24 45-51: Luke 12 41-48; 16 10-12]

Matt. 25 14-30

14 For *it is* as *when* a man, going into another country [*cp.* 21 33],
cp. 18 23; 22 2 *ff.*; 25 34, 40.

called his own [1] servants,

and delivered unto them his goods. **15** And unto one he gave five talents [*cp.* 18 24], to another two, to another one; to each according to his several ability;

Mark 13 **34** *It is* as *when* a man, sojourning in another country [*cp.* 12 1],
having left his house, and given authority to his [1] servants, to each one his work, commanded also the porter to watch.

[1] Gr. *bondservants.*

Luke 19 12-27

12 He said therefore, A certain nobleman went into a far [*cp.* 15 13] country [*cp.* 20 9], to receive for himself a kingdom, and to return. **13** And he called ten [1] servants of his,

and gave them ten [2] pounds,

and said unto them, Trade ye *herewith* till I come.

---

cp. 21 22, 23.

and he went on his journey [cp. 21 33].

cp. 12 1.

cp. 20 9.

14 But his citizens hated him, and sent an ambassage [cp. 14 32] after him, saying, We will not that this man reign over us.

16 Straightway he that received the five talents went and traded with them, and made other five talents. 17 In like manner he also that *received* the two gained other two. 18 But he that received the one went away and digged in the earth, and hid his lord's [cp. 18 25, *etc.*] money. 19 Now　　　　after a long time　　　the lord of those ¹ servants [cp. 18 27; 24 50] cometh,

15 And it came to pass,
when he
[cp. 12 46]　　　was come back again, having received the kingdom, that he commanded these ¹ servants, unto whom he had given the money, to be called to him, that he might know what they had gained by trading. 16 And the first
came before him,

and maketh a reckoning with them [cp. 18 23]. 20 And he that received the five talents came　　　　and brought other five talents, saying, Lord, thou deliveredst unto me five talents: lo, I have gained other five　　talents.

saying, Lord,
　　　　　　　　　thy pound
　　hath made　　　ten
pounds more. 17 And he said unto him, Well done, thou good
　　[cp. 12 42] ³ servant: because thou wast found faithful in a very little [cp. 16 10: *also* 12 26], have thou authority over [cp. 12 44 *and* 42] ten cities.　　　　cp. 13 24; *etc.*

cp. 9 43; *etc.*

21 His lord said unto him, Well done,　　good and faithful [cp. 24 45] ² servant:　　thou hast been faithful over a few things, 　　　　　　　　I will set thee over [cp. 24 47 *and* 45] 　　many things: enter [cp. 7 13; *etc.*] thou into the joy of thy lord. 22 And he also that *received* the two talents came and said, Lord, thou deliveredst unto me two talents: lo, I have gained other two talents. 23 His lord said unto him,　　Well done, good and faithful [cp. 24 45] ² servant; thou hast been faithful over a few things, I will set thee over [cp. 24 47 *and* 45] 　　many things: enter [cp. 7 13; *etc.*] thou into the joy of thy lord. 24 And he also that had received the one talent came and said, Lord,
　　　　　　　　　　　　　I knew thee　　　　that thou art a hard man,
　　　　　　　　　reaping where thou didst not sow, and gathering where thou didst not scatter: 25 and I was afraid, and went away and hid thy talent in the earth: lo, thou hast thine own. 26 But his lord answered and said unto him,
　　Thou wicked [cp. 18 32: *also* 24 48] and slothful ² servant, thou knewest that I

cp. 9 43; *etc.*

18 And the second
　　　　came, saying, Thy pound,
Lord,
　　　　hath made　　　five
　　pounds. 19 And he
said unto him also,
　　cp. 12 42.
　　cp. 16 10: *also* 12 26.
Be thou also over [cp. 12 44 *and* 42] five cities.
　　cp. 13 24; *etc.*
20 And ⁴ another
　　　　came, saying, Lord, behold, *here is* thy pound, which I kept laid up in a napkin: 21 for I feared thee, because thou art an austere man: thou takest up that thou layedst not down, and reapest that thou didst not sow.

cp. 3 5; 10 1, 2, 9: *and* 15 11; 17 13.

cp. 3 5; 10 1, 2, 9: *and* 15 11; 17 13.

22 He　　　　　　saith unto him, Out of thine own mouth will I judge thee, thou wicked
　　　　　　　　³ servant.
Thou knewest that I am an austere man, taking up that I laid not down, and reaping that I did not sow;
　　　　　　　23 then
　　wherefore gavest thou not my money into the bank,　　and ⁵ I at my coming　　should have required it　　with interest? 24 And he said unto them that stood by [cp. 9 27], Take　　away
from him the pound, and give it unto him that hath the ten
pounds. 25 And they said unto him,

reap where I sowed not, and gather where I did not scatter; 27 thou oughtest therefore to have put　　my money to the bankers, and　　at my coming I should have received back mine own with interest.
　　cp. 16 28; 26 73; 27 47.
28 Take ye away therefore the talent from him,　　　and give it unto him that hath the ten talents [cp. 21 43].

cp. 9 1; 11 5; 14 47, 69, 70; 15 35, 39.

cp. 12 29.

29 For unto every one that hath shall be given, and he shall have abundance: but from him that hath not, even that which he hath shall be taken away.

Matt. 13 12 For whosoever hath, to him shall be given, and he shall have abundance: but whosoever hath not, from him shall be taken away even that which he hath.

Mark 4 25 For he that hath, to him shall be given:

and he that hath not, from him shall be taken away even that which he hath.

30 And cast ye out the unprofitable [2] servant into the outer darkness [*cp.* 8 12; 22 13]:

there shall be the weeping and gnashing of teeth [*cp.* 8 12; 13 42, 50; 22 13; 24 51].

[1] Gr. *bondservants.*   [2] Gr. *bondservant.*

Lord, he hath ten pounds.   **26** I say unto you, that unto every one that hath shall be given;

but from him that hath not, even that which he hath shall be taken away from him.

Luke 8 18 For whosoever hath, to him shall be given;

and whosoever hath not, from him shall be taken away even that which he [6] thinketh he hath.

cp. 17 10.

27 Howbeit these mine enemies, which would not that I should reign over them, bring hither, and slay them before me.

cp. 13 28.

[1] Gr. *bondservants.*
[2] *Mina,* here translated a pound, is equal to one hundred drachmas. See ch. 15 8.
[3] Gr. *bondservant.*   [4] Gr. *the other.*
[5] Or, *I should have gone and required*
[6] Or, *seemeth to have*

§ 223. The Parable of the Sheep and the Goats

Matt. 25 31-46

31 But when the Son of man shall come in his glory [*cp.* 16 27; 24 30; 26 64], and all the angels with him [*cp.* 16 27: *also* 13 41, 49; 24 31], then shall he sit on the throne of his glory [*cp.* 19 28]: **32** and before him shall be gathered all the nations: and he shall separate them one from another [*cp.* 3 12; 13 30, 47-50: *also* 22 10], as the shepherd separateth the sheep from the [1] goats: **33** and he shall set the sheep on his right hand, but the [1] goats on the left. **34** Then shall the King [*cp.* 18 23; 22 2, 7, 11, 13; 25 40] say [*cp.* 7 23] unto them on his right hand, Come, ye blessed of my Father, inherit the kingdom prepared [*cp.* 20 23] for you from the foundation of the world [*cp.* 13 35]: **35** for I was an hungred, and ye gave me meat: I was thirsty, and ye gave me drink: I was a stranger, and ye took me in; **36** naked, and ye clothed me: I was sick, and ye visited me: I was in prison, and ye came unto me. **37** Then shall the righteous answer him, saying, Lord, when saw we thee an hungred, and fed thee? or athirst, and gave thee drink? **38** And when saw we thee a stranger, and took thee in? or naked, and clothed thee? **39** And when saw we thee sick, or in prison, and came unto thee? **40** And the King [*see verse* 34 *above*] shall answer and say unto them, Verily I say unto you, Inasmuch as ye did it unto one of these my brethren, *even* these least, ye did it unto me [*cp.* 10 40-42]. **41** Then shall he say [*cp.* 7 23] also unto them on the left hand, [2] Depart from me [*cp.* 7 23], ye cursed, into the eternal fire [*cp.* 18 8 *and* 25 46: *also* 3 12; 5 22; 13 42, 50; 18 9: *and* 5 29, 30; 10 28; 23 33] which is prepared for the devil and his angels: **42** for I was an hungred, and ye gave me no meat: I was thirsty, and ye gave me no drink: **43** I was a stranger, and ye took me not in; naked, and ye clothed me not; sick, and in prison, and ye visited me not. **44** Then shall they also answer, saying, Lord, when saw we thee an hungred, or athirst, or a stranger, or naked, or sick, or in prison, and did not minister unto thee? **45** Then shall he answer them, saying, Verily I say unto you, Inasmuch as ye did it not unto one of these least, ye did it not unto me. **46** And these shall go away into eternal punishment [*see verse* 41 *above*]: but the righteous into eternal life [*cp.* 19 16, 29].

[1] Gr, *kids.*   [2] Or. *Depart from me under a curse*

cp. 8 38; 13 26, 27; 14 62: *also* 10 37.	*cp.* 9 26; 21 27: *also* 12 8, 9: *and* 9 32; 24 26.	*cp.* 1 14; 2 11; 12 41; 17 5, 22, 24.
	cp. 3 17.	
	cp. 19 12, 15, 27: *and* 13 27.	
cp. 10 40.	*cp.* 11 50.	*cp.* 17 24.
	cp. 19 12, 15, 27.	
cp. 9 41.	*cp.* 13 27.	
	cp. 13 27.	
cp. 9 43, 45, 47.	*cp.* 3 17: *also* 12 5.	*cp.* 15 6.
cp. 3 29.		*cp.* 5 29.
cp. 10 17, 30.	*cp.* 10 25; 18 18, 30: *also* 16 9.	*cp.* 3 15; *etc.*

(iv) Summary (§ 224)

§ 224. The Jerusalem Ministry in Retrospect

	Mark 11 19	Luke 21 37-38	
cp. 26 55: *also* 21 23.		37 And every day he was teaching in the temple [*cp.* 19 47; 22 53: *also* 20 1]; and every night he went	*cp.* 18 20: *also* 7 28; 8 20.
cp. 21 17; 26 30.	*cp.* 14 49 : *also* 12 35. 19 And [1] every evening [2] he went forth out [*cp.* 11 11 ; 14 26] of the city.	out [*cp.* 22 39], and lodged in the mount that is	*cp.* 18 1-2.
cp. 24 3; 26 30.	*cp.* 13 3 ; 14 26.	called *the mount* of Olives [*cp.* 22 39]. 38 And all the people came early in the morning to him in the temple, to	*cp.* 8 1.
	cp. 12 37.	hear him [*cp.* 19 48].	*cp.* 8 2.

[1] Gr. *whenever evening came.*
[2] Some ancient authorities read *they.*

F. The Passion and Resurrection (§§ 225-259)

(i) The Prologue to the Passion (§§ 225-228)

§ 225. The Plot to destroy Jesus

Matt. 26 1-5	Mark 14 1-2	Luke 22 1-2	John 11 55, 47-53
1 And it came to pass, when Jesus had finished all these words [*cp.* 7 28; 11 1; 13 53; 19 1], he said unto his disciples, 2 Ye know that after two days the passover *cp.* 26 17. cometh,		*cp.* 7 1.	
and the Son of man is delivered up to be crucified [*cp.* 16 21; 17 12, 22-23; 20 18-19: *also* 20 28; 26 24, 25].	1 Now after two days was *the feast of* the passover and the un-leavened bread[*cp.* 14 12]: *cp.* 8 31; 9 12, 31; 10 33-34: *also* 10 45; 14 21, 41.	1 Now the feast of un-leavened bread [*cp.* 22 7] drew nigh, which is called the Passover. *cp.* 9 22, 44; 18 31-33; 24 7: *also* 13 32-33; 17 25; 22 22.	55 Now the passover of the Jews was at hand. *cp.* 2 19; 3 14; 12 32-33.
3 Then were gathered to-gether the chief priests, and the elders of the people, unto the court [*cp.* 26 57, 58: *also* 26 69: *and* John 18 15]	and the chief priests and the scribes *cp.* 14 53, 54: *also* 14 66.	2 And the chief priests and the scribes *cp.* 22 55.	47 The chief priests therefore and the Pharisees gathered a council, and said, What do we ? for this man doeth many signs. 48 If we let him thus alone, all men will believe on him : and the Romans will come and take away both our place and our nation. 49 But a certain one of them,
of the high priest, who was called Caiaphas [*cp.* 26 57];		*cp.* 3 2.	Caiaphas [*cp.* 18 13, 14, 24, 28], being high priest that year, said unto them, Ye know nothing at all, 50 nor do ye take account that it is expedient for you that one man should die for the people, and that the whole nation perish not. 51 Now this he said not of himself : but being high priest that year, he prophesied that Jesus should die for the nation [*cp.* 10 11, 15, 17]; 52 and not
cp. 20 28.	*cp.* 10 45.		

cp. 8 11; 10 18; 21 31, 41, 43; 22 7-10; 24 14; 26 13; 28 19. cp. 5 9: also 5 45; and 8 12; 13 38.	cp. 12 9; 13 10; 14 9; 16 15.	cp. 2 30-32; 3 6; 13 29; 14 21-24; 20 16; 24 47. cp. 20 36: also 6 35; 16 8.	for the nation only [cp. 10 16], but that he might also gather together into one the children of God [cp. 1 12: also 12 36] that are scattered abroad. **53** So from that day forth they took counsel that they might
4 and they took counsel together that they might take Jesus by subtilty, and kill him [cp. 12 14; 21 46; 27 1: also 22 15; and 12 10]. **5** But they said, Not during the feast, lest a tumult [cp. 27 24] arise among the people [cp. 21 26, 46: so 14 5].	sought how they might take him with subtilty, and kill him [cp. 3 6; 11 18; 12 12: also 12 13; and 3 2]: **2** for they said, Not during the feast, lest haply there shall be a tumult of the people [cp. 11 18, 32; 12 12].	sought how they might put him to death [cp. 6 11; 19 47; 20 19, 20: also 11 53-54; and 6 7]; for they feared the people [cp. 19 48; 20 6, 19].	put him to death [cp. 5 16, 18; 7 30, 32: also 8 6].

§ 226. The Anointing in Bethany

Matt. 26 6-13	**Mark 14** 3-9	Luke 7 36-50	John 12 1-8
		36 And one of the Pharisees desired him that he would eat [cp. 7 34] with him. And he entered into the Pharisee's house,	
6 Now when Jesus was in Bethany, in the house of Simon the leper,	**3** And while he was in Bethany in the house of Simon the leper,	cp. 7 40, 43, 44. cp. 10 40.	**1** Jesus therefore six days before the passover came to Bethany, where Lazarus was, whom Jesus raised from the dead. **2** So they made him a supper there: and Martha served; but Lazarus was one of them that sat at meat with him.
7 there came unto him a woman	as he sat at meat, there came a woman	and sat down to meat [cp. 11 37; 14 1]. **37** And behold, a woman which was in the city, a sinner [cp. 7 34]; and when she knew that he was sitting at meat in the Pharisee's house, she brought 1 an alabaster cruse of ointment,	**3** Mary therefore
having 1 an alabaster cruse of exceeding precious ointment, and she poured it upon his head, as he sat at meat.	having 1 an alabaster cruse of ointment of 2 spikenard very costly; and she brake the cruse, and poured it over his head.	**38** and standing behind at his feet [cp. 8 35; 10 39], weeping, she began to wet his feet with her tears, and wiped them with the hair of her head, and 2 kissed his feet, and anointed them with the ointment.	took a pound of ointment of 1 spikenard, very precious, and anointed the feet of Jesus, and wiped his feet with her hair: and the house was filled with the odour of the ointment. **4** But
8 But when the disciples saw it, they had indignation, saying,	**4** But there were some that had indignation among themselves, saying,	**39** Now when the Pharisee which had bidden him saw it, he spake within himself [cp. 11 38], saying,	Judas Iscariot, one of his disciples, which should betray him, saith

Matthew	Mark		Luke
To what purpose is this waste ?	To what purpose hath this waste of the ointment been made ? **5** For this ointment might have been sold for above three hundred ³pence, and given to the poor. And they murmured against her [*cp.* 10 13].		5 Why was not this ointment sold for three hundred ² pence, and given to the poor?
9 For this *ointment* might have been sold for much, and given to the poor. *cp.* 15 23; 19 13.		*cp.* 18 15.	6 Now this he said, not because he cared for the poor ; but because he was a thief, and having the ³ bag [*cp.* 13 29] ⁴ took away what was put therein. 7 Jesus therefore *cp.* 5 6; 6 15. said,
10 But Jesus perceiving it [*cp.* 12 15; 16 8; 22 18] said unto them, Why trouble ye the woman? for she hath wrought a good work upon me. *cp.* 19 14.	**6** But Jesus *cp.* 8 17. said, Let her alone; why trouble ye her ? she hath wrought a good work on me. *cp.* 10 14.	*cp.* 18 16.	5 Suffer her to keep it against the day of my burying. 8 For the poor ye have always with you ;
11 For ye have the poor always with you ; but me ye have not always. **12** For in that she ² poured this ointment upon my body, she did it to prepare me for burial. **13** Verily I say unto you, Wheresoever ³ this gospel [*cp.* 4 23; 9 35; 24 14] shall be preached in the whole world [*cp.* 24 14: *also* 8 11; 10 18: 21 31, 41, 43; 22 7-10; 28 19], that also which this woman hath done shall be spoken of for a memorial of her.	**7** For ye have the poor always with you, and whensover ye will ye can do them good: but me ye have not always. 8 She hath done what she could: she hath anointed my body aforehand for the burying. **9** And verily I say unto you, Wheresoever the gospel [*cp.* 1 1, 14, 15; 8 35; 10 29; 13 10; 16 15] shall be preached throughout the whole world [*cp.* 13 10: *also* 12 9; 16 15], that also which this woman hath done shall be spoken of for a memorial of her.	*cp.* 2 30-32; 3 6; *etc.*	but me ye have not always. *cp.* 10 16; 11 52.

Matthew footnotes:
¹ Or, *a flask*   ² Gr. *cast.*
³ Or, *these good tidings*

Mark footnotes:
¹ Or, *a flask*
² Gr. *pistic nard,* pistic being perhaps a local name. Others take it to mean *genuine* ; others, *liquid.*
³ See marginal note on Matt. 18 28.

Luke footnotes:
¹ See marginal note on Mark 14 3.
² See marginal note on Matt. 18 28.
³ Or, *box*
⁴ Or, *carried what was put therein*
⁵ Or, *Let her alone: it was that she might keep it*

		Luke (continued)	
cp. 13 57; 21 11, 46.	*cp.* 6 4, 15.	This man, if he were ³ a prophet [*cp.* 4 24 ; 7 16 ; 13 33 ; 24 19], would have perceived who and what manner of woman this is which toucheth [*cp.* 6 19 ; 8 44: Matt. 9 20; 14 36: Mark 3 10; 5 27; 6 56: John 20 17] him, that she is a sinner [*cp.* 5 30; 15 2; 19 7]. **40** And Jesus answering said unto him, Simon, I have some-what to say unto thee. And he saith, ⁴ Master, say on. **41** A certain lender had two debtors: the one owed five hundred ⁵ pence, and the other fifty. **42** When they had not *wherewith* to pay, he forgave them both. Which of them therefore will love him most ? **43** Simon answered and said, He, I suppose, to whom he forgave the most. And he said unto him, Thou hast rightly judged [*cp.* 10 28]. **44** And	*cp.* 4 19, 44; 6 14; 7 40; 9 17.
cp. 9 11; 11 19. *cp.* 26 6.	*cp.* 2 16. *cp.* 14 3.		
cp. 18 23-34. *cp.* 18 25.			
cp. 9 22; 16 23.	*cp.* 5 30; 8 33.	turning [*cp.* 7 9 ; 9 55 ; 10 23 ; 14 25 ; 22 61 ; 23 28] to the woman, he said unto Simon, Seest thou this woman ? I entered into thine house, thou gavest me no water for my feet : but she hath wetted my feet with her tears, and wiped them with her hair. **45** Thou gavest me no kiss : but she, since the time I came in, hath not ceased to ⁶ kiss my feet. **46** My head with oil thou didst not anoint : but she hath anointed my feet with ointment. **47** Wherefore I say unto thee, Her sins, which are many, are forgiven ; for she loved much : but to whom little is forgiven, *the same* loveth little [*cp.* 5 32 ; 7 29, 30 ; 15 7, 10 ; 18 14 ; 19 10]. **48** And he said unto her,	*cp.* 1 38.
cp. 9 13; 21 31. *cp.* 9 2. *cp.* 8 27; 21 10. *cp.* 9 22.	*cp.* 2 17. *cp.* 2 5. *cp.* 1 27; 2 7; 4 41. *cp.* 5 34; 10 52.	Thy sins are forgiven [*cp.* 5 20]. **49** And they that sat at meat with him began to say ⁷ within themselves, Who is this [*cp.* 5 21 : *also* 4 36 ; 8 25 ; 9 9] that even forgiveth sins ? **50** And he said unto the woman, Thy faith hath saved thee [*cp.* 8 48 ; 17 19 ; 18 42] ; go in peace [*cp.* 8 48].	*cp.* 5 12: *also* 12 34.

Luke footnotes:
¹ Or, *a flask*   ² Gr. *kissed much.*
³ Some ancient authorities read *the prophet.* See John 1 21, 25.   ⁴ Or, *Teacher*
⁵ See footnote on Matt. 18 28.   ⁶ Gr. *kiss much.*
⁷ Or, *among*

§ 227. The Treachery of Judas

Matt. 26 14-16	**Mark 14** 10-11	**Luke 22** 3-6	*cp.* 13 2, 27.
14 Then one of the twelve, who was called Judas Iscariot, went unto the chief priests, **15** and said, What are ye willing to give me, and I will deliver him unto you? And they weighed unto him thirty pieces of silver [*cp.* 27 3]. **16** And from that time he sought opportunity to deliver him *unto them*. *cp.* 26 5.	**10** And Judas Iscariot, [1] he that was one of the twelve, went away unto the chief priests, that he might deliver him unto them. **11** And they, when they heard it, were glad, and promised to give him money. And he sought how he might conveniently deliver him *unto them*. *cp.* 14 2.	**3** And Satan [*cp.* 22 31] entered into Judas who was called Iscariot, being of the number of the twelve. **4** And he went away, and communed with the chief priests and captains [*cp.* 22 52], how he might deliver him unto them. **5** And they were glad, and covenanted to give him money. **6** And he consented, and sought opportunity to deliver him unto them [1] in the absence of the multitude [*cp.* 22 2].	
	[1] Gr. *the one of the twelve.*	[1] Or, *without tumult*	

Matt. 26 15: *cp.* Zech. 11 12.

§ 228. The Preparation for the Passover

Matt. 26 17-19	**Mark 14** 12-16	**Luke 22** 7-13	
17 Now on the first *day* of unleavened bread *cp.* 26 1. the disciples came [*cp.* 5 1; 13 10, 36; 14 15; 15 12, 23; 17 19; 18 1; 24 1, 3] to Jesus, saying, Where wilt thou that we make ready for thee to eat the passover? *cp.* 21 1. **18** And he said, Go into the city to such a man, and say unto him, The [1] Master saith, My time is at hand [*cp.* 26 45]; I keep the passover at thy house with my disciples. **19** And	**12** And on the first day of unleavened bread, when they sacrificed the passover [*cp.* 14 1], his disciples *cp.* 6 35. say unto him, Where wilt thou that we go and make ready that thou mayest eat the passover? **13** And he sendeth two [*cp.* 11 1: *also* 6 7] of his disciples, and saith unto them, Go into the city, and there shall meet you a man bearing a pitcher of water: follow him; **14** and wheresoever he shall enter in, say to the goodman of the house, The [1] Master saith, [*cp.* 14 41: *also* 14 35] Where is my guest-chamber, where I shall eat the passover with my disciples? **15** And he will himself shew you a large upper room furnished *and* ready: and there make ready for us. **16** And	**7** And the day of unleavened bread came, on which the passover [*cp.* 22 1] must be sacrificed. *cp.* 9 12. **8** And he sent [*cp.* 19 29: *also* 10 1] Peter and John, saying, Go and make ready for us the passover, that we may eat. **9** And they said unto him, Where wilt thou that we make ready? **10** And he said unto them, Behold, when ye are entered into the city, there shall meet you a man bearing a pitcher of water; follow him into the house whereinto he goeth. **11** And ye shall say unto the goodman of the house, The [1] Master saith unto thee, [*cp.* 22 14] Where is the guest-chamber, where I shall eat the passover with my disciples? **12** And he will shew you a large upper room furnished: there make ready. **13** And	*cp.* 11 28. *cp.* 12 23; 13 1; 17 1: *also* 12 27: *and* 2 4; 7 6, 8, 30; 8 20.

the disciples did	the disciples went forth, and came into the city, and found	they went,
as Jesus appointed them [*cp.* 21 6]; and they made ready the passover.	as he had said unto them: and they made ready the passover.	and found as he had said unto them [*cp.* 19 32]: and they made ready the passover.
¹ Or, *Teacher*	¹ Or, *Teacher*	¹ Or, *Teacher*

(ii) In the Upper Room (§§ 229-234)

§ 229. **The Prophecy of the Betrayal** (Matt. and Mark)

Matt. 26 20-25	**Mark 14** 17-21	**Luke 22** 14 (21-23)	**John 13** 21, 18-19, 22-30
20 Now when even [*cp.* 26 45: *also* 26 18] was come,	**17** And when it was evening [*cp.* 14 35, 41] he cometh with the twelve. **18** And as they ¹ sat *cp.* 6 30.	**14** And when the hour [*cp.* 22 53] was come,	*cp.* 12 23, 27 ; 13 1 ; 17 1 : *also* 2 4 ; 7 6, 8, 30 ; 8 20.
he was sitting at meat *cp.* 10 2. with the twelve ¹ disciples; **21** and as they were eating [*cp.* 26 26], he said, Verily I say unto you, that one of you shall betray me.	and were eating [*cp.* 14 22], Jesus said, Verily I say unto you, One of you shall betray me, *even*	he sat down, and the apostles [*cp.* 6 13 ; 9 10 ; 17 5 ; 24 10] with him. **21** But behold, the hand of him that betrayeth me	**21** When Jesus had thus said, he was troubled in the spirit, and testified, and said, Verily, verily, I say unto you, that one of you shall betray me. . . . **18** I speak not of you all: I know whom I ¹ have chosen [*cp.* 6 70]: but that the scripture may be fulfilled, He that eateth ² my bread lifted up his heel against me. **19** From henceforth I tell you before it come to pass, that, when it is come to pass, ye may believe that ³ I am *he.* . . . **22** The disciples looked [*cp.* 16 6, 20, 22] one on another, doubting of whom he spake. **23** There was at the table reclining in Jesus' bosom one of his disciples, whom Jesus loved. **24** Simon Peter therefore beckoneth to him, and saith unto him, Tell *us* who it is of whom he speaketh. **25** He leaning back, as he was, on Jesus' breast saith unto him, Lord, who is it? **26** Jesus therefore answereth, He it is, for whom I shall dip the sop, and give it him.
verse 24	*verse* 21 he that eateth with me.	*verse* 22 is with me on the table.	
22 And they were exceeding sorrowful [*cp.* 17 23 ; 18 31: *also* 26 37], and began	**19** They began to be sorrowful, and	*cp.* 22 45.	
to say unto him every one, Is it I, Lord? **23** And he answered and said, He that dipped his hand with me in the dish, the same shall betray me.	to say unto him one by one, Is it I? **20** And he said unto them, *It is* one of the twelve, he that dippeth with me in the dish.	*verse* 23	
24 The Son of man goeth, even as it is written of him [*cp.* 16 21-23 ; 17 12, 22-23 ; 20 17-19, 28 ; 26 2, 45: *also* 26 12, 18; *and* 21 42 ; 26 31, 54, 56]: but woe [*cp.* 18 7: *also* 23 13 *ff.*] unto that man through whom the Son of man is be-	**21** For the Son of man goeth, even as it is written of him [*cp.* 8 31-33 ; 9 12, 30-32 ; 10 32-34, 45 ; 14 41: *also* 14 8; *and* 12 10 ; 14 27, 49]: but woe unto that man through whom the Son of man is be-	**22** For the Son of man indeed goeth, as it hath been determined [*cp.* 9 22, 43-45 ; 13 32-33 ; 17 25 ; 18 31-34 ; 24 7, 44: *also* 20 17 ; 22 37 ; 24 25-27, 46]: but woe [*cp.* 17 1: *also* 11 42 *ff.*] unto that man through whom he is be-	*verse* 18 *cp.* 2 19, 22 ; 3 14 ; 12 32, 33: *also* 5 39 ; 15 25 ; 17 12.

trayed ! good were it ² for that man if he had not been born.	trayed ! good were it ² for that man if he had not been born.	trayed !	
verse 22	*verse 19*	**23** And they began to question among themselves, which of them it was that should do this thing.	*verse 22* So when he had dipped the sop, he taketh and giveth it to Judas, *the son* of Simon Iscariot.
25 And Judas, which betrayed him, answered and said, Is it I, Rabbi [*cp.* 26 49: *also* 23 7, 8]? He saith unto him, Thou has said [*cp.* 26 64: *also* 27 11].	*cp.* 9 5; 11 21; 14 45: *also* 10 51. *cp.* 15 2.	*cp.* 23 3: *also* 22 70. *cp.* 22 3.	*cp.* 1 38, 49; *etc.*: *also* 20 16. *cp.* 18 37. **27** And after the sop, then entered Satan into him. Jesus therefore saith unto him,
¹ Many authorities, some ancient, omit *disciples.* ² Gr. *for him if that man.*	¹ Gr. *reclined.* ² Gr. *for him if that man.*		

That thou doest, do quickly. **28** Now no man at the table knew for what intent he spake this unto him. **29** For some thought, because Judas had the ⁴ bag, that Jesus said unto him, Buy what things we have need of for the feast ; or, that he should give something to the poor. **30** He then having received the sop went out straightway : and it was night.

¹ Or, *chose*
² Many ancient authorities read *his bread with me.*
³ Or, *I am*　　　⁴ Or, *box*

§ 230. The Institution of the Eucharist

[*Cp.* John 6 48-59]

Matt. 26 26-29	**Mark 14** 22-25	**Luke 22** 15-20	1 Corinthians 11 23-25
26 And as they were eating [*cp.* 26 21], Jesus	**22** And as they were eating [*cp.* 14 18], he	**15** And he said unto them, With desire I have desired to eat this passover with you before I suffer : **16** for I say unto you, I will not eat [*cp.* 22 30: *also* 13 29; 14 15] it, until it be fulfilled in the kingdom of God. **17** And he received a cup, and when he had given thanks [*cp. verse* 19], he said, Take [*cp.* Matt. 26 26 *and* Mark 14 22] this, and divide it among yourselves : **18** for I say unto you, I will not drink [*cp.* 22 30: *also* 13 29; 14 15] from henceforth [*cp.* 1 48; 5 10; 12 52; 22 69] of the fruit of the vine, until the kingdom of God shall come. **19** And he took ¹ bread, and when he had given thanks [*cp. verse* 17], [*cp.* 9 16; 24 30] he brake it, and gave to them,	
cp. 15 36; 26 27.	*cp.* 8 6; 14 23.	*cp.* 6 11.	
verse 29	*verse 25*		
			23 For I received of the Lord that which also I delivered unto you, how that the Lord Jesus in the night in which he was betrayed took bread ; **24** and when he had given thanks,
took ¹ bread, and [*cp.* 15 36; 26 27] blessed [*cp.* 14 19], and brake it; and he gave to the disciples,	took ¹ bread, and when he had [*cp.* 8 6; 14 23] blessed [*cp.* 6 41; 8 7], he brake it, and gave to them,	*cp.* 6 11.	he brake it,

Matthew

and said, Take, eat; this is my body.

27 And he took 2 a cup,

and gave thanks [cp. 15 36], and gave to them,

saying, Drink ye all of it; **28** for this is my blood of 3 the 4 covenant,

which is shed for many [cp. 20 28] unto remission of sins. **29** But I say unto you, I will not drink [cp. 8 11] henceforth [cp. 23 39; 26 64] of this fruit of the vine, until that day [cp. 7 22; 24 36] when I drink it new with you in my Father's [cp. 13 43] kingdom.

1 Or, *a loaf*
2 Some ancient authorities read *the cup.*
3 Or, *the testament*
4 Many ancient authorities insert *new.*

Mark

and said, Take ye: this is my body.

23 And he took a cup,

and when he had given thanks [cp. 8 6], he gave to them: and they all drank of it. **24** And he said unto them,

This is my blood of 2 the 3 covenant, which is shed for many [cp. 10 45]. *cp.* 1 4. **25** Verily I say unto you, I will no more drink

of the fruit of the vine, until that day [cp. 13 32] when I drink it new in the kingdom of God.

1 Or, *a loaf*
2 Or, *the testament*
3 Some ancient authorities insert *new.*

Luke

saying [*cp. verse* 17], This is my body 2 which is given for you: this do in remembrance of me. **20** And the cup in like manner after supper,

cp. verses 17 *and* 19.

saying,

This cup is the new 3 covenant in my blood, *even that* which is poured out for you. *cp.* 3 3: *also* 1 77; 24 47.

verse 18; *cp.* 16. *cp.* 10 12; 17 31; 21 34.

1 Or, *a loaf*
2 Some ancient authorities omit *which is given for you . . . which is poured out for you.*
3 Or, *testament*

(center cross-references)

cp. 6 11.

cp. 13 19; 14 7. *cp.* 14 20; 16 23, 26.

John

and said, This is my body, which 1 is for you: this do in remembrance of me. **25** In like manner also the cup, after supper,

saying,

This cup is the new 2 covenant in my blood:

this do, as oft as ye drink *it*, in remembrance of me.

1 Many ancient authorities read *is broken for you.*
2 Or, *testament*

Matt. 26 28 || Mark 14 24 || Luke 22 20 ; *cp.* Is. 52 15 ; 53 4-6, 8, 11-12.

§ 231. The Prophecy of the Betrayal (Luke)

Matt. 26 20-25	Mark 14 17-21	Luke 22 (14) 21-23	John 13 21, 18-19, 22-30

Matt. 26 20-25

20 Now when even [*cp.* 26 45: *also* 26 18] was come,

he was sitting at meat *cp.* 10 2.

with the twelve 1 disciples; **21** and as they were eating [*cp.* 26 26], he said, Verily I say unto you, that one of you shall betray me.

verse 24

22 And they were exceeding sorrowful [*cp.* 17 23; 18 31: *also* 26 37], **and began**

Mark 14 17-21

17 And when it was evening [*cp.* 14 35, 41] he cometh with the twelve. **18** And as they 1 sat *cp.* 6 30.

and were eating [*cp.* 14 22], Jesus said, Verily I say unto you, One of you shall betray me, *even*

verse 21 he that eateth with me.

19 They began to be sorrowful, and

Luke 22 (14) 21-23

14 And when the hour [*cp.* 22 53] was come,

he sat down, and the apostles [*cp.* 6 13; 9 10 17 5; 24 10] with him.

21 But behold, the hand of him that betrayeth me

verse 22 is with me on the table.

cp. 22 45.

John 13 21, 18-19, 22-30

cp. 12 23, 27; 13 1; 17 1: *also* 2 4; 7 6, 8, 30; 8 20.

21 When Jesus had thus said, he was troubled in the spirit, and testified, and said, Verily, verily, I say unto you, that one of you shall betray me. . . . **18** I speak not of you all: I know whom I 1 have chosen [*cp.* 6 70]: but that the scripture may be fulfilled, He that eateth 2 my bread lifted up his heel against me. **19** From henceforth I tell you before it come to pass, that, when it is come to pass, ye may believe that 3 I am *he.* . . . **22** The disciples looked [*cp.* 16 6, 20, 22] one on another, doubting of whom he spake. **23** There was at

Matt.	Mark		Luke

the table reclining in Jesus' bosom one of his disciples, whom Jesus loved. **24** Simon Peter therefore beckoneth to him, and saith unto him, Tell *us* who it is of whom he speaketh. **25** He leaning back, as he was, on Jesus' breast saith unto him,
Lord, who is it? **26** Jesus therefore answereth,

to say
unto him every one,
Is it I, Lord? **23** And he
answered and
said,

to say
unto him one by one,
Is it I? **20** And he

said unto them, *It is*
one of the twelve,
he that dippeth
with me in the dish.

verse 23

He it is,
for whom
I shall   dip

the sop, and give it him.

He that dipped his
hand with me in the dish,

the same shall betray me.
24 The Son of man
goeth, even as it
is written of him [*cp.* 16
21-23; 17 12, 22-23; 20
17-19, 28; 26 2, 45: *also* 26
12, 18; *and* 21 42; 26
31, 54, 56]: but woe [*cp.*
18 7: *also* 23 13 *ff.*] unto
that man through whom
the Son of man is be-
trayed! good were it
² for that man if he had
not been born.

21 For the Son of man
goeth, even as it
is written of him [*cp.* 8
31-33; 9 12, 30-32; 10
32-34, 45; 14 41: *also* 14
8; *and* 12 10; 14 27, 49]:
but woe
unto
that man through whom
the Son of man is be-
trayed! good were it
² for that man if he had
not been born.

22 For the Son of man
indeed goeth,   as it
hath been determined [*cp.*
9 22, 43-45; 13 32-33;
17 25; 18 31-34; 24 7,
44: *also* 20 17; 22 37; 24
25-27, 46]: but woe [*cp.*
17 1: *also* 11 42 *ff.*] unto
that man through whom
he   is be-
trayed!

23 And they
began to question among
themselves, which of
them it was that should
do this thing.

verse 18
cp. 2 19, 22; 3 14; 12 32,
33: *also* 5 39; 15 25
17 12.

verse 22

verse 19

25 And

Judas,
which betrayed him,
answered and said, Is it
I, Rabbi [*cp.* 26 49: *also*
23 7, 8]? He saith unto
him, Thou hast said [*cp.*
26 64: *also* 27 11].

verse 22

So when
he had dipped the sop, he
taketh and giveth it to
Judas, *the son* of Simon
Iscariot.

cp. 9 5; 11 21; 14 45:
also 10 51.
cp. 15 2.

cp. 23 3: *also* 22 70.

cp. 1 38, 49; *etc.*: *also*
20 16.
cp. 18 37.

27 And
after the sop, then entered
Satan into him. Jesus
therefore saith unto him,

cp. 22 3.

¹ Many authorities, some
ancient, omit *disciples*.
² Gr. *for him if that man*.

¹ Gr. *reclined*.
² Gr. *for him if that man*.

That thou doest, do quickly. **28** Now no man at the table knew for what intent he spake this unto him. **29** For some thought, because Judas had the ⁴ bag, that Jesus said unto him, Buy what things we have need of for the feast; or, that he should give something to the poor. **30** He then having received the sop went out straightway: and it was night.

¹ Or, *chose*   ³ Many ancient authorities read *his bread with me*.
³ Or, *I am*   ⁴ Or, *box*

§ 232. **Rivalry among the Disciples and Sayings of Rebuke: the Necessity and Rewards of Service: the Prophecy of Peter's Denial** (Luke)

[*Cp.* Matt. 18 1-5: Mark 9 33-37: Luke 9 46-48]
[*Cp.* Matt. 10 16-42; 16 24-28: Mark 8 34-9 1; 13 9-13: Luke 9 23-27; 21 12-19:
John 12 26; 14 2-3; 15 18-21; 16 2-3, 33]

Matt. 20 24-28; 23 11; 19 27-29; 26 33-35	Mark 10 41-45; 9 35; 10 28-30; 14 29-31	Luke 22 24-34
cp. 18 1.	*cp.* 9 33-34.	**24** And there arose also a contention among them [*cp.* 9 46], which of them is accounted to be ¹ greatest.

20 24 And when the ten heard it, they were moved with indignation concerning the two brethren. 25 But Jesus called them unto him, and said, Ye know that the rulers of the Gentiles lord it over them, and their great ones exercise authority over them.

26 Not so shall it be among you : but whosoever would become great among you shall be your [1] minister ; 27 and whosoever would be first among you shall be your [2] servant :

23 11 But he that is [3] greatest among you shall be your [4] servant.

20 28 even as the Son of man came [cp. 18 11] not to be ministered unto, but to minister, and to give his life a ransom for many [cp. 26 28]. 19 27 Then answered Peter [cp. 14 28 ; 15 15 ; 16 22 ; 17 4 ; 18 21 ; 26 33 : also 16 16 ; 17 24] and said unto him, Lo, we have left all, and followed thee [cp. 4 20, 22 ; 9 9] ; what then shall we have ? 28 And Jesus said unto them, Verily I say unto you, that ye which have followed me, in the regeneration when the Son of man shall sit on the throne of his glory [cp. 25 31 : also 16 27],

cp. 8 11 ; 26 29.

[cp. 16 28 ; 20 21] ye also shall sit upon twelve thrones, judging the twelve tribes of Israel. 29 And every one that hath left houses, or brethren, or sisters, or father, or mother, [5] or children [cp. 10 37], or lands, for my name's sake [cp. 10 22 ; 24 9 : also 5 11 ; 10 18, 39 ; 16 25],

cp. 4 23 ; 9 35 ; 24 14 ; 26 13.

shall

---

10 41 And when the ten heard it, they began to be moved with indignation concerning James and John. 42 And Jesus called them to him, and saith unto them, Ye know that they which are accounted to rule over the Gentiles lord it over them ; and their great ones exercise authority over them.

43 But it is not so among you : but whosoever would become great among you, shall be your [1] minister : 44 and whosoever would be first among you, shall be [2] servant of all.

9 35 If any man would be first, he shall be last of all, and minister of all.

10 45 For verily the Son of man came not to be ministered unto, but to minister, and to give his life a ransom for many [cp. 14 24]. 10 28 Peter [cp. 8 32 ; 9 5 ; 11 21 ; 14 29 : also 8 29] began to say unto him, Lo, we have left all, and have followed thee [cp. 1 18, 20 ; 2 14].

29 Jesus said, Verily I say unto you,

cp. 10 37 : also 8 38.

cp. 14 25.

There is no man that hath left house, or brethren, or sisters, or mother, or father, or children, or lands, for my sake [cp. 8 35 ; 13 9 : also 13 13], and for the gospel's sake [cp. 8 35 : also 1 1, 14, 15 ; 13 10 ; 14 9 ; 16 15],

30 but he shall

---

25 And he said unto them,

The kings of the Gentiles have lordship over them ; and they that have authority over them are called Benefactors. 26 But ye shall not be so : but he that is the greater among you, let him become as the younger ; and he that is chief, as he that doth serve.

9 48 For he that is [2] least among you all, the same is great.

27 For whether is greater, he that [3] sitteth at meat, or he that serveth ? is not he that [3] sitteth at meat [cp. 17 7, 8] ? but I am in the midst [cp. 9 55 ; 19 10]

of you as he that serveth [cp. 12 37].

18 28 And Peter [cp 8 45 ; 9 33 ; 12 41 : also 5 8 ; 9 20] said, Lo, we have left [cp. 5 11, 28 ; 14 33] [4] our own, and followed thee [cp. 5 11, 28].

29 And he said unto them, Verily I say unto you,

28 But ye are they which have continued with me in my temptations [cp. 4 13 ; 8 13] ;

[cp. 9 26, 32 ; 24 26] 29 and [5] I appoint unto you a kingdom, even as my Father appointed unto me, 30 that ye may eat and drink at my table [cp. 13 29 ; 14 15 ; 22 16, 18] in my kingdom [cp. 23 42] ; and ye shall sit on thrones judging the twelve tribes of Israel.

There is no man that hath left house, or wife [cp. 14 26], or brethren, or parents, or children [cp. 14 26],

cp. 6 22 ; 9 24 ; 21 12, 17.

for the kingdom of God's sake, 30 who shall not

---

cp. John 13 2-17

cp. 10 11, 15, 17 ; 11 51, 52.

cp. 13 36, 37 ; 21 21 : also 6 68.

cp. 1 14 ; 2 11 ; 12 41 ; 17 5, 22, 24.

cp. John 13 36-1

cp. 18 36.

cp. 15 21.

receive [6] a hundredfold [cp. 13 8, 23: and 6 33],

cp. 13 21.
and
[cp. 12 32] shall inherit eternal life [cp. 19 16: also 25 46].

Matt. 26 33 But Peter [cp. 14 28; 15 15; 16 22; 17 4; 18 21; 19 27: also 16 16; 17 24] answered and said unto him,
If all shall be [7] offended in thee,   I will never be [7] offended.

cp. 16 17; 17 25.

cp. 8 26; 14 31; 16 8; 17 20; 21 21; 28 17.

cp. 16 18-19.

verse 35
34 Jesus said unto him,
Verily I say unto thee, that this night, before the cock   crow, thou shalt deny
cp. 26 70, 72, 74.
me thrice [cp. 26 75].
35 Peter saith unto him,
Even if I must die with thee, yet will I not deny thee.
Likewise also said   all the disciples.

[1] Or, servant   [2] Gr. bondservant.
[3] Gr. greater.   [4] Or, minister
[5] Many ancient authorities add or wife: as in Luke 18 29.
[6] Some ancient authorities read manifold.
[7] Gr. caused to stumble.

---

receive a hundredfold [cp. 4 8, 20, and 24]
now in this time, houses, and brethren, and sisters, and mothers, and children, and lands, with persecutions [cp. 4 17]; and in the [3] world to come   eternal life [cp. 10 17].

Mark 14 29 But Peter [cp. 8 32; 9 5; 10 28; 11 21: also 8 29]

said unto him,
Although all shall be [4] offended, yet will not I.

cp. 14 37.

cp. 4 40; 11 22; 16 11, 13, 14.

verse 31
30 And Jesus saith unto him,
Verily I say unto thee, that thou to-day, even this night, before the cock   crow twice [cp. 14 68, 72], shalt deny
cp. 14 68, 71.
me thrice [cp. 14 72].
31 But he spake exceeding vehemently,   If I must die with thee, I will not deny thee. And in like manner also said they all.

[1] Or, servant
[2] Gr. bondservant.
[3] Or, age
[4] Gr. caused to stumble.

---

receive   [cp. 8 8] manifold more [cp. 12 31] in this time,

and in the [6] world to come   eternal life [cp. 18 18: also 10 25].

cp. 8 45; 9 33; 12 41; 18 28: also 5 8; 9 20.

31 Simon, Simon, behold, Satan [cp. 22 3] [7] asked to have you, that he might sift you as wheat: 32 but I made supplication for thee, that thy faith [cp. 8 25; 12 28; 17 5, 6: also 24 11, 12, 38, 41: and 24 25] fail not: and do thou, when once thou hast   turned   again, stablish thy brethren. 33 And he said unto him, Lord, with thee I am ready to go both to prison and to death. 34 And he said,

I tell   thee, Peter,

the cock shall not crow this day, until thou shalt thrice deny that thou knowest [cp. 22 57, 60] me [cp. 22 61].

verse 33

[1] Gr. greater.
[2] Gr. lesser.   [3] Gr. reclineth.
[4] Or, our own homes
[5] Or, I appoint unto you, even as my Father appointed unto me a kingdom, that ye may eat and drink &c.
[6] Or, age
[7] Or, obtained you by asking

John 13 36 Simon Peter [cp. 21 21: also 6 68]

saith unto him, Lord, whither goest thou?

Jesus answered, Whither I go, thou canst not follow me now; but thou shalt follow afterwards [cp. 21 18-19].
cp. 1 42; 21 15, 16, 17.

cp. 3 12; 6 64; 14 10 20 25, 27.

cp. 21 15-17.
37 Peter saith unto him, Lord, why cannot I follow thee even now? I will lay down   my life for thee.
38 Jesus answereth, Wilt thou lay down thy life for me? Verily, verily, I say unto thee,

The cock shall not crow,

till thou hast denied

me thrice [cp. 18 27].

verse 37

cp. 3 15; etc.

Matt. 20 28 ‖ Mark 10 45: cp. Is. 52 15; 53 4-6, 8, 11, 12.

§ 233. Reflection on the Designs of Providence

Luke 22 35-38

cp. 10 10.		
cp. 19 21.	cp. 10 21.	
cp. 21 42; 26 24, 31, 54, 56.	cp. 9 12; 12 10; 14 21, 27, 49.	
cp. 26 51.	cp. 14 47.	

35 And he said unto them, When I sent you forth without purse, and wallet, and shoes [cp. 10 4], lacked ye anything? And they said, Nothing. **36** And he said unto them, But now, he that hath a purse, let him take it, and likewise a wallet: [1] and he that hath none, let him sell [cp. 12 33; 18 22] his cloke, and buy a sword. **37** For I say unto you, that this which is written must be fulfilled [cp. 18 31; 20 17; 24 25-27, 44-46: also 12 50; and 13 32] in me, And he was reckoned with transgressors: for that which concerneth me hath [2] fulfilment. **38** And they said, Lord, behold, here are two swords [cp. 22 49, 50: John 18 10]. And he said unto them, It is enough.

cp. 5 39; 13 18; 15 25; 17 12: also 4 34; 5 36; 17 4; 19 28, 30.

[1] Or, and he that hath no sword, let him sell his cloke, and buy one.
[2] Gr. end.

Luke 22 37 = Is. 53 12.

§ 234. The Concluding Hymn and Departure to the Mount of Olives

Matt. 26 30	Mark 14 26	Luke 22 39	John 18 1
30 And when they had sung a hymn, they went out [cp. 21 17] unto the mount of Olives [cp. 24 3].	**26** And when they had sung a hymn, they went out [cp. 11 11, 19] unto the mount of Olives [cp. 13 3].	**39** And he came out, and went, [cp. 21 37] as his custom was [cp. 21 37: also 4 16; and 1 9; 2 42], unto the mount of Olives [cp. 21 37]; and the disciples also followed him.	1 When Jesus had spoken these words, he went forth cp. 18 2. cp. 8 1. with his disciples over the [1] brook [2] Kidron.

[1] Or, ravine Gr. winter-torrent.
[2] Or, of the Cedars

(iii) On the Way to Gethsemane (§ 235)

§ 235. Prophecies of the Flight of the Disciples, of the Resurrection, and of Peter's Denial
(Matt. and Mark)

Matt. 26 31-35	Mark 14 27-31	Luke 22 31-34	John 16 32; 13 36-38
31 Then saith Jesus unto them, All ye shall be [1] offended [cp. 11 6; 13 57; 15 12: also 13 21; 24 10] in me this night [cp. verse 34]: for it is written [cp. 21 42; 26 24, 54, 56], I will smite the shepherd, and the sheep [cp. 9 36; 10 6; 15 24] of the flock shall be scattered abroad [cp. 26 56].	**27** And Jesus saith unto them, All ye shall be [1] offended [cp. 6 3: also 4 17]: for it is written [cp. 9 12; 12 10; 14 21, 49], I will smite the shepherd, and the sheep [cp. 6 34] shall be scattered abroad [cp. 14 50].	cp. 7 23. cp. 18 31; 20 17; 22 37; 24 25-27, 44-46.	16 **32** Behold, the hour cometh, yea, is come, cp. 6 61: also 16 1. cp. 5 39; 13 18; 15 25; 17 12. cp. 10 11-16. that ye shall be scattered, every man to his own, and shall leave me alone [cp. 8 16, 29]. cp. 2 19-22.
32 But after I am raised up [cp. 16 21; 17 9, 23; 20 19], I will go before you into Galilee [cp. 28 7]. **33** But Peter [cp. 14 28; 15 15; 16 22; 17 4; 18 21; 19 27: also 16 16; 17 24] answered and said unto him,	**28** Howbeit, after I am raised up [cp. 8 31; 9 9, 31; 10 34], I will go before you into Galilee [cp. 16 7]. **29** But Peter [cp. 8 32; 9 5; 10 28; 11 21: also 8 29] said unto him,	cp. 9 22; 13 32; 18 33; 24 7, 26, 46. cp. 8 45; 9 33; 12 41; 18 28: also 5 8; 9 20.	13 **36** Simon Peter [cp. 21 21: also 6 68] saith unto him, Lord, whither goest

Matt.	Mark	Luke	John
If all shall be ¹ offended in thee, I will never be ¹ offended.	Although all shall be ¹ offended, yet will not I.		thou ?

Jesus answered, Whither I go, thou canst not follow me now ; but thou shalt follow afterwards [cp. 21 18-19].

| cp. 16 17; 17 25. | cp. 14 37. | 31 Simon, Simon, behold, Satan [cp. 22 3] ¹asked to have you, that he might sift you as wheat : 32 but I made supplication for thee, that thy faith [cp. 8 25 ; 12 28 ; 17 5, 6 : also 24 11, 12, 38, 41 : and 24 25] fail not : and do thou, when once thou hast turned again, stablish thy brethren. 33 And he said unto him, Lord, | cp. 1 42; 21 15, 16, 17. |

| cp. 8 26; 14 31; 16 8; 17 20; 21 21; 28 17. | cp. 4 40; 11 22; 16 11, 13, 14. | | cp. 3 12; 6 64; 14 10; 20 25, 27. |

(Luke column continued:)
with thee I am ready to go both to prison and to death. 34 And he said,

cp. 21 15-17.
37 Peter saith unto him, Lord, why cannot I follow thee even now ? I will lay down my life for thee. 38 Jesus answereth,

| cp. 16 18-19. | | | |

verse 35	*verse* 31		
34 Jesus said unto him,	30 And Jesus saith unto him,		Wilt thou lay down thy life for me ? Verily, verily, I say unto thee,
Verily I say unto thee, that this night, before the cock crow, thou shalt deny	Verily I say unto thee, that thou to-day, *even* this night, before the cock crow twice [cp. 14 68, 72], shalt deny	I tell thee, Peter, the cock shall not crow this day, until thou shalt thrice deny that thou knowest [cp. 22 57, 60]	The cock shall not crow, till thou hast denied
cp. 26 70, 72, 74. me thrice [cp. 26 75].	cp. 14 68, 71. me thrice [cp. 14 72].	me [cp. 22 61].	me thrice [cp. 18 27].
35 Peter saith unto him, Even if I must die with thee, *yet* will I not deny thee. Likewise also said all the disciples.	31 But he spake exceedingly vehemently, If I must die with thee, I will not deny thee. And in like manner also said they all.	*verse* 33	*verse* 37

¹ Gr. *caused to stumble.*   ¹ Gr. *caused to stumble.*   ¹ Or, *obtained you by asking*

Matt. 26 31 ‖ Mark 14 27 = Zech. 13 7.

(iv) In Gethsemane (§§ 236-238)

§ 236. **The Agony**

Matt. 26 36-46	Mark 14 32-42	Luke 22 40-46	John 18 1; 12 27; 14 31
cp. 26 30.	cp. 14 26.	cp. 22 39.	18 1 When Jesus had spoken these words, he went forth with his disciples over the ¹ brook ² Kidron, where was a garden, into the which he entered, himself and his disciples.
36 Then cometh Jesus with them unto ¹ a place called Gethsemane, and saith unto his disciples, Sit ye here, while I go yonder and pray.	32 And they come unto ¹a place which was named Gethsemane : and he saith unto his disciples, Sit ye here, while I pray.	40 And when he was at the place, he said unto them, Pray that ye enter not into temptation [cp. *verse* 46].	cp. 18 2.
37 And he took with him Peter and the two sons of Zebedee [cp. 17 1],	33 And he taketh with him Peter and James and John [cp. 1 29; 5 37;	cp. 8 51; 9 28.	

and began to be sorrowful [*cp. verse* 38: *also* 17 23; 18 31; 26 22] and sore troubled. **38** Then saith he unto them, My soul is exceeding sorrowful, even unto death: abide ye here, and watch [*cp.* 24 42; 25 13; 26 41] with me.	9 2; 13 3], and began to be greatly amazed, and sore troubled. **34** And he saith unto them, My soul is exceeding sorrowful even unto death: abide ye here, and watch [*cp.* 13 33, 35, 37; 14 38].		**12 27** Now is my sou troubled;
39 And he went forward a little, and fell on his face, and prayed [*cp.* 14 23; 19 13; 26 36, 42, 44: *also* 11 25],	**35** And he went forward a little, and fell on the ground, and prayed [*cp.* 1 35; 6 46; 14 32, 39]	*cp.* 12 37; 21 36. **41** And he was parted from them about a stone's cast; and he kneeled down and prayed [*cp.* 3 21; 5 16; 6 12; 9 18, 28, 29; 11 1; 22 44: *also* 10 21],	and what shall I say ? *cp.* 11 41; 12 27-28; 17 1-26.
	that, if it were possible,		Father [*cp.* 11 41; 12 28; 17 1, 5, 11, 21, 24, 25], save me from this ³ hour [*cp.* 12 23; 13 1; 17 1: *also* 2 4; 7 6, 8, 30; 8 20].
cp. 26 45: *also* 26 18.	the hour [*cp. verse* 41] might pass away from him.	*cp.* 22 14, 53.	But for this cause, came I unto this hour.
saying, O my Father [*cp. verse* 42 *and* 11 25, 26: *also* 6 9], if it be possible, *cp.* 19 26. let this cup [*cp.* 20 22, 23] pass away from me: nevertheless, not as I will, but as thou wilt [*cp. verse* 42 *and* 6 10: *also* 7 21; 12 50; 21 31].	**36** And he said, Abba, Father, all things are possible unto thee [*cp.* 10 27]; remove this cup [*cp.* 10 38, 39] from me: howbeit not what I will, but what thou wilt [*cp.* 3 35].	**42** saying, Father [*cp.* 10 21, 22; 23 34, 46: *also* 11 2], if thou be willing, *cp.* 1 37; 18 27. remove this cup from me: nevertheless not my will, but thine, be done.	*cp.* 18 11.
cp. 4 11; 26 53.	*cp.* 1 13.	**43** ¹ And there appeared unto him an angel from heaven, strengthening him. **44** And being in an agony he prayed more earnestly: and his sweat became as it were great drops of blood falling down upon the ground. **45** And when he rose up from his prayer, he came unto the disciples, and found them sleeping [*cp.* 9 32] for sorrow, **46** and said unto them, [*cp.* 22 31] Why sleep ye?	*cp.* 4 34; 5 30; 6 38; 7 17; 9 31. *cp.* 1 51; 12 29.
40 And he cometh unto the disciples, and findeth them sleeping [*cp. verse* 43: *also* 25 5], [*cp. verse* 38: *also* 17 23; 26 22] and saith unto Peter, *cp.* 16 17; 17 25. What, could ye not watch with me one hour? **41** ² Watch [*cp. verse* 38] and pray, that ye enter not into temptation [*cp.* 6 13]: the spirit indeed is willing, but the flesh is weak. **42** Again a second time he went away, and prayed, saying [*verse* 44], O my Father [*cp. verse* 39], if this cannot pass away, except I drink it, thy will be done [*cp. verse* 39]. **43** And he	**37** And he cometh, and findeth them sleeping [*cp. verse* 40: *also* 13 36], [*cp. verse* 34: *also* 14 19] and saith unto Peter, Simon, sleepest thou? couldest thou not watch one hour? **38** ² Watch [*cp. verse* 34] and pray [*cp.* 13 33], that ye enter not into temptation: the spirit indeed is willing, but the flesh is weak. **39** And again he went away, and prayed, saying the same words.	*cp.* 12 37; 21 36. rise and pray [*cp.* 21 36], that ye enter not into temptation [*cp. verse* 40 *and* 11 4].	*cp.* 16 6, 20, 22. *cp.* 1 42; 21 15, 16, 17.
43 And he	**40** And again he	*cp. verse* 42.	

Matt.	Mark	Luke	John
came again and found them sleeping [*cp. verse* 40], for their eyes were heavy.	came, and found them sleeping [*cp. verse* 37], for their eyes were very heavy; and they wist not what to answer him [*cp.* 9 6]. **41** And he	*cp. verse* 45.	
		cp. 9 32.	
44 And he left them again, and went away, and prayed a third time, saying again the same words. **45** Then cometh	*verse* 39	*cp.* 9 33.	
he to the disciples, and saith unto them, Sleep on now, and take your rest: behold, the hour [*cp.* 26 18] is at hand, and the Son of man is betrayed into the hands of sinners [*cp.* 17 22-23; 20 18-19; 26 2: *also* 16 21; 17 12; 26 24]. **46** Arise, let us be going: behold, he is at hand that betrayeth me.	cometh the third time, and saith unto them, Sleep on now, and take your rest: it is enough; the hour [*cp. verse* 35] is come; behold, the Son of man is betrayed into the hands of sinners [*cp.* 9 31; 10 33: *also* 8 31; 9 12; 14 21]. **42** Arise, let us be going: behold, he that betrayeth me is at hand.	*cp.* 22 14, 53. *cp.* 9 44; 18 31-33; 24 7; *also* 9 22; 13 32-33; 17 25; 22 22.	*cp.* 12 23, 27; 13 1; 17 1: *also* 2 4; 7 6, 8, 30; 8 20. **14** **31** Arise, let us go hence.

§ 237. The Arrest

Matt. 26 47-56	Mark 14 43-50	Luke 22 47-53	John 18 2-11, 20
cp. 26 36.	*cp.* 14 32.	*cp.* 22 40.	**2** Now Judas also, which betrayed him, knew the place: for Jesus oft-times resorted thither with his disciples.
47 And while he yet spake [*cp.* 12 46; 17 5], lo,	**43** And straightway, while he yet spake [*cp.* 5 35], cometh	**47** While he yet spake [*cp.* 8 49; 22 60], behold, a multitude, and he that was called Judas, one of the twelve, went before them;	**3** Judas then,
Judas, one of the twelve, came, and with him a great multitude with swords and staves, from the chief priests and elders of the people.	Judas, one of the twelve, and with him a multitude with swords and staves, from the chief priests and the scribes and the elders.	*verse* 52	having received the ¹ band *of soldiers,* and officers from the chief priests and the Pharisees, cometh thither with lanterns and torches and weapons. **4** Jesus therefore, knowing all the things that were coming upon him, went forth, and saith unto them, Whom seek ye? **5** They answered him, Jesus of Nazareth [*cp. verse* 7: *also* 1 45; 19 19]. Jesus saith unto them, I am *he.* And Judas also, which betrayed him, was standing with them.
cp. 2 23; 26 71: *also* 21 11.	*cp.* 1 24; 10 47; 14 67; 16 6.	*cp.* 4 34; 18 37; 24 19.	
48 Now he that betrayed him	**44** Now *he* that betrayed him		
gave them a sign, saying, Whomsoever I shall kiss, that is he: take him. **49** And	had given them a token, saying, Whomsoever I shall kiss, that is he; take him, and lead him away safely. **45** And when he was come,	and	
straightway he came to Jesus, and said, Hail	straightway he came to him, and saith,	he drew near unto Jesus	

[*cp.* 27 29; 28 9], Rabbi; and ¹ kissed him. **50** And Jesus said unto him,	[*cp.* 15 18] **Rabbi**; and ¹ kissed him.	*cp.* 1 28. to kiss him. **48** But Jesus said unto him, Judas, betrayest thou the Son of man with a kiss?	*cp.* 19 3.
Friend [*cp.* 20 13; 22 12], *do* that for which thou art come.			*cp.* 13 27. 6 When therefore he said unto them, I am *he*, they went backward, and fell to the ground. 7 Again therefore he asked them, Whom seek ye? And they said, Jesus of Nazareth [*cp. verse* 5]. 8 Jesus answered, I told you that I am *he*: if therefore ye seek me, let these go their way: 9 that the word might be fulfilled which he spake, Of those whom thou hast given me I lost not one.
		49 And when they that were about him saw what would follow, they said, Lord, shall we smite with the sword?	
Then they came and laid hands on Jesus, and took him. **51** And behold, one of them that were with [*cp.* 16 28; 27 47: *also* 26 73] Jesus	**46** And they laid hands on him, and took him. **47** But a certain one of them that stood by [*cp.* 9 1; 11 5; 15 35: *also* 14 69, 70; 15 39]	**50** And a certain one of them *cp.* 9 27: *also* 19 24.	10 Simon Peter therefore *cp.* 12 29.
stretched out his hand, and drew his sword, and smote the ² servant of the high priest, and struck off his [*cp.* 5 29, 30, 39; 27 29] ear.	drew his sword, and smote the ² servant of the high priest, and struck off his ear.	*cp.* 22 36, 38. smote the ¹ servant of the high priest, and struck off his right [*cp.* 6 6] ear.	having a sword drew it, and struck the high priest's ²servant, and cut off his right ear. Now the ² servant's name was Malchus.
52 Then saith Jesus unto him,	**48** And Jesus answered	**51** But Jesus answered and said, Suffer ye thus far. And he	11 Jesus therefore said unto Peter,
cp. 8 3, 15; 9 18, 25, 29; 14 31; 17 7; 19 13, 15; 20 34: *also* 9 20; 14 36.	*cp.* 1 31, 41; 5 23, 41; 6 2, 5; 7 33; 8 22, 23, 25; 9 27; 10 13, 16: *also* 3 10; 5 27; 6 56.	touched [*cp.* 4 40; 5 13; 7 14; 8 54; 13 13; 14 4; 18 15: *also* 6 19; 7 39; 8 44] his ear, and healed [*cp.* 6 19; 9 2, 11, 42; 14 4] him.	*cp.* 9 6: *also* 20 17.
Put up again thy sword into its place: *cp.* 26 39: *also* 20 22, 23.	*cp.* 14 36: *also* 10 38, 39.	*cp.* 22 42.	Put up the sword into the sheath: the cup which the Father hath given me, shall I not drink it?
for all they that take the sword shall perish with the sword. **53** Or thinkest thou that I cannot beseech my Father, and he shall even now send me more than twelve legions of angels [*cp.* 4 11]? **54** How then should the scriptures be fulfilled. that thus it must be [*cp. verse* 56]? **55** In that hour [*cp.* 18 1] said Jesus to the multitudes,	*cp.* 1 13. and said unto them,	*cp.* 22 43. **52** And *cp.* 7 21; 10 21; 13 31. Jesus said unto the chief priests, and captains [*cp.* 22 4] of the temple, and elders, which were come against him, Are ye come out, as against a	*cp.* 1 51; 12 29. 20 Jesus answered him,
verse 47 Are ye come out as against a robber with swords and	*verse* 43 Are ye come out, as against a robber, with swords and	robber, with swords and	*verse* 3

act opposite and await a full study of
the future of the electric bus.

"They are simply defying council," said Councillor Lois Griffin (Rexdale Mistletown), a commission member who voted against the trolleys' return.

Colle told Leach yesterday that an earlier 4-3 decision of the commission stands and he should continue hiring staff and inspect the overhead wires needed to bring back the buses on the y St. and Annette St. routes.

"He's the boss. They'll be back on the road by Sept. 9, unless I hear different," Leach said yesterday.

Colle said he respects the council request but can't abide by it — just yet. He's had word from the transportation ministry that it will give the TTC the 85,000 needed to fund the trolleys' return for the last four months this year. If he gets the money, Colle said, then council can forget the matter.

Several councillors disagree.

"If they keep going along this track, we'll have four new commissioners at the TTC in October," said Councillor Scott Cavalier (Scarborough Agincourt) referring to a plan to remove the four pro-trolley councillors from the TTC.

The four — Howard Moscoe, Bev Salmon, Paul Christie and Colle — have been dubbed the "Trolley Jolleys."

Metro solicitor Ossie Doyle has told council its only control over the TTC is appointing or recalling councillors from the commission. Also, while Metro pays about $113 million of the TTC's 35 million budget (69 per cent comes from the farebox), it cannot legally tell the TTC where to spend it.

During this year's tough budget debate, council directed all boards and commissions and departments not to bring in any new programs, or even move money around from one budgeted program to another without approval from council's budget committee.

Council and the commission specifically cut out the trolley service for a year to save $2 million.

The TTC's trolley fleet numbered 120 on nine routes.

The Star's view/A20

---

tional coalition — like that which drove Iraqi forces from Kuwait last year — to come to the aid of the Bosnian government, diplomats said.

Nor was there a response to Bosnian pleas for the council to authorize arms sales or shipments so the government of the newly independent former Yugoslav republic can defend itself.

"This resolution does not prescribe the use of force, it merely authorizes it as a last resort," British Ambassador David Hannay said. "It is very important we try every means possible to get supply through without the use of force."

Bosnian U.N. representative Muhamed Sacirbey told reporters the resolutions "address some of the symptoms — but not the basic problem at all.

"We have become the modern world's Warsaw Ghetto of 50 years ago, abandoned by many, deprived, but together . . . resisting a fascist philosophy of an ethnically cleansed, morally soiled Greater Serbia," Sacirbey said.

U.S. pol
to sham

By Linda I
TORONTO

WASHINGTON
administration is
few months, to en
Minister Brian Mul
North American
Agreement.

Nobody, least of
President George I
do it to Mulroney a
vative government
has a choice.

It's politics.

The problem wil
critical issue: Wh
government do for
lose their jobs be
trade with Mexico.

Because of the

UV RISK high 7.4 low

METRO WEATHER
Cloudy, shower, cool
High 19°C
Details — A25

SCOREBOARD

BASEBALL
Jays 4 Orioles 2
Toronto up by 2

FOOTBALL
Bombers 32 Argos 17

Bones may be of man who held Jesus's trial

By David Briggs
ASSOCIATED PRESS

JERUSALEM (AP) — The bones of a first-century man named Caiaphas have been discovered in an ancient burial cave in Jerusalem, and archaeological evidence indicates they may be the remains of the high priest who tried Jesus.

The age of the bones, the elaborateness of the ossuary in which they were found and the inscriptions with the name Caiaphas found on the side of the casket-like box point to the man described in the Gospels, although the Israeli archaeologists who found them say they cannot make a positive identification.

The finding, to be reported in a coming issue of *Biblical Archaeology Review* is particularly striking since it represents the first archaeological evidence of the remains of any major figure in the New Testament, Ronny Reich, of the Israeli antiquities authority, said in an interview yesterday.

Reich said it's also one of only a few figures from the late Second Temple period.

"Now, to that small list, we may add in all probability the high priest who presided at Jesus' trial," Reich writes in the magazine's September-October issue.

Archaeologists happened on the bones in November, 1990, during the building of a water park in Peace Forest, on the outskirts of Jerusalem.

The burial cave's roof had collapsed, and archaeologists discovered 12 ossuaries, or boxes, usually made of limestone, in which the bones of the dead were stored, said Zvi Greenhut, Jerusalem's city archaeologist.

In the late Second Temple period (1st century B.C. to 1st century A.D.), bodies were often laid out in a niche of burial caves. After the flesh had decomposed, the bones were collected in an ossuary, apparently reflecting a belief in resurrection, Greenhut wrote.

On the outside of a particularly ornate ossuary — decorated in what Greenhut said was a rare, intricate pattern of rosettes — the inscription "Joseph, son of Caiaphas" was in two places. Inside were a 60-year-old man's bones.

A person named Joseph, nicknamed Caiaphas, was the high priest in Jerusalem from the years 18 to 36 A.D.

Reich said that the New Testament provides the nickname only in Greek form, but the first-century Jewish historian Flavius Josephus described him as "Joseph who was called Caiaphas of the high priesthood."

Further evidence that indicates the ossuary dates to the first-century century came with a bronze coin minted in the years 42 and 43 during the reign of Herod Agrippa I, found in another ossuary.

So, are the bones of the 60-year-old man those of Caiaphas, the high priest who is said in the Gospel of Matthew to have found Jesus guilty of blasphemy before handing him over to the Roman governor Pilate for execution?

"I have no answer for this question," Greenhut said in a telephone interview from his home.

The inscriptions and the age and the elaborateness of the ossuary all point to the bones being those of Caiaphas, but the bones were not identified as his and the relative simplicity of the burial cave also raises doubts, Greenhut said.

Reich also said he couldn't be positive it's Caiaphas, but it is the first time the name Caiaphas has been found on an inscription.

"This is a considerable step forward to one of the main figures of the Bible," he said.

After the archaeological study was made, Greenhut said, the bones were given over to the religious affairs ministry, which reburied them on the Mount of Olives.

staves to seize me ?	staves to seize me ?	staves ?　　　cp. 22 54.	cp. 18 12. I have spoken openly to the world ; I ever taught
I sat daily	**49** I was daily with you	**53** When I was daily with you	
in the temple [cp. 21 23]	in the temple [cp. 12 35]	in the temple [cp. 19 47; 20 1; 21 37],	in ³ synagogues, and in the temple [cp. 7 28 ; 8 20], where all the Jews come together ; and in secret spake I nothing.
teach-ing, and ye took me not.	teach-ing, and ye took me not :	ye stretched not forth your hands against me : but　this is your hour [cp. 22 14], and the power of dark-ness.	
56 But all this is cp. 26 18, 45.	but　　　*this is* cp. 14 35, 41.	cp. 18 31; 20 17; 22 37; 24 25-27, 44-46.	cp. 12 23, 27 ; 13 1 ; 17 1 : also 2 4 ; 7 6, 8, 30 ; 8 20.
come to pass, that the scriptures of the pro-phets might be fulfilled [cp. *verse 54*: also 21 42; 26 24, 31]. Then all the disciples left him, and fled [cp. 26 31].	*done*　　　that the scriptures might be fulfilled [cp. 9 12; 12 10; 14 21, 27]. **50** And they all left him, and fled [cp. 14 27].		cp. 5 39 ; 13 18 ; 15 25 ; 17 12.
			cp. 16 32 : also 8 16, 29.
¹ Gr. *kissed him much.* ² Gr. *bondservant.*	¹ Gr. *kissed him much.* ² Gr. *bondservant.*	¹ Gr. *bondservant.*	¹ Or, *cohort*　² Gr. *bondservant.* ³ Gr. *synagogue.*

§ 238. The Young Man who escaped

Mark 14 51-52

51 And a certain young man followed with him, having a linen cloth cast about him, over *his* naked *body*: and they lay hold on him ; **52** but he left the linen cloth, and fled naked.

(v) The Trial (§§ 239-249)

§ 239. Jesus led to the High Priest's House

Matt. 26 57-58	Mark 14 53-54	Luke 22 54-55	John 18 12-13, 24, 15-16, 1
57 And they that had taken Jesus led him away	**53** And they cp. 14 48 *and* Matt. 26 55. led Jesus away	**54** And they　seized him, and led him *away*,	**12** So the ¹ band and the ² chief captain, and the officers of the Jews, seized Jesus and bound him, **13** and led him to Annas first ; for he was father in law to Caiaphas, which was high priest that year. . . . **24** Annas there-fore sent him bound unto Caiaphas [cp. 11 49] the high priest. . . .
to *the house of* Caiaphas [cp. 26 3] the high priest, where	to the high priest: and there come together with him all the chief priests and the elders and the scribes.	cp. 3 2. and brought him into cp. 3 2. the high priest's house.	
the scribes and the elders were gathered to-gether [cp. 26 3]. **58** But Peter followed him afar off,	**54** And Peter had followed him afar off,	cp. 22 66. But Peter followed afar off.	**15** And Simon Peter followed Jesus, and *so did* another disciple. Now that disciple was known unto the high priest, and entered in with Jesus into the court of the high priest ; **16** but Peter was standing at the door with-out. So the other disciple, which was known unto the high priest, went out and spake unto her that kept
unto the court [cp. 26 3, 69] of the high priest,			

and entered in,

and sat with the officers,

to see the end.

even within, into the court [cp. 14 66: *also* 15 16] of the high priest;

and he was sitting with the officers, and warming himself [cp. 14 67] in the light *of the fire.*

55 And when they had kindled a fire in the midst of the court, and had sat down together, Peter sat in the midst of them.

cp. 22 56.

the door, and brought in Peter ....
18 Now the [3] servants and the officers were standing *there,* having made [4] a fire of coals; for it was cold; and they were warming themselves: and Peter also was with them, standing and warming himself [cp. 18 25].

[1] Or, *cohort*
[2] Or, *military tribune* Gr. *chiliarch.*
[3] Gr. *bondservants.*
[4] Gr. *a fire of charcoal.*

§ 240. Peter's Denial (Luke)

Matt. 26 69-75	Mark 14 66-72	Luke 22 56-62	John 18 17, 25-27
69 Now Peter was sitting without in the court [cp. 26 58]: and a maid	**66** And as Peter was beneath in the court [cp. 14 54], there cometh one of the maids of the high priest;	cp. 22 55. **56** And a certain maid	cp. 18 15. **17** The maid therefore that kept the door
came unto him, saying, Thou also wast with cp. verse 71. Jesus the Galilæan.	**67** and seeing Peter cp. 14 54. warming himself [cp. 14 54], she looked upon him, and saith, Thou also wast with the Nazarene [cp. 1 24; 10 47; 16 6], *even* Jesus. cp. verse 70.	seeing him as he sat in the light *of the fire,* and looking stedfastly upon him, said, This man also was with him. [cp. 4 34; 18 37; 24 19] cp. verse 59.	cp. 18 18, 25. saith un to Peter Art thou also *one* of cp. 18 5, 7; 19 19: *also* 1 45. this man's disciples? He saith,
70 But he denied before them all, saying, I know not what thou sayest. **71** And when he was gone out into the porch,	**68** But he denied, saying, [1] I neither know, nor understand what thou sayest: and he went out into the [2] porch; [3] and the cock crew, **69** And	**57** But he denied, saying, Woman, I know him not.	I am not.
another *maid* saw him, and saith unto them that were there, This man also was with Jesus the Nazarene [cp. 2 23: *also* 21 11]. **72** And again he denied with an oath, I know not the man. **73** And after a little while	cp. 14 54, 67. the maid saw him, and began again to say to them that stood by [cp. verse 70], This is *one* of them. cp. verse 67. **70** But he again denied it.	**58** And after a little while another saw him, and said, Thou also art *one* of them. cp. 4 34; 18 37; 24 19. But Peter said, Man, I am not. **59** And after the space of about one hour	**25** Now Simon Peter was standing and warming himself [cp. 18 18] They said therefore unto him, Art thou also *one* of his disciples? cp. 18 5, 7; 19 19: *also* 1 45. He denied, and said, I am not.
they that stood by [cp. 16 28; 27 47]	And after a little while again they that stood by [cp. 9 1; 11 5; 14 47, 69; 15 35, 39]	cp. 9 27; 19 24.	cp. 12 29. **26** One of the [1] servants of the high priest, being a kinsman of him whose ear Peter cut off,
came and said to Peter, Of a truth thou also art	said to Peter, Of a truth thou art	another confidently affirmed, saying, Of a truth this man also was with him:	saith,

Matt.

one of them ;
[*cp. verse* 69] for thy speech
bewrayeth thee.

74 Then
began he to curse
and to swear,   I
know not the man.
                        And
straightway
    cp. 12 46 ; 17 5 ; 26 47.
                        the
cock crew.

cp. 9 22 ; 16 23.

75 And
Peter remembered
    the word
    which Jesus had said,
            Before the
cock crow,
            thou shalt
deny me thrice [*cp.* 26
34]. And
            he went
out, and wept bitterly.

Mark.

one of them; for thou art
a Galilæan.

71 But he
began   to curse,
and to swear,   I
know not this man of
whom ye speak. **72** And
straightway
    cp. 5 35 ; 14 43.
the second   time   the
cock crew.
    cp. 16 19, 20.

cp. 5 30 ; 8 33.

                        And
Peter called to mind
    the word,
    how that Jesus said
unto him, Before the
cock crow   twice
[*cp.* 14 68, 72], thou shalt
deny me thrice [*cp.* 14
30]. ⁴And when he
thought thereon, he
wept.

¹ Or, *I neither know, nor understand:
thou, what sayest thou ?*
² Gr. *forecourt.*
³ Many ancient authorities omit
and the cock crew.
⁴ Or, *And he began to weep.*

Luke.

                        for he is
a Galilæan.

60 But Peter
    said, Man, I
know not
what thou sayest. And
immediately, while he yet
spake [*cp.* 8 49 ; 22 47],
            the
cock crew. **61** And the
Lord [*cp.* 7 13, 19 ; 10
1, 39, 41 ; 11 39 ; 12 42 ;
13 15 ; 17 5, 6 ; 18 6 ;
19 8 ; 24 3, 34] turned
[*cp.* 7 9, 44 ; 9 55 ; 10
23 ; 14 25 ; 23 28], and
looked upon Peter. And
Peter remembered [*cp.*
24 6, 8] the word of the
Lord, how that he said
unto him, Before the
cock crow this day,
            thou shalt
deny me thrice [*cp.* 22
34]. **62** And
            he went
out, and wept bitterly.

¹ Gr. *bondservants.*

John.

                        Did not
I see thee in the garden with
him ?   **27** Peter
therefore

denied again :

                        and
straightway

                        the
cock crew.
    cp. 4 1 ; 6 23 ; 11 2 ;
20 2, 18, 20, 25 ; 21 7, 12.

    cp. 1 38.

    cp. 2 22 ; 12 16.

    cp. 13 38.

§ 241. **The Mockery in the High Priest's House** (Luke)

[*Cp.* Matt. 27 27-31 ‖ Mark 15 16-20 ‖ John 19 2-3; Matt. 27 39-44 ‖ Mark 15 29-32 ‖ Luke 23 35-39;
Luke 23 11 : *also* Matt. 20 19 ‖ Mark 10 34 ‖ Luke 18 32]

Matt. 26 67-68

cp. 27 29, 31, 41 : *also* 20 19.

67 Then did they spit [*cp.*
27 30]   in
            his
face   and   buffet
him : and some smote him
¹ with the palms of their
hands,
68 saying,   Prophesy unto us, thou Christ
[*cp.* 27 17, 22 : *also* 26 63 :
and 16 16] :
who   is   he   that   struck
thee ?

¹ Or, *with rods*

Mark 14 65

65 And some
cp. 15 20, 31 : *also* 10 34.

            began to spit [*cp.*
15 19 : *also* 10 34] on
him, and to cover his
face,   and   to buffet
him,

            and
to say unto him, Prophesy :
cp. 15 32 : *also* 14 61 :
    and 8 29.

            and   the officers
            received him
with   ¹ blows of their
hands.

¹ Or, *strokes of rods*

Luke 22 63-65

63 And the men that
held ¹ *Jesus* mocked [*cp.*
23 11, 35, 36 : *also* 18
32] him, and beat him.
    cp. 18 32.

64 And they blind-
folded him,

                        and asked him,
saying,   Pro-
phesy :
cp. 23 35, 39 : *also* 22
    67 ; 23 2 : *and* 9 20.
who   is   he   that   struck
thee ?

65 And
many other [*cp.* 3 18]
things spake they against
him, reviling him.

¹ Gr. *him.*

John 18 22-23

22 And when he had said
this,

    cp. 19 3.

cp. 1 41 ; 4 25, 26, 29 ; 7 26,
    41 ; 9 22 ; 10 24 ; 11 27.

            one of the officers
standing by struck Jesus
¹ with   his
hand [*cp.* 19 3], saying,
Answerest thou the high
priest so ? **23** Jesus answered him, If I have
spoken evil, bear witness of
the evil : but if well, why
smitest thou me ?

¹ Or, *with a rod*

§ 242. Jesus before the Council

Matt. 26 59-68	**Mark 14** 55-65	**Luke 22** 66-71 (63-64)	**John 18** 19-23 ; 2 18-19 ; 10 24-25 ; 1 51
cp. 27 1.	*cp.* 15 1.	**66** And as soon as it was day, the assembly of the elders of the people was gathered together, both chief priests and scribes; and they led him away into their council,	*cp.* 18 28.

cp. 26 57.
59 Now the chief priests and
                      the whole council sought false witness against Jesus, that they might put him to death; **60** and they found it not, though many   false witnesses came.
	cp. 14 53.
	55 Now the chief priests and
	                      the whole council sought witness against Jesus to put him to death; and found it not. **56** For many bare false witness against him, and their witness agreed not together. **57** And there stood up certain, and bare false witness against him, saying, **58** We heard him say,
			cp. 10 25 (*below*).

But afterward came two,
61 and said,
        This man said, I am able to destroy the ¹ temple of God,
        and to build it in three days [*cp.* 27 40: *also* 12 40; 16 21; 17 23; 20 19; 27 63, 64].
	I will destroy this ¹ temple that is made with hands, and in three days [*cp.* 15 29: *also* 8 31; 9 31; 10 34]
	
	I will build another made without hands. **59** And not even so did their witness agree together. **60** And the high priest stood up in the midst, and asked Jesus,
		cp. 9 22; 13 32; 18 33; 24 7, 21, 46.	**2 18** The Jews therefore answered and said unto him, What sign shewest thou unto us, seeing that thou doest these things? **19** Jesus answered and said unto them, Destroy this ¹ temple,
			
			and in three days
			
			I will raise it up.

62 And the high priest   stood up,
 	
        and said unto him, Answerest thou nothing? what is it which these   witness against thee? **63** But Jesus held his peace.
cp. 27 12, 14: *also* 15 23.
	saying, Answerest thou nothing? what is it which these witness against thee? **61** But he held his peace, and answered nothing [*cp.* 15 5].	*cp.* 23 9.	**18 19** The high priest therefore
			        asked Jesus of his disciples, and of his teaching.
			cp. 19 10.
			
			20 Jesus answered [*cp.* 19 9] him, I have spoken openly to the world; I ever taught in ² synagogues, and in the temple [*cp.* 7 28; 8 20], where all the Jews come together; and in secret spake I nothing. **21** Why askest thou me? ask them that have heard *me*, what I spake unto them: behold, these know the things which I said.

cp. 26 55: *also* 21 23.	*cp.* 14 49: *also* 12 35.	*cp.* 22 53: *also* 19 47; 20 1; 21 37.	**10 24** The Jews therefore came round about him, and said unto him, How long dost thou hold us in suspense?
And the high priest said unto him, I adjure thee by the living [*cp.* 16 16] God, that thou tell us whether thou be the Christ [*cp.* 16 16: *also* 26 68; 27 17, 22],	Again the high priest asked him, and saith unto him, *cp.* 5 7. Art thou the Christ [*cp.* 8 29: *also* 15 32],	saying, **67** If thou art the Christ [*cp.* 9 20: *also* 23 2, 35, 39], tell us. But he said unto them, If I tell you, ye will not believe:	If thou art the Christ [*cp.* 1 41; 4 25, 26, 29; 7 26, 41; 9 22; 11 27], tell us plainly. **25** Jesus answered them, I told you, and ye believe not: the works that I do in my Father's name,

cp. verses 59 and 60.

cp. verses 55 and 56.

verse 64

verse 62

the Son of God [cp. 4 3, 6; 8 29; 14 33; 16 16; 27 40, 43, 54: also 3 17; 17 5]. **64** Jesus saith unto him, Thou hast said [cp. 26 25: also 27 11]: [cp. 24 5] nevertheless I say unto you, Henceforth [cp. 23 39; 26 29] ye shall see [cp. 16 28]

the Son of the Blessed? [cp. 1 1; 3 11; 5 7; 15 39: also 1 11; 9 7] **62** And Jesus said, cp. 15 2. I am [cp. 13 6]: and ye shall see [cp. 9 1]

68 and if I ask *you*, ye will not answer. **69** But from henceforth [cp. 1 48; 5 10; 12 52; 22 18] shall the Son of man be seated at the right hand of the power of God. **70** And they all said, Art thou then the Son of God [cp. 1 35; 4 3, 9, 41; 8 28: also 3 22; 9 35]? And he said unto them, cp. 23 3. ¹ Ye say that I am [cp. 21 8].

these bear witness of me.

cp. 10 36: also 1 34; etc.

1 51 And he saith unto him, cp. 18 37. cp. 8 24, 28; 13 19. Verily, verily, I say unto you, cp. 13 19; 14 7. Ye shall see the heaven opened, and the angels of God ascending and descending upon the Son of man.

the Son of man sitting at the right hand of power, and coming on the clouds of heaven [cp. 16 27-28; 24 30-31; 25 31]. **65** Then the high priest rent his garments, saying, He hath spoken blasphemy [cp. 9 3]: what further need have we of witnesses? behold, now ye have heard the blasphemy: **66** what think ye [cp. 17 25; 18 12; 21 28; 22 17, 42]? They answered and said, He is ² worthy of death. **67** Then cp. 27 29, 31, 41: also 20 19. did they spit [cp. 27 30] in his face and buffet him: and some smote him ³ with the palms of their hands, **68** saying, Prophesy unto us, thou Christ [cp. 27 17, 22: also 26 63: and 16 16]: who is he that struck thee?

the Son of man sitting at the right hand of power [cp. 16 19], and coming with the clouds of heaven [cp. 8 38; 13 26-27]. **63** And the high priest rent his clothes, and saith, cp. 2 7. What further need have we of witnesses? **64** Ye have heard the blasphemy: what think ye? And they all condemned him to be ² worthy of death. **65** And some cp. 15 20, 31: also 10 34. began to spit [cp. 15 19: also 10 34] on him, and to cover his face, and to buffet him, and to say unto him, Prophesy: cp. 15 32: also 14 61: and 8 29. and the officers received him with ³ blows of their hands.

cp. 9 27.

verse 69

cp. 9 26; 21 27.

71 And they said, cp. 5 21. What further need have we of witness? for we ourselves have heard from his own mouth.

18 22 And when he had said this, cp. 10 33, 36. cp. 11 56.

63 And the men that held ² Jesus mocked [cp. 23 11, 35, 36: also 18 32] him, and beat him. cp. 18 32. **64** And they blindfolded him, and asked him, saying, Prophesy: [cp. 23 35, 39: also 22 67; 23 2: and 9 20] who is he that struck thee?

cp. 19 3.

cp. 1 41; 4 25, 26, 29; 7 26, 41; 9 22; 10 24; 11 27. one of the officers standing by struck Jesus ³ with his hand [cp. 19 3], saying, Answerest thou the high priest so? **23** Jesus answered him, If I have spoken evil, bear witness of the evil: but if well, why smitest thou me?

---

¹ Or, *sanctuary*: as in ch. 23 35; 27 5. ² Gr. *liable to.* ³ Or, *with rods*

¹ Or, *sanctuary* ² Gr. *liable to.* ³ Or, *strokes of rods*

¹ Or, *Ye say it, because I am.* ² Gr. *him.*

¹ Or, *sanctuary* ² Gr. *synagogue.* ³ Or, *with a rod*

Mark 14 59: cp. Num. 35 30.   Matt. 26 64 || Mark 14 62 || Luke 22 69: cp. Ps. 110 1 *and* Dan. 7 13.

§ 243. **Peter's Denial** (Matt. and Mark)

Matt. 26 69-75	Mark 14 66-72	Luke 22 56-62	John 18 17, 25-27
69 Now Peter was sitting without in the court [cp. 26 58]: and a maid	**66** And as Peter was beneath in the court [cp. 14 54], there cometh one of the maids of the high priest; **67** and seeing Peter cp. 14 54. warming himself [cp. 14 54], she looked upon him, and saith,	cp. 22 55. **56** And a certain maid seeing him as he sat in the light of the fire, and looking stedfastly upon him, said,	cp. 18 15. **17** The maid therefore that kept the door cp. 18 18, 25. saith unto Peter,
came unto him, saying, Thou also wast with cp. verse 71. Jesus the Galilæan.	Thou also wast with the Nazarene [cp. 1 24; 10 47; 16 6], even Jesus. cp. verse 70.	This man also was with him. [cp. 4 34; 18 37; 24 19] cp. verse 59.	Art thou also one of cp. 18 5, 7; 19 19: also 1 45. this man's disciples ?
70 But he denied before them all, saying, I know not what thou sayest. **71** And when he was gone out into the porch,	**68** But he denied, saying, 1 I neither know, nor understand what thou sayest: and he went out into the 2 porch; 3 and the cock crew. **69** And	**57** But he denied, saying, Woman, I know him not.	He saith, I am not.
another maid saw him, and saith unto them that were there, This man also was with Jesus the Nazarene [cp. 2 23: also 21 11]. **72** And again he denied with an oath, I know not the man. **73** And after a little while	cp. 14 54, 67. the maid saw him, and began again to say to them that stood by [cp. verse 70], This is one of them. cp. verse 67. **70** But he again denied it.	**58** And after a little while another saw him, and said, Thou also art one of them. cp. 4 34; 18 37; 24 19. But Peter said, Man, I am not. **59** And	**25** Now Simon Peter was standing and warming himself [cp. 18 18]. They said therefore unto him, Art thou also one of his disciples ? cp. 18 5, 7; 19 19: also 1 45. He denied, and said, I am not.
they that stood by [cp. 16 28; 27 47]	And after a little while again they that stood by [cp. 9 1; 11 5; 14 47, 69; 15 35, 39]	after the space of about one hour cp. 9 27; 19 24.	cp. 12 29. **26** One of the 1 servants of the high priest, being a kinsman of him whose ear Peter cut off, saith,
came and said to Peter, Of a truth thou also art one of them; [cp. verse 69] for thy speech bewrayeth thee.	said to Peter, Of a truth thou art one of them; for thou art a Galilæan.	another confidently affirmed, saying, Of a truth this man also was with him: for he is a Galilæan.	Did not I see thee in the garden with him ? **27** Peter therefore
74 Then began he to curse and to swear, I know not the man. And straightway cp. 12 46; 17 5; 26 47. the cock crew.	**71** But he began to curse, and to swear, I know not this man of whom ye speak. **72** And straightway cp. 5 35; 14 43. the second time the cock crew. cp. 16 19, 20.	**60** But Peter said, Man, I know not what thou sayest. And immediately, while he yet spake [cp. 8 49; 22 47], the cock crew. **61** And the Lord [cp. 7 13, 19; 10 1, 39, 41; 11 39; 12 42; 13 15; 17 5, 6; 18 6; 19 8; 24 3, 34] turned	denied again: and straightway the cock crew. cp. 4 1; 6 23; 11 2; 20 2, 18, 20, 25; 21 7, 12.

cp. 9 22; 16 23.	cp. 5 30; 8 33.	[cp. 7 9, 44; 9 55; 10 23; 14 25; 23 28], and looked upon Peter. And	cp. 1 38.

75 And Peter remembered the word which Jesus had said, Before the cock crow, thou shalt deny me thrice [cp. 26 34]. And he went out, and wept bitterly.

And Peter called to mind the word, how that Jesus said unto him, Before the cock crow twice [cp. 14 68, 72], thou shalt deny me thrice [cp. 14 30]. [4] And when he thought thereon, he wept.

Peter remembered [cp. 24 6, 8] the word of the Lord, how that he said unto him, Before the cock crow this day, thou shalt deny me thrice [cp. 22 34]. **62** And he went out, and wept bitterly.

cp. 2 22; 12 16.

cp. 13 38.

[1] Or, *I neither know, nor understand: thou, what sayest thou?*
[2] Gr. *forecourt.*
[3] Many ancient authorities omit *and the cock crew.*
[4] Or, *And he began to weep.*

[1] Gr. *bondservants.*

§ 244. Jesus brought to Pilate

Matt. 27 1-2	**Mark 15** 1	**Luke 23** 1	**John 18** 28

1 Now when morning was come, all the chief priests and the elders of the people took counsel [cp. 12 14; 22 15; 27 7; 28 12] against Jesus to put him to death: **2** and they bound him, and led him away, and delivered him up to Pilate the governor [cp. 27 11, 14, 15, 21, 27; 28 14].
cp. 27 27.

1 And straightway in the morning the chief priests with the elders and scribes, and the whole council, held a consultation [cp. 3 6], and bound Jesus, and carried him away, and delivered him up to Pilate.

cp. 15 16.

1 And
cp. 22 66.
the whole company of them rose up, and brought him before Pilate.
cp. 20 20.

28 They lead Jesus therefore from Caiaphas into the [1] palace [cp. 18 33; 19 9] and it was early . . .

[1] Gr. *Praetorium.*

§ 245. The Death of Judas

Matt. 27 3-10

3 Then Judas, which betrayed him, when he saw that he was condemned, repented himself, and brought back the thirty pieces of silver to the chief priests and elders, **4** saying, I have sinned in that I betrayed [1] innocent [cp. 27 24] blood. But they said, What is that to us? see thou *to it* [cp. 27 24]. **5** And he cast down the pieces of silver into the sanctuary, and departed; and he went away and hanged himself. **6** And the chief priests took the pieces of silver, and said, It is not lawful to put them into the [2] treasury, since it is the price of blood. **7** And they took counsel [cp. 12 14; 22 15; 27 1; 28 12], and bought with them the potter's field, to bury strangers in.

cp. 3 6; 15 1.

8 Wherefore that field was called, The field of blood, unto this day [cp. 11 23; 28 15]. **9** Then was fulfilled that which was spoken [3] by Jeremiah the prophet, saying, And [4] they took the thirty pieces of silver, the price of him that was priced, [5] whom *certain* of the

cp. 21 22, 23.

Acts 1 18 Now this man obtained a field with the reward of his iniquity; and falling headlong, he burst asunder in the midst, and all his bowels gushed out. **19** And it became known to all the dwellers at Jerusalem; insomuch that in their language that field was called Akeldama, that is, The field of blood.

children of Israel did price; **10** and ⁶ they gave them for the potter's field, as the Lord appointed me.

¹ Many ancient authorities read *righteous*.
² Gr. *corbanas*, that is, *sacred treasury*.   Compare Mark 7 11.
³ Or, *through*   ⁴ Or, *I took*
⁵ Or, *whom they priced on the part of the sons of Israel*
⁶ Some ancient authorities read *I gave*.

Matt. 27 6 : *cp.* Deut. 23 18 ?   **Matt. 27 7** : *cp.* Jer. 19 11.   **Matt. 27 9-10** : Zech. 11 12-13—*cp.* Jer. 32 6-15 : *also* 18 1-12 ; 19 1-13.

§ 246. Jesus before Pilate (i)

Matt. 27 11-14	**Mark 15** 2-5	**Luke 23** 2-7	John 18 28-38 ; 19 8-10
			18 28 And they themselves entered not into the ¹palace, that they might not be defiled, but might eat the passover. **29** Pilate therefore went out unto them, and saith, What accusation bring ye against this man ? **30** They answered and said unto him, If this man
verse 12	*verse* 3	**2** And they began to accuse him, saying, We found this man perverting [*cp.* 23 14] our nation, and forbidding to give tribute [*cp.* 20 20-26] to Cæsar, and saying that he himself is ¹ Christ [*cp.* 22 67 : *also* 23 35, 39 : *and* 9 20] a king [*cp. verse* 3].	
cp. 22 15-22.	*cp.* 12 13-17.		*cp.* 19 12.
cp. 26 63-64 : *also* 26 68 ; 27 17, 22 : *and* 16 16.	*cp.* 14 61-62 : *also* 15 32 : *and* 8 29.		*cp.* 4 25, 26 : *also* 1 41 ; 4 29 ; 7 26, 41 ; 9 22 ; 11 27. were not

an evil-doer, we should not have delivered him up unto thee. **31** Pilate therefore said unto them, Take him yourselves, and judge him according to your law. The Jews said unto him, It is not lawful for us to put any man to death : **32** that the word of Jesus might be fulfilled, which he spake, signifying by what manner of death he should die. **33** Pilate therefore entered again into the ¹ palace, and called Jesus,

Matt. 27 11-14	**Mark 15** 2-5	**Luke 23** 2-7	John 18 28-38 ; 19 8-10
11 Now Jesus stood before the governor [*cp.* 27 2, 14, 15, 21, 27; 28 14] : and the governor asked him, saying, Art thou the King of the Jews [*cp.* 2 2 ; 27 29, 37 : *also* 27 42 : *and* 21 5] ?	**2** And Pilate asked him, Art thou the King of the Jews [*cp.* 15 9, 12, 18, 26 : *also* 15 32] ?	*cp.* 20 20. **3** And Pilate asked him, saying, Art thou the King of the Jews [*cp.* 23 37, 38 : *and* 19 38 ; 23 2] ?	and said unto him, Art thou the King of the Jews [*cp.* 18 39 ; 19 3, 19, 21 : *also* 1 49 ; 12 13 : *and*

6 15 ; 12 15 ; 18 37 ; 19 12, 14, 15] ? **34** Jesus answered, Sayest thou this of thyself, or did others tell it thee concerning me ? **35** Pilate answered, Am I a Jew ? Thine own nation and the chief priests delivered thee unto me : what hast thou done ? **36** Jesus answered, My kingdom is not of this world : if my kingdom were of this world, then would my ² servants fight, that I should not be delivered to the Jews : but now is my kingdom not from hence. **37** Pilate therefore said unto him, Art thou a king then ?

Matt. 27 11-14	**Mark 15** 2-5	**Luke 23** 2-7	John 18 28-38 ; 19 8-10
And Jesus said unto him, Thou sayest [*cp.* 26 25, 64].	And he answering saith unto him, Thou sayest.	And he answered him and said, Thou sayest [*cp.* 22 70].	Jesus answered,

king. To this end have I been born, and to this end am I come into the world, that I should bear witness unto the truth. Every one that is of the truth heareth my voice. **38** Pilate saith unto him, What is truth ? And when he had said this, he went out again unto the Jews, and saith unto them,

Matt. 27 11-14	**Mark 15** 2-5	**Luke 23** 2-7	John 18 28-38 ; 19 8-10
cp. 27 24. **12** And when he was accused by the chief priests and elders,	**3** And the chief priests accused him of many things.	**4** And Pilate said unto the chief priests and the multitudes, I find no fault [*cp.* 23 14, 22] in this man. **5** But they were the more urgent, *cp.* 23 2, 10. saying, He stirreth up the people, teaching throughout all Judæa, and beginning	**3** Thou sayest that I am a king. I find no crime [*cp.* 19 4, 6] in him. *cp.* 18 29, 30.
	cp. 15 11.		

he answered nothing [*cp.* 26 63; 27 14: *also* 15 23].	*cp.* 14 61; 15 5.	from Galilee even unto this place. *cp.* 23 9. **6** But when Pilate heard it,	*cp.* 19 9.
13 Then　saith Pilate unto him,	**4** And Pilate again asked him, saying,	he asked　whether the man were a Galilæan.	19 **8** When Pilate therefore heard this saying, he was the more afraid ; **9** and he entered into the [1] palace again, and　saith unto Jesus, Whence art thou ?
Hearest thou not how many things they witness against thee ?　**14** And he　gave him no answer [*cp.* 26 63; 27 12: *also* 15 23], not even to one word : insomuch that the governor [*cp. verse* 11 ; *etc.*] marvelled greatly.	Answerest thou nothing? behold　how many things they accuse thee of. **5** But Jesus no more answered [*cp.* 14 61] anything ;　insomuch that Pilate　marvelled.	*cp.* 23 9.	But Jesus　gave him no answer.
			10 Pilate therefore saith unto him, Speakest thou not unto me ? knowest thou not that I have [4] power to release thee, and have [4] power to crucify thee ?
		7 And when he knew that he was of Herod's jurisdiction, he sent him unto Herod, who himself also was at Jerusalem in these days.	
		[1] Or, *an anointed king*	[1] Gr. *Praetorium.* [2] Or, *officers* [3] Or, *Thou sayest it, because I am a king.* [4] Or, *authority*

§ 247. **Jesus before Herod**

Luke 23 8-12

cp. 26 63; 27 12, 14: *also* 15 23. *cp.* 26 67-68; 27 27-31, 39-44: *also* 20 19.	*cp.* 14 61; 15 5. *cp.* 14 65; 15 16-20, 29-32: *also* 10 34.	**8** Now when Herod saw Jesus, he was exceeding glad : for he was of a long time desirous to see him [*cp.* 9 9], because he had heard concerning him [*cp.* 9 7, 9] ; and he hoped to see some [1] miracle done by him. **9** And he questioned him in many words ; but he answered him nothing. **10** And the chief priests and the scribes stood, vehemently accusing him [*cp.* 23 2, 5: Matt. 27 12: Mark 15 3: John 18 29, 30]. **11** And Herod with his soldiers set him at nought, and mocked [*cp.* 22 63-65; 23 35-39: *also* 18 32] him, and arraying him in gorgeous apparel [*cp.* Matt. 27 28: Mark 15 17: John 19 2] sent him back to Pilate. **12** And Herod and Pilate became friends with each other that very day : for before they were at enmity between themselves.	*cp.* 19 9. *cp.* 19 2-3.

[1] Gr. *sign.*

§ 248. **Jesus before Pilate** (ii)

Matt. 27 15-26	**Mark 15** 6-15	**Luke 23** 13-25	**John 18** 39-40; 19 1, 4-6, 12-16
15 Now at [1] the feast the governor [*cp.* 27 2, 11, 14, 21, 27; 28 14]　was wont to release unto the multitude one prisoner,	**6** Now at [1] the feast he　used to release unto them one prisoner,	*cp.* 20 20.	18 **39** But ye have a custom, that I should release unto you one　at the pass-

whom they would.
16 And they had then a notable prisoner, called Barabbas.

17 When therefore they were gathered together,

Pilate said unto them,

cp. 27 24.

cp. verse 26.

Whom will ye that I release unto you?
cp. 2 2; 27 11, 29, 37: *also* 27 42: *and* 21 5.

Barabbas, or Jesus which is called Christ [*cp.* 1 16; 27 22: *also* 26 63, 64, 68: *and* 16 16]? **18** For he knew that for envy they had delivered him up. **19** And while he was sitting on the judgement-seat, his wife sent unto him, saying, Have thou nothing to do with that righteous man [*cp. verse* 24]: for I have suffered many things this day in a dream [*cp.* 1 20; 2 12, 13, 19, 22] because of him. **20** Now the chief priests and the elders persuaded the multitudes that they should ask for Barabbas, and destroy Jesus. **21** But the governor [*cp. verse* 15] answered and said unto them, Whether of the twain will ye that I release unto you? And they

said,

Barabbas.

---

whom they asked of him. **7** And there was one called Barabbas, *lying* bound with them that had made insurrection, men who in the insurrection had committed murder. **8** And the multitude went up and began to ask him *to do* as he was wont to do unto them. **9** And Pilate answered them, saying,

cp. verse 15.

Will ye that I release unto you the King of the Jews [*cp.* 15 2, 12, 18, 26: *also* 15 32]?

cp. 14 61, 62; 15 32: *and* 8 29.
10 For he perceived that for envy the chief priests had delivered him up.

11 But the chief priests stirred up the multitude, that he should rather release Barabbas unto them.

---

verse 19

13 And Pilate called together the chief priests and the rulers and the people, **14** and said unto them, Ye brought unto me this man, as one that perverteth [*cp.* 23 2] the people: and behold, I, having examined him before you, found no fault [*cp.* 23 4, 22] in this man touching those things whereof ye accuse him: **15** no, nor yet Herod: for he sent him back unto us; and behold, nothing worthy of death hath been done by him. **16** I will therefore chastise him, and release him [*cp. verse* 22].[1]

cp. 23 3, 37, 38: *and* 19 38; 23 2.

cp. 22 67; 23 2, 35, 39: *and* 9 20.

cp. 23 47.

cp. 23 5.

18 But they cried out all together, saying, Away with this man, and release unto us Barabbas: **19** one who for a certain insur-

---

over.

cp. 18 40.

19 4 And Pilate went out again,

and saith unto them, Behold, I bring him out to you, that ye may know that I find no crime [*cp.* 18 38; 19 6] in him. **5** Jesus therefore came out, wearing the crown of thorns and the purple garment. And *Pilate* saith unto them, Behold, the man [*cp.* 19 14]!

cp. 19 1.

18 39 b Will ye therefore that I release unto you the King of the Jews [*cp.* 18 33; 19 3, 19, 21: *also* 1 49; 12 13: *and* 6 15; 12 15; 18 37; 19 12, 14, 15]?

cp. 4 25, 26: *also* 1 41; 4 29; 7 26, 41; 9 22; 11 27.

18 40 They cried out there-fore again, saying, [*cp.* 19 15] Not this man, but Barabbas. Now Barabbas

Matthew

22 Pilate saith unto them, What then shall I do unto Jesus which is called Christ [cp. verse 17]?

They all say, Let him be crucified. 23 And he said,

Why, what evil hath he done?

cp. 27 24.

cp. verse 26.

cp. 23 2.

cp. 27 62. cp. 15 42. cp. 23 54.
cp. 27 45. cp. 15 33. cp. 23 44.

But they cried out exceedingly, saying,

Let him be crucified.

24 So when Pilate saw that he prevailed nothing, but rather that a tumult [cp. 26 5] was arising, he took water, and washed his hands before the multitude, saying, I am innocent [cp. 27 4] ² of the blood of this righteous man [cp. verse 19]: see ye to it [cp. 27 4]. 25 And all the people answered and said, His blood be on us, and on our children.

26 Then released he unto them Barabbas:

but Jesus he scourged and delivered

Mark

verse 7

12 And Pilate again answered and said unto them, What then shall I do unto him whom ye call the King of the Jews [cp. verse 9]?

13 And they cried out again, Crucify him. 14 And Pilate said unto them, Why, what evil hath he done?

cp. verse 15.

But they cried out exceedingly,

Crucify him.

15 And Pilate,

wishing to content the multitude,

released unto them Barabbas,

and delivered Jesus, when he had scourged

Luke

rection made in the city, and for murder, was cast into prison. 20 And Pilate spake unto them again,

desiring to release Jesus; 21 but they shouted, saying, Crucify, crucify him. 22 And he said unto them the third time, Why, what evil hath this man done [cp. 23 41]?

I have found no cause [cp. 23 4, 14] of death in him: I will therefore chastise him and release him [cp. verse 16].

cp. verse 20.

23 But they were instant with loud voices, asking that he might

cp. 23 18.

be crucified.

And their voices prevailed. 24 And Pilate

cp. 23 47.

gave sentence that what they asked for should be done. 25 And he released him that for insurrection and murder had been cast into prison, whom they asked for; but Jesus

cp. verse 16 and 22.

he delivered up

John

was a robber.

cp. 19 12.

19 6 When therefore the chief priests and the officers saw him, they cried out, saying, Crucify him, crucify him. Pilate saith unto them,

Take him yourselves, and crucify him: for I find no crime [cp. 18 38; 19 4] in him. . . .

cp. 19 1.

12 Upon this Pilate sought to release him: but the Jews cried out, saying, If thou release this man, thou art not Cæsar's friend: every one that maketh himself a king ¹ speaketh against Cæsar. 13 When Pilate therefore heard these words, he brought Jesus out, and sat down on the judgement-seat at a place called The Pavement, but in Hebrew, Gabbatha. 14 Now it was the Preparation [cp. 19 31, 42] of the passover: it was about the sixth hour. And he saith unto the Jews, Behold, your King [cp. 19 5]! 15 They therefore cried out,

Away with him, away with him, crucify him. Pilate saith unto them, Shall I crucify your King? The chief priests answered, We have no king but Cæsar.

19 1 Then Pilate therefore took Jesus, and scourged him. . . . 16 Then therefore he delivered him

to be crucified.	him, crucified.	to be will.	unto them to be crucified.
to their			

to be
crucified.

¹ Or, *a feast*
² Some ancient authorities read of this blood: *see ye &c.*

him,
crucified.

to be

¹ Or, *a feast*

to their
will.

¹ Many ancient authorities insert ver. 17 *Now he must needs release unto them at the feast one* prisoner. Others add the same words after ver. 19.

unto them to be
crucified.

¹ Or, *opposeth Caesar*

Matt. 27 24 : *cp*. Deut. 21 6-9 ; Susanna 46.

§ 249. The Mockery in the Prætorium

[*Cp*. Matt. 26 67-68 ‖ Mark 14 65 ‖ Luke 22 63-65 ; Matt. 27 39-44 ‖ Mark 15 29-32 ‖ Luke 23 35-39 ;
Luke 23 11 : *also* Matt. 20 19 ‖ Mark 10 34 ‖ Luke 18 32]

Matt. 27 27-31	**Mark 15** 16-20		John 19 2-3
27 Then the soldiers of the governor [*cp*. 27 1, *etc*.] took Jesus into the ¹ palace, and gathered unto him the whole ² band. **28** And they ³ stripped him, and put on him a scarlet robe. **29** And they plaited a crown of thorns and put it upon his head, and a reed in his right [*cp*. 5 29, 30, 39] hand ; and they kneeled down before him, and mocked [*cp*. 27 31, 41 : *also* 20 19] him, saying, Hail, King of the Jews [*cp*. 2 2 ; 27 11, 37 : *also* 27 42 : *and* 21 5] ! **30** And they spat [*cp*. 26 67] upon him, and took the reed and smote him on the head. **31** And when they had mocked [*cp*. 27 29, 41 : *also* 20 19] him, they took off from him the robe, and put on him his garments, and led him away to crucify him.	**16** And the soldiers led him away within the court [*cp*. 14 54, 66], which is the ¹ Prætorium ; and they call together the whole ² band. **17** And they clothe him with purple, and plaiting a crown of thorns, they put it on him ; **18** and they began to salute him, Hail, King of the Jews [*cp*. 15 2, 9, 12, 26 : *also* 15 32] ! **19** And they smote his head with a reed, [*cp*. 14 65] and did spit [*cp*. 14 65 : *also* 10 34] upon him, and bowing their knees worshipped him. **20** And when they had mocked [*cp*. 15 31 : *also* 10 34] him, they took off from him the purple, and put on him his garments. And they lead him out to crucify him.	*cp*. 20 20. *cp*. 22 55. *cp*. 23 11. *cp*. 6 6 ; 22 50. *cp*. 22 63 ; 23 11, 35, 36 : *also* 18 32. *cp*. 23 3, 37, 38 : *and* 19 38 ; 23 2. *cp*. 18 32. *cp*. 22 63 ; 23 11, 35, 36 : *also* 18 32. *cp*. 23 26.	**2** And the soldiers *cp*. 18 15. *cp*. 18 28, 33 ; 19 9. plaited a crown of thorns, and put it on his head, and arrayed him in a purple garment ; *cp*. 18 10. **3** and they came unto him, and said, Hail, King of the Jews [*cp*. 18 33, 39 ; 19 19, 21 : *also* 1 49 ; 12 13 : *and* 6 15 ; 12 15 ; 18 37 ; 19 12, 14, 15] ! and they struck him ¹ with their hands [*cp*. 18 22]. *cp*. 19 16b.

¹ Gr. *Prætorium*. See Mark 15 16.
² Or, *cohort*
³ Some ancient authorities read *clothed*.

¹ Or, *palace*   ² Or, *cohort*

¹ Or, *with rods*

(vi) On the Way to Golgotha (§§ 250-252)

§ 250. Simon of Cyrene compelled to bear the Cross

Matt 27 32	**Mark 15** 21	**Luke 23** 26	John 19 16-17
cp. 27 31.	*cp*. 15 20.	**26** And when they led him away,	
32 And as they came out, they found a man of Cyrene, Simon by name :	**21** And they ¹ compel one passing by, Simon of Cyrene, coming from the country, the father of Alexander	they laid hold upon one Simon of Cyrene, coming from the country,	**16** They took Jesus therefore : **17** and he went out,

him they ¹ compelled to go *with them*,	and Rufus, to go *with them*,			
that he might bear his cross.	that he might bear his cross.	and laid on him the cross, to bear it after Jesus.	the cross himself.	bearing for
¹ Gr. *impressed*.	¹ Gr. *impress*.			

§ 251. A Lament over the Daughters of Jerusalem

[*Cp.* Matt. 23 37-39 ‖ Luke 13 34-35: *also* Luke 19 41-44 *and* 21 20]

Luke 23 27-31

cp. 9 22; 16 23. cp. 9 15.	cp. 5 30; 8 33. cp. 2 20.	**27** And there followed him a great multitude of the people [*cp.* 23 35, 48], and of women who bewailed and lamented him. **28** But Jesus turning [*cp.* 7 9, 44; 9 55; 10 23; 14 25; 22 61] unto them said, Daughters of Jerusalem, weep not [*cp.* 7 13; 8 52] for me, but weep for yourselves [*cp.* 19 41], and for your children. **29** For behold, the days are coming [*cp.* 5 35; 17 22; 19 43; 21 6], in which they shall say, Blessed are the barren, and the wombs that never bare, and the breasts that never gave suck. **30** Then shall they begin to say to the mountains, Fall on us; and to the hills, Cover us. **31** For if they do these things in the green tree, what shall be done in the dry?	cp. 1 38.

Luke 23 30 : Hos. 10 8.

§ 252. Two Malefactors led out with Jesus

Luke 23 32

cp. 27 38.	cp. 15 27.	**32** And there were also two others, malefactors, led with him to be put to death [*cp.* 23 33].	cp. 19 18.

(vii) On Golgotha (§§ 253-255)

§ 253. The Crucifixion

Matt. 27 33-44	**Mark 15** 22-32	**Luke 23** 33-38	John 19 16-18, 23-24, 19-22
			16 They took Jesus therefore : **17** and he went out, bearing the cross for himself,
33 And when they were come unto a place called Golgotha, that is to say, The place of a skull,	**22** And they bring him unto the place Golgotha, which is, being interpreted, The place of a skull.	**33** And when they came unto the place which is called ¹ The skull,	unto the place called The place of a skull, which is called in Hebrew Golgotha;
34 they gave him wine to drink mingled with gall [*cp.* 27 48]: and when he had tasted it, he would not drink. **35** And when they had crucified him, *verse* 38	**23** And they offered him wine mingled with myrrh [*cp.* 15 36]: but he received it not. **24** And they crucify him, *verse* 27	*verse 36* there they crucified him, and the malefactors, one on the right hand and the other on the left.	cp. 19 29-30. **18** where they crucified him, and with him two others, on either side one, and Jesus in the midst.
cp. 11 25, 26; 26 39, 42: *also* 6 9. cp. 5 44. they	cp. 14 36. and	**34** ²And Jesus said, Father [*cp.* 10 21, 22; 22 42; 23 46: *also* 11 2], forgive them [*cp.* 6 28]; for they know not what they do. And	cp. 11 41; 12 27, 28; 17 1, 5, 11, 21, 24, 25. **23** The soldiers therefore, when they had crucified Jesus

[Matthew]

parted his garments among them,

casting lots:

36 and they sat and watched [*cp.* 27 54] him there. **37** And they set up over his head his accusation written, THIS IS JESUS THE KING OF THE JEWS [*cp.* 2 2; 27 11, 29: *also* 27 42: *and* 21 5].

38 Then are there crucified with him two robbers, one on the right hand, and one on the left. *cp. verse* 36.

39 And they that passed by railed on him, wagging their heads, **40** and saying, Thou that destroyest the ¹ temple, and buildest it in three days [*cp.* 26 61: *also* 12 40; 16 21; 17 23; 20 19; 27 63, 64], save thyself: if thou art the Son of God [*cp.* 4 3, 6: *also* 8 29; 14 33; 16 16; 26 63; 27 43, 54: *and* 3 17; 17 5], come down from the cross. **41** In like manner also the chief priests mocking *him*, with the scribes and elders, said, **42** He saved others; ² himself he cannot save. *cp.* 26 68; 27 17, 22: *also* 26 63: *and* 16 16.

He is the King of Israel

[Mark]

part his garments among them,

casting lots upon them, what each should take.

25 And it was the third hour, and they crucified him.

26 And the superscription of his accusation was written over, THE KING OF THE JEWS [*cp.* 15 2, 9, 12, 18: *also* 15 32].

27 And with him they crucify two robbers; one on his right hand, and one on his left.¹

29 And they that passed by railed on him, wagging their heads, and saying, Ha! thou that destroyest the ² temple, and buildest it in three days [*cp.* 14 58: *also* 8 31; 9 31; 10 34], **30** save thyself, *cp.* 1 1; 3 11; 5 7; 15 39: *and* 1 11; 9 7. and come down from the cross. **31** In like manner also the chief priests mocking *him* among themselves with the scribes said, He saved others; ³ himself he cannot save. **32** Let the Christ, [*cp.* 14 61: *and* 8 29],

the King of Israel

[Luke]

parting his garments among them,

they cast lots.

cp. verse 35.

verse 38

verse 33

35 And the people stood beholding [*cp.* 23 27, 48].

cp. 9 22; 13 32; 18 33; 24 7, 21, 46.

verse 37

cp. 4 3, 9: *also* 1 35; 4 41; 8 28; 22 70: *and* 3 22; 9 35.

And the rulers also scoffed [*cp.* 16 14] at him, saying, He saved others; let him save himself, if this is the Christ [*cp.* 23 39: *also* 22 67; 23 2: *and* 9 20] of God [*cp.* 9 20], his chosen [*cp.* 9 35].

[John]

took his garments, and made four parts, to every soldier a part; and also the ¹ coat: now the ¹ coat was without seam, woven from the top throughout. **24** They said therefore one to another, Let us not rend it, but cast lots for it, whose it shall be: that the scripture might be fulfilled, which saith, They parted my garments among them, And upon my vesture did they cast lots. These things therefore the soldiers did.

19 And Pilate wrote a title also, and put it on the cross.

And there was written JESUS OF NAZARETH, THE KING OF THE JEWS [*cp.* 18 33, 39; 19 3, 21: *also* 1 49; 12 13: *and* 6 15; 12 15; 18 37

verse 18

cp. 2 19.

cp. 1 34; *etc.*

cp. 1 41; 4 25, 26, 29; 7 26, 41; 9 22; 10 24; 11 27.

[center, full width]

19 12, 14, 15]. **20** This title therefore read many of the Jews: ² for the place where Jesus was crucified was nigh to the city: and it was written in Hebrew, *and* in Latin, *and* in Greek. **21** The chief priests of the Jews therefore said to Pilate, Write not, The King of the Jews; but, that he said, I am King of the Jews. **22** Pilate answered, What I have written I have written.

[left margin]

Cp. Matt. 26 67-68 || Mark 14 65 || Luke 22 63-65 || Matt. 27 27-31 || Mark 15 16-20 || John 19 2-3; Luke 23 11: *also* Matt. 20 19 || Mark 10 34 || Luke 18 32.

Cp. Matt. 26 67-68 || Mark 14 65 || Luke 22 63-65; Matt. 27 27-31 || Mark 15 16-20 || John 19 2-3; Luke 23 11: also Matt. 20 19 || Mark 10 34 || Luke 18 32.

Matthew

[cp. verse 37, etc.]; let him now come down from the cross, and we will believe on him. **43** He trusteth on God; let him deliver him now, if he desireth him: for he said, I am the Son of God [cp. 26 63, 64: also 4 3, 6; 8 29; 14 33; 16 16; 27 40, 54: and 3 17; 17 5].

verse 34: cp. 27 48.

verse 40

verse 37

44 And the robbers also that were crucified with him cast upon him the same reproach.

1 Or, sanctuary
2 Or, can he not save himself?

Mark

[cp. verse 26, etc.], now come down from the cross, that we may see and believe.

cp. 1 1; 3 11; 5 7; 15 39: and 1 11; 9 7.

verse 23: cp. 15 36.

verse 30

verse 26

And they that were crucified with him reproached him.

1 Many ancient authorities insert ver. 28 And the scripture was fulfilled, which saith, And he was reckoned with transgressors. See Luke 22 37.
2 Or, sanctuary
3 Or, can he not save himself?

Luke

cp. verse 38, etc.

cp. 22 70: also 1 35; 4 3, 9, 41; 8 28: and 3 22; 9 35.

36 And the soldiers also mocked him, coming to him, offering him vinegar, **37** and saying, If thou art the King of the Jews [see below], save thyself [cp. 23 39: also 4 23]. **38** And there was also a superscription over him, THIS IS THE KING OF THE JEWS [cp. 23 3, 37: and 19 38; 23 2].

23 39.

1 According to the Latin, Calvary, which has the same meaning.
2 Some ancient authorities omit And Jesus said, Father, forgive them; for they know not what they do.

John

cp. 1 49; 12 13: and 19 19; etc.

cp. 1 34; etc.

cp. 19 29-30.

verse 19

1 Or, tunic
2 Or, for the place of the city where Jesus was crucified was nigh at hand

Matt. 27 34 || Mark 15 23 || Luke 23 36: cp. Ps. 69 21.   Luke 23 34: cp. Is. 53 12.   Matt. 27 35 || Mark 15 24 || Luke 23 34 || John 19 23-24: cp. Ps. 22 18.   Matt. 27 36: cp. Ps. 22 17.   Matt. 27 38 || Mark 15 27 || Luke 23 33 || John 19 18: cp. Is. 53 12.   Luke 23 35: cp. Ps. 22 17.   Matt. 27 39-44 || Mark 15 29-32 || Luke 23 35-39: cp. Ps. 22 6-8.   Matt. 27 43: Ps. 22 8   cp. Wisd. 2 13, 16-18.

§ 254. The Penitent Malefactor

Luke 23 39-43

27 44
cp. 27 40.

15 32
cp. 15 30.

cp. 16 28; 20 21.

39 And one of the malefactors which were hanged railed on him, saying, Art not thou the Christ? save thyself [cp. 23 37: also 4 23] and us. **40** But the other answered, and rebuking him said, Dost thou not even fear God, seeing thou art in the same condemnation? **41** And we indeed justly; for we receive the due reward of our deeds: but this man hath done nothing amiss [cp. 23 22]. **42** And he said, Jesus, remember me when thou comest 1 in thy kingdom [cp. 22 29, 30]. **43** And he said unto him, Verily I say unto thee, To-day shalt thou be with me in Paradise.

cp. 18 36.

1 Some ancient authorities read into thy kingdom.

Luke 23 43: cp. Is. 53 12.

§ 255. The Death of Jesus

Matt. 27 45-56	Mark 15 33-41	Luke 23 44-49	John 19 28-30, 25-27
45 Now from the sixth hour there was darkness over all the 1 land until the ninth hour.	**33** And when the sixth hour was come, there was darkness over the whole 1 land until the ninth hour.	**44** And it was now about the sixth hour, and a darkness came over the whole 1 land until the ninth hour, **45** 2 the sun's light failing: and the veil of the 3 temple was rent in the midst. **46** 4 And when	cp. 19 14.
verse 51	verse 38		
46 And about	**34** And		**28** After this

the ninth hour Jesus

                cried with a loud voice, saying, Eli, Eli, lama sabachthani? that is,
            My God, my God, ² why hast thou forsaken me?
47 And some of them that stood there [*cp.* 16 28: *also* 26 73],
      when they heard it, said,   This man calleth Elijah.
      48 And straightway one of them ran, and took a sponge, and filled it with vinegar [*cp.* 27 34], and put it on a reed, and gave him to drink. **49** And the rest said, Let be; let us see whether Elijah cometh to save   him.³
50 And Jesus

cried again with a loud voice,
cp. 11 25, 26; 26 39, 42: *also* 6 9.

         and yielded up his spirit. **51** And behold, the veil of the ⁴ temple was rent in twain from the top to the bottom; and the earth did quake; and the rocks were rent; **52** and the tombs were opened; and many bodies of the saints that had fallen asleep were raised; **53** and coming forth out of the tombs after his resurrection they entered into the holy city [*cp.* 4 5] and appeared unto many. **54** Now the centurion,

               and they that were with him watching [*cp.* 27 36] Jesus, when they saw

the earthquake, and the things that were done, feared [*cp.* 9 8; 17 6; 28 4, 8]

exceedingly,
cp. 9 8; 15 31: *also* 5 16.

         saying, Truly this
       was ⁵ the Son of God [*cp.* 14 33; 16 16:

---

at the ninth hour Jesus

             cried with a loud voice,   Eloi, Eloi, lama sabachthani? which is, being interpreted, My God, my God, ² why hast thou forsaken me?
35 And some of them that stood by [*cp.* 9 1; 11 5: *also* 14 47, 69, 70; 15 39], when they heard it, said, Behold, he calleth Elijah.
        36 And one ran, and filling a sponge   full   of   vinegar [*cp.* 15 23],   put it on a reed, and gave him to drink, saying, Let be; let us see whether Elijah cometh to   take him down.
37 And Jesus

uttered   a loud voice
     cp. 14 36.

            and gave up the ghost. **38** And   the veil of the ³ temple was rent in twain from the top to the bottom.

        39 And when the centurion, which stood by [*cp. verse* 35] over against him,

        saw that he ⁴ so gave up the ghost,

          he
    cp. 2 12.

          said, Truly this
man was ⁵ the Son of God [*cp.* 3 11: *also* 1 1;

               Jesus

            had cried with a loud voice,

         cp. 9 27: *also* 19 24.

        cp. 23 36.

          he said, Father [*cp.* 10 21, 22; 22 42; 23 34: *also* 11 2], into thy hands I commend my spirit:
and having said this, he   gave up the ghost.

       verse 45

        47 And when the centurion

         saw

        what was done,
cp. 1 12, 65; 2 9; 5 26; 7 16; 8 25, 35, 37, 47; 9 34, 45; 24 5, 37.
         he glorified God [*cp.* 2 20; 5 25, 26; 7 16; 13 13; 17 15; 18 43], saying, Certainly this was a righteous man.
cp. 4 41: *also* 1 35; 4 3,

              Jesus, knowing that all things are now finished, that the scripture might be accomplished,
       saith,

           I thirst.

     cp. 12 29.

       29 There was set there a vessel full of vinegar: so they   put a sponge full   of the vinegar   upon hyssop, and brought it to his mouth.

       30 When Jesus therefore had received the vinegar,

       he said,
cp. 11 41; 12 27, 28; 17 1, 5, 11, 21, 24 25.

         It is finished:
and   he bowed his head, and gave up his spirit.

         cp. 9 24.

       cp. 1 34; *etc.*

also 4 3, 6; 8 29; 26 63; 27 40, 43: *and* 3 17; 17 5].

5 7: *and* 1 11; 9 7].

9; 8 28; 22 70: *and* 3 22; 9 35.

48 And all the multitudes that came together to this sight [*cp.* 23 27, 35], when they beheld the things that were done, returned smiting their breasts [*cp.* 18 13]. 49 And all his acquaintance, and the women [*cp.* 8 2; 23 55; 24 1, 10, 22, 24] that followed with him from Galilee [*cp.* 23 55] stood afar off,

55 And many women were there

40 And there were also women

25 But there were

standing

by the cross of Jesus

beholding from afar, which had followed Jesus from Galilee, ministering unto him:
56 among whom was

beholding from afar:

verse 41

among whom *were* both

cp. 8 3.
seeing these things.

his mother, and his mother's sister, Mary the *wife* of Clopas, and Mary Magdalene [*cp.* 20 1, 18].

Mary Magdalene [*cp.* 27 61; 28 1], and Mary the mother of James and Joses [*cp.* 27 61; 28 1], and the mother [*cp.* 20 20] of the sons of Zebedee [*cp.* 20 20].
verse 55

Mary Magdalene [*cp.* 15 47; 16 1, 9], and Mary the mother of James the 6 less and of Joses [*cp.* 15 47; 16 1], and Salome [*cp.* 16 1];

cp. 8 2; 24 10.

cp. 24 10.

41 who, when he was in Galilee, followed him, and ministered unto him; and many other women which came up with him unto Jerusalem.

verse 49
cp. 8 3.

26 When Jesus therefore saw his mother, and the disciple standing by, whom he loved, he saith unto his mother, Woman, behold, thy son! 27 Then saith he to the disciple, Behold, thy mother! And from that hour the disciple took her unto his own *home.*

---

1 Or, *earth*
2 Or, *why didst thou forsake me?*
3 Many ancient authorities add *And another took a spear and pierced his side, and there came out water and blood.* See John 19 34.
4 Or, *sanctuary*
5 Or, *a son of God*

1 Or, *earth*
2 Or, *why didst thou forsake me?*
3 Or, *sanctuary*
4 Many ancient authorities read *so cried out, and gave up the ghost.*
5 Or, *a son of God*
6 Gr. *little.*

1 Or, *earth*
2 Gr. *the sun failing.*
3 Or, *sanctuary*
4 Or, *And Jesus, crying with a loud voice, said*

Matt. 27 46 || Mark 15 34: Ps. 22 1.   Matt. 27 48 || Mark 15 36 || John 19 29: *cp.* Ps. 69 21.   Luke 23 46: *cp.* Ps. 31 5.
Matt. 27 55 || Mark 15 40 || Luke 23 49: *cp.* Ps. 31 11; 88 8.

(viii) The Burial (§§ 256-257)

§ 256. The Body of Jesus laid in the Tomb

Matt. 27 57-61 | **Mark 15** 42-47 | **Luke 23** 50-56 | John 19 31, 38-42

57 And when even was come,

cp. 27 62.

42 And when even was now come, because it was the Preparation, that is, the day before the sabbath,

verse 54

31 The Jews therefore, because it was the Preparation [*cp.* 19 14, 42], that

the

Matthew

there came a rich man from Arimathæa, named Joseph,

who also himself

was Jesus' disciple [cp. 13 52; 28 19]: 58 this man went to Pilate, and asked for the body of Jesus.

Then Pilate commanded it to be given up. 59 And Joseph

took the body,

and wrapped it in a clean linen cloth,

60 and laid it in his own new tomb, which he had hewn out in the rock:

and he rolled a great stone [cp. 27 66; 28 2] to the door of the tomb, and departed.

cp. 27 62.

61 And

cp. 27 55.

Mark

43 there came Joseph of Arimathæa, a councillor of honourable estate,

who also himself was looking for the kingdom of God;

and he boldly went in unto Pilate, and asked for the body of Jesus. 44 And Pilate marvelled if he were already dead: and calling unto him the centurion, he asked him whether he ¹ had been any while dead. 45 And when he learned it of the centurion, he granted the corpse to Joseph. 46 And he bought a linen cloth, and taking him down,

cp. 16 1.

wound him in the linen cloth,

and laid him in a tomb which had been hewn out of a rock;

and he rolled a [cp. 16 4] stone [cp. 16 3, 4] against the door of the tomb.

verse 42

47 And

cp. 15 40.

Luke

50 And behold, a man named Joseph, who was a councillor, a good man and a righteous 51 (he had not consented to their counsel and deed), a man of Arimathæa, a city of the Jews, who was looking [cp. 2 25, 38] for the kingdom of God:

52 this man went to Pilate, and asked for the body of Jesus.

53 And he took it down,

cp. verse 56.

and wrapped it in a linen cloth,

and laid him in a tomb that was hewn in stone, where never man had yet lain [cp. 19 30].

cp. 24 2.

54 And it was the day of the Preparation,

and the sabbath ¹ drew on. 55 And the women [cp. 8 2; 23

John

bodies should not remain on the cross upon the sabbath (for the day of that sabbath was a high *day*), asked of Pilate that their legs might be broken, and *that* they might be taken away. . . . 38 And after these things

Joseph of Arimathæa,

being a disciple of Jesus, but secretly for fear of the Jews, asked of Pilate that he might take away the body of Jesus:

cp. 19 33.

and Pilate gave *him* leave. He came therefore, and took away his body. 39 And there came also Nicodemus, he who at the first came to him by night [cp. 3 2; 7 50], bringing a ¹mixture of myrrh and aloes, about a hundred pound *weight*. 40 So they took the body of Jesus, and bound it in linen cloths with the spices, as the custom of the Jews is to bury. 41 Now in the place where he was crucified there was a garden; and in the garden a new tomb wherein was never man yet laid.

cp. 20 1.

42 There then because of the Jews' Preparation [cp. 19 14, 31] (for the tomb was nigh at hand) they laid Jesus.

cp. 27 55.
Mary Magdalene
[*cp.* 27 56; 28 1] was
there, and the other
Mary,
  cp. 27 56; 28 1.
sitting over against
the sepulchre.
	cp. 15 41.
	  Mary Magdalene
	[*cp.* 15 40; 16 1, 9]
	    and
	Mary the *mother* of Joses
	[*cp.* 15 40; 16 1]
	
	       beheld
	      where he
	was laid.
	
	  cp. 16 1.
		49; 24 1, 10, 22, 24],
		which had come with
		him out of Galilee [*cp.*
		23 49],
		  cp. 8 2; 24 10.
		
		  cp. 24 10.
		      followed
		after,
		    and beheld
		the tomb, and how his
		body was laid. **56** And
		they returned, and pre-
		pared spices [*cp.* 24 1],
		and ointments. And on
		the sabbath they rested
		according to the com-
		mandment.
			cp. 19 25; 20 1, 18.
			
			  cp. 19 25.
			
			  cp. verses 39 *and* 40.

[1] Many ancient authorities read *were already dead.*	[1] Gr. *began to dawn.*	[1] Some ancient authorities read *roll.*	

Luke 23 56 (*cp.* John 19 31) : Exod. 12 16 ; 20 9-10 ; Deut. 5 13-14.

§ 257. **The Posting of the Guard**

Matt. 27 62-66

62 Now on the morrow, which is *the day* after the Preparation, the chief priests and the Pharisees were gathered together unto Pilate, **63** saying, Sir, we remember that that deceiver said, while he was yet alive, After three days [Mark 8 31 ; 9 31 ; 10 34 : *cp.* Matt. 16 21 ; 17 23 ; 20 19 : *also* 12 40 ; 26 61 ; 27 40] I rise again [*cp.* 16 21 ; 17 9, 23 ; 20 19 ; 26 32]. **64** Command therefore that the sepulchre be made sure until the third day, lest haply his disciples come and steal him away [*cp.* 28 13], and say unto the people, He is risen from the dead [*cp.* 28 6, 7] : and the last error will be worse than the first. **65** Pilate said unto them, [1] Ye have a guard : go your way, [2] make it *as* sure as ye can. **66** So they went, and made the sepulchre sure, sealing the stone [*cp.* 27 60 ; 28 2], the guard being with them.	*cp.* 15 42. *cp.* 14 58 ; 15 29 : *also* 8 31 ; 9 9, 31 ; 10 34 ; 14 28. *cp.* 16 6. *cp.* 15 46 ; 16 3, 4.	*cp.* 23 54. *cp.* 9 22 ; 13 32 ; 18 33 : *also* 24 7, 21, 26, 46. *cp.* 24 6, 34. *cp.* 24 2.	*cp.* 19 14, 31, 42. *cp.* 2 19-22. *cp.* 20 1.
[1] Or, *Take a guard* [2] Gr. *make it sure, as ye know.*			

(ix) The Resurrection (§§ 258-259)

§ 258. **The Empty Tomb**

Matt. 28 1-10	**Mark 16** 1-8	**Luke 24** 1-12	John 20 1-18
1 Now late on the sab- bath day,	**1** And when the sab- bath was past, Mary Magdalene [*cp.* 15 40, 47 ; 16 9], and Mary the *mother* of James [*cp.* 15 40, 47], and Salome [*cp.* 15 40], bought spices, that they might come and anoint him.	*verse* 10 *cp.* 23 56.	*cp.* 19 25. *cp.* 19 39, 40.

as it began to dawn
toward the first *day* of the
week,
    came Mary Mag-
dalene [*cp.* 27 56, 61]
and the other Mary
[*cp.* 27 56, 61]
        to see
the sepulchre.
	2 And very early
	on the first day of the
	week,
	they come
	
	       to
	the tomb when the
	sun was risen.
	  cp. verse 1.
	
	     3 And
		1 But
		on the first day of the
		week, at early dawn,
		they came
		
		     unto
		the tomb,
		    bringing the
		spices [*cp.* 23 56] which
		they had prepared.
			1 Now
			on the first *day* of the
			week
			    cometh Mary Mag-
			dalene [*cp.* 19 25 ; 20 18]
			  cp. 19 25.
			    early, while
			it was yet dark, unto
			the tomb,
			
			  cp. 19 39, 40.

[Matthew]

2 And behold, there was a great earthquake; for an angel of the Lord descended from heaven, and came and rolled away the stone [cp. 27 60, 66], and sat upon it. **3** His appearance was as lightning, and his raiment white as snow [cp. 17 2]: **4** and for fear [cp. verse 8] of him the watchers did quake, and became as dead men.

cp. 27 60.

cp. verse 3.

cp. 8 27; 9 33; 12 23; 15 31; 21 20; 27 14: also 7 28; etc.

cp. 9 8; 17 6; 27 54; 28 4, 8.

5 And the angel answered and said unto the women, Fear not ye: for I know that ye seek Jesus, [cp. 2 23; 26 71: also 21 11] which hath been crucified.

6 He is not here; for he is risen, even as he said.

Come, see the place ¹ where the Lord lay. **7** And go quickly, and tell his disciples, He is risen from the dead [cp. 27 64]; and lo, he goeth before you into Galilee [cp. 26 32]; there shall ye see him [cp. verse 10]:

[Mark]

they were saying among themselves, Who shall roll us away the stone [cp. 15 46; 16 4] from the door of the tomb?

cp. verse 5.

cp. 9 26. **4** and looking up, they see that the stone [cp. 15 46; 16 3] is rolled back: for it was exceeding great. **5** And entering into the tomb,

cp. 16 19, 20.

they saw a young man sitting on the right side, arrayed in a white [cp. 9 3] robe; and they were amazed [cp. 1 27; 2 12; 5 20, 42; 6 51; 7 37; 10 32; 15 5; 16 8: also 1 22; etc.].

cp. 4 41; 5 15, 33; 9 6, 32; 10 32; 16 8.

6 And he saith unto them, Be not amazed: ye seek Jesus, the Nazarene [cp. 1 24; 10 47; 14 67], which hath been crucified:

he is risen; he is not here:

cp. verse 7.

behold, the place where they laid him! **7** But go, tell his disciples and Peter,

He goeth before you into Galilee [cp. 14 28]: there shall ye see him

[Luke]

2 And they found the stone rolled away from the tomb. **3** And they entered in, and found not the body [cp. 24 23] ¹ of the Lord [cp. 7 13, 19; 10 1, 39, 41; 11 39; 12 42; 13 15; 17 5, 6; 18 6; 19 8; 22 61; 24 34] Jesus. **4** And it came to pass, while they were perplexed thereabout, behold, two men [cp. 24 23] stood by them in dazzling [cp. 9 29] apparel: **5** and as they were [cp. 5 9, 26; 8 25, 56; 9 43; 11 14; 24 12, 41: also 2 47, 48; etc.] affrighted [cp. 1 12, 65; 2 9; 5 26; 7 16; 8 25, 35, 37, 47; 9 34, 45; 24 37], and bowed down their faces to the earth, they said unto them,

cp. 4 34; 18 37; 24 19.

Why seek ye ² the living among the dead? **6** ³ He is not here, but is risen: remember [cp. verse 8] how he spake unto you when he was yet

cp. 24 34.

in Galilee,

[John]

cp. verse 12.

cp. verse 12.

and seeth the stone taken away from the tomb.

cp. verses 6-8.

cp. 4 1; 6 23; 11 2; 20 2, 18, 20, 25; 21 7, 12.

cp. verse 12.

cp. 7 15, 21, 46.

cp. verses 12 and 13.

cp. 18 5, 7; 19 19: also 1 45.

lo, I have told you.
cp. verse 6.

cp. 26 45.
cp. 20 19: *also* 23 34.

cp. 16 21; *etc.*

cp. 26 75.

8 And they departed quickly from the tomb

with fear [*cp. verse* 4: *also* 9 8; 17 6; 27 54] and great joy, and ran to bring his disciples word. **9** And behold, Jesus met them, saying, All hail [*cp.* 26 49; 27 29]. And they came and took hold of his feet, and worshipped him [*cp.* 2 11; 8 2; 9 18; 14 33; 15 25; 20 20; 28 17: *also* 17 14]. **10** Then saith Jesus unto them, Fear not [*cp.* 14 27; 17 7]: go tell my brethren that they depart into Galilee, and there shall they see me [*cp. verse* 7 *and* 28 16-20].

verse 1

cp. 27 55.

cp. 10 2.

cp. 28 17.

---

as he said unto you.

cp. 14 41.

cp. 8 31; *etc.*

cp. 14 72.

8 And they went out, and fled from the tomb; for trembling and astonishment [*cp. verse* 5] had come upon them: and they said nothing to any one; for they were afraid [*cp.* 4 41; 5 15, 33; 9 6, 32; 10 32].

cp. 15 18.

cp. 5 6: *also* 1 40; 3 11; 5 22, 33; 7 25; 10 17.

cp. 6 50.

cp. verse 7.

cp. 16 10.

verse 1

cp. 15 40-41.

cp. 6 30.

cp. 16 11, 13, 14.

---

7 saying that the Son of man must be delivered up into the hands of sinful men, and be crucified, and the third day rise again [*cp.* 9 22, 43-44; 18 31-33: *also* 13 32, 33; 17 25; 22 22: *and* 24 26, 44, 46]. **8** And they remembered [*cp.* 22 61] his words, **9** and returned 4 from the tomb,

cp. 1 12, 65; 2 9; 5 26; 7 16; 8 25; *etc.*
cp. 24 41, 52.

cp. 1 28.

cp. 24 52: *also* 5 8, 12; 8 28, 41, 47; 17 16.

and told all these things [*cp. verses* 10 *and* 23] to the eleven, and to all the rest. **10** Now they were Mary Magdalene [*cp.* 8 2], and Joanna [*cp.* 8 3], and Mary the *mother* of James: and the other women [*cp.* 8 2, 3; 23 49, 55; 24 22, 24] with them told these things unto the apostles [*cp.* 6 13; 9 10; 17 5; 22 14].
see verse 3.

11 And these words appeared in their sight as idle talk; and they disbelieved [*cp.* 24 38, 41: *also* 24 25] them. **12** 5 But Peter arose,

and ran

---

cp. 2 19-22; 3 14; 12 32-33.

cp. 2 22; 12 16.

cp. 20 20: *also* 16 22.
2 She runneth therefore,

cp. 19 3.

cp. 9 38: *also* 11 32; 18 6.

cp. 6 20.
cp. verse 17.

and cometh to Simon Peter, and to the other disciple, whom Jesus loved,

cp. verse 18.

cp. 19 25.

cp. 19 25.

and

saith unto them,

They have taken away the Lord [*cp.* 4 1; 6 23; 11 2; 20 18, 20, 25; 21 7, 12] out of the tomb, and we know not where they have laid him.

cp. 20 25.

3 Peter therefore went forth, and the other disciple, and they went toward the tomb. **4** And they ran both together: and the other unto the tomb; and stooping and looking in, he seeth the linen cloths

disciple outran Peter, and came first to the tomb; 5 and stooping and looking in, he seeth the linen cloths lying; yet entered he not in. 6 Simon Peter therefore also cometh, following him, and entered into the tomb; and he beholdeth the linen cloths lying, 7 and the napkin, that was upon his head, not lying with the linen cloths, but rolled up in a place by itself. 8 Then entered in therefore the other disciple also, which came first to the tomb, and he saw, and believed. 9 For as yet they knew not the scripture, that he must rise again from the dead. 10 So the disciples went away again unto their own home.

cp. verse 5.   *cp. verse 3.*

by themselves;
cp. verse 5.   *cp. verse 3.*

and
he   6 departed
to his   home,
wondering at that which
was come to pass [*cp.
verse 5*].

11 But Mary was standing without at the tomb weeping: so, as she wept, she stooped and looked into the tomb; 12 and she beholdeth two angels in white sitting, one at the head, and one at the feet, where the body of Jesus had lain. 13 And they say unto her, Woman, why weepest thou? She saith unto them, Because they have taken away my Lord, and I know not where they have laid him. 14 When she had thus said, she turned herself back, and

cp. 28 2, 3, 5.   *cp. 16 5.*   *cp. 24 4.*

[1] Many ancient authorities read *where he lay.*

[1] Some ancient authorities omit *of the Lord Jesus.*
[2] Gr. *him that liveth.*
[3] Some ancient authorities omit *He is not here, but is risen.*
[4] Some ancient authorities omit *from the tomb.*
[5] Some ancient authorities omit ver. 12.
[6] Or, *departed, wondering with himself*

cp. 16 9.

cp. 28 10.
cp. 28 8.   *cp. 16 10.*   *cp. 24 9, 10, 23.*

beholdeth Jesus standing, and knew not that it was Jesus. 15 Jesus saith unto her, Woman, why weepest thou? whom seekest thou? She, supposing him to be the gardener, saith unto him, Sir, if thou hast borne him hence, tell me where thou hast laid him, and I will take him away. 16 Jesus saith unto her, Mary. She turneth herself, and saith unto him in Hebrew, Rabboni; which is to say, [1] Master. 17 Jesus saith to her, [2] Touch me not; for I am not yet ascended unto the Father: but go unto my brethren, and say to them, I ascend unto my Father and your Father, and my God and your God. 18 Mary Magdalene cometh and telleth the disciples, I have seen the Lord; and *how that* he had said these things unto her.

[1] Or, *Teacher*   [2] Or, *Take not hold on me*

§ 259. The Report of the Guard

Matt. 28 11-15

11 Now while they were going, behold, some of the guard came into the city, and told unto the chief priests all the things that were come to pass. 12 And when they were assembled with the elders, and had taken counsel [*cp.* 12 14; 22 15; 27 1, 7], they gave large money unto the soldiers, 13 saying, Say ye, His disciples came by night, and stole him away [*cp.* 27 64] while we slept. 14 And if this [1] come to the governor's [*cp.* 27 2, 11, 14, 15, 21, 27] ears, we will persuade him, and rid you of care. 15 So they took the money, and did as they were taught: and this saying was spread abroad among the Jews, *and continueth* until this day [*cp.* 11 23; 27 8].

cp. 3 6; 15 1.

cp. 20 20.

[1] Or, *come to a hearing before the governor*

G. The Appearances after the Resurrection and the Commissioning of the Eleven
(§§ 260-268).

(i) The Appearance and Commission according to Matthew (§ 260)

§ 260. **To the Eleven on the Mount in Galilee**

Matt. 28 16-20	Mark 16 15-16	Luke 24 46-49	John 20 21-23
16 But the eleven disciples went into Galilee, unto the mountain [*cp.* 5 1; 14 23; 15 29; 17 1: *also* 24 3] where Jesus had appointed them [*cp.* 28 10]. **17** And when they saw him, they worshipped *him* [*cp.* 2 11; 8 2; 9 18; 14 33; 15 25; 20 20; 28 9: *also* 17 14]: but some doubted [*cp.* 14 31]. **18** And Jesus came to them and spake unto them, saying,	*cp.* 3 13; 6 46; 9 2: *also* 13 3. *cp.* 5 6: *also* 1 40; 3 11; 5 22, 33; 7 25; 10 17. *cp.* 16 11, 13, 14. 15 And he said unto them,	*cp.* 6 12; 9 28. *cp.* 24 52: *also* 5 8, 12; 8 28, 41, 47; 17 16. *cp.* 24 11, 38, 41. 46 And he said unto them, Thus it is written [*cp.* 24 26: *also* 18 31-33; 20 17; 22 37: *and* 9 22, *etc.*], that the Christ should suffer, and rise again from the dead the third day;	*cp.* 6 3, 15. *cp.* 9 38: *also* 11 32; 18 6. *cp.* 20 25. 21 Jesus therefore said to them again, Peace *be* unto you: *cp.* 5 39; 13 18; 15 25; 17 12.
cp. 21 42; 26 24, 31, 54, 56: *also* 16 21, *etc.*	*cp.* 9 12; 12 10; 14 21, 27, 49: *also* 8 31, *etc.*		
All authority [*cp.* 7 29; 9 6, 8; 21 23-27: *also* 11 27] hath been given unto me in heaven and on earth.	*cp.* 1 22, 27; 2 10; 11 27-33.	*cp.* 4 32, 36; 5 24; 20 1-8: *also* 10 22.	*cp.* 5 27; 17 2: *also* 3 35; 13 3.
cp. 26 28.	*cp.* 1 4.	47 and that repentance [1] and remission of sins [*cp.* 1 77; 3 3] should be preached in his name [*cp.* 9 48, 49; 10 17; 21 8]	*cp.* 14 13, 14, 26; 15 16; 16 23, 24, 26.
[*cp. verse* 19: *also* 7 22; 18 5, 20; 24 5] **19** Go ye therefore, and make disciples [*cp.* 13 52; 27 57] of all the nations [*cp.* 24 14; 26 13: *also* 8 11; 10 18; 21 31, 41-43; 22 7-10], *cp.* 4 23; 9 35; 24 14; 26 13.	[*cp.* 16 17: *also* 9 37, 38, 39; 13 6] Go ye into all the world, and *cp.* 13 10; 14 9: *also* 12 9. preach the gospel [*cp.* 1 1, 14, 15; 8 35; 10 29; 13 10; 14 9] to the whole creation [*cp.* 10 6; 13 19].	unto all the [2] nations [*cp.* 2 30-32; 3 6: *also* 13 29; 14 21-24; 20 16],	*cp.* 10 16; 11 52.
baptizing them into the name of the Father and of the Son and of the Holy Ghost:	16 He that believeth and is baptized shall be saved; but he that disbelieveth shall be condemned.	beginning from Jerusalem. *cp. verse* 47.	
20 teaching them to observe all things whatsoever I commanded you:			*cp.* 14 15, 23.
		48 Ye are witnesses of these things. 49 And behold, I send forth the promise of my Father upon you: but tarry ye in the city,	*cp.* 15 27. as the Father hath sent me, even so send I *cp.* 14 16, 26 15 26; 16 7. you.

cp. 5 30.

until ye be clothed with power [cp. 1 17, 35 ; 4 14, 36 ; 5 17 ; 6 19 ; 8 46 ; 9 1] from on high [cp. 1 78].

22 And when he had said this, he breathed on them, and saith unto them, Receive ye the ¹ Holy Ghost : 23 whose soever sins ye forgive, they are forgiven unto them ; whose soever *sins* ye retain, they are retained.

cp. 14 23.

cp. 16 19 ; 18 18.

and lo, I am with you [cp. 1 23] ¹ alway [cp. 18 20], even unto ² the end of the world [cp. 13 39, 40, 49 ; 24 3].

Gr. *all the days.*
² Or, *the consummation of the age*

¹ Some ancient authorities read *unto.*
² Or, *nations. Beginning from Jerusalem, ye are witnesses*

¹ Or, *Holy Spirit*

(ii) The Appearances and Commission according to Luke (§§ 261-264)

§ 261. The Appearance to Two Disciples on the Way to Emmaus

		Mark 16 12-13	Luke 24 13-35	
		12 And after these things he was manifested in another form unto two of them, as they walked, on their way into the country.	13 And behold, two of them were going that very day to a village named Emmaus, which was threescore furlongs from Jerusalem. 14 And they communed with each other of all these things which had happened. 15 And it came to pass, while they communed and questioned together, that Jesus himself drew near, and went with them. 16 But their eyes were holden that they should not know him. 17 And he said unto them, ¹ What communications are these that ye have one with another, as ye walk ? And they stood still, looking sad. 18 And one of them, named Cleopas, answering said unto him, ² Dost thou alone sojourn in Jerusalem and not know the things which are come to pass there in these days ? 19 And he said unto them, What things ? And they said unto him, The things concerning Jesus of Nazareth [cp. 4 34 ; 18 37], which was a prophet [cp. 4 24 ; 7 16, 39 ; 13 33] mighty in deed and word before God and all the people : 20 and how the chief priests and our rulers delivered him up to be condemned to death, and crucified him. 21 But we hoped that it was he which should redeem [cp. 1 68 ; 2 38 ; 21 28] Israel. Yea and beside all this, it is now the third day [cp. 9 22 ; 13 32 ; 18 33 ; 24 7, 46] since these things came to pass. 22 Moreover certain women of our company amazed us, having been early at the tomb ; 23 and when they found not his body [cp. 24 3], they came, saying, that they had also seen a vision of angels, which said that he was alive [cp. 24 4-10]. 24 And certain of them that were with us went to the tomb, and found it even so as the women had said : but him they saw not [cp. 24 11, 12]. 25 And he said unto them, O foolish men, and slow of heart to believe [cp. 24 11, 38, 41] ³ in all that the prophets have spoken ! 26 Behoved it not the Christ to suffer these things [cp. 24 46: *also* 18 31-33 ; 20 17 ; 22 37: *and* 9 22, 44 ; 13 32, 33 ; 17 25 ; 22 22 ; 24 7], and to enter [cp. 11 52 ; 13 24 ; 18 17, 24, 25] into his glory [cp. 9 26, 32: *and* John 1 14 ; 2 11 ; 12 41 ; 17 5, 22, 24] ? 27 And beginning from Moses and from all the prophets [cp. 16 29, 31], he interpreted to them in all the scriptures the things concerning himself [cp. 24 44]. 28 And they drew nigh unto the village, whither they were going : and he made as though he would go further. 29 And they constrained him, saying, Abide with us : for it is toward evening, and the day is now far spent [cp. 9 12]. And he went in to abide with	
cp. 2 23 ; etc. cp. 13 57 ; 21 11, 46.	cp. 1 24 ; etc. cp. 6 4, 15.			cp. 20 14 ; 21 4.
				cp. 18 5 ; etc. cp. 4 19, 44 ; 6 14 ; 7 40 ; 9 17.
cp. 16 21 ; etc.	cp. 8 31 ; etc.			cp. 2 19.
cp. 28 5-8.	cp. 16 5-7.			cp. 20 11-18.
cp. 28 17.	cp. 16 11, 13, 14.			cp. 20 3-10. cp. 20 25, 27.
cp. 26 24 ; etc.	cp. 14 21 ; etc.			
cp. 5 20 ; etc. cp. 19 28 ; 25 31.	cp. 9 43 ; etc. cp. 10 37.			cp. 3 5 ; 10 1, 2, 9.
				cp. 1 45 ; 5 46.
cp. 14 15.	cp. 6 35.			

Matt.	Mark	Luke	John
cp. 14 19; 15 36; 26 26.	cp. 6 41; 8 6; 14 22.	them. **30** And it came to pass, when he had sat down with them to meat, he took the 4 bread, and blessed it, and brake, and gave to them [cp. 9 16; 22 19]. **31** And their eyes were opened, and they knew him; and he vanished out of their sight. **32** And they said one to another, Was not our heart burning within us, while he spake to us in the way, while he opened to us the scriptures [cp. 24 45]?	cp. 6 11.
	13 And they went away	**33** And they rose up that very hour, and returned to Jerusalem, and found the eleven gathered together, and them that were with them, **34** saying, The Lord [cp. 7 13, 19; 10 1, 39, 41; 11 39; 12 42; 13 15; 17 5, 6; 18 6; 19 8; 22 61; 24 3] is risen [cp. 24 6] indeed, and hath appeared to Simon. **35** And they rehearsed the things *that happened* in the way, and how he was known of them in the breaking of the bread.	cp. 4 1; 6 23; 11 2; 20 2, 18, 20, 25; 21 7, 12.
	cp. 16 19, 20.		
cp. 27 64; 28 6, 7.	cp. 16 6. and		
	told it		
cp. 28 17.	unto the rest : neither believed they them [cp. 16 11, 14].	cp. 24 11, 38, 41: also 24 25.	cp. 20 25.

1 Gr. *What words are these that ye exchange one with another.*
2 Or, *Dost thou sojourn alone in Jerusalem, and knowest thou not the things*
3 Or, *after*   4 Or, *loaf*

§ 262. **The Appearance to the Eleven in Jerusalem**

Matt.	Mark 16 14	Luke 24 36-43	John 20 19-20
	14 And afterward	**36** And as they spake these things,	19 When therefore it was evening, on that day, the first *day* of the week, and when the doors were shut where the disciples were, for fear of the Jews, Jesus
	he was manifested unto the eleven themselves as they sat at meat;	he himself	
cp. 9 8; 17 6; 27 54; 28 4, 8. cp. 14 26.	cp. 4 41; 5 15, 33; 9 6, 32; 10 32; 16 8. cp. 6 49.	stood in the midst of them, 1 and saith unto them, Peace *be* unto you. **37** But they were terrified and affrighted [cp. 1 12, 65; 2 9; 5 26; 7 16; 8 25, 35, 37, 47; 9 34, 45; 24 5], and supposed that they beheld a spirit. **38** And he said unto them,	came and stood in the midst, and saith unto them, Peace *be* unto you.
cp. 28 17: also 13 58. cp. 19 8.	and he upbraided them with their unbelief [cp. 16 11, 13 : *also* 6 6] and hardness of heart [cp. 6 52; 8 17 : *also* 3 5; 10 5], because they believed not them which had seen him after he was risen.		cp. 20 25, 27. cp. 12 40.
cp. 28 17.		Why are ye troubled ? and wherefore do reasonings arise in your heart [cp. 24 11, 41 : *also* 25] ? **39** See my hands and my feet, that it is I myself : handle me, and see; for a spirit hath not flesh and bones, as ye behold me having. **40** 2 And when he had said this, he shewed them his hands and his feet.	cp. 20 25, 27. cp. 20 27. 20 And when he had said this, he shewed unto them his hands and his side. The disciples therefore were
cp. 28 17. cp. 28 8.	cp. 16 11, 13, 14.	**41** And while they still disbelieved [cp. 24 11, 38 : *also* 24 25] for joy [cp. 24 52],	cp. 20 25, 27. glad [cp. 16 22],

		and wondered, he said unto them, Have ye here anything to eat ? **42** And they gave him a piece of a broiled fish.[3] **43** And he took it, and did eat before them.	when they saw the Lord.

cp. 21 5. |

[1] Some ancient authorities omit *and saith unto them, Peace be unto you.*
[2] Some ancient authorities omit ver. 40.
[3] Many ancient authorities add *and a honeycomb.*

§ 263. The Commission to the Eleven in Jerusalem

Matt. 28 18-20	Mark 16 15-16	**Luke 24** 44-49	John 20 21-23
18 And Jesus came to them and spake unto them, saying,	**15** And he said unto them,	**44** And he said unto them, These are my words which I spake unto you, while I was yet with you, how that all things must needs be fulfilled, which are written in the law of Moses, and the prophets, and the psalms [*cp.* 16 29, 31; 24 27: *also* 20 42], concerning me [*cp.* 24 27]. **45** Then opened he their mind, that they might understand the scriptures [*cp.* 24 32]; **46** and he said unto them, Thus it is written	**21** Jesus therefore said to them again, Peace *be* unto you :

cp. 14 25 ; 16 4.

cp. 1 45 ; 5 46. |
| cp. 21 42 ; 26 24, 31, 54, 56 : *also* 16 21 ; *etc.* | cp. 9 12 ; 12 10 ; 14 21, 27, 49 : *also* 8 31 ; *etc.* | [*cp.* 24 26: *also* 18 31-33; 20 17; 22 37: *and* 9 22; *etc.*], that the Christ should suffer, and rise again from the dead the third day; | cp. 5 39; 13 18; 15 25; 17 12. |
| All authority [*cp.* 7 29 ; 9 6, 8 ; 21 23-27: *also* 11 27] hath been given unto me in heaven and on earth.

cp. 26 28. | cp. 1 22, 27 ; 2 10 ; 11 27-33.

cp. 1 4. | cp. 4 32, 36 ; 5 24 ; 20 1-8: *also* 10 22. | cp. 5 27; 17 2: *also* 3 35; 13 3. |
| [*cp. verse* 19: *also* 7 22 ; 18 5, 20 ; 24 5] **19** Go ye therefore, and make disciples [*cp.* 13 52 ; 27 57] of all the nations [*cp.* 24 14 ; 26 13: *also* 8 11 ; 10 18; 21 31, 41-43 ; 22 7-10], cp. 4 23 ; 9 35 ; 24 14 ; 26 13. | [*cp.* 16 17 : *also* 9 37, 38, 39 ; 13 6] Go ye into all the world, and

cp. 13 10 ; 14 9: *also* 12 9. | **47** and that repentance [1] and remission of sins [*cp.* 1 77; 3 3] should be preached in his name [*cp.* 9 48, 49; 10 17; 21 8] unto all the [2] nations [*cp.* 2 30-32; 3 6: *also* 13 29; 14 21-24; 20 16], | cp. 14 13, 14, 26; 15 16; 16 23, 24, 26.

cp. 10 16 ; 11 52. |
| baptizing them into the name of the Father and of the Son and of the Holy Ghost : | preach the gospel [*cp.* 1 1, 14, 15 ; 8 35 ; 10 29 ; 13 10 ; 14 9] to the whole creation [*cp.* 10 6 ; 13 19]. **16** He that believeth and is baptized shall be saved ; but he that disbelieveth | beginning from Jerusalem.

cp. *verse* 47. | |

	shall be condemned.		
20 teaching them to observe all things whatsoever I commanded you :		**48** Ye are witnesses of these things. **49** And behold, I send forth the promise of my Father upon you : but tarry ye in the city, until ye be clothed with power [*cp.* 1 17, 35; 4 14, 36; 5 17; 6 19; 8 46; 9 1] from on high [*cp.* 1 78].	*cp.* 14 15, 23. *cp.* 15 27. as the Father hath sent me, even so send I *cp.* 14 16, 26 15 26 ; 16 7. you.
	cp. 5 30.		**22** And when he had said this, he breathed on them, and saith unto them, Receive ye the [1] Holy Ghost : **23** whose soever sins ye forgive, they are forgiven unto them ; whose soever *sins* ye retain, they are retained. *cp.* 14 23.
cp. 16 19 ; 18 18. and lo, I am with you [*cp.* 1 23] [1] alway [*cp.* 18 20], even unto [2] the end of the world [*cp.* 13 39, 40, 49 ; 24 3].			
[1] Gr. *all the days.* [2] Or, *the consummation of the age*		[1] Some ancient authorities read *unto.* [2] Or, *nations. Beginning from Jerusalem, ye are witnesses*	[1] Or, *Holy Spirit*

§ 264. **The Parting at Bethany**

	Mark 16 19-20	Luke 24 50-53	
		50 And he led them out until *they were* over against Bethany : and he lifted up his hands, and blessed them. *cp.* 7 13, 19 ; 10 1, 39, 41 ; 11 39 ; *etc.*	*cp.* 4 1 ; 6 23 ; 11 2 ; 20 2, 18, 20, 25 ; 21 7, 12.
	19 So then the Lord [*cp. verse* 20] Jesus, after he had spoken unto them,		
cp. 28 17 : *also* 2 11 ; *etc.* *cp.* 28 8.	was received up into heaven, and sat down at the right hand of God. *cp.* 5 6 : *also* 1 40 ; 3 11 ; 5 22, 33 ; 7 25 ; 10 17.	**51** And it came to pass, while he blessed them, he parted from them, [1] and was carried up into heaven. **52** And they [2] worshipped him [*cp.* 5 8, 12 ; 8 28, 41, 47 ; 17 16], and returned to Jerusalem with great joy [*cp.* 24 41] : **53** and were continually in the temple, blessing God [*cp.* 1 64 ; 2 28].	*cp.* 9 38 : *also* 11 32 ; 18 6. *cp.* 16 22 ; 20 20.
cp. 13 19-23.	**20** And they went forth, and preached everywhere, the Lord [*see above*] working with them, and confirming the word [*cp.* 2 2 ; 4 14-20, 33] by the signs that followed [*cp.* 16 17-18]. Amen.	*cp.* 1 2 ; 4 32 ; 8 12-15 : *also* 5 1 ; 8 11, 21 ; 11 28.	*cp.* 4 41 ; 5 24, 38 ; *etc.*
		[1] Some ancient authorities omit *and was carried up into heaven.* [2] Some ancient authorities omit *worshipped him, and.*	

(iii) The Appearances and Commission according to Mark (§§ 265-268)

§ 265. **The Appearance to Mary Magdalene**

	Mark 16 9-11		
cp. 28 1, 9, 10.	**9** [1] Now when he was risen early on the first day of the week [*cp.* 16 2], he appeared first to Mary Magdalene [*cp.* 16 1], from whom he had cast out seven [2] devils. **10** She went and told	*cp.* 24 1, 10. *cp.* 8 2.	*cp.* 20 1, 14-17.

cp. 28 8. cp. 28 17.	them that had been with him, as they mourned and wept. **11** And they, when they heard that he was alive, and had been seen of her, disbelieved [cp. 16 13, 14].	cp. 24 9, 10, 23. cp. 24 11, 38, 41: also 25.	cp. 20 18. cp. 20 25, 27.

¹ The two oldest Greek manuscripts, and some other authorities, omit from ver. 9 to the end. Some other authorities have a different ending to the Gospel.
² Gr. *demons*.

§ 266. The Appearance to Two Disciples on their way into the Country

	Mark 16 12-13	Luke 24 13-35	
	12 And after these things he was manifested in another form unto two of them, as they walked, on their way into the country.	**13** And behold, two of them were going that very day to a village named Emmaus, which was threescore furlongs from Jerusalem.	
	13 And they went away	**33** And they rose up that very hour, and returned to Jerusalem, and found the eleven gathered together, and them that were with them, **34** saying, The Lord [cp. 7 13, 19; 10 1, 39, 41; 11 39; 12 42; 13 15; 17 5, 6; 18 6; 19 8; 22 61; 24 3] is risen [cp. 24 6] indeed, and hath appeared to Simon. **35** And they rehearsed the things *that happened* in the way, and how he was known of them in the breaking of the bread.	cp. 4 1; 6 23; 11 2; 20 2, 18, 20, 25; 21 7, 12.
cp. 27 64; 28 6, 7.	cp. 16 19, 20. cp. 16 6. and told it		
cp. 28 17.	unto the rest: neither believed they them [cp. 16 11, 14].	cp. 24 11, 38, 41: also 25.	cp. 20 25, 27.

§ 267. The Appearance and Commission to the Eleven as they sat at Meat

Matt. 28 18-20	**Mark 16** 14-18	Luke 24 36-49 10 17-19	John 20 19-23	John 20 26-29
18 And	**14** And afterward	**36** And as they spake these things,	**19** When therefore it was evening, on that day, the first *day* of the week, and when the doors were shut where the disciples were, for fear of the Jews,	**26** And after eight days again
Jesus came to them	he was manifested unto the eleven themselves as they sat at meat;	he himself stood in the midst of them,	Jesus came and stood in the midst,	his disciples were within, and Thomas with them. Jesus cometh, the doors being shut, and stood in the midst,
cp. 9 8; 17 6; 27 54; 28 4, 8. cp. 14 26.	cp. 4 41; 5 15, 33; 9 6, 32; 10 32; 16 8. cp. 6 49. and he upbraided them	¹ and saith unto them, Peace *be* unto you. **37** But they were terrified and affrighted [cp. 1 12, 65; 2 9; 5 26; 7 16; 8 25, 35, 37, 47; 9 34, 35; 24 5], and supposed that they beheld a spirit. **38** And he said unto them, Why are ye troubled? and wherefore do reasonings arise in your heart [cp. verse 41]?	and saith unto them, Peace *be* unto you.	and said, Peace *be* unto you.
				27 Then saith he to

[Matthew column]

cp. 28 17 : also 13 58.

cp. 19 8.

cp. 28 8.

and spake unto them, saying,
cp. 21 42 ; 26 24, 31, 54, 56 : also 16 21 ; etc.

All authority [cp. 7 29 ; 9 6, 8 ; 21 23-27 : also 11 27] hath been given unto me in heaven and on earth.

cp. 26 28.
cp. verse 19 : also 7 22 ; 18 5, 20 ; 24 5.
19 Go ye therefore, and make disciples [cp. 13 52 ; 27 57] of all the nations [cp. 24 14 ; 26 13 : also 8 11 ; 10 18 ; 21 31, 41-43 ; 22 7-10],
cp. 4 23 ; 9 35 ; 24 14 ; 26 13.
baptizing them into the name of the Father and of the Son and

with their unbelief [cp. 16 11, 13 : also 6 6] and hardness of heart [cp. 6 52 ; 8 17 : also 3 5 ; 10 5],

because they believed not them which had seen him after he was risen.

15 And he said unto them,
cp. 9 12 ; 12 10 ; 14 21, 27, 49 : also 8 31 ; etc.

cp. 1 22, 27 ; 2 10 ; 11 27-33.

cp. 1 4.
cp. verse 17 : also 9 37, 38, 39 ; 13 6.
Go ye into all the world, and

cp. 13 10 ; 14 9 : also 12 9.

preach the gospel [cp. 1 1, 14, 15 ; 8 35 ; 10 29 ; 13 10 ; 14 9] to the whole creation [cp. 10 6 ; 13 19].
16 He that believeth and is baptized

39 See my hands and my feet, that it is I myself :

handle me, and see ; for a spirit hath not flesh and bones, as ye behold me having.
40 2 And when he had said this, he shewed them his hands and his feet.
41 And while they still disbelieved [cp. 24 11, 38 : also 25]

for joy [cp. 24 52],

and wondered, he said unto them, Have ye here anything to eat ? 42 And they gave him a piece of a broiled fish.3
43 And he took it, and did eat before them. . . .

46 And he said unto them, Thus it is written [cp. 24 26 : also 18 31-33 ; 20 17 ; 22 37 : and 9 22 ; etc.], that the Christ should suffer, and rise again from the dead the third day ;
cp. 4 32, 36 ; 5 24 ; 20 1-8 : also 10 22.

47 and that repentance 4 and remission of sins [cp. 1 77 ; 3 3] should be preached in his name [cp. 9 48, 49 ; 10 17 ; 21 8]

unto all the 5 nations [cp. 2 30-32 ; 3 6 : also 13 29 ; 14 21-24 ; 20 16],

beginning from Jerusalem.

cp. verse 47.

20 And when he had said this, he shewed unto them his hands and his side. The disciples therefore [cp. 20 25]

cp. 12 40.

were glad [cp. 16 22], when they saw the Lord.

cp. 21 5.

Thomas, Reach hither thy finger, and see my hands ;

and reach hither thy hand, and put it into

my side : and be not faithless, but believing.

28 Thomas answered and said unto him, My Lord and my God. 29 Jesus saith unto him, Because thou hast seen me, 1 thou hast believed : blessed are they that have not seen,

and yet have believed.
21 Jesus therefore said to them again,
cp. 5 39 ; 13 18 ; 15 25 ; 17 12.

cp. 5 27 ; 17 2 ; also 3 35 ; 13 3.

cp. 14 13, 14, 26 ; 15 16 ; 16 23, 24, 26.

cp. 10 16 ; 11 52.

of the Holy Ghost :

20 teaching them to observe all things whatsoever I commanded you :

              shall be saved ; but he that disbelieveth shall be condemned.

48 Ye are witnesses of these things. **49** And behold,

     I send forth the promise of my Father upon you : but tarry ye in the city, until ye be clothed with power [*cp.* 1 17, 35 ; 4 14, 36 ; 5 17 ; 6 19 ; 8 46 ; 9 1] from on high [*cp.* 1 78].

cp. 14 15, 23.

cp. 15 27.

     Peace *be* unto you : as the Father hath sent me, even so send I [*cp.* 14 16, 26 ; 15 26 ; 16 7] you.

cp. 5 30.

22 And when he had said this, he breathed on them, and saith unto them, Receive ye the [2] Holy Ghost : **23** whose soever sins ye forgive, they are forgiven unto them ; whose soever *sins* ye retain, they are retained. *cp.* 14 23.

cp. 16 19 ; 18 18. and lo, I am with you [*cp.* 1 23] [1] alway [*cp.* 18 20], even unto [2] the end of the world [*cp.* 13 39, 40, 49 ; 24 3].

17 And these signs shall follow [*cp.* 16 20] them that believe :

     in my name [*cp.* 9 37, 38, 39 ; 13 6] shall they cast out [1] devils ; they shall speak with [2] new tongues ; **18** they shall

10 17 And the seventy returned with joy, saying,

     Lord, even the [6] devils are subject unto us in thy name [*cp.* 24 47 : *also* 9 48, 49 ; 21 8].

cp. verse 19 : *also* 7 22 ; 18 5, 20 ; 24 5.

cp. 14 13, 14, 26 ; 15 16 ; 16 23, 24, 26.

18 And he said unto them, I beheld Satan fallen as lightning from heaven. **19** Behold, I have given you authority [*cp.* 10 9 ; 9 1 : *also* 9 6, 40] to tread upon serpents and scorpions, and over all the power of the enemy : and   nothing shall in any wise hurt you.

cp. 10 1, 8 : *also* 17 16.

[*cp.* 3 15 ; 6 7 : *also* 6 13 ; 9 18] take up serpents,

     and if they drink any deadly   thing, it shall in no wise hurt them ; they shall lay hands on the sick, and they shall recover.

[1] Gr. *all the days.*
[2] Or, *the consummation of the age*

[1] Gr. *demons.*
[2] Some ancient authorities omit *new.*

[1] Some ancient authorities omit *and saith unto them, Peace be unto you.*
[2] Some ancient authorities omit ver. 40.
[3] Many ancient authorities add *and a honeycomb.*
[4] Some ancient authorities read *unto.*
[5] Or, *nations. Beginning from Jerusalem, ye are witnesses*
[6] Gr. *demons.*

[1] Or, *hast thou believed ?*
[2] Or, *Holy Spirit*

§ 268. **The Reception into Heaven and the Mission which followed**

	Mark 16 19-20	Luke 24 50-53	
	19 So then the Lord [*cp. verse 20*] Jesus, after he had spoken unto them,	*cp.* 7 13, 19 ; 10 1, 39, 41 ; 11 39 ; *etc.*	*cp.* 4 1 ; 6 23 ; 11 2 ; 20 2, 18, 20, 25 ; 21 7, 12.
		50 And he led them out until *they were* over against Bethany : and he lifted up his hands, and blessed them. **51** And it came to pass, while he blessed them, he parted from them, [1] and was carried up into heaven.	
cp. 28 17: *also* 2 11 ; *etc.* *cp.* 28 8.	was received up into heaven, and sat down at the right hand of God. *cp.* 5 6: *also* 1 40 ; 3 11 ; 5 22, 33 ; 7 25 ; 10 17.	**52** And they [2] worshipped him [*cp.* 5 8, 12 ; 8 28, 41, 47 ; 17 16], and returned to Jerusalem with great joy [*cp.* 24 41]: **53** and were continually in the temple, blessing God [*cp.* 1 64 ; 2 28].	*cp.* 9 38: *also* 11 32 ; 18 6. *cp.* 16 22 ; 20 20.
cp. 13 19-23.	**20** And they went forth, and preached everywhere, the Lord [*see above*] working with them, and confirming the word [*cp.* 2 2 ; 4 14-20, 33] by the signs that followed [*cp.* 16 17-18]. Amen.	*cp.* 1 2 ; 4 32 ; 8 12-15 : *also* 5 1 ; 8 11, 21 ; 11 28.	*cp.* 4 41 ; 5 24, 38 ; *etc.*

[1] Some ancient authorities omit *and was carried up into heaven.*
[2] Some ancient authorities omit *worshipped him, and.*

INDEX OF JOHANNINE PARALLELS
printed in the text in full

INDEX TO SECTION HEADINGS